Population Policy in Developed Countries

AUTHORS

Brendan M. Walsh, *Ireland*
Dov Friedlander, *Israel*
Paavo Piepponen, *Finland*
Lena Jonsson, *Sweden*
Ivan Stefanov, Nicola Naoumov, *Bulgaria*
N. Louros, J. Danezis, D. Trichopoulos, *Greece*
Louis Lohlé-Tart, *Belgium*
Andras Klinger, *Hungary*
W. D. Borrie, *Australia*
Philip van Praag, Louis Lohlé-Tart, *The Netherlands*
Zdenek Pavlik, Vladimir Wynnyczuk, *Czechoslovakia*
Petre Muresan, Ioan M. Copil, *Romania*
L. T. Badenhorst, *South Africa*
Jacques Henripin, Hervé Gauthier, *Canada*
Horacio D. Gregoratti, Carlos Luzzetti, *Argentina*
Janusz A. Ziolkowski, *Poland*
Salustiano del Campo, *Spain*
Jean Bourgeois-Pichat, *France*
John Simons, *Great Britain*
Massimo Livi Bacci, *Italy*
Hermann Schubnell, *West Germany*
Minoru Muramatsu, Toshio Kuroda, *Japan*
Charles F. Westoff, *United States*
Dmitri I. Valentei, *Soviet Union*

Population Policy in Developed Countries

EDITED BY **Bernard Berelson**

A POPULATION COUNCIL BOOK

McGRAW-HILL BOOK COMPANY

New York   St. Louis   San Francisco   Düsseldorf   London
Sydney   Toronto   Mexico   Panama   Kuala Lumpur
Montreal   New Delhi   São Paulo   Singapore

Library of Congress Cataloging in Publication Data

Berelson, Bernard, 1912–
   Population policy in developed countries.

   "A Population Council book."
   Includes bibliographies.
   1. Population—Addresses, essays, lectures.
I. Walsh, Brendan M. II. Population Council,
New York. III. Title.
HB851.B45   301.32   73–18368
ISBN 0–07–004833–4

123456789 KPKP 7987654

Contents

CONTENTS

Preface

This project began in connection with the work of the Commission on Population Growth and the American Future. At an early period in its tenure, Charles Westoff, as Executive Director, and I, as a member, considered whether a review of population policy in a few developed countries would be useful as counterpoint to the commission's own deliberations. Because of other pressures on the commission's time, however, that review was not carried out under its auspices, and later the idea was taken up by the Population Council as an independent and much larger project. This volume is the outcome.

In the course of putting together this collection of papers, I was assisted by a number of people to whom I take this opportunity, once more, of expressing thanks. First of all, I am indebted to the collaborators themselves who made time in busy schedules to prepare these reports on population policy in their countries. As initiator and editor, I was always impressed by the friendly cooperation that existed across this range of countries.

I owe a special debt of thanks to Dr. Westoff for his early advice as the project got under way and for his encouragement to expand the scope from a few countries to essentially the developed world. At the Population Council, I benefited from consultation with several colleagues, particularly Parker Mauldin, Thomas Burch, Dorothy Nortman, and Tomas Frejka; from the editorial work of Susan Robbins and Ethel Churchill; and of life-saving quality, from the management of manuscript and office, with both skill and good humor, by Joyce Tait and Marianne Rein.

In October 1972, several of the collaborators met together in Belgrade to review the then available reports and the first draft of my introduction and summary. I am grateful to the Economic Institute and its Director, Dr. Dusan Bjelogrlic, for serving as our host on that occasion and to Dr. Milos Macura and Ranka Raos for handling the local arrangements in so efficient and pleasant a manner.

At the outset, the collaborators were given a common outline as guide to the topics to be addressed, but each author was free to prepare his report in his own manner. Thus the papers represent the views of the several authors and not necessarily those of the Population Council or myself as editor. And I add, on the authors' behalf, that they write here in their individual professional capacities and not necessarily in the official positions that many of them hold.

These years population policy is usually understood as applying to the developing countries and their struggle toward a better life under the burden of a rapid rate of population growth. Yet it is also relevant to the goals of the developed world, as these papers make clear. It is with that sense of balance that the Population Council is glad to offer this symposium as a contribution to the deliberations of World Population Year 1974 and the World Population Conference.

BERNARD BERELSON

New York, New York
June 1973

The Authors

Bernard Berelson. President of the Population Council, New York.

IRELAND
Brendan M. Walsh. Senior Research Officer at the Economic and Social Research Institute in Dublin.

ISRAEL
Dov Friedlander. Associate Professor in Demography and Statistics and Chairman of the Department of Demography at the Hebrew University of Jerusalem.

FINLAND
Paavo Piepponen. Associate Professor of Sociology at the University of Kuopio.

SWEDEN
Lena Jonsson. Ministry of Health and Social Affairs in Stockholm.

BULGARIA
Ivan Stefanov. Member of the Bulgarian Academy of Sciences.
Nicola Naoumov. Director of the Scientific Research Institute of Statistics, Sofia.

GREECE
Nicolas C. Louros. Member of the Academy of Athens, Professor Emeritus of Obstetrics and Gynecology of the University of Athens, and President-Elect of the International College of Surgeons.
John Danezis. Director of Premarital and Marriage Counseling Center of the Hellenic Eugenic Society, Athens, and Assistant Professor of Obstetrics and Gynecology at the University of Athens.
Dimitrios Trichopoulos. Professor and Head of the Department of Hygiene and Epidemiology of the University of Athens Medical School.

BELGIUM
Louis Lohlé-Tart. Research Assistant in the Department of Demography
of the Catholic University of Louvain.

HUNGARY
Andras Klinger. Chief of the Population Statistics Department at the
Hungarian Central Statistical Office in Budapest and a member of
the IUSSP Council.

AUSTRALIA
W. D. Borrie. Director of the Research School of Social Sciences of the
Australian National University in Canberra.

THE NETHERLANDS
Philip van Praag. Professor of Demography and Political Science at
the Free University of Brussels.
Louis Lohlé-Tart. See Belgium.

CZECHOSLOVAKIA
Zdenek Pavlik. Associate Professor of Demography at Charles University
in Prague.
Vladimir Wynnyczuk. Head of the Department of Population Problems of
the Research Institute of Social Affairs in Prague.

ROMANIA
Petre Muresan. Director of the Computing and Health Statistics of the
Ministry of Health, Bucharest, and member of the Romanian National
Commission of Demography.
Ioan M. Copil. Doctor in economic sciences, Adviser in the Secretariat
and member of the National Commission of Demography.

SOUTH AFRICA
L. T. Badenhorst. Research Manager at SANLAM Life Assurance Company
in Sanlamhof.

CANADA
Jacques Henripin. Professor at the Department of Demography at the
University of Montreal.
Hervé Gauthier. Population and Health Sciences Division of the
International Development Research Centre in Ottawa.

ARGENTINA
Horacio David Gregoratti. Professor of Economic History at the Argentine
Museum University.
Carlos Luzzetti. Dean of the School of Economics of the National
University of Cuyo, Mendoza.

POLAND
Janusz A. Ziolkowski. Professor of Sociology at the University of Poznan.

SPAIN
Salustiano del Campo. Professor of Sociology at the University of Madrid.

FRANCE
Jean Bourgeois-Pichat. Chairman of the Committee for International Coordination of National Research in Demography (CICRED).

GREAT BRITAIN
John Simons. Sociologist with the population studies group of the London School of Hygiene and Tropical Medicine.

ITALY
Massimo Livi Bacci. Professor of Demography on the Faculty of Economics, University of Florence, and Director of the Department of Statistics.

WEST GERMANY
Hermann Schubnell. Director of the Federal Institute for Population Research in Wiesbaden.

JAPAN
Minoru Muramatsu. Chief of the Department of Public Health Demography at the Institute of Public Health in Tokyo.
Toshio Kuroda. Director of the Population Policy Division of the Institute of Population Problems in Tokyo.

UNITED STATES
Charles F. Westoff. Professor of Sociology and Demographic Studies, Associate Director of the Office of Population Research at Princeton University, and President of the Population Association of America.

SOVIET UNION
Dmitri I. Valentei. Professor at the University Center on the study of Population Problems, Faculty of Economics, Moscow State University.

Population Policy in Developed Countries

CHAPTER 1

Introduction

In recent years the "population problem" has become well-known. What is not so well-known is that the "population problem" has been recognized not only in developing countries but in developed as well. For the most part population issues have been identified with traditional, agrarian, poor countries like India rather than modern, industrial, rich countries like the United States. But there is now concern and attention in the latter too, not the same but still there. This is a report on population policy in twenty-four developed countries, prepared in each case by a national specialist.

Neither of the key terms in the title is easy to define with full precision, but their core meanings are reasonably clear. On the whole, "developed countries" is easier than "population policy."

DEVELOPED COUNTRIES

By "developed countries" we mean the industrialized, healthier, better educated, better off, more "modernized" societies—as a rough measure, those countries with annual per-capita incomes on the order of US$1,000 and above. As it happens, such countries also are distinguished by low fertility. There may be a few problems of classification at the margin but, given the complexity of the concept, not many; and in any case the "developed countries" in this volume are defined by enumeration.

1

The countries are included on two bases. First, the volume includes every one of the thirteen developed countries with 20 million or more population. Second, the volume includes eleven smaller countries of special interest in this connection: Australia on immigration grounds, Belgium for its ethnic division, Finland as a recently declining population, Greece for low fertility coupled with high emigration, Ireland for its distinctive demographic history, Israel on both immigration and ethnic grounds, the Netherlands in view of population density, Sweden as a pioneer in population policy, and the eastern European countries of Bulgaria, Czechoslovakia, and Hungary as socialist countries with low fertility. This is not to say that these countries are dealt with only in these special regards; they are considered more generally, just as the larger countries, but these are matters of particular demographic interest that led to their selection for this volume.

Taken together, these countries have a population of over one billion people, or about 95 percent of the total population of the developed world. From this standpoint they *are* the developed world.[1] They vary not only in size and density but also in national culture, religious practice, and political system. Moreover, they are geographically dispersed, on every continent.

Despite their variability in other respects, the countries do have a common demography: low growth rates and among the lowest birth and death rates in the world, especially in comparison with the developing countries, though more crowded than the latter (Table 1). They have consistently high life expectancies at birth (well over seventy years for females); high urbanization (the local definitions vary but about 70 percent "urban" in the median country); high levels of popular education (with virtually all of the children in primary school and large proportions in secondary school); higher age at marriage than the developing countries (early twenties as against the mid- or late teens); and high per-capita incomes (with a median of something over $2,000 per year, omitting a few for which comparative data are not available). Thus in standard of living, in education, and in health as well as in demography, these are the favored nations in the world today.

With regard to fertility these countries lead the world on the down side. Their total fertility rates[2] are, with a few exceptions, both low and

---

[1] For information, the only developed countries not included with populations of 4 million or more are East Germany (16.3), Portugal (9.7), Austria (7.5), Switzerland (6.4), Denmark (5.0), and Norway (4.0). East Germany was invited to participate in this collection of reports.

[2] The total fertility rate (TFR) is a measure of the average number of children a woman would have if she experienced the fertility of a cross-section of women at the time of measurement—that is, a rough approximation of completed family size. Replacement for most of these countries is about 2.1 or 2.2. I am indebted to Michael Teitelbaum of Princeton University for most of the data on TFRs for these countries.

TABLE 1.

Country Characteristics (latest available data, 1970–1972)

Country	Population (millions)	Density (pop./sq. km.)	Birth Rate (per 1,000 pop.)	Death Rate (per 1,000 pop.)
Ireland	3.0	43	22.8	10.6
Israel	3.1	152	28.2	7.0
Finland	4.6	14	12.7	9.6
Sweden	8.1	19	14.1	10.2
Bulgaria	8.7	77	16.3	9.1
Greece	8.8	68	16.3	8.3
Belgium	9.7	340	14.4	12.3
Hungary	10.3	111	14.5	11.9
Australia	12.7	2	21.7	8.7
Netherlands	13.4	394	16.2	8.5
Czechoslovakia	14.3	113	17.0	10.9
Romania	20.7	87	18.8	9.1
South Africa	21.5	18	38.2	13.7
Canada	21.6	2.4	16.7	7.4
Argentina	23.4	8	20.9	8.4
Poland	32.8	105	17.2	8.7
Spain	34.0	62	19.6	8.9
France	51.3	93	17.1	10.7
Great Britain	53.8	235	16.1	11.6
Italy	55.2	178	16.8	9.7
West Germany	61.7	248	11.3	11.7
Japan	105.0	284	19.7	6.6
United States	210.0	22	15.4	9.4
Soviet Union	248.6	11	17.8	8.2
Median country (approx.)	20	90	17	9
Developing world (approx.)	6	35	40	15

apparently still declining in 1970 (Figure 1). The postwar rates are remarkably similar by various groupings: in western Europe, reasonably steady to the mid-1960s and then uniformly down; in eastern Europe, sharply down since the 1950s but with a recent upturn, particularly as a result of the sudden withdrawal of legalized abortion in Romania; the baby boom and then down in Australia, Canada, and the United States; and the distinctive residual case of Japan. Overall, the differences tend to be narrowing and a rough convergence on low rates seems in process, with at least a third of the countries at or below replacement in the early 1970s.

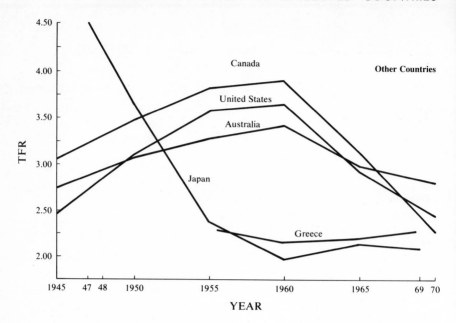

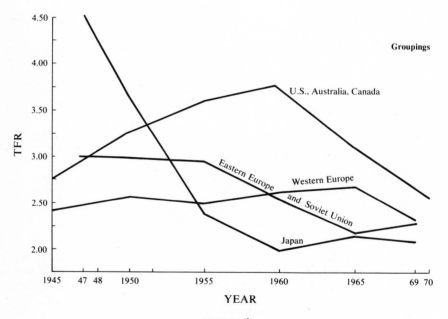

FIGURE 1

Total Fertility Rates (TFR)

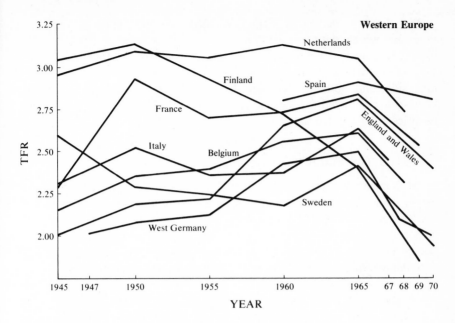

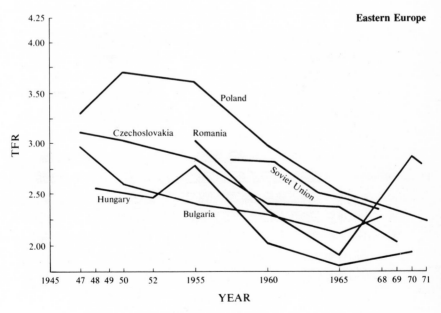

FIGURE 1 (continued)

And that is reflected in births by parity. In the median country (of those for which data are available) about 40 percent of annual births these years are first births and only about 15 percent are fourth or higher (Figure 2), with only Ireland and Israel as the major exceptions on the high side, and both of them are declining. And that means that childbearing is completed for most women at a relatively early age, in the late twenties or early thirties.

POPULATION POLICY

What is meant by "population policy?" As noted, that is more difficult to define than development. There can be a narrow definition referring only to the policies explicitly adopted by governments for their (presumed) demographic consequences; and there can be a broad definition referring not only to such policies but also to those policies that actually do influence demographic events, or even those that are perceived to do so.

The narrow definition of explicit intent is reasonably clear and relatively easy to apply, but in most countries it misses the major demographic consequences of governmental actions. The broad definition, on the other

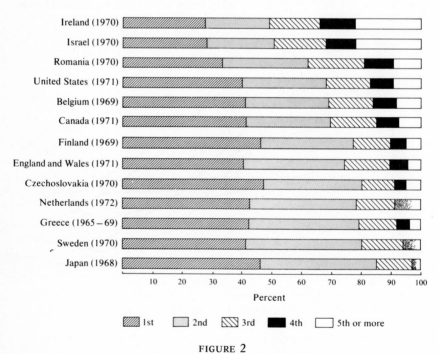

FIGURE 2

Annual Births by Birth Order

hand, runs the danger of including virtually all governmental actions—for example, education policy or military service that can affect marital age and hence birth rates, health policies that can affect mortality rates, housing policies that can affect nuptiality as well as family size, highway construction that can influence the distribution of population, civil rights programs to equalize ethnic differentials that can affect demographic performance, policies on women's employment that can influence birth rates up or down, and so on through a long list. It is not easy to draw a sharp or consistently applicable line between the too narrow and the too broad, and in any case it is probably not necessary to do so.

In the main, we deal with governmental policies that are directly intended to affect demographic events (for example, the subsidized dispersal of industry to build up certain areas and relieve others, the provision of children's allowances in some countries, the withdrawal of legalized abortion); governmental policies that are taken primarily for other reasons but with demographic factors taken into some account (for example, regulations on the availability of modern contraception); and governmental policies taken without explicit demographic intent but with nontrivial demographic consequences, actual or perceived (for example, the limited provision of public housing, children's assistance programs in other countries, laws on age at marriage). And by "demographic events" we refer to population size, rates of population change (births, deaths, and migration), the internal distribution of population, and population composition or structure.

Based on that core, the individual papers adapt the definitional boundaries to their own situations, and somewhat differing definitions do show through the following papers, based on local circumstances. Finally, these reports are limited to domestic population policies. Although several of the countries have governmental programs to assist developing countries in the population field, they are not covered here.

In view of the coverage, the current population policies of these twenty-four countries comprise, in effect, the population policy of the developed world as of the early 1970s. This last phrase perhaps needs underlining, for in the nature of the case the situations described in this volume represent a cross-section in time, subject to change with changing conditions. Thus there is some topicality in this series of presentations that is inevitable on a subject of this character. Demographic and demographic-related matters do change and policies change with them—these days, rather rapidly. This is the picture as of this time.

The following chapters, then, report on the current state of "population policy" in the several countries, arranged in order of size from the smallest to the largest. Those presentations are then followed by a summary chapter that tries to present an overall picture.

CHAPTER 2

Ireland

Brendan M. Walsh

ABSTRACT

A century of declining population, caused by high emigration, has colored Irish thinking on population issues. The basic criterion by which economic policies have been judged since the foundation of an independent Irish state in 1922 has been the ability to lower the emigration rate and reverse the population decline. The disadvantages attendant on low population density combined with a reduction in total numbers are always emphasized by Irish commentators; these include high overhead costs in the provision of many social and economic services, limited opportunities for economic growth based on the domestic market, and a general lack of optimism about the country's prospects. This last factor may be attributed to the low marriage rate which, in view of Ireland's high marriage fertility, served as an important check on the birth rate. The fact that one-quarter to one-third of each cohort of Irish men and women remained in lifelong celibacy was seen both as a reflection of the restricted economic prospects available to young people in Ireland and as a factor generating pessimism and an atmosphere not conducive to economic growth.

The most important element in an Irish "population policy" has, therefore, been the effort to develop the economy. Other measures, more readily identifiable as demographic in nature, have been of secondary importance. Chief among these has been a strict ban on the sale or importation of contraceptives* or literature relating to contraception and an absolute pro-

---

* See note on page 22.

hibition on abortion and divorce. Welfare payments, public housing subsidies, and the income tax system all embody many features designed to provide financial support to parents. Of these, income tax concessions are the most significant, but their impact is somewhat curtailed by the relatively unimportant role of taxes on income in the Irish fiscal system. The effect of these measures on demographic behavior is probably not very great and certainly was not an important consideration.

In recent years, Ireland's demographic development has given rise to new emphases in debates on population questions. The rise in the marriage rate and the fall in emigration since 1960 have reduced concern with stagnation. The regional concentration of the population in the Dublin area has provoked a limited government response in the form of an effort to decentralize industrial growth. The acceptance of the pill by apparently large numbers of married women as a means of contraception has been accompanied by widespread demands for a change in the laws prohibiting all other forms of contraception in Ireland. The changed structure of the population—especially the growing proportion of young married couples—seems to have generated a climate favorable to new social policies affecting demographic behavior. The growing number of Irish women making use of Britain's liberalized abortion facilities has drawn attention to the need for family planning services in Ireland. It is likely that in the coming years laws and policies will gradually be altered to reflect the new realities.

INTRODUCTION: HISTORICAL BACKGROUND

The burden of history seems to weigh heavily on Irish thinking about population problems. A fascination with the "uniqueness" of the Irish experience over the last 150 years has tended to distract attention from the extent to which our demographic history has elements in common with that of the rest of western Europe. Since the mid-nineteenth century, Irish[1] population has become increasingly concentrated in urban areas; both the Irish birth and death rates have declined, with the birth rate tending (until recently, at least) to fall more rapidly than the death rate, thus leading to a decline in the rate of natural increase; average family size is no longer near the natural maximum, as it was in early nineteenth-century Ireland; and as the fertility of marriage has declined, differentials have emerged between socioeconomic groups within the country. All these developments

[1] Throughout this paper, unless otherwise specified, the terms "Ireland" and "Irish" refer to the area that is now the Republic of Ireland. The remaining six counties of the island are referred to as "Northern Ireland." The island was partitioned into these areas in 1922.

have occurred in Ireland at about the same time and to the same extent as they occurred in other parts of Europe.

Nonetheless, there are several aspects of Ireland's demographic development that are unique, and the manner in which the general trends were achieved in Ireland has colored thinking on population problems. Urbanization has been caused more by a drastic decline in the rural Irish population than by a growth of urban centers in Ireland; even in 1844, Engels could write about the condition of the working classes in England by studying the Irish in Manchester, and after the famines of 1846–1849, a steady stream of emigrants from rural Ireland ensured that urbanization of the Irish took place to a large extent in British and American cities. The depopulation of the Irish countryside was severe and was not offset, at least over the period 1841–1936, by any concomitant growth in the urban population of Ireland. (In Northern Ireland, the Belfast region is an example of the growth of a new metropolis caused by the industrialization of an area.) These trends are reflected in the fact that, in 1971, the population of the predominantly rural province of Connacht was only 28 percent of its level

TABLE 1.

Population in 1971 as Percentage of Population
in 1841, Ireland (by county)

County	Percentage	County	Percentage
Leinster	75.9	**Connacht**	27.6
Carlow	39.7	Galway	33.9
Dublin	228.6	Leitrim	18.3
Kildare	62.9	Mayo	28.2
Kilkenny	30.4	Roscommon	21.1
Laois	29.4	Sligo	27.8
Longford	24.5		
Louth	58.4	**Ulster (3 counties)**	28.0
Meath	39.0	Cavan	21.6
Offaly	35.3	Donegal	36.5
Westmeath	37.9	Monaghan	23.1
Wexford	42.7		
Wicklow	52.6	**Republic of Ireland**	45.6
		Antrim	121.3
		Armagh	57.2
Munster	36.8	Down	85.9
Clare	26.2	Belfast City	503.1
Cork	41.3	Fermanagh	31.9
Kerry	38.4	(London) Derry	81.9
Limerick	42.6	Tyrone	44.4
Tipperary	28.4		
Waterford	39.4	**Northern Ireland**	92.8

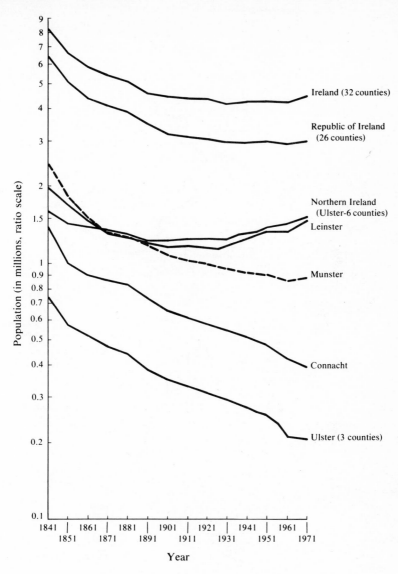

FIGURE 1

Population of Ireland by Province, 1841–1971

in 1841 (see Table 1 and Figures 1 and 2). The county and city of Dublin, however, have grown, if not spectacularly at least steadily, and in 1971, the population was over twice their 1841 level. This combination of moderate growth in the Dublin region and severe depopulation in the west has led to a very rapid rise in the concentration of national popula-

FIGURE 2

Population of Ireland in 1971 as a Percentage of the Population
in 1841, by County

tion in Dublin. In 1841, only 5.7 percent of the population lived in the Dublin region, compared with 28.6 percent in 1971.

The fall of the Irish birth rate was caused by some very idiosyncratic features of Irish population history. Irish marriage rates declined steadily (although not uniformly throughout the country) from a fairly high level at the beginning of the nineteenth century until a nadir was reached in the 1930s (see Table 2). At this time, about one-quarter of each cohort of Irishwomen and one-third of each cohort of Irishmen remained unmarried throughout their lives, while the average age of those who married was about thirty-four for grooms and twenty-eight for brides.[2] In the farming community, the marriage rate was even lower than suggested by these figures. This remarkable record of low nuptiality was not accompanied by high illegitimacy rates, and the evidence suggests that Ireland emerged from the nineteenth century exemplifying to an extraordinary degree the Malthusian "preventative check" on population growth, namely, "restraint from marriage which is not followed by irregular gratifications" [1].[3] Fertility of marriage declined in Ireland from a level near the natural maximum at the beginning of the nineteenth century, but toward the end of the century, British fertility was falling more rapidly than Irish, and at the turn of the twentieth century, Ireland was remarkable not only for its low nuptiality but also for its relatively high fertility. This combination of marriage and fertility patterns led to a decline in the birth rate from an average of 26 per 1,000 per year in the 1860s to less than 20 per 1,000 per year in the 1930s (see Table 2). The Irish death rate was already fairly low by European standards in the late nineteenth century, since the absence of vast urban slums moderated the incidence of infectious diseases, and Ireland's infant mortality rate was lower than Britain's until the 1930s. However, the decline in the birth rate outpaced the decline in the death rate, and consequently, the rate of natural increase fell from almost 10 per 1,000 per year in the 1860s to only 5 per 1,000 per year in the 1930s. In the 1930s, the net reproduction rate stood at 1.19, not much above replacement, thus illustrating the effectiveness of a very low marriage rate in counteracting high fertility of marriage. Neither the marriage nor fertility rates were, however, crucial to the rate of change of the population; throughout the century preceding 1961, the emigration rate consistently exceeded the rate of natural increase, and consequently, the population of the country declined steadily. This decline in national population is the

---

[2] These figures relate, of course, to those who remained in Ireland and, since emigration was very heavy, therefore exclude a sizable proportion of each birth cohort.

[3] Some of the cultural and social aspects of the adjustment to the low marriage rate have been explored in Connell's fascinating essays [2].

TABLE 2.

Average Annual Vital Rates, Ireland, 1871–1971
(per 1,000 population in twenty-six counties)

Period	Marriage Rate (1)	Birth Rate (2)	Death Rate (3)	Rate of Natural Increase (2) − (3) = (4)	Rate of Population Growth (5)	Estimated Net Emigration Rate (4) − (5) = (6)
1871–1880	4.5	26.3	18.1	8.3	−4.7	13.0
1881–1890	4.0	22.9	17.6	5.3	−11.6	16.9
1891–1900	4.5	22.2	17.7	4.5	−7.7	12.2
1901–1911	4.8	22.4	16.8	5.6	−2.6	8.2
1911–1926	5.0	21.1	16.0	5.2	−3.7	8.8
1926–1936	4.6	19.6	14.2	5.5	−0.1	5.6
1936–1946	5.4	20.3	14.5	5.9	−0.4	6.3
1946–1951	5.5	22.2	13.6	8.6	+0.4	8.2
1951–1956	5.4	21.3	12.2	9.2	−4.3	13.4
1956–1961	5.4	21.2	11.9	9.2	−5.6	14.8
1961–1966	5.7	21.9	11.7	10.3	+4.6	5.7
1966–1971	6.5	21.3	11.2	10.1	+6.4	3.7

most extraordinary aspect of Ireland's demographic history and is without parallel in modern history.[4] One possible interpretation of this period is to regard the decline in Irish population as part of the redistribution of population within a western European/North American labor market. It has been argued by Crotty that the adjustment of the Irish economy to a rise in the relative profitability of cattle grazing, as opposed to tillage, played a key role in these developments [3].

Since the 1930s, the historical trend of many demographic variables has been reversed in Ireland. Nuptiality has risen; fertility has declined; and with the exception of the years 1951–1961, the emigration rate has fallen. Since 1961, a sustained growth in population has occurred for the first time in 120 years. The pace of this transformation has accelerated in recent years.[5] The record of the century following the famine must, however, be kept in mind when examining contemporary Irish attitudes and policies toward demographic issues.

ATTITUDES TOWARD THE IRISH EXPERIENCE

A consensus exists among commentators that the demographic history of Ireland since 1841 is an indictment of the administrators, politicians, and political economists who tried to deal with the fundamental economic weaknesses of the country. Above all, the continued decline of population after the formation of an independent Irish state in 1922 raised the question in some minds as to whether or not Ireland was "economically viable" outside some larger economic unit. One historian, in a commentary on the economic policies of the newly formed state, noted "worst of all, the government had not succeeded in arresting the decline in population" [4, p. 598]. The continuing decline of the rural and especially of the farming population was in stark contrast with the general social objectives of the new state. Article 45, 2.v, of the Constitution enacted in 1937 laid down that:

The State shall, in particular, direct its policy toward securing that there may be established on the land in economic security as many families as in the circumstances shall be practicable.

Even more optimistic aims were expressed by the leaders of the Nationalist movement. Two weeks before the 1916 rising, Patrick Pearse wrote:

[4] East Germany is now experiencing a decline in population and a comparison of its experience with the Irish would be instructive.
[5] These developments are discussed in more detail below.

In a free Ireland . . . gracious and useful rural industries will supplement an improved agriculture, the population will expand in a century to 20 million and it may even in time go up to 30 million (quoted by Meenan [5, p. 332]).

After independence, however, the decline in population and in the farm labor force continued unabated. The population of the state fell from almost exactly 3 million in 1922 to its lowest level of 2.8 million in 1961. The numbers engaged in agriculture fell from 644,000 in 1926 to 331,000 in 1966.

Whereas, in other countries, population growth might be sought as a source of military strength or political influence, in Ireland, a growing population was avidly desired as evidence that the experiment of nationalism and independence had not failed. We may surmise the impact of demographic events on Ireland's role in European affairs simply by recalling that, in 1800, the population of all Ireland equaled about 50 percent that of Britain, but by 1961, it had fallen to a mere 9 percent of the British total. In the 1950s, the political unimportance of Ireland to any but the Irish and their immediate neighbors was taken for granted, even welcomed, in Ireland, and the public was concerned lest the demographic weakness which had led to eclipse would result in extinction. (One popular set of essays published in 1954 was entitled *The Vanishing Irish*.) The only reassuring corollary of these developments was the awareness of the strength and influence of the emigrant Irish and their descendants.[6]

We are fortunate in having the *Reports* of the Commission on Emigration and Other Population Problems, 1948–1954 [6], as a compendium of views on the causes and consequences of Irish population patterns. Writing in the immediate postwar period, the members of this commission were naturally influenced by the demographic situation of that time. The authors of the *Reports* not only distilled the main elements in the debate on Ireland's problems, they also provided a statistical survey that has won this document a permanent place in world demographic literature.

The establishment of the commission was an admission of the seriousness with which the Irish government viewed the continuing heavy emigration and decline in population. The commission was asked "to consider the desirability of formulating a national population policy," but this was clearly taken to refer primarily to a policy in regard to "emigration as the principal cause of the decline in population during the past century and of the failure of the population to increase appreciably in recent years"

---

[6] It has been estimated that total net emigration from Ireland since the 1840s amounts to almost 6 millon people. In 1931, there were 1.6 million Irish-born people living outside Ireland, compared with the 4.2 million living in Ireland (both parts) [6, table 95].

[6 (1)].⁷ The majority report stated "in our view a strongly increasing population should occupy a high place among the criteria by which the success of a national economic policy should be judged" [6 (472)]. The *Reports* contain ample discussion of why a declining population, especially when it is the consequence of low nuptiality and high emigration, is undesirable. The main themes stressed (especially in Chapter 9) were:

(1) Population growth encourages a "dominant attitude" of "buoyancy and activity rather than inertia." The "demographic background of Ireland tended rather to retard progress and to induce in the minds of many people an attitude of helplessness and hopelessness" [6 (462, 463)]. Nonetheless, the view that "the survival of the nation was in jeopardy" due to existing demographic trends was firmly rejected [6 (459)].

(2) A declining population leads to high overhead costs in the provision of many social services and discourages investment and economic risk-taking. An increasing population, on the other hand, "broadens the scope for progress in every section of human activity." However, these benefits are mentioned only in the context of a country that is not "over populated," as the commissioners clearly believe Ireland was not [6 (462)]. The absence in Ireland "of the pressure of an increasing population operating to force the pace of development" was regretted [6 (308)].

(3) Heavy emigration distorts the age structure of the population by raising the proportion in the "old dependent" age group. The greater propensity of young women to leave the rural areas distorted the sex ratio of these areas, further depressing the marriage rate. Emigration also reduced the sense of urgency concerning economic development and tended to produce an environment "unfavourable to the development of the latent potentialities of the population" [6 (314)]. It is interesting, however, that in this section the commissioners rejected any suggestion that a "brain drain" was occurring, stating their belief (in the absence of statistical evidence on the subject) that "the intrinsic quality of those who in each generation remain in the country is at least as high as that of those that emigrate." Both sides of the complex "brain drain" debate were argued with great subtlety by the commissioners long before this issue became commonplace in the economic and demographic literature. Concern was expressed that many Irish emigrants, from a rural background and relatively uneducated, suffered serious hardship in adjusting to the environment outside Ireland.

(4) The low marriage rate and late age at marriage were considered "undesirable," symptomatic either "of a wrong attitude among the people toward marriage or of material conditions unfavourable to marriage" [6 (457)]. "Ireland's low marriage rate over such a long period has had an unfavourable effect on the outlook of young people and has contributed to discontent, unsettlement, and emigration" [6 (161)] and led to an "insufficient development of the community's sense of responsibility" [6 (162, 163)]. Encouragement of the marriage rate was, thus,

---

⁷ Numbers in parentheses refer to paragraphs in the majority report [6].

high on the list of priorities for a population policy as seen by the commissioners.

Some aspects of these viewpoints call for comment. In the first place, it is interesting to see that the commissioners rejected any suggestion that emigration should be curbed forcibly. They acknowledged the extent to which higher standards of living among both the migrant and nonmigrant populations were attributable to emigration: Reduced unemployment, higher wages, and increased average farm size were among the benefits to the nonmigrant population cited [6 (313)]. The economic motivation was clearly acknowledged, emigration being viewed as an intelligent response to low wages and poor prospects at home and ready access to the wealthy economies of the United States and Britain.[8] The solution to the emigration problem favored by the commission was not a ban on movement out of the country but rather the achievement of higher standards of living in Ireland through "intensive economic development within the country" [6 (471)].

The report emphasized the contrast between the (static) benefits to the country from the high emigration rate (reduced unemployment, higher wages, and so forth) and the (dynamic) disadvantages it entailed (reduced chances of successful intensive economic development). The most urgent task of Irish policy makers was seen as the need to break the vicious circle whereby poverty bred emigration and emigration hindered economic development. No attempt was made to define an "optimum" population for Ireland, but any idea that there was a "natural" limit in the region of 3 million people was firmly rejected by the commissioners [6 (436)].

In connection with the commissioners' sense of urgency in regard to raising the marriage rate, their views on marriage fertility require careful study. The ideal of the large family is implicit throughout the majority report and explicit in several passages. Commenting on the (relatively mild) decline in Irish family size since 1911, the commissioners stated "this downward trend in size of family is unwelcome and every effort should be made to arrest it" [6 (211)]. It was felt that the existing system of children's allowances and income tax relief helped to ease the burden of a large family (in any event, "for a comparatively short period in a man's whole earning life"). The idea that "our family pattern imposes an undue strain on mothers in general" was rejected [6 (212)]. Above all, notions of family planning or fertility control "either from selfish or purely materi-

---

[8] In his reservation to the report, A. Fitzgerald could not "accept that a high rate of emigration is necessarily a sign of national decline or that policy should be over-anxious to reduce it. . . . High emigration . . . releases social tensions that would otherwise explode and makes possible a stability of manners and customs which would otherwise be the subject of radical change."

alistic motives which are morally indefensible, or by the use of contraceptives or artificial means, or by other methods which are contrary to the natural law" were utterly condemned [6 (458)]. The possibility that the fear of large families and the prohibition on divorce deterred many people from marriage was considered and rejected: "No convincing evidence has been put before us in support of this view" [6 (166)].

The measures suggested by the majority report to stimulate the marriage rate do not appear, in retrospect, very significant in relation to the urgency with which the low marriage rate was discussed. Increased housing subsidies and the removal of any ban on the employment of married women were the only direct measures suggested to encourage marriages. Beyond these measures, the commission looked to its general rcommendations concerning the economic development of the country to help break down the age-old reluctance to marry. It is interesting that much of the evidence cited in the majority report on social-class differentials in marriage and fertility rates has subsequently been used in support of the hypothesis of a causal link between large family size and low marriage rates [7]. The consequences for emigration and/or unemployment of maintaining (or even increasing) average family size while at the same time attaining a more normal proportion living in the married state were not seriously discussed in the majority report. In some of the reservations and addenda, especially those by Collis and Marsh, some of these issues were raised, and one voice (that of A. A. Luce) was raised in favor of at least considering the case for contraception.

The commission's skepticism concerning the existence of a "brain drain" might be less easy to maintain if the report were being written today. Although the issue remains an unsettled and controversial one, the association between high emigration and high rates of hospitalization for mental illness is now well-documented in Ireland [8], and this finding may be cited as a further reason why high emigration rates should not be tolerated.

In some more detailed aspects of the problems raised, the commissioners failed to draw inferences that seem very important today. The question of the impact of high fertility on the proportion in the "young dependent" age groups was not discussed, although the impact of emigration on the "old dependent" group was considered. Ireland now has the highest level of dependency in Europe, due to an unusual combination of moderately high old dependency and very high young dependency. The implications of a high burden of dependency on savings and capital formation were not spelled out. The adverse effects of a low population density were not always clearly distinguished from those of a stable or declining population. The possibility of a healthy export trade's allowing a country to gain the benefits otherwise only conferred by a large domestic market was not adequately discussed.

On the question of mortality, the commission drew attention to the relatively high life expectancy enjoyed by the Irish population, especially in rural areas. Attention was drawn, however, to the comparatively small differential between male and female mortality, a point that has recently been explored at length by Kennedy, who believes that "the high female mortality compared with male was due, at least in part, to the subordinate status of females in the rural areas, and of daughters in the Irish family system" [9, Chap. 3]. Infant mortality is currently 18 per 1,000 live births per year, and although by no means the lowest in western Europe, it has been falling steadily, and its level does not attract a great deal of attention in policy statements on health matters.

The Commission on Emigration and Other Population Problems had a unique opportunity to review Irish attitudes toward population problems in the immediate postwar years. No comparable source is available in connection with contemporary attitudes, and to the extent that change has occurred, this must be inferred from a variety of sources. It is unquestionable that change has occurred on the economic front and in the broader environment. The years immediately after the publication of the commission's *Reports* in 1954 were marked, ironically, by a sharp rise in emigration (see Table 2). Employment declined not only in agriculture but also in industries and services. The old question of the "viability" of the Irish economy was raised with renewed cogency. The publication by the government of a report on *Economic Development* [10], in response to this crisis and to the longer-term issue of promoting economic growth, is generally cited as a watershed in Irish history. This document advocated a new departure in economic policy, to be based on a vigorous expansion of export markets, increased foreign investment in Irish industry, and a shift of public expenditure from "social" to "directly productive" investment. Once again, the need to reduce emigration and to provide all with a chance to obtain acceptable employment in Ireland was stressed:

After 35 years of native government, people are asking whether we can achieve an acceptable degree of economic progress. The common talk among parents in the towns, as in rural Ireland, is of their children having to emigrate as soon as their education is completed in order to be sure of a reasonable livelihood. . . . There is therefore a real need at present to buttress confidence in the country's future and to stimulate the interest and enthusiasm of the young in particular [*10*, chap. 1, par. 12].

LAWS AND POLICIES OF DEMOGRAPHIC RELEVANCE

¶ THE CONSTITUTION

Before turning to the course of economic and demographic events since 1958, it will be helpful to summarize the contemporary legal and institutional framework as far as it impinges explicitly or implicitly on demographic matters. The 1937 Constitution contains a provision that "no law shall be enacted providing for the grant of a dissolution of marriage" (Article 41.3.2°). In addition, one section stresses the family as the "natural, primary, and fundamental unit group of Society" (Article 41.1.1°), and another stresses that, ideally, mothers should not have to work outside the home: "The State shall endeavour to ensure that mothers shall not be obliged by economic necessity to engage in labour to the neglect of their duties in the home" (Article 41.2.2°).

In December 1972, the fifth amendment to the Constitution was approved by 84 percent of those voting in the referendum. This amendment deleted two sections of Article 44, the most important provision of which was to recognize the "special position" of the Roman Catholic church as the "guardian of the Faith professed by the great majority of the citizens." The significance of this amendment in general, and for population policies in particular, is hard to foresee, but it is unlikely to be very great, since these sections had never been invoked in support of legislation affecting population.

¶ ABORTION
Under the existing criminal law, induced abortion is regulated by the Offenses Against the Person Act of 1861 (enacted by the British government when Ireland was part of the United Kingdom and carried over into Irish law). Under this act, any attempt to induce abortion by any means is a felony and on conviction punishable by penal servitude for life. Any person who supplies or procures the means of abortion is guilty of a misdemeanor. Prosecutions for induced abortion are exceedingly rare in Ireland: Only one case each in 1968 and 1969 is reported as known to the police [11]. There is no reason to believe that illegal abortion is anything other than rare. No deaths have been registered as occurring from the side effects of induced abortion in recent years [12; 13]. The question of abortion among the Irish in Britain is discussed below.

¶ CONTRACEPTION
By far the most conspicuous Irish law relating to demographic matters is the Criminal Law (Amendment) Act of 1935. Section 17 of this act makes it unlawful to "sell or expose, offer, advertise or keep for sale, or to import or attempt to import into the State for sale any contraceptive." A contraceptive is defined for the purposes of the act as "any appliance, instrument, drug, preparation or thing designed, prepared or intended to prevent pregnancy resulting from sexual intercourse between human beings." This

section of the act also added contraceptives to the list of items prohibited under the Customs Consolidation Act of 1876, so that importation for personal use is also illegal. Allied to these provisions, the Censorship of Publications Acts of 1929 and 1946 prohibit the publishing, sale, and distribution of books or periodicals that "advocate the unnatural prevention of conception." Taken together, these laws constitute a very strict and comprehensive prohibition on the importation and sale of contraceptives or literature relating to contraception.* It should, however, be noted that the law does not deal with the use of contraceptives.

The background to Section 17 of the 1935 act remains somewhat obscure. The author of the standard study of church-state relations in modern Ireland considers this act as one where "consultation between government and the [Roman Catholic] hierarchy would appear to have been probable, but where I have no evidence that it actually took place" [14, p. 365]. The main purpose of the act was to "make further and better provision for the protection of young girls and the suppression of brothels and prostitution." Section 17 contained the only wholly new provision in the act, and the impetus to include this section appears to have come from a report of a committee on vice that has never been published [see 15].

¶ SOCIAL WELFARE POLICY

Children's allowances were introduced in Ireland in 1944, a year earlier than their introduction in the United Kingdom. In the early years, they were payable only for third and subsequent children, but they have been extended to second children since 1952 and to first children since 1963. They are payable to all parents, without an income qualification. The allowance is £2.00 per month for the first child, £3.00 for the second, and £3.75 for each subsequent eligible child; thus, a married man with four young children receives £12.50 per month in allowances, which is about a 9 percent increase in his gross earnings if he is a typical industrial worker.[9] Similarly, old-age pensions, unemployment benefits and assistance, and other welfare payments are related to the number of children dependent on the recipient. A married person entitled to unemployment insurance benefits, for example, receives (as of July 1973) £43.20 per month if he has no dependent children and £70.00 if he has four dependent children (or a total of £82.50 including children's allowances). It is probably accurate

---

* NOTE: In mid-December 1973 the Irish Supreme Court held unconstitutional the 40-year-old ban on importation of contraceptives. Advertising and sale remain illegal, although the Senate is considering a bill to permit both.

[9] In June 1972, the average monthly earnings of an adult male industrial worker were £120. As of January 1, 1973, £1 equaled approximately US$2.35.

to say that these allowances were introduced, and continue to be paid, not with a view to their impact on family size but rather as an attempt to provide economic support to parents, especially those with large families.

Despite its emphasis on the need to raise the marriage rate, the Commission on Emigration and Other Population Problems did not favor the payment of cash grants on marriage, believing that such grants were "largely ineffective" [6 (174)]. Nonetheless, since 1929, a small benefit (at present £10.00 maximum) is payable to insured women on marriage. Some employers (notably in the public sector) have a policy of giving a grant proportional to years of service to women retiring to get married. In the public service, married men are generally paid at a higher rate than single men in the same grade.[10] The state also pays a maternity grant of £4.00 and a maternity allowance of £22.20 a month for three months to insured women on their confinement. "This allowance is intended to relieve her of the necessity of working immediately prior and subsequent to the confinement" [16, p. 45]. (The average monthly earnings of female industrial workers was £57.60 in March 1972.)

¶ INCOME TAX

The income tax code takes into account the marital status of the taxpayer and the number of children in the household. An evaluation of these allowances is complex, since the possible effect of marriage on the labor force status of the woman must also be considered. An illustration of the tax and social welfare system is shown in Table 3.

It may be seen that, if both husband and wife continue to work after marriage, their combined net income will be slightly lower than if they had remained single (compare line 6 with line 3 in Table 3). This feature of the Irish tax laws is criticized frequently by those interested in raising the present very low participation rate among married women. Even when there are four children, a wife in paid employment raises the net income of the household by only two-thirds of her gross earnings.

On the other hand, the presence of four children in the family considerably reduces the tax liability of the married couple. In the case where the wife is not working, the net income of the family with four children is 22 percent higher than that of the childless family (line 15 as percent of line 9). If the wife is working, the presence of four children raises the net income of the household by 16 percent (line 12 as percent of line 6). If we take the combined net incomes of a single man and woman as 100, the fol-

---

[10] But this system is now being phased out with the implementation of an equal-pay policy. There is also an increase of £100 in the income tax allowance for the year in which a man marries.

TABLE 3.

Effect of Income Tax and Social Welfare Contributions and
Benefits on Income, Ireland, October 1972 (in £)

	Gross Income[a]	Net Income[b]
Single persons		
1. Man	1,500	1,156
2. Woman	700	570
3. Combined	2,200	1,726
Married couple		
No children, wife working full time		
4. Husband	1,500	1,263
5. Wife	700	430
6. Combined	2,200	1,698
No children, wife not working		
7. Husband	1,500	1,225
8. Wife	—	—
9. Combined	1,500	1,225
Four children, wife working full time		
10. Husband	1,500	1,515
11. Wife	700	457
12. Combined	2,200	1,972
Four children, wife not working		
13. Husband	1,500	1,498
14. Wife	—	—
15. Combined	1,500	1,498

[a] The gross income figures are based on the average earnings of adult industrial workers, December 1971.

[b] Net income is gross income less income tax and social welfare contributions, but including social welfare benefits. All children assumed to be less than eleven years old.

lowing are the net incomes of families in the various circumstances of Table 3:

	Wife Working Full Time	Wife Not Working
No children	98	71
Four children	114	87

Thus, it may be seen that in Ireland, as in most European countries, the income tax system takes account of family size in assessing income tax liability, and this results in a significant increase in the take-home income of those with children. It is probably accurate to say that this arrangement reflects a desire to link tax liability to some notion of "ability to pay" rather than representing an attempt to influence demographic behavior by fiscal incentives. The effectiveness of these income tax concessions must be evaluated in the light of the fact that an unusually low proportion (less than 30 percent) of the Irish central government's current revenue is derived from taxes on income. Receipts from taxes on expenditures (principally, customs duties and value-added tax) exceed receipts from income taxes by 75 percent, but no concessions of a demographic nature (such as zero rating for food or children's clothes) are made in the administration of taxes on expenditures.[11]

¶ HEALTH

The various health acts contain numerous provisions that are, at least indirectly, relevant to population policy. The most famous controversy involving the Roman Catholic hierarchy and the Irish government centered on the implementation of certain provisions of the 1947 Health Act. In 1950, the Minister of Health put forward a "mother and child scheme" for providing maternity and child-care facilities to all, free of charge, by the public health authorities. After the annual meeting of the Roman Catholic hierarchy in October a letter was sent to the *Taoiseach* (Prime Minister) protesting against certain aspects of the proposed scheme. The main objections derived from broad principles of social policy, in particular that "the right to provide for the health of children belongs to parents, not to the State." Objections were also raised to state clinics because "gynaecological care may be, and in some countries is, interpreted to include provision for birth limitation and abortion. We have no guarantee that State officials will respect Catholic principles in regard to these matters" [*14*, p. 404]. The Irish Medical Association also opposed the scheme. Eventually, this scheme was abandoned and the minister resigned. In 1953, a new government, after intricate consultation with the hierarchy, passed a new health act which gave the health authorities substantially the same powers sought earlier. However, guarantees were built into the act that no patient need submit himself to anything "contrary to the teaching of his religion." A choice of doctors was also explicitly guaranteed. Since 1954, the scope of the public health services has expanded considerably, especially in the

---

[11] After the general election of March 1973, which resulted in a change of government, zero rating for food was introduced.

areas of child care and preventative medicine, and there has been no recurrence of the controversies that were so bitter in 1950.

¶ HOUSING

Housing policy has obvious demographic implications. One of the changes in emphasis that occurred in Irish economic policy after 1958 was a reduced emphasis on the housing program. Heavy emigration and a declining population even in urban areas had led to the belief that a slowing down in "housing and certain other forms of social investment will occur from now on because needs are virtually satisfied over wide areas of the State" [10, par. 9]. Between 1955 and 1961, public authority expenditures on housing declined from 3.4 to 2.0 percent of gross national product [17]. The belief that needs were "virtually satisfied" proved illusory, in part, perhaps, because of the success of the government's new economic policies. In particular, the accelerated expansion of the city and suburbs of Dublin (at a rate of almost 2 percent per year between 1961–1966) was sufficient to create severe shortages in the availability of housing units. In the 1960s, Ireland's rate of new housing construction was among the lowest in Europe, although the units being built were, on average, larger than those in other countries [see 18]. At the present time, there is a considerable shortage of public housing, especially in the Dublin area. In order to ration the available supply of public housing, family size is taken into account in allocating units. It is generally the case that a family with fewer than two children would not be allocated public housing in Dublin today, other than special units built for old-age pensioners. Once again, the philosophy behind this policy is not explicitly demographic but rather reflects the desire to help the neediest cases first. However, this policy does create an incentive for newly married couples to have two children as quickly as possible. The importance of this possibility from a national viewpoint may be gauged from the fact that about one-third of the urban population lives in public authority housing.[12] On the other hand, a person who purchases a (private) house can benefit in full from government building grants, property-tax relief, and income tax relief on mortgage interest paid, without regard to marital status or family size.[13] In fact, inasmuch as the single man or the couple with no children is likely to be paying high marginal

---

[12] In what appears to be significant change in policy on this issue, the Minister for Local Government, in a statement of December 13, 1972, told local authorities "that not less than 10 per cent of their housing output from 1973–74 onwards must be special dwellings suitable for small families, whose housing needs cannot normally be met within the existing schemes."

[13] Both the initial grant and the property tax relief are, however, no longer available for houses above a certain size limit.

income tax rates, the subsidy to private house purchase is inversely related to family size.

On the whole, specifically demographic issues have played a minor role in the evolution of Irish social welfare policy. With some exceptions, the philosophy of the Irish "welfare state" has been very strongly influenced by the British example. Within the constraints imposed by a lower level of economic development and an unfavorable population age structure, Ireland has followed the British model fairly closely. Membership in the European Economic Community implies that Ireland will be increasingly influenced by the philosophy and standards prevailing in the enlarged community.

CHANGE AND CONTROVERSY: THE 1960s

¶ ECONOMIC CHANGE

The annual average rate of net emigration declined from 14.8 per 1,000 in the period 1956–1961 to 5.7 between 1961–1966 and 3.7 per 1,000 between 1966–1971. At present, there is probably a net balance of zero between in and out movement. In the early and mid-1960s, this decline in emigration was due to the depletion of the numbers unemployed in Ireland by the heavy emigration of the 1950s combined with the expansion in Irish nonagricultural employment after 1958. In recent years, however, rising unemployment in Britain has played a major role in discouraging Irish workers from emigrating, and the growth of the population in Ireland has not been matched by an expansion of the labor force. Between 1961–1971, the population grew by 5.7 percent, but the numbers employed by only 1.8 percent. Table 4 gives a more detailed picture of these develop-

TABLE 4.

Labor Force in Ireland, 1961 and 1971 (in thousands)

	1961	1971
Total at work in agricultural occupations	379.5	282.0
Total at work in nonagricultural occupations	673.0	789.0
Total at work	1,052.5	1,071.0
Unemployed	55.6	68.0
Total labor force	1,108.1	1,139.0
Total not in labor force	1,710.2	1,839.0
Total population	2,818.3	2,978.2

SOURCE: See [12; 19].

ments. Thus, of the total population growth of 160,000 between 1961–1971, 129,000 (or 80 percent) appears to have been caused by the growth of the numbers not in the labor force. There may be as many as 40,000 more young people, aged 15–18 years, at school because of a change in the financing of postprimary education in 1968. The proportion of the population in the labor force declined from 39.3 to 38.2 percent between 1961 and 1971 and is now very low by European standards (the comparable figure in the United Kingdom is 45.7 percent). Although differences in definitions of the labor force influence these comparisons, the most important reason for Ireland's low rate is the high proportion of young people in the population. Despite this aspect of recent Irish population growth, the improvement in living standards that has accompanied the growth in population has been substantial: Between 1965–1970, for example, the annual average growth rate of gross national product per person (in constant prices) was 3.3 percent. The unemployment rate, however, has remained high, currently at almost 8 percent and above 5 percent in every year since 1960.

¶ REGIONAL POPULATION BALANCE

The proportion of the population of Ireland living in the Dublin area has grown in every intercensal period since 1841. The main reason for this concentration in the capital city has been its low rate of net emigration compared with the rest of the country (only in a few periods, notably 1961–1966, has Dublin experienced a net in-movement of population). However, the more favorable demographic experience of Dublin has over time given it a "healthier" age structure, resulting in a low death rate and a high birth rate. Thus, while almost one-third of the country's population now lives in the Dublin region, over 40 percent of the country's natural increase occurs among Dublin residents. (Some of the poorest counties in Ireland have, in recent years, recorded an excess of deaths over births.) The government's response to this imbalance has been a firm declaration of intent to hold Dublin's actual population growth to its rate of natural increase, thereby committing itself to a policy of zero net in-movement to the area. This would still allow Dublin to grow at an annual rate of 1.6 percent, 50 percent faster than the growth rate of the rest of the country, if it grew at its rate of natural increase.

In order to influence regional population growth patterns, the Industrial Development Authority (IDA), the main governmental agency responsible for industrial investment incentives, has, since 1969, accepted among its objectives "a substantial reduction in regional imbalances to be achieved by a greater dispersal of economic activity among the regions." To this end a strategy is adopted of providing employment opportunities within commuting distance of the job seeker's home community. . . . The development of small scale industry outside the major centres will play a key role in this regional development strategy [20, p. 3].

In order to achieve these goals, the IDA has adopted the tactic of using its incentive schemes "to send industry to depressed areas and as far as possible to keep the rural population where it is" [20, p. 9]. The most important regional incentive that the IDA uses is a nonrepayable cash grant equal to 60 percent of the project's establishment and development costs to industries locating in the designated areas of the west, compared with no grant for a Dublin location. One of the most important incentives offered to industrialists by the Irish government is tax relief on profits from exports, but this incentive is available regardless of where in Ireland the industry is located. Commercial and office developments are not affected by the IDA's regional policy, and no system of tax penalties or controls on location in the Dublin region has been introduced. The central government is itself highly localized in Dublin, with 74 percent of its employees residing in that city according to the 1966 census of population.

One of the factors militating against the success of efforts to correct regional imbalances in Ireland is the absence of a tradition of internal movements of population other than to Dublin or to contiguous counties. In 1961, 82.4 percent of the population was born in the county in which it was resident, and outside Dublin this proportion rises to 84.7 percent [21]. It often is remarked that a migrant from the west of Ireland would be more likely to join relatives or friends in Boston or Birmingham than to face the unknown by moving to Cork or Waterford.

¶ CHANGES IN MARRIAGE AND FERTILITY PATTERNS
Ireland's marriage patterns, already undergoing gradual change in the immediate postwar years, had been virtually transformed by the end of the 1960s. Between 1946 and 1969, the median age of grooms fell from thirty-two to twenty-six and of brides from twenty-seven to twenty-four years. The marriage rate per 1,000 unmarried population aged 15–64 rose from 18.5 in 1961 to 24.2 in 1969. As may be seen from Table 5, even by 1966, there had been a radical fall in the proportions of single persons in the age group 25–34. There can be little doubt that these changes mark the end of Ireland's formerly unique marriage patterns.

Simultaneously with these changes in marriage patterns, there has been an almost equally dramatic change in regard to marriage fertility. In 1963, there was a downturn in the number of higher-order births occurring, and by 1970, the number of sixth or later births was almost 30 percent below the 1963 level. The changes are shown in Table 6. Whereas, on the basis

TABLE 5.

Measures of Fertility and Nuptiality, Ireland,
1861–1966 (twenty-six counties)

Fertility
(legitimate births per 1,000 married women aged 15–44 at census date)

Three-year Period	Number
1870–1872	307
1880–1882	284
1890–1892	287
1900–1902	292
1910–1912	305
1925–1927	271
1935–1937	256
1945–1947	270
1950–1952	248
1960–1962	251
1965–1972	243

Nuptiality
(proportion of males and females single in certain age groups)

	Age					
	25–34		35–44		45–54	
Year	Males	Females	Males	Females	Males	Females
1861	56.8	39.1	23.9	18.5	14.3	13.5
1871	57.3	38.2	25.5	19.8	16.4	15.2
1881	62.0	41.2	27.1	19.2	16.4	15.5
1891	67.3	48.1	33.0	23.1	19.7	16.6
1901	71.8	52.9	38.3	27.8	23.8	20.0
1911	74.5	55.5	44.5	31.0	28.6	24.0
1926	71.7	52.6	45.0	29.5	31.4	23.9
1936	73.8	54.8	44.2	30.2	33.5	25.1
1946	70.4	48.3	43.0	30.0	32.1	25.6
1951	67.4	45.6	40.5	27.6	31.0	25.7
1961	58.0	37.1	36.2	22.7	29.7	23.1
1966	49.8	31.0	33.4	20.4	29.1	20.8

of the 1963 fertility patterns, for every 1,000 families with at least one child about 400 would eventually have had at least six children, on the basis of the 1970 patterns, this proportion has fallen to 234 out of every 1,000 [22]. Although the decline in fertility has been sudden, it must be kept in mind that Irish family size remains very high by European stand-

TABLE 6.

Marriage Fertility Patterns, Ireland, 1963–1970

Number of Previous Children	0	1	2	3	4	5+	Total
Percentage increase or decrease in births recorded, 1963–1970	+25.2	+21.1	+2.9	−3.8	−18.0	−29.2	+1.4
As percentage of total births in							
1963	22.0	18.0	16.3	12.5	9.6	21.6	100.0
1970	27.0	21.6	16.6	11.8	7.8	15.2	100.0

ards: In 1970, 15 percent of Irish live births were to mothers who had five or more children, compared with 2.9 percent in England and Wales.

The increase in the marriage rate in the 1960s has been linked with the decline in fertility on the basis of the argument (mentioned above) that the traditionally high fertility of Irish marriages acted as a deterrent to young people when contemplating marriage; according to this interpretation, a reduction in family size implies a reduction in the economic costs of the married state and, hence, tends to stimulate the marriage rate. This hypothesis sheds light on the paradoxical chain of events in Ireland between 1963 and 1971, when a decline in fertility of marriage occurred at the same time as a rise in the birth rate because of the sharp rise in the marriage rate that accompanied the fall in fertility. The Irish birth rate in 1971 was 22.8 compared with its low point of 18.7 in the 1930s. Similarly, the net reproduction rate is now the highest in western Europe, and although this measure of natural increase is obviously an unreliable guide to the future in a period of rapid change, it is clear that the rate of natural increase of the Irish population is likely to remain high for a considerable time to come. The key determinant of the future of Irish fertility will be the final family size of the couples who are currently marrying at what is by Irish standards an early age. We have no indicators (from studies of family formation intentions or otherwise) of the likely future course of this variable.

¶ CONTROVERSY ON BIRTH CONTROL

The dramatic change in fertility patterns in the 1960s is generally attributed to the spread in the use of the pill. The pill became available in Ireland, on medical prescription, in the guise of a cycle regulator. No prosecution has been brought under the 1935 act against anyone for selling or distributing the pill. The impact of the pill on fertility has been considerable even in countries where no legal restrictions existed on other forms of birth control, and it is not surprising to see the significant effect of its introduction in Ireland. This especially is true in the light of the ambiguity believed by many to have existed before 1968 in Roman Catholic teaching on birth control.

Publication of *Humanae Vitae* naturally led to widespread discussion and debate on contraception in Ireland. The Roman Catholic hierarchy in Ireland were notable for their enthusiastic endorsement of the Pope's letter. There were, however, some voices of dissent among the clergy, and the less enthusiastic welcome given the document among Roman Catholic theologians elsewhere did not pass unnoticed [23]. The birth statistics for the period since 1969 are not yet available in sufficient detail to allow definitive conclusions to be drawn, but it seems that, at most, the encyclical occasioned a slowing down in, or a cessation of, the rate of decline of higher-order births. There was no sudden reversion to the pre-1963 fertility patterns [24]. Isolating the net effects of the encyclical is complicated by the various medical reports concerning possible adverse side effects from the pill which appeared in 1968 and 1969.

Birth control and Irish laws on the subject became more and more frequently a center of controversy after 1968. The fact that illegal importation (especially across the border from Northern Ireland) acted as a safety valve and reduced pressure on the government to change the law was viewed increasingly as a hypocritical and discriminatory situation, favoring those who traveled frequently, tending to create a black market in smuggled goods, and forcing otherwise law-abiding citizens to break the law in order to obtain contraceptives. In May 1971, a group of members of the Irish Women's Liberation Movement made a trip to Belfast and back by train and declared quantities of contraceptives to the Irish customs on their return, inviting prosecution for illegal importation. No prosecution resulted from this incident, although the matter was raised in Parliament on June 2 and June 9, 1971, when the Minister of Finance stated that any contraceptives that were declared had been confiscated. Protracted discussion on the issue of the legal ban on contraceptives was also provoked by public meetings held by the newly formed Irish Family Planning Rights Association.[14] On March 11, 1971, the Roman Catholic hierarchy issued a joint statement expressing the belief that the majority of the population was opposed to a change in the law. On March 22, however, the Church of Ireland (Protestant) Archbishop of Dublin issued a statement in favor of change. This was followed one week later by a strong state-

[14] The author of this chapter has been chairman of the association since its founding in 1970.

ment against change by the Roman Catholic Archbishop of Dublin, whose pastoral letter of March 28 contained these passages:

> To speak in this context of a right to contraception on the part of the individual, be he Christian or non-Christian or atheist, or on the part of a minority or a majority, is to speak of a right that cannot even exist. . . . Legislation legalizing contraception would prove gravely damaging to morality, private and public; it would be, and would remain, a curse on our country.

Three senators had tried repeatedly during the early months of 1971 to introduce a private members' bill to change the law. Finally, in July, the bill was denied a first reading (which is required in order that the Senate may see the published bill). After the failure of this attempt, two medical doctors (both Labour party members of Parliament) tried to secure a first reading for the same bill in the lower house, but failed by a vote of 75 to 44. Both major opposition parties have now endorsed the need for change.[15]

The public discussion that centered on contraception, which is still continuing, rarely involved explicitly demographic arguments. Proponents of change have stated their case in terms of the right of the individual to make a free choice in an area of private morality, the adverse social effects of ignorance of birth control especially among the lower socioeconomic groups, and the sectarian nature of the existing legislation (believed especially relevant in view of the religious element in the Northern Ireland conflict). Those who oppose change have generally stressed the belief that legalized contraception would undermine the traditional values of Irish family life and sexual morality, opening a "floodgate" to permissiveness, and eventually lead to demands for legalized abortion, divorce, and euthanasia. In the words of the March 1971 letter by the Roman Catholic Archbishop of Dublin:

> Given the proneness of our human nature to evil . . . it must be evident that an access, hitherto unlawful, to contraceptive devices will prove a most certain occasion of sin, especially to immature persons. The public consequences of immorality that must follow for our whole society are too clearly seen in other countries.

The repercussions of the availability of contraceptives on the birth rate are not generally raised in this debate, and it seems that there is a general awareness that the long-term decline in Ireland's population cannot be blamed on either a low birth rate or low fertility of marriage. The pro-

---

[15] These two parties now form a coalition government. No move had been made to change the law by July 1973.

ponents of change do, however, stress that some, at least, of the existing marked social-class differentials in Irish fertility derive from the relative ease with which middle- and upper-income groups can evade the law. An interesting aspect of the debate is the discussion of the effect of the availability of contraceptives on the demographic behavior of the Roman Catholic minority in Northern Ireland. The fact that Roman Catholic fertility is almost the same in the two parts of Ireland, despite the contrast in the legislation regarding contraception, has been interpreted variously as showing that legislation has little or no effect on demographic behavior or as a reflection of the impact of minority status on fertility [see 25].

In 1969, a private nonprofit company with a grant from the International Planned Parenthood Federation opened a family planning clinic in Dublin, and a second clinic was opened in 1971. By 1972, over 7,000 patients had passed through these clinics. Advice is given on all forms of birth control in these clinics, but patients generally have to make their own arrangements to obtain the supplies necessary to implement the advice obtained. There are now eighteen Roman Catholic Marriage Advisory Centers in Ireland, which deal with all aspects of marriage counseling, but advice is given only on church-approved methods of family planning. In November 1972, the Cork center was closed by the Bishop of Cork, apparently because of a statement by a doctor working there who claimed that 93 percent of those using the center were seeking advice on family planning.

Two opinion polls have been conducted on the issue of legalizing contraception. In June 1971, *This Week* magazine published the results of a national poll that asked whether or not the sale of contraceptives should be permitted: 34 percent answered "yes," 63 percent "no," and 3 percent had no views on the subject. Higher proportions in favor of change were recorded among younger people, urban residents, and the middle/professional classes. In April 1971, an opinion poll conducted by the *Irish Medical Times* that obtained a response from 45 percent of the registered doctors in Ireland showed 73 percent in favor of change, of whom a majority were not in favor of availability on prescription only. Finally, in October 1972, the executive council of the Irish Medical Association voted unanimously to recommend a change in the law.

The law also has been challenged in the courts. In 1971, a Dublin housewife named Mrs. McGee had some contraceptive supplies intercepted in the mail and confiscated by the revenue commissioners. She brought suit against the revenue commissioners and the Attorney General, seeking a declaration that Section 17 of the 1935 act was repugnant to the Constitution. She based her case on the articles of the Constitution that safeguard religious freedom and guarantee the family as the necessary basis of the social order. Medical evidence at the hearing established that Mrs. McGee (a mother of four who has had thrombosis) would be ill-advised to become pregnant again and had contraindications to taking the pill. The case failed in the High Court (in August 1972) and an appeal is awaiting hearing in the Supreme Court. In his judgment on the case, the President of the High Court stated:

One must accept that the plaintiff in the circumstances in which she found herself had decided the correct course for her to adopt in the interests of her husband and her family was to take effective steps to ensure that she would not again conceive and put her life in jeopardy, while at the same time not to deny her husband and herself the natural right of a married couple [26].

But he added that he felt the 1935 act did not violate the articles of the Constitution to which appeal had been made. However, he went on to point out that his judgment

does not involve any declaration that legislation cannot be enacted by the Oireachtas [Parliament] which would have the effect of repealing the relevant sections of the Act [26].

During the last three years, there has been an unprecedented interest in the contraception issue. The voices in favor of change have become more numerous, and action on the legislative, judicial, and propagandistic fronts has been considerable. It remains to be seen whether these efforts will finally bear fruit, either in governmental action or in a favorable verdict from the Supreme Court appeal during 1973.

¶ ABORTION

Despite the assertion by those opposed to a change in the ban on contraception that a clamor for liberalized abortion laws will follow success on the birth control issue, there is no public demand or pressure in Ireland for a change in the absolute prohibition on induced abortion. Nonetheless, evidence has become available that, since the 1968 Abortion Act in Britain, Irish women have in increasing numbers gone to Britain to procure abortion. (The 1968 act does not apply in Northern Ireland.) On June 13, 1972, the Minister of Health was asked in the Dail (lower house) whether he was aware of this trend and if he would try to alleviate the problem by introducing a family planning service under the public health authorities. The minister replied that it was not his intention to introduce such a service and that "the facts show that in countries where national family planning has been advanced to a tremendous extent, the abortion rate has risen."

On November 2, 1972, in reply to another question on the same topic, the minister quoted the following data, obtained from the British Office of Population Censuses and Surveys, on the number of abortions performed in England and Wales on women who give the Republic of Ireland as their usual residence (the Abortion Act came into force in April 1968):

1968	64
1969	122
1970	261
1971	577

In the first six months of 1972, a total of 391 was recorded. In reply to questions about the government's policy on this issue, the minister answered:

Everything is being done to help women who are to have illegitimate children; facilities are provided for them; arrangements are made for them to stay with families. . . . The voluntary organization (dealing with unmarried mothers) is working very well [27].

It is not known, however, what proportion of the Irish women seeking abortion in Britain are unmarried. It may also be suspected that the data understates the extent of the problem, since many Irish women who seek abortion undoubtedly establish British residence. One study of a London hospital in 1970 revealed that 15 of 155 applicants for abortion were born in Ireland but resided in Britain [28].

INTERCOMMUNITY DEMOGRAPHIC PROBLEMS

¶ RELIGIOUS GROUPS

The partitioning of Ireland divided the country into two areas with very different religious compositions. In 1926, 79 percent of the Protestant population of the whole country was living in Northern Ireland.[16] In 1926, 93 percent of the population of the republic was Roman Catholic, and by 1961, this had risen to 95 percent. In Northern Ireland, the proportion that was Roman Catholic rose from 33.5 to 34.9 percent between 1926 and 1961. Because Northern Ireland's total population grew at a more rapid rate than that of the republic, a higher proportion of the Roman Catholic population of all Ireland was concentrated in Northern Ireland

---

[16] This figure reflects the fall in the non-Catholic population of the twenty-six counties following partition.

at the end of this period than at the beginning: 15.7 percent compared with 13.3. The net outcome of all of these forces has been almost total stability in the proportion of all Ireland's population that is Roman Catholic: 75.0 percent in 1926, 74.7 percent in 1961 [25].

In the last few years, the question of the religious balance of the population in both parts of Ireland has been raised in public debate. In the republic, the idea that the non-Catholic minority is being pressured out of the country is sometimes expressed, while in the north, the notion of a *revanche du berceau* and an eventual Roman Catholic majority is feared by some. The data, however, show that the non-Catholic minority in the republic has had a lower net emigration rate than the Catholic majority since 1946. The demographic weakness of the minority community derives from an abnormally old-age structure (caused by heavy emigration in the past), moderately low marriage and birth rates, and hence, over the years 1946–1961, a natural decrease of population. There is evidence to suggest that an important factor in the low birth rate among the Protestant community of the republic has been the impact of "mixed marriages" in which children with one Protestant and one Roman Catholic parent are raised as Roman Catholics [25].

In Northern Ireland, the relatively small increase in the Roman Catholic share in total population is the net outcome of a number of separate differentials: The average Roman Catholic family is considerably larger than that of the rest of the population (even when socioeconomic class is considered), and the Roman Catholic birth rate is estimated to be in the region of 28 per 1,000 per year compared with a non-Catholic rate of 20 per 1,000. The birth rate differential is, however, almost entirely offset by an emigration differential: The Roman Catholic emigration rate for the period 1951–1961 was over twice the rate of the rest of the population. This, in turn, is caused by the concentration of the Roman Catholic population in occupations particularly prone to unemployment and low income (farming, farm laboring, and unskilled manual laboring) and their underrepresentation in the professional, employer, and skilled manual worker groups.

¶ LINGUISTIC GROUPS

Demographic factors have played an important role in the decline of the Gaelic-speaking community in Ireland. Even in 1851, less than 25 percent of the population was listed in the census as Gaelic speaking, and only 5 percent was classified as monolingual Gaelic speakers. The depopulation of certain regions by the famines of 1846–1849 took an exceptionally heavy toll among Gaelic speakers. The further decline of the language during the nineteenth century was accelerated by a change from Gaelic to

English, encouraged by the impact of an English-language national school system, the growth of a commercial economy, and the improvement in communications in remote rural areas. But the fact that Gaelic speakers were concentrated in the poorer western areas also meant that they were most prone to emigrate, and a high rate of emigration among Gaelic speakers has probably been the most important reason for the decline of the language and the decay of those areas most typical of the old customs and way of life.[17] Between 1961 and 1971, the total (Gaelic and non-Gaelic speaking) population of the *Gaeltacht* areas (areas defined by the government as having an especially high concentration of population whose mother tongue is Gaelic) declined by 11 percent, while the population of the country rose by 5.7 percent. *Gaeltacht* areas now contain only 2.4 percent of the population of the republic and 1.6 percent of the population of all Ireland.

CONCLUSION

Ireland's demographic history has forced commentators to raise some basic questions of population policy more explicitly than has been customary in other countries until very recently. To see in Irish experience since the early nineteenth century merely a confirmation of a simple Malthusian model of the interaction between population growth and economic development is to oversimplify the train of events. Nonetheless, Malthusians find more support for their hypotheses in Irish history than in most of the other countries. Certainly, extreme population pressure resulted in severe and widespread poverty in the decades leading to the famines of the 1840s, and the reduction in population brought about by starvation, emigration, and low nuptiality played a considerable role in raising the material living standards of the average Irishman to the present relatively high level. However, those who do not accept the Malthusian interpretation may erect a counterfactual model in which no emigration occurred, population pressure continued to build, thereby inducing fundamental reforms in land tenure and in the whole structure of the economy and eventually leading to rising living standards based on intensive economic development. The key element in this alternative vision of history is, of course, enterprise, and proponents of this vision hold that it was precisely this factor whose supply was most severely curtailed by the actual pattern of demographic events in nineteenth-century Ireland. If it is believed that the more enter-

---

[17] Popular interest since the end of the nineteenth century and official policy since 1922 have compensated, at least in part, for this decline by fostering the use of the language in a bilingual contest in all the schools and some government departments in the republic.

prising persons emigrated and that a low marriage rate induced pessimism and lack of initiative, then the logic of this alternative interpretation is enhanced. But even granting these premises, obvious implausibilities remain, not least of which is the dubiousness of the assertion that a curb on emigration or a radical land reform would actually have stimulated the supply of enterprise within the country sufficiently to overcome the obvious problems posed by the rapid rate of population growth. The obstacles to have been removed were enormous and, as one historian comments, "even in the age of Keynes and Mao the chances of success could not be guaranteed. In the early nineteenth century they were nil" [29, p. 145].

The lessons of the Irish experience for other countries may not, at first sight, seem evident. In an era when "zero population growth" achieved by small average family size combined with a high marriage rate is increasingly common as an ideal among demographers, it may be felt that the history of a country that achieved a substantial reduction in its population through combining high fertility of marriage with a very low marriage rate and high emigration rate is largely irrelevant. What is of interest in the Irish case, however, is the extent to which the adverse effects of a declining population may have been independent of the manner in which this decline was achieved. It is also relevant that, in the Irish case, the traditional models and analytical techniques of demographers do not appear to shed a great deal of light on the exact nature of the interaction between demographic and socioeconomic variables. Nonetheless, the hypothesis that looks most acceptable in the light of available evidence is that the long-term swings in Irish emigration and marriage rates were primarily induced by variations in the economic conditions, rather than vice versa. This interpretation of Irish demographic history is similar to the interpretation of various aspects of the American experience advanced by Easterlin [30].

Turning from the past to the demographic future of Ireland, one is struck by the rapidity with which fundamental changes of emphasis have occurred in public discussion of demographic issues. From an obsession with the need to achieve population growth, public attention has, in less than a decade, concentrated increasingly on newer themes, such as the urgency of correcting the regional imbalance of the population's development and the need to abandon laws and attitudes that were more appropriate to the marriage and fertility patterns of previous generations. Apart from a general concern with economic development and an implicit belief that emigration would fall and the marriage rate rise in response to brighter economic prospects at home, Irish governments have not, in the past, involved themselves to any serious degree in formulating a "population policy." Recent attempts to influence the regional distribution of the population represent a major innovation in this respect. The buildup of pressure to change the law that bans the importation and sale of contraceptives may soon lead to a curtailment of the state's role in this aspect of demographic behavior. It may well be a long time before an Irish "population policy" advances beyond these stages. It is likely, however, that the policies of governments in other Western nations will exercise increasing influence on Irish thinking on these matters.

REFERENCES

1. T. R. Malthus. *Essay on Population.* "New edition." London: privately printed, 1803, Part 1, Chap. 2.

2. K. H. Connell. *Irish Peasant Society: Four Historical Essays.* Oxford: Clarendon Press, 1968.

3. Raymond D. Crotty. *Irish Agricultural Production: Its Volume and Structure.* Cork: Cork University Press, 1966.

4. F. S. L. Lyons. *Ireland since the Famine: 1850 to the Present.* London: Weidenfeld and Nicholson, 1971.

5. James Meenan. *The Irish Economy since 1922.* Liverpool: Liverpool University Press, 1970.

6. Commission on Emigration and Other Population Problems, 1948–1954. *Reports.* Dublin: The Stationery Office, 1954.

7. Brendan M. Walsh. *Some Irish Population Problems Reconsidered.* Paper No. 48. Dublin: Economic and Social Research Institute, 1968.

8. D. Walsh and B. M. Walsh. "Some influences on the intercounty variation in Irish psychiatric hospitalization rates." *British Journal of Psychiatry,* January 1968.

9. R. E. Kennedy, Jr. *The Irish: Emigration, Marriage, and Fertility, 1841–1966.* Berkeley: University of California Press, 1972.

10. Department of Finance. *Economic Development.* Dublin: The Stationery Office, 1958.

11. Gárda Siochána. *Reports on Crime, 1968, 1969.* Dublin: The Stationery Office, 1970 and 1971.

12. Central Statistics Office. *Report on Vital Statistics.* Dublin: The Stationery Office, 1963–1973.

13. *Census of Population, 1971.* Vol. 1. Dublin: The Stationery Office, 1972.

14. J. H. Whyte. *Church and State in Modern Ireland, 1923–1970.* Dublin: Gill and Macmillan, 1971.

15. P. Mac Aonghusa. *The Sunday Press,* April 4, 1971.

16. Department of Social Welfare. *Summary of Social Insurance and Services, 1972/3.* Dublin, 1972.

17. Fionala Kennedy. "Social expenditure of public authorities and economic growth, 1947–1966." *Economic and Social Review,* April 1970.

18. Department of Local Government. *Quarterly Bulletin of Housing Statistics.* Dublin, 1973.

19. *Review of 1971 and Outlook for 1972.* Dublin: The Stationery Office, 1972.

20. Industrial Development Authority. *Regional Industrial Plans, 1973–1977.* Part 1. Dublin: IDA, 1972.

21. R. C. Geary and J. G. Hughes. *Internal Migration in Ireland.* Dublin: Economic and Social Research Institute, 1970.

22. Brendan M. Walsh. "Ireland's demographic transformation, 1958–1970." *Economic and Social Review,* January 1972.

23. Austin Flannery. "Chronicle: Humanae Vitae." *Doctrine and Life,* November 1968.

24. Garret Fitzgerald. "What's happening to people?" *Irish Times,* February 14, 1972.

25. Brendan M. Walsh. *Religion and Demographic Behaviour in Ireland.* Paper no. 55. Dublin: Economic and Social Research Institute, May 1970.

26. *Irish Times,* August 1, 1972.

27. Parliamentary Debates, vol. 263, no. 3, col. 515.

28. C. Ingham and M. Simms. "Study of applicants for abortion at the Royal Northern Hospital, London." *Journal of Biosocial Science,* vol. 4 (1972): 351–369.

29. Gearóid Ó Tuaithaigh. *Ireland before the Famine, 1798–1848.* Dublin: Gill and Macmillan, 1972.

30. Richard A. Easterlin. *Population, Labor Force, and Long Swings in Economic Growth.* New York: National Bureau of Economic Research, 1968.

CHAPTER 3

Israel

Dov Friedlander

Acknowledgments: The author is indebted to Ruhama Yitzhaki who assisted in compiling much of the statistical data as well as other information that has been used in this study. The author is also indebted to Yudah Matras, Helmut Muhsam, Efraim Kleinman, Calvin Goldscheider, and all the others who have read earlier versions of this study and offered very useful comments.

ABSTRACT

The focus of population concern, first in Palestine and now in Israel, has always been political. The Jewish community in Palestine aimed at increasing the size of the Jewish population as rapidly as possible, since this was considered to be an important issue in determining the country's political future. Conflicting political ambitions of the two communities—Jews and Arabs—in Palestine, restrictions imposed on Jewish immigration by the British, and the fate of European Jewry were three important elements in the Jewish community's concern about the declining birth rates before the founding of the state of Israel. After independence, the political-demographic situation changed completely. One of the first laws passed by the Israeli government was the Law of Return, whereby every Jewish person was entitled to immigrate to Israel, and hundreds of thousands of Jews did so from 1948 to 1951. During this time, Israel's population more than doubled.

After 1952, immigration declined because of a reduction in the number of potential immigrants and Israel's economic difficulties. The consequent pressures from various political quarters to establish a pronatal policy resulted in the April 1962 appointment of a Natality Committee to study the problems connected with Israel's demographic patterns: the differential fertility between the Arabs, who constituted 12 percent of Israel's total population and had a growth rate of 4 percent per year, and the Jews, who had a growth rate of 1.5 percent per year; the large proportion of economically deprived families, generally of Afro-Asian origin, whose fertility was high; and the difference in population size and growth rate between Israel and its neighboring Arab countries, in view of the persistent political-military conflict. Two other considerations were (1) the possibility that Israel's population growth rate was too low from an economic point of view and (2) the desire for a demographic revival of world Jewry. In April 1966, the Natality Committee submitted a report recommending a pronatal policy including the granting of financial aid to large families, restrictions on induced abortions, and the establishment of a Demographic Center to initiate, devise, and coordinate pronatal action.

The author, however, believes that a pronatalist policy for Israel is not at all useful. Given the incentives that can possibly be granted, a meaningful increase in Jewish fertility is most unlikely. But even if such an increase were to occur, it would still contribute very little toward the elimination of Israel's problems. Increased immigration, which can help to reduce the extent of the problems, should be encouraged, in addition to increased support to deprived families and to the establishment of a public family clinics system which would be beneficial to all.

MAJOR DEMOGRAPHIC TRENDS

¶ IMMIGRATION
The history of population concern in Israel antedates the present political state and was developed by a movement originating outside of the Middle East region. One of the main features of Zionist ideology, which emerged as a national movement toward the end of the nineteenth century in Europe, was to stimulate mass immigration of Jews to Palestine. Populating Palestine by Jews became one of the major goals of Zionism and a focus of its policies and action programs. Leaders of the Zionist movement acted through diplomatic channels to secure the support of governments for mass Jewish migration to Palestine and, indeed, for their support to establish a Jewish state. In addition to such diplomatic efforts, offices for the promotion of Jewish immigration to Palestine were opened in various cities by the Zionist organization, and over the years funds were established to support Jewish immigration to and settlement in Palestine. This was the beginning of population policies of the Jewish people in the modern period —to resettle the land of Israel. They proved to be quite successful. The

Jewish population in Palestine increased from merely 50,000 at the beginning of the century to 650,000 just before the establishment of the state of Israel (in 1948), mostly as a result of mass immigration. This success occurred despite the great difficulties and severe restrictions imposed periodically by Turkish and British rulers of the area.

In 1920, the British had acquired Palestine as a mandate of the League of Nations. Although by the terms of that mandate and of the British Balfour Declaration (of 1917), Palestine was marked as the place for the establishment of a Jewish national home (with due regard for the rights of the non-Jewish population), the British did very little to carry out that mandate. The Jews were represented by the Jewish Agency whose main concern at the time was to maximize immigration. The Arab position was one of fear of the consequences of large-scale Jewish immigration. Therefore, the British authorities led what seemed to them to be a "balanced" policy of immigration, that is, they restricted it, at times most severely. Thus, the British migration policy and the Jewish struggle against it were a consequence of the contradictory political-demographic objectives of the two communities in Palestine. It is in large part correct to see the recent concern over natality levels and attempts to establish a pronatalist policy as part of the historical continuity of political and ideological issues.

To be more specific, until 1948 (the year of the foundation of the state of Israel), the population objective of the Jewish community was to reach a balance (at least) in the size and rate of growth between the Jewish and the Arab communities, so that the establishment of a Jewish state in Palestine would not be hindered by its being a minority population. To illustrate the political significance of differential demographic patterns, it is sufficient to read the reports of one of the many committees on the future of the country set up by the British government or international organizations. For instance, special population projects were prepared for the Palestine Royal Commission of 1937 to show the likely future development of the population in the Jewish and Arab communities according to various demographic assumptions, in particular assumptions concerning future Jewish immigration. One table in that report shows, for illustrative purposes, the year when the Jewish and Arab populations would be equal in size as a function of the annual volume of Jewish immigration. It is not surprising, therefore, that the internal political authorities of the Jewish community always aimed at maximizing the number of Jews in Palestine. It was, in fact, the struggle between the British authorities and the Jewish community in Palestine during the post-World War II period over the immigration issue that was at the center of the events that eventually led to the 1948–1949 independence war and the establishment of Israel. Jews in Israel (and elsewhere) felt that Palestine should become a Jewish state and the homeland for the Jews in Europe and in Arab states. The Palestinian Arabs and the Arab states objected to the establishment of a Jewish state in Palestine and to further immigration. During this period, the British government had almost stopped immigration and convened the Anglo-American Commission which recommended (in April 1946) allowing 100,000 displaced European Jews to immigrate to Palestine. However, the British government decided subsequently to admit just 2,000 Jews a month; in response to this decision, bitter anti-British violence began in Palestine, and Jewish immigration (even if illegal) to Palestine became a huge and powerful national movement. The British intercepted many illegal ships and sent thousands of Jewish immigrants to camps in Cyprus. Subsequently, a session of the General Assembly of the United Nations was called and established the UN Special Committee on Palestine (April 1947). They submitted, in August 1947, a plan to divide Palestine into two states, one Jewish and one Arab. The plan was accepted by a two-thirds majority of the General Assembly on November 29, 1947. Consequently, the British began to withdraw from Palestine in early 1948, and Arabs and Jews prepared for what turned into the 1948–1949 Israel Independence War.

The war and the independence of Israel changed the political-demographic map considerably. The newly established state was only part of the former area consisting mostly of the Jewish settled areas.[1] This and the exodus of over 500,000 Arabs, formerly residents of areas that were now included in the new state of Israel, were responsible for the important change in the demographic map. In particular, the new state of Israel had a majority of Jewish people. However, the objective of achieving a high rate of population growth in Israel remained, for the state now had to survive in the heart of the Arab world, whose population numbered well over 70 million (see Table 1). Perhaps even more important was the fact that the new state contained a 14-percent Arab minority with a high rate of natural increase.

¶ JEWISH-ARAB DEMOGRAPHIC DIFFERENTIALS

After the establishment of the state of Israel, the volume of Jewish immigration was under Jewish control. Indeed, one of the first laws to be passed by the Knesset (the Israeli Parliament) was the Law of Return. According to this law, every Jewish person had the right to immigrate and settle in Israel with the aid and assistance of the state. The law gave formal expres-

---

[1] In what follows, Israel's territory will mean the areas that were included in Israel at the cease-fire agreements after the 1948–1949 Israel Independence War. However, in the population projections to be presented in a later section, the population of East Jerusalem also is included.

TABLE 1.

Population Size and Rates of Population Growth,
Various Arab Countries and Israel, 1968

Country	Population Size (in millions)	Rate of Population Growth (percent)
Lebanon	2.5	2.5
Syria	5.5	3.0
Iraq	8.3	3.1
Jordan	2.0	3.2
Egypt	30.2	2.5
Sudan	13.9	2.8
Algeria	12.2	2.0
Total	74.6	2.6
Israel	2.4	2.1

SOURCE: See [1].

sion to public sentiment about the settlement of Jews in Israel and provided the legal basis for an active pro-immigration policy. This law enabled and encouraged hundreds of thousands of Jews from many countries to immigrate to Israel in the subsequent years. The impact of immigration on population growth before and after the foundation of Israel and, in particular, on Jewish-Arab differential growth is illustrated in Table 2. While, in 1922, the ratio of Arabs to Jews was about 7 to 1, it was only slightly over 2 to 1 in 1945 and 1.9 to 1 just before the founding of Israel. As mentioned earlier, Israel contained mainly the Jewish settled areas of what was formerly Palestine and consisted of a population of 650,000 Jews and just over 150,000 Arabs. However, the ratio of Jews to Arabs in Israel increased in time even further. In fact, both the Jewish and the Arab communities experienced enormous growth during the past fifty years. The Jewish community had a growth rate of about 10 percent per annum (on average) to 1948 and a rate of about 7 percent per annum after the foundation of the state (to 1967). The Arab population was growing at a rate of over 3 percent per annum before 1948 and at a rate of 4 percent thereafter. What were the relative contributions of migration balance and of natural increase to the very considerable population growth in these two communities? This is shown in Tables 3 and 4. Jewish immigration was high before World War II and almost ceased during that war. It increased sharply in the postwar period and reached its peak volume during the years 1948–1951, when, in 1949, 266 migrants per 1,000 (of the mean population) arrived in just one single year [3]. Subsequently, the volume

TABLE 2.

Development of the Jewish and Arab Populations,
Palestine and Israel, 1922–1968 (in 1,000s)

Year	Total Population	Jewish Population	Arab Population	Percent Jewish
	Palestine			
1922	649	84	565	12.9
1925	757	122	635	16.1
1930	922	165	757	17.9
1935	1,196	322	874	26.9
1940	1,461	456	1,005	31.2
1945	1,708	541	1,167	31.7
May 14, 1948	1,885	650	1,235	34.5
	Israel			
May 15, 1948	806	650	156	80.6
1951	1,577	1,404	173	89.0
1954	1,718	1,526	192	88.8
1957	1,976	1,763	213	89.2
May 22, 1961	2,179	1,932	247	88.7
1964	2,525	2,239	286	88.7
1967	2,777	2,384	393	85.8
1968	2,841	2,435	406	85.7

SOURCE: See [2].
NOTES: (1) Mid-year population: 1922, 1925, and 1930. (2) Mean population: 1935, 1940, and 1945. (3) Population at end of year: 1951, 1954, 1957, 1964, 1967, and 1968.

of migration declined considerably, and in some years, it was slight, for example, in the years 1952–1954, 1958–1960, and 1965–1968. Table 3 shows also the rates of natural growth and total growth of the Jewish community in Israel. It can be seen that the contribution of natural increase to the development of the Jewish population was very slight. Clearly the enormous population growth among Jews in Israel was, in large part, the direct result of the very substantial immigration over the past fifty years. Indeed, in some years, immigration contributed over 90 percent to the total growth of the Jewish population. One important point concerning the effectiveness of immigration policies should, however, be made. Jewish immigration to Israel was strongly motivated by both a "pull" factor (from Israel) and a very powerful "push" factor. Israel's immigration policies were successful not only because of governmental encouragements and aid extended to Jewish migrants but also because of the desire of hundreds

TABLE 3.

Components of Population Growth, Jewish Population,
Palestine and Israel, 1936–1968

Period	Absolute Numbers (in 1,000s)			Rates per 100 Population			Percentage Growth Due to Natural Increase
	Migration Balance	Natural Increase	Total Growth	Migration Balance	Natural Increase	Total Growth	
1936–1940	19.3			4.7	1.8	6.5	28
1941–1945	9.9			2.0	1.9	3.9	49
1946–1947	20.4			3.4	2.3	5.7	40
Jan. 1, 1948– May 14, 1948	17.2			7.3			
May 15, 1948– Dec. 31, 1948	104.4	4.7	109.1	16.1	0.7	16.8	4
1949	234.9	20.3	255.2	31.0	2.6	33.6	8
1950	160.1	29.0	189.1	15.8	2.9	18.7	15
1951	166.9	34.5	201.4	13.9	2.8	16.7	17
1952	10.7	35.1	45.8	0.8	2.5	3.3	76
1953	−1.6	35.0	33.4	−0.1	2.4	2.3	100
1954	11.1	31.3	42.4	0.8	2.1	2.9	72
1955	31.2	33.3	64.5	2.0	2.2	4.2	52
1956	43.8	33.2	77.0	2.8	2.0	4.8	42
1957	61.1	34.1	95.2	3.7	2.0	5.7	35
1958	14.5	32.9	47.4	0.8	1.9	2.7	70
1959	14.7	34.0	48.7	0.8	1.9	2.7	70
1960	17.8	34.6	52.4	1.0	1.8	2.8	64
1961	37.8	32.7	70.5	2.0	1.7	3.7	46
1962	55.0	32.2	87.2	2.8	1.6	4.4	36
1963	53.0	33.7	86.7	2.6	1.6	4.2	38
1964	48.0	35.6	83.6	2.2	1.7	3.9	44
1965	22.9	37.0	59.9	1.0	1.7	2.7	63
1966	8.3	37.5	45.8	0.4	1.6	2.0	80
1967	4.3	34.4	38.7	0.2	1.5	1.7	88
1968	12.7	38.5	51.2	0.5	1.6	2.1	76

SOURCE: Various tables from [2] and some other official sources.

of thousands of Jewish people to leave their former countries of residence.
Of course, many arrived as refugees. These factors help explain the tremendous effectiveness of migration policies in Israel.

In addition to variations in the volume of migration over time, there was
another aspect of much significance, that is, their changing composition by
origin. Data shown in Table 5 indicate that, until the establishment of the
state of Israel, the majority of migrants came from European countries.
However, after the founding of Israel, there was a gradual shift toward
migration of those of Afro-Asian origins.

TABLE 4.

Population Growth and Natural Growth, Arabs, Palestine and Israel,
1951–1968 (rates per 100)

Period	Total Growth	Natural Increase	Percentage Growth Due to Natural Increase
1951	3.8	3.5	92
1955	3.5	3.5	100
1960	4.1	4.1	100
1965	4.5	4.5	100
1968	3.5	3.7	106

SOURCE: See [2].

TABLE 5.

Jewish Immigration and Population by Continent of Origin, Israel,
1919–1968 (absolute figures, in 1,000s)

Period	Migrants during the Period (by origin)			Population at the Beginning of the Period (by origin)			
	All	European	Afro-Asian	All	European	Afro-Asian	Israel
			Absolute figures				
1919–1931	116.8[a]	97.7	11.2				
1932–1948	335.5[a]	287.4	33.7	174.6	81.3	19.9	73.4
1949–1951	582.4[a]	258.0	317.5	716.7[b]	393.0[b]	70.0[b]	253.7[b]
1952–1964	504.9	194.0	310.2	1,404.4	659.1	387.6	357.7
1965–1968	72.3	31.3	41.0	2,239.2	714.6	643.1	881.5
			Percentages				
1919–1931	100.0	83.6	9.6				
1932–1948	100.0	85.7	10.0	100.0	46.6	11.4	42.0
1949–1951	100.0	44.3	54.5	100.0	54.8	9.8	35.4
1952–1964	100.0	38.4	61.4	100.0	46.9	27.6	25.5
1965–1968	100.0	43.3	56.7	100.0	31.9	28.7	39.4

SOURCE: See [2].
[a] Totals include migrants of unknown origin.
[b] Figures relate to November 8, 1948.

A different picture can be observed of the development of the Arab population (see Table 4). Their high growth rate (though not as high as that of the Jews) was almost exclusively caused by very high natural increase. This, in turn, was a result of extremely high fertility coupled with rapidly declining mortality (see also Table 6).

TABLE 6.

Gross Reproduction and Net Reproduction Rates of Jews and Arabs,
Israel, 1944–1966 (by origin)

	Jewish Population								Arab Population	
	Total		Of European Origin		Of Afro-Asian Origin		Israeli Born			
Period	GRR	NRR	GRR	NRR	GRR	NRR	GRR	NRR	GRR	NRR
1944–1945	1.69	1.52	1.38	1.21	2.28	2.00	1.75	1.53		
1949	1.66	1.53	1.55	1.46	2.17	1.89	1.73	1.63		
1950	1.89	1.75	1.59	1.52	2.76	2.41	1.91	1.82		
1951	1.95	1.81	1.54	1.47	3.06	2.72	1.73	1.64		
1952	1.95	1.79	1.48	1.41	3.02	2.74	1.63	1.55		
1953	1.88	1.77	1.39	1.32	2.74	2.52	1.56	1.48		
1954	1.74	1.66	1.28	1.22	2.75	2.55	1.40	1.33		
1955	1.77	1.67	1.28	1.22	2.77	2.60	1.38	1.31	3.55	3.07
1956	1.77	1.68	1.27	1.21	2.73	2.58	1.35	1.28	3.54	3.06
1957	1.76	1.67	1.26	1.20	2.64	2.50	1.37	1.30	3.39	2.93
1958	1.65	1.57	1.20	1.14	2.40	2.28	1.32	1.26	3.55	3.07
1959	1.69	1.62	1.13	1.08	2.56	2.44	1.35	1.28	3.58	3.09
1960	1.69	1.62	1.15	1.10	2.48	2.38	1.34	1.27	3.88	3.36
1961	1.63	1.57	1.16	1.12	2.35	2.26	1.31	1.27	3.70	3.24
1962	1.60	1.54	1.13	1.09	2.27	2.18	1.26	1.21	3.72	3.25
1963	1.63	1.57	1.16	1.11	2.24	2.15	1.34	1.29	3.79	3.31
1964	1.66	1.60	1.24	1.19	2.22	2.13	1.38	1.32	4.10	3.58
1965	1.68	1.62	1.26	1.21	2.23	2.14	1.41	1.35	4.07	3.56
1966	1.65	1.59	1.19	1.04	2.17	2.08	1.35	1.30	4.00	3.50

SOURCES: See [2] and [4].

Thus, although population growth during the past fifty years was, on the whole, very much higher among the Jewish population than among the Arab population it was fundamentally of a temporary nature and could not be expected to last indefinitely. This was because the Jewish population growth rate depended mainly on immigration, which had limited sources, while natural increase was only a small fraction of total Jewish population growth. Consequently, it generally was assumed in Israel that, if fertility among Jews could not be increased substantially, the growth rate of the Jewish population in Israel would decline. What were the prospects for the future growth of the Arab population? In almost all demographic writings on the subject and in the press (whenever the subject received attention), it was assumed implicitly, and often explicitly, that the rate of growth of the Arab population (which was equivalent to natural increase) would remain at its very high levels for many years to come. An early and interesting example illustrating this kind of thinking that has been mentioned is the report of the Palestine Royal Commission of 1937.

If these assessments concerning the future growth rates of these two subcommittees were realistic (that is, a future of 1 percent growth among the Jewish community and 3.5 percent growth among the Arab community), significant demographic and political implications would be involved, particularly in view of the long-standing political conflict between the Arab world and the Jewish community in Israel. The belief in the likelihood of such demographic prospects was perhaps the most important element in the background under which the Natality Committee was appointed by the government in 1962.

¶ DIFFERENTIALS BETWEEN JEWISH GROUPS
There was another important element of a sociopolitical-demographic nature in the development of the population of Israel. The Jewish population in Israel, as a result of immigration patterns noted earlier, is rather heterogeneous in its social-economic-demographic characteristics. Broadly speaking, the population can be divided into two major groups: (1) Jewish people of Afro-Asian origins[2] and their Israeli-born descendants and (2) people of European origins and their Israeli-born descendants. Members of the first group are, on the average, less affluent and have lower educational levels and larger families. (Their total fertility rate fell from six to four children per woman in fifteen years.) The second group can be characterized as more affluent, better educated, and having relatively small families (see Table 6).

Thus, given these differentials in family size, the fertility of the Jewish population as a whole depends on the relative size of these two socioeconomic (and ethnic) groups. Indeed, future fertility levels of the Jewish population in Israel will depend in large part on the degree of convergence in the fertility patterns of Western and Eastern Jews. There appear to be two conflicting results of these trends: First, further reductions in the fertility of Asian-African Jews may contribute to an increase in their social and economic level. On the other hand, a decline in fertility for this group portends the reduction in total growth of the Jewish sector.

¶ TWO MAJOR "POPULATION" PROBLEMS IN ISRAEL
To sum up the discussion on differentials in natural increase *between* the Jewish and Arab communities on the one hand and *within* the Jewish community on the other, we have shown (in Table 6) net production rate

[2] This is what often is referred to as the group of Oriental Jewry. The origins of these Jews are mainly Moslem countries in the Middle East and North Africa.

(NRR) values, which show the demographic implications (in terms of population growth) of the continuation of present patterns in fertility and mortality. Within the Jewish population, it is the Afro-Asian population that is still reproducing fast, while that of European origins is almost stationary in terms of natural growth. The social implications are clear. Assuming the continuation of these patterns even for a limited period would imply that the less affluent, the less educated, the socially deprived section of the population would grow fast, while the affluent section would grow extremely slowly.

Within the total population, natural increase differentials between the Jewish and Arab communities are of great significance. These differentials were, in fact, increasing since the early 1950s as a result of the considerable increase in expectation of life among the Arabs. The demographic implications are quite clear. The Arab population in Israel, which consists of nearly 15 percent of the total population, will increase rapidly and be equal in size to the Jewish population in less than three generations, assuming the continuation of current fertility and also assuming that no further substantial Jewish immigration takes place. Against this background, a pronatalist position for the Jewish population becomes understandable.

PRONATALIST ATTITUDES
BEFORE THE FOUNDING OF ISRAEL

Immigration policies in Palestine began early in this century. These can be understood against the political-demographic background of the Jewish-Arab conflict. Although immigration policies were on the whole effective, there were periods when the restrictions imposed were so severe that Jewish immigration was very limited. It was in such periods that the need for pronatal policies was stressed. However, among some segments of the Jewish community, the possibility of increasing Jewish fertility to achieve more rapid population growth was an important consideration even during periods of heavy immigration.

Population problems and the need for pronatal action have been discussed by political leaders, members of the Knesset, and other public figures, both in the press and in public speeches, for over thirty years. It is evident that open discussions about and political pressures toward the formulation of an official pronatal policy in Israel during the 1950s and the 1960s were a direct continuation of discussions and public debate during the British rule in Palestine, in the late 1930s and the 1940s. We are concerned in this section with these early activities before the founding of Israel.

The earliest pronatal discussions that can be traced in the literature relate to 1939, but their appearance, at first, was rare. It was only in the following years that the frequency of such discussions increased. First, as was shown, Jewish migration declined considerably since the beginning of World War II, thus increasing the relative importance of natality in the growth of the Jewish population in Palestine. Second, the decline in the birth rate among Jews in Palestine which began prior to World War II (which also, of course, occurred in other Western populations), together with the decline in migration during the war, resulted in a low rate of population growth during the war period. Third, in the early 1940s, the first news about the destruction of European Jewry began to be publicized. Thus, discussions on the population problem during the early 1940s should be understood in this context.

It appears that David Ben-Gurion was the first to stress publicly the importance of increased natality. In the background was Professor Roberto Bachi (then statistician for the Hadassah Medical Institute, later Professor of Statistics and Demography at the Hebrew University, Jerusalem) who drew Ben-Gurion's attention to the problem. The fact was that the Jewish population did not have a particularly low birth rate. It was over 30 per 1,000 between 1930 and 1935, over 25 per 1,000 in the period 1935–1940, and just over 20 per 1,000 in the early 1940s. But these relatively high birth rates resulted mainly from a very favorable age structure, while age-specific fertility rates were not high at all. The gross reproduction rate (GRR) was 1.4 between 1931–1935 and 1.2 between 1936–1940. These GRR values with Israel's current mortality levels would imply birth rates well under 20, given a "stable" age distribution, and not of the order of nearly 30, as experienced. Thus, Bachi, in a number of meetings in the late 1930s, drew Ben-Gurion's attention to the fact that the relatively high crude birth rates among Jews in Palestine by no means reflected high fertility levels. The birth and fertility rates of the Jewish population then became one of the subjects which received Ben-Gurion's attention during the subsequent thirty years.

On many occasions during these thirty years, he called on parents to fulfill their "demographic duty" toward the nation and regarded the issue as one of the "highest importance." One of Ben-Gurion's early statements on the natality issue was at a conference on "Labor Force" organized by the Mapai party (socialist and the largest Jewish political party in Palestine) in 1943. Ben-Gurion posed the question of whether the majority of Jewish people did, in fact, fulfill their reproductive commitments to the nation. He said that an average of 2.2 children per family was inadequate and that such a fertility level, if there was no immigration (and there was only little immigration at that time), implied that the Jewish community would die out. He added that the Jewish population in Palestine was, as western European nations in general were, in a state of demographic and moral decay [5]. On another occasion, Ben-Gurion pointed out that, without a Jewish majority in Palestine, a Jewish state, and even the survival of the existing Jewish community, would be impossible. Since the volume of immigration at that time was small and was under strict British control, Ben-Gurion suggested that the number of births, which, of course, was exclusively under Jewish parents' control, should be increased. Although no attempt was made during those years to formulate policies with the object of increasing Jewish natality, Ben-Gurion took an active interest in the subject. He was not the only one active on the pronatal issue. In a series of articles published between 1939 and 1944, attention was called by Professor Bachi to the implications of the continuation of differential natural increase between the Jewish and Arab communities in Palestine. In one article [6], he suggested that the Jewish authorities should take whatever action was necessary to encourage and stimulate families to have more than two or three children. At the same time, he argued that further attempts should be made to control mortality.

In another article [7], he emphasized that the demographic and political survival of the Jewish community in Palestine was now of even greater importance. But the demographic situation was, in fact, such that the number of Moslem births was four times as high as the number of Jewish births, although the Arab population was only twice as large as the Jewish. The result was, he argued, that, in years with no significant Jewish immigration, the proportion of Jews in the total population declined. This was considered inconsistent with the political objectives of the Jewish community. Hence, the call for the formulation of a population policy to curb the fertility decline among Jews in Palestine. The argument was that the ideal number of children should be three to four and even more. Specifically, fiscal policies were suggested to allow easier credit facilities for families, family allowances, and the like. Several of the suggestions made in 1943 were considered some twenty years later, by the Natality Committee headed by Professor Bachi and appointed by Prime Minister Ben-Gurion.

In addition to this national-political position, there was also the religious section of the population, who viewed population objectives from a religious-nationalistic point of view. A good example of the religious attitude is the call made in 1943 by the then Chief Rabbi I. H. Herzog of Palestine to Jewish families to increase the number of their offspring. In his call, Rabbi Herzog mentioned first the terrible news of the fate of European Jewry. He suggested then that this might have been a consequence, "by the will of God," of the "modern" style of living that had spread throughout the nation. One aspect of this kind of life was family limitation which is, according to Jewish religion, one of the worst sins. The Jews should number not just 11 million but tens of millions and should "be fruitful and multiply, and replenish the earth" [8]. One of the earliest pronatal advocators of the orthodox section in Palestine, whose views were widely publicized, was the late A. H. Fraenkel, a distinguished Professor of Mathematics at the Hebrew University, Jerusalem. As a mathematician, he was concerned (even more so than demographers) at the demographic and political implications of the *indefinite continuation* of differential demographic patterns between Jews and Arabs in Palestine. He expressed his views in a number of articles in the period 1942–1944. Fraenkel not only contended that families ought to have more children, but he also suggested definite policies to achieve this objective. For example, he proposed that a "total war" be declared against those gynecologists performing induced abortions [9, p. 31]. Not only was it immoral, a terrible crime and murder, according to Fraenkel, but it was a major reason for the low birth rate among Jews in Palestine. There was no doubt in his mind that controlling the number of abortions would automatically and effectively increase the birth rate. It is interesting that this inference was based on no other country than Nazi Germany. Fraenkel states that in that country, "among the many means by which Hitler attempted in 1933 to increase the German birth rate, the one effective measure was the war against abortions." Fraenkel proposed, therefore, that heavy penalties be imposed on surgeons and other persons involved in an illegal act of induced abortion [9, p. 32]. Naturally, Fraenkel objected to any kind of family planning. Fraenkel's views on population could well represent those of the leadership of the orthodox section of the population in Palestine and Israel, while Professor Bachi's views could represent the more liberal, nonreligious approach which was more or less adopted by Ben-Gurion and perhaps a few others among the political establishment. These two different approaches to the problem remained after the foundation of the state and are, in fact, still present today. Although later developments were shaped mainly according to the more liberal pronatal view, they were supported, stimulated, and encouraged by public figures from the religious section.

PRONATALIST ACTIVITIES AFTER THE FOUNDING OF ISRAEL

The state of Israel was founded on May 15, 1948. It might have been expected that, since some aspects of the population problem were now no longer relevant, in the short run at least, and since immigration had been resumed, the subject of pronatal policies would be dropped, particularly since the new state had to deal with various other problems. Was this, in fact, so? An indication of population activities in the early period of the state of Israel may be obtained through a comparison of the frequency of appearance of the subject in the press in that period with the frequency in earlier and later periods. Although this frequency was, in fact, much lower in the early years of the state than it was in both the years before independence and the period after 1953, yet there was some activity. The fact that there was now only little interest in the subject is hardly surprising in view of the very substantial immigration to Israel during 1948–1953. This made the problem of population growth through increased natality more or less irrelevant. The variation in the frequency of the appearance of the population issue can also be found in discussions in the Knesset. Indeed, until 1953, the issue was raised in the Knesset only occasionally and then mainly by members of the religious parties. Since 1953, however, the subject has gradually started to receive more frequent attention, and no doubt this was associated with the constant decline in the volume of immigration to Israel. As before 1953, members of the religious parties were clearly the enthusiastic advocators of granting pronatal incentives as were a few members of the right-wing, nationalist party Herut, but to a much lesser extent. Among members of the left-center Mapai party (the ruling party), there was not much active interest in the pronatal issue except, of course, for Ben-Gurion. This difference in attitude can again be demonstrated through the frequency with which members of the various political parties raised the issue. Indeed, during the period 1954–1962, requests by Knesset members to the government to act more vigorously on the pronatal issue were made on about twenty occasions, with fourteen of them made by members of the various religious parties. And even when the population problem was raised or discussed by members of the left-wing political parties, it was in most cases from its social welfare rather than its pronatal aspect. Some examples of such discussion are shown below.

Already in September 1948, when the new state was just four months old, the then Minister of Health (who was a member of the National Religious party) announced in the Knesset that he had appointed a public committee to consider the population question. One-and-a-half years later, the same minister announced in the Knesset that his public committee had studied various possible pronatal incentives and that a proposal had been submitted to the Prime Minister. This had, however, no practical consequences.

Of more importance, at least because of the wide publicity it received and the number of occasions on which it was raised in the Knesset and in the press, was Ben-Gurion's initiative in paying a fL 100 (approximately US$24 at the exchange rate of January 1, 1973) cash prize to every woman bearing her tenth child. It was in 1949 that he sent the first check. In that year, a budget of fL 35,000 was allocated to enable Ben-Gurion to proceed with his small-scale pronatal cash gift scheme. The Ben-Gurion prize was finally abolished in 1959, and one of the reasons was apparently that many Arab women received it. We have no statistics to show how many Jewish and how many Arab mothers did, in fact, receive the prize during the period, nor is it of much importance. No doubt, in relative terms and possibly even in absolute terms, Arab women received it more frequently. But one aspect was significant. In many cases, the fact that an Arab woman received the Ben-Gurion prize was reported more widely than its importance deserved. It has never been argued openly that Arab women should not have received the prize on the grounds that a population with a birth rate of over 50 per 1,000 hardly needed pronatal incentives; yet this was indeed the case. This anomaly arose because the prize that was clearly instituted as a symbolic act to encourage *Jewish* families to have more children was, in fact, so frequently granted to Arab women. This is indicative of a more general and important problem, namely, the possible undesirable "side effects" that are likely to result from a population policy that aims at a desired objective. It is perhaps not surprising that it was Ben-Gurion who suggested, over fifteen years later, that any pronatal measures in Israel ought to be administered by the Jewish Agency (which is a Jewish, not a state, organization), and not by the government (see his articles [10; 11]). However, as mentioned, the Ben-Gurion prize was finally abolished in 1959, whether for these or other reasons.

Natality issues have been raised on other occasions in the Knesset, mostly by members of religious parties, but only one more example is presented here. It was a member of the National Religious party who, on July 15, 1959, claimed that Israel's Women's Enrollment Act (whereby every woman aged eighteen must join the armed forces for a specified period) was a significant factor in the decline of the birth rate. As evidence, he attempted to show that the birth rate had been declining since the enrollment act was passed. He asked the Defense Minister in what way the latter intended to act on this problem. Prime Minister Ben-Gurion, serving also as Defense Minister, replied that the decline in the birth rate was causing much concern, although he did not share the view that the enrollment act was an important factor. He said that the demographic problem needed discussions and, even more so, urgent action. (Ben-Gurion did not forget to remind his audience that he had drawn attention to the demographic problem some twenty years earlier.)

It is interesting how, for the religious sector, various issues related to the demographic problem as they saw it: campaigns against the existing abortion regulations, against women's national service in the armed forces, and even against the establishment of public family planning services, and so forth. The pressures that they brought to bear were on all levels, that is, on public opinion, in the Knesset and its committees, and, in particular, in the administrative machine, in which they had considerable power as partners in most government coalitions since the establishment of the state in 1948.

As mentioned earlier, some members of the right-wing parties also pressed for pronatal measures but not nearly as vigorously and as frequently as the religious members. There were members of other parties, too, who raised the population question but never so insistently as the orthodox or the right-wing members. Even antinatal views were occasionally heard in the Knesset, but these were clearly exceptions.

Discussions or questions in the Knesset on the population problems were, occasionally, more specific, in that various aspects of the "population problem" were considered. For instance, two such aspects were social welfare for deprived *large* families and the declining Jewish birth rate. These two distinct (though certainly not independent) issues were quite often considered together, and in time, they were hardly ever considered separately. Indeed, when in 1962, Prime Minister Ben-Gurion appointed the Natality Committee, it was asked to deal with the various aspects of both these issues. It seems to us that the integration of these two aspects into one "demographic problem" has contributed much, though perhaps unintentionally, to the almost general acceptance of the pronatal issue as *one* of the two aspects of the demographic problem that required governmental action. This is because, on the one hand, there has never been strong objection among Knesset members to pronatal action, although there was no general active interest over the question. On the other hand, there was general interest and strong support for social welfare policies to assist large families. This kind of approach to the two issues seems to be quite typical. Among various persons that we have interviewed who have some connection with these problems, some were in favor of pronatal action, while others were strongly opposed. However, all of them, without exception, strongly favored more governmental support for large families on social welfare grounds.

To sum up this discussion on pronatal activities during the first fifteen years of the Knesset, we may say that, throughout, there were persistent voices demanding the formulation of pronatal policies and action, although these came from only a relatively small number of members, particularly from the orthodox and the right-wing sections. There was practically no objection, except from one or two members of the house. Most members of the left-wing parties seemed to be more or less indifferent, though no doubt sympathetic, to the subject. It seems that the integration of the pronatal and the social welfare issues into one population problem made it even more acceptable. Consequently, the government was in a position to work in the direction of formulating a pronatal policy and acting upon it if and when it considered it appropriate.

¶ ESTABLISHMENT OF THE NATALITY COMMITTEE

Political Background.
The demographic problem was discussed not only in the Knesset. At times, it received the attention of the press in editorials and articles. The attitudes have mostly been favorable toward action that would be likely to increase Jewish fertility, although in a few cases, the possible undesirable consequences of such action have been emphasized. While the demographic problem continued to receive attention occasionally in the Knesset, in the press, and from time to time in public appearances by public figures, Ben-Gurion's government decided to appoint in 1962 a special committee to inquire into the demographic problem. What seems clear from the foregoing discussion is that Prime Minister Ben-Gurion himself had a long-standing interest in the population problem and that it was his conviction that this was one of Israel's major problems, requiring urgent attention. It has also been shown that, not only was there no real objection within Ben-Gurion's own party, but there was even enthusiastic support both from the right and from the various religious political parties. During this period, Ben-Gurion, from time to time, held consultations and discussions with various people on the subject, among them Professor Roberto Bachi. Ben-Gurion appointed Bachi as chairman of the Committee for Natality Problems (referred to as the "Natality Committee") on April 1, 1962. Of the eight members of the committee, at least three could be regarded as enthusiastic pronatalists, and three more as sympathizers. The charges to the committee were: to enquire and to advise the government on matters concerning natality policies and, in particular, to consider means by which large and deprived families could be assisted. The recommendations of the committee were submitted to the government in the form of a report in April 1966.

Status of Family Planning.
A proper assessment of this report can only be made against the background of the status of family planning, induced abortions, and family allowances at the time of the appointment of the Natality Committee. In common with most countries that have no officially declared natality policy, Israel has, and has had in the past, regulations that relate to fertility. In particular, the status of family planning facilities, regulations concerning

induced abortions, and various child allowances are relevant factors since their possible change might affect patterns of future fertility. The accessibility of family planning services and of induced abortions is of particular importance in Israel. This is because nearly half of Israel's population (that is, those of Afro-Asian descent) has been in the process of transition from its former high fertility levels to moderate or low fertility levels. The availability of such services could speed up their transition which, in turn, could have significant consequences on future population growth and composition.

Generally speaking, all the different kinds of contraceptives are available, including oral contraceptives and IUDs. The use of modern contraceptives requires a physician's advice, which is obtainable in Israel but on a strictly private basis. Thus family planning services are conspicuously absent from general public health services, which include almost the entire range of medical assistance. It is not suggested that there has been a deliberate and conscious governmental policy against the provision of family planning services in Israel, but that this is one consequence of political, demographic, and religious factors that have been discussed, in that no ministry, governmental agency, or public organization of any significance has considered it of sufficient importance to take the initiative to change the status quo.

Because of the lack of a nonprofit family planning service, only a relatively small percentage of families use effective contraceptives. For instance, only 43 percent of adults in the urban population have described themselves as family planners [12], and there seems to be much public ignorance in Israel about family planning. At the same time, a family limitation method that is used extensively is induced abortions, apparently because the contraceptives that are in common use are so ineffective (due to ignorance).

Formally, induced abortions were illegal in Israel, except for the "purpose of preserving the women's health," but in practice, they can be performed with relative ease, although their cost by local standards is relatively high. This has been the case since 1952, when the then Attorney General recommended that the police should not prosecute a complaint concerning an induced abortion, with the exception of some special circumstances, such as abortions terminating in the death of the woman. One consequence is that, in general, the performance of induced abortions in Israel is under high medical standards. The frequency of induced abortions in Israel is believed to be high, but there are no direct statistics on their annual number. Various estimates of the frequency of induced abortions have been made [13]. According to one of these, 46.7 percent of women aged forty and over had had at least one induced abortion (25, 30, and 52 percent, respectively, among women of Afro-Asian, Israeli, and European origins). Thus, induced abortions are used as a means of birth control in Israel, yet Israel is certainly not unique in this respect.

Israel is perhaps different from other countries in its odd combination of fairly liberal regulations concerning induced abortions, on the one hand, and an illiberal state concerning family planning, on the other. There are, of course, pressures from various quarters, particularly from religious parties, to alter legally the regulations concerning induced abortions so as to restrict their number, but these have so far been of no consequence.

Like many other countries that have no official population policies, Israel has a system of family allowances, and these obviously vary with family size. Do these have a pronatal effect? A study of income tax regulations shows clearly that income tax has, in practice, neither a pronatalist nor an antinatalist effect. In terms of percentages of total income, marginal benefits for an additional child are relatively low, that is, mostly in the range of 2–3 percent of total income. A similar conclusion is drawn if national insurance allowances for children are studied; that is, these, too, have no significant pronatal effect.

Thus, three aspects related to fertility and birth rates, which are under governmental or public control, have been mentioned briefly: family planning, induced abortion, and children's allowances. Of these aspects, only family planning, or rather the lack thereof, may have (at least in the short run) pronatal effects.

¶ REPORT OF THE COMMITTEE FOR NATALITY PROBLEMS
The report of the Natality Committee was submitted to the then Prime Minister Levi Eshkol in April 1966. Its content is summarized here under three main headings.[3]

The Demographic Situation.
The report summarizes the findings of studies on the demography of Jews in Israel as well as the Diaspora (the Jews living outside Israel).

Generally speaking, the fertility of Jews in Western countries is described as being highly controlled and low. According to the report, the low Jewish fertility, the holocaust suffered by European Jewry, and the high frequency of mixed marriages (between Jews and non-Jews) had led to a demographic recession of Western Jewry. The demographic situation among Jews in the Soviet Union was said to be very similar.

---

[3] The content of these sections attempts to summarize the main findings and recommendations of the Natality Committee and consists *entirely* of translations or summaries in English of appropriate sections of the report, which appeared in Hebrew [*14*], except for a few footnotes. A critical evaluation of these findings and recommendations is presented in following sections.

As for fertility levels of the Jewish population in Israel, the different sectors (says the report) should be considered separately. The report states that, among women of European origins, family size is in the order of 2.3–2.4 children per woman. This leaves just a very slight margin of population growth, which is stated to be not only bad in itself but also indicative of the probable future fertility levels of the Afro-Asian section of the population. Families of European origins control their fertility through the use of contraceptives and a very high frequency of induced abortions. (In a further section, the report gives more details on the nature and frequency of induced abortions in Israel.) As for women of Afro-Asian origins, the report states that they are in the first stage of fertility control which becomes more pronounced the greater the length of residence in Israel. Consequently, the birth rate among Jews in Israel has been declining continuously, and at the time of the report (1966) was less than half the fertility level of the Arab community in the country.

The socioeconomic problems of large families in Israel make up an important part of the report. It is shown that the frequency of large families is high among the Afro-Asian sector, and that family size and the achievements of school children in Israel are inversely related. Since some 44 percent of the total number of children grow up in large families, it follows that, on average, the educational levels of the population are likely to deteriorate. The fact that a high percentage of these large families are of Afro-Asian origins makes this social problem even more acute. It is clear, therefore, says the report, that, on average, educational achievements in the country as a whole are much lower than they would have been if there were no such fertility differentials among the various sections of the Israeli population, that is, if the fertility of women of European origins had been higher.[4] The report concludes the section by stating that differential fertility in Israel creates a very serious problem as to the quality of the younger generations and might have important bearings on the future development of the country.

Major Demographic Problems in Israel.
The Natality Committee, after analyzing sociodemographic patterns in Israel, concluded that three aspects of the demographic situation in Israel caused particular concern:

[4] This last sentence, within the present context, obviously implies that closing the educational gap should come as a result of a combination of "more education for the poor and more children for the rich" rather than *more* education and *less* children for the poor. This, again, is characteristic of the conflict between socioeconomic aims, on the one hand, and demographic aims, on the other.

(1) A reduction in the rate of growth of the population in the future seems undesirable from several viewpoints. The demographic-economic condition is such that an increase in the present size of the population and a substantial rate of population growth might stimulate economic development. Population growth could also increase Israel's capacity to absorb further immigration. Should there be no large-scale immigration, then significant population growth can come about only through higher natural increase. By means of an increased birth rate, the Jewish population of Israel would make an important contribution toward the rebuilding of world Jewry, whose general demographic situation is very unfavorable at present. A high rate of population growth seems most desirable from the standpoint of political and national security factors; however, while these factors are often dealt with by Israel's statesmen, the committee felt itself unqualified to consider them.

(2) There is social inequality in the demographic sphere. It is easier for the affluent and the educated to obtain information about, and the means of, birth control. These affluent families limit their fertility to a great extent and refrain from having large families, although they could raise and support more children under favorable economic conditions and without sacrificing too much. In contrast, poor families with low educational levels have many children who are often brought up in unfavorable economic conditions, and they constitute a heavy economic burden. These factors have important bearings on the quality of the younger generation growing up in Israel.

(3) Family planning in Israel is, to a very large extent, achieved through the use of primitive, unsophisticated contraceptives and through the practice of induced abortions. The extent of the practice of induced abortions in Israel has harmful implications from moral, health, and demographic points of view.

The report adds at this stage that future declines in natural increase might result from the gradual spread of family planning among families in Israel. The committee considered whether it would be desirable to attempt a restriction of the spread of family planning in Israel. It concluded, however, that such an attempt would not only be unfeasible but also undesirable for moral as well as for other reasons. It is important, according to the report, that the transition toward controlled fertility in Israel should not bring about "exaggerated" reductions in fertility, but rather it should become a trend toward "responsible parenthood" that would take into consideration, apart from private preferences, the "national interest" also.

In accordance with these general considerations, specific suggestions were made by the Natality Committee, and these will be noted below.

Recommendations for a Population Policy.

The *first* recommendation concerns the establishment of a special body, within the government framework, to deal with general questions of natality and with problems connected with the welfare of the family. This body would be responsible for carrying out the demographic policy recommended by the committee. The body, which should not be a ministry, would act as a coordinator between the appropriate organizations to ensure the carrying out of the recommended policies. Specifically, it would be responsible for:

(1) Expressing opinion on new legislation proposed by the various ministries concerning population in general and the welfare of the family in particular.
(2) Examining and studying demographic problems in Israel and attempting to make the public aware of these through educational means. This should be done, as far as possible, through existing governmental machinery.
(3) Proposing action with the aim of closing the socioeconomic gap between children brought up in small families and those brought up in large families.
(4) Initiating research on population problems and on family welfare.
(5) Advising the government, through the Prime Minister, on all matters concerning population and family welfare and encouraging voluntary organizations to act in these fields.

It was agreed that the offices were to be located in the office of the Prime Minister, although at least one member of the Natality Committee suggested that the Jewish Agency (which represents world Jewry and is not an Israeli governmental organization) might be a more appropriate location because the policy was intended to increase Jewish fertility, rather than that of the total population.

The *second* recommendation of the Natality Committee concerns governmental action in initiating psychological stimulants, designed to increase natality and to reorientate families toward having more children. The report states that the education of the public (and, in particular, those of child-bearing ages) on the responsibility of the family for the welfare of their children, on the one hand, and for the future of the nation, on the other, is of vital importance. In this respect, the public should be aware of where its duty lies. From a purely national point of view, each family should aim at having the maximum number of children that it can raise with the support of the state. But it is understood that the national interest is only one aspect of this very complex matter. Indeed, desired family size is determined according to the individual and legitimate preferences of each family. However, for information purposes, the committee considered that it might be advisable to state clearly that: "If all families bore two children only, a dangerous demographic recession would follow. Families of three contribute just marginally, and only families of four or more children make a real contribution toward the demographic revival of the nation" [*14*]. Some more specific recommendations follow. For example, it is suggested that education for "responsible parenthood" should be transmitted through various media, such as radio and television, at the public clinics for natal care, at the Kupat Holim Health Service clinics, and so on. Such education should also attempt to explain the "great risks" involved in performing induced abortions, on the one hand, and provide information on birth control on the other. But when information on birth control and family planning is provided, the "national interest" in higher natality should be stressed too. The committee also considered that social workers, physicians, and nurses working among families for whom further increase would be a great handicap may inform them about the possibility of obtaining free family planning advice.[5]

The *third* recommendation of the Natality Committee concerns financial and economic incentives for natality. For various reasons, mainly of an economic and social nature, the committee did not consider it desirable to allocate direct monthly family grants as natality incentives. However, it recommended other pronatal incentives. For example, the committee considered the conflict between the aim of increased family size and the existing tendency among Israeli women to participate increasingly in the labor force. So as to minimize the conflict between these, the committee recommended that employers should enable women to work on a part-time basis and enable them to work during convenient working hours. Some other suggestions regarding special facilities for employed women and their children also were considered. The committee dealt, too, with the problem of appropriate housing conditions for "growing" families. It felt strongly that, very often, families who actually wished to have additional children refrained from doing so because their housing conditions were inadequate. Since it becomes increasingly difficult for these families to acquire larger apartments, the committee recommended that state assistance should be granted in such cases as a pronatal incentive.[6]

Another direction in which the Natality Committee recommended indirect children's benefits was high schools as well as higher education. The suggestion was that tuition fees should be inversely related to family size.

The committee also recommended that fiscal policies and, in particular,

[5] The report does not specify where such free advice can be obtained, nor does it make any specific suggestions concerning the establishment of a free family planning service system.

[6] As a matter of fact, the committee was more specific on this point in its attempts to restrict such assistance as a pronatal incentive. The report states that such assistance (in the form of a loan) should be granted subject to various conditions. One of these was that the family would have an additional child within ten months to three years from the date on which an application had been submitted.

income tax regulations should be reexamined. It suggested that income tax allowances should increase progressively from the first to the fourth child and remain constant thereafter.

The *fourth* recommendation of the Natality Committee concerns grants intended to improve the socioeconomic condition of large families in Israel. The committee felt very strongly about the urgent need for real assistance to large families. A subcommittee studied various forms of assistance and concluded that it was advisable to assist such families through the provision of direct services for their children, in particular in education and housing. However, in addition to such support, direct financial support should also be given to such families according to the number of children and family income.

The *fifth* recommendation of the Natality Committee deals with the reduction in the number of induced abortions. In view of the high frequency of induced abortions and their possible negative effects on health, as well as from the demographic point of view, the committee unanimously agreed that it was a serious problem that required attention. However, as far as a solution was concerned, the committee's views were sharply divided.

One view, supported by four of the eight-member committee including the chairman (which is referred to in the report as the majority view), was that induced abortions should not be permitted, except in authorized public hospitals and under strict control. Committees would be appointed at these hospitals to consider each case. The main purpose of these committees would be to reduce considerably the number of induced abortions. However, they would act not only on medical indications but on social and family indications too. In those cases where the request for an abortion was approved, it would be performed free of charge. The committees would have appropriate facilities and funds at their disposal to help and assist those women whose requests for abortion were rejected. The performance of an abortion in any place other than in an authorized public hospital should be prohibited under penalty. As mentioned earlier, these views on abortions were supported by four members of the Natality Committee. Three members (out of the eight) felt that, although there were certainly great advantages in restricting the performance of abortions to authorized public hospitals only, thus ensuring that they would be carried out by specialized physicians, "they could not support the restrictions proposed by the Natality Committee's majority."

Several arguments were put forward by these three members. They felt that the majority proposal would tend to make illegal induced abortions more costly, rather than significantly to reduce their number, and thus create even greater inequality between the rich and the poor in this respect. They also felt that such new regulations would tend to "push" the performance of abortions to "back streets," while, at present, they were being performed under relatively favorable conditions.[7]

Another member of the committee who disagreed with the majority proposal was the Director General of the Ministry of Health, and he, too, submitted his own proposals. He stated that the majority proposal was intended mainly to increase natural growth and was based on the assumption that a reduction in the number of abortions could achieve this. He did not believe, however, that through legal action the frequency of abortions could be reduced. Experience in Israel showed that induced abortions were performed under satisfactory medical conditions, and this was probably the reason for the relatively low incidence of complications. He was convinced that induced abortions were unacceptable as a means of birth control, and he concluded that the best way to reduce the number of abortions in Israel was to educate the public in the use of effective and sophisticated contraceptives and to make these widely available.

The *sixth* item in the Natality Committee recommendations deals with the financial problems connected with a population policy. The committee felt that it could not, at that stage, make a specific statement concerning financial requirements, but it believed that there would be no hope for an effective policy without the allocation of substantial funds for the purpose. The committee made this statement in spite of the great financial stresses on Israel and its government. Nevertheless, it felt that the problems of population growth and quality might become crucial for Israel politically, economically, and socially. Israel has invested enormous amounts in its immigration policies, and there was no doubt that achieving population growth through immigration was much more costly than through increased natality.[8]

In the *seventh* recommendation, it is suggested that the body to be established (see recommendation 1) should initiate research on topics connected with pronatal policies.

The *eighth* recommendation mainly reemphasizes the great difficulties and problems involved in the formulation and establishment of pronatal policies and action but does not add much to the more specific recommendations 1–7.

---

[7] The report also contains the reaction of the "majority" to these qualifications.

[8] It seems odd how categorically this last statement was made. There is no doubt that, without a thorough study of these two kinds of costs, even accepting the general assumption that it is rational policy for Israel to invest in population growth, this statement cannot be substantiated.

¶ THE DEMOGRAPHIC CENTER

The establishment of a governmental body to deal with natality problems was proposed in the first recommendation of the Natality Committee. Accordingly, the government, at its meeting of April 9, 1967, decided to establish the "Demographic Center" to act as an administrative unit at the Prime Minister's office. It was stated in the government's decision that the aim of the center would be "to act systematically in carrying out a natality policy intended to create a psychologically favorable climate, such that natality will be encouraged and stimulated, an increase in natality in Israel being crucial for the whole future of the Jewish people" [15].

The administrative framework within which the center would act was drawn. There would be a public committee of about 100 members, representing the various governmental departments, public organizations, and nongovernmental departments, as well as members of the general public. This public committee was to meet several times a year for the purpose of obtaining information, exchanging views, and proposing the general policy direction.

There was to be an executive council of some twenty members to direct the center's work and policies. The members of the executive council would represent the various ministries and selected public organizations, and they would meet frequently.[9]

The Demographic Center was also to have committees of experts to give advice on various subjects. So there were to be committees to deal with research, induced abortions, information, and so on.

The center's permanent staff were to carry out the policies as formulated by the executive council and to coordinate between ministries, obtain information and data, and carry on the routine operations.

According to this general outline, the Demographic Center was established on June 1, 1968, and its first director was Zena Harman, qualified in social work, formerly an official at United Nations headquarters (UNICEF). The public committee's inauguration ceremony took place on July 1, 1968, in the presence of Prime Minister Levi Eshkol. Among the main speakers were the Prime Minister himself, Professor Bachi, and Mrs. Harman.

In his address, Prime Minister Eshkol emphasized the great importance of increased natality for the Jewish people as a whole, because so many millions had been lost in the Holocaust. However, no less important was the labor shortage in Israel and this, too, demanded a higher rate growth.

---

[9] Incidentally, six of the eight members of the Natality Committee (including the chairman) joined the executive council of the Demographic Center.

He concluded by presenting his good wishes and appreciation to the members of the public committee.

Professor Bachi mainly summarized the population problems of Israel as outlined in the report of the Natality Committee.

In her address, Mrs. Harman said, among other things, that it was necessary to encourage an increase in the size of smaller families, on the one hand, and to look after the welfare of the larger families, on the other. She also stated that: "We cannot refrain from the necessity of deciding what should be the optimum number of children per family in Israel, taking into consideration the welfare of these children. We might decide on five or four children per family as the optimum average." She added that, in her view, "long-term policies should aim at the maximum number of children per family raised under favorable economic conditions" [16]. Mrs. Harman also mentioned the committees of experts, some already appointed and others soon to be appointed. These included committees on finance, housing, health and abortions, education, information, problems concerned with the employment of women, and research.

Subsequently, a few more meetings of the public committee of the Demographic Center took place in which reports of the center and its research groups were read.

Activities of the center to date have been in three areas: research, publicity, and experimentation. Research has been initiated on Israeli attitudes toward having a third and fourth child. The center has promoted large families through various public channels such as radio and television. It has also initiated a small-scale program through which couples intending to have another child may, under certain conditions, apply for a low-interest loan for the purpose of acquiring a larger apartment. There are various other programs under consideration; however, nothing of significance has been done toward their implementation nor does it seem likely that any large-scale action will be attempted in the foreseeable future because of Israel's current economic difficulties.

In conclusion, it seems fair to say that Israel had a Natality Committee whose recommendations were accepted. Although governmental machinery has been available to deal with demographic problems, it has not carried out in a systematic way the recommendations of that committee.

¶ A CRITIQUE OF THE RECOMMENDATIONS

Lack of Attention to Immigration.
The Natality Committee at its appointment was charged to advise the government on matters concerning natality policies and to consider means

to assist large and deprived families. Keeping in mind the political, social, and demographic background against which the committee was appointed, this charge seems to have been far too narrowly defined. This is so because at least some of the problems that have been quoted as justifying a pronatal policy for Israel were problems resulting from differential rates in population growth (for instance, between ethnic groups within the Jewish population, between national groups in the total population of the country, and so forth). Such imbalances in population growth rates can, in principle, be reduced either through increases in natural growth—that is, in fertility— (because expectation of life is high for all population groups) or through increases in immigration balances. But considerations concerning immigration policies were almost excluded from the committee's dealings. Thus, even assuming that the achievement of higher rates of population growth among Jews in Israel is a desirable goal (which in itself needs demonstration), this still leaves open the question as to the relative merit of immigration or fertility as possible means to achieving that goal.

Omission of Demographic Targets.

Another important omission of Israel's Natality Committee was clear and specific fertility targets that would eliminate, or substantially reduce, the social-political-economic problems that have been identified in its analysis. In its report, the Natality Committee reached the conclusion that "some aspects and problems in the demographic trends in Israel were causing concern" [14], and these led it to formulate its pronatal recommendations. But, in terms of a specific statement concerning optimal fertility goals, the committee's report was rather vague.

In one section of the report, though, it was stated that for "publicity purposes it should be declared that, from a national point of view, every family should aim at the maximum number of children that it could bring up and educate properly." The conclusion of that section was that "only families with four or more children make their full contribution to the demographic revival of the nation" [14, p. 30]. Was an average family size of 4+ really considered only for publicity purposes, or was it, after all, a fertility objective? In an address given by the first director of the Demographic Center a few years later, an optimum family size of 4–5 children was mentioned. Can this be taken as the fertility objective? But if Israel's problems, which called for the establishment of a policy, required adjustments in the growth rate of various population subgroups, then fertility targets alone are certainly inadequate. Indeed, a rational policy should have stated specific targets both in terms of fertility and immigration, which brings us back to the previous point. Also, though of less importance, without stating specific targets, it becomes difficult to make an assessment as to the kind of policies that are required, nor is it easy to evaluate, when the time comes, the effectiveness of the policies that have been adopted.

Failure to Examine Fertility Trends More Fully.
Implicit in the committee's report were a number of assumptions about fertility trends, differentials, and the possible future direction of fertility processes within Israel. Some of these assumptions were empirical, but the committee did not test them adequately. These relate to fertility trends and differentials among Jews and between Jews and Arabs. In the next section, we will attempt to evaluate these fertility patterns, starting with fertility trends among Jews.

FERTILITY PATTERNS

The report of the Natality Committee, in its analysis of fertility changes among Jewish people of European origins in Israel, states that fertility was high in the period before the British rule of Palestine, declined during the 1920s, and reached its minimum level toward the late 1930s. Then came the "baby boom" which lasted until the early 1950s. Since then, says the report, fertility has declined again to its low pre-baby-boom levels. The report concludes that, in recent years, fertility has stabilized at a low level, that is, to total fertility rates of 2.3–2.4 children per woman. This was one of the reasons, according to the committee, that necessitated a pronatal policy in Israel. It seems, however, that fertility indices in terms of "current measurements" are inadequate for the purpose of assessing whether or not higher fertility should be encouraged through appropriate policies. For instance, the fact that there has been a significant fertility decline since the early 1950s, in terms of "current measures," cannot be considered as convincing evidence of a significant decline in *family size* in recent years. The concepts of number of births per woman or per family of cohorts seems to be of much greater significance in the present context. Unfortunately, the committee did not have the kind of data at its disposal that would permit a proper cohort analysis of fertility trends in Israel, which may explain the use of unsuitable measures. However, it must be realized, as many studies have shown, that the use of current fertility measures might be misleading when trends in family size are of interest. Cohort studies for other modernized societies have demonstrated, and this will also be shown through some rough calculations for one population group in Israel, that fundamentally there has been one simple and dominating trend in fertility and family size in the present century: the transition from a relatively large family size toward a relatively small family size. It was found in such studies that fertility patterns were subject to fewer variations around this main trend when cohort fertility indices were used rather than current indices.

An attempt to reconstruct fertility estimates based on birth cohorts for one population subgroup in Israel has been made, which may enable an examination of trends in family size by age for a few birth cohorts of that group. This might also provide a basis for a more realistic assessment of projected family size for the younger cohorts of women, when completing their fertility histories in the next few decades. Thus, Table 7 presents estimates of cohort fertility for the Israeli-born population group which have been calculated somewhat roughly from current vital statistics data. There are two reasons why the cohort estimates were made for this particular group. The first is that, as this group is not affected by immigration, the problems of the bias which may be introduced by migration, when current fertility rates are accumulated for a given cohort, does not arise.[10] But the second reason is perhaps more important. The relative importance of the Israeli-born group does increase from one generation to the next,[11] and their fertility patterns will no doubt dominate in the future.

The upper part of Table 7 shows the number of children born, by birth cohort and by age. The right-hand lower part of the table shows *projected* values.[12] Two interesting features of the figures in Table 7 deserve attention. The first is that the number of children per woman has declined by one child between the 1915 and the 1930 birth cohorts. The second is that, since the 1930 cohort, fertility has been fairly stable at the level of an average of 2.75 children per woman, in spite of the considerable changes shown by current fertility indices. It should perhaps be added that, although these figures are rough estimates, their general validity is congruent with results of 1961 census data.

The projected average family-size values in Table 7 suggest a value of 2.50–2.75 children per woman for the coming cohorts, in the absence of effective pronatal incentives. Thus, for purposes of illustration, we will consider 2.6 children per woman as an average that, it may be assumed, will establish itself in the future for this population group in the absence

---

[10] For a more detailed discussion of these biases, see [17].

[11] For instance, from projections made by the Israeli Central Bureau of Statistics, it can be seen that by 1985 the 15–29 age group will consist of nearly 95 percent Israeli-born.

[12] Basically, these were calculated under the assumption that the ratio between the number of children born of a given cohort to a given age and five years younger will equal the same ratio for a cohort born five years earlier. However, a modification was introduced to allow for the changing composition between cohorts of women by origin of their fathers (that is, Western or Afro-Asian), which is an important variable in fertility levels' variations.

TABLE 7.

Average Number of Children Born per Woman to Age X, Israel,
1915–1950 (by birth cohort of women)

Age X	Cohort of Women Born around the Year:							
	1915	1920	1925	1930	1935	1940	1945	1950
20	0.12	0.12	0.12	0.12	0.13	1.10	0.08	0.07
25	1.09	1.02	1.01	1.02	0.87	0.89	0.85	(0.81)
30	2.25	2.13	2.02	1.92	1.81	1.86	(1.89)	(1.71)
35	3.15	2.90	2.61	2.48	2.47	(2.52)	(2.42)	(2.33)
40	3.58	3.25	2.88	2.77	(2.71)	(2.78)	(2.67)	(2.58)
45	3.66	3.32	2.94	(2.82)	(2.76)	(2.84)	(2.70)	(2.60)

NOTE: Figures in parentheses are projected values.

of effective fertility incentives. However, it is perhaps more important to consider what increases in family size are likely to result if the government will, in fact, act seriously in the direction of establishing a pronatal policy in line with the recommendations submitted.

¶ PROBABLE EFFECTS OF POLICIES ON BEHAVIOR

Effects on Fertility and Family Size.

The understanding of social processes has not yet reached such an advanced stage that the kind and the extent of demographic responses to specific policies can be predicted, except in a very general manner. Therefore, the discussion that follows is based upon general theoretical considerations and on experiences in other societies. It must be admitted that the validity and relevancy of these experiences for the Israeli case may, in some instances, be open to question. The main question we pose is this: "To what extent can the fertility of the Jewish population in Israel be expected to increase through the pronatal policies that have been recommended recently?" The answer to this question is of such importance in the present context that even an answer based mainly upon assessments is preferable to no answer at all. This is because, if it is unlikely that significant fertility increases can be expected from the proposed policies, important implications follow at once. It is not only that there might be no returns to investments into the proposed policies (which may or may not be high), but there might be, in addition, the costs involved in not following alternative policies. If, on the other hand, it appears likely that a significant fertility increase can be expected in response to the proposed pronatal policies, it still does not follow necessarily that such policies are, in fact, rational. For in that case, the effect of increased fertility upon such problems as have been identified ("political," "social," and so forth) must be considered. But we leave such questions to a later section, while in this we consider the likelihood of achieving a significant increase in fertility and family size in response to a pronatal policy.

Several sample surveys of the Jewish population have been taken in recent years in Israel to study, among other things, attitudes toward family size ideals and preferences. In particular, the attitudes of people toward increasing their families in response to fertility incentives have been studied [18; 12]. On the question of whether the respondent thought that in his/her case pronatal policies of various kinds would affect his/her fertility behavior, only a minority replied positively (25–40 percent of such groups that currently have low fertility). This only shows that Israeli families (as those in other societies) do not reproduce for the "benefit of the nation" (whatever this means) even if the nation does provide some assistance. It is, of course, possible that, through a pronatal publicity campaign, the number of people who are willing to respond positively to fertility incentives might increase. Let us assume, therefore, that as many as 50 percent of families might be willing to increase the number of their children in response to policies. Then with a fertility level of 2.6 children per woman,[13] an average *increase* of 3–4 children per woman (that is, 3–4 in addition to the current average) among those families who are "willing" to increase their fertility in response to policies would be necessary in order to achieve a national average family size of 4–5 children.[14] Even reaching a modestly large national average family size of only 3.5 children would, under these assumptions, imply that those families who are willing to increase the number of their children (say, 50 percent) would have to bear nearly 2 extra children on average. Are changes of such magnitude likely to occur? Taking as examples other countries that have had pronatal policies, it would be quite correct to state that there is no precedent, anywhere, for policies that have achieved even 1 extra child on average, in a substantial portion of the population, let alone 2, 3, or 4 extra children.

Thus, there seems to be a very substantial gap between present fertility trends in the Jewish population in Israel and the average family size that has been mentioned as "required" or as an "optimum" from the point of view of "national needs." This, and the fact that only a minority of families in Israel are, at present, prepared to change their productive behavior

---

[13] This is the fertility level that seems to establish itself among Israeli women, whose fertility patterns will, no doubt, dominate in the future.

[14] As mentioned earlier, this is the mean number of children per family considered as optimum by the Demographic Center. The committee has mentioned families with four or more children as fulfilling national needs.

in response to fertility incentives, means that this minority would have to increase their fertility behavior by an enormous extent in order to achieve a significant increase in the national average family size. It seems inconceivable, therefore, that such family size objectives as have been mentioned could be achieved with the policies proposed or even with those fertility incentives that are known to be under consideration at present. As will be suggested, there have been similar, though not identical situations, either where very substantial economic incentives were offered or where there were almost no economic barriers to having more children, in addition to attempts to create and spread a pronatal ideology. In all of these situations, the increments in family size were insignificant or nonexistent. One such example was, of course, in France.

It is strange how, among certain circles in Israel, the myth of "the very effective pronatal policies of France" has been accepted. It is, of course, certain that France has invested a very great deal in her pronatal policies, and there is no doubt that Israel could not afford a pronatal investment on such a scale which, according to calculations made for the Natality Committee, would cost about 12 percent of Israel's gross national product in 1969 [14, p. 63]. However, the available evidence indicates that French pronatal policies have not been really effective. The minimum completed average family size was recorded for the 1945 marriage cohort in France, with a slight increase for the 1955 marriage cohort of the order of 0.20 child. This is not a very impressive increase even if it can be wholly attributed to the policies.

Glass, in his article on "Fertility Trends in Europe since the Second World War," states that "even where fertility has risen somewhat as compared with the position of the marriages of the 1930s there is no evidence of a return to large families. On the contrary, the proportions of married women having 4 or more live births have generally continued to fall" [19]. The author refers, of course, to all west European countries irrespective of whether or not they had pronatal policies. Is Israel likely to achieve very much more than France, in terms of additional children per married woman, with a very much lower pronatal investment? Of course, there are differences between Israel and west European countries that attempted pronatal policies, in that Israel has political problems that the others did not have. Indeed, one of the recommendations of the Natality Committee dealt with a publicity campaign which should be carried out as an instrument for achieving increases in fertility. The question of the extent to which such a campaign can be at all effective may be open to different opinions, and in the Israeli case, the results of such a campaign remain to be seen.

Another second example of a situation in which pronatalist efforts did not seem to affect fertility can be drawn from the kibbutz community in Israel. For years, until the early 1950s, the kibbutz community had somewhat lower fertility levels compared with the population at large [20, pp. 158–159]. This phenomenon and the kibbutz family and its functions and roles have been analyzed extensively [21]. The relatively low fertility levels in the kibbutz were consistent, according to the author, with the family functions in the kibbutz, on the one hand, and with the then economic situation in the kibbutz, on the other. For these two reasons, fertility levels in the kibbutz were depressed for years. However, since the early 1950s, a radical change has taken place. The kibbutz society became gradually more differentiated, and the functions of the family have widened. One aspect of this was that the raising of children began to occupy a more important place in the kibbutz family. Moreover, the whole ideology concerning reproductive behavior has changed. In the early days of the kibbutz, children were a heavy economic burden on the community in the sense that an increase in their number implied a higher dependency ratio. It was now realized that higher reproduction levels formed the main instrument to secure the continuation and, indeed, the survival, of the kibbutz community. Faster population growth became a vital issue in the kibbutz, because of the acute labor shortage, but also for other social-demographic reasons. Consequently, various measures intended to reduce some of the burdens of women in pregnancy and after confinement were initiated. In an attitude survey, taken in the late 1950s, positive attitudes toward larger families were expressed by the majority of the sample of kibbutz respondents [22]. Among the reasons for change in these attitudes, both particular ones relating to the kibbutz itself and more general, national-political reasons were quoted as being important.

Thus, fertility levels in the kibbutz might have been expected to rise over the last two decades for several reasons. A new pronatal ideology has been substituted for the traditional antinatalistic ideology that prevailed in the kibbutz for years; the burdens of pregnancy and parenthood have eased; and children occupy a more important place in the family with the shift in its functions. In addition to all these, there were, of course, the same ideological national and political factors (whether they are or are not likely to affect family size preferences) that are common to the population at large. It should also be remembered that, in the kibbutz, an additional child does not constitute an additional economic burden on the family directly. What was the response of kibbutz families to the changes just described? It is difficult to assess real changes in family size in the absence of a cohort fertility analysis. However, we do know that current fertility measures show definite increases in the 1950s and the 1960s. These increases (in current fertility) were in the order of less than 0.50 child, in terms of the total fertility rate. However, there are no signs so far of any spectacular fertility increases, certainly not a return to the "large family."

Is there any inference that can be drawn from the kibbutz fertility experience? Families in the kibbutz and elsewhere in Israel have in common the same national-political and ideological motivations to increase their reproductive levels. Families in the kibbutz, however, have some additional ideological and socioeconomic motivations for an increase in family size. Even if substantial pronatal incentives are one day granted in Israel, an additional child will still be a heavy burden on most families. This hardly applies to families on the kibbutz, at least in its present structure. Is it likely that more significant fertility increases will be achieved in the population at large than have been achieved so far in the kibbutz, through pronatal incentives that have been present in the kibbutz for many years? It is possible, but not likely. It is admitted, however, that this is not strong evidence, but merely lends some additional support to the hypothesis that fertility and family size in Israel cannot be expected to increase significantly in response to the pronatal policies that have been recommended, and there seems to be no chance whatsoever for a return to the large family.

Effects of Restrictions on Induced Abortions
on Family Size.

The foregoing discussion suggested that the pronatal incentives that have been recommended for Israel are unlikely to bring about a major increase in family size preferences. However, besides the efforts to influence family size preferences, there was also one recommendation of the Natality Committee that dealt with the problem of induced abortions. The committee felt strongly that the number of such abortions should be considerably reduced for "moral, health, as well as demographic reasons" [14]. Considering, for the time being, only demographic effects, the purpose behind this recommendation was clearly to increase the number of live births by reducing the number of abortions. Are fertility and family size likely to be affected by regulations concerning the performance of induced abortions? This would clearly be an attempt to increase people's families *against* their own preferences. Could it succeed? Drawing on examples elsewhere, there is no doubt that birth rates have been altered following changes in abortion regulations. For instance, birth rates in Japan were reduced considerably following the liberalization of the abortion laws in the late 1940s and early 1950s. But this was at a time when *preferences* for the small family had already spread in Japan, and it was not the new abortion regulations that brought the birth rate down. Abortions have been used by families, in many countries, as an effective means of reducing fertility in the process of spreading preferences for the small family system. Through recommendations of the Natality Committee, it is hoped to achieve in Israel the opposite of that which occurred in such countries, that is, the achievement of sustaining increase in fertility and family size.[15] Is such a policy likely to succeed? Romania is an interesting example, where current birth rates have twice changed substantially following alterations in abortion regulations.[16] As was typical of eastern European countries, fertility in Romania in the 1930s was still high (crude birth rates of over 30 per 1,000) but subsequently fell quite rapidly. In September 1957, new regulations were issued, allowing abortions to be performed upon request regardless of indication. The birth rate continued to drop, from 22.9 per 1,000 in 1957 to 15.7 in 1963 and to only 14.3 in 1966. In October 1966, a new decree was issued, limiting abortions to a list, which still, however, contained over 100 indications. It included such items as pregnancies endangering life, pregnancies resulting from rape, pregnancies of older women, and others. As a result, the birth rate, which was only 14.5 per 1,000 in the month when the new changes were introduced (October 1966), ten months later reached a level of 39.9 per 1,000 (September 1967). This is no doubt a very impressive and probably unprecedented increase in such a short period, and if it was the end of the story, it could have been a very encouraging case in support of restrictions on abortion as a means of increasing fertility levels. However, it has been shown that, after September 1967, birth rates began to drop again and reached levels of just over 20 per 1,000 toward the end of 1968 [23]. Whether or not the birth rate continued its decline during 1969–1970, and at what level it will stabilize eventually, remains to be seen. To date, there is no evidence anywhere, the Romanian example included, in which a *sustained* increase in fertility has been achieved as a result of regulations restricting the performance of abortions. The report of the Natality Committee considered the practice of induced abortions to be harmful not only in its demographic effects but also in its moral and health aspects. The moral issue obviously depends on one's point of view, and cannot be subject to a rational argument. As for health factors, it is worthwhile, perhaps, to return to the Romanian example. David states that following the revision of the abortion laws in Romania in October 1966:

> The incidence of so-called spontaneous abortions and complications is rising. It was reported at the 1968 Budapest Conference of the European and Near East Region of the International Planned Parenthood Federation that in the

---

[15] Increases in fertility and family size in this context should not be confused with short-term increases in birth rates.

[16] This discussion of the Romanian case is based on [23].

region of the hospital in Baco there were before the change in law about 15,000 induced abortions per year, with no cases of mortality. In the two years after the revision, five deaths occurred due to complications from illegal abortions. In the Filantropia Hospital in Bucharest, there were about 12,000 induced abortions without mortality before the decree of 1966. In the subsequent year there were 1,200 spontaneous abortion cases and two deaths [23, p. 130].

Actually, similar predictions of this nature have been made by the Director General of the Israel Ministry of Health in his memorandum to the Natality Committee [14, p. 71]. Thus, both general theoretical considerations and experience in other societies do not lend support to the hypothesis that fertility and average family size in Israel can be expected to increase significantly as a result of a change in abortion regulations.

In conclusion, it seems that a substantial increase in long-term fertility and family size among the Jewish population in Israel, in response to the pronatal incentives and/or the restrictions on induced abortions that have been recommended by Israel's Natality Committee, is very unlikely. At most, small or short-run fertility increases can be expected that will hardly affect social, political, or national problems in Israel.

In its analysis of demographic processes that are taking place in Israel, the Natality Committee considered the widening gap between Jewish and Arab natural increase resulting from low declining fertility levels among Jews, on the one hand, and from high stable fertility levels among Arabs, on the other. The foregoing discussion attempted to illustrate that continued low fertility among the Jewish population can probably be expected, irrespective of whether or not a pronatal policy will be followed. Is the implicit assumption of future "stability" in the very high fertility levels among Arabs (and particularly among Moslems) realistic? Obviously, the extent of at least one potential source of population concern in Israel will be reduced the earlier a fertility transition among Moslems in Israel begins, and the faster such transition proceeds over time. It is important, therefore, to consider the likelihood of such a transition's taking place among Israel's Arab population in the near future.

THE FERTILITY OF ARABS IN ISRAEL

It has already been shown that the fertility of the Arab community in Israel is high. The Natality Committee dealt with the subject and stated that:

The fertility of Moslems has tended to increase for some time and it is currently very high indeed. For instance, according to the 1961 census, a Moslem woman aged 45–49 at the time of the census had 8.2 children and a Christian woman had 7.2 children (on average). Current fertility data indicate that the fertility of Arabs in Israel is 2.2 times higher than Jewish fertility [14, pp. 16–17].

Since mortality is relatively low among Israeli Arabs, it follows that their current rate of natural increase is high (currently over 45 per 1,000 per year). This is, indeed, an impressive rate of growth implying the doubling of the population every fifteen years. The continuation of such growth depends on the continuation of the very high fertility levels. However, the observation that Moslem women aged 45–49 at the time of the 1961 census had 8.2 children on average is not very revealing. These data relate, of course, to the fertility experience of an older cohort of women. To be sure, current fertility rates are quite high (consistent with over 8 children per woman), but these measures are too crude to determine whether or not this population is in the beginning of a fertility transition. Nevertheless, an abundance of evidence on social and economic changes that have been taking place in recent years in the Arab community in Israel can be cited that makes the assumption of a fertility decline in the near future most likely and the assumption of fertility stability unreasonable. Indeed, such a fertility decline may already have started. From the time of the foundation of the state of Israel until the late 1950s, there was very little interaction between the Jewish and the Arab economic sectors [24]. However, after 1958, this situation started to change when regulations limiting the free movements of Israeli Arabs began to be liberalized by the Israeli authorities, leading eventually to their total freedom of movement. One of the consequences was that the labor market open to Arabs increased substantially. Arabs could now find temporary or even permanent employment in the Jewish economic sector. This development was not restricted to mixed residential towns and cities. Many thousands of Arabs, formerly engaged in agriculture in rural villages, changed their employment to other industries, particularly building and construction. This did not mean that those Arabs who took employment in the Jewish sector transferred their home there. It was, in fact, labor mobility; that is, villagers commuted to work just for the day (or for the week), returning to their home villages at night (or over the weekend). There was clearly a two-way interchange—not only was rural labor imported from the villages to the cities, but elements of modernization and urban life were imported from the cities to those villages.

This labor mobility has intensified over time, for two main reasons. The first was the continuous increase in the man-land ratio in the Arab rural sector which resulted from past rapid population growth [24, pp. 48–49]. Consequently, the pressure on people to seek alternative employment became increasingly strong. Second, such alternative employment also provided much higher income. This kind of labor mobility has increased and intensified, particularly since 1967, and currently tens of thousands of Arabs, men and women, are employed in the Jewish economic sector. These changes in economic activity were associated, as could be expected, with significant increases in participation rates in the labor force of both males and females in the Arab community. For example, between 1958 and 1963, the labor force participation rate of the 14–17 age group increased from 41.5 to 60.6 percent (both sexes). Somewhat smaller but still impressive increases occurred for other age groups. Arab occupational structure changed as well; in particular, there was a significant shift away from rural-agricultural to nonagricultural occupations. Indeed, during 1958–1963, the percentage in agricultural occupations dropped by 50 percent, while participation in nonagricultural occupations doubled. Such changes could be expected to have far-reaching effects in many respects, not the least in family structure and functions. The high rate of labor migration that has developed among Arabs in Israel since 1958 may be viewed as a demographic response to the changes that had taken place in their economic structure in the 1950s and 1960s. Increasing densities and the developing of new economic opportunities were just two aspects of these changes. However, the basic question in the present context is: "Was increased labor migration among Arabs in Israel the only response to the changes discussed?" Have they also responded, as have other societies in the process of modernization, by raising the age at marriage and by reducing marital fertility? And if not, are there any signs that such responses are to follow in the near future? As stated earlier, there are, as yet, no definite answers to these questions. But, we will attempt to examine what little demographic evidence there is in order to arrive at a tentative conclusion.

It may be argued that fertility differences *within* the Arab community are first indicators of future change processes, although such data are far from conclusive evidence. Family size among Arab Christian women was, according to the 1961 census, only 70 percent that of Arab Moslem women. Or considerable fertility differentials can be found according to rural-urban residence, educational levels, and other variables [25]. This does not necessarily mean that in the very near future rapid and significant fertility reduction among the Arab minority in Israel is assured. It does mean, however, that fertility aspirations and family size preferences are not indifferent to changes in other demographic and socioeconomic variables. Indeed, the spread of such elements of modernization, as mentioned above, has a cumulative effect, and these should not be ignored in considering future fertility patterns.

Some evidence on fertility change among Arabs in Israel is available from current fertility data, but this, too, is inconclusive. For example, there has been a notable decline in age-specific fertility rates at the *younger age groups* for both Moslems and Druze in recent years. Declines on the order of 50 percent over a period of five years for the 15–19 age group can be noted. And declines on the order of 15 percent can be noted for the 20–24 age group. Did these declines result from the spread of family limitation within marriages, or did they result from a rise in age at marriage? A definite answer must await the next general census when it may become possible to study changes in marital status composition in these two communities during the 1960s. In the present context, we may draw an inconclusive inference: Both census and current registration data indicate that age at first marriage has been increasing in recent years. Estimates of age-marital status composition, prepared by the Israeli Central Bureau of Statistics, suggest that, since 1961, increases have taken place in the percentage "single" in the younger age groups among Arabs in Israel. Rough calculations based on these estimates have shown that all the declines in age-specific fertility rates among these younger age groups *could have* resulted from changes in nuptiality only. If correct, this may have important social and demographic implications. Couldn't such increases in age at marriage represent a second phase in the response pattern of the younger generations of Arabs in Israel to changes that have been described above (the first phase being labor migration)? And if so, might not one expect (as evidenced elsewhere) a third phase in response, that is, a decline in the number of children born per family?

In conclusion, it seems that any projections or recommended policy that are based on the assumption of the indefinite continuation of the very high fertility levels among Israeli Arabs ignores the powerful forces of social and economic change as well as processes of modernization and demographic change which have occurred elsewhere. The question, "How fast will fertility decline?" is, of course, a vital one, and to that question no definite answer can be offered. Therefore, it seems that the assumption of a long-term continuation of present differentials in natural increase between the Jewish majority and the Arab minority (the source of the "political problem") is totally unrealistic.

We have argued that a substantial increase in long-term fertility and family size among the Jewish population in Israel is most unlikely to result from the pronatal policy that has been recommended to the government. As for the Arab section of the population (particularly Moslem Arabs), we have suggested that their fertility seems likely to decline in the near future if, indeed, such decline has not, in fact, started. If these assessments are realistic, it would imply that the pronatal policy recommended to the government needs considerable revision. It means that such a policy is unsuitable if only because its objective (of increasing fertility) cannot be achieved. However, it is clear that there are also other reasons that make such a policy unsuitable. It is, of course, possible, though unlikely, that the assessments made here are unrealistic and that Jewish fertility and family size in Israel can be increased through pronatal incentives. Such a possibility should be considered and the implications worked out. To be more specific, it is important to work out the socioeconomic and political implications of the possibility of an effective pronatal policy for Israel, although such a possibility seems unlikely.

THE PROBABLE IMPACT OF CHANGES
IN FERTILITY AND IMMIGRATION

The Natality Committee, in its report, identified three "problems" that called for the formulation of a pronatal policy in Israel. It hinted at two other "problems." The proposed policies, which are intended to bring about a substantial rise in fertility, are discussed here from the point of view of their probable effect in eliminating these problems. In other words, an attempt is made here to consider the impact of a significant increase in fertility (although such an increase is most unlikely, as has been discussed in previous sections) in eliminating these problems. However, it might be worthwhile first to restate and summarize the nature of these problems.

¶ THE PROBLEMS

It was argued in the report that from an economic point of view the slowing down of population growth in Israel was undesirable. This will be referred to as *the economic problem*.

It was argued that increased natality would contribute to the demographic revival of world Jewry. This will be referred to as *the Jewish demographic problem*.

Another problem mentioned was the contrast between differential fertility and differentials in economic opportunities. That is, those people (a high proportion of whom are of European origins) who could afford to bring up many children under favorable conditions have, in fact, only few. In contrast, the less affluent (a high proportion of whom are of Afro-Asian origins) have many children. This will be referred to as *the social problem*.

There were two other problems only hinted at in the report, for which a slowdown of population growth was said to be desirable. Both are of political and national security aspects. To be more specific, the first problem is concerned with the Arab minority in Israel whose natural increase is very high. It easily can be calculated that the *indefinite* continuation of such differentials (if these persist!) could cause serious political difficulties. This problem will be referred to as *the political problem*.

The last problem is caused by the difference in population size (as well as rates of natural increase) between Israel and its neighboring Arab countries, in view of the persistent political-military conflict between them. This will be referred to as *the national security problem*.

Apparently, the objective of the natality policies proposed by the committee was to eliminate entirely or reduce significantly the extent and severity of some if not all of these problems. Thus, the questions that will be asked for each of these problems are: "What is the likely effect of a significant increase in fertility and family size in the Jewish population (assuming for argument's sake that such an increase can be achieved in practice) in eliminating these problems?" "And what could be the expected effect of only a modest increase in family size?" To answer these questions, it may be useful first to work out the demographic implications associated with various fertility levels that might develop in the future. However, to permit a comparison of the relative merits of fertility and/or immigration in their effects on these "problems," the demographic effects of immigration should be considered as well. Toward this goal, projections of the Jewish population have been prepared, according to several fertility and migration assumptions. In addition, a population projection for the Arab community has also been prepared.

The results of these projections are presented in summary form in Table 8. The migration volume assumptions are not arbitrary; they have been selected in accordance with plans for future immigration made by two authorities—the Ministry of Immigration and Absorption and the Jewish Agency's Department of Immigration. Indeed, Table 3 suggests that the medium immigration assumption (of 25,000 immigrants annually) is not at all unrealistic. The four fertility assumptions were also not selected arbitrarily. The highest fertility is in accordance with the Demographic Center's declaration of the "optimum family size," that is, a gradual fertility shift to 4.5 children per woman. (This fertility level has been termed as a "return to the large family.") The lowest assumption is the continuation of current trends (that is, 2.6 children per woman), which is equivalent to an assumption that the pronatal policies were either completely ineffective or had never been followed. And there are two intermediate assumptions: a gradual shift to an average family size of 3.0 and 3.5 children per woman respectively, indicating partial effectiveness of the proposed pronatal policies. No major changes were assumed for mortality levels.

It can be seen from Table 8 that, in the absence of any immigration in

TABLE 8.

Actual Jewish Population Size in 1968 and Projected Jewish Population Size in 1985 and 2000, Israel (by fertility levels, according to the effectiveness of policies, and net annual immigration)

Year	Assumptions concerning Future Fertility according to the Effectiveness of the Policies	Actual Population	Projected Population according to Various Assumptions on Future Annual Net Immigration			
			None	15,000	25,000	40,000
Actual 1968		2,435				
1985	Continuation of present fertility patterns, i.e., pronatal policies are ineffective (2.6 children per woman)		3,072	3,435	3,654	4,038
	The proposed policies have marginal or moderate effect — Fertility will stabilize at 3.0 children per woman		3,107	3,474	3,726	4,084
	Fertility will stabilize at 3.5 children per woman		3,159	3,531	3,786	4,149
	Proposed policies are effective: a return to the "large family" (4.5 children per woman)		3,252	3,633	3,894	4,269
2000	Continuation of present fertility patterns, i.e., pronatal policies are ineffective (2.6 children per woman)		3,708	4,417	4,890	5,579
	The proposed policies have marginal or moderate effect — Fertility will stabilize at 3.0 children per woman		3,873	4,604	5,089	5,802
	Fertility will stabilize at 3.5 children per woman		4,127	4,881	5,365	6,125
	Proposed policies are effective: a return to the "large family" (4.5 children per woman)		4,623	5,426	5,971	6,770

the future, the difference in total population size in 1985 would be of the order of 200,000 between the two extreme alternative fertility assumptions, that is, between completely ineffective policies and effective policies that would bring about a "return to the large family." This difference shrinks to less than 100,000 if a transition to only a moderately large family size (of 3.5 children per woman) is assumed. However, by the year 2000, the effects of a return to the large family (4.5 children per woman) and to moderately large families (3.5 children per woman) would be 900,000 and 400,000, respectively. If, instead, we consider projections with higher immigration assumptions, only slightly larger differences in population size, due to a transition to higher fertility, would result. In other words, these *differences* remain almost of the same magnitude irrespective of the particular immigration assumption. This was the effect of the increase in fertility on population size. What would be the effect of immigration on total population size in 1985 and the year 2000? It can be seen that, irrespective of future fertility levels, a considerable effect can be achieved in terms of population growth by an increase in annual immigration. Indeed, a rough (and very much oversimplified) calculation shows that, in terms of population growth in the short run, an equivalent effect resulting from a "return to the large family" (for example) can be achieved through the immigration of less than 20,000 annually. This is, of course, very significant indeed. For, if it is accepted that the probability of Israeli society to "return to the large family" is practically nil, then a shifting of *all* efforts from pronatal policies to the encouragement of more immigration would be wise and rational. Of course, everything depends on the validity of the argument presented in previous sections, namely, that significant increases in fertility and family sizes in response to pronatal policies are most unlikely. According to this argument, not only do pronatal policies in Israel have only a very slight chance of succeeding in bringing about a shift toward larger families, but even in the unlikely event of their success, only a relatively small and minor effect can be expected in terms of population growth in the relatively short run (15–30 years). This almost eliminates the need for an answer to the complicated question of the relative costs involved in the attempt to achieve a higher population growth through either increased fertility or alternatively, through immigration.

However, it still leaves undecided the more general question of whether or not it is at all rational for Israel to invest resources for the purpose of achieving a higher rate of population growth.[17] It may probably be

---

[17] This point should not be misinterpreted. Even if it can be shown that investment in faster population growth is not a good policy, investment in immigration may still be desirable for ideological reasons, even if the extra population growth resulting from immigration involves heavy costs. This has always been accepted in Israel and is probably an essential feature of Zionism.

accepted, in any event, that population growth as such has no value on its own. Population growth may, however, have value as being an instrument for achieving other ends and goals—such as the elimination (or partial elimination) of the five problems defined above. The question of whether or not this is so in the Israeli case is dealt with below.

¶ THE IMPACT ON THE ECONOMIC PROBLEM

Can it be argued seriously, at the present time, that Israel will be significantly better off in economic terms if its population size increases 10–15 percent larger within thirty years (see Table 8)? It may be accepted that faster population growth has certain advantages, but it certainly has disadvantages too. Unfortunately, the costs to society involved in population growth have not even been mentioned in the report submitted by the Natality Committee. The economic advantages to Israel of having a larger population may be divided into two kinds. In an economic system, people are both producers and consumers; Israel has, for some years, suffered from an acute shortage of labor, and it has long been realized in Israel that its relatively small consumer market is a great handicap to industrial expansion. Does it follow, then, that pronatal policies can alter this situation? Even if pronatal policies in Israel could be assumed to have a good chance of being effective, what would be the expected effect on the labor force? In absolute terms, it will begin to grow *faster* only after 20–25 years (when the first generations of the increased fertility reach working ages). However, there is an important factor that should be borne in mind. One of the implications of an increase in fertility is its effects on the age structure. Other things being equal, a rise in fertility would bring about an increase in the dependency ratio, that is, an increase in the young age groups relative to working age groups. The more detailed results of the projections (which are not shown here) suggest that, in the year 2000, the percentage of the age groups 20–64 would be 54.5, if present fertility patterns continue. On the other hand, a "return to the large family" (a gradual shift to 4.5 children per family) would imply a decline in that percentage to only 45.6 percent in the year 2000. Thus, to say the least, increased fertility (if this can be achieved at all through policies) cannot improve the labor force situation in Israel in any sense. Immigration is, of course, a different matter, in the sense that it can increase the labor force in absolute terms *in the short run* and, at the same time, decrease the dependency ratio (as most migrations tend to do).

Can Israel increase its consumer population significantly through pronatal policies? The answer is given in Table 8. Even a 100 percent success in raising fertility (which is most unlikely) would contribute not much more than marginally to Israel's total population size within the next thirty years. In the long run, the effect would, of course, be very substantial. But can anyone seriously advocate, at present, a *long-term* rate of population growth of the order of 2.7 percent per annum (the long-term rate of population growth implied in a "return to the large family") in order to gain (possibly!) some economic advantages in the distant future? There is, of course, extensive literature dealing with economic, environmental, and other consequences of fast population growth [26; 27], and there is no need, therefore, to go into this in more detail here. Nevertheless, it is clear that population growth involves not only economic benefits but also costs of various kinds, and these might be very high in relation to the benefits.

In conclusion, a substantial increase in fertility and family size, even if it can be achieved (which is, of course, most unlikely), can hardly contribute to Israel's economic situation in the short run (within thirty years). This is because neither the labor force situation nor the size of the consumer market can be expected to change significantly as a result of an increase (and even a considerable one) in family size. However, a more significant change could be achieved through increased immigration.

¶ THE IMPACT ON THE JEWISH DEMOGRAPHIC PROBLEM

It is difficult to argue with the rationale of increased fertility as a means for a demographic revival of world Jewry. It is, of course, true that world Jewry lost millions of people during World War II, but this can obviously not be reversed in any way. It may also be true that a substantial number of Jews are lost to Judaism every year (for instance, through mixed marriages as claimed in the committee's report). But the relevant question in the present context is: "To what extent can pronatal policies in Israel contribute to faster population growth of the Jewish nation (assuming this to be a desirable goal)?" Estimates of the number of Jews during the post-World War II period show an annual rate of growth on the order of 1 percent (28, Table B/3]. The same table also shows that the percentage of Jews residing in Israel is approximately 18 percent. Because this percentage is relatively small, Israel simply cannot contribute more than marginally to a faster growth of the Jewish population in the world. A very simple calculation shows that to achieve an *increment* of only 0.25 percent in the annual rate of growth of the Jewish world population within the next thirty years would require an *increment* of nearly 1.5 percent in the growth rate of the Jewish population in Israel. This, in turn, would imply that average family size in Israel would have to increase over and above the "large family" of 4.5 children per woman, which is, of course, most unlikely. In conclusion, it does not seem obvious how a very much faster growth of the world Jewish population would serve a very useful and important purpose. In any event, even if it did, a significantly faster growth of world Jewish population could hardly be achieved through an increase in Jewish fertility in Israel, even if this was a very great increase (which could not be expected anyway). This is because the percentage of the world's Jewish population living in Israel is relatively small.

¶ THE IMPACT ON THE POLITICAL PROBLEM

The "political" problem is undoubtedly very serious and will clearly be even more so in the future. Israel is not the only country having to face the political consequences of differential population growth between minority and majority population groups which may be said to have conflicting political aims. Typical examples are the United States, Canada, Thailand, and others. Israel is different, perhaps, in the way she is trying to deal with the problem. Table 9 shows that, at the end of the year 1968, 86 percent of the population of Israel was Jewish and the remaining 14 percent was non-Jewish, mainly Arabs. Since the extent of the problem depends strongly upon the size of the minority group, it is quite clear that, as long as the political conflict between these groups remains, the problem is likely to become more acute. This is because, in the coming years, the Arab minority in Israel will grow faster than the Jewish majority (even if Arab fertility declines). Moreover, Table 9 suggests that the percentage of the Jewish majority will decline in the next thirty years, almost irrespective of whether or not pronatal policies succeed or not. In fact, it can be seen that, in the absence of any immigration, the percentage of Jews in Israel will decline in the year 2000 to 82 percent (from the present 86 percent), even in the very unlikely event of a "return to the large family" in the Jewish sector. On the other hand, the percentage of the Jewish majority will decline from the current 86 percent to 79 percent if it is assumed that Jewish fertility will continue its present patterns (that is, an average family size of 2.6 per woman). This means that, while the percentage of Jews in Israel will probably continue to decline, an increase in Jewish fertility can do very little to change this expected trend in the coming thirty years. It can be seen, however, that an annual immigration of the order of 40,000 can stop the decline in the percentage of Jews (and this is also the case with a combination of 25,000 immigrants annually *with* a "return to the large family"). Thus, as before, substantial immigration is a much more effective means than is increased fertility to cope with the political problem. However, the "political problem" is unlikely to be eliminated solely through demographic means, in general, or through pronatal policies, in particular.

¶ THE IMPACT ON THE NATIONAL SECURITY PROBLEM

The national security problem is caused by the fact that Israel's population consists of a very small minority in the Middle East region. This and the long-standing political conflict between Israel and her Arab neighbors makes this problem one of the most important issues. Can the extent of the

TABLE 9.

Percentage of the Jewish Population, Israel and Occupied Areas, and the Middle East, Actual Percentage for 1968 Compared to Projected Percentages for 1985 and 2000[a]

(by various assumptions on future migration and fertility according to "minimum projection of Arabs")

Assumption Concerning Future Patterns of:		End 1985			End 2000		
Number of Annual Immigrants	Number of Children per Woman	Percent of Jewish Population in Israel	Percent of Jewish Population in Israel and in Occupied Areas	Percent of Jewish Population in Middle East	Percent of Jewish Population in Israel	Percent of Jewish Population in Israel and in Occupied Areas	Percent of Jewish Population in Middle East
		End 1968[a]			End 1968[a]		
		86	63	3.4	86	63	3.4
None	No change (2.6)	82	57	2.9	78	53	2.8
	3.0	82	57	2.9	79	54	2.9
	3.5	83	57	3.0	80	56	3.1
	4.5	83	58	3.0	82	59	3.5
15,000	No change (2.6)	84	59	3.2	81	58	3.3
	3.0	84	60	3.3	82	59	3.4
	3.5	84	60	3.3	83	60	3.6
	4.5	85	61	3.4	84	63	4.0
25,000	No change (2.6)	85	61	3.5	83	60	3.7
	3.0	85	61	3.5	83	61	3.8
	3.5	85	62	3.5	84	62	4.0
	4.5	86	62	3.6	85	64	4.4
40,000	No change (2.6)	86	63	3.8	85	63	4.1
	3.0	86	63	3.8	85	64	4.3
	3.5	86	64	3.9	86	65	4.5
	4.5	87	64	4.0	87	68	5.0

a Values for the end of 1968 are actual figures for that year. The projections for the years 1985 and 2000 are based on the assumption that the growth of the Arab population in: (1) Israel will experience only a modest decline in fertility according to CBS projections. (2) Occupied areas will experience a modest decline in fertility so that the annual growth rate will be 1.5 percent. (3) The Middle East will be the same as in occupied areas.

problem be reduced through demographic means? The last column of Table 9 shows beyond any doubt that pronatal policies can accomplish nothing in this area. Israel is an ethnic and political minority in the Middle East and will remain so regardless of any population policies that she might want to undertake. Again, the political implications of this problem can be removed only through political and social change and not through demographic change. However, an important qualification should be made here. Since the efforts needed for the defense of a given territory depend mainly on the military strength of the "enemy," then for any given "enemy strength" the burden of defense per person in that territory will be less, other things being equal, the larger the population. Therefore, it would seem that even a 10 percent or 20 percent larger population in Israel in the year 2000 would imply a smaller defense burden per person if other things do remain equal.[18] But, do they? Even ignoring more complicated factors, such as economic and environmental ones (which certainly do not remain equal), it is sufficient here to consider one simple demographic factor. Do persons of different ages contribute equally to defense efforts? For instance, children contribute very little, if anything, and this brings us back to the "labor force" argument that was discussed earlier. In fact, it can be calculated from the projections that a population of 3.7 million or 4.6 million in the year 2000 with the continuation of present family patterns and of a "return to the large family" (of 4.5 children per woman) will have almost *the same absolute size* in the age range 20–64. This is so because an assumption of a gradual "return to the large family" would imply a substantial increase in the proportion of children in the population particularly in the short run (by the year 2000, only a small number of the "increased births" will have reached age twenty). Thus, it is not inconceivable that an increased population in the year 2000, as a result of a significant increase in family size, will, in fact, have a smaller defense capability compared with a smaller population resulting from the continuation of present fertility patterns. Again, it may be argued that immigration can make a positive contribution to national security in the short run. In conclusion, it is difficult to see how an increase in family size can contribute in any way toward the reduction of the extent of Israel's national security problem.

¶ THE IMPACT ON THE SOCIAL PROBLEM

The social problem is a consequence of the prevailing differentials in social economic opportunities, on the one hand, and in fertility, on the other, between the "Afro-Asian" and the "European" sections of the Jewish pop-

---

[18] For a simplified model analyzing the relationship between the "power" and "population," see for instance [29].

ulation in Israel. The Natality Committee was, of course, aware that granting pronatal incentives to those groups currently having large families
(mostly of Afro-Asian origin) makes no positive contribution either to this
group specifically or from a national point of view generally. Therefore,
the Natality Committee recommended both pronatal incentives to small
families for demographic reasons and aid to large families for social welfare reasons. In other words, the policy calls for investments on a massive
scale toward both demographic (pronatal) ends and social ends. Since the
resources that can be made available for these two purposes are necessarily
limited, a rational allocation between the two seems essential. Not only has
no such allocation been considered, but no guidelines have been formulated. However, the question of optimum allocation does not seem to be
too difficult, if the analysis presented here in respect to four other "problems" is accepted as valid. This analysis clearly leads to the conclusion that
no resources at all should be allocated toward the pronatal end because,
even in the unlikely event of a substantial increase in family size in
response to a pronatal policy, there will be no positive contribution toward
reducing the extent of the Jewish demographic, political, national, and
economic problems. On the other hand, since direct investments toward
increasing the standards of living of large families have no doubt a good
chance of making a positive contribution to reducing the socioeconomic
gap, this is certainly a more useful purpose. Consequently, at least as a
guideline, the resources that are made available for both purposes should
all be invested in social aid to large families.

It must be mentioned, however, that high immigration policy is also a
competing goal to "social welfare" from the point of view of available
resources. Nevertheless, contrary to "increased fertility," "increased immigration" contributes positively to at least three of the "problems," in addition to its being the most important element in Zionist ideology. The
analysis in this and the previous sections clearly suggests that, not only have
the recommended pronatal policies in Israel almost no chance of being
effective in raising the fertility of Jews in Israel, but even if fertility could
be increased significantly through policies, this would still contribute only
marginally (if at all) to the elimination of the problems that have been
mentioned by the Natality Committee as justifying the recommended policy. Does it follow that Israel does not need a population policy? Not
necessarily. All that is implied in the above analysis is that the kind of
policy which is being attempted currently is probably not a good one.

DOES ISRAEL NEED A POPULATION POLICY?

Israel has to face problems of various kinds, and some of these are related
to her particular population characteristics. The analysis presented here

attempted to demonstrate that almost none of these problems can be solved, even partially, through a pronatal policy. This is the reason why some of the recommendations contained in the recently formulated pronatal policy do not seem likely to fulfill any useful purposes. It is probably a great advantage if certain aspects of a policy can be shown a priori to be doomed to fail, in which case not only may the policy costs involved in these aspects be saved, but even more important, a possible alternative policy—a useful one—can be sought. It should be borne in mind, too, that, at least theoretically, the major costs of an inappropriate policy may be the losses in not following a more suitable policy. This brings us to the crucial question of whether or not there can be a more useful alternative policy than that recommended. Such a policy must clearly have a high probability of being sufficiently beneficial for the society as a whole and for a good proportion of its members. In suggesting an alternative policy, only the "social problem" will be considered specifically, as this is an example where an appropriate population policy can contribute significantly toward the elimination of a problem, even if it cannot by itself solve the problem. In addition, this alternative policy can also be shown to be more effective in dealing with the other "problems," although it can by no means contribute very much toward their elimination; in these respects, the principles for a policy to be suggested here differ from the official policy that has been adopted by the government.

It seems that a rational policy concerning fertility could contribute significantly to the elimination of the "social problem," that is to say, the problem of the socioeconomic gap between the population of Afro-Asian and that of European origins. Strictly speaking, this problem can only be alleviated through the more equitable distribution of economic means between the two sections, but this aspect requires no further discussion since there is almost no argument on this point. However, such transfers are obviously limited, for economic as well as for political reasons. Therefore, other things being equal, at a given level of such transfer, the closing of the socioeconomic gap between these two population groups is likely to come sooner the earlier and the faster the fertility of the Afro-Asian group declines. It has been shown that fertility levels of the Afro-Asian group have, in fact, been declining since the 1950s, which only shows that the transition to the small family system in this population group is under way. This means that a policy whose aim is the speeding up of this process has a high chance of success and, in turn, is likely to contribute to the solution of the social problem.

Thus, it follows that a more rational policy for Israel would be to invest resources in an efficient system of free family planning services rather than in a pronatal policy. In addition to its likely contribution toward the closing of the socioeconomic gap, such a policy may have some other merits too (which could be considered a bonus). For instance, such a policy is likely to help many couples (from whatever population group) to substitute efficient contraceptives for inefficient ones and, by this, reduce the number of induced abortions. Further, there is some likelihood that such services would be increasingly used by Israel's Arab minority and, thus, contribute to the solution of the "political problem" in the long run. This policy might help families to space their confinements more efficiently according to their own choices and preferences and, thus, make an indirect contribution to an increase in the amount of female employment in *the short run*. Not least important, such a policy is clearly in the public interest, in the sense that it would contribute toward the improvement of the present situation in the family planning market in Israel.

It should be made clear that it is not suggested here that the recommended pronatal policy should be replaced by an antinatal policy. It is merely suggested that a deliberate pronatal policy, of which one aspect is practically (though not officially) an anti-family planning policy, is not only inconsistent with the aims and preferences of many families and individuals, but it contributes almost nothing to national or social interests. A pro-family planning policy, on the other hand, is consistent with the individual aims of people, in the sense that everybody may use the service but nobody is obliged to do so.

The second aspect of the population policy suggested here is the diversion of efforts and means currently invested or intended to be invested in a pronatal policy toward the task of increasing Jewish immigration to Israel. There is no need to repeat in detail the merits of immigration to Israel from a national point of view or from the point of view of the immigrants themselves. Much has been written on this for over half a century; however, to mention just a few specific points that have been analyzed previously, it should be repeated that it is high (but not unrealistically high!) immigration that possibly can achieve a nondeteriorating balance between Jews and Arabs in Israel (the "political problem") or in the Middle East (the "national security problem"). Such a situation could not even be hoped to be achieved by the most optimistic future fertility levels that might result from massive pronatal incentives. Since most migrations have a high proportion in the relatively young-adult age groups, a high immigration volume is likely to contribute, in *the short run,* toward an increase in the labor force (both in absolute and in relative terms) and also increase the Israeli consumer market more efficiently (as compared with higher fertility). Even from the point of view of world Jewry (the "Jewish demographic problem"), more immigration seems to make a more important contribution compared with marginally higher fertility rates in Israel. In addition to these, immigration has probably been the most impor-

tant element of Zionist ideology for over half a century, which even adds
to its utility from practical considerations. However, a policy that aims at
high immigration is problematic, too, and calls for some qualifying remarks. First, one obvious fact that has already been mentioned is that,
similar to increased fertility, increased immigration involves high costs in
terms of alternative goals. And it should be reemphasized that the foregoing analysis attempted to demonstrate one important point, namely, that
it is more rational to invest in a high immigration policy, not because the
costs per one "additional" immigrant are necessarily less than per one
"additional" birth, but merely because increased fertility simply cannot
solve any of the problems that have been mentioned as giving rise to the
need for a pronatal policy. Second, there is of course the question of the
feasibility of long-term high immigration to Israel. Two preconditions
should be satisfied for such immigration to be feasible: There must be a
large enough number of potential immigrants able and willing to immigrate
to Israel, under given appropriate conditions; and Israel must be able and
willing to create such conditions so as to attract these potential immigrants.
As for the first point, it seems that a long-term average net immigration
stream of the order of 40,000 a year (as our maximum assumption in the
projections) is unlikely, unless the Soviet Union will allow the continuation of out-migration of Jews. This is so simply because the number of
Jews that are still left in Afro-Asian countries is relatively small. On the
other hand, the number of Jews in Western countries who can be attracted
(under present conditions there) to Israel is not very large. As for the second point, experience in the last two decades, and particularly in the last
few years, has shown that, from a social and economic point of view, an
average *long-term* immigration much over that which has been experienced
recently (just over 30,000 immigrants net per year since 1963, or 1.0–1.5
percent of the population per year) is almost impossible. Hence, a constant
stream (of 40,000 immigrants per year, as assumed in our maximum
assumption for the next thirty years) may well be the practical upper limit.
Nevertheless, a constant immigration on such a scale and even on a somewhat lower one (which seems feasible enough) can contribute positively
toward reducing the impact of some of the "problems."

Thus, it seems that, instead of having a pronatal population policy, as
Israel attempts to have, she could only gain by allocating these resources
to a combination of pro-family planning policy and increased immigration.
In other words, given a fixed amount of resources to be invested over the
coming years in population policies, it would make more sense to invest
in a family planning service system combined with a high immigration
policy (in addition, of course, to social welfare to large families on a socioeconomic basis). Such a combination would appear to have more merit

from a social, national, economic, political, and, not least important, from a moral point of view.

REFERENCES

1. United Nations. *Demographic Yearbook*. New York, 1968.

2. Central Bureau of Statistics. *Statistical Abstracts of Israel*. Jerusalem. Various annual volumes.

3. M. Sicron. *Immigration to Israel, 1948–1953*. Falk Project for Economic Research in Israel and Central Bureau of Statistics. Jerusalem, 1957.

4. K. R. Gabriel. *Nuptiality and Fertility in Israel*. Jerusalem: Hebrew University, 1960.

5. D. Ben-Gurion. "Three issues." *Hapoel Hazair*, vol. 27. (In Hebrew.)

6. R. Bachi. "The decline in fertility: A national danger." *Haaretz*, August 5, 1940.

7. R. Bachi. "More children and more for children." In *Havaad Haleumi*. Child and Welfare Institute, 1943. (In Hebrew.)

8. I. H. Herzog. "A call to the nation by the Chief Rabbi of Palestine." A message circulated at the *B'nei Brit* Chamber, Jerusalem, 1943.

9. A. H. Fraenkel. *Fertility in the Jewish Community in Palestine*. Aharonson Publication, 1944. (In Hebrew.)

10. D. Ben-Gurion. "How to increase Jewish fertility." First article. *Haaretz*, November 23, 1967.

11. D. Ben-Gurion. "How to increase Jewish fertility." Concluding article. *Haaretz*, December 8, 1967.

12. D. Friedlander. "Family planning in Israel: Irrationality and ignorance." *Journal of Marriage and the Family*, vol. 35, no. 1 (February 1973): 117–124.

13. R. Bachi. "Induced abortions in Israel." Paper presented to the International Conference of the Association for the Study of Abortions, 1968.

14. Israel. "Report of the Committee for Natality Problems (the Natality Committee), presented to the Prime Minister." 1966.

15. Israel. Office of the Prime Minister, Demographic Center. "Report on activities." January 4, 1970. (In Hebrew.)

16. Israel. Office of the Prime Minister, Demographic Center. "The Public Committee." July 1, 1968. (In Hebrew.)

17. D. Friedlander. "Generation fertility and some other demographic characteristics of the population of Israel," Ph.D. thesis. University of London, 1962.

18. Z. Peled. "Problems and attitudes in family planning in Israel." The Israel Institute of Applied Social Research, 1969. (Mimeographed.)

19. D. V. Glass. "Fertility trends in Europe since the Second World War." *Population Studies*, vol. 22, no. 1 (March 1968).

20. R. Bachi (with D. Gurevich and A. Gertz). *The Jewish Population of Palestine*. Jerusalem: Department of Statistics of the Jewish Agency for Palestine, 1944. (In Hebrew.)

21. Y. Talmon-Garber. *The Kibbutz: Sociological Studies.* Jerusalem: Magnes Press, 1970. (In Hebrew.)

22. Y. Talmon-Garber. "Social change and family structure." *International Social Science Journal,* vol. 14, no. 3 (1962).

23. H. P. David. *Family planning and abortion in the socialist countries of central and eastern Europe.* New York: The Population Council, 1970.

24. Y. Ben Porat. *The Arabic Labour Force in Israel.* Falk Project for Economic Research in Israel, 1966. (In Hebrew.)

25. Central Bureau of Statistics. *Moslems, Christians, and Druze in Israel.* Data from the 1961 population census, publication no. 17, 1964.

26. P. Demeny. *The Economics of Population Control.* International Population Conference, London: IUSSP, 1969, vol. 3.

27. D. Kiefer. "Population: Technology's desperate race with fertility," Parts I and II, A.C. and EN. *Feature,* October 7 and October 14, 1968.

28. Central Bureau of Statistics. *Statistical Abstract of Israel, 1970.* Jerusalem, 1970.

29. A. Sauvy. *General Theory of Population.* London: Weidenfeld and Nicolson, 1969.

BIBLIOGRAPHY

Anglo-American Committee. "Report of the Anglo-American Committee of Enquiry regarding the problem of European Jewry and Palestine." Lausanne, 1946.

Bachi, R., and J. Matras. "Contraception and induced abortions among Jewish maternity cases in Israel." *Milbank Memorial Fund Quarterly,* vol. 60, no. 2 (April 1962).

Central Bureau of Statistics. *Marriage and Fertility.* Data from the 1961 population census, publication no. 32, 1964.

Central Bureau of Statistics. *Projection of the Population in Israel up to 1985.* Jerusalem, 1968.

Divrei Haknesset. Various volumes. (In Hebrew.)

Feldman, D. M. *Birth Control in Jewish Law.* New York: New York University Press, 1968.

Friedlander, D. "The fertility of three Oriental immigration groups in Israel: Stability and change." *Fifth World Congress of Jewish Studies,* Papers in Jewish Demography, Jerusalem, 1969.

Goldscheider, C. "Ideological factors in Jewish fertility differentials." *The Jewish Journal of Sociology,* vol. 7 (June 1965).

Levi, H. "Differential wages," M.A. thesis. Jerusalem: Hebrew University, 1963.

Matras, J. *Social Change in Israel.* Chicago: Aldine, 1965.

———. "Demographic perspective in the assimilation process in Israel." In *Integration of Immigrants from Different Countries of Origin in Israel—A Symposium.* Jerusalem: Magnes Press, 1969.

Ministry of Health. *Health Services in Israel: Mother and Child Care.* Jerusalem, 1968.

Royal Commission on Palestine. *Report.* London: HMSO, 1937.

CHAPTER 4

Finland

Paavo Piepponen

ABSTRACT

Every now and then, the "population problem" arouses public discussion in Finland. The discussion seems to stem from unusual demographic situations and trends. Thus, in the 1930s, when fertility declined rapidly and fell below 20 per 1,000, population development was given considerable attention. A population committee was appointed, and the first population projections were made. They showed that under the prevailing conditions the population of Finland would never reach 4 million persons.

After World War II, fertility began to rise and produced an entirely different situation. The large number of children who were born from 1945 to 1950 needed, as they grew older, public expenditures for services such as maternity wards, mother-and-child clinics, schools, job opportunities, housing, and so forth. Yet, these populous age groups never were considered a threat to overpopulation. On the contrary, in Finland, these large groups were considered a wealth which later would contribute positively to the welfare of the country. These two examples show that a pronatalist public opinion prevailed during times of both low and high fertility.

The "baby boom" did not last long, and fertility declined almost annually during the following twenty-five years. In the beginning of this period, public discussion about fertility was almost nonexistent. By the end of the 1960s and especially during early years of the 1970s, individuals, the press, interest groups, political parties, and so forth took stands in regard to fertility. Emigration to Sweden, which increased during the 1960s to a peak in 1970, is another "population problem" that has stimulated public discussion. As a result of low fertility and high emigration, the Finnish population decreased in 1969 and 1970. The population question is again before the country, and quite different and opposing views are expressed, some optimistic and others pessimistic.

As a response to the decline of fertility in the 1930s and even before that period, some measures were taken by the government that were aimed at compensating a few of the expenses of family and children. In the beginning, tax reductions—classifying taxpayers and taxes according to family status—and maternity benefits were introduced. These methods for leveling family expenses still are used, and many other measures were adopted later.

Low fertility and concern about families were factors that motivated the founders of the Finnish Population and Family Welfare League (*Vaestö-liitto*), founded in 1941, to function as a pressure group in population and family matters. Although the league has rejected some of its older functions and adopted newer ones, its aim has always been to stress the importance of planned population policy.

POPULATION POLICY MEASURES

Direct, or explicit, population policy is sometimes understood to mean measures that influence demographic processes—fertility, mortality, family formation, migration, and population growth—in such a way as to achieve, from the societal point of view, a "desirable" result. This definition of population policy presumes that the goals of "desirable" population development are fixed by the government or some other body with power to control social development. In some countries, this control could be exercised by a local community or a joint community designed for specific action. In most countries, however, if population goals are defined at all, they are fixed at the national level.

In Finland, direct population goals are lacking. The measures taken by the government are not the objectives of a population policy but have, in most cases, economic, social, or humanitarian goals. On the other hand, these measures, at the same time, can have implicit effects upon population change and redistribution. These measures, in Finland, are considered population policy or family policy even if their stated goals lie in economic, social, educational, housing, or development policy.

FAMILY POLICY

Family policy in Finland started during the 1930s with the introduction of tax reductions for married couples and families with children. These reductions are, one way or another, available in both the local and state taxation systems. They purport to lessen the tax burden of families. This advantage is partially reduced by the system of joint taxation of husband and wife. If both work outside the home, the amount to be paid to the state is defined according to their combined income, and since taxation is progressive, they pay more together than if they were taxed according to each individual's income. This disadvantage to families has been recognized by the government for almost twenty years, but so far, no tax reform has been accomplished.

Several family welfare allowances were introduced before 1960. First among them were *maternity benefits* (birth payments), paid by the state to every mother in cash (US$20) or as a parcel of supplies for the mother and the baby (including condoms). The only condition for the maternity benefit is that the mother visit a mother-child clinic where she is examined by a doctor or a midwife. The purpose of the maternity benefit is to help a family meet the costs that arise from childbirth. It had a value in 1960 of 13 percent of the average monthly wage paid by manufacturing industries. Compared to many other European countries, the benefit was small [1, p. 92]. Its value compared to wages is now even smaller, perhaps 6 percent.

A *family allowance* has been paid since 1943 from state funds to families with at least four children under sixteen years of age. This allowance is restricted to families with low incomes. The amount per child is US$32 per year.

In 1948, during the baby boom, the first *children's allowance* was introduced. Paid by the state but financed primarily by employers, every child under sixteen years of age is entitled to receive this allowance. In 1969, the children's allowance in a family with two children under age sixteen was 9 percent of the average monthly wage paid by the manufacturing industries. Its relative share has now declined to about 4 percent of the monthly wage, a decline partly explained by the rise of wages. Since 1962, the government has had the power to raise the children's allowance according to the cost of living. Although this has been done, the buying power of this allowance is now much lower than in 1962. Another amendment made in 1962 stated that the allowance would increase by parity. The first child receives the least; the second child, somewhat more; and the third and the subsequent children earn the most (US$67, $80, and $95 per year, respectively). The "steps" indicated as percentages of the first are 100, 120, and 142. In 1961, a new so-called *special child allowance* was introduced. It is paid to families with children who need special economic support for subsistence, care, and education (US$58 per year). In 1970, *special care subsidies* were adopted. They are paid to parents of children who need continuous care because of illness or injury (US$58 per year). Further, if the helpless child is cared for at home or if the child lacks both parents, the special child allowance is doubled (US$116 per year).

Another family policy is the *housing subsidy,* which, since 1963, has been paid to all families of small means as a form of rent reduction. The purpose of this subsidy is to raise the housing standard of families with children under sixteen years of age. The subsidy is at least 20 percent of gross income.

Similarly, since 1967, the *communal home help service* has functioned as a form of equalization of family expenses. A family may obtain this service if the housewife is prevented from caring for the home.

One neglected area in family policy measures is *children's day care* in kindergartens and day care homes. The increasing number of working wives has led to a growing demand for children's day care centers. The organization of day care is a problem that requires both state and community efforts. The Day Care Act has been in effect since 1973.

The acts that govern Finnish family policy date back to a time when conditions were very different from those prevailing now. During the last thirty years, population development has changed from high fertility to very low, from a rather high infant mortality to a very low one. Population redistribution is dynamic. Nevertheless, the main principles of population policy—or family policy—have remained unchanged. The government has not become involved directly with fertility. However, the present government coalition has adopted a program to improve the security of families with children by unifying the systems of family allowances and raising the level of allowances.

CONTRACEPTIVE POLICY AND PROGRAMS

Unlike the situation in many countries, there has never been a law in Finland that prohibited the sale of contraceptives. Consequently, all new and modern methods of contraception are available. Public officials have not, however, actively disseminated information about birth control. The idea of family planning has come from the people themselves who want to limit family size. Even before modern methods of contraception had been introduced or were available on a large scale, fertility control was practiced by traditional methods (coitus interruptus, abortion, and the condom). A birth rate of less than 20 per 1,000 (as Finland experienced in the 1930s) cannot be reached without effective birth control.

It was not until the 1960s that the commercial distribution and sale of condoms increased considerably. They are advertised in newspapers and magazines; they went from hidden boxes to places in the open where they can easily be seen and bought by anyone who visits a tobacco shop, a supermarket, a gasoline station, or a public toilet. But as late as the early 1960s, the Finnish Population and Family Welfare League, in its statement to the medical board, took a negative attitude to the request by the Anti-VD Association to place automatic condom-delivery apparatuses in restaurant toilets. Less than ten years later, the league began selling condoms by mail. However, in its own marriage guidance clinics, the league used other methods of contraception: foam, diaphragms, and later pills and IUDs. Condoms are easily available, prices have decreased, and quality is good. All condoms are imported.

Foams and other chemical means of contraception are available in pharmacies, but their popularity is decreasing, as is happening with diaphragms, which are prescribed by doctors. Doctors also insert IUDs and prescribe pills. In 1969, about 11 percent of women aged 18–50 in the Helsinki region used pills. The figure for the whole country in the previous year was 8 percent. Since then, the pill has gained more popularity, and the proportion of acceptors is estimated to be much higher. Most pill users were married women (14 percent) and in the age group 25–34 (17 percent); users, however, did not appear to vary according to social group. Domestic production covers about two-thirds of the sales [2].

While availability of contraceptives has improved, birth control has become a popular topic in the mass media, beginning in the mid-1960s in weeklies and on radio and television. It seems that this phase of giving information in the mass media is over. These "programs" coincided with changes in the abortion law (to be discussed later). The whole question of birth control has become "public" at a societal level, in small groups, and in families.

Official programs before 1972 were of minor importance. Birth control advice has been given by doctors and by midwives in maternity advice clinics. This service reached only those women who had already delivered their babies. Whether such advice was given or not depended on the interest of the midwives or doctors and the mothers. Also, some semiofficial organizations such as the Finnish Population and Family Welfare League ran clinics in large cities, where information on birth control was available. But only a small proportion of the population who needed such information visited these clinics.

The turning point in official family planning—if abortion is excluded—was the Public Health Act, which came into effect in 1972. According to this law, it is the community's task to organize and disseminate "pregnancy prevention advice." Thus, family planning is an integrated part of other public health services provided for citizens. The government has accepted the action program for the years 1974–1978. According to this program, local health centers are obliged to organize family planning services, including contraceptive devices, which can be distributed free of charge to visitors to the centers. The Public Health Act states that "birth control will be taken as a natural part of social needs and life situations of the visitors." The maternity guidance clinics will be expected to turn this official program into practice.

It is significant that an effective government program on family planning was formed at the time when Finnish fertility rates were decreasing and, indeed, were among the lowest in Europe. This shows that the government does not want to control population development. On the contrary, it leaves to the people the decision of whether or not to "multiply." This program also indicates that the government is more willing to provide effective services to those who will not have babies than to those who will have babies.

Sex education has been given in connection with hygiene, biology, or other subjects. This has been more or less voluntary and has varied from school to school. New plans make sex education compulsory in the new comprehensive school system. Sex education is taught generally under the subject "civic education."

ABORTION POLICY AND PROGRAMS

It was not until 1950 that the first abortion law was passed by the Parliament. This law included social indications as a valid reason for abortion, but restricted this to cases where, in addition to illness, "serious living circumstances" prevailed. A team of two doctors granted the abortion. In the beginning, from 1951 to 1967, only 21–30 percent of the cases reviewed were permitted to have abortions. At the end of the decade, doctors were more permissive, perhaps because of the public discussion and the preparation of a new abortion law.

The new law was adopted in 1970. Under this law, social indications were included as one of the reasons for an abortion. Other new reasons were the age of the woman (under seventeen and over forty) and the number of children in the family (four or more births). The social indications make permissible almost all reasons for abortion. The official goals of the new abortion law are to diminish illegal abortions and eliminate the inequality arising from social and regional reasons.

The total number of abortions increased fourfold from 1964 to 1971. The rate of abortions to live births has increased fivefold at the same time. This relatively higher increase is explained by the decrease in fertility. Table 1 presents data on legal abortions in Finland.

It is too early to say to what extent the official goals have been reached.

TABLE 1.

Legal Abortions, Live Births, and Abortions, Finland, 1951–1972
(per 1,000 live births)

Year	Abortions	Live Births	Abortions per 1,000 Live Births
1951	3,007	93,063	32
1952	3,327	94,314	35
1953	3,802	90,866	42
1954	3,699	89,845	41
1955	3,659	89,740	41
1956	4,090	88,896	46
1957	4,553	86,985	52
1958	5,274	81,148	65
1959	5,773	83,253	69
1960	6,188	82,129	75
1961	5,867	81,996	72
1962	6,015	81,454	74
1963	5,616	82,251	68
1964	4,919	82,428	61
1965	4,782	77,885	61
1966	5,219	77,697	67
1967	5,618	77,289	73
1968	6,288	73,654	85
1969	8,175	67,450	121
1970	14,757	64,559	229
1971[a]	20,622	61,531	335
1972[a]	22,146	58,831	376

[a] Preliminary data.

According to one estimate, however, the number of illegal abortions has diminished. In the less developed regions and in lower social groups of Finland where induced abortions were less numerous before the 1970 law, there has been an increase among the poorly developed regions and in the middle social groups. Yet, regional and social differences prevail, although the number of doctors who have the right to give permission for abortion and the number of hospital beds available for abortion patients have increased considerably.

One effect has become apparent during the short duration of the new law: Instead of using contraception, people seem to use abortion as a birth control method [3]. This situation is not so unusual, since the organization of effective and free family planning services has just started. The logical order of steps should have been reversed. However, government measures were introduced in Finland in the same order as in countries with similar population problems: first, abortion law; then, effective family planning services; and last—when fertility has dropped—effective family policy measures.

A new law on sterilization also was passed in 1970. The official goals of this law are: (1) to increase the number of those who would adopt sterilization as a means of birth control and (2) to decrease sterilization by force or pressure. Toward the first goal, it was thought that men would make more use of this possibility, even though sterilization is not generally used by men as a birth control method. Similarly, there has been no rise in female sterilizations to equal the rise in abortions. Table 2 shows the number of sterilizations performed in recent years.

While before the new abortion law about 30 percent of aborting women also underwent sterilization, under the new law, this share has dropped to about 15 percent, which is much the same as in other Scandinavian countries [3].

MIGRATION AND INTERNAL DISTRIBUTION POLICIES AND PROGRAMS

In Finland, people are free to choose their places of residence. Despite heavy migration to cities, the government has not checked population influx. The only restrictive factor is the housing shortage. At the same time, job opportunities in cities are better than in rural areas. In recent years, both urban and rural communities have set target populations, which are used in economic and social planning. The targets are flexible and are changed and fixed anew if actual economic or social events considerably change the situation.

Regional planning bodies recently have approved population targets instead of population projections as guides in planning. It is believed that, in some regions, population losses will be increased if only negative population growth figures (as in projections) are available to entrepreneurs.

TABLE 2.

Male and Female Sterilizations, Finland, 1967–1970

Year	Number	Males	Females
1967	4,022	12	4,010
1968	4,294	18	4,276
1969	5,449	12	5,437
1970	5,727	50	5,677

Thus, population projections would be "self-fulfilling prophecies." If, however, communities or regional planning units set the targets, there are no guarantees that they will be reached. Planning units might have a tendency to be too optimistic in their pursuit of development.

Because of the imbalance of labor force supply and demand, Finland's governments since the 1960s have shaped regional policy. The internal migration streams flow to the areas where secondary and tertiary economic activities are more developed. There is less unemployment in the southern part of the country than in the northern and eastern parts, which are called "developing" areas.

At least three kinds of measures attempt to interfere with the ongoing process of population concentration in the southern areas: (1) Vocational courses are arranged for unemployed persons in the developing areas of the north and east. Of course, those who pass the courses are free to move. However, the courses give them better opportunities to enter the labor force in nonagricultural enterprises in the developing areas. (2) Economic support is given to the enterprises in the developing areas, which consists of tax reductions, low-interest loans, subsidies for the cost of transportation, and so forth. (3) State-owned enterprises are established in the developing areas, and plans have been formulated by a government committee to move some government offices from Helsinki to other cities.

The present governmental program contains some points on population and its distribution, including a regional plan covering the entire country which outlines regional population and industrial goals. In designing regional development plans, the goal is to supply the highest possible service that, according to the governmental program, presumes a varied population and economic structure. To realize these goals, the government has reshaped the organization of economic and national planning.

With regard to agrarian population, the government has promised in its program to take measures that secure the income of farmers with small holdings in developing areas. The purpose of this measure is to prevent the desolation of the rural areas.

One of the most serious and much discussed population problems during recent years has been the Finnish emigration to Sweden. Two things should be mentioned in this connection. Since 1954, citizens of the Scandinavian countries, including Finland, have had common labor markets within Scandinavia, which also allows for free travel between the countries. No passport, only an identification card, is needed to pass across the borders. Since the emigration statistics were based on passports granted, the number of migrants to the Scandinavian countries has been unknown until recent years. Another reason for migration to Sweden has been the labor shortage there and the surplus population in rural Finland. Emigration to

Sweden increases during boom periods in Sweden. Migrants predominantly are young adults whose general education is good but who lack vocational training. In highly automated industries such as those that exist in Sweden, this kind of labor force is in demand.

As Table 3 shows, net emigration to Sweden was heaviest in 1969 and 1970. The result was that the population of Finland *decreased* during these years. But suddenly, the return migration increased in such volume that, in the year 1971, the number of migrants between Finland and Sweden was about equal, and in 1972, the stream *to* Finland was greater than that *from* Finland. The population, thus, started to increase again, but this increase remained very small because of low fertility.

The government had been concerned about the emigration situation and had established a committee to investigate the problem. As a result of the committee proposals, an Emigration Council was established to direct an extensive investigation of the situation. The council has awarded money for various sociological and economic studies to be conducted at universities and research institutions. The government has promised to take into consideration the results of the investigations and to make use of them in the

TABLE 3.

Migration between Finland and Sweden, 1960–1972

| Year | Number of Migrants[a] | | | |
	From Finland to Sweden	From Sweden to Finland	Net	Rate (per thousand)
1960	12,311	3,166	− 9,145	−2.1
1961	12,830	3,768	− 9,062	−2.0
1962	9,770	4,271	− 5,499	−1.2
1963	10,385	4,071	− 6,314	−1.4
1964	19,302	3,824	−15,478	−3.4
1965	21,852	4,540	−17,312	−3.8
1966	16,617	6,378	−10,239	−2.2
1967	10,616	6,061	− 4,555	−1.0
1968	17,338	6,108	−11,230	−2.4
1969	38,607	5,858	−32,749	−7.0
1970	39,745	8,910	−30,835	−6.7
1971[b]	17,479	17,187	− 292	−0.1
1972[b]	11,094	16,121	+ 5,027	+1.1

SOURCE: See [4] and *Official Statistics of Finland.*

[a] The number of emigrants outside Scandinavia is 1,000–2,000 persons per year, most of whom leave for Australia.

[b] Preliminary data. Includes also migrants between Finland and other Scandinavian countries.

long-range planning of employment policy. Employment officials in Finland and Sweden have made their services more effective, toward a goal of an employment service for migrants.

MORTALITY AND MORBIDITY POLICIES

The standard of medical care in Finland has increased considerably over the last two decades. Special attention has been given to the creation of a central hospital system to service the whole country. These large hospitals are supported by communes or by joint communes and the state. At the local level, there are hospitals for the treatment of minor diseases and the prevention of morbidity.

An example of effective preventive medicine is the mother-child care program. It was created some thirty years ago and encompasses all mothers and their babies free of charge. As a result of this program, infant mortality rates are now among the lowest in the world. The figures in Table 4 show the rapid decline. Table 4 also reveals that differences in infant mortality rates no longer exist between urban and rural communities. This result might be regarded as a success of the total coverage of the preventive public health program.

One of the major policies in public health is the Sickness Insurance Act adopted in 1963. This act covers the whole resident population. According to the law, *medical treatment* is compensated to a certain amount. This includes the doctor's fee, medicine, medical examination, out-patient hospital care, and travel expenses. *Daily allowances* are paid during sickness. The amount of compensation depends on the family's income, but a mini-

TABLE 4.

Infant Mortality Rates, Finland, 1941–1972
(per 1,000 live births)

Year	Whole Country	Urban	Rural
1941–1950[a]	56.0	50.7	57.5
1951	35.4	30.6	37.4
1956	25.7	23.3	27.0
1961	20.8	20.5	21.0
1966	15.0	14.3	15.7
1970	13.2	13.4	13.0
1972	11.3[b]		

[a] Annual mean.
[b] Preliminary rate.

mum of 10 marks (US$2.50) is given to everyone. This act also covers the *maternity allowance*, which is paid for seventy-two working days (twelve weeks). Hospital care is not included in this policy, since it has long been paid by the state and the community. A patient pays only a nominal daily fee (10 marks) in the hospital. Ninety percent of all hospital beds are in state and community hospitals.

A study that was done before and after the Sickness Insurance Act went into effect showed that health services were used especially by those groups and individuals who were in the most unfavorable position in relation to sickness and care. Thus, the goal of the policy—increasing the use of medical care by groups who did not make use of it before the act—was reached. Some groups still use fewer of the medical services than do others. Among them, both before and after the passage of the act, are those living in rural areas, having large families, and earning small incomes. The discrepancy between need and use of medical services was especially great among men living in rural areas [5].

The new Public Health Act, discussed earlier in connection with birth control, forms a frame of reference for public health services at the local level. One of the goals is to shift the emphasis from a hospital care to an open care system. It is the duty of every community or joint community to provide a variety of public health services. They should include: (1) health guidance, birth control guidance, and health inspection; (2) organization of the care of the sick; (3) organization of ambulance service; (4) dental care service; (5) organization of health services in schools and other educational institutions; and (6) prevention and care of serious diseases. Although many of these functions are already performed by local health authorities, the new law introduces new functions, like birth control, to be administered and financed by local authorities.

The national health budget for the year 1973 is 1,253 million marks (approximately US$300 million), which is 8.4 percent of the national budget. Of this, 0.6 percent is for administration, 24.6 percent is for health services, and 74.8 percent is for the care of the sick and for hospitals. If we add to the health budget the sickness insurance expenses, the health budget increases to 1,348 million marks, and the share of health services increases to 30 percent.

Despite the developed hospital system and public health system, the mortality and especially the morbidity of the population are not at "satisfactory" levels. There are regional differences in favor of southern developed and urban areas, and there prevails a high male overmortality and morbidity. The difference in mean expectation of life between women and men is more than seven years: For females, life expectation is 72.6 years, and for males, 65.4 years (1961–1965). Effective measures are needed to increase the health of the male population. The Public Health Act offers a chance for the realization of this goal.

POPULATION GROWTH

As mentioned earlier, an interesting feature in the population development of Finland was the decrease during two successive years, in 1969 and 1970. Table 5 gives the number of population, the percentage living in urban communities, and females per 1,000 males. The proportion of population who live in urban communities has increased during the 1960s, caused partially by administrative changes of communities from one category to another. In the whole country, there are more females than males, especially in the urban communities. The sex ratio (females per 1,000 males) has decreased during the last years.

Vital rates for Finland are given in Table 6. Live births have decreased so much that the birth rate is now one of the lowest in the world. Death rates have remained about the same or increased to around 10 per 1,000 because of the increase of the aging population. As a result of these contradictory trends, the natural increase of population has diminished from

TABLE 5.

Population Data, Finland, 1960–1972

Year	Number	Population Change over Previous Year	Percent Urban	Females per 1,000 Males Whole Country	Urban
1960	4,446,200	33,200	38.4	1,075	1,186
1961	4,479,300	33,100	39.1	1,074	1,181
1962	4,512,800	33,500	39.8	1,073	1,175
1963	4,547,000	34,200	42.1	1,072	1,168
1964	4,570,800	23,800	43.2	1,072	1,165
1965	4,588,600	17,800	44.3	1,071	1,160
1966	4,611,900	23,300	45.5	1,070	1,156
1967	4,638,400	26,500	47.8	1,070	1,149
1968	4,653,100	14,700	48.7	1,069	1,148
1969	4,636,700	−16,400	50.3	1,070	1,145
1970	4,622,300	−14,400	50.9	1,069	1,140
1971[a]	4,632,000	9,700	51.6	1,071	1,139
1972[a]	4,634,000	2,000	55.1		

[a] Preliminary data.

FINLAND

FINLAND 111

TABLE 6.

Vital Rates, Finland, 1960–1972 (per 1,000)

Year	Live Births	Deaths	Natural Increase	Population Growth
1960	18.5	9.0	9.6	7.5
1961	18.4	9.1	9.3	7.4
1962	18.1	9.5	8.6	7.4
1963	18.2	9.3	8.9	7.6
1964	17.6	9.3	8.3	5.2
1965	17.0	9.7	7.3	3.9
1966	16.9	9.5	7.4	5.1
1967	16.7	9.5	7.2	5.7
1968	15.9	9.7	6.2	3.2
1969	14.5	9.9	4.6	−3.6
1970	13.9	9.5	4.4	−3.1
1971[a]	13.4	10.0	3.4	3.4
1972[a]	12.7	9.6	3.2	4.3

[a] Preliminary data.

nearly 10 per 1,000 to just above 3 per 1,000.[1] Because of international migration patterns, primarily to Sweden, the population growth has been very small or even negative as the rates for the years 1969 and 1970 show. Preliminary data from 1971 and 1972 show that the growth rate is positive, because of return migration from Sweden. If immigration continues to grow, the population will continue to increase, although the birth rate will still go down.

Reasons for the fertility decline are not known. A surprise to many observers has been the fact that the large age groups do not produce large families, which, in Finland, should have started in the late 1960s and continued to the middle of the 1970s. However, there is still a possibility for fertility to recover. Bigger age groups may have a new model of family growth with longer spacing between births.

Also, other possibilities have been suggested. In discussing fertility and family in the United States and Finland, Sweetser and Piepponen present an hypothesis of the trend toward the end of the 1960s:

During these years the children born after the war have grown up to adulthood and have experienced the disadvantages of the rapidly growing families, being themselves more apt to form a smaller family. Perhaps even more

[1] It seems evident that Finland is approaching zero population growth.

112   POPULATION POLICY IN DEVELOPED COUNTRIES

important might be that they are members of a large generation, for which the economic competition might be difficult, for it fills up the jobs at the same time when automation decreases the needs for workers in many branches of industry [6, pp. 16–17].

REFERENCES

1. Jarl Lindgren. "The economic significance of the equalization of costs of family maintenance." *Väestöntutkimuksen vuosikirja*, vol. 8, 1964. (In Finnish with English summary.)

2. Kaudo Nyman. "Pills in Finland in 1968." *Sosiaalivakuutus* 1, 1971. (In Finnish.)

3. Raimo Lahti. "The effects of new abortion and sterilization laws in our country." *Suomen lääkärilehti* 5, 1973. (In Finnish.)

4. *Population and Development in Finland.* Reply to the UN Second Inquiry on Population and Development. The Population Research Institute, Series A14, 1973.

5. Tapani Purola, Kaudo Nyman, Esko Kalimo, and Kai Sievers. "Sickness insurance, morbidity and use of medical services." 1971. (In Finnish.)

6. Frank Sweetser and Paavo Piepponen. "The youthful population of Finland and the United States." *Väestöntutkimuksen vuosikirja*, vol. 8, 1964. (In Finnish with English summary.) Also in Frank Sweetser and Paavo Piepponen. "Postwar fertility trends and their consequences in Finland and the United States." *Journal of Social History*, vol. 1, no. 2 (winter, 1967).

CHAPTER 5

Sweden

Lena Jonsson

ABSTRACT

The birth rate in Sweden is one of the lowest in the world. Today, there is little public concern about a possible eventual decline in the Swedish population, and there is no official population policy.

The Swedish social welfare system is not based on demographic grounds but on social and humanitarian grounds. It is based on fostering solidarity between and within the generations.

Planned parenthood is considered to be of the utmost importance. The basic assumption behind family planning in Sweden is that every child should be wanted and well cared for. Information and education on sexual questions are openly supplied, and sex education is compulsory in the schools. All methods of contraception are readily available.

The high immigration rate during the last decade is one of the most important features of the Swedish demographic situation. The long-range impact can not yet be determined since immigration is very much influenced by labor market conditions. That Sweden still has not experienced a decline in population is, in part, caused by the effects of immigration. Also, the high immigration rate will affect the age structure of the population.

BRIEF HISTORY OF POPULATION POLICY

As recently as the late nineteenth century, Sweden was a fairly poor, agrarian country. At the time of the 1870 census, about 72 percent of the entire population depended upon agriculture and related occupations for a livelihood. The dominant family pattern was the three-generation family, in which both husband and wife worked in the home and on the farm. The children took part in working life at an early age, and they and older family members helped look after smaller children.

At this time, families often were large, and the population growth rate was fairly high. During most of the latter nineteenth and early twentieth centuries, the natural population increase amounted to over 1 percent per year. The actual population increase, however, was limited by considerable emigration until the outbreak of World War I. The main reasons for emigration were poverty and the lack of job opportunities within the country. In the 1880s, when emigration reached its peak, the natural population increase—which amounted to 1.2 percent per year—was reduced by about two-thirds. The birth rate—the annual number of live births per 1,000 population—had stayed at a little above 30 throughout the nineteenth century. During the 1880s, however, the birth rate slowly began to decline, a tendency that was accentuated in the 1920s and early 1930s. During 1931–1935, the birth rate was as low as 14, and the natural population increase amounted to only 0.25 percent per year.

The declining birth rate coincides in time with a rapid and radical transformation of Swedish society brought about by industrialization and urbanization. The industrialization process in Sweden did not start until the latter half of the nineteenth century, but it developed rapidly. The transition was facilitated by several factors. Opportunities for emigration reduced pressures on the job market. No wars or other major crises disrupted industrialization. The entire population enjoyed from the start a fairly good standard of schooling, since compulsory public education had been introduced in 1842. And there was also a tradition that fostered the early vigorous growth of organizations promoting the interest of working people.

Some people soon realized the importance of increased knowledge of birth control as a weapon in the fight against poverty. Birth control began to be discussed in the late 1880s. This entire movement was privately organized. However, no public action was taken to promote family planning; on the contrary, publicity and advertising for contraceptives were prohibited legally in 1911.

Industrialization and urbanization led to a reduction in the numbers of children born. Industrialization was accompanied by a general effort to raise the family's standard of living, and children presented an obstacle to this aim. Thus, desire to keep down the number of births existed among large segments of the population at an early period. Although this desire was expressed rarely, it provided a natural starting point for a discussion of means. Information on family planning was spread privately by persons devoted to the cause. No deliberate state policy on family planning underlay the declining birth statistics in the late nineteenth and early twentieth centuries. Only in the mid-1930s did the state pursue any deliberate policy on population. By this time, birth figures were so low that interest was concentrated on strengthening the economic status of families with children and making it easier for parents to have as many children as they desired.

The Swedish birth figures have remained consistently low since the 1930s, although they have varied with economic conditions and other factors. In the 1930s, fear of an eventual decline of the Swedish population helped to stimulate reform of the family policy. Two government population commissions were established in 1935 and 1939 to study family assistance. Only for a brief period, however, were fears of population decline the main reason for extending public support to families with children. The motive for such support shifted increasingly from reasons of population policy to the requirements of justice in the social welfare system. In the 1940s and 1950s, Sweden's social welfare system made great gains. Allowances were given to parents for all children, and free schooling, free school meals, and free textbooks were introduced. A system of free child care and maternity care was developed. Rent subsidies were introduced to enable families with children to obtain good housing at a reasonable cost. During the 1960s, reinforcement of public support for children concentrated on improved services for families with children and on specially designed measures of support for low-income groups.

Parallel with the development of family support, family planning information and services were provided in an attempt to remove the obstacles to planned parenthood, that is, to make parenthood voluntary. The 1911 act prohibiting contraceptives was abolished in 1938; in 1946, chemists were obliged to provide contraceptives to all who requested them, including teenagers. Sexual instruction was introduced in the schools in the 1940s and became compulsory in 1956. Since the 1940s, there have been maternity care centers to provide mothers with advice on birth control.

Although today there is no official population policy, the government makes it economically possible for those who want children to have them, and it helps those who want to limit their families to learn how to do so. Policy is based on social rather than demographic grounds. More and more, the purpose of support to families and birth control services has been to increase the individual's freedom of choice, rather than to manipulate the number of births.

POPULATION GROWTH PATTERNS[1]

¶ FLUCTUATIONS IN THE NUMBER OF ANNUAL BIRTHS

In the study of the number of live births in Sweden during the twentieth century, it is possible to recognize, on the one hand, a long-range develop-

---

[1] This section is mainly extracted from Appendix 5 by Erland Hofsten in [1].

ment toward smaller and smaller birth cohorts per year and, on the other, periodic fluctuations of more and fewer children (see Table 1). The short-range fluctuations in the annual number of births complicate the understanding of long-range population trends.

Figures from separate years seem to indicate that, in certain years, more children have been born in Sweden than are necessary for replacement, while in other years, the number of births has been much lower than that needed in the long run to keep the population static. (Actually, Swedish fertility has been at or slightly below replacement level from roughly the 1895 cohort onward. Nevertheless, Sweden still has a surplus of births over deaths.)

Figure 1 shows that the age-specific fertility rates for all age groups except those aged 15–19 declined markedly to the mid-1930s. But during the 1940s, the rate increased in all age groups. In the youngest age groups, this increase has continued to the mid-1960s. In the age groups over thirty years, the increase during the 1940s was of short duration. From the mid-

TABLE 1.

Live Births and Birth Rate, Sweden, 1921–1971

Year	Live Births per Year	Birth Rate
1921–1925	114,690	19.1
1926–1930	96,990	15.9
1931–1935	87,374	14.1
1936–1940	93,283	14.8
1941–1945	121,889	18.8
1946–1950	124,949	18.2
1951–1955	108,581	15.2
1956–1960	105,518	14.3
1960	102,200	13.7
1961	104,500	13.9
1962	107,300	14.2
1963	112,900	14.9
1964	122,700	16.0
1965	122,800	15.9
1966	123,400	15.8
1967	121,360	15.4
1968	113,193	14.3
1969	107,314	13.5
1970	110,000	13.7
1971	114,500	14.1

SOURCE: See [1].

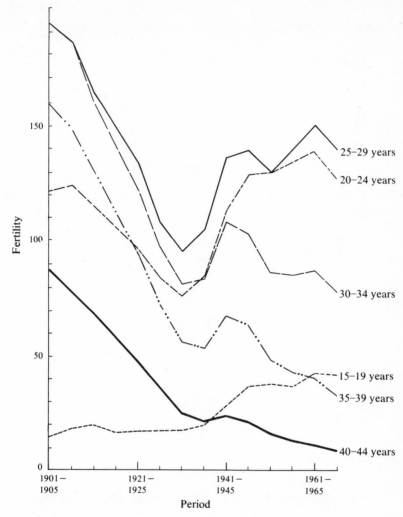

SOURCE: See [1].

FIGURE 1

Age-Specific Fertility Rates by Age Groups, Sweden

1940s, there has been a decline in these age groups, and fertility is now lower than it was in the mid-1930s.

Adding the fertility rates for different age groups gives the total fertility rate (TFR). The continuous curve in Figure 2 shows the development of the period TFR.

Both the age-specific fertility rate and the period TFR show marked fluc-

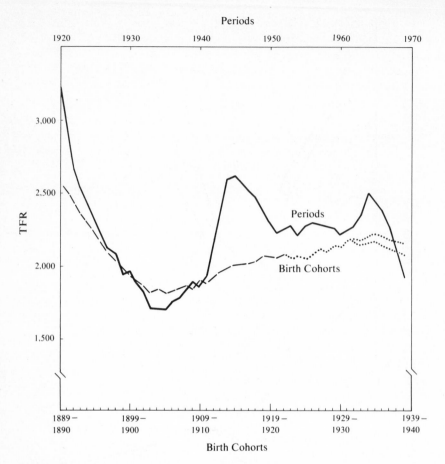

SOURCE: See [1].

FIGURE 2

Total Fertility Rate (TFR) for Birth Cohorts and for Periods, Sweden

tuations during the twentieth century. In countries such as Sweden, where birth control is practiced, it is not possible to restrict the study of fertility to a few separate years. Changes in childbearing between different periods of the women's reproductive ages can have great influence on the number of children born in a certain year. When studying the fertility development it is, therefore, necessary to look at the fertility for birth cohorts of women.

¶ LONG-RANGE DEVELOPMENT OF FERTILITY

The long-range fertility development is best illustrated by the total number of children born per woman in different birth cohorts. The TFR for birth cohorts is shown by the dotted line in Figure 2.

For women born in 1889–1890, the TFR amounted to more than 2,500. It declined rapidly, and for women born in 1900–1909, it did not amount to more than 1,800. A certain increase occurred afterward, and for the youngest cohorts who can be followed to the end of their reproductive period—women born during the latter part of the 1920s—the TFR amounted to about 2,100. The latest cohorts have not yet finished their reproductive period. The development of these cohorts has been projected according to two different assumptions. According to the upper curve, fertility in the higher age groups will be as high as in 1969; according to the lower curve, it will continue to decline as it has during recent years. Both curves give a completed fertility for women born in 1938–1939 of about 2,100.

The heavy fluctuations that appear when summarizing the fertility for periods in Figure 2 disappear entirely when one looks instead at the TFR for birth cohorts.

If the number of children that a cohort bears as a consequence of birth control is kept far below the maximum, it is of utmost importance whether the children are born mostly at the beginning or at the end of the reproductive period. With a reliable contraceptive, the number of children most women have is very much less than the possible maximum: Generally in Sweden it is one, two, or three. Not only the first but also subsequent children can be planned at different periods in a woman's life. The number of children born in a certain year, therefore, depends on how many children have already been born and how many will be born later to the cohorts that are in the fertile ages in that year.

The birth rate differs very much for individual birth cohorts. During the 1940s, the fertility for all birth cohorts peaked, and an increase in the number of births resulted. On the one hand, this pattern occurred because of births to older women who normally would have had their children in the war-torn 1930s; on the other hand, it occurred because young women in the 1940s started their childbearing period at an earlier age than had been customary. Also, in the 1940s there was a higher frequency of marriage. Interestingly, there was no essential increase in completed family size in the 1940s. Figure 3 shows the age pattern of fertility for five birth cohorts.

¶ REPLACEMENT LEVEL

In Figure 4, the TFR for the birth cohorts 1879–1880 to 1939–1940 is compared with the TFR that would have resulted in replacement-level fertility over the same years. The actual curve of TFR for these birth cohorts is identical with the cohort curve in Figure 2. The upper curve in Figure 4 shows the total fertility that, with the prevailing death rate, should

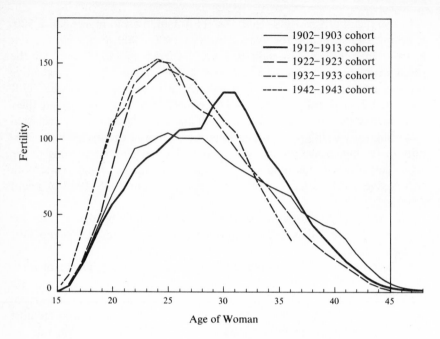

SOURCE: See [1].

FIGURE 3

Age Pattern of Fertility for Five Birth Cohorts, Sweden

have been needed to reach replacement. A comparison of the two curves shows that the fertility of no birth cohort born since 1885 has reached replacement.

If the replacement level is not reached and if there is no immigration, the population of Sweden would decline. But in Sweden, there is an excess of births over deaths, caused by three main factors: First, there is a time lag in the effects of changes in the reproduction situation; second, there has been large-scale immigration to Sweden during the postwar period; and third, the death rate has been declining.

In 1969, there were 108,000 live births and 83,000 deaths. Thus, the excess of births over deaths amounted to 25,000 or 0.3 percent. Nearly 9,000 of the children born in 1969 had a mother of foreign citizenship. Practically all these women must have immigrated to Sweden during the postwar years. In addition to this, we must include children born to women who have received Swedish citizenship during the postwar years. Their number is unknown but may amount to several thousand. Without emigration during the postwar period, the number of births in 1969 would not have amounted to more than 95,000–100,000. Also, the declining death rate

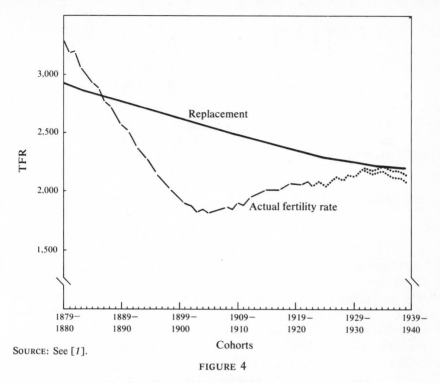

SOURCE: See [1].

Cohorts

FIGURE 4

Total Fertility Rate (TFR) for the Birth Cohorts 1879–1880
to 1939–1940, Sweden

during the postwar period has helped maintain the excess of births over
deaths. Thus, without postwar immigration and a declining death rate, the
surplus of births over deaths would have been reduced to a few thousand.
In the long run, Sweden would have had a decreasing population.

In this connection, it is of interest to look at the fertility of the immigrant population. If it is higher than that of the native population, it will
help explain why Sweden still has an excess of births over deaths. Figures
about the fertility of foreign citizens during recent years show that the age-
specific fertility rates are about 20 percent higher for foreign citizens than
for the rest of the population. Also, the young age structure of the immigrants contributes to the high number of children born to foreign citizens.

¶ CURRENT FERTILITY DEVELOPMENT
Table 2 shows the age-specific fertility rates for several years, with a
marked decline in the number of births in all age groups from 1966–1969.

TABLE 2.

Age-Specific Fertility Rates, Sweden, 1956–1970

Age of Woman	Live Births (per 1,000 women)			
	1956–1960	1966	1969	1970
15–19	36.7	50.2	35.0	33.9
20–24	132.5	139.1	117.2	120.3
25–29	136.9	149.9	129.2	129.4
30–34	85.5	86.6	71.7	70.1
35–39	42.3	37.8	28.2	27.4
40–44	12.9	9.1	6.9	6.1

SOURCE: See [1].

¶ FUTURE FERTILITY AND NUMBER OF CHILDREN

The latest cohorts to complete reproduction have reached a completed fertility of 2,100 per 1,000. The younger cohorts born about 1940 do not appear as if they will reach a completed fertility of more than 2,000 per 1,000. But there is no indication that this number will decline further. The new young cohorts have, at ages twenty, twenty-five, and thirty, reached a fertility that is as high as that of the cohorts ten years their senior.

It is well-known that the long-term trend toward smaller family size has been associated with industrialization, with children constituting an economic burden. It also is known that the economic depression during the 1930s caused the extremely low fertility in those cohorts who were in the most reproductive age groups at that time. It is also true that good conditions on the labor market during the 1940s in connection with certain measures in the field of family policy led, on the one hand, to the older cohorts giving birth to children who would normally have been born ten years earlier and, on the other, to the younger cohorts starting childbearing earlier than their older counterparts.

The increase in births during the earlier part of the 1960s and the subsequent decline toward the end of the decade are more difficult to explain. Favorable economic conditions made it possible for a lot of couples to have children at earlier ages than the nearest preceding cohorts. But why, then, did this tendency cease rather suddenly without any worsening of the economic conditions? It is difficult to say anything definite about the decline at the end of the 1960s, but there are two hypotheses: It could be caused, first, by new and more effective contraceptives (the pill and IUD) and, second, by a liberalized enforcement of the abortion law.

If the decline in fertility continues, especially in the youngest age groups, it simply may mean young cohorts are tending to have children later than did the earlier cohorts. They may catch up with the earlier cohorts by the end of their fertile period, but it is also possible that a decreased fertility in the younger ages means that total fertility declines for that cohort.

The changed marriage pattern may be a contributing factor in the postponement of childbearing. During the 1940s, the increased frequency of marriages explained most of the increase in fertility, and thus it was not actually an increase in the number of children per married woman. The situation has changed, and it is now more common for young couples to live together without marriage. In 1966, for example, the number of marriages amounted to around 60,000, while by 1971 it had dropped to around 40,000. There are no figures to predict what effects this will have on fertility. Table 3 shows the age at marriage for men and women in Sweden in 1968.

¶ PROGNOSIS
In 1971, the National Central Bureau of Statistics presented an estimate of population growth to the year 2000. The estimate was made according to two different hypotheses about the number of immigrants. In the one case, the immigration is assumed to be zero; in the other case, it is assumed to amount to 20,000 per year. Table 4 shows the number of live births according to the estimate. Without immigration, the number of births declines. With a net immigration of 20,000 per year, a smooth increase in the number of births is anticipated.

TABLE 3.

Age at Marriage, Sweden, 1968

Age Group	Men		Women	
	Number	Percent	Number	Percent
15–19	930	1.7	7,320	14.0
20–24	24,657	47.4	29,380	56.2
25–29	15,521	29.8	8,910	17.0
30–34	4,460	8.6	2,479	4.7
35–39	2,158	4.2	1,268	2.4
40–49	2,489	4.8	1,890	3.6
50–59	1,252	2.4	787	1.5
60–69	417	0.8	205	0.5
70+	132	0.3	52	0.1
Total	52,016	100.0	52,291	100.0

SOURCE: See [1].

TABLE 4.

Estimated Number of Live Births, Sweden, 1971–2000

Year	Net Immigration = 0	Net Immigration = 20,000
1971	115,811	116,075
1975	115,963	118,939
1980	110,909	117,604
1985	109,145	118,669
1990	109,815	121,455
1995	110,344	124,154
2000	109,549	126,042

SOURCE: See [1].

Table 5 shows the expected distribution of the population by age groups in the year 1975 and every fifth year to the year 2000 (at net immigration of 20,000 per year).

The changes in the age group below nineteen are relatively small with a tendency to decline smoothly. The largest fluctuations are in the age group above sixty-five where a rather marked increase is expected until 1990. After 1990, a rather strong decrease in the number of people aged sixty-five and older is expected. This is because the small birth cohorts in the 1930s will be reaching the age groups above sixty-five. The age group 20–64, where the majority of the gainfully employed people in the country are found, is expected to be relatively smaller during the 1970s (as during the 1960s), to be relatively constant during the 1980s, and then to increase during the 1990s.

TABLE 5.

Distribution of Population by Age Groups, Sweden, 1975–2000
(net immigration = 20,000 per year)

Year	Total Population	Age Group (percent)			
		0–19	20–64	65+	Total
1975	8,334,598	27.5	57.6	14.9	100.0
1980	8,560,170	27.6	56.8	15.6	100.0
1985	8,758,217	27.3	56.7	16.0	100.0
1990	8,948,724	26.9	56.9	16.2	100.0
1995	9,141,672	26.7	57.7	15.6	100.0
2000	9,340,724	26.5	58.7	14.8	100.0

SOURCE: See [1].

The age structure of the population is shown in Table 6 for selected years from 1900 projected to the year 2000. The proportion of the population under age fifteen declined a great deal between 1920 and 1940. The proportion of people aged sixty-five and older has increased consistently since 1920. In addition, the age group 40–64 has hitherto increased steadily, while the proportion belonging to the age group 15–39 has fluctuated. The future distribution of age groups depends very much on the development of fertility.

The social and economic consequences of the changed age group distribution are apparent. The increased proportion of people aged sixty-five and older will mean an increased burden on the population in the working-age group.

FAMILY PLANNING AND BIRTH CONTROL

Even in a country like Sweden, where the birth rate is one of the lowest in the world, planned parenthood is considered to be of the utmost importance, although obviously for reasons other than that of avoiding a population increase. The basic assumption behind family planning in Sweden is that every child should be wanted and taken care of properly. Any restriction in family planning opportunities would be regarded by both men and women in Sweden as a terrible encroachment upon their personal freedom and integrity.

¶ BRIEF HISTORY

A shift in the attitude toward birth control occurred in Sweden in the 1930s. In 1929, a bill was introduced into Parliament to enable measures

TABLE 6.

Age Structure of the Population, Sweden, 1900–2000

| Year | Percentage of Population in Age Group | | | | |
	0–14	15–39	40–64	65+	Total
1900	32.4	36.6	22.6	8.4	100.0
1920	29.3	39.9	23.3	8.4	100.0
1940	20.4	41.5	28.7	9.4	100.0
1960	22.0	33.3	32.7	12.0	100.0
1970	20.9	34.4	31.0	13.8	100.0
1980	20.5	35.9	27.9	15.6	100.0
2000	19.6	34.0	31.5	14.8	100.0

SOURCE: See [1].

to be taken to give people information and education on sexual matters.

Parallel with the development of family support, information and services were provided in an attempt to remove the obstacles to family planning and birth control, that is, to make parenthood voluntary. Until as recently as 1938, the law forbade the public provision of knowledge about contraception. Now such information is supplied openly to everyone. Maternal health centers provide information regardless of marital status and make diaphragms, pills, and IUDs available to women requesting them. All contraceptive devices sold are quality controlled, and contraceptive advertising is permitted.

Official interest in family planning dates from 1935, when the first government commission on population was appointed specifically to examine the facts and issues preparatory to drafting legislation. This commission proposed that information on general sexual questions should be given to children, young people, and adults; that information on contraception should be given also to young people; and that adults should get individual advice on contraception.

Concurrent with governmental activities were those of the privately run and financed Swedish Association for Sex Education (RFSU), founded in 1933. It provides extensive information services aimed at the general public and—above all—at those coming into contact with sexual questions in the course of their work, such as doctors, nurses, social workers, teachers, journalists, youth leaders, and so on.

Courses for doctors, nurses, social workers, and teachers are also given by the voluntary study organizations associated with the universities of Uppsala and Stockholm and at the medical faculties. Courses for the general public are arranged by the family advice bureaus and the popular education associations.

¶ CONTRACEPTIVE PRACTICE IN SWEDEN

It is difficult to get a good idea of how extensive birth control is in Sweden; however, several rough estimates are available. According to an investigation by the recent Abortion Commission, the number of children born in Sweden in 1969 would have been between 400,000 and 500,000 had no contraceptives been used, whereas the actual number of births that year was 108,000.

A 1967 survey asked, "At the time of your last sexual intercourse, did you do anything to prevent pregnancy?" About 60 percent said they used a relatively reliable contraceptive. Among those not using contraceptives, 6 percent were already pregnant, 9 percent wanted to get pregnant, 20 percent—mostly elderly—could not have children. Five percent used less reliable methods of birth control.

According to sales statistics in the report from the Abortion Commission, an expected 400,000–450,000 women, or about 25–28 percent of the 15–44 age group, were taking the pill in 1969. About 260,000 packages of chemicals were sold, and approximately 30,000 women were using IUDs. In 1968, about 30 million condoms and about 24,000 diaphragms were sold.

Sterilization usually is not recommended as a birth control method. In Sweden, only women can receive permission for sterilization on "medico-social" grounds. A man can be sterilized only for eugenic or medical reasons. In 1968, 1,573 people were sterilized, of whom only 5 were male. The Swedish Parliament has recently asked for an investigation regarding liberalization of the present law to make sterilization available also for family planning purposes.

¶ DISSEMINATION OF CONTRACEPTIVES
Condoms, which can be obtained at supermarkets, gas stations, and coin-operated dispensers, are the most readily available contraceptives. Chemical devices also are sold freely at pharmacies. Pills and IUDs must be prescribed by a doctor.

Contraceptives are, in principle, available for anyone regardless of marital status and age, although sexual relations are illegal for persons under fifteen years of age (to prevent sexual exploitation).

All contraceptives must be approved by the National Board of Health and Welfare before they are released on the market. The government recognizes condoms, diaphragms, chemical methods, IUDs, and pills as legitimate contraceptives. Sales and importation are controlled by specific governmental regulations.

¶ MATERNAL AND CHILD HEALTH SERVICES
The government program to promote family planning includes maternal health care centers that are, in principle, responsible for contraceptive services. Personal advice on family planning also can be obtained at a limited number of counseling bureaus. Often, women are assisted only after childbirth or an abortion.

¶ SEX EDUCATION IN THE SCHOOLS
Sex education was introduced in the schools in Sweden in the 1940s and made compulsory in 1956. The National Board of Education has published recommendations concerning the structure and content of teaching.

In 1964, a government commission was appointed to revise and improve the entire sex education program—both at the school and at the adult level. The pluralistic approach in Swedish sex education is underlined in recent proposals (1971) by the Sex Education Commission. The objective of sex education is to inform people about anatomy, physiology, and sexual life so that shortcomings arising from ignorance are counteracted and harmonious relations between two people are promoted. Instruction starts in the first grade when the children are seven years old. The initial discussion is limited to how the sexes differ; where children come from, including the role of the father; how they develop before birth; how they are born; and in what ways they are dependent on their mothers, fathers, and homes. These fundamental facts are reviewed in the following two grades.

Between the ages of eleven and thirteen, instruction continues with the structure and function of the sexual organs, puberty, menstruation, nocturnal emission (wet dreams), masturbation, conception, pregnancy and "traumatic experiences" during pregnancy, development of the fetus, determination of sex or of twins, and so on.

The subject matter covered between the ages of fourteen and sixteen is as follows: a review of previous items as required; sex and youth (moral considerations, as abstention from sexual relations during adolescence); children born out of wedlock; spontaneous and induced abortions; venereal diseases; contraceptives; sterilization; the climacteric, or menopause; sexual abnormalities; moral and social aspects of sex; welfare measures to help in establishing a family; welfare measures during pregnancy, confinement, and nursing; welfare measures for the care and training of children and adolescents.

Compulsory education ends in Sweden with the ninth school year. Those students who continue with their education—usually between the ages of seventeen and twenty—are given a review of what has already been covered, followed by more comprehensive information on various sexual questions. According to a 1965 amendment of the National Board of Education, contraceptive techniques and venereal diseases should be given special emphasis.

Thus, sex education is a part of the school curriculum for all age groups. But still, the sex education program does not work as well as it should. Many circumstances contribute to inadequate treatment of the subject in some of the schools; the subject is relatively new and difficult; and the teachers' training is not sufficient. Many efforts have been made to improve the training of teachers in sex education. The National Swedish Association for Sex Education and the National Board of Education among others arrange workshops for teachers.

¶ PRESENT REFORMS
In recent years, many people have pointed out that society should increase its role in giving information about sexual life and contraceptives. In 1968,

the National Board of Health and Welfare presented a program of measures to provide information and individual counseling in these areas. The board proposed that sex education in schools should be expanded, that counseling about contraceptives and information about sexual life at the maternal care centers should be improved, and that counseling about contraceptives to men ought to be expanded as far as resources permit.

Also in 1968, a special group was appointed by the National Board of Education to deal with the questions of how contraceptive advice could be fitted into health—and medical care—with respect to administration and of what steps should be taken to provide better service in this field. They, too, pointed out, in their report in 1971, that the contraceptive counseling ought to be broadened in Sweden. They proposed that contraceptive advice be made available in particular for certain groups (for example, for mothers of newborn babies), that advice to young people of school age should be increased, that contraceptive counseling organized by society should be free of charge; and that the charge for a medicine prescribed as a contraceptive should be the same as for other prescribed medicines.

Questions dealing with sex education in schools and general sex information to both young people and adults are currently being investigated by a government commission.

INDUCED ABORTION

¶ LAWS

Until 1921, abortion was illegal. In 1921, an amendment of the penal code permitted abortion on "medical grounds" if the woman's life or health were in serious danger. In 1938, a special abortion law was passed, chiefly to combat illegal abortions. Under the act of 1938, amended in 1946 and 1963, a pregnancy may be interrupted in the following cases:

(1) If childbirth would entail serious danger to life or health of a woman suffering from illness, a physical defect, or weakness as indicated by medical and medicosocial authorities.
(2) If there is reason to assume that childbirth and child care would seriously damage a woman's physical or psychic strength in view of her living conditions and other special circumstances.
(3) If a woman has become pregnant as a result of rape, other criminal coercion, or incestual sexual intercourse or if she is mentally retarded, legally insane, or under fifteen years of age at the time of impregnation.
(4) If there is reason to assume that either parent of the expected child might transmit to the offspring hereditary insanity, imbecility, serious disease, or a serious physical handicap.

(5) If there is reason to assume that the expected child will suffer from serious disease or deformity resulting from injury during fetal life.

In 1945, state subsidies were allocated, and instructions were given for community abortion advice centers, staffed by doctors and social workers. There are, at present, approximately thirty of these distributed throughout the country.

As can be seen from the formulation of the law, particularly item (2), considerable flexibility of interpretation is allowed. This has been the subject of extensive public debate, and this again has been reflected by large variations in the yearly number of applicants as well as in the percentage of applications granted. Thus, the number of applications in 1960 was around 4,000, of which a little more than 60 percent were granted, whereas the corresponding figures for 1967 were over 10,000 applications, of which 90 percent were granted. Such fluctuations in the implementation of the law have caused a demand for a new formulation, securing a better uniformity of interpretation and with due consideration to the prevailing public opinion in favor of a greater decisive role on the part of the concerned woman.

In 1965, a government commission was appointed to study the abortion law. The report of the commission was released in 1971. Although the commission did not promote the notion of abortion "on demand," it did recommend that every woman resident of Sweden should be entitled to an abortion (1) if it can be assumed that her health will be threatened or her strength seriously reduced by a continuation of pregnancy, or (2) if it can be assumed that the child to be born would suffer from a serious illness or defect, or (3) if for another reason it is an unreasonable hardship for her to continue her pregnancy. "Unreasonable hardship" has been interpreted as including a large number of children, advanced age, immaturity, economic difficulties, various conflicting situations, and other personal reasons.

Today, a Swedish woman considering abortion will go to one of the special advisory centers on abortion. Authorization is granted either by a specially appointed committee of the National Board of Health and Welfare after an investigation or by two doctors (unless it is a eugenic or fetal injury case). In an emergency, the physician performing the abortion makes the authorization.

Until recently, most cases were decided by a committee of the National Board of Health and Welfare. According to this procedure, the woman submits an application to the board with one certificate from a physician and another from a social worker. The committee then decides whether or not there are grounds for abortion and whether the investigation should be supplemented by further examinations, which, as a result, would further extend the waiting period. Today, more than half of the legal abortions are authorized by the two-doctor procedure. One of the doctors has to be the physician performing the abortion. In every case, a report has to be sent to the board.

¶ NUMBER OF ABORTIONS

Among the approximately 300,000–400,000 births averted in 1969, a maximum of 20,000, and probably less, were averted through abortion. About 14,000 women had legal abortions, and a maximum of 6,000, and probably much fewer, had illegal abortions. That so few women apply to have an abortion can be explained by the fact that, in Sweden, the practice of birth control was widespread as early as the 1930s.

The number of induced abortions per year has grown steadily from 6,600 in 1965 to 11,000 in 1968, 14,000 in 1969, and 16,000 in 1970. The ratio of applications granted has also risen sharply: 62 percent in 1960, 93 percent in 1969, and an estimated 97 percent during 1970. The abortion rate for 1970 was 145 per 1,000 live births.

The most common grounds for abortion are "medicosocial" reasons. In 1966, these grounds represented almost 80 percent and, in 1968, 88 percent of the total number of abortions. The next largest category was medical (about 20 percent in 1966 and nearly 10 percent in 1968). Table 7 gives the statistics pertaining to abortions in Sweden.

¶ PUBLIC OPINION

Criticism of the present abortion law has been leveled particularly by those groups who believe that a woman should have a right to decide for herself whether or not she shall have an abortion. No recent official stand has been taken by the church. At a bishops' meeting in 1951 (which was supported by a subsequent meeting in 1964), abortions for other than medical grounds were condemned. This view is not shared by all pastors or by a majority of the population. In 1967, a survey showed that 50 percent of the general public favored a liberal policy of abortion (that is, lifting present restrictions), 13 percent were uncertain, and 36 percent were against.

Another survey of young women found that 54 percent of those who had never been pregnant favored liberal abortion; 58 percent of those who had had a desired pregnancy and 61 percent of those who had had an undesired pregnancy felt that the law should be relaxed.

TABLE 7.

Induced Abortions, Sweden, 1950–1970

Year	Number of Births	Number of Applications for Abortions Received	Applications Granted		Number of Legally Sanctioned Abortions Performed				Grounds for Abortions					
			Number	Per cent	Authorized by Official Board	Authorized by Two Doctors	Emer-gency	Total	Dis-ease	Weak-ness	Antic-ipated Weak-ness	Human-itarian	Eugenic	Increased Risk of Injury to Fetus
1950	117,754	6,361	5,149	81	4,786	1,096	7	5,889	1,790	2,965	565	18	544	
1960	103,637	4,085	2,552	62	2,377	414	1	2,792	1,141	1,425	138	68	19	
1962	108,632	4,257	2,957	69	2,772	431	2	3,205	1,265	1,675	162	89	12	
1964	124,055	5,469	4,314	79	4,073	596	2	4,671	1,393	2,840	207	99	14	116
1966	124,591	6,499	5,782	89	5,375	1,876	3	7,254	1,467	4,433	1,205	78	9	59
1968	114,017	7,554	7,072	93	6,499	4,441		10,940	1,025	5,186	4,521	128	4	76
1970	111,079	7,548	7,220	97	6,604	9,496		16,100	1,004	5,861	8,874	227	3	69

REGIONAL POLICY

In the last few decades, many changes have been brought about in the Swedish economy by industrial development. The shift from farming and forestry to manufacturing and service industries has resulted in heavy migration from rural to urban areas. Whereas only 33 percent of the population lived in cities and towns in 1900, the proportion in 1965 was about 75 percent, and an urban share of about 90 percent is predicted by the year 2000. Sweden has an average density of 19 inhabitants per square kilometer. A closer look reveals considerable variations, ranging from 160 people per square kilometer in the south to 3 in the northern counties. In Sweden, migration has been mostly from north to south; today, 90 percent of the population and most industry are concentrated in the southern half of the country. Sweden's regional development policies derive largely from a concern with maintaining full employment.

¶ REGIONAL DEVELOPMENT POLICY, 1945–1965
Official attempts to influence industrial location date back to the 1940s. In 1945, the National Labor Market Board opened a counseling and information service in designated areas and communities. The object was to promote locations that best provided for both the private and public interest. In 1951, a government commission of inquiry published a report that analyzed the economic, social, and strategic reasons for having the government conduct a policy of regional development. Until 1963, national activities in this field were limited mainly to giving advice and information.

From early 1963 until 1965, this service was augmented by different forms of relocation assistance. New goals were formulated in 1963 when a government commission on regional policy was appointed and in 1965 with the introduction of a parliamentary decision about the trial period, explained below.

¶ GOALS OF REGIONAL DEVELOPMENT POLICY AFTER 1965
Current policy is based on the objectives that Parliament defined for Swedish regional policy in 1964 when a new program of government-supported regional development got under way in the form of a five-year trial period. In this parliamentary decision, the objective was to promote a regional policy:

(1) So that the country's resources of capital and labor are fully exploited and are distributed in such a way as to encourage rapid economic progress.
(2) So that the increasing wealth is distributed in such a way that people

in different parts of the country get satisfactory economic, social, and cultural conditions.

(3) So that structural changes and economic expansion continue in such a way and at a pace that protects the safety of the individual.

The goals were worded in general terms, but the 1970 Parliament ordered that these be made more specific. Even now, however, it is clear that the different counties as well as the central government want to give priority to areas with a good potential for spontaneous growth, while efforts are made to keep the growth of large urban areas in check. Every county should have at least one urban region, which should have a diversified corporate structure and labor market that can serve as a base for the region's urban hierarchy and, at the same time, offer an alternative to the large cities.

¶ INSTRUMENTS OF REGIONAL DEVELOPMENT POLICY

To achieve a better balance between population and economic activity in different parts of Sweden, the 1964 Parliament voted to offer direct financial assistance to new firms or existing firms that expand their industrial operations in designated areas with acute change-over problems. Although continuing to provide industrial firms with information about plant location opportunities in different parts of the country was considered a valuable role, it was felt that regional development should be based on active and long-range community planning.

Rendering assistance to individual firms for investments in plant and equipment still ranks high as a goal of regional policy. A firm's application for assistance is evaluated in terms of a community's geographic location and the firm's prospects for success. Financial aid is to be granted on a one-time-only basis so that the firm can operate on commercial principles without the need of subsidies. Assistance is given on the condition that the firm's investment will have a lasting and positive effect on employment.

The means that are used today in the regional policy to achieve the objectives are of three main types:

(1) Government support to the so-called depressed areas, especially the northern part of Sweden. This support, among others, consists of: (a) measures to facilitate geographical and occupational mobility (including labor market training), (b) location grants and loans, (c) education grants, (d) transport grants.

(2) Consultation and information: In the metropolitan areas, for example, firms that are planning to enlarge, rebuild, or build new factories of a certain size have to consult the National Labor Market Board about possibilities of relocation in other parts of the country.

(3) Enlargement of the infrastructure in different areas (dwellings, social services, and so on).

¶ REGIONAL PLANNING

The 1964 parliamentary decision explicitly stated that the chief emphasis of the new regional development policy would be placed on an intensification of community planning. The economic segment of community planning has two main purposes. The first is to coordinate those decisions that are taken in different sectors and at different levels of central government. The second is to work toward a better integration of actions by central government and local authorities to move toward a common goal of regional policy.

In order to arrive at a common data base for assessing regional development with reference to demographic, economic, and other factors, the government, in 1967, commissioned the county administrative boards and their affiliated county planning councils to make a tentative assessment of growth in each county to 1980. This project, known as "County Planning, 1967," had two ends in view: first, given the background of prevailing demographic and economic trends, to forecast the development in each county, with special attention given to how the population might be distributed within the county; and second, given the constraints defined by the population sizes, to indicate the extent to which the county authorities were prepared to accept the spontaneous development. Among other things, this project is supposed to identify specific communities as growth points that merit development inputs by the central government.

The plans are to be regularly updated and to result in concrete proposals and action programs. The concrete plans and action programs called for by the 1964 Parliament are met by County Planning, 1967, only in part. In 1969, the government commissioned the county administrations and their planning councils to take the county planning study as a starting point for preparing concrete action programs of regional policy and to specify the measures necessary to achieve the goals proposed.

¶ GOVERNMENT BILL OF 1972

In October 1972, a regional development program for the counties was presented to Parliament. Until then, both municipal planning and the sector planning conducted by various government departments had, to a certain extent, proceeded independently of each other and of government objectives. The national regional planning aims, among other things, to produce a common objective for the work of all these bodies, together with a coordination of their deliberations and decisions.

The goals of regional planning are, according to the 1972 government bill, equal opportunities for employment; equal social, commercial, and cultural services; and a good environment for the people in the different regions. As has earlier been the case, most of the efforts will go to the depressed areas, especially the northern part of Sweden. In regard to metropolitan areas, a slower population growth than before is assumed. The program aims at providing a certain amount of places or districts in every region that are big enough to give the people alternatives for employment and so on.

According to the government bill, internal migration has been, in the long run, comparatively constant in proportion to the total population. In an average year, about 700,000 people in Sweden move, that is, change parish. About 70 percent of these remain in the same municipality or county. The long-distance migrations—over a county boundary—involve between 10 percent and 15 percent of all migrants. Most of these migra- tions are to and from regions where the labor market is in balance or where there is excess demand, such as between the metropolitan areas. Only about 2 percent of all long-distance migrations among people over the age of thirty is from counties with unemployment. It is this type of migration that should be reduced through regional policy measures. About 85 percent of the people moving are 35–40 years old. Long-distance migra- tions are made mainly by young people. This means continuing deteriora- tion of the age structure in regions from which a large number of people move.

Among the people moving, there is a very high proportion with rather large incomes. This is especially true for people moving to the metro- politan areas.

In the period 1965–1972, funds for industrial relocation have been granted to 920 firms, totaling 1,850 million kronor (skr) (about US$390 million).[2] More than 75 percent of this has been granted to firms in the depressed areas, for example, the northern part of Sweden. This will create about 23,500 new jobs.

IMMIGRATION

¶ THE DEVELOPMENT OF IMMIGRATION
About one person in every thirteen living in Sweden is either a foreign national or a naturalized Swedish citizen. This ratio explains why the community at large has become increasingly concerned with minority problems.

Sweden has not always been a country of immigration. During the latter

---

[2] One hundred kronor equaled approximately US$21.40 as of January 1, 1973.

part of the nineteenth century and until World War I, it was an emigrant country. The net emigration during the fifty years of the great emigration period was more than 1 million people, or about one-fifth of the Swedish population at that time—at a rate of more than 20,000 per year. Since the 1930s, immigration has exceeded emigration, and as Table 8 shows, the flow increased markedly during the 1960s. The extremely high immigration rates for 1969 and 1970—practically as high as the peak emigration figures during the 1800s—may be the most important feature of the Swedish demographic situation during the last decade. The long-range impact of recent immigration cannot yet be determined. However, if the annual number of live births is less than 100,000, the consequence of the number of immigrants to Sweden in 1969 and 1970 will be—after one generation—that about one-third of all young people are immigrants or children of immigrants.

During the years 1946–1970, the total net immigration amounted to 442,000. During 1971, immigration dropped sharply and only amounted to 3,055 persons for the whole year. This low net immigration was not, on the whole, caused by a small number of immigrants but rather by a high rate of emigration.

At the end of 1971, the number of foreign nationals and naturalized citizens living in Sweden amounted to 416,000, or about 5 percent of the total population. Most of them came to Sweden during the postwar period.

TABLE 8.

Immigration, Sweden, 1945–1971

Year	Net Immigration
1945	12,865
1950	15,080
1955	17,394
1960	11,005
1965	33,609
1966	27,249
1967	10,004[a]
1968	12,816
1969	44,143
1970	48,710
1971	3,055

SOURCE: See [1].

[a] The sharp decrease in net immigration between 1966 and 1967–1968 was caused mainly by a recession in the years 1967–1968. Net immigration again increased in 1969 due to a boom in the years 1969–1970 and again decreased drastically because of a recession in 1971.

In recent years, about 10,000 persons have adopted Swedish citizenship every year.

The marked increase in immigration, particularly in the 1960s, has been in response to the growing demand for industrial workers. And there is every indication that this demand will continue in the future.

In the earlier part of the century, the growing need for manpower in industries could be met through the excess population in farming. The labor reserves from farming were used up at the same time as the small birth cohorts in the 1920s reached the labor force. In addition to this, the then young cohorts received a much longer education than earlier cohorts had been given and entered the labor market at a later age.

The birth cohorts in the 1950s and 1960s are—apart from a few cohorts in the 1960s—as small as those in the 1920s and 1930s. Moreover, there is nothing to indicate that the cohorts of the 1970s will be any bigger, and these younger cohorts also will be more occupied with their education.

By far, the majority of immigrants to Sweden are young persons. As such, they have provided valuable increments to the country's labor force and have also partially offset the decline in certain age groups that resulted from the low Swedish birth rates in the 1930s. Table 9 shows the age structure for the foreign citizens and for the whole population in 1971.

The table shows that more than 140,000 children under the age of eighteen in Sweden are foreign citizens. About 33 percent of the foreign citizens were under the age of eighteen, compared with 25 percent for the whole population. About 55 percent of the foreign citizens were 18–44 years old, compared with 36 percent for the whole population.

In 1971, the alien portion of Sweden's total labor force stood at about 6 percent. Two-thirds of this foreign labor force come from the other Nordic countries. As of April 1972, a total of about 220,000 aliens were

TABLE 9.

Age Structure of Population, Sweden, 1971

	Foreign Citizens		Total Population	
Age	Number	Percent	Number	Percent
Under 6	71,886	17.2	813,329	10.0
7–17	68,458	16.4	1,196,343	14.7
18–24	65,905	15.8	857,043	10.6
25–44	164,629	39.6	2,079,102	25.6
45–66	40,816	9.8	2,200,664	27.1
67+	4,873	1.2	968,945	12.0
Total	416,567	100.0	8,115,426	100.0

SOURCE: See [1].

registered as being gainfully employed in Sweden. As a consequence of the differing age structures of the two populations, there is a higher percentage of gainfully employed immigrants than Swedes.

The curve in Figure 5 shows the number of immigrants in the labor force between 1947 and 1970 and largely reflects the economic trends of postwar Sweden. Higher levels of output have created many new job openings that have been filled partly by immigrants. However, the alien labor force also declined twice during this period, in 1954–1955 and 1958–1959, which were years of recession or stagnation. The years 1969 and 1970 showed a record-high immigration with a very heavy proportion of Scandinavians. Many immigrants returned to their native countries in 1971, when business conditions again slackened.

¶ IMMIGRATION LAWS
Until 1915, an alien could enter Sweden freely and work without special permission. During World War I, however, many restrictions were im-

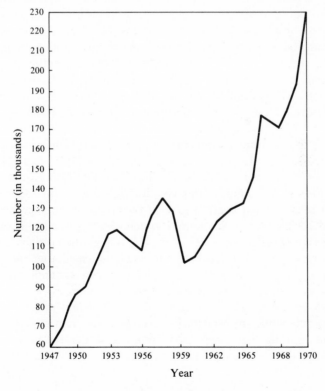

FIGURE 5

Number of Immigrants in the Labor Force, Sweden, 1947–1970

posed because of prevailing shortages in food and housing, the necessity for security precautions, and other reasons. Among other measures adopted was the requirement that an alien have an entry permit before being allowed to enter Sweden.

In time, increasing importance was attached to the labor-market aspects of immigration. A new law was passed during the interwar period, which required that aliens obtain work and residency permits. The same law granted broad powers to refuse admission to aliens and to test their rights to reside and work in Sweden. Its main purpose was to protect the Swedish labor market by preserving it for the domestic labor force. Later, in 1937, the law was amended to guarantee greater security to political refugees. During World War II, the work-permit requirement was waived for Nordic citizens and refugees from the Baltic states.

A new Aliens Act was passed in 1954. This law, which is still in force, is based essentially on the principle of free movement of peoples between nations. It includes (1) a permanent system of rules for deporting criminal or antisocial aliens and (2) provisions of a general, nonpermanent nature to regulate the flow of aliens with reference to such matters as prevailing labor market and housing conditions and the adequacy of resources. As in other countries, the principal determinant of immigration policy is the manpower situation. The act strengthens the legal protection of refugees.

Immigration into Sweden increased strikingly and almost without interruption during the first five years of the 1960s. The complications caused by completely unrestricted immigration became a matter of public debate.

In 1961, the government appointed a parliamentary commission to study immigration policy. Its report was published in 1967, and the debate following it constitutes the basis of a new law that applies only to non-Nordic citizens. According to this law, immigration is still controlled, but increased consideration is given to such factors as the immigrants' adjustment and social needs. The control system within Sweden is simplified and a permanent residence permit (which grants unlimited rights to assume employment and establish residence) normally is issued after the applicant has lived in Sweden for two years. Under a further regulation adopted in 1967, immigrants from other than the Nordic countries[3] are required to have work permits before coming to Sweden. It is not possible to obtain a work permit while in Sweden, for example, as a tourist. This was one method of limiting the immigration permitted under the general control provisions of the 1954 act. At present, a work permit is not issued unless

[3] Work and residency permits are not required of the two-thirds of the foreign labor force coming from the other Nordic countries. People from the Nordic countries are free to take employment in any member country without special formalities.

housing accommodation is also arranged, with consideration given to the views of employers and trade unions.

A new government agency, the Immigration and Naturalization Board, established in 1969, attends to matters of permits and controls. It is given wide responsibility for aliens' adjustment and is empowered to pass on applications for Swedish citizenship.

¶ ADJUSTMENT PROBLEMS

The problems connected with immigration have been fiercely debated in Sweden. Prevailing opinion today seems to agree that planned immigration is beneficial, but opinions differ where matters of adjustment are concerned. According to one school of thought, the best solution to problems of adjustment is to have the newcomers abandon their traditional cultural patterns and adopt the Swedish way of life (assimilation). Another school holds that the immigrants should be permitted to retain their own cultural patterns as they adapt to Swedish customs (integration). Sweden hopes to offer the immigrant a choice between integration and assimilation.

A government commission on the social adjustment of immigrants was appointed in 1968 to investigate the situation of immigrants and ethnic minorities in Sweden and to present a plan for various social measures for these groups. The local authorities of some forty communities have established information centers with interpreter services for immigrants. However, in accordance with the principle of nondiscrimination, no other special institutions for immigrants have been established.

The Immigration and Naturalization Board has a special division to deal with adjustment matters, another division concerned with permits and supervision, a third division for citizenship matters, and a secretariat. The division for adjustment matters performs coordinating, expediting, and initiating functions in public services to immigrants.

¶ RIGHTS AND OBLIGATIONS OF IMMIGRANTS

Immigrants largely enjoy the same rights under law as Swedish citizens and receive equal treatment. Insofar as no restrictions are explicitly stated, this is a main guiding rule. Other Nordic nationals living in Sweden are on virtually the same footing as Swedish citizens with respect to social benefits, education, and so on. Under law, however, nationals from countries outside the Nordic area are not on the same level. Swedish citizenship may be acquired after a residency of three years for Nordic nationals and seven years for other nationals.

¶ SOCIAL BENEFITS

As a part of an international drive to promote equality in social benefits, Sweden has signed a number of reciprocity conventions. However, these agreements cover benefits which, generally, have already been enjoyed by aliens living in Sweden. Thus, for example, aliens already receive the following benefits, on the same grounds as Swedish nationals or with only partial restrictions: general children's allowance, financial aid for students, industrial injuries insurance, unemployment insurance, unemployment assistance, and public assistance.

¶ MEDICAL SERVICES

Treatment is provided in hospitals, surgeries, and homes irrespective of nationality. Prenatal and postnatal services are also available free of charge to alien women and children whose names appear on Swedish census rolls. As soon as aliens establish residence in Sweden, they become members of a local social insurance office, which reimburses the costs of hospitalization, pays toward income lost from work through illness, and provides financial assistance during pregnancy.

¶ PENSIONS

The national basic pension, though limited in principle to Swedish nationals who are registered in Sweden for census purposes, has been extended under reciprocity conventions to immigrants from most of the other European countries. Immigrants from these countries receive the national basic pension after having established legal residence in Sweden for a specified period. Eligibility for the national supplementary pension is open to aliens and Swedes on equal terms.

¶ EDUCATION

Aliens qualify under the same general conditions as Swedish nationals for the education offered in the basic school, secondary school, and university, where tuition is free or nominal fees are charged. School attendance is mandatory for children between the ages of seven and sixteen. Immigrant children are given special instruction in Swedish and other subjects for a transitional period. They also can receive instruction in their native language. Aliens who have come to Sweden to pursue their education are not entitled to financial aid under the same conditions as Swedish students.

¶ INSTRUCTION IN THE SWEDISH LANGUAGE

The immigrants are encouraged to enroll in Swedish language courses, which are free of charge because of a government subsidy. The number of classroom hours rose from 110,000 in the 1965–1966 academic year to 780,000 in 1970–1971, when the expenditure amounted to 49 million skr (about US$10 million). Extended efforts are now being made to improve textbooks and give additional training to teachers. Teaching Swedish and civics to the immigrants ranks high in the educational programing of the Swedish Broadcasting Corporation.

The need to train immigrants in the Swedish language also is recognized by the labor market organizations. In 1970, the Swedish Employers' Confederation (SAF) and the Swedish Confederation of Trade Unions (LO) reached an agreement that urges firms with immigrant employees to pay wages for sixty hours of Swedish language teaching, twenty of them during working hours. The agreement proposes the payment of state bonuses to immigrants who complete 200 hours of instruction.

A 1972 government bill proposes giving all immigrants a basic course in Swedish and elementary civics. Immigrants starting their first employment in Sweden after January 1, 1973, will, according to the bill, have a legal right to a 240-hour basic course in Swedish without loss of wages.

SUPPORT TO FAMILIES WITH CHILDREN

Support by the public sector to families with children is provided in the form of both cash benefits and services.

¶ GENERAL CHILDREN'S ALLOWANCE

The main form of financial support to families is the general children's allowances, which all children under the age of sixteen living in Sweden, regardless of nationality, receive. It amounts to 1,320 skr per year (about US$280). This allowance is not taxed, nor is it subject to any means test. Children who continue to study after the age of sixteen can obtain study allowances, which correspond to the previous children's allowances.

¶ HOUSING ALLOWANCES

Central and local government housing allowances are an important supplement to the children's allowances for families with low incomes and for those with several children. Almost half of Swedish families with children receive some level of state housing allowances. Some 90 percent of single parents receive such allowances. Housing allowances are subject to a means test and can be paid to families living in Sweden with one or more children under seventeen living at home.

The state housing allowance is 75 skr (about US$16) per month for each child. The full grant is paid if the family income is about 20,000 skr (about $4,200) or below. The sum is reduced as income increases, ceasing entirely in the case of a family with only one child and an annual income of 27,000 skr (about $5,700).

Municipal housing allowances are designed to relieve the situation of families confronted with high housing costs, especially in recently built housing. These allowances cover 80 percent of the cost of rent above 400 skr (about $85) per month to a certain upper limit. The state makes a grant covering 60 percent of the municipality's actual costs.

¶ MATERNITY BENEFITS

The national insurance system incorporates numerous features dictated by family policy. Every woman giving birth to a child is entitled to a maternity benefit of 1,080 skr (about $227). It is available to all women living in Sweden. The maternity benefit is designed mainly to cover expenditures on new items necessitated by the birth of a child.

In addition, a daily benefit is paid to a gainfully employed woman at childbirth, according to her income for as long as she refrains from gainful employment, for a maximum of six months. Such compensation is paid according to the rules for the ordinary sickness benefit, although it is somewhat lower than the benefit.

A woman cannot be dismissed from a steady job because of pregnancy or giving birth to a child. She also has the right to six months' leave of absence in connection with the birth of a child.

The mother receives free advice and care at the maternity center both before and after delivery. Obstetric care is free. Practically all Swedish children are born in hospitals. About 90 percent of expectant mothers make use of maternity centers, and almost 100 percent of the children are given checkups at these centers during their first year. The frequency declines as the child grows older so that a general four-year checkup is now being introduced.

As a result of the family Policy Committee the maternity benefit will from January 1, 1974 be replaced by a parent-insurance system covering both parents. Within the framework of a total six months' leave of absence in connection with, and subsequent to, the birth of a child, it will be possible for both parents to alternate in caring for the infant after childbirth, with compensation. It will be up to the parents to decide which of them is to stay at home with the child and thus draw compensation. At the same time new rules will be introduced that permit a parent in gainful employment, whether father or mother, to remain home from work, with sick benefits, in order to care for a sick child. Also, a father will be entitled to sick leave with sick benefits if he needs to care for older children in his family while the mother is hospitalized in connection with a pregnancy or childbirth.

¶ HOME-FURNISHING LOANS

To facilitate initial homemaking, loans for young couples are available to a maximum of 6,000 skr (about $1,260). Unmarried mothers or fathers with the custody of a small child can also obtain such a loan.

¶ CHILDREN OF UNMARRIED AND DIVORCED PARENTS

If a child's parents are separated, the parent who does not have custody of the child normally pays maintenance. To prevent the child from suffering if the person required to pay maintenance fails to meet the obligations, the community pays an "advance maintenance grant," which amounted to approximately 3,000 skr (about $630) per year in 1972. Single persons providing for the care of children also enjoy certain tax reliefs.

¶ CHILDREN'S PENSIONS

Widows with custody of a child under sixteen receive, under the national basic pensions scheme, a widow's pension, which is identical to the old-age pension paid to a single pensioner. The widow's pension is paid without a means test to women widowed after June 30, 1960. If the husband died prior to July 1960, the size of the widow's pension depends upon her income. The national basic pensions scheme also provides a children's pension of about 2,000 skr (about $445) per year for each child under sixteen who has lost its father or mother. The widow's pension and children's pension, under the national basic pensions scheme, often are supplemented by corresponding pensions under the national supplementary pensions scheme. Such pensions are related to the deceased's previous income.

¶ DISABILITY ALLOWANCES

The national basic pensions scheme provides a disability allowance payable to any severely handicapped child under sixteen. This grant, about 4,500 skr per year (about $1,000), is paid, in principle, only if the child is cared for at home.

¶ CHILD HEALTH

Children are also entitled to the benefits of national health insurance for care by a doctor, hospital care, free and subsidized medical preparations, and so forth without any special charge to parents. Free supervision of the child's health to school age is provided by child welfare centers.

¶ SOCIAL WELFARE EXPENDITURES

In 1972, social welfare expenditures constituted about 35,000 million kronor ($7,000 million), or 18 percent of the gross national product. Support of the old and disabled and the Public Health Service costs are the largest expenditures. Next comes assistance to families and children, which, in 1972, totaled about $1,200 million. The general children allowances represented about 40 percent of the total expense in this category (about $450 million). Assistance to families and children, thus, represented approximately 17 percent of all social expenditures in 1972.

¶ PRESCHOOL AND FREE-TIME CENTERS

Steadily increasing efforts are being made to provide preschool and free-time centers, and these have developed in Sweden as an integral part of the child welfare system. The preschool program has two parts: the day nurseries, which are open 11–12 hours a day, 5–6 days per week; and the play schools, which provide children with three hours of activity per day for five days a week. The free-time centers are day nurseries for schoolchildren, primarily those in the 7–9 age group.

The day nurseries can receive children from the age of six months until they start school at the age of seven. The play schools offer places primarily to six year olds. The free-time centers accept children at the junior level (7–9 years old).

The common task of the preschools and free-time centers is to provide, by their educational activities, favorable conditions for the intellectual, social, and emotional development of the children. Apart from providing educational activities, the day nurseries and free-time centers are to remain open a sufficient number of hours per day for parents to be able to undertake gainful employment.

Because the preschools and free-time centers are a part of the child welfare system, priority is given to children in particular need of a place. Priority has been given to the children of single parents and others dependent on gainful employment. In recent years, the social care system has tried, to an increasing extent, to use preschools for children with social, mental, and physical handicaps.

The number of places at preschools and free-time centers has risen sharply during the 1960s (see Table 10), and the interest in these centers has increased greatly. The most important reasons for this are the altered status of women in the labor market and a new attitude toward bringing up children in groups. An underlying factor is also the new realization that both men and women have roles to play both in the family and in the

TABLE 10.

Preschools and Free-Time Centers, Sweden, 1950–1972

Year	Day Nurseries[a]	Play Schools	Free-Time Centers	Family Day Nurseries
1950	9,700	18,700	2,400	1,500
1965	11,900	52,100	3,000	8,000
1970	33,000	86,000	6,500	32,000
1972 (est.)	52,000	105,000	10,000	45,000

[a] Run by the municipalities.

community. This presupposes greatly increased support from the community in the form of preschool activities for children.

¶ TAXES

Swedish income taxes are steeply progressive. Since 1971, the tax system has changed in several ways. The main ideas behind the reforms were to

TABLE 11.

Gainfully Employed Women with Children under Seventeen, Sweden, 1971

Number of Children	Average Hours of Work	Number of Women in Labor Force (as percent of all women)
Youngest child under the age of 3		
1	29.5	57.7
2	27.5	42.4
3+	23.8	32.9
Total	28.0	47.2
Youngest child 3–6 years old		
1	31.8	71.6
2	27.1	53.2
3+	25.2	51.3
Total	28.5	58.5
Youngest child 7–10 years old		
1	31.2	70.4
2	27.9	67.8
3+	29.2	68.0
Total	29.2	68.7
Youngest child 11–16 years old		
1	30.6	74.5
2	30.7	74.1
3+	28.6	75.9
Total	30.6	74.5
Total		
1	30.7	68.8
2	28.1	56.6
3+	26.3	49.5
Total	29.2	61.1

SOURCE: See [1].

redistribute the tax burden from low-income groups and to introduce the principle of individual taxation of spouses; there are, however, exceptions to this latter rule. Individual taxation applies only to income from work. Husband and wife are only aggregated for tax purposes as regards income from net wealth. Smaller deductions are allowed for married persons if only one spouse earns income while the other takes care of children. If both the spouses are gainfully employed or if, in a one-parent family, the only parent is gainfully employed and if they have children under sixteen years old, a special allowance is granted. The allowance is meant to compensate, in part, for the cost of child care.

¶ WOMEN IN THE LABOR FORCE

As in other industrial countries, women with children of preschool age have, during the 1960s, begun to undertake gainful employment to a much greater extent. This trend has been particularly marked since the mid-1960s in Sweden. As a result, there were in Sweden in 1971 about 220,000 preschool children with gainfully employed parents. Table 11 gives statistics about women with children under the age of seventeen who were in the labor force in 1971.

REFERENCE

1. Ministry of Health and Social Affairs. *Family Support.* Governmental Commission Report, 34, 1972.

BIBLIOGRAPHY

Fors, Ake. *Social Policy and How It Works.* Stockholm: The Swedish Institute, 1972.
Linner, Birgitta. *Society and Sex in Sweden.* Stockholm: The Swedish Institute, 1971.
Ministry of Education. *Sexual Life in Sweden.* Governmental Commission Report, 2. Stockholm, 1969. (In Swedish.)
Ministry of Health and Social Affairs. *Family Planning and the Status of Women in Sweden.* Report by the government of Sweden to the United Nations. Stockholm, 1970.
Ministry of Justice. *Right to Abortion.* Governmental Commission Report, 58. Stockholm, 1971. (In Swedish.)
Ministry of Labor and Housing. *Regional Economic Development.* Governmental Commission Report, 15. Stockholm, 1970. (In Swedish.)
Ministry of Physical Planning and Local Government. *Administration of Land and Water.* Governmental Commission Report, 75. Stockholm, 1971. (In Swedish.)
National Board of Health and Welfare. *Proposed Organization of Advice on Contraception.* Stockholm, 1971. (In Swedish.)
Svala, Gertrud. "Sweden." *Country Profile.* New York: The Population Council, July 1972.
Sweden. Proposition (Governmental Bill) 1972:111. (In Swedish.)

CHAPTER 6

Bulgaria

Ivan Stefanov
Nicola Naoumov

ABSTRACT

In the People's Republic of Bulgaria, demographic policy is viewed as a component of the state's overall social policy; its objective is to promote childbirth, while preserving individual freedom to determine family size.

Natality, which has declined fairly steadily since 1950, is low, with the net reproduction rate around one. Mortality, after falling sharply in this century, is leveling off at a low level and even showing a slight tendency to rise because of the aging of the population. Prior to World War II, emigration and immigration were considerable, as a result of political unrest and fluctuating economic trends; however, both have been low in recent years. Internal migration is predominantly from rural to urban areas.

Since World War II, Bulgaria has enjoyed unprecedented economic growth, with the state playing a major role in the development of agricultural and industrial cooperatives.

Against this background, the government has established a pronatalist population policy based on specific ideological concepts and on specific socioeconomic and demographic conditions. Policy is implemented through a number of measures to promote the well-being of the married couple, the family, maternity, and infancy. Benefits to reduce the costs of childbearing and childrearing include: labor laws to protect the health of pregnant women; paid maternity leave; public health policies and programs; and a tax structure beneficial to families. Graduated birth allowances and monthly child allowances are paid to families for first, second, and third children; the benefits for fourth and subsequent children revert to the level for one child. Contraceptive devices are available throughout the country, and abortion is also available.

DEMOGRAPHIC TRENDS

¶ VITAL RATES

The demographic transition in Bulgaria in the twentieth century followed the general European pattern. In the period 1920–1925, tendencies toward parallel fertility and mortality declines emerged. This trend was arrested during World War II when fertility and mortality remained at about their 1939 levels, and it was temporarily reversed during the period 1944–1950, with a comparatively high level of fertility coupled with continued reduction in mortality (particularly child mortality). Table 1 shows the main demographic trends in Bulgaria since 1920.

The demographic trends after 1950, when the postwar compensation period came to an end, are of great importance for the demographic policy. Natality has been steadily declining during this period, except for 1968 and 1969 when a certain rise can be noted. On several occasions between 1961 and 1967, when natality attained its lowest level, the net reproduction rate dropped below unity.

Natality has been declining in all parts of the country, among the urban as well as among the rural population. Up until 1965 it was always higher in the villages than in the towns. (For example, in 1945 the urban birth rath was 21.6 per 1,000 and the rural birth rate, 24.8 per 1,000.) Along with the general downward trend, the difference between urban and rural

TABLE 1.

Demographic Trends, Bulgaria, 1920–1971

Year	Total Population (in thousands)	Natality	Mortality	Natural Increase	Child Mortality	Net Reproduction Rate
		per 1,000				
1920	4,847	39.9	21.4	18.5	146.0	1.69
1925	5,368	36.9	19.2	17.7	152.1	1.51
1939	6,319	21.4	13.4	8.0	138.9	1.24
1945	6,971	24.0	14.9	9.1	144.5	1.11
1950	7,273	25.2	10.2	15.0	94.5	1.14
1955	7,538	20.1	9.0	11.1	82.4	1.01
1960	7,906	17.8	8.1	9.7	45.1	1.01
1965	8,231	15.3	8.1	7.2	30.8	0.95
1966	8,285	14.9	8.3	6.6	32.2	0.91
1967	8,335	15.0	9.0	6.0	33.1	0.93
1968	8,404	16.9	8.6	8.3	28.3	1.06
1969	8,464	17.0	9.5	7.5	30.5	1.08
1970	8,515	16.3	9.1	7.2	27.3	1.03
1971	8,558	15.9	9.7	6.2	24.9	1.01

natality decreased gradually, and in 1965, the rate was 14.7 per 1,000 in the towns and 15.9 per 1,000 in the villages. Since then urban natality has tended to gradually exceed and outdistance rural natality, and in 1970 it was 18.0 per 1,000 as compared with 14.6 per 1,000 in the countryside.

Mortality has declined substantially since 1945. This is true in particular of child mortality, which dropped from 144.5 per 1,000 in 1945 to 24.9 per 1,000 in 1971. Mortality in all the other age groups, too, has decreased appreciably during this period, with the average life expectancy advancing from 53.3 for men and 56.4 for women in 1946–1947 to 70.0 and 73.5 respectively in 1969–1970. The aging of the population, a process that started at the beginning of the century, has been gaining momentum since World War II. This accounts for the recent halt in the downward trend of mortality, which since 1964 has tended to increase somewhat.

The changes in the age structure during the 1920–1970 period (Table 2) illustrate the aging of the population.

MIGRATION

¶ EXTERNAL MIGRATION

External migration, shown in Table 3 for 1927–1971, has played a considerable role in Bulgaria, assuming during certain periods a predominantly political character and during others an economic character. Frequently these two aspects would intermingle. The determining causes of political migration were the wars and the serious political crises in different countries, which found an expression in sharp clashes between the progressive and the reactionary forces, compelling some of those who had lost out to emigrate.

The Russo-Turkish War of 1877–1878, which led to Bulgaria's reemergence as an independent nation, caused a mass exodus of the Turkish population. But the bulk of that national minority remained within the confines of the new state, where it enjoyed absolute equality of rights, as had been proclaimed by the fighters for Bulgaria's national liberation.

TABLE 2.

Age Structure of the Population, Bulgaria, 1920–1970

	Percentage of Total Population		
Age Group	1920	1946	1970
0–19	47	38	31
20–59	44	53	54
60 and over	9	9	15
Total	100	100	100

TABLE 3.

External Migration, Bulgaria, 1927–1971 (in thousands)

Year	Immigration	Emigration	Migration Growth
1927–1930			−10.4
1931–1943	37.1	272.5	−235.4
1944–1946			
1947–1951	1.1	195.4	−194.3
1952–1971	1.3	27.3	−26.0

On the other hand, quite a few Bulgarians whose homes remained outside the confines of the newly established state immigrated to Bulgaria. The Bulgaro-Serbian War of 1885 produced no appreciable migration flows, but the two Balkan Wars of 1912–1913 brought about major shifts in the population of the Balkan states.

Even more pronounced were the population shifts that occurred during and after World War I. The number of Bulgarian refugees was so large that the then League of Nations intervened, floating and guaranteeing a special Refugee Loan so as to somewhat alleviate their fate. After World War II quite a few Bulgarian Jews and Turks emigrated. Between 1956 and 1969 there was practically no migration from or to Bulgaria. In 1970–1972 Turks emigrated on the basis of a special agreement between the Bulgarian and Turkish governments providing for the voluntary emigration of Turks from Bulgaria.

The military-fascist coup of June 9, 1923 and the September 1923 anti-fascist uprising resulted in a regime of white terror that compelled tens of thousands of communists, agrarians, and other anti-fascists to leave their homeland.

Socioeconomic factors have also played a major role in internal and external migration. As early as the beginning of this century many market gardeners emigrated to different countries, where they cultivated rented land intensively and provided the local market with vegetables. This was followed somewhat later by an economic emigration to the so-called New World. Special travel agencies organized the emigration primarily to North America, where the influx of European capital gave rise to a corresponding demand for manpower. The emigrants were primarily well-to-do and middle-income peasants who could afford to defray the rather high traveling expenses. The Great Depression of 1929–1934 likewise intensified emigration.

After World War II, the emigration of Bulgarians was only sporadic. In 1948 and 1949 some 33,000 Jews, constituting 92 percent of all emigrants in those two years, left Bulgaria. Another minority exodus followed in 1949–1951, when about 155,000 Turks left. After a lapse of eighteen years there followed a second and much smaller wave of Turkish emigration in 1970–1972, when some 35,000 left.

Summing up, in the 1930s a total of 254,000 persons left Bulgaria, while the number of immigrants was only 35,000, representing a net population decrease of 219,000. In the 1931–1971 period the number of emigrants approached 700,000 and that of immigrants was less than 40,000, representing a population loss of over 650,000.

¶ INTERNAL MIGRATION

Internal migration is primarily conditioned by two factors: a) industrialization and its repercussions on the other sectors of the nation's economy and b) the broading of the state's functions leading to an extension of its administrative apparatus.

Industrialization in Bulgaria was a relatively slow process prior to World War II. It was confined mainly to the traditional branches of the processing industry: food and tobacco, textile, leather and fur, and woodworking. The building up of the new state absorbed quite a few highly qualified cadres and ordinary employees as well as a considerable number of men for the army and the police.

The excessive protectionism of the home industry maintained high prices of finished products and low prices of agricultural raw materials. This policy compelled the peasants, who up to World War II constituted 80 percent of the total population, to continue processing their raw materials at home and thus impeded the development of the home market. As a result, up to World War II the percentage of the urban population remained constant, about 20. It was only in the postwar years, when industrialization assumed major proportions and became many-sided and when a people's democratic state began to be built that internal migration picked up momentum (see Table 4).

Far and away first ranking migratory patterns are from the villages and into the towns—which incidentally are interconnected patterns, for practically every urban immigration is at the cost of rural emigration. Much less important is the reverse flow, from towns to villages. During the entire twenty-six-year period, 1947–1972, migration into towns amounted to 2,579,000 and migration from towns to 944,000. The net urban surplus was, therefore, 1,635,000. In the villages we have the reverse picture, with out-migration (2,811,000) far surpassing the in-migration (1,240,000), resulting in a population loss of 1,635,000— precisely as much as the towns gained during that period.

When the in-migration and out-migration flows are differentiated by direction, the biggest flow is from villages to towns, which is fairly stable, attaining an annual average of 80,000–90,000. Intervillage migration ranked second up to 1965, when it was displaced by intertown migration.

TABLE 4.

Internal Migration from and to Villages and Towns,
Bulgaria, 1947–1972

Year	Out-Migration		In-Migration		Total Flow
	Villages	Towns	Villages	Towns	
Annual Average (in thousands)					
1947–1950	84.2	33.8	67.0	51.0	118.0
1956–1960	131.2	26.2	100.0	58.0	158.0
1969	107.1	49.6	122.3	34.4	156.7
1972	95.4	55.3	118.7	32.0	150.7
Percent of Total					
1947–1950	71.4	28.6	53.4	46.6	100.0
1956–1960	83.0	17.0	63.3	36.7	100.0
1969	68.3	31.7	78.1	21.9	100.0
1972	70.0	30.7	78.0	22.0	100.0

Intervillage migration shows a steady downward trend, because the total rural population is declining because of the flight from the countryside and because a growing number of villages are acquiring the status of towns, while intertown migration shows an upward trend, mainly because of the growing migration from smaller to bigger towns.

The flow from towns to villages ranks last, but in the past few years it has tended to increase because of the need for specialists and machine operators for farming operations, on the one hand, and for doctors, teachers, and cultural workers to meet the rising rural living standards, on the other. This flow keeps increasing despite the constant decline of the rural population because of emigration and the growing evolution of villages into towns, a phenomenon that has become fairly typical of late.

Intervillage migration is influenced by various factors. The concentration of agriculture makes for an increase of intervillage migration, while the growing mechanization of production releases ever more manpower from agriculture. On the one hand, there is an increase in the processing of part of the agricultural produce in the village and, on the other, there is a growing concentration of industrial activity into ever larger units which attracts the processing of part of the agricultural produce into the towns. This latter movement is the trend of development in the advanced capitalist countries. In comparison with them, Bulgarian agriculture is still able to retain a fairly large part of the active population. In the United States and even in Denmark the percentage of farmers is much smaller than in Bulgaria.

The different development of the four migration flows by destination has also changed correspondingly the structure of the total migration flow.

Migration from villages to towns accounts almost invariably for about half of the total flow. From 1960–1962 to 1972, the percentage of inter-village migration dropped from 33 percent to 13 percent, while that of intertown migration went up from 12 percent to 27 percent. Migration from towns to villages is below 10 percent, varying somewhere in the neighborhood of 8 percent.

A particularly important feature of internal migration in Bulgaria is its decentralization (there are data only from 1960 on). Whereas in most countries migration is directed immediately toward the capital and the larger cities, in Bulgaria it is directed toward the closest town or central village where there are communal authorities.

The decentralization of migration is apparent from the following data. Bulgaria has twenty-eight districts with an average population of 300,000 each. These are very small territorial units. In spite of this, almost half of the migrations occur within the same district. One quarter of the migrations take place between neighboring districts and often are less in distance than the within-district migrations. Only about one-quarter of these migrations are over a distance exceeding that between neighboring districts, but in quite a few cases even that distance is not considerable.

Migrations always considerably influence demographic processes mainly because they lead to substantial changes in the population's age and sex structure. Practically all the migrants are young people who have to adapt themselves to the new residence, to find work and make a living, then marry and expect progeny. In the inhabited localities from which people emigrate there likewise occur changes in the population's age and sex structure, and adverse ones at that, leading to an aging of the population. Migration also affects mortality by the passage of part of the population to an environment offering better health conditions. The marriage rate too is affected by migration, inasmuch as primarily young people emigrate. In Bulgaria, internal migration by sex is balanced by an almost equal participation of young men and women.

SOCIOECONOMIC TRENDS

The rapid development of the Bulgarian economy and especially of the new socialist relations of production has brought about profound changes in the social structure of the population (Table 5). The latest census data cover the 1956–1965 decade, during which the process of the socialist reconstruction of agriculture which started in the early 1950s continued. Over the period 1956–1965, the percentage of industrial workers increased by 70, that of office workers by 34, and that of cooperated craftsmen more than doubled; the percentage of cooperative farmers, on the other hand, went down by 3, although their absolute number increased. Private pro-

TABLE 5.

Percent Distribution of Employed Population,
Bulgaria, 1956 and 1965

Category	1956	1965
Workers[a]	24.6	41.8
Employees[a]	12.1	16.2
Cooperative		
Farmers	41.6	38.2
Artisans	1.1	2.4
Others	20.6	1.4
Total	100.0	100.0

[a] Including those employed in state farms.

ducers, who in 1956 constituted more than 5 percent of the population, have practically disappeared.

The overall change of socioeconomic conditions in Bulgaria is partly illustrated by the data in Table 6. The national income reveals an economic expansion of almost 150 percent during the past twelve years. Fixed capital shows a similar increase. The number of industrial and office workers, however, has increased only by 65 percent, which is quite comprehensible in view of the greatly increased labor productivity. The percentage of women employed in all sectors of the economy also shows a substantial increase. As a matter of fact, in some sectors of material production and especially in the sphere of services more than half of all the industrial and office workers are women.

The doubling of the number of specialists and the almost trebling of the number of research workers likewise deserve attention. Intensive electrification is an important indicator showing that economic growth has a secure and durable foundation. Total electric power consumed has quintupled, and the power consumed in agriculture attains about the same growth rate. The adequate increase in the capital invested every year is likewise an indicator of the stability of Bulgaria's economic expansion.

POPULATION POLICY

The ideological bases of the demographic policy of the People's Republic of Bulgaria are the communist ideology and the Marxist-Leninist demographic doctrine. Proceeding from clear and well-defined positions, the policy may be defined as one that consistently promotes childbirth while preserving individual freedom to determine the number of children and the time of their birth. Moreover, the policy is not confined to

TABLE 6.

Chief Parameters of Socioeconomic Growth,
Bulgaria, 1960–1972

Item	1960	1965	1972
National income (1960=100)	100	138	240
National per capita income (1960=100)	100	133	220
Fixed capital (in billions of leva)	9	12	23
Annual capital investments (1960=100)	100	146	280
Industrial and office workers (in thousands)	1,774	2,197	2,920
Percent female among industrial and office workers	33	39	45
Specialists (in thousands)	145	196	319
Research workers (in thousands)	2.7	4.2	8.0
Electrical power consumed (in billions of kilowatt hours)	3.3	8.0	17.6
Electrical power consumed in agriculture (in millions of kilowatt hours)	164	455	795

measures regulating the quantitative reproduction of the population but also tries to affect its qualitative composition, and thereby spreads out within wide limits as a component of the state's overall social policy.

The principles governing the state's social policy are to be found in a number of decisions of the Bulgarian Communist party. Proceeding from them, the government organizations work out and apply concrete measures of demographic policy. The principles governing this policy were formulated in some of the most recent decisions of the Bulgarian Communist party, particularly the decisions of the December 1972 Plenum of its Central Committee on the further improvement of the general standard of living and the Politburo decision of March 1973 on the role of women in the construction of a developed socialist society. These decisions, on the basis of which the normative documents of the nation's demographic policy are being gradually elaborated, confirm the principles governing this policy, while at the same time develop them further in consonance with the attained stage in social evolution and the experience gained from the demographic policy pursued so far. Policy and the broad means of implementing it in major areas are summarized below; details of implementation of policies on marriage and the family are discussed in a later section.

¶ POLICY TOWARD CHILDBEARING AND CHILDREARING

The pronatalist policy of the government of the People's Republic of Bulgaria does not aim at maintaining a high birth rate and a high growth rate. The dominant view on this question is one of moderation, as revealed by the whole system of measures aimed at promoting the birth rate. The aim is to maintain a moderate growth, to have families with two to three children on the average. A special tax is imposed on those who have no children (men up to age 50, women up to age 45). Those who have only one child receive a minimal family allowance. The leave of absence granted to mothers for the rearing of the first child is shorter than that granted for a second or third child. The allowances given at the birth of a fourth, fifth, and following child are the same in amount as those for a first child, while allowances for a second and third child are greater.

A woman's freedom to decide how many children she wants to have and when is ensured by a policy that permits abortions in accordance with social considerations. The restrictive stipulations in the decrees regulating abortion have almost no practical significance and actually do not limit this freedom. In the aforementioned Politburo decision of March 1973 there is a text that clearly and explicitly states that it is up to the families to decide how many children they want to have and when they want to have them.

¶ POLICY TOWARD WOMEN'S ROLES

A salient feature of the nation's demographic policy is the high recognition of woman's maternal role as a socially useful function of prime importance. On this recognition are based a series of measures of demographic and social policy for the protection and alleviation of female labor and of the labor of mothers, for facilitating the rearing of children and the maternal functions, for easing of household chores, and so on. At the same time, emphasis is also placed on woman's other social functions, such as active participation in the different spheres of economic and social life, and there is a manifest endeavor to combine harmoniously the maternal with all the other functions.

With the establishment of complete equality between men and women, as consecrated by the Constitution and all the special laws and as carried out in practice, a social conflict has arisen that profoundly affects women in modern Bulgarian society. Women have come into their own not only in production, trade, and the service branch but also in the nation's political and cultural life. It has become necessary for women to attain and maintain high professional proficiency. On the other hand, their functions as mother and housewife have not been sufficiently alleviated, in spite of the great progress made in the development of the service industry during the last two decades on the basis of large enterprises, mechanization of household chores, public catering, and establishments for children.

An inevitable consequence of this social conflict has been a decline in the birth rate to the level of a mere reproduction of the population in the long run. The net reproduction rate has in some years been ranging around unity. The government is now taking ever broader and more comprehensive measures to alleviate the tasks of the mother in the rearing of small children. Paid leave of absence for motherhood has been prolonged to three years. The scope of housing construction is to be extended, with priority being given to young families. More kindergartens, nurseries, and other establishments for children are to be opened, and more baby food, garments, and other necessities for children are to be produced. Mother and child care is becoming ever more all-encompassing.

The goal that the Bulgarian state has set itself is to secure for women real equality with men in the next few years, an equality that is not distorted by the performance of maternal functions, by offering her optimal opportunities for the attainment of high professional proficiency and for maintaining it throughout her career.

The measures of demographic policy now being elaborated and carried out proceed from the principle that the cost of bringing up the younger generations should increasingly be assumed by society as a whole, the long-range goal being their complete defrayal by social welfare funds. This goal has already been attained to a considerable degree, for in addition to family allowances for children, paid leave-of-absence for motherhood, and so on, free school and university education, including free textbooks and school utensils for a large part of the pupils, fellowships for many students, low-cost canteens, free medicare, and similar measures have already been introduced. All this by no means implies a separation of the children from their families to be raised in specialized establishments. On the contrary, it is fully realized that there can be no real substitute for maternal and parental care in the upbringing of children, and all that is being done by the state along these lines merely pursues the aim of facilitating the job of the parents in their highly responsible social function.

¶ PUBLIC HEALTH AND EDUCATION POLICY
The public health scheme is of particular importance in the state's overall demographic policy. Free medicare, the development of a system of health protection, the curative and preventive care activities of the health organizations, the training of cadres necessary for health protection, and similar undertakings are subordinated to one supreme goal: to reduce mortality to a minimum, that is, to protect human life, the vitality and the health of the people, and to create optimum conditions for a steadily

rising life expectancy. Considerable attention is paid to the active population in connection with reducing accidents and disabilities to a minimum, while preserving the vitality and working capacity of the people.

The social policy of Bulgaria as a whole is directed toward the creation of conditions necessary for the improvement of the qualitative composition of the population. The supreme aim is to meet ever more fully and comprehensively the material and cultural requirements of all members of society, as a prerequisite for the harmonious and versatile development of the individual, so that each and everyone may fully realize himself. The educational policy aims to create conditions for the formation of men with a broad cultural background, of highly skilled manpower in accordance with the growing needs of socioeconomic development. The social policy pursued is leading to an increasing homogeneity of the population from all parts of the country as regards professional qualification, living and cultural standards, health protection, and so on.

¶ MIGRATION POLICY

The internal migration policy is based on the principle of the individual's complete freedom of movement and residence in all parts of the country. The provisional measures restricting permanent residence in some of the larger towns now in force are motivated by the desire to surmount as quickly as possible the difficulties ensuing from the overpopulation and congestion existing in those towns. As to the external migration policy, permission to emigrate or immigrate is given whenever the reasons are considered as well-founded. The current economic emigration is regulated by normative documents settling the sending of workers and specialists to other countries for temporary work there.

The demographic and social policy pursued applies in the same manner to all citizens, regardless of sex, age, family status, nationality, or social status. It derives from the basic principle of complete equality for all citizens of the country.

In conclusion, it may be said that the entire demographic and social policy of Bulgaria is based on a principle that has been proclaimed as the supreme law of the nation's social development: care of man.

PROTECTION OF MARRIAGE, THE FAMILY, MATERNITY, AND INFANCY

Marriage, the family, maternity, and infancy are given special protection by the state. This protection is proclaimed in the Constitution of the People's Republic of Bulgaria:

Article 37. The mother enjoys special protection from the State and care by the State and by economic and social organizations. She receives a paid leave before and after delivery, free obstetrical and medical care, the use of maternity homes; work is eased for her. An expanding network of institutions for infants is becoming available as well as enterprises for providing everyday necessities and food consumption.

Article 38. The family and marriage are both under the protection of the State.

Civil marriage is the only legal marriage.

Both members of a couple have equal rights and equal responsibilities in marriage and in the family. The parents have the right as well as the responsibility to care for the raising and communist education of their children.

Children born out of wedlock have the same rights as children born in wedlock.

Article 47. The State gives the people comprehensive health care through medical-prophylactic and other institutions and public health services.

State and social organizations facilitate the dissemination of health information and education and encourage physical culture and tourism.

Each citizen has a right to free medical assistance.

State and social organizations provide special care for the health of children and youths.

The family is the basic unit of society in Bulgaria. The bonds of marriage are an essential prerequisite for population replacement (out of total births per year only approximately 8.0 percent are out of wedlock). The family is considered the most important environment for preparing children for the socialist society.

All normative acts directly or indirectly related to the family and marriage are permeated with a spirit of assistance and protection. The family and marriage are revered in Bulgaria; and it is in this spirit that the rising generations are being educated.

¶ MARRIAGE

Legally, only civil marriage is valid. The legal age of marriage is 18. The marriage may be concluded on the couple's mutual consent. There are no limitations to marriage from the standpoint of social affiliation, nationality, racial group, and so on.

Marriage is dissolved by divorce or death. In the event of divorce proceedings, the court gives full consideration to the dissolution of the marriage and attempts to bring about a reconciliation of the parties to close the case. However, no pressure is brought to bear on the couple: in the end the decision is theirs.

From a social standpoint, and in the spirit of the law, if there are young children at the time of the dissolution of the marriage, the court is responsible for providing the children with the necessary moral and material conditions for their upbringing until they reach maturity. The court determines the rights and duties of each party toward the children. In certain circumstances of particular hardship, the state remands custody of the children of the dissolved marriage to special state homes or makes arrangements for their adoption.

When a marriage is dissolved by the death of one party, the other becomes responsible for the upbringing of the children; moreover, the children are provided with a pension for their deceased parent until they reach a determined age.

Moreover, widowed parents with one or more infants may receive aid from the state in bringing up the children by placing them in special state homes. The state takes particular care of orphaned infants. When these children are not adopted or when nobody assumes the responsibility for their upbringing, they are placed in orphanages, where they are brought up and educated at the cost of the state until maturity.

PUBLIC HEALTH POLICIES

The public health policy of the People's Republic of Bulgaria may be viewed as an element of its demographic policy, insofar as it has a direct effect on the regulation of mortality and the reproduction of the population. The direct aim of public health policy is to help steadily reduce mortality and morbidity, to increase life expectancy, and to preserve as long as possible the physical, mental, and intellectual capacity of man.

Free medicare for everybody was introduced in 1951. All health institutions are state-owned and hospitalization is free. The Decree on Free Medicare of March 17, 1951 states:

Free medicare is implemented by the state health establishments and includes:

a) all examinations at home, in out-patient clinics and polyclinics, surgical interventions, manipulations, investigations, performed for a diagnostic, medical and prophylactic purpose;

b) hospitalization and child-bearing in medical-prophylactic establishments, hospitals, sanatoria for tuberculosis, maternity homes, etc., including surgical interventions, manipulations, examinations, and dressing;

c) treatment of teeth and of the oral cavity except false teeth for which the cost of the material is paid;

d) all X-ray, laboratory and other examinations;

e) drugs and dressing material provided by the health establishments during hospitalization or examination of patients;

f) meals during hospitalization;

g) prophylactic examinations, vaccinations, quininizations, anti-epidemical disinfections, and all prophylactic measures taken in accordace with the prescription of sanitary organs; and

h) sera and vaccines against contagious diseases, as well as medical preparations against malaria.

The state considers it its duty to promote and perfect public health services in all parts of the country by securing for the population free and universally accessible highly qualified medical assistance in accordance with the modern achievements of medical science. Great efforts have been made in developing public health services so as to attain the goals of the public health policies. Just a few examples. The number of doctors per inhabitant has almost quadrupled since 1939 (one per 520 in 1971 as' against one per 2,020 in 1939), while that of dentists has almost doubled, the respective figures being 2,730 and 5,240. The public health network has been considerably extended by the construction of new hospitals, sanatoria, out-patient clinics, polyclinics, and other health establishments. The number of available hospital beds has more than quadrupled: in 1939 there was one bed per 590 inhabitants and in 1971 one bed per 145 inhabitants. The adduced data on mortality are an illustration of the results of Bulgaria's postwar public health policies.

The public health policies put particular stress on the protection of motherhood, infants, and, in general, the growing generations. The aim is to preserve woman's childbearing faculties and to rear young generations healthy in mind, body, and spirit, by employing all the modern means of medicine.

A wide network of obstetrical health establishments of different categories and types covering all parts of the country engages in medical, prophylactic, informational and educational activities connected with the health of women and children. Whereas in 1939 only one-third of the childbirths were performed with the assistance of qualified medical workers, in 1971 a mere 1 percent was deprived of that assistance. In 1939, about 5 percent of the children were born in health establishments, and in 1971 no less than 98 percent.

The so-called womens' consultation offices, special establishments keeping track of the health condition of the female population, are of particular importance in the sphere of this health activity. Their many-sided activity pursues the aim of making sure that a woman's reproductive and sexual functions proceed normally at the different stages of her life and of protecting the health and work capacity of the female population. These consultation offices try to encompass in their activity all pregnant and lying-in women, as well as the newborn, so as to ensure a normal development of pregnancy and to preserve the health and life of the mother and the fetus, so that a viable and healthy child may be born. Their principal function is to protect the health and treat the female population whenever necessary in connection with gynecologic disturbances, anomalies, and disorders in sexual development, as well as to combat sterility, pre-cancerous and cancerous diseases, and so on. The consultation offices do not perform their work merely at request but are duty-bound to locate all pregnant women in the third month of pregnancy, mothers, and newborns, and to lend them all the necessary medical assistance, carrying out systematic prophylactic examinations, keeping track of their health and sending more complicated cases for examination and treatment to the respective specialized health establishments. It is their duty to periodically subject all women above the age of 14 living in their region to prophylactic gynecological examinations.

Along with medical-prophylactic activities, these institutions are active in raising the health standards of the female population. In order to ensure female health and fertility, and the proper growth of children, programs are set up to teach women hygiene during pregnancy, birth, and the post-partum period. These classes on maternity and child care also discuss social problems, describing the country's demographic problems as well as the psychological basis for low fertility, the sociopsychological analysis of one-child families, the harm and danger of abortion, the problems of educating and properly feeding the growing generation, family interrelationships, the psychohygiene of early childhood, and so on. The demographic policy of the country is explained.

The country's labor laws contain a number of provisions for the protection of female laborers. Women are excluded from jobs that might have an adverse influence on fertility. If a pregnant woman's job involves activity that might result in a complication in pregnancy, she is transferred to a job more suited to her condition. Should this transfer be to a lower paying position, she retains her previous salary.

Specialized medical institutions implement maternity welfare services on the basis of a series of statements in the codex of labor laws; they control job transfers of pregnant women, carry out inspection of spontaneous abortions and premature births, and provide general welfare services. Furthermore, the law prohibits females from certain types of work that might impair woman's childbearing capacity by producing temporary or permanent sterility.

The country's public health policy is oriented toward reducing mortality and morbidity. The activities most directly related to demographic policy are those directed at further reduction of infant and child mortality. All children, from birth until maturity, are registered in the country's health service institutions where their health and physical and psychological development are checked. The health establishments are quite active in protecting the health of children of preschool age. Since in Bulgaria education from age 7 to age 14 is compulsory, all children of this age group are covered by the health network of schools. Those who continue to study, including up to university graduation, also remain under the supervision of the health network of the educational establishments, which systematically carry out prophylactic examinations of young people, and engage in information and education activity, as well as in medical work.

MEASURES TO ENCOURAGE REPRODUCTION

The government has instituted a variety of measures to alleviate the economic costs of childbearing and childrearing. These measures are of two kinds: money given directly to parents, and provision of goods and services connected with rearing children either free or at reduced prices.

    In the first category are sums of money given at the time of a live birth and monthly family allowances. These benefits are proportional to the number of live births in the family rather than to the income of the parents. The values are presented below:

Live-Birth Order	Allowance for Live Birth	Monthly
1	20 lv.	5 lv.
2	200 lv.	15 lv.
3	500 lv.	35 lv.
4 or higher	20 lv.	5 lv.

    The one-time benefit for the first child represents approximately one-sixth of the average 1970 monthly salary; that for the second child, approximately one and a half times the monthly salary; and for the third child, approximately four months' salary.

    The monthly family allowances represent a percentage increase over the average 1970 monthly salary, as follows: for the one-child family, an increase of 4 percent; for the two-child family, 16 percent; for the three-child family, 44 percent.

    The monthly family increases are provided until the child reaches age 16 and are provided to only one of the parents if both are employed.

    During pregnancy and the postpartum period, employed women are entitled to a paid leave that varies in duration according to the number of live births, as follows:

For the first child	= 120 days
For the second child	= 150 days
For the third child	= 180 days
For the fourth and following children	= 120 days

In addition, besides the above leaves of absence, additional paid and non-paid leaves are granted at the request of the interested parties. Immediately after a maternity leave of absence, a mother may ask for an additional leave to look after her infant. The duration of this leave is six months for the first child, seven months for the second child, eight months for the third child, and six months for every following child. This leave is granted if the child has not been placed in a state establishment and if the leave is paid in accordance with the fixed minimum wage.

A mother may also ask for an additional leave to look after her child up to the age of three. This leave, over and above the fixed months of paid leave, is unpaid but counts as length of service.

The law provides for a paid leave to look after a sick child. This leave is granted to the mother or father, whichever looks after the sick child. A paid leave is also granted a parent for accompanying a child to another locality within the country or abroad in connection with medical examinations, investigations, and treatment. The paid leave in these cases can amount to a maximum of sixty days per annum and is given for children up to the age of sixteen. It should be noted that these sixty days do not include leaves for looking after a sick child suffering from an infectious disease, a suckling in a hospital, a child under quarantine, or a sick member of the family above the age of sixteen.

To facilitate the raising of infants and to provide nourishing food, the state has organized kitchens throughout the country where food for children up to one year of age is available at low cost. The food industry produces a variety of foods for older children at low prices.

Employed mothers can place their children in nurseries, kindergartens, and other specialized institutions at a low cost. The state is constantly expanding its network of institutions for children, as a means of facilitating childrearing.

All citizens are entitled to free education in all the types and degrees of educational institutions. All educational institutions are state-run. Elementary education is compulsory, and high school education will soon be also. Many students receive state grants.

The state also organizes vacation programs for chlidren. A network of specialized institutions—sanatoria, camps, student rest homes, and so on, are available at a minimal cost. The state is concentrating its energies on the expansion of a network of health resorts for youths.

Families with three or more children receive priority treatment when applying for a state dwelling, for a loan to build a dwelling, or for a job. They receive more state grants for payment for the use of child institutions. Some families that have raised three or more children receive medals as a social expression of gratitude.

Children born out of wedlock are protected by the country's laws. As citizens, they have equal rights with the other members of society and enjoy all the state benefits that accrue to children. Of course, births out of wedlock are not encouraged. The appropriate institutions deal with the social problems of births out of wedlock and arbitrate questions concerning the upbringing of such children.

TAX STRUCTURE

With certain exceptions, citizens pay tax for as long as they are employed. For those aged 21–30 the tax is 5 percent of total income, for those aged 31 and older it is 10 percent.

A couple pays no tax for the first two years of marriage. After that, the couple pays the 5 percent tax for four years, and the 10 percent tax subsequently.

A family in which a child has died pays the tax for childlessness starting two years after the child's death. The tax is not paid by families where the child died after becoming of age.

Generally speaking, although this tax is insufficient to encourage fertility, it nonetheless introduces a measure of social fairness by separating families that raise children for society from those that do not carry out these personal and social functions.

In addition to social programs to facilitate childbearing and rearing, the government stresses education of children in the school system on the importance of the family and maternity. In the people's consciousness, maternity is elevated, and the rearing of children has gained general recognition as a socially beneficial work and as a duty toward the nation.

CONTRACEPTIVE DEVICES AND ABORTIONS

In conformity with the principle of the individual's right to determine the number of children he wants, a variety of contraceptive devices produced both domestically and abroad are available in the country, and abortion is legal on many grounds.

Contraceptive devices are available throughout the country at drugstores and at centers specializing in the distribution of hygienic and medical products. These centers also provide contraceptive information and education. The production and distribution of contraceptive devices is controlled by public health services, which withdraw from the market those products harmful to health and reproductive capabilities. Contraceptives are priced low enough to be within the means of those with minimal incomes.

Of particular importance from the point of view of demographic policy is the legalization of abortion on request for social indications. On the basis of the existing free medical assistance in the People's Republic of Bulgaria, abortions performed by the social public health service are free.

In order to minimize possible undesirable consequences for the woman's health, regulations ensure that abortions be performed by highly qualified personnel in specialized obstetrical institutions. All abortions undertaken outside the regulations are punishable by law.

The woman wishing to undergo an abortion must apply to a special committee appointed by the Ministry of Public Health Service. Committee members include official functionaries who have the competence necessary for an appraisal of the social and medical aspects of each case.

The committees attempt to discourage the woman from choosing abortion; they explain the possible adverse consequences of abortion and enumerate the advantages of large families for the parents, the children, and society.

As evidence that the committees do not employ coercion or refuse permission to applicants, in recent years the number of abortions per year has almost equalled the number of live births. Only in certain circumstances do the committees not permit abortions; for example, abortion is not granted for young childless couples who have no impediment to raising children.

In the rare case in which permission for abortion is denied, the pregnant women must register at a health service institution, which conducts follow-up to ensure the normal development of pregnancy. In this way criminal abortion practices are discouraged.

Abortions are permitted during the period preceding the fifth month and —in exceptional cases—in the sixth month. Needless to say, abortion is only allowed if there is no medical contra-indication.

The work of the committees is confidential. When necessary, the committees review official documents submitted for the purpose of strengthening the reasons for the desired abortion. Employed women who have been given an abortion receive a sick-leave certificate.

In the spirit of the country's population policies, contraceptive devices and abortions as well as means for birth regulation are available, but their adoption is not encouraged as it is in countries whose demographic policy is to reduce population.

NETWORK FOR POLICY IMPLEMENTATION

The demographic policy of the country is the policy of the Bulgarian Communist party, which in cooperation with the Bulgarian Agrarian party directs the construction of a developed socialist society in Bulgaria. The Committee of Bulgarian Women and the professional unions participate actively in shaping concepts and in applying measures. At the same time, these organizations help various branches of the government implement demographic policy and inform the public of policy. Although fertility is low, popular opinion favors higher fertility. To attain this goal, it is necessary to create the social and economic prerequisites. There are virtually no opponents to the country's demographic policy, but, of course, there is controversy over the most effective ways to achieve the goal of greater growth.

The problems related to the country's demographic development are at the center of the government's attention. In 1971, at the time of the adoption of the new Constitution, a council dealing with reproduction was founded at the State Council.

The government's demographic policy remains oriented toward fertility stimulation and mortality reduction, and it includes measures to achieve these goals. For the future the problem will not be one of excessive fertility, but rather of attaining a higher level of fertility.

The most important governmental documents and normative acts that have a direct or indirect bearing on demographic policy are:

1. The decree of general free medical assistance, 1968.
2. Resolution no. 61 of the Central Committee of the Bulgarian Communist party and of the Council of Ministers of the People's Republic of Bulgaria concerning encouragement of reproduction, 1967.
3. The decree for encouragement of reproduction, 1968.
4. The rules for the application of the decree for encouragement of reproduction, 1968.
5. The codex of family laws, 1968.
6. Order no. 187 of the Ministry of Public Health Service and Social Maintenance concerning the execution of Resolution no. 61 and the provision of improved maternal and child health care in public health services, 1968.
7. Instructions on the regulations for abortions, and the repression of criminal abortion practices, 1968.
8. The rules of social maintenance for agricultural cooperative owners, 1968.
9. The codex of labor laws, 1969.
10. The Constitution of the People's Republic of Bulgaria, 1971.
11. Decisions of the December Plenum of the Central Committee of the Bulgarian Communist party, 1972.
12. Decisions of the Politburo of the Central Committee of the Bulgarian Communist party of March 6, 1973.

BIBLIOGRAPHY

Atanassov, M. *Fertility and Social Employment of Women.* Sofia, 1968.

Genovski, M. *Juristic Regulation of the Demographic Phenomena in the People's Republic of Bulgaria.* Sofia, 1968.

Ilieva, N. *Education of Women and Its Influence upon Fertility.* Sofia, 1968.

Petkov, Khr., M. Apostolov, and G. Borissov. *Medico-Social Measures for Fertility Stimulation.* Sofia, 1968.

Petkov, P. *Family Budget and Fertility.* Sofia, 1967.

Popov, Kiril. *Economic Bulgaria.* Sofia: Bulgarian Academy of Sciences, 1915.

Ribarksi, Encheva, Pashova. *Measures of State Social Maintenance Influencing Fertility Rise.* Sofia, 1968.

Stefanov, I., Z. Sougarev, and N. Naoumov. *Demography of Bulgaria.* Sofia, 1973.

Stoimenov, G., and N. Chochkova. *Comparative Study of Some Medico-Social Factors Influencing Fertility Rise during the Last Decade.* Sofia, 1968.

Vassilev, D. *Studies of the Problem of Medico-Social Indications for Abortions upon Request in Bulgaria.* Sofia, 1968.

Vassilev, D., and M. Popov. *Survey Study of Opinions of Women in Bulgaria about the Optimal Number of Children in Their Families.* Sofia, 1968.

CHAPTER 7

Greece

N. Louros, M.D.
J. Danezis, M.D.
D. Trichopoulos, M.D.

ABSTRACT

Fertility in Greece declined during the last thirty-five years from about 30 to about 18 live births per 1,000 population. A number of studies undertaken since 1963 have shown that the low birth rate was achieved mainly through the wide practice of illegal abortions and to a lesser extent through the general—but inefficient—practice of contraception. Infant and childhood mortality rates are declining also but they are still relatively high. By contrast, mortality rates of adults in Greece, particularly in the rural areas, are among the lowest in Europe, mainly because of the comparatively low mortality from cardiovascular diseases.

International emigration has always been a potent factor in Greece. Since 1960, however, it has reached unprecedented dimensions, causing a virtual stagnation in the rate of population growth. At the same time, huge waves of rural migrants flooded the cities, increasing the urban population from 38 percent of the total in 1951 to 53 percent of the total in 1971.

The objectives of the official population policy in today's Greece are: higher birth rate; high immigration and lower emigration rates; decentralization and redistribution of the population.

In order to combat subfertility, the government recently has enacted a law according to which every child born to a family having at least two other children would bring to his family a monthly allowance of 500 drachmas and has introduced substantial tax benefits for families with three or more children. With respect to international migration, no official action has been taken but the short-term and long-term consequences are now being studied intensively and various measures are being considered (for example, labor contracts, higher salaries, social security, and housing benefits). Finally, in order to promote decentralization and to slow down the wave of internal migration toward cities, the government has divided the country into seven areas with a high degree of administrative autonomy, and it has taken measures for the decentralization of the health services and higher education.

THE DEMOGRAPHIC BACKGROUND

¶ QUALITY AND GENERAL PATTERN OF VITAL STATISTICS

In Greece, correct data on vital statistics exist for the years 1930–1938 and after 1956. Even for these periods, the analysis reveals a number of systematic errors, mainly underregistration of perinatal deaths and misstatements in the reported cause of death. However, in spite of these limitations, population statistics provide a fairly clear picture of the trends of fertility and mortality. Furthermore, data are not classified by educational level, social class, economic status, and so forth, and therefore differences in fertility and mortality can only be studied between urban and rural populations. Table 1 provides a summary of vital statistics in Greece since 1930.

¶ FETAL MORTALITY

The registration of late fetal deaths (that is, of stillborn after the twenty-eighth week of pregnancy) is compulsory in Greece. However, in spite of the legal obligation, registration is incomplete, particularly in the rural areas of the country. This incompleteness accounts for the peculiar time

TABLE 1.

Summary of Vital Statistics, Greece, since 1930

Period	Population (in thousands)	Births (per 1,000 population)	Deaths (per 1,000 population)	Infant Deaths (per 1,000 live births)
1930–1934	6,545	30.0	16.7	128
1935–1939	7,029	26.6	14.4	114
1950–1954	7,731	19.5	7.2	41
1955–1959	8,105	19.3	7.3	41
1960–1964	8,434	18.1	7.8	39
1965–1969	8,704	18.0	8.1	34

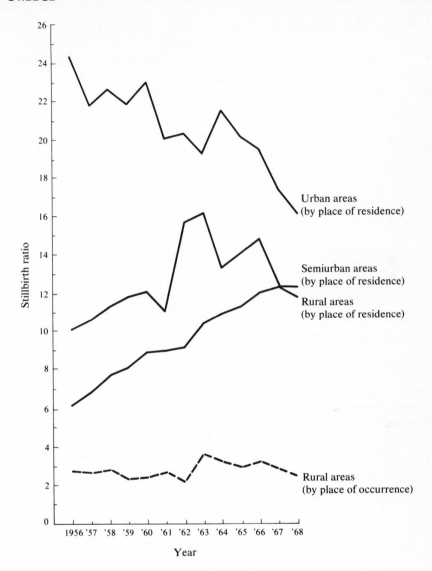

FIGURE 1

Stillborn per 1,000 Live Births in Urban and Semiurban Areas
(by place of residence of mother) and in Rural Areas
(by place of residence of mother *and* by place of occurrence),
Greece, 1956–1968

trends of stillbirth ratio in urban (10,000+), semiurban (2,000–9,999), and rural (under 1,999) areas of the country (Figure 1). It seems likely that in urban areas there is an actual decline of late fetal mortality, whereas for the semiurban and rural areas the observed pattern is dictated mainly by the improvement in the completeness of registration.

¶ INFANT MORTALITY

Infant mortality has fallen significantly during the last forty years from about 130 per 1,000 live births to about 32 per 1,000 live births (Table 2 and Figure 2). In spite of this remarkable improvement, the Greek rate is still among the highest in Europe, being about 2.5 times higher than that of the Scandinavian countries. Approximately two-thirds of all infant deaths in this country occur within the first four weeks of life (neonatal mortality). Nevertheless, in proportional terms, late infant mortality is particularly high in Greece, being about four times that of the Scandinavian countries.

The excessive infant mortality in Greece is mainly attributable to infective diseases, to various ill-defined diseases of early infancy, and to a lesser degree, to postnatal asphyxia and atelectasis.

TABLE 2.

Reported Infant Mortality, Greece, during the Periods 1931–1939 and 1949–1969

Year	Infant Deaths (per 1,000 live births)	Year	Infant Deaths (per 1,000 live births)
1931	133.8	1954	42.4
1932	128.7	1955	43.5
1933	122.7	1956	38.7
1934	111.7	1957	44.2
1935	112.8	1958	39.0
1936	114.2	1959	40.6
1937	122.2	1960	40.1
1938	99.4	1961	39.9
1939	118.2	1962	40.4
		1963	39.3
		1964	35.8
1949	41.9	1965	34.3
1950	35.5	1966	34.0
1951	43.6	1967	34.3
1952	40.5	1968	34.4
1953	42.5	1969	31.8

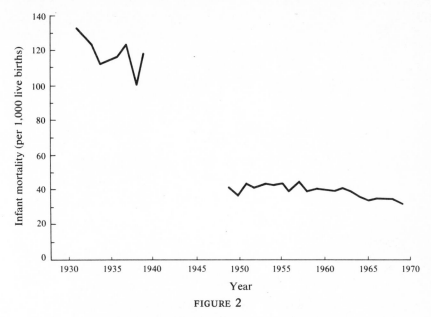

FIGURE 2

Infant Mortality (per 1,000 live births),
Greece, 1931–1939 and 1949–1969

SOURCE: Table 2

The postwar trends of neonatal and late infant mortality in urban, semiurban, and rural areas of Greece by place of residence are shown in Figure 3.

The following main conclusions may be drawn from the study of these rather peculiar time trends: (1) Neonatal mortality in urban areas is high, whereas the actual level of this mortality in rural areas is unknown because of the apparent incompleteness of registration of neonatal deaths. Underregistration is also responsible for the unreliability of the shown trends of neonatal mortality. (2) Late infant mortality declines clearly and steadily in the urban and semiurban areas; by contrast, in rural areas the decline of this rate is slower and rather irregular. It should be noted (in Figure 3) that since 1964 infant mortality has been higher in urban areas than in rural ones—a pattern reminiscent of the prewar experience. The single most important factor responsible for this rapid increase of neonatal mortality in urban areas may possibly be the improvement of the registration system in these areas.

¶ GENERAL MORTALITY

The ranks of age-specific mortality rates in Greece among the corresponding rates of all twenty-four European countries for which data are avail-

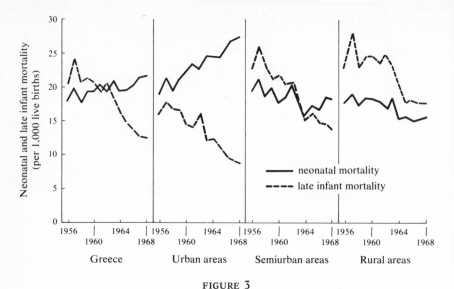

FIGURE 3

Neonatal and Late Infant Mortality in the Urban, Semiurban and Rural Population, Greece, 1956–1968 (by place of residence)

able (rank 1 indicates the lowest and rank 24 the highest rate) are shown below:

Age	0	1–4	5–14	15–34	35–54	55–74	75+
Rank	19	19	8	5	1	2	10

It is of particular significance that the infant and childhood mortality of Greece are among the highest in Europe, whereas the mortality of adults of this country is among the lowest in Europe and, indeed, in the whole world. The excessive premature mortality in Greece as compared to that of other European countries is attributable mainly to infective and parasitic diseases, while the comparatively low mortality of adults in Greece is due mainly to the apparently low prevalence of cardiovascular diseases in the country. However, international comparisons by cause of death are hindered by the fact that approximately 12 percent of all deaths in Greece are attributed to senility or ill-defined and unknown causes (the corresponding figures for Sweden and England-Wales are both less than 1 percent).

A comparison of age-specific death rates in the urban (10,000+) and in the rural (under 1,999) population reveals that up to the age of forty-five years mortality is higher in rural areas, while the opposite is true for the older ages (Figure 4).

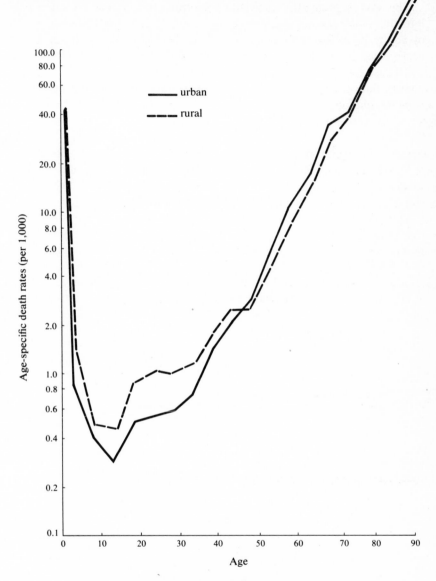

FIGURE 4

Annual Age-Specific Death Rates per 1,000 Population in Urban
and Rural Areas, Greece, 1966–1968 (infant deaths per 1,000
live births; infant mortality of rural population rectified)

The excess premature mortality in rural areas is caused mainly by infective and parasitic diseases; on the other hand, the higher mortality of adults in urban areas is accounted for by the correspondingly higher death rates from cardiovascular diseases and malignant neoplasms. Age- and cause-specific mortality rates of semiurban population hold usually intermediate positions between the corresponding rates of the urban and rural population.

¶ FERTILITY

Fertility trends are shown in Tables 3 and 4. The reduction of fertility has occurred especially in mothers over the age of thirty-five, and in birth orders beyond the third child. These data, however, throw no light on the ways and means by which the reduction in fertility was achieved.

The postwar decline of fertility and the simultaneous wave of emigra- tion have created serious concern among both government officials and the public. The concern became stronger in 1963, when the net reproduction rate dropped below the value of 1, and around 1970, when fertility rates, after a temporary increase between 1963 and 1967, again began to decline.

In order to clarify the ways by which the reduction in fertility came

TABLE 3.

Age-Specific Fertility Rates, Greece, since 1933 (per 1,000 women)

Period	Age-Specific Fertility							Net Repro- duction Rate
	15–19	20–24	25–29	30–34	35–39	40–44	45–49	
1933–1937	18.2	129.4	205.5	178.5	141.1	51.6	12.6	1.26
1956–1959	15.5	100.6	154.2	110.4	54.6	16.6	3.0	1.01
1960–1964	17.9	109.1	145.4	103.9	46.4	12.6	1.6	0.98
1965–1969	30.4	128.2	154.5	98.7	44.1	10.2	1.2	1.05

TABLE 4.

Fertility Rates by Birth Order, Greece, since 1936
(per 1,000 women aged 15–49)

Period	Birth Order					
	1	2	3	4	5	6+
1936	26.3	22.5	19.2	16.0	11.7	15.7
1956–1959	28.8	21.4	10.1	4.9	2.7	3.2
1960–1964	28.6	22.8	9.3	3.9	1.9	2.3
1965–1969	29.4	25.8	9.0	3.1	1.2	1.3

about, a field survey was conducted in 1962–1963 by the Department of
Hygiene and Epidemiology of the University of Athens [1]. It was found
that the average desired family size was 2.6 children in urban and 2.9
children in rural areas. Of the urban and rural married women interviewed, 87 and 79 percent, respectively, reported practicing some method
of birth control (Table 5), primarily coitus interruptus (withdrawal) or
the condom (Table 6). The contraceptive pill and the intrauterine device
were almost unknown to the sample interviewed.

In view of the rather low effectiveness of the reported birth control
methods, these findings could not fully explain the drastic curtailment in
the number of live births in Greece. Thus, a new field survey was undertaken in 1966–1967 in order to evaluate the frequency and reveal the
epidemiologic background of induced abortions, which are illegal in
Greece but thought to have been the factor responsible for the reduction

TABLE 5.

Percentage of Urban and Rural Married Women Practicing
Birth Control, Greece, 1962–1963 (by age)

| | Percent Practicing | |
Age	Urban	Rural
20	74.4	53.8
20–24	82.5	80.6
25–29	84.8	81.2
30–34	92.0	85.5
35–39	95.1	86.0
40–44	90.5	74.4
45+	75.0	69.6
All ages	87.1	78.7

TABLE 6.

Percent Distributions of Urban and Rural
Contraceptive Users by Method, Greece, 1962–1963

Method	Urban	Rural
Withdrawal	41.7	67.4
Condom	33.2	19.3
Other	25.1	13.3
Total	100.0	100.0

in live births. The study was carried out by the Department of Hygiene and Epidemiology of the University of Athens [2]. Approximately one-third of the married women interviewed reported one or more induced illegal abortions. On the average, there was a correspondence of 75 induced abortions per 100 married women of reproductive age, or of 34 induced abortions per 100 live births. The findings of the abortion survey by age of mother, duration of marriage, schooling of the mother, urban or rural population, as well as by order of pregnancy, are given in Tables 7, 8, 9, and 10 respectively. With the use of the available data, Polychronopoulou and Trichopoulos later estimated that induced illegal abortions were responsible for about 40 percent of the recent reduction of the fertility of the Greek population [3].

¶ MIGRATION

Since 1922, when an exchange of population minorities between Greece and Turkey took place, the population of Greece has been practically homogeneous. Thus, no ethnic or religious differentials are of importance,

TABLE 7.

Live Births and Induced Abortions, Greece, 1966–1967
(by age of mother and duration of marriage)

		Per 100 Interviewed		
Item	Number Interviewed	Live Births	Admitting Abortion	Total Abortions
Age group				
Under 25	485	113	15	20
25–29	1,044	174	28	50
30–34	1,533	205	34	69
35–39	1,446	234	40	93
40–44	1,070	245	42	101
45+	924	308	38	86
Total	6,502			
Years of marriage				
0–4	1,281	113	14	18
5–9	1,806	195	31	53
10–14	1,478	235	43	89
15–19	1,041	271	45	115
20+	882	346	49	134
Total	6,488			

SOURCE: See [2].

TABLE 8.

Induced Abortions, Greece, 1966–1967
(by years of school attendance of mother)

School Years	Number Interviewed	Abortions per 100 Interviewed
0	545	94
1–3	2,242	91
4–7	2,639	65
8–12	943	60
13+	113	38
Total	6,482	

SOURCE: See [2].

TABLE 9.

The Frequency of Abortion in Rural (under 10,000 inhabitants),
Urban (10,000–100,000 inhabitants), and Two Metropolitan
Populations, Greece, 1966–1967

Population	Number Interviewed	Per 100 Interviewed	
		Admitters	Abortions
Rural	3,606	31	59
Urban	2,382	37	77
Athens and Salonica	514	52	180
Total	6,502		

SOURCE: See [2].

TABLE 10.

Outcome of Pregnancies, Greece, 1966–1967 (by order)

Order of Pregnancy	Number of Pregnancies	Percent Outcome of Pregnancy			
		Live Births	Still-births	Spontaneous Abortions	Induced Abortions
1	6,252	88.8	1.8	6.6	2.8
2	5,227	80.1	1.3	7.7	10.9
3	3,460	60.5	1.8	9.0	28.7
4	2,133	50.5	1.5	9.0	39.0
5	1,325	42.2	1.0	9.0	47.8
6+	1,644	32.6	1.0	9.1	57.3
Total	20,041				

SOURCE: See [2].

TABLE 11.

Factors in Population Growth, Greece, since 1955

Year	Excess of Births over Deaths	Emigrants	Immigrants	Emigrants minus Immigrants	Emigrants Aged 15–44 Years (as percent of total emigrants)	Emigrants (per 1,000 population)
1955	99,482	29,787			77.0	3.74
1956	98,746	35,349			76.6	4.40
1957	94,276	30,428			81.4	3.76
1958	97,199	24,521			77.4	3.00
1959	99,347	23,684			80.0	2.87
1960	96,676	47,768			86.6	5.69
1961	86,761	58,837			88.8	7.01
1962	85,604	84,054			90.4	9.95
1963	81,436	100,072			89.2	11.80
1964	83,681	105,569			88.7	12.40
1965	84,179	117,167			85.3	13.70
1966	86,701	86,896			80.7	10.09
1967	90,864	42,730			71.1	4.90
1968	87,029	50,866	18,882	31,984	73.3	5.82
1969	82,252	91,552	18,132	74,420	83.5	10.44
1970	70,919	92,681	22,665	70,016	82.1	10.54

TABLE 12.

Percentage Distribution of Rural (under 10,000 inhabitants) and
Urban (10,000 + inhabitants) Populations, Greece, 1928, 1940,
1951, 1961, and 1971 (censuses)

	Percent Distribution	
Census Year	Rural	Urban
1928	68.9	31.1
1940	67.2	32.8
1951	62.3	37.7
1961	56.7	43.3
1971	46.8	53.2

since about 97 percent of the population are Greek-speaking and belong
to the Greek Orthodox church.

International emigration has always been a potent factor shaping the
profile of the Greek population. Since 1960, however, the wave of emigration, mainly toward Germany and other European countries, reached
unprecedented dimensions. The excess of emigrants over immigrants became almost as large as the excess of births over deaths, thus causing a
virtual stagnation in the rate of population growth (Table 11). The
emigration rate has been higher in rural areas, and it has been partly
responsible for the more pronounced decline of fertility in the rural population. Most emigrants are between fifteen and forty-four years of age,
thus depleting seriously the labor force of the country.

Internal migration had begun to intensify in Greece during the postwar
period. After 1945, huge waves of rural migrants flooded the cities, which
were not ready to absorb them. The rapid postwar urbanization is demonstrated in Table 12, which summarizes the relevant data from five consecutive censuses.

According to the latest available data (census of 1971), women represent 27.84 percent of the economically active population of Greece
(914,140 of 3,283,880).

THE DEVELOPMENT OF POPULATION POLICY

¶ POSITION OF THE CHURCH
The Greek Orthodox church prohibits, condemns, and punishes not only
the practice of abortion but also the avoidance of procreation.[1] The church
does not allow abortion even on medical grounds.

[1] Following the Old Testament, Chapter 38 (Genesis), lines 8–10.

According to the ξγ' Rule of the Elvira's Synod, the woman who induces abortion is punished with prohibition from the holy communion for a lifetime until her last moments before death. Then she is allowed to receive it. The punishment of a ten-year prohibition from the holy communion is imposed by the Rules of Ka' anchor as well as by B' Basil the Great and ya' Arch of Synods, while according to Fasting John, five-year and three-year penalties are imposed on married and unmarried women respectively. The penalty not only condemns the pregnant woman but includes also the physician who performs the abortion and all those who participate in any aspect of it.

The Greek Orthodox church believes that every human being and even the fetus itself is entitled to life. Children are God's gifts according to the Old Testament (Psalm ρκζ' 3). Only God can give life, and nobody, therefore, has the right to take life away, not even from the fetus. According to the moral rules, in very exceptional cases when the life of the pregnant woman is in danger and when the physician faces the so-called confrontation of duties, he is permitted to save the life of the mother by sacrificing the life of the fetus. In other cases regarding any human need or justification, the church raises the inviolable and eternal law of God that commands, "Thou shalt not kill."

The Greek church prohibits and condemns the use of abortifacient drugs as well as the means of controlling conception. The woman who takes measures to prevent conception is punished by a three-year forced abstention from the holy communion (twenty-first rule of Fasting John). The pregnant woman who uses abortifacient drugs, as well as her physician or anybody else who provides them, is condemned to a ten-year abstention from the holy communion (ninety-first rule of the Penthektis Synod).

Eunuchism is prohibited and condemned also according to the eighth rule of the Protosecond Synod. A legendary example is that of Origenes (185–254 A.D.) who as a teacher of young women castrated himself for reasons of self-control and was condemned by the church.

The prohibition and condemnation of all those who avoid childbearing is illustrated in Chapter 38 of Genesis of the Old Testament:

Judah said to his son Avnan: You shall take as a wife Thamar the widow of your own brother; come into union with her and let her bear a child for the sake of your childless brother. Avnan, aware that the child product of his union with his brother's wife will not be his own, purposely let his seed pour on to the earth. God considered that as an evil deed and punished him with death.

The Greek word "avnanismos," a synonym for masturbation, has its etymology from the name of Avnan and this biblical episode.

Despite the general strictures of the Greek Orthodox church against abortion and contraception, many religious leaders feel that because of the number of abortions in Greece they may have to be more realistic about contraception. Of course, abstinence is openly accepted and the rhythm method is not condemned. Among enlightened priests there seems to be a widespread attitude to advise that, instead of ending with an abortion, God gave you the mind to prevent conception. Such advice, however, does not extend to a discussion of what method, if any, is permitted by the church.

After the publicity given in recent years to the findings of the field survey of abortions in Greece [2], the church has been greatly concerned with the subject. Through a special committee created within the Holy Synod, the problem of abortions was reviewed and examined in detail. An enlightening encyclical, which was distributed among the priests, provided the necessary information and stated the position of the church on abortion. The encyclical stressed mainly the following point:

> Many couples, in our country, are being carried away by this epidemic and murderous trend of inducing abortion. Not only are they committing a sinful act but by threatening the nucleus of the family unit they actually endanger the survival of our nation.

Other points were also considered: the financial problem, the psychological consequences, and finally, the medical complications. The encyclical urged the believer against "this destructive trend" and asked them "to repent and realize that children in a family are a blessing and not a curse."

¶ CONTRACEPTION, CONTRACEPTIVES, AND ABORTION LAWS

There is no legislation concerning the importation and distribution of contraceptives in Greece. All pharmaceutical products have to be approved by a governmental committee known as State Laboratory for the Control of Pharmaceutical Products, acting similarly to the Food and Drug Administration of the United States government. Although most of the oral contraceptives are available in Greece, none is manufactured by Greek pharmaceutical industries or tested by government or private organizations.

Condoms are sold freely throughout Greece. Diaphragms and spermicides have been introduced recently in limited quantities. The only intrauterine device available is Saf-T-Coil. Oral contraceptives were introduced in 1963; they are advertised not as contraceptives but rather for their gynecological effects and can be obtained without a physician's prescription.

Male sterilization is not practiced. Female sterilization is practiced on a limited number of women on strictly medical grounds.

The modern aspects of control of conception are not included officially in the medical curriculum, and no legal fertility control services are provided as yet in governmental programs of public health. Therefore, knowledge among practicing physicians about family planning and contraception frequently is limited. As a result, only a small proportion of women make use of the modern and reliable methods of contraception, and the effectiveness and side effects of these methods usually are unknown. The contraceptives available in Greece are listed in the appendix to this chapter.

Abortions are illegal in Greece. According to Articles 304 and 305 of the criminal code:

A pregnant woman who purposefully destroys by abortion or otherwise the embryo she is bearing, or who allows someone else to do so, is punishable by imprisonment of up to three years.

Whoever, with the approval of the pregnant woman, brings about the embryo's death or provides to her the means for doing so is punishable by imprisonment of at least six months. If, furthermore, he performs abortions on a regular basis he is punishable by imprisonment of ten years maximum. Whoever, without the knowledge of the pregnant woman or against her desires, purposefully brings about the embryo's death, is punishable by imprisonment of a minimum of five years.

The act is not unjust and remains unpunished when performed by a physician with the purpose of avoiding an otherwise unavoidable threat to the life, or a serious and permanent damage to the health of the pregnant woman, provided that the need for abortion is also certified by a second physician.

Also unpunishable is abortion performed by a physician, with the approval of the pregnant woman, when conception took place subsequent to rape, to violation of a woman unable to resist, or of a girl under sixteen years of age, or incest. . . .

Whoever, in public, or by circulating pamphlets, pictures, or designs, proclaims or advertises, even if subtly, drugs or other objects, as capable of causing abortion, or similarly makes available his own or someone else's services for performing or assisting in an abortion, is punishable by imprisonment of one year maximum.

In spite of this legal definition and the great number of abortions performed, only about twenty cases are brought to court every year, and then only if the woman aborted dies or a disagreement arises among the persons involved.

¶ POPULATION POLICY ISSUES

The rate of population growth has never been considered a catastrophic threat in Greece. One reason for this relaxed attitude is that, during the last 150 years, the Greeks have been obliged to fight several wars for their independence, thus experiencing losses through war. Another reason is that emigration has always been relatively high. In fact, the rapid decline, not increase, of fertility recently has turned the attention of officials and the public to the problems of population.

Environmental concerns have been expressed in Greece only recently. They are linked to industrialization and the concentration of the population in the cities (mainly in the area of greater Athens), rather than to the fairly small rate of population growth.

Fertility rates began to decline in the 1930s, but it was not until about 1960 that the extent of the reduction was fully realized.[2] A number of field surveys and scientific studies [1; 2; 3; 4], undertaken during the next few years, showed that the low birth rate was achieved mainly through the wide practice of illegal abortions and to a lesser extent through the general—but inefficient—practice of contraception. Therefore, the major demographic issues in Greece after the mid-1960s were: low fertility rates, high frequency of abortions, high emigration rates, and uncontrolled urbanization.

The demographic situation in Greece has been covered extensively during recent years by the mass media, particularly the press. Demographic problems have received sufficient attention from both government officials and the general public. It is not difficult to account for this expressed interest in view of the very large number of abortions performed every year (about 75,000 among married women and about as many among unmarried women) and the huge wave of emigration. Furthermore, many Greeks believe that the present fertility rates are too low and the wave of migration from certain regions is too high for a country with the geopolitical position of Greece.

The interest of the scientific community in the demographic problems has been expressed in many ways. Besides field surveys, a number of theoretical studies about the population trends and future projections were undertaken [5; 6; 7], as well as several projects on basic research in the field of contraception and abortion [8; 9]. Furthermore, many round-table discussions [10; 11] and review articles have contributed to the enlightenment of the medical community and the public.

Several institutions and university departments were responsible for scientific activities in the field of demography in Greece after 1965. Among those institutions and departments that have contributed substantially to the scientific movement and the public education and eventually to the formation of an official policy in the field of population were the following [12; 13]: Hellenic Eugenic Society; National Statistical Service of Greece, Population Division; National Center of Social Research; Technical University of Athens, Department of Economics; Athens School of Hygiene, Department of Epidemiology and Biostatistics; University of Athens Medical Schools, First Department of Obstetrics and Gynecology, Division of

---

[2] During the period 1940–1954, the registration of vital events was very incomplete and in some areas of the country nonexistent, because of the war (1940–1945) and the Communist uprising (1946–1949).

Fertility and Sterility; University of Athens Medical School, Department of Hygiene and Epidemiology; University of Thessaloniki Medical School, Department of Hygiene.

Governmental concern was expressed in 1968 with the appointment, by the Minister of Coordination, of an ad hoc Committee on Demographic Policy, consisting mainly of governmental officers and a few experts from the medical community. The committee was asked to study the nature, dimensions, and probable causes of the problems of Greek population and to propose ethically, socially, and economically acceptable corrective measures. The following were some of the proposals of the committee:

(1) Foundation of family planning units throughout the country. Each unit organized as a consultation center for marriage, birth, fertility and sterility, and related family conditions.
(2) Education of the public on basic aspects of human reproduction.
(3) Decentralization of the health services. Creation of additional units for protection of maternity and child health in the rural areas of the country.
(4) Prevention of migration through decentralization, creation of new job opportunities, and various economic measures.
(5) New legislation favoring an increase of the birth rate of the Greek population.

In 1968, there was no legislation with explicit demographic objectives. There had been before World War II a number of laws for the protection of maternal and child health (for example, maternal leave of about four months), but they were based on humanitarian rather than demographic grounds. Furthermore, these laws provided for the unmarried pregnant woman or mother and for the unprotected or illegitimate child. They also guaranteed for the "large" families (those with five or more children):

(1) Free education of all children at all levels.
(2) Free medical care.
(3) Special tax exemptions.
(4) Exemption of the first born from the obligatory military service.
(5) Housing accommodations.

Since World War II, a variety of family assistance measures have been introduced in Greece. They include marriage payments (an allowance between 5–10 percent of the salary), maternity benefits (between US$40 and $200 for each delivery irrespective of parity), children allowances (between 3 and 6 percent of salary), and various tax benefits. Housing is not a major problem in Greece, since houses are available for rent at relatively low prices, and furthermore it is easy to obtain long-term, low-interest bank loans for housing.

Two additional official studies, undertaken in 1968 and 1970 by the (governmental) Center of Planning and Economic Research and the Ministry of Coordination, have confirmed the findings of earlier studies and have reached similar conclusions. These later studies have stressed particularly, however, the decay of the rural population, brought about by the huge internal migration and emigration and by the alarming subfertility of that segment of the population.

When the statistical data for the year 1970 were assembled and calculated, it became apparent that the birth rate had reached the lowest point in the demographic history of modern Greece and the emigration rate one of the highest (see Table 11). Furthermore, the 1971 census plainly demonstrated the uncontrolled growth of the population of Athens and the hopeless shrinkage of the rural population. It was under these conditions that official population policy was developed and formulated in the fall of 1971.

The objectives of the official population policy in Greece today are a higher birth rate, higher immigration and lower emigration rates, and decentralization and redistribution of the population.

In order to promote the decentralization and to slow down the wave of internal migration toward the two larger cities (Athens and Salonica), the government has divided the country into seven geographical areas, with a high degree of administrative and executive autonomy, and has taken measures for the decentralization of the health service and higher education. There have been few objections against the theoretical value of these measures, but many people are skeptical about their effectiveness.

In order to combat subfertility, the government enacted a law according to which every child born to a family with at least two other children would bring to his family a monthly allowance of 500 drachmas (approximately US$17).[3] Additional and substantial tax benefits were introduced for families with three or more children. These decisions have been well received by most concerned parties, notably the church and the army, and they have been favorably editorialized in the mass media. Some people have argued, however, that the population problem in Greece is, in fact, an emigration problem and that only an emigration-oriented solution would have been satisfactory. Others have noted that children of large families and particularly those born in birth orders beyond the third child come behind the other children of the same sex, age, and even social class with respect to both physical development and intellectual performance [14]. Nevertheless, the opinion of most people in Greece was that it was indeed

---

[3] US$1 equaled approximately 30 drachmas on January 1, 1973. The average income per capita per year in Greece is approximately $1,200.

necessary to take some measures, and that those already enacted had to prove their effectiveness before any change would be considered.

With respect to the two other major population issues, that is, emigration and illegal abortions, no official action has been taken as yet. The short-term and long-term consequences of emigration are being intensively studied, with particular attention paid to subfertility and the lack of sufficient labor force to meet the demands of the rapidly expanding industry. There have been hints from high-ranking officials that some sort of action should be expected. Among the proposed measures are the creation of socioeconomic motives to encourage immigration (labor contracts, higher salaries, social security, and housing benefits). The complexity of the problem, however, allows little optimism about a generally acceptable solution.

The problem of induced abortions seems even more complicated. On the one hand, there can be no question of legalization; on the other hand, the enforcement of the existing prohibited legislation would have serious and unpredictable consequences. The other visible alternative, that is, the establishment of a state-supported population planning program involving a national system of consultation centers, has to overcome the objections of the Greek Orthodox church and of many conservative Greek sociologists and physicians.

APPENDIX. Contraceptives Available in Greece

I. Caps
  A. Diaphragms
    1. Coromex
II. Condoms
  A. Dry
    1. Durex
    2. Fromms transparent
    3. Million Gold
    4. R_3
    5. Super Tex
    6. Thinex
  B. Lubricated
    1. Durex Fetherlite
    2. Durex Gossamer
    3. Fromms Feuchtfilm
    4. R_3 feucht
    5. Thins
  C. Shaped
    1. Durex Nu-form
III. Spermicides
  A. Aerosols
    1. Patentex Foam

B. Foaming Tablets
  1. Speton
IV. Oral Contraceptives
  A. Combined
    1. Enavid
    2. Enavid-E
    3. Eugynon
    4. Lyndiol 2, 5
    5. Norlestrin
    6. Ovral
    7. Ovulen
    8. Ovulen 50
    9. Volidan
  B. Sequential
    1. Sequental
V. IUDs
  A. Saf-T-Coil

REFERENCES

1. V. Valaoras, A. Polychronopoulou, and D. Trichopoulos. "Control of family size in Greece: The results of a field survey." *Population Studies*, vol. 18 (1965): 265–278.

2. V. Valaoras, A. Polychronopoulou, and D. Trichopoulos. "Abortion in Greece." *Social Demography and Medical Responsibility*. Proceedings of the Sixth Conference of the International Planned Parenthood Federation, Europe and Near East Region, Budapest, 1969. London: IPPF, 1970, pp. 31–44.

3. A. Polychronopoulou and D. Trichopoulos. "The effect of induced abortions on the reduction of birth rate in Greece." *Archives of Hygiene*, vol. 19 (1969): 105–113. (In Greek, with English summary.)

4. J. Danezis. "Induced abortions as an international and Greek problem." *Iatriki*, vol. 15 (1969): 195–205. (In Greek, with English summary.)

5. National Statistical Service of Greece. *Demographic Trends and Population Projections of Greece, 1960–1985*. Athens, 1966. (In Greek, with English summary.)

6. V. Katsouyiannopoulos. *Natality in Greece during the Years 1956–1967*. Doctoral thesis. Thessaloniki, 1970. (In Greek, with English summary.)

7. G. Siampos. *Demographic Trends in Greece, 1950–1980*. Athens: Ministry of Coordination, 1969. (In Greek, with English summary.)

8. J. Danezis. *The Effect of Low-Dose Lynestrenol on the Cervical Mucus and Sperm Migration*. Proceedings of the Seventh World Congress on Fertility and Sterility, Tokyo, October 17–25, 1971.

9. P. Panayotou, D. Kaskarelis, O. Miettinen, D. Trichopoulos, and A. Kalandidi. "Induced abortion and ectopic pregnancy." *American Journal of Obstetrics and Gynecology*, vol. 114, no. 4 (October 15, 1972): 507–510.

10. Hellenic Eugenic Society. *The Problem of Induced Abortions in Greece*. Proceedings of HES, round-table discussion, Athens, March 1967. (In Greek.)

11. Helenic Eugenic Society and Greek Endocrine Society. *Social and Medical Aspects of Oral Contraceptives.* Proceedings of HES, round-table discussion, Athens, May 1967. (In Greek.) Also, *Organorama,* no. 4 (1967).

12. R. Pressat. *Advances in Demographic Teaching and Research in Europe.* Council of Europe. Second European Conference on Demography. Strasbourg, September 1971. (In French.)

13. A. Stavropoulos. *Analytical and Critical Evaluation of the Experimental Center for Premarital and Marital Counseling of the Hellenic Eugenic Society of Athens.* Psychology dissertation. Louvain: Catholic University of Louvain, 1970. (In French.)

14. G. Papoutsakis, E. Pimenidou, V. Kalapothaki, A. Kalandidi, G. Papageorgiou, and D. Trichopoulos. "Height and weight of schoolchildren in Greece, by place of residence, parents' education, sibship size, and birth order." *Bulletin of Pediatric Clinic of the University of Athens,* vol. 19 (1972): 172–181. (In Greek, with English summary.)

CHAPTER 8

Belgium

Louis Lohlé-Tart

Acknowledgments: Much valuable information on natality and fertility policies is from Mrs. F. Coulon, Secretary, National Belgian Federation of Associations for Family Planning and Sex Education (Brussels) and Mrs. J. Geairain-Dedeken, Lawyer, Brussels. For a comprehensive view of the mechanics of Belgian policy making and for other information, we are deeply indebted to A. Delpérée, General Secretary at the Ministry of Social Security, who is not responsible for the critical appraisal of the policies that is partially based on data gathered by interviewing him.

ABSTRACT

There is no real population policy in Belgium, although there has been legislation related to population. The population of Belgium has three main characteristics: a very old age structure, a low rate of natality, and a high mortality rate. (However, mortality—except for road accidents—does not seem to be a preoccupation in the country.) Important ethnic differentials are gradually disappearing.

Various legislative measures could be considered favorable to natality. For example, a high-rate family allowance system exists, which largely covers the population under the age of twenty-five. Legislation concerning contraception and abortion also adds to this seemingly pronatalist attitude. Although contraception is not prohibited, no advertisement or even dissemination of contraceptive information is permitted by law. (Presently, a private bill is attempting to change this situation.) Family planning centers, however, are officially recognized. Abortion, even for therapeutic reasons, is forbidden under the law; no change can be expected in the near future. In actual fact, though, many abortions (probably about 50,000) do take place each year. In all these instances, government policy seems to have little effect on the country's rate of natural increase.

Regarding welfare measures in Belgium, social security is well-organized and compulsory. Other financial aspects, however, such as old-age retirement pensions and sickness indemnities, are poor and require improvement.

A very important aspect of Belgium's population evolution has been international immigration. Several legislative measures have been passed that favor such migration.

In general, it can be said that public opinion seems little concerned with population problems.

INTRODUCTORY REMARKS

¶ WHAT IS BELGIUM?

A small country (33,000 square kilometers) in western Europe, Belgium is surrounded by France (on the south), Germany and Luxembourg (east), and the Netherlands (north), and faces the United Kingdom (on the western coast). Since its creation as an independent political entity in 1830, Belgium has been a nonfederal state established as a constitutional monarchy; nevertheless, it is divided mainly into two large communities, easily distinguishable by several aspects. The northern part of the country, Flanders, is a region where the Dutch language is spoken; traditionally, Flemish people are Roman Catholic—both as a religion and a political affiliation—and work in agriculture and connected activities. Intensive industrialization in the north has occurred only since World War II. By contrast, the southern part of the country (Wallony) is a French-speaking region, less Christianized, and socialistic in its political orientation. Moreover, Wallony has a very long history of industrialization—one of the oldest in the world.

Economic and social evolution, of course, has deeply changed the actual picture of the two communities; it has, however, not modified their contrasting characters. We shall see that there are also region-bound demographic differentials. Since the constitutional amendments of 1970–1971, the formal structure of the country is being modified to recognize the two communities officially; the present political evolution seems to be leading to a kind of federal state.

In addition to Flanders and Wallony, there are also two special regions: First, Brussels, the capital of the country, which becomes in the new Belgian structure a "city-state" (similar to Washington, D.C.) enclosed in Flanders, near the border of Wallony; though Brussels is predominantly French-speaking, it is considered legally as a neutral and bilingual territory.

The second special region is a small area in the east of the country, which is German-speaking. It is known as "the redeemed cantons," because it was gained from Germany after World War I.

¶ BELGIAN POLICY MAKING

Since the end of World War II, two successive problems have prevailed in Belgium's political life. Until 1950, there was a monarchic crisis that ended in the retirement of King Leopold III; the present king is his son Baudouin. Since about 1955, it is the "linguistic problem" (that is, the relations between the two communities) that prevails in political life.

In comparison to these, all other problems appear to be minor, at least in the minds of the policy makers (except, perhaps, the construction of the European Economic Community, the loss of the African colony, and the reformation of fiscal laws). Consequently, one may say that the Belgian government rules but *does not make policies*. An arising question is treated as a minor problem whose *specific* solution must be found. There is *no* large decision-making attempt to cover an extended field of problems; there is *no* deep study of probable long-term consequences of the decisions; there is *no* integrated set of laws aiming at the future orientation of social life. In brief, Belgian political life is ruled by a kind of elementary stimulus-response process. As we shall see in this chapter, population questions are a typical example of this process.

¶ STATISTICAL DATA AVAILABLE FOR BELGIUM

Generally speaking, Belgian published data are scarce, outdated, and rather inadequate. For example, the government has no official knowledge of the recent statistical distribution of incomes; in 1972, the last official figures are for 1965–1966. Similarly, it is very difficult to obtain any reliable estimation of demographic trends in each community (except for raw data), and even the most common information is problematic. Seventeen months were needed to receive the first unofficial results of the 1970 census. This explains the relatively low quality of data used in this chapter.

PAST AND PRESENT TRENDS OF BELGIAN POPULATION

¶ INTRODUCTION

To understand decisions (or lack of decisions), it is usually crucial to estimate the pressure on political institutions exerted by events—the facts themselves or the development of public opinion in response to them. This is especially true when there is no explicit political will to anticipate the events, as is the case in Belgium.

In the field of demography, there are no genuine facts but only constructs. Generally speaking, population changes are perceived as absolute figures or as crude rates. For example, an increase in the number of live births could be, for the demographer, an epiphenomenon related to some irregularities in the age structure or to any slight modification in the timing of natality or nuptiality. But in public opinion, the press, and the governmental agencies, "more births" means "greater fertility." Thus, a good understanding of the population policy requires greater knowledge of the unsophisticated rates and figures than of the good demographic tools; satisfactory for the demographer, they bear no evidence at the decision level.

¶ NONDEMOGRAPHIC FACTS INFLUENCING POPULATION CHANGES

Territorial Changes.
By the Versailles Treaty, which concluded World War I, Belgium received a small portion of former German territories—the "redeemed cantons"—containing in 1920 only about 60,000 inhabitants. These districts were returned to Germany only during the Nazi occupation between 1940 and 1944.

Wars and Vital Rates.
During World War I, Belgium's war losses were not very serious in comparison with those of some other countries. However, the natural growth of the population decreased, due to a strong negative effect of war conditions on natality. Table 1 shows the vital demographic rates in Belgium during five-year periods beginning in 1906. It is significant that there are few fluctuations in average crude death rates during this period.

Throughout the years of War II, the same pattern of sensitivity of the natality rate to extraneous pressures appears. However, available data seem unreliable and we could hardly make any computations.[1]

Migratory movements were frozen during each world war (except for the forced emigration of workers to other German-controlled areas). The World War II period also greatly influenced the number of marriages, which dropped 40 to 70 percent. Divorce data do not exist or are unverifiable.

[1] For information purposes, one can find here the general fertility rate (number of births per 1,000 women in reproductive ages) and crude death rate (per 1,000 inhabitants), for each of these years:

Year	1939	1940	1941	1942	1943	1944	1945
GFR	68.06	58.97	52.84	57.29	65.24	67.43	68.82
CDR	13.77	16.12	14.67	14.73	13.45	15.74	14.72

SOURCE: From [1, pp. 18, 20].

TABLE 1.

Vital Rates, Belgium, 1906–1971

Period	Crude Death Rate (1)[a]	Live Birth Rate (2)[a]	Crude Rate of Natural Increase (3)[b]	Annual Growth (per 1,000) (4)[c]	Infant Mortality Rates (5)[d]
1906–1910	15.9	24.7	8.8	6.3	141
1911–1915	14.6	20.9	6.3	7.6	125 (1911–1913)
1916–1920	15.8	14.7	−1.1	−4.1	103 (1919–1920)
1921–1925	13.4	20.5	7.1	6.8	100
1926–1930	13.7	18.6	4.9	6.7	97
1931–1935	13.0	16.9	3.9	5.5	89
1936–1939	13.2	15.4	2.2	2.7	75
1940–1944				−2.4	
1945–1949	13.4	17.3	3.9	7.7	71.2
1950–1954	12.2	16.7	4.5	4.7	46.3
1955–1959	11.9	17.0	5.1	6.4	35.4
1960–1964	12.1	17.1	5.0	5.9	27.8
1965–1969	12.3	15.4	3.1	5.7	23.1
1970	12.3	14.6	2.3	3.2	19.8
1971	12.3	14.4	2.1	4.6	

[a] Number of events by 1,000 inhabitants.
[b] (2) − (1).
[c] Computed (except for 1970 and 1971) from $P(t)$ and $P(t+5)$, estimates of the population at the beginning and the end of the period, according to $(1+x)^5 = P(t+5)/P(t)$.
[d] Number of deaths among children under the age of one, by 1,000 births.

Other Events.

The world economic crisis of the 1930s resulted in a demographic pattern similar to that of the wars: a slowing of natality and migration rates and fewer marriages.

In 1960, the independence of the Congo (a Belgian territory) and its subsequent civil troubles involved an important process of repatriation of citizens (estimated at about 50,000).[2]

¶ ABSOLUTE POPULATION FIGURES AND POPULATION GROWTH
The population growth in Belgium is very slow, as shown in Table 2. The natural growth of the Belgian population is still slower—as shown in Table 1—than the total growth, due to a systematic positive migratory balance.

[2] Many Belgians living in the Congo remained on registers as Belgian residents and, thus, do not appear in migratory statistics.

TABLE 2.

Population Growth, Belgium, 1800–1971 (in thousands)

Year	Mid-year Estimate	Census Data (end of year)[a]
1800	3,000	
1846		4,337
1850	4,426	
1900	6,659	6,694
1910	7,392	7,424
1920	7,552	7,406
1930	8,076	8,092
1940	8,301	
1947		8,512
1950	8,639	
1960	9,153	
1961		9,189
1970	9,675	9,651
1971	9,673	

[a] Census data are corrected by elimination of registration errors (intercensus excess of about 40,000 persons for 1961 and 1970); next estimated data follow these corrected census data. For 1920, the corrections also take into account the war-bound errors (and do not include extended territory).

¶ MORTALITY

Decrease in mortality is one of the most prominent features in past demographic trends; Belgium follows the general pattern. However, Belgian crude mortality rates are among the highest in the developed world. As a rule, they fluctuated between 25 and 20 per 1,000 (with a few exceptions) during the entire second half of the nineteenth century. But since the beginning of the twentieth century, when the decrease was very fast, the changes were slow and alternatively increase and decrease: 14.9 per 1,000 in 1910, between 13.9 and 12.4 per 1,000 in the 1920s and 1930s. Its absolute lowest figure was 11.34 per 1,000 in 1959 (12.26 per 1,000 in 1971 or about 119,000 deaths).

Evidently, this does not exactly reflect the genuine trend of the mortality in Belgium, due to a high (and rising) proportion of older people. The age-specific rates of mortality show that deaths become more and more scarce in the youngest part of the population; the infant mortality rate has strongly diminished, although remaining rather high (See Table 1). However, the death rates for men do not decrease very much after the age of fifty, and even increase at older ages (seventy-five and over). For women, the trend seems to be the same but with a delay of about twenty years. While older male mortality rates have been approximately stationary since World War II (for example, specific rates for males aged 60–65 were 29.8 per 1,000 just before World War II, 26.6 per 1,000 in 1950, 25.7 per 1,000 in 1955, 29.8 per 1,000 in 1960, and 28.0 per 1,000 in 1968), female mortality has been leveling off since about 1965. The life expectancy gives a good synthetic picture of this evolution, as shown in Table 3. By contrast with some other countries, male life expectancy at birth does not yet decrease; this is probably due to the fact that Belgium still has a long way to go before attaining the same level.

¶ NATALITY

The natality trends are obvious. However, two facts are important: First, coming from a rather medium value (average around 30 per 1,000), the crude birth rate has decreased since the very early years of this century (rates of 29.0 per 1,000 in 1890 and 28.9 per 1,000 in 1900 but 23.7 per 1,000 in 1910), that is, simultaneously with the mortality rates; but its decline was at least as large, which explains the continuing low natural increase of the population. Second, as noted elsewhere earlier, any modification in life conditions (war, economic crisis, and so on) causes important changes in natality. From 1945 to 1965, natality rates fluctuated between 17.5 and 16.5 per 1,000; then, suddenly, they dropped to around 14.6 per 1,000 (1968–1970) and 14.4 per 1,000 in 1971 (or about 139,000 births). Here also, as for mortality, a more precise analysis—by age, by parity and/or by marriage duration—shows the internal variation of the phenomenon.

Comparing 1959 and 1969 (Table 4), one sees that the legitimate fertility remains approximately constant under twenty-five years of age but

TABLE 3.

Life Expectancy, Belgium, 1891–1966 (in years)[a]

Period	Male		Female	
	At Birth	At 1 Year	At Birth	At 1 Year
1891–1900	45.39	53.51	48.84	55.88
1928–1932	56.02	61.25	59.79	63.84
1946–1949	62.04	68.25	67.26	69.72
1959–1963	67.73	68.39	73.51	73.90
1963–1966 (estimate)	68.18		74.19	

[a] These figures come from the only official life tables computed since 1900. Computation *excludes* children who died just after birth (before registration). By including them, the last figures became: at birth, 1959–1963—67.15 for men, 73.04 for women; for 1963–1966, respectively 67.61 and 73.69.

TABLE 4.

Legitimate Fertility Rates by Age Group, Belgium,
1959 and 1969 (per 1,000)

Age	Rates in 1959	Rates in 1969
15–19	24.21	28.09
20–24	147.30	143.76
25–29	163.58	142.88
30–34	100.58	78.79
35–39	49.81	36.01
40–44	15.72	9.86
45+	1.20	0.70

SOURCE: See [2, p. 40].

falls uniformly for all durations of marriage and all parities after age twenty-five. Table 4 clearly shows the shift in natality, which is more and more concentrated at lower ages. Table 5 gives the latest detailed data presently available. The children born out of wedlock must be added to this total; 3,779 were born in the same year (the absolute figure of births for 1969 is thus 141,799), which constitutes an illegitimacy rate of about 26.7 per 1,000 live births. We must underline that illegitimacy is rather rare in Belgium and does not show any consistent trend to increase (Table 6), except for the very few years (1964–1969). This increase in the number of illegitimate births is only due to the decrease in legitimate fertility. The number of illegitimate children varies only by 10 to 40 each year, but at the same time, the total number of births decreases by 19,000 (−12 percent).

¶ AGE AND SEX STRUCTURES OF THE POPULATION
Figure 1a–e shows the evolution in population structure by age and sex according to five censuses of this century (1910, 1920, 1930, 1947, and 1961). Data of the sixth census of December 31, 1970, are not yet available, more than two full years later.

The general aspect of the 1910 pyramid (Figure 1a) is a "young" one. Nevertheless, one can see the narrowing of the base, a consequence of the sharp decline in natality noted earlier; this is the first sign of an unavoidable aging of the population (even without any other disturbance in its future history).

Just after World War I, in 1920 (Figure 1b), the age pyramid exhibits the demographic results of this war: the deep gap of the age group 1–4 is highly noticeable. The slight increase in mortality has mainly affected the male classes between 25 and 34—the war casualties—but also the older age groups (because of war restrictions and the pandemic flu in 1918).

TABLE 5.

Legitimate Natality by Age Groups of Mothers and Parity, Belgium, 1969, Raw Data (data in parentheses are the corresponding rates per 1,000 married women)

Age Group	Parity									Total
	0[a]	1	2	3	4	5	6	7	8 and over	
15–19	8,430	1,333	161	16[b]	1[b]					9,942
	(23.8)	(3.8)	(0.5)							(28.1)
20–24	30,338	14,291	4,104	1,046	272	61	5[b]	1[b]	1[b]	50,119
	(87.0)	(41.0)	(11.8)	(3.0)	(0.8)	(0.2)				(143.8)
25–29	12,698	14,288	7,441	3,086	1,184	478	162	57	19	39,411
	(46.0)	(51.8)	(27.0)	(11.2)	(4.3)	(1.7)	(0.6)	(0.2)	(0.1)	(142.9)
30–34	3,948	6,440	5,674	3,746	1,858	881	490	228	221	23,486
	(13.2)	(21.6)	(19.0)	(12.6)	(6.2)	(3.0)	(1.6)	(0.8)	(0.7)	(78.8)
35–39	1,406	2,060	2,300	2,057	1,451	947	546	346	496	11,609
	(4.4)	(6.4)	(7.1)	(6.4)	(4.5)	(3.0)	(1.7)	(1.1)	(1.5)	(36.0)
40–44	348	429	487	451	408	345	234	186	314	3,202
	(1.1)	(1.3)	(1.5)	(1.4)	(1.3)	(1.1)	(0.7)	(0.6)	(1.0)	(9.9)
45+	33	30	28	24	35	23	22	18[b]	38	251
	(0.1)	(0.1)	(0.1)	(0.1)	(0.1)	(0.1)	(0.1)		(0.1)	(0.7)
Total	57,199	38,871	20,195	10,426	5,209	2,735	1,460	836	1,089	138,020

SOURCE: See [2, p. 40].
[a] No previous births.
[b] Under 0.05.

TABLE 6.

Illegitimate Births, Belgium, 1930–1969

Year	Rate (per 1,000 live births)	Number
1930	40.4	6,164
1939	24.6	3,200
1950	25.9	3,777
1955	21.2	3,169
1960	20.7	3,200
1965	23.6	3,677
1969	26.7	3,779

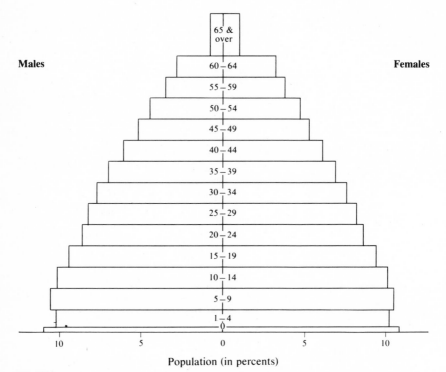

(a) 1910

FIGURE 1

Age and Sex Structure of the Belgian Population in
Five Different Years (percents calculated separately for each sex):
(a) 1910; (b) 1920; (c) 1930; (d) 1947; (e) 1961

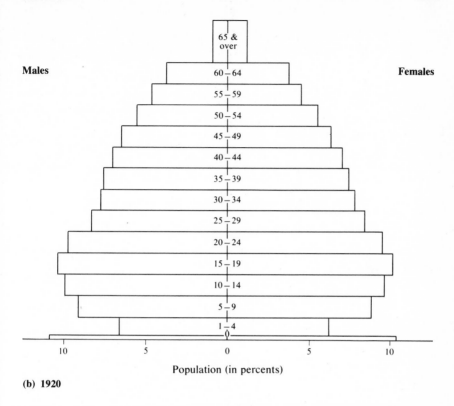

Males

Females

| 65 & over |
| 60 – 64 |
| 55 – 59 |
| 50 – 54 |
| 45 – 49 |
| 40 – 44 |
| 35 – 39 |
| 30 – 34 |
| 25 – 29 |
| 20 – 24 |
| 15 – 19 |
| 10 – 14 |
| 5 – 9 |
| 1 – 4 |

10   5   0   5   10

Population (in percents)

(b) 1920

In 1930 (Figure 1c), the decline of natality is confirmed, with the small bulge (ages 5–9) due to the postwar "catching up" of delayed births and the short increase that followed it.

The pyramid of 1947 (Figure 1d) is drawn just after World War II, and presents many similarities with the structure of 1920; the consequences of war casualties are largely masked by falling precisely around the reduced age groups born during World War I.

Finally, the age pyramid of 1951 (Figure 1e) shows its typical aspect of an old population with traces of severe disturbances. Nevertheless, one must notice that the base of the pyramid remains rather large, in spite of the fact that the most fertile female groups (between 20 and 29) are among the reduced age classes.

For 1970 (detailed data not yet available), the general trend is toward a decrease in the proportion of the young classes (0–14, due primarily to those under age six years) and of the adult ones (15–64) and a consider-able increase in the older groups (sixty-five and over) [2, p. 12].

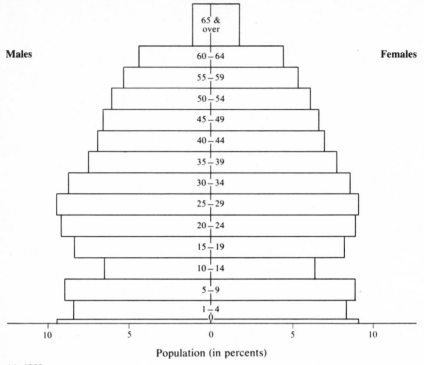

Males

Females

| 65 & over |
| 60 — 64 |
| 55 — 59 |
| 50 — 54 |
| 45 — 49 |
| 40 — 44 |
| 35 — 39 |
| 30 — 34 |
| 25 — 29 |
| 20 — 24 |
| 15 — 19 |
| 10 — 14 |
| 5 — 9 |
| 1 — 4 |
| 0 |

10   5   0   5   10

Population (in percents)

(c) 1930

¶ NUPTIALITY

There is no noticeable disparity in the distribution of population by sexes and, consequently, no particular pressure on some segment of the "marriage market." At the present time, for each sex, the rate of celibacy is about 9 percent; there is, thus, no significant tendency toward a low nuptiality.

Generally speaking, the Belgian population has always had a high proportion of marriages (1970 crude nuptiality rate: 7.56 percent; absolute number: 73,241). This rate has remained very stable since the beginning of the century, in long-term analysis. However, since the proportion of young people in the total population is decreasing, this means a greater frequency of marriage at these ages. Simultaneously, the nuptiality occurs at younger ages; for example, the proportion of women marrying under the age of twenty-one goes from 21.0 percent in 1910 to 24 percent in 1930, 25.3 percent in 1950, and 38.5 percent in 1969 (at the same time, the proportion of men marrying under twenty-five rises from 40.5 to 65.6 percent). These features, together with the fertility trends noted above, help to limit the natality decline.

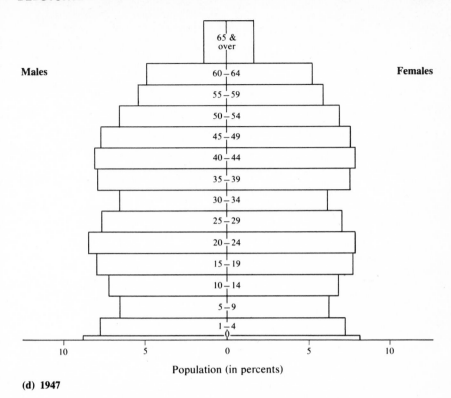

Population (in percents)

(d) 1947

Divorces were very rare before World War I; between the wars, there were about 3 to 6 divorces annually for every 100 marriages. These figures were 7.1 per 100 in 1950 and 7.0 per 100 in 1960, but rose to 8.9 in 1970 (absolute figure: 6,532).

¶ MIGRATION

Belgium is traditionally a country of immigration, and in effect, the total balance computed over a long span of time is positive in favor of the country. However, migration is a very sensitive phenomenon that fluctuates largely year by year, following a complex pattern of causes, including the economic and social situation of Belgium and of the country of origin as well as the political evolution of the world.

We have seen that the annual growth of the population was always larger than its natural increase, due to the excess of immigration over emigration. It is especially true for some years where the two sources of increase were about equal, such as 1964, and even more so in 1971. By contrast, exemplifying the short-term variations, the migratory balance

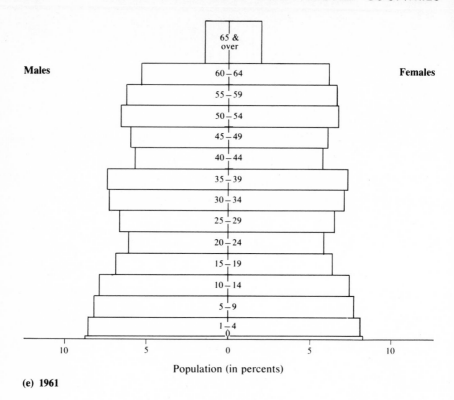

Males   **Females**

Population (in percents)

(e) 1961

accounted for less than 25 percent of the total increase in 1969 and about 30 percent in 1970.

However, as is shown here, the migratory flow became significant only after World War I (during the 1920s) and more so after 1950. The economic crisis of the 1930s and the war froze migrations (with a slight trend toward net out-migration).

¶ THE FOREIGN POPULATION OF BELGIUM

The migratory balance (its highest absolute value was 48,945 persons in 1964) is only a measure of the excess of immigration. Consequently, it does not show the importance, in proportion to the total population, of the foreigners (see Table 7).

The latest available structure of the foreign population, for 1961 (Figure 2), shows striking differences with the total population (Figure 1e): sex disequilibrium of the adult population, very low proportion of older ages, and important proportion of children. The spectacular gap around age twenty may be explained in several ways. The migrant is often a young

Foreign Population, Belgium, 1920–1970

Year	Number (in thousands)	Proportion of Total Population (per 1,000)
1920	150	20.2
1930	319	39.4
1947	368	39.8
1961	453	49.4
1970 (est.)	716	73.8

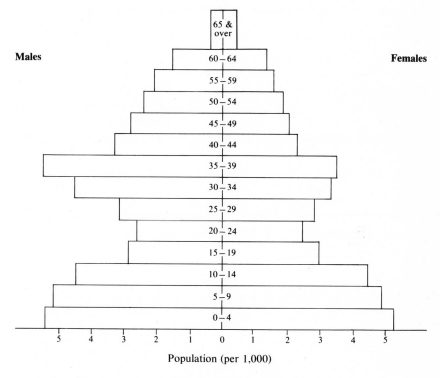

FIGURE 2

Age and Sex Structure of the Foreign Population in Belgium, 1961
(per 1,000). The Percentage of Some Groups of the Foreign Population
in 1961 Were as Follows: Children 0–14 Years = 35.3 Percent;
Married = 43.6 Percent; Single = 16.3 Percent; Widows = 4 Percent;
Divorced = 0.8 Percent.

SOURCE: Based on data from the Ministry of Public Health and the Family, Center for
Studies on Population and the Family

adult. Many are single and marry in Belgium. If he is married, he then comes with young children. Since the large migratory flow was a rather recent trend at the time of this computation and since the stabilization of the foreigners was a still more recent trend, one can easily understand that the Belgium-born children of foreigners have not yet reached adult age. Moreover, while before 1950 migrants were predominantly males, a considerable number of women, even single women, have emigrated in recent years, thus providing more opportunities for the single male migrants to marry.

Remaining sociologically akin to their country of origin, most foreigners have a higher fertility than the Belgian population, which, together with their younger age structure, explains their high natality (about 8 percent of births were due to about 5 percent of the population in 1961; estimates for 1970 are 12 percent of births for 7.4 percent of the population).

¶ DEMOGRAPHIC DIFFERENTIALS IN BELGIUM

The most significant differences between Belgian subgroups are based on regional grounds: Flanders versus Wallony with a distinct mention of the district of Brussels. This is not only a geographical criterion; it is also a linguistic, occupational, religious, and political one, that is, truly an ethnic differentiation.

On demographic grounds, differentials have existed for a very long time, centuries even. The general trend is a lower natality and a higher mortality in Wallony with as a consequence—and also as a cause during this evolution—an older age structure. It is easy to see that the proportion of Walloons in the Belgian population can only decrease, as it does (Table 8).

TABLE 8.

Proportional Population of the Regions, Belgium, 1930–1971
(in percents)

Year	Flanders	Wallony	Brussels
1930	51.14	37.17	11.02
1947	53.48	34.65	11.23
1961	55.10	33.14	11.13
1971 (est.)	56.23	32.05	11.08

SOURCE: See [2, p. 75].
NOTES: Totals do not add up to 100 percent because the small German-speaking region (about 0.65 percent) is excluded here.
This table shows the figures computed recently, after a new administrative distribution of the regions (law of August 2, 1963); early published statistics were computed on the basis of the old limits of the provinces, which did not exactly overlap the cultural limits of the communities. Flanders thus "gains" some 3.5 to 4 percent by reference to older figures.

Using the crude birth rates, the four Flemish provinces have always exceeded the four Walloons (Brabant[3] being the ninth). This is changing rapidly. The decline in natality during the last years is due mainly to a decrease in Flemish natality and we can expect, in the short run, the differential to disappear (Table 9). This table shows the evidence that the trend is to homogeneity of natality: the higher the natality, the greater the decline. It is interesting to notice that illegitimacy rates follow a distribution roughly inverse to that of total natality, Brabant ranking first, before the Walloon provinces.

The crude death rates follow the same regional pattern, with Flemish mortality lower than Walloon mortality. This is, however, mainly caused by the older age structure of Wallony. Nevertheless, this fact evidently does not explain why *infant* mortality is also significantly higher in Wallony than in Flanders.

The differences are still more significant when we consider only the Belgian population, since the foreigners (younger and more fertile) are mainly concentrated in the two Walloon provinces of Liege (15.3 percent of the population) and Hainaut (12.3 percent).

[3] Brussels is included in the province of Brabant, which also is divided into a Flemish and a Walloon part.

TABLE 9.

Regional Evolution of Natality, Belgium, 1963–1970 (crude birth rates per 1,000; ranks are within parentheses)

Province	1963	1970	Percentage Difference 1963–1970
Flanders			
Antwerp	18.5 (3)	14.6 (5)	−21.1 (2)
Limburg	23.3 (1)	17.5 (1)	−24.9 (1)
Eastern Flanders	17.5 (4)	14.9 (4)	−14.9 (5)
Western Flanders	18.8 (2)	15.4 (2)	−18.1 (3)
Wallony			
Hainaut	15.3 (8)	14.4 (6)	− 5.9 (9)
Liege	15.4 (7)	13.6 (8)	−11.7 (7)
Luxembourg	17.1 (5)	14.4 (7)	−15.8 (4)
Namur	17.1 (6)	15.0 (3)	−12.3 (6)
Brabant	15.1 (9)	13.5 (9)	−10.6 (8)

¶ INTERNAL MIGRATION

Each year, about 5 percent of the population moves across the border of local circumscriptions. There is, nevertheless, no consistent trend of migration toward or from specific regions, and the study of internal flows does not seem of any interest here. In fact, since Belgium is a small country, commuting is very much more important than is true migration: about 1,250,000 workers (or 37 percent of the active population) are commuters.

¶ SUMMARY AND CONCLUSIONS

The trends outlined above are summarized graphically in Figure 3. The following are only the most salient features of Belgian demography:

(1) Old-age population.
(2) Low natality because of this age structure and a specifically low fertility.
(3) Relatively high mortality.
(4) Important contribution of foreigners to the total evolution of the population.
(5) High sensitivity of demographic parameters to crises (war, economic depression).
(6) Major ethnic differentials, but with a recent trend toward lessening differentials.

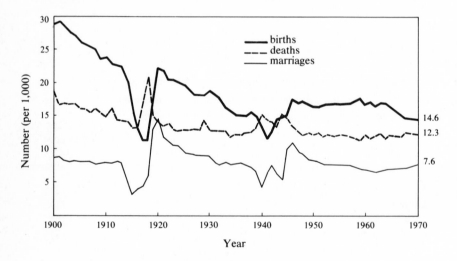

FIGURE 3

Summary of Belgian Demography: (a) Births, Deaths, and Marriages, 1900–1970 (per 1,000 inhabitants); (b) Evolution of the Age Structure, 1880–1969 (per 100,000); (c) Age Structure, 1969 (per 100,000)

SOURCE: See [3, p. 50]

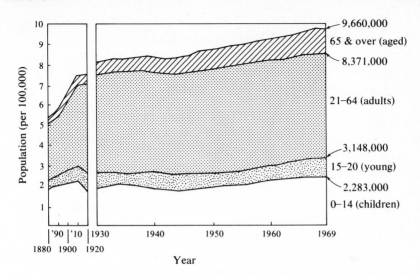

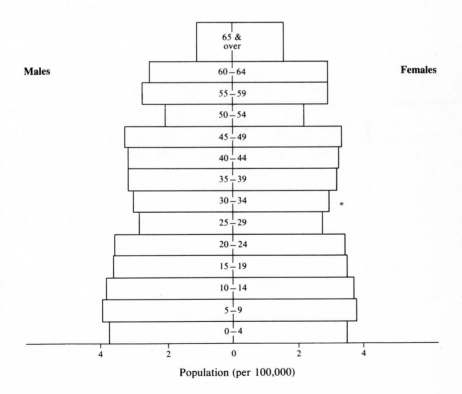

(7) From the demographic point of view, stability of the traditional family structure (low rates of illegitimacy and divorce).

POPULATION POLICY AND POPULATION-DIRECTED LEGISLATION

¶ INTRODUCTION

As mentioned earlier, we can hardly speak of a population *policy* in Belgium since there is no consistent and systematic attempt to direct or influence population growth or population structure. However, there are several laws that have social, moral, or other juridical objectives, are related to the population problems, and could have some demographic consequences. We shall review separately the main areas in which laws are related to population.

¶ POPULATION PROBLEMS IN THE PUBLIC OPINION

Usually, demography has no reference in the mass media. There is a sharp contrast between, for example, the French or Dutch newspapers and those of Belgium; papers on Belgian population problems are very scarce except in some intellectual journals of rather limited distribution. The only instance where population questions appeared in the general press was, in 1962, when the Sauvy and Delpérée reports were issued (see the following section) and were greatly commented upon in the press. Other demographic features treated by mass media are generally connected with external events or viewed as specific, nondemographic questions. For example, contraceptives, mainly the oral ones (the pill), are frequently spoken about, and the discussion deals with the moral aspects or the (often spurious) counter effects of the pill. Typically, this topic was important in 1968, after the encyclical *Humanae Vitae*. Also often treated are the questions of abortion (mainly ethically) and of the overcrowding of the world (as a political and economical problem for the third world). Presently, however, public interest in a question such as "zero population growth" does not seem probable.

¶ ATTEMPT TO MAKE A POLICY FOR WALLONY:
THE SAUVY AND DELPÉRÉE REPORTS

We have discussed the rather difficult situation of the Walloon population. During World War II, the industrial infrastructure of Wallony was not damaged too much. The postwar recovery was, thus, relatively easy but, with a very old infrastructure, more and more obsolete. This partially explains the economic stagnation of the region during the 1950s. Moreover, the mining industries, traditional backbone of Walloon industry, were collapsing, which further increased unemployment. Finally, several social and political conflicts arose, culminating in a violent three-week general strike at the end of 1960. Only this sort of serious crisis could make the problems perceptible to the leading circles of Wallony.

In 1961, the Economic Council for Wallony[4] appointed two experts, the well-known French demographers Alfred Sauvy and Roland Pressat, to study the population problem and suggest provisional solutions. The result, known as the "Sauvy Report" [4], was issued in March 1962. Pressat wrote the analysis of the past and present trends of the Walloon population and made detailed forecasts of the total and active population. Sauvy's paper was devoted to a large group of suggestions aimed at promoting an "overall renewal."

Estimating that the present Walloon situation was very near to the French one of some years ago, Sauvy thought the successful experience of France could be transferred to Belgian conditions. Thus, his essential suggestions were fiscal and financial measures: a greater decrease in taxation according to family size, more allowances for all children (or only for the second and following children, while almost all couples do have at least one child), and a greater increase in allowances for higher birth ranks. Moreover, the report mentioned various actions of indirect assistance (exemption from military service, apportionment of housing, and psychological measures), the suggestion of a coherent immigration policy, the proposal that the age of retirement be changed for those who wished to continue to work, and the call for the creation of centers of research and information on demographic problems.

On the national political level, however, the main point of the report was that a "federal" distribution of social security programs be adopted, these being autonomous programs in Flanders and Wallony. In 1962, this proposal was unacceptable because, at that time, the official doctrine absolutely refused to consider any attempt of any kind to divide the country.[5] Consequently, one month later, the Belgian government assigned a commission to draw up, within nine weeks, a report on the directions to be followed with regard to population. In spite of the extremely short time allotted, a ninety-page mimeographed document was issued in June 1962. This was the "Delpérée Report,"[6] named for the General Secretary of the Ministry of Social Security, the president of and principal figure on the commission. This report was a remarkable attempt of rational policy. Without lingering to describe a situation too well known, the author took up, this time within a national framework, the principal conclusions of Sauvy,

[4] An unofficial but influential organization composed of political, social, administrative, and industrial leaders of the region.

[5] We have seen that the community problem of Belgium is now being solved, precisely in a "federal" way.

[6] Its most important parts were published; see [5].

which he integrated into a comprehensive group of measures constituting a true family and population policy. Suggestions concerning assistance to families and the sociocultural integration of foreigners completed immigration policy proposals. New methods of financial aid were matched with a plan for the coordination and decentralization of the responsible organs. The "Delpérée Report" never neglected human factors such as personalized administration, qualitative and quantitative adaptation of housing, individual assistance by social workers for problem solving,[7] and so forth. In short, this report was a series of proposals to improve the "quality of life."

The plan as a whole was never put into action. The financial measures were taken because money was available and it is popular to give allowances. It must be emphasized that these social security benefits were implemented without any relationship to population policy but rather in connection with the regional origin of the minister in charge. It is dubiously coincidental that increases in allowances for higher birth ranks were settled by Flemish ministers (Flanders having higher parity children than Wallony), with an inverse action taken when Walloon ministers were in office.

Concerning Delpérée's other proposals, only partial measures were taken, often at the level of the small communities (cities). As a reaction to the Walloon population problems, a new ministry was created to deal with family and population affairs. But, until the short-lived last government (January to November 1972), all ministers were Flemish! The suggestion to create centers for studies and information on demography was followed partially. The bilingual Center for the Study of Population and the Family was founded under government responsibility, but it has few staff members and no large practical preoccupations. Its publications— including a journal *Population et Famille* published in two languages—are very little disseminated.[8] Other centers (including the Department of Demography of the University of Louvain) were organized without the initiative of the government.

¶ GENERAL NATALITY AND FERTILITY POLICY

We can speak of "pronatalist" or "antinatalist" when referring to the orientation of a policy. But when there is no policy, as is the case in

---

[7] We have mentioned that Belgian laws are not integrated and, thus, are more and more difficult for citizens to follow. Moreover, the persons are scarce who know what rights they have. Aware of this, a Minister of Social Affairs had, on a broadcast, invited the people with social or legal problems to write him personally.

[8] The center and its publications are being reorganized on a wider scale, including national and international cooperation with other demographic institutions.

Belgium, these qualifications are not useful. Many legislative acts have a (possible) effect that can be described only as favorable or unfavorable to natality. And one measure can be qualified when it is taken with an integrated set of decisions and *not* when it is taken alone. For example, to liberalize abortion is an antinatalist measure when it is done together with laws organizing abortive clinics, regulating liberal use of contraceptives, and so forth. But, when taken alone, only as a fight against the consequences of illegal abortions, we think it is more a way to replace these illegal abortions by legal ones than it is a true antinatalist measure.

Considering this, one may say that Belgium is neither pronatalist nor antinatalist: laws are promulgated with possible effects in one or the other direction, but there is no clear will and probably no true effect on demographic evolution. We shall, thus, use the word "legislation," *not* "policy," when discussing the various governmental actions.

¶ LEGISLATION ON ABORTION

Since its writing in 1867, the penal code (criminal law) prohibits all forms of abortion, including therapeutic abortion (Articles 348–353). It provides for the following penalties: If the woman is convicted, she faces two to five years of imprisonment and severe fines; the performer of the abortion receives at least the same penalties and, if the person is a physician or medical worker, double. Similarly, the medical authorities prohibit the performance of abortion (except in the very rare case of ultimate life-saving attempts, and even this practice is theoretically not permitted by law).

The actual situation is quite different. Since abortion is a criminal offense, it is impossible to give better figures than estimates. According to the general opinion, the annual number of performed *abortus provocatus* varies from about 30,000 up to 200,000 (or between 22 and 140 abortions for each 100 live births). We personally think that the true number probably is around 50,000 annual cases (35 per 100 live births), on the basis of the (estimated) number of medical complications known by hospitals. By comparison, the number of trials for abortion is surprisingly low; there have been less than 200 since 1960 (about 0.5 percent of the cases of the most "optimistic" estimate), of which 15 to 30 percent ended without conviction. In the other cases, a trend to forgiveness is appearing, with the motive that present legislation is socially discriminative; the upper class can easily get an abortion in another country, whereas a female factory worker cannot.

Since 1970, a campaign has been launched by the Belgian League for the Legalization of Abortion, headed by some jurists and journalists and supported by one of the most influential magazines in the country. The basic argument is the same social one, together with considerations about health, nondesired children, and the moral responsibility of each person, but never about demographic consequences.

A law project (the Callewaert Project), introduced in the Senate on February 18, 1971, is attempting to attain in Belgium the state of liberalization reached in the 1950s in Scandinavian countries. Thus, to have an abortion would never again be a crime; there also would be no crime committed when a physician performs the abortion in the first fifteen weeks of pregnancy after positive reactions from two (or three if social motives are advocated) other physicians. A strong opposition against this project comes from the government, the church, and chiefly, from medical associations, which are extremely conservative both politically and morally.

Finally, we must mention that free and easy abortion is among the demands of the women's liberation groups which are, in Belgium, as active as they are small.

¶ LEGISLATION ON STERILIZATION

Vasectomy and tubectomy seem to be rare; no figures are available because these procedures are not authorized (or prohibited) by law; only the criminal law on "noncurative voluntary bodily lesions" is applicable in these situations.

¶ LEGISLATION ON CONTRACEPTION

Contraception is a matter of individual choice and behavior and is not subject to the law. Nevertheless, the criminal law (Article 383, modifications promulgated in 1923) is established in such a way as to prevent the use of contraceptives. Indeed, it prohibits all forms of advertisement (including dissemination of contraceptive information or visible exposure in pharmacies), which, in the law, is equated with pornography. This law is generally followed. Nevertheless, as is shown by a recent survey,[9] the use of contraceptive methods is very important in Belgium, which helps to explain so low a natality rate. The distribution of contraceptive methods in use (see Table 10) is rather typical with its preeminence of noninstrumental methods (psychologically better accepted but often less efficient). But, as noted by the authors, this is *not* representative of the current practice of young married people, since the sample was drawn in 1966 and, thus, does not count couples with less than five years of conjugal life in 1971.

---

[9] National sample of 1,032 married persons; 3 percent of answers are not usable; 7 percent are not users of contraceptives; the remaining 90 percent are users (see Table 10). The sample was studied two times, in 1966 and 1971.

TABLE 10.

Contraceptive Methods Used, Belgium, 1966 and 1971 (in percents)
(on users only: N = 921)

| | 1966 | 1971 | |
Method	Ever Used[a]	Presently Used[b]	Ever Used[a]
Coitus interruptus	74	64	77
Rhythm	34	23	35
Oral contraceptives	12	13	26
Vaginal spooling	3	2	3
Chemical and/or mechanical contraceptives (jelly, condom, pessary)	11	8	13

SOURCE: See [6, p. 147].
[a] Total adds up to more than 100 percent because more than one method could have been used.
[b] Total adds up to more than 100 percent because about 8 percent of the sample use both the rhythm method and coitus interruptus.

On February 8, 1966, a law project (the Cudell Project) was introduced for the first time in the House of Representatives. It aimed at rejecting all mention of "pregnancy-preventive means" in the criminal law. The government objected immediately and entered a more restrictive counter project. Until 1971, the two law projects were reintroduced each year without any further evolution. In May 1971, the Parliamentary Commission of Justice approved a modified version, forbidding only commercial advertisement and free distribution of contraceptives. Unfortunately, this modified version did not go any further because of a political crisis (November 1971). One year later, the law was ready, but a new government crisis froze it. At present, then, all contraceptives except the oral ones (for which, due to their hormonal nature, a medical prescription is needed) are sold, but nothing can be said, published, advertised, or shown about contraception.

¶ LEGISLATION ON FAMILY PLANNING
The legal status of family planning associations could only be very precarious, in view of the legislation on contraception. Indeed, these organizations were slow to develop. Ten years ago, there was a federation grouping the only three centers then existing in Belgium. Now, the National Belgian Federation of the Movements for Family Planning and Sexual Education has about twenty centers, a rather small number for an entire country. It

has had many difficulties because of an opposition between centers of the two ethnic communities.

Repressive legislation does not affect these institutions in practice, since the legislation aims at the *lucrative* exploitation and advertisement of contraception, while family planning centers are conceived on a nonprofit basis and are not publicized. But with the governmental opposition to liberalized contraception in mind, it is rather paradoxical that a decree (April 3, 1970) recognized and subsidizes the centers of family planning; these centers are officially known as Centers for Pre-Matrimonial, Conjugal, and Family Counseling and are intended to provide information to couples.

¶ LEGISLATION ON FAMILY ALLOWANCES

As a consequence partially of the Sauvy and Delpérée reports and partially of some social policy, the family allowances system has been largely expanded. Belgium is one of the countries devoting the greatest part of its gross national product to allowances (more than 3.2 percent of the GNP). However, the system is rather complicated: There are separate rates for independent workers and for others; orphans and the disabled also benefit from special rates. The basic rates (for children of employees and workers) vary according to the age and the rank of birth of the child (Table 11).

All children under fourteen receive allowances automatically; these are given until age twenty-five if the child is a student or apprentice. There are also birth payments: $239.50[10] for the first delivery, $165 for the second,

[10] As of January 1, 1973, US$1 equaled approximately 44 Belgian francs (B. fr.).

TABLE 11.

Basic Monthly Rates of Family Allowances, Belgium, 1973 (in US$)[a]
(Rate: US$1 = 44 B. fr.)

	Rank Order of Birth		
Age	1	2	3 and Over
Under 6	$16.00	$27.00	$38.00
6–9	19.50	30.50	41.50
10–13	22.00	33.00	44.00
14–24	26.00	37.00	48.00

[a] These amounts change frequently because they are linked to the cost of living index (presently rising rapidly).

and $89 for all subsequent births. Since independent workers have a less favorable allowance pattern, the official policy tends to equate the rates.

One must note that Belgium is a typical example of the discrepancy between possible pronatalist effects and true effects of a measure. In Belgium, we find very high and increasing family allowances, together with a very low and decreasing natality.

¶ LEGISLATION ABOUT AGE AT MARRIAGE

Since 1807 (the French *Code Napoléon* being the origin of the present Belgian civil law), legal age at marriage has been fifteen for women and eighteen for men. The King can, by royal decree, authorize earlier marriage; but this happens rather infrequently (between 100 and 200 per year, of which more than 90 percent are given to young men seventeen years old).

¶ LEGISLATION ON DIVORCE

There are two kinds of divorces in Belgium: divorce against one of the spouses ("divorce for determined cause") and divorce by mutual consent. The acknowledged causes are mainly severe cruelty and adultery. The latter is an example of discrimination between the sexes: Legally, any female adultery is grounds for divorce, but in the case of the male, it is necessary to prove continued adultery in the family house. The mutual consent procedure is only used by 20–25 percent of the couples because it is a considerably longer one.

Finally, there is also a procedure of spouse separation with all effects of divorce except that the marital bonds still exist; this is very rarely used (about 2 separations for every 100 divorces) and, probably, only by Roman Catholic couples who cannot accept divorce.

¶ HOUSING POLICIES AND DEMOGRAPHIC FEATURES

Belgium has no shortage of dwellings. Nevertheless, there is a *qualitative* housing problem: About 35 percent of the Belgian homes are considered as obsolete houses or, even, as slums. There is no consistent national policy aiming at a radical renovation in this field. Apparently, no significant relationship between housing and demographic features can be found.

¶ MORTALITY POLICY

There is no policy on general mortality as such, only policies on public health. Nevertheless, specific mortality through road accidents is explicitly the target of several laws and is a constant preoccupation when developing the highway network.

¶ LEGISLATION ON SOCIAL SECURITY AND PUBLIC HEALTH

Sickness funds are compulsory, giving an insurance coverage to a large part of the expenses in the field of health (hospitalization, medicine, medical treatments). However, as with family allowances, the independent workers have less favorable coverage.

Hospitals are distributed widely, providing for most needs. So, more than 95 percent of the births occur in clinics with rather good medical help, and severe sicknesses or accidents can be treated satisfactorily in wards.

Nevertheless, the financial protection of the disabled worker is not effective: Wages are only continued for a short time (seven days for "blue collar" workmen, one month for clerical, or "white-collar," employees). After this time, sickness funds give an indemnity of 60 percent of the basic salary, the latter being limited to about US$365 per month (that is, the maximum indemnity is about $220 a month). Maternity leaves, which are compulsory for fourteen weeks, are subject to the same restrictions. We may thus conclude that the birth payment allowed by the government is often simply a way of correcting the loss of salary due to the leave.

The social security system is financed largely by subscriptions of workers and employers. Retirement and old-age assistance are parts of the social security system. The age of retirement is sixty for women and sixty-five for men (with a possibility of retiring at sixty). Retirement pensions are very low. The maximum pension for couples is $2,500 a year for employees and about $1,950 for workmen when the worker was already retired in 1961; more recently retired persons benefit from a better rate, based on individual circumstances, following several legal measures.

Assistance to aged persons is provided by social workers, municipal institutions, or private ones (which are often very costly). Much remains to be done, however, to insure efficient aid to the aged.

¶ INTERNATIONAL MIGRATION POLICY

After the "freeze" on migrations between 1930 and 1945, Belgium wanted to encourage the immigration of foreign workers, especially into those areas of the economy where there was a shortage of Belgian manpower (unskilled manual labor, colliers, and so forth). Nevertheless, this remained an unstable population (reemigration represented up to 80 percent of the immigrations). In view of stabilizing manpower, the orientation in the 1950s had been toward mobility of entire families. Between 1947 and 1961, the foreign population in Belgium increased by 23 percent, but the male foreign population in the working age group diminished by 8 percent, the adult female population increased by 16 percent, and the number of children increased by 110 percent. A factor that undeniably played an important role is the considerable development of social policy (family allowances, relatively high salaries, and so forth). But this role cannot be understood fully without taking into account recruitment (the census of 1961 shows that 44 percent of the foreign population living in Belgium was of Italian nationality). To the population of the most underdeveloped areas of Europe, suffering endemic unemployment and precarious living conditions, Belgium may have seemed a land of plenty. In the course of the 1960s, an attempt was made to stabilize the foreign population by means of other economic motivation. Since then, family allowances have been given, at the Belgian rate, to the family living in the country of origin.[11]

At present, however, recruitment is changing without any explicit policy formulated on this subject, and increasingly, there is the trend to turn toward a *temporary* immigration of nationals of countries outside Europe (the Arab countries, central Africa) in the hope that they will return to their countries at the end of two to five years with a certain amount of professional experience, not very specialized but sufficient to give the impression of indirect assistance toward their development. In this context, it is indicative that greater facilities are offered to single persons in particular and to migrants without their dependents (the only social effort on the part of Belgium being the payment of allowances abroad).

Illegal immigration seems rather exceptional, at least among foreign workers. Indeed, every foreigner needs an official permit to take a job. This permit is given only to those who have established residence. The control on employers to prevent the hiring of illegally resident workers is apparently strong.

¶ POLICY ON INTERNAL DISTRIBUTION OF FOREIGNERS
The geographic distribution of foreigners has tended to become more uniform, while earlier it was concentrated in the industrial basin of Wallony, where 53 percent of the foreigners lived in 1961. The reasons for this change are of a strictly political nature and are related to the conflict between the communities. Representatives and Senators are distributed according to the number of inhabitants, foreigners included. Since there is one representative for each 40,000 inhabitants, the relative excess of foreigners in Wallony gave four to five additional deputies to the French-speaking region.

---

[11] One must notice that the high level of Belgian allowances makes it a very important revenue for a family staying in countries with low price levels. It may even have a pronatalist effect on these persons.

There is, however, no explicit legislation on this point. But it is with this preoccupation in mind that some specific factory implantations are favored, attracting foreign workers.

¶ POLICY ON WORKING WOMEN

In spite of an explicit disavowal of wage differences,[12] women earn less than men. Moreover, there is no legislation about part-time work; the legislation on maternity leaves is a disadvantage to young mothers; and, above all, fiscal measures impair the cumulation of wages in a family.

Indeed, all members of the household benefit from the social security when there is at least one wage earner. But each worker contributes to the security funds. Thus, all wage earners other than the first contribute without any additional benefit. Moreover, the income tax is progressive (its *rate* being higher when income rises) and it is applied not on individuals but on households. Thus, all salaries must be added, and the total tax is well above that of the total amount of taxes on each *separate* salary.

With her low salary, the female worker would have to spend virtually all her income to compensate (in services, helpers, electrical appliances for the household, and so forth) for her absence from home.

¶ OTHER POLICY FEATURES

One may further mention innumerable policy measures related to demographic facts, such as the regulations in matters of inheritance that especially favor direct descendants, the exemption of military service for fathers of several children, the reductions granted in fees for public services (transportation, and so forth) to the members of large families. These considerations, however, are too far removed from demographic facts, strictly speaking. To treat all that relates to sex and age distribution, to spatial distribution, to demographic events—birth, marriage, migration, death—would lead us to consider virtually all the legislation, the precedents, and the sociocultural consequences, which would exceed the objectives of the present report.

¶ A COMMISSION ON POPULATION?

In contrast to many other countries, there is no Belgian commission on population problems. The Delpérée commission was in existence for the nine weeks needed to complete its report. It does not seem probable that a new attempt will be made in this direction in the near future.

---

[12] But the official unemployment indemnities are less for women than for men.

¶ INTERNATIONAL POPULATION POLICIES

The Belgian government has never signed the "Declaration on Population" of the United Nations. In the assistance given to the third world, family planning and related topics are not included.

¶ CONCLUSIONS

After this brief overview of the population policies in Belgium, we can conclude that the fundamental components of population structure and movement are somewhat influenced by legislation. Yet there is no true demographic policy, for legislation is not coordinated and, generally, is drawn up for reasons that are by no means demographic. Often, policies are made in complete ignorance of the demographic problems and the possible consequences of the legislation. Nonetheless, in the rather rare cases where legislation is directed to demographic features, there is hardly any perceptible effect. The case of family allowances is typical of this.

To summarize, let us say again that there is *no* population policy in Belgium. Only morality and health are considered with regard to contraception and abortion, social welfare with regard to morbidity and mortality, and the labor market with regard to migration. Population as such is never considered.

REFERENCES

1. *Demography of Belgium, 1940–1945.* Brussels: Institut National de Statistique, 1947. (In French.)
2. *Demographic Statistics*, no. 3. Brussels: Institut National de Statistique, 1972. (In French.)
3. *Belgium Statistical Annual*, vol. 91. Brussels: Institut National de Statistique, 1971. (In French.)
4. *Review of the Economic Council of Wallony*, no. 1 (1962). (In French.)
5. Belgian Social Security Review, no. 7 (1962). (In French.)
6. J. Morsa and G. Julémont. "A national survey on fertility, 3: Contraceptive practice, 1966–1971." *Population et Famille*, no. 25 (1971). (In French.)

BIBLIOGRAPHY

Belgium Statistical Annual. Brussels: Institut National de Statistique. Published annually since 1960. (In French.)
Statistical Annual of Belgium and the Belgian Congo. Brussels: Institut National de Statistique. Published annually prior to 1960. (In French.)
The Census of the Population. Brussels: Institut National de Statistique. Several vol-

umes spread over the years following the censuses of 1910, 1920, 1930, 1947, and 1961.

Creutz, E. "Demographic evolution and policy on family allowances in Belgium." *Revue Belge del Sécurité Sociale*, June–July 1966. (In French.)

The Demography of Belgium, 1921–1939. Brussels: Office Central de Statistique, 1943. (In French.)

"Belgium." In *Population and Law*, Luke T. Lee and Arthur Larson, eds. Durham, N.C.: Rule of Law Press; Leiden: A. W. Sijthoff, 1971. Pp. 157–176.

Koeune, J. C. "Political migration in Belgium." *Revue Nouvelle*, October 1965. (In French.)

The Natural Movement of Population in the World, 1906–1936. Paris: Institut National d'Etudes Démographiques, 1954. (In French.)

Belgian Population in . . . . Brussels: Institut National de Statistique. Annual issue of the *Bulletin de Statistique.* (In French.)

Demographic Statistics. Brussels: Institut National de Statistique. Published quarterly since 1969. (In French.)

CHAPTER 9

Hungary

Andras Klinger

A B S T R A C T

In Hungary, the main factor of population change is the great decline in fertility. Because of the lateness of the industrial revolution in Hungary, fertility began to decrease later than in most countries of western Europe. The fall in fertility, however, could be observed since the middle of the last century. After World War II, fertility increased for some years; then in 1951, it began to decline. In the following years, fertility was influenced primarily by measures relating to the prohibition of induced abortion. In 1956, interruption of pregnancy was permitted, and from this year, the number of births began to fall to its lowest level of 12.9 per 1,000 in 1962. From 1963, first a plateau, then a greater increase could be observed in number of live births. The rise in fertility beginning in 1967–1968 is due partly to the pronatalist measures taken by the government, partly to the growth in the number of women of reproductive age. The analysis of fertility shows that the decline in the rate of live births is, first of all, the consequence of the lower fertility of older women. Also, the average parity decreased in a similar way. At present, in Hungary, the ratio of families with two children is the highest.

Beside the decline in mortality that could be observed for a longer period, in recent years, the crude death rate grew because of the gradual aging of the population. Although this increase is mostly the consequence of the change in age structure, mortality actually rose to a certain extent. In 1971, of the total number of deaths, the ratio of infants was under 5

225

percent and that of children, under 1 percent, while the proportion of the old amounted to 77 percent.

The internal movement of the population is characterized by the migration from communes to towns. At present, 47 percent of the population live in towns. In the last ten years, the urbanization process slowed.

The structure of the population changed. Illiteracy practically does not exist. The number of economically active persons reached 5 million in 1970. Of the total number of economically active persons, the number of women is over 2 million. This means that about 66 percent of women of 20–54 years are working. Forty-four percent of economically active persons are working in industry, building, and construction; 26 percent in agriculture; and the other 30 percent are distributed among the other branches of the national economy. In 1970, about 75 percent of economically active persons were manual workers.

Of the legislation relating to population policy, the basic laws generally exert rather an indirect influence on population phenomena, while special legislation directly affects the development of fertility and the practice of birth control and family planning. The latter ones are connected with pregnancy and childbirth, infant and child care, family allowance system, children's institutions, housing, birth control, and consultation for the protection of women.

The declining birth rate aroused very great interest in the wide society. Many published articles expressed a desire to increase the low live birth rate. Demographers agreed that the present number of births is very low, that its stabilization would give much trouble in the future, and that an efficient and deliberate population policy would be necessary. Political views stress the necessity of an increase in the birth rate and add that, because this is a question relating to many aspects of human life, expedient measures can be developed only on the basis of careful investigation and consultation with the interested parties.

In Hungary, in recent years, many investigations were performed to identify family planning and birth control attitudes. Research plans to be realized in the future embrace the different aspects and results of family planning, birth control, and population policy.

The future population policy ideas purport to contribute to a gradual increase in the number of births to ensure at least the replacement of the population and to improve the age structure of the population.

In Hungary, in the past and especially in the last decade, some governmental measures have exerted a direct effect on population processes even when they were not originally designed for that purpose. The view that long-range state planning must take into account population policy in a coordinated form, as opposed to single independent laws, is becoming more widespread. It was accepted at first by demographers, then by sociologists, economists, and health specialists, and most recently by the Commission for Long-Range Planning of the Labor Force and Standard of Living which received a working group study in January 1971 incorporating a fifteen-year plan of population policy measures.[1] The Central Planning Office has already taken into consideration the principles of the study in connection with its planning of population, employment, and fertility.

The major parts of relevant past legislation and of the future comprehensive system of population policy measures are restricted to the areas of fertility and birth control. This chapter will focus on those areas, presenting a short review of the demographic situation—particularly fertility trends—a consideration of the most important laws and their efficacy, a summary of generally held views about the demographic situation, a brief overview of past and planned research, and a discussion of the principles of population policy for the future.

DEMOGRAPHIC CHARACTERISTICS

Hungary is situated in the eastern part of central Europe. Its territory amounts to 93,000 square kilometers. At the time of the census of January 1, 1970, the population was 10,316,000, 3.6 percent larger than on January 1, 1960. Density was 111 persons per square kilometer, 4 persons more than ten years previously.

Except for the decade of the 1940s, when war losses influenced the rates, average annual population growth in Hungary was the lowest between 1960 and 1969 of any 10-year period in the past 100 years. This is a consequence of both a decrease in the number of births and an increase in the number of deaths, related to the growing ratio of older persons in the population (Table 1).

¶ FERTILITY

In Hungary, as in other countries of central and eastern Europe, the decline in the birth rate began later than in western Europe. This was because of a delayed industrial revolution and, as a consequence, the development of a different socioeconomic structure.

The decline of fertility in Hungary began in the middle of the last century and was already significant before World War I. In the interwar period, births continued to fall even faster following a temporary increase

---

[1] The study was prepared by Dr. Rudolf Andorka, Dr. Andras Klinger, Zsuzsa Mausetz, Dr. Karoly Miltenyi, and Dr. Jozsef Tamasy under the direction of Dr. Egon Szabady.

TABLE 1.

Selected Demographic Data, Hungary, 1870–1970

Year	Population (in thousands)	Density (population per km.^{2})	Increase or Decrease (in thousands)	Population as Percentage of Population in Specified Year 1870	Previous	Annual Increase or Decrease[a] (in percents)
1870	5,011	54		100		
1880	5,329	57	318	106	106	0.56
1890	6,009	65	680	120	113	1.21
1900	6,854	74	794	137	113	1.25
1910	7,612	82	758	152	111	1.05
1920	7,987	86	375	159	105	0.48
1930	8,685	93	698	173	109	0.84
1941	9,316	100	631	186	107	0.70
1949	9,205	99	−111	184	99	−0.15
1960	9,961	107	756	199	108	0.72
1970	10,322	111	361	206	104	0.36

[a] Based on geometrical mean.

in the early 1920s that compensated for the low fertility of the war years. Thus, the birth rate declined in Hungary from about 40 per 1,000 at the end of the last century, one of the highest rates at that time, to about 20 per 1,000 before World War II, an average rate for European countries for that period.

After World War II, the birth rate continued to decline, except for a slight rise immediately following the war and an increase between 1954 and 1956 to 23 per 1,000 as a result of the prohibition of induced abortion. The overall decline in fertility continued after 1956, when abortion was legalized, to a low of 12.9 per 1,000 in 1962. Since 1962, when Hungary had the lowest birth rate in Europe, fertility has increased somewhat. Estimates for 1971 indicate that general fertility is approximately 5 percent higher than in 1962, although it is 6 percent lower than the maximum observed in 1968 (Table 2).

The recent slight increase in the number of live births derives from several factors. Government provisions contributing to the desire to bear children are the most important. In 1967, child care leave for working women was introduced, insuring paid leave until the child was two-and-one-half years old, a period that was extended in 1968 to three years. The increase in the number of live births was also caused by the increase in

TABLE 2.

Trend in Births, Hungary, 1938–1972

			Birth Rate						
			Per 1,000 Women of Specified Age						
Year	Number of Live Births	Per 1,000 Population	15–19	20–24	25–29	30–34	35–39	40–49	15–49
1938	182,206	19.9	42.1	146.6	134.6	92.9	57.6	13.2	73.6
1949	190,398	20.6	47.3	162.6	140.7	84.0	52.7	10.9	75.4
1960	146,461	14.7	52.5	159.2	105.6	52.9	25.0	3.6	58.9
1965	133,009	13.1	41.9	147.9	100.6	47.8	18.2	3.0	53.2
1970	151,819	14.7	50.1	158.7	109.3	51.2	18.4	2.2	56.4
1971	150,640	14.5	50.4	157.4	102.9	49.5	17.9	2.1	55.8
1972[a]	152,909	14.7							

[a] Preliminary estimate.

the number of women of reproductive age within the population. In the period 1965–1968, general fertility—the number of live births per woman aged 15–49—grew by 10 percent, whereas the number of live births increased by 16 percent and the crude birth rate by 15 percent. In other words, one-third of the increase in the number of births was due to the change in age structure of the population.

For a long time in Hungary, fertility among older women has been falling, and younger women have increased as a proportion of all mothers. The proportion of the women aged 20–24 among all childbearing women has risen from just over 15 percent at the beginning of the century to 41 percent in 1965. At the same time, the ratio of older women has decreased, for example, from 33 percent aged 30–39 at the beginning of the century to only 16 percent of that age in 1970–1971.

While fertility has been declining steadily among older women, for instance, from 170 births per 1,000 women aged 30–39 in 1910 to 37 per 1,000 in 1968, the trend among the youngest age groups was the opposite. The age-specific birth rate for women 15–19 rose from 41 per 1,000 in 1930 to 50 per 1,000 in 1971.

The average birth order has declined also, from 3.05 in 1938 to 1.88 in 1971 (Table 3). Whereas before World War II, 14 percent of the total number of live births were sixth or higher birth orders, only 3 percent were in this category in 1971.

The rate of first-born and second-born children has increased, as the proportion of third and higher birth orders has decreased. First-born children, who in 1938 equaled 33 percent of the total number of live-born children, represented 50 percent of total live births in 1971. Second-born

TABLE 3.

Percentage Distribution of Live Births, Hungary, 1938–1971
(by birth order)

	Percentage Distribution by Birth Order						
Year	First	Second	Third	Fourth and Fifth	Sixth and Higher	All Births	Average Birth Order
1938	33.1	22.1	14.6	16.3	13.9	100	3.05
1949	40.6	26.6	13.2	11.1	8.5	100	2.51
1960	44.0	29.3	12.7	8.9	5.1	100	2.18
1965	48.8	29.9	10.1	7.0	4.2	100	2.01
1970	49.0	33.6	9.0	5.3	3.1	100	1.88
1971	49.5	33.8	8.8	5.0	2.9	100	1.88

children increased from 22 percent of total births in 1938 to 34 percent in 1971.

The average number of children per married woman of reproductive age decreased from 222 in 1960 to 198 in 1970, a phenomenon that derives from the decrease in the number of women bearing three or more children. Between 1960 and 1970, the number of women with three children declined by 3 percent, women with four or five children, by 20 percent, and those with six or more, by 43 percent (Table 4).

¶ MORTALITY

Mortality has declined rapidly and steadily in Hungary from a crude death rate of 35–39 per 1,000 at the end of the 1870s to 11.7 per 1,000 in 1971, with a low point of 9.6 in 1961 (Table 5).

The slight increase in the crude death rate in the last decade results from changes in the age structure of the population (Table 6). The ratio of older people has increased gradually, with people of sixty years and older presently accounting for 17 percent of the total population. Because of the decline in fertility, the ratio of persons under fifteen has decreased. The actual improvement in mortality is better expressed by age-standardized death rates which show, for example, that, if the age structure in 1968 were the same as in 1910, mortality would have decreased 73 percent as against 54 percent and would be at a level of 6.5 per 1,000 as against 11.2 per 1,000. Similarly, the 10-percent increase in mortality shown for crude

TABLE 4.

Percentage Distribution of Number of Children Born, Hungary, 1960 and 1970

Number of Children Born	Percentage Distribution		1970 as Percent of 1960
	1960	1970	
0	15	14	101
1	25	30	126
2	26	31	129
3	14	12	97
4–5	12	9	80
6+	8	4	57
Total	100	100	108
Average number of children per 100 married women of reproductive age	232	198	85

TABLE 5.

Trend in Deaths, Hungary, 1876–1972[a]

| | | | Death Rate | |
| | | | Age-Standardized on the Population of Specified Year | |
Year	Number of Deaths	Per 1,000 Population	1910	1960
1876	178,610	34.9		
1901	166,662	24.2		
1911	184,009	24.1	24.1	
1921	170,059	21.2		
1931	144,968	16.6		
1938	130,628	14.2	14.0	16.1
1941	123,349	13.2		
1949	105,718	11.4	10.1	12.4
1960	101,525	10.2	7.0	10.1
1965	108,119	10.7	6.6	9.7
1970	120,197	11.7	6.5	9.8
1971	123,009	11.9	6.6	9.8
1972[b]	118,548	11.4		

[a] All data relate to the present territory of the country.
[b] Preliminary estimate.

TABLE 6.

Percentage Distribution of Population, Hungary, 1949, 1960, and 1970 (by age group)

| Age Group | Percentage Distribution | | | 1960 as Percent of 1949 | 1970 as Percent of 1960 |
	1949	1960	1970		
0–14	25	25	21	110	86
15–39	39	37	37	103	105
40–59	25	24	25	105	107
60+	11	14	17	128	128
All ages	100	100	100	108	104

rates between 1960 and 1968 can be represented as a 4 percent decrease in age-standardized rates.

The improvement in mortality has been different for different age groups, with the decrease in crude death rates declining with increasing age. Infant and child mortality, representing 32 percent of deaths at the beginning of the century, accounted for over 4.5 percent of deaths in 1970 (Table 7). Conversely, older people, who accounted for 22 percent of deaths in 1900, now account for 77 percent. At the present time, even if infant mortality in Hungary declined to the level of countries having the lowest rate, overall mortality would be improved by only 2 percent.

¶ MARRIAGE RATES AND AGE AT MARRIAGE
As in other parts of Europe, in Hungary, too, marriage rates have been relatively stable for some decades, and the changes that occurred were not as great as those with respect to births and deaths.

TABLE 7.

Trend in Deaths, Hungary, 1900–1971 (by age group)

Year	Percentage Distribution of Deaths, by Age Group					
	0[a]	1–14	15–39	40–59	60+	All Ages
1900–1901[b]	31.8	22.0	12.4	12.2	21.6	100.0
1910–1911[b]	29.3	20.9	12.5	12.4	24.9	100.0
1920–1921	28.6	14.9	15.1	12.5	28.9	100.0
1930–1931	24.0	9.9	14.8	14.2	37.1	100.0
1938	18.3	7.3	12.7	16.2	45.5	100.0
1941	16.6	6.4	12.7	16.5	47.8	100.0
1948–1949	16.7	4.5	10.8	18.0	50.0	100.0
1959–1960	7.3	1.9	5.1	16.4	69.3	100.0
1965	4.8	1.3	4.2	14.8	74.9	100.0
1970	4.5	1.0	4.1	13.9	76.5	100.0
1971	4.3	0.9	4.1	14.1	76.6	100.0
	Mortality per 1,000 Population					
1900–1901[b]	215.1	17.7	8.5	16.6	73.4	26.0
1910–1911[b]	201.2	15.6	8.0	15.9	73.2	24.1
1920–1921	192.8	11.3	7.8	14.0	68.0	21.3
1930–1931	157.0	6.3	5.6	11.4	61.0	16.1
1938	131.4	4.1	4.4	10.6	62.2	14.2
1941	115.6	3.5	4.1	9.5	58.7	13.2
1948–1949	92.5	2.2	3.2	8.4	49.3	11.5
1959–1960	50.1	0.8	1.4	7.0	51.9	10.3
1965	38.8	0.6	1.3	6.3	51.1	10.7
1970	35.9	0.6	1.3	6.5	51.8	11.7
1971	35.1	0.5	1.3	6.8	52.0	11.9

[a] Per 1,000 live births.
[b] Based on the territory of Hungary before 1920.

In World War I in four years, for well-known reasons, the number and percent of marriages decreased to a very low level. After the war, marriages that had been delayed were contracted, and after that, the percentage of marriages remained stable at the old level until World War II. During World War II, the number of marriages did not decrease as much as during the previous war; consequently, the rise after the war was not so great either. However, because of the changed social conditions, the increase lasted much longer. For about a decade, marriage rates were among the highest on an international scale. From the middle of the 1950s, marriage rates began to decrease slowly, returned to their original level, and have been equal to 9.1–9.4 percent for some years.

The age structure of persons marrying became much younger as a result of the change in the socioeconomic conditions after World War II. While after World Wars I and II, 25 percent of the brides were 19 years old or younger, at present this ratio amounts to about 36 percent (Table 8). The ratio of bridegrooms aged 20–24 years was equal to 34 percent in 1920. At present, nearly 50 percent of bridegrooms are in this age group (Table 9). The same sudden rejuvenation can be observed also in respect to single men or women who marry the first time (Table 10).

¶ REGIONAL DISTRIBUTION OF POPULATION
Significant internal movement of the Hungarian population, particularly from villages to towns, influences its distribution (Table 11). One hundred years ago, 26 percent of the population lived in towns; 46 percent do now.

TABLE 8.

Marriage by Age Groups of Women, Hungary, 1920–1970 (in percents)

Years	19 or Younger	20–24	25–29	30–34	35–39	40+	Total	Average Age of Women at Marriage (in years)
1920[a]	25.3	42.7	18.1		9.7	4.2	100.0	24.9
1930	28.5	40.7	15.1	6.7	3.7	5.3	100.0	23.9
1938	30.0	28.7	21.2	9.0	4.7	6.4	100.0	24.9
1941	28.7	34.7	17.4	9.0	4.2	6.0	100.0	24.5
1948	26.0	40.1	17.4	5.4	4.5	6.6	100.0	24.5
1961	33.4	36.1	10.6	6.0	4.4	9.5	100.0	24.9
1965	32.6	40.3	10.3	4.8	3.5	8.5	100.0	24.3
1970	36.6	39.1	10.3	4.3	2.6	7.1	100.0	23.6

[a] Based on the 1920 area of Hungary.

TABLE 9.

Marriage by Age Groups of Men, Hungary, 1920–1970 (in percents)

Years	19 or Younger	20–24	25–29	30–34	35–39	40+	Total	Average Age of Men at Marriage (in years)
1920[a]	4.4	33.7	33.1	19.9		8.9	100.0	29.0
1930	3.5	38.1	32.1	11.8	5.1	9.4	100.0	28.1
1938	3.2	22.6	39.7	16.6	7.7	10.2	100.0	29.5
1941	3.6	19.0	41.3	18.2	7.7	10.2	100.0	29.6
1948	3.3	34.7	32.6	10.2	7.7	11.5	100.0	28.8
1961	5.3	40.6	25.8	9.7	5.6	13.0	100.0	29.0
1965	5.0	47.3	23.7	7.7	4.7	11.6	100.0	28.0
1970	6.1	49.6	23.7	6.9	3.8	9.9	100.0	27.1

[a] Based on the 1920 area of Hungary.

TABLE 10.

Marriage by Age Groups of Persons Who Marry the First Time, Hungary, 1941–1970 (in percents)

Years	19 or Younger	20–24	25–29	30–34	35–39	40+	Total	Average Age (in years)
			Single women					
1941	31.8	37.9	17.4	7.6	2.9	2.4	100.0	23.0
1948	29.6	44.6	16.7	3.9	2.7	2.5	100.0	22.8
1961	40.7	41.6	9.0	3.7	2.3	2.7	100.0	21.9
1965	39.6	45.8	8.4	2.4	1.5	2.3	100.0	21.6
1970	44.0	43.8	7.7	2.0	0.9	1.6	100.0	21.1
			Single men					
1941	4.2	22.0	46.3	17.9	6.0	3.6	100.0	27.5
1948	3.9	40.2	36.5	9.7	5.7	4.0	100.0	26.5
1961	6.8	50.7	29.0	7.5	3.0	3.0	100.0	25.3
1965	6.3	57.9	26.0	5.4	2.1	2.3	100.0	24.5
1970	7.6	59.8	24.9	4.7	1.4	1.6	100.0	24.0

In the last decade, the population of Budapest grew 12 percent, that of other towns increased by 19 percent, and that of villages decreased by 5 percent. It was the first time in 100 years that both the rate and the number of the rural population decreased. Natural increase no longer compensated

TABLE 11.

Internal Migration, Hungary, 1960–1969 and 1970–1971

Residence	Resident Population, January 1960	Natural Increase or Decrease	Migration Difference Total/Permanent/Temporary 1960–1969			Actual Increase or Decrease	Resident Population, January 1970	Resident Population, January 1971
			Total	Permanent	Temporary			
			Number (in thousands)					
Budapest	1,783	−18	236	155	81	218	2,001	2,020
Other towns	2,360	110	343	275	68	453	2,813	2,871
Villages	5,806	260	−579	−430	−149	−319	5,487	5,442
Total	9,949	352				352	10,301	10,333
		Change as percent of 1960 population						
Budapest		−1.0	13.2	8.7	4.5	12.2		
Other towns		4.7	14.5	11.6	2.9	19.2		
Villages		4.5	−10.0	−7.4	−2.6	−5.5		
Total		3.5				3.5		

for the loss to the rural population caused by migration. Although most of the migration is permanent, more than 500,000 persons had a temporary or second residence in 1970.

¶ EDUCATION

Education and economic activity are both significant determinants of demographic attitudes that contribute to fertility decline. Literacy is almost universal in Hungary. Of the population aged ten and over, only 1.8 percent had not attended school in 1970. More than half of the population aged fifteen and over has completed at least eight forms of primary school, and over 15 percent of those aged eighteen and over have completed scondary school (Table 12).

Educational attainment by women has increased faster than that by men, although more men are still reaching higher educational levels. Among the population aged eighteen and over, twice as many men and four times as many women have passed the secondary school leaving examination as was the case twenty years ago. Nevertheless, the rate of men obtaining a diploma is two and one-half times as high as that of women.

¶ ECONOMIC ACTIVITY

Changes in the educational level of the population influence its economic activity. The labor force increased throughout the decade of the 1960s, with a major increase in 1968–1969, when the number of persons born at the beginning of the 1950s became active, and reached 5 million in 1970, an increase of 1.2 million over 1930.

The increase in the labor force has occurred differentially by sex (Table 13). The number of working men in 1970 was 4 percent smaller than in

TABLE 12.

Educational Level, Hungary, 1930–1970

Year	Percent of Population of Specified Age and Over Who Have Attained Specified Educational Level		
	Fifteen: Completion of at Least Eight Forms of Primary School	Eighteen: Secondary School Leaving Certificate	Twenty-five: Third-Level Education Diploma (graduates)
1930	12.9		1.7
1949	20.6	5.5	1.7
1960	32.8	8.8	2.7
1970	51.4	15.5	4.6

TABLE 13.

Economic Activity, Hungary, 1930–1970 (by sex)

| | Percentage Distribution | | | | | | | |
| | Male | | | | Female | | | |
Economic Activity	1930	1949	1960	1970	1930	1949	1960	1970
Economically active	65	65	64	59	22	25	33	39
Inactive earner	2	3	5	12	2	3	4	14
Dependent	33	32	31	29	76	72	63	47
Total	100	100	100	100	100	100	100	100

1960. For women, labor-force participation increased from 22 percent (1 million) in 1930 to 39 percent (2 million) in 1970. Of the 14 percent of women who are inactive earners, 3 percent receive a child care allowance and 11 percent are pensioners. If young women presently taking advantage of child care leave, introduced in 1967, were participating in the labor force, the proportion of active earners among women aged 15–54 would be 69 percent. In 1970, about 66 percent of women aged 20–54 were working, with the highest rate (70 percent) among those aged 30–39.

¶ ECONOMIC SECTOR

Among the various changes transforming Hungary, the most important is the radical difference, breaking the tradition of 1,000 years, in the structure of the economy by sector. This demonstrates the total transformation of economic life that has occurred in the last twenty years. Whereas in 1949, more than 50 percent of the labor force worked in agriculture; in 1970, a mere 26 percent did (Table 14). Of these, 15 percent worked only part of the year.

At the same time, the number of earners working in industry has grown by 36 percent since 1960. In building and construction, the number has increased by 27 percent. The labor force engaged in transport is 20 percent higher than it was ten years ago; it is 32 percent higher in trade. Industry and agriculture have effectively changed places. Of those working in trade, 60 percent are women. Between 1960 and 1970, the number of women working in building and construction increased by 84 percent, in industry, by 72 percent, and in transport, by 54 percent. The number of women in agriculture, corresponding to the general decline in that sector, fell by 30 percent. The relative importance of manual workers has also declined, from 83 percent of active earners in 1963 to 75 percent in 1970.

TABLE 14.

Percentage Distribution of Economically Active Population, Hungary,
1930–1970 (by sector)

| | Percentage Distribution | | | |
Sector	1930	1949	1960	1970
Industry	18	20	28	37
Building and construction	3	2	6	7
Agriculture	54	54	39	26
Transport	3	4	6	7
Trade	6	5	6	8
Other	16	15	15	15
Total	100	100	100	100
Number (in thousands)	3,737	4,085	4,760	4,989

LEGISLATION

We introduce this section with a short description of the general basic
measures that determine the rights of women and mothers. The balance of
the section gives details of other special provisions that exert a direct or
indirect influence on fertility, birth control, and family planning practice.
Measures include acts of the Parliament, law decrees of the Presidential
Council, resolutions of the Council of Ministers, governmental regulations,
and ministerial orders or directives of interested ministers.

¶ BASIC LEGISLATION

The Constitution of Hungary (Law 20 of 1949) forms the basis of its
population policy. The Constitution includes among the rights and obligations of Hungarian citizens equality between men and women, protection
of the institution of marriage and the family, assurance of similar working
conditions by sex, paid leave for women in case of pregnancy, and maternity
and child protection.

Starting with this basic law, the law on marriage, family, and guardianship (Law 4 of 1952) is designed "to protect the institution of marriage
and the family, to ensure the equal rights of women in marriage and
family life, to protect children's interests, and to promote the development
and growth of youth." It states, among other things, that spouses have
equal rights and obligations in "the questions of married life."

The Constitution stipulates that working conditions be regulated by the labor code (Law 2 of 1967) or governmental decree (Governmental Decree 34/1967/X.8/Korm./enacting clause). The basic dispositions of statutes outlining the rights of working women, pregnant women, and women with small children (to be considered in greater detail later) are as follows: Job discrimination by sex is illegal: job preference should be given to pregnant women and mothers of small children; women and youth are not permitted to do work that might have deleterious consequences for their health. In regard to job termination, the law states that it is illegal to dismiss a female worker during pregnancy or breast feeding until the end of the sixth month after confinement. When a woman has been transferred to sick pay in order to nurse a sick child or takes unpaid leave for the same purpose, a dismissal notice can be given "only in justified cases" to an employee with four or more family dependents or no other employed person in the family and to the single woman before her child is eighteen years old.

In 1953, the Council of Ministers adopted a law (Decision no. 1,004/1953/II.8) to further protect mothers and children. For a long time, this was the only law regulating population policy. Its aim was to increase the desire to bear a child, and it was issued simultaneously with the prohibition of induced abortion. Although legal abortion was reinstated in 1956 and although in the period since 1953 most of the concrete aspects of the Council of Ministers' decision have become outdated, its basic principles remain valid even now. These relate to increasing the protection of pregnant women and mothers, granting free baby clothing for the newborn, reducing confinement costs, and increasing household services for mothers and children. They are discussed more fully below.

Another more comprehensive government decision (no. 1,013/1970/V.10/Korm.) was made in 1970. It prescribed the improvement of the socioeconomic status of women and advocated such measures as improving working conditions for women, developing service branches to facilitate household work, and increasing the production of goods that would facilitate household work.

Measures also were taken to develop institutions for children, particularly kindergartens and daytime homes, during the Fourth Five-Year Plan. Financial assistance to families with many children, as well as to single women raising children, was urged. The Minister of Health was charged with developing health protection for women, particularly in family planning. The mass media, specifically the daily press, journals, radio, and television, were urged to discuss ways to improve the socioeconomic status of women.

Pregnancy and Confinement.

Legislation passed to protect pregnant women or their special work and home conditions can be considered as having a direct population effect. The 1953 order (no. 8,100-1/1953/Eü, M.) of the Minister of Health was designed to improve the organization of health care for pregnant women. It prescribed that health institutions should give notice of any pregnancies diagnosed so that health visitors could visit the pregnant woman within a week thereafter and she could be invited to appear at the medical consultation for the protection of mothers. The order provided that the health visitor give constant care to the pregnant woman during the course of her pregnancy and that the National Health Service provide free medical examinations at least three times during the pregnancy.

The effect of this order is evident in the fact that 98–99 percent of pregnant women appeared at the consultations in 1970, as opposed to 94 percent in 1960. Additional orders increased the number of obligatory consultations from three to six, meaning one each month after the third month of pregnancy. In fact, the number of actual consultations was higher, averaging 7.6 appearances by pregnant women in 1970 compared with 5.1 in 1960.

Additional labor legislation further protects the working conditions of pregnant women by stating that it is illegal to employ a pregnant woman in a job "unbeneficial to her health." From the beginning of the fourth month of pregnancy to the first birthday of the child, she cannot be obliged to work in another place without her consent. Overtime, except with the consent of the mother, is prohibited for the same time period. Women do not have to work at night until the child is one year old. If possible, women should work the morning shift after their four month of pregnancy.

Childbirth services are the subject of many decrees, most important of which is the law relating to social insurance (Decree of Legal Force no. 39 of 1955 and its enacting clause, Decree no. 71/1955/XII.3MT). These specify that hospital treatment is free without a time limitation to workers with social insurance. In 1971, a new order (Decree of Legal Force no. 10 of 1970) extended the right to family members of workers with valid social insurance. Free hospital care had previously been limited to ninety days for members of the immediate family.

In 1970, 97 percent of the Hungarian population was included under social insurance, either by their own right as an employee or as a family member of an employee, compared with 60 percent in 1955 and 85 percent in 1960. The percentage of deliveries taking place in institutions increased from 85 in 1960 to 99 in 1970.

The social insurance decree stipulates that workers receive aid in case of pregnancy, child care, or disease. Working women may obtain free medical treatment for pregnancy and childbirth and receive a pregnancy or confinement benefit, which ranges from 50 to 100 percent of their wage, depending on how long they are insured beforehand.

Duration of maternity leave, stipulated as eighty-four days by the former labor code (Law no. 7 of 1951), was modified in 1962 (Decree of Legal Force no. 26 of 1962) to last for twenty weeks, with an addition of four weeks in the case of an abnormal confinement. Four weeks of maternity leave may be taken before the confinement if the woman so desires, a ruling that was repeated in the enacting clause of the labor code.

The maternity benefit, according to the Central Council of the Hungarian Trade Unions (SZOT) in 1968, which supervises social insurance, ranges from 700 forints (Ft)[2] for the first live-born child to 600 Ft for each subsequent child, provided the woman was examined by a physician at least three times during her pregnancy. The sum of 120 Ft is issued for a stillborn child.

Modifications to the maternity benefit appeared in the 1960s. Maternity aid to members of agricultural cooperatives, which had been lower than the figures mentioned previously, was raised by a 1967 order, which was published in the trade unions' *Bulletin* in 1968, to the same as that of other insured persons. A second modification provided that, if a nonworking woman is confined, the working father receives maternity aid in the amount of 450 Ft for each child.

Those women who receive agricultural insurance have a different legal status. They receive a uniform maternity benefit that includes the pregnancy-confinement and the maternity benefits (Rule no. 1/1958/II.23/SZOT). Following the 1955 order, the amount of this aid was increased several times in 1962 (Rule no. 3/1962/XII.24/SZOT) and in 1968 (Rule no. 3/1968/VI.30/SZOT). In 1969, it amounted to 4,000 Ft for the first live-born child and 3,900 Ft for each additional child, provided the woman had at least three medical examinations during pregnancy or at least one if the child was premature, and 3,420 Ft for a stillborn child.

Mothers of many children receive an additional benefit, according to a Decree of Legal Force (no. 21 of 1957) that invalidated the earlier "maternity order and medal" (Decree of Legal Force no. 9 of 1951); mothers bearing six or more children are awarded 1,000 Ft, and those bearing eleven or more receive 2,000 Ft.

[2] US$10 was equal to approximately 276 Ft on January 1, 1973.

A special maternity allowance is given to the childbearing woman who is a member of the trade union or to her husband if she does not work, the amount depending upon the period of membership.[3]

A 1953 decision (no. 1,004/1953/II.8/of the Council of Ministers), regarding protection of mothers and children, stipulated that the state supply to the parent a layette free of charge for each newborn, along with certain baby items, provided the mother participated in three medical examinations. Subsequent decisions in 1957 (no. 1,032/1957/III.22/Korm.) and 1970 (no. 1,007/1970/IV.12/Korm.) modified the order, and from January 1, 1971, 400 Ft in cash was given instead of a layette, primarily to those women entitled to insurance.

The number of women using maternity services has increased considerably in the last decade as a consequence of increases in the number of people covered by social insurance, in the rate of working women, and in the rate of confinements to working women among total confinements. Between 1960 and 1970, the increase in the rate of women obtaining pregnancy-confinement benefits was 115 percent; of women receiving maternity aid, 23 percent, of which 158 percent was based on the women's own rights; and of those obtaining a layette, 9 percent (Table 15). At present, 92 percent of childbearing women receive maternity aid; in 1960, 77 percent did. Among working women, the rate increased from 85 percent in 1960 to 95 percent now. The total sum of the three benefits (pregnancy-confinement aid, maternity aid, layette) was 3.5 times as high in 1970 as in 1960 (Table 16). This is due primarily to the increase in the pregnancy-

---

[3] Information of the Central Council of the Hungarian Trade Unions of 1968. Those who obtain maternity aid through their own rights are employees; the others are wives or family members of employees.

TABLE 15.

Number of Women Receiving Maternity Aid and Pregnancy-Confinement Aid, Hungary, 1960–1971 (in thousands)

| | Maternity Aid | | | | | Pregnancy-Confinement Aid |
| | On Own Right | | | As a Family Member | Total | |
Year	General	Agricultural	Subtotal			
1960	41	2	43	72	115	40
1965	63	2	65	49	114	61
1969	95	6	101	41	142	94
1970	101	7	108	33	141	99
1971	105	7	112	31	143	

TABLE 16.

Social Insurance Allowance Paid to Childbearing Women,
Hungary, 1960–1971

Type of Allowance	1960	1965	1969	1970	1971
	(numbers are in millions of forints)[a]				
Pregnancy-confinement aid	119	340	604	673	706
Maternity aid	60	67	86	88	92
Layette	55	52	60	60	60

[a] Official exchange rate US$100 = 2,760 Ft, January 1, 1973.

confinement aid because of the growth in the number of participants caused by the lengthening of the period of services and by the increase in women's wages.

Infant and Child Care.

Labor and social insurance laws in Hungary guarantee help to working women in caring for infants and under-aged children, especially in the case of illness.

Pay for care of a sick child, according to the basic social insurance disposition (Decree no. 71/1955/XXI.3/MT), is given to women who have returned to work after maternity leave and who have no convenient family member living with them to care for the child. This applies to working mothers of any children under one year old and, for sixty days, to single mothers with a sick child between one and two years old. "Sick pay" is equal to 65 percent of the salary in most cases. A woman who has been employed by the same employer without interruption is entitled to sick pay of 75 percent of her salary (Decree of Legal Force no. 60 of 1957, § 1).

Leave without pay, an additional advantage to working women, is insured by the enacting clause of the labor code (Decision no. 1, 004/1953/II.8/of the Council of Ministers), which provides that the working woman and the father raising a child alone are entitled to leave without pay until the child is two years old or, in the case of the need for home nursing, ten years old.

Working women are entitled to a reduction in the working day in order to have time for breast feeding, according to the labor code, specifically two 45-minute periods daily during the first six months of breast feeding and one similar period, subsequently, to the end of the ninth month. For those women working only four to six hours, the reduction is granted once a day for the first six months only.

Supplementary leave is available to working mothers of many children in the amount of two working days for three children and two more for each additional child, up to a limit of twelve working days a year. Unemployed children under eighteen are counted.

A new institution, the child care allowance, was introduced at the Ninth Congress of the Hungarian Socialist Workers party in 1966. The purpose of the order (no. 3/1967/I.29/Korm.) was to provide state financial aid to mothers of small children and, thereby, to stimulate the birth rate. It grants to working women a child care allowance of up to 600 Ft monthly for each child under thirty months, including adopted, step-, and foster children, provided the woman has worked (1) full time, (2) for twelve months immediately before confinement, or (3) for a total of twelve months within the previous year and a half, or provided she takes leave without pay to care for her child. In 1969 (decree no. 5/1969/I.28/ Korm.), this was modified to include children to the age of three.

Since 1967, more and more women have made use of this allowance, reaching a total of 280,000 in a four-year period (Table 17). According to September 1971 data, 175,000 women were on child care leave.

Within the framework of social insurance for child care, the following allowances were paid:

Year	Forints (in millions)
1967	64
1968	449
1969	870
1970	1,191
1971	1,319

Family Allowance System.

Hungary has a long tradition of a family allowance system that serves as a basis for the state's contribution to the expenses of child raising. Family allowances were paid to civil servants in 1912, to industrial workers in places employing twenty or more workers in 1938, and in 1946, to all workers and employees covered by obligatory sickness insurance and to agricultural workers in state enterprises. A 1953 disposition eliminated the discrimination between different groups of employed persons and granted the rights to members of agricultural cooperatives. The governmental decree (no. 38/1959/VIII.15/Korm.) valid at the beginning of the decade of the 1960s has changed since then in many respects, particularly by the broadening of the definition of persons entitled to family allowance

TABLE 17.

Data on Child Care Allowances, Hungary, 1967–1970

	1967	1968	1969	1970
Total number of live births	148,886	154,419	154,318	151,819
Live births to working women	85,585	97,390	105,150	110,050
Live births to working women as percent of total live births	57.5	63.1	68.1	72.5
Number of women using child care allowance	61,385	68,225	69,100	80,000[a]
Number of women using child care allowance as percent of childbearing women who work	71.7	70.1	65.7	72.7[a]
Females using child care allowance as percent of working women receiving maternity aid	75.2	72.6	68.5	74.2[a]

[a] Estimate.

and the increasing amounts stipulated for the family allowance. In the following, the system is described on the basis of valid law, and the modifications that have occurred in the last decade are indicated.

The legal basis of the Hungarian family allowance system is the labor code (Governmental Decree no. 34/1967/X.8/Korm./enacting clause), which states "workers and employees shall receive a family allowance for their dependent children."

Different orders have extended the right to a family allowance to different categories of workers. The last governmental decree (no. 20/1968/ V.21/Korm.) lists the following groups eligible for a family allowance of different amounts and under somewhat different conditions: workers and employees on payroll, members of agricultural and fishing cooperatives, members of more simple agricultural cooperatives, members of the armed forces, members of artisans' cooperatives, home workers, old age and disability pensioners, students on a social scholarship, and apprentices "of the last year."

The following description of the family allowance system applies to workers and employees on payroll and to members of cooperatives, who together represent the majority of employed persons.

Eligible workers are those on payroll covered by insurance, working at least half the time stipulated for their particular type of work, who have at least two dependent children—defined as children by blood, adopted, foster, stepchild, brother, sister, stepbrother, stepsister, and grandchild.

Children are considered who are: under sixteen; under nineteen and studying by day at a primary or secondary school or serving as apprentices of the first or second year; and under nineteen who have lost at least two-thirds of their working capacity through a physical or mental deficiency, a conditions that has lasted at least one year and will probably not cease within one year.

The single worker, the blind worker, and the worker whose spouse is blind have the right to a family allowance even if the worker has only one child. The important element of this order is that it broadens the 1959 ruling relating to the single working female to include the single worker, that is, the single father. The enacting clause relating to the family allowance defines "single person" as follows:

(1) That worker or employee who is unmarried, widowed, divorced, or separated from the spouse.
(2) One whose husband is serving as a regular soldier.
(3) One whose spouse is arrested; imprisoned; a student in high school; incapable of working for at least six months because of physical or mental deficiency; receives a pension; is undergoing medical treatment ordered by the court; or whose salary, income, or pension is not more than 500 Ft a month.
(4) One who lives under one of two conditions: A divorce suit is in process; alimony is being paid for the spouse or by the spouse or for the child as a result of a divorce based on a court settlement.

The dependent child is defined by the same enacting clause as: (1) one who is living in the household of the worker or employee even if the child is placed in a creche, kindergarten, or day-time home; and (2) one who is placed in an educational establishment, students' home, either primary or secondary school, health institution, creche or children's home, institution for the education of mentally defective children, social institute, or the home of a private person or relative.

The monthly amount of the family allowance is shown in Table 18. Minimum working time required for payment of the family allowance is at least eighteen working days a month.

If both parents work, only one of them, namely, the father, has the right to family allowance. The mother gets the family allowance only if she works and (1) if she is considered to be single, in which case she is entitled to a higher allowance than would have been paid by the father's right; (2) if the father has not taken care of his children for at least two months; or (3) if the father is not entitled to family allowance.

As a consequence of the extension of the sphere of persons entitled to family allowance and as a result of the gradual increase in the sum of the

TABLE 18.

Monthly Family Allowance, Hungary, 1959–1973
(by type of recipient)

Type of Recipient and Number of Children	Monthly allowance (in forints)					
	1959[a]	1965[b]	1966[c]	1968[d]	1972[e]	1973[f]
Workers and employees						
For 1 child						
For 2 children	75	200	300	300	300	400
For 3 children	360	360	510	510	810	960
For 4 children	480	480	680	680	1,080	1,280
For 5 children	600	600	850	860	1,360	1,610
For 6 children	720	720	1,020	1,020	1,620	1,920
Single females						
For 1 child	90	90	140	140	240	290
For 2 children	240	240	340	340	540	640
Single males						
For 1 child				140	240	290
For 2 children				340	540	640
Members of agricultural cooperatives						
For 1 child						
For 2 children			140	200	400	500
For 3 children	210	210	210	360	660	810
For 4 children	280	280	280	480	880	1,080
For 5 children	350	350	350	600	1,100	1,350
For 6 children	420	420	420	720	1,320	1,620
Single females						
For 1 child	70	70	70	120[g]	220[g]	270[g]
For 2 children	140	140	140	240[g]	440[g]	540[g]
Single males						
For 1 child				120	220	270
For 2 children				240	440	540

[a] Decree No. 15/1959/III.27/Korm.
[b] Decree No. 8/1965/VI.13/Korm.
[c] Decree No. 16/1966/VI.1/Korm.
[d] Decree No. 20/1968/V.21/Korm.
[e] Decree No. 50/1971/XII.29/Korm.
[f] Decree No. 44/1972/XII.27/of the Council of Ministers.
[g] The same sum for children with a physical or mental disability.

allowance, the number of receiving families and the sums paid for this purpose grew considerably in the 1960s. The amount paid in 1970 was more than twice as high as in 1960. During the same period, the number of families covered by family allowance increased by one-third (Table 19).

In 1970, a total of 1.6 million children received a family allowance, representing two-thirds of a total number of children under sixteen and 11 percent more than the number who received the allowance in 1960. This occurred in the context of a fertility decrease that meant that the number of families with children under sixteen dropped by approximately 25 percent in the ten-year period. Whereas in 1960, a little more than half of the families with at least two children under sixteen and single persons with at least one child in this age received a family allowance, this proportion had reached 90 percent in 1970. Table 20 shows the distribution of families receiving family allowance by number of children.

Children's Institutions.

Organizations that provide day care for infants and children have a population policy aim: to help those working women with many children to raise them by providing health care, food, and education.

The institutions can be divided into three groups according to the age of the children.

(1) Creches: for children under three.
(2) Kindergartens: for children over three but not yet in school (under six).
(3) Day-time homes of primary schools: for primary school pupils of 6–14 during that part of the day when there is no teaching.

The task of the creches, as stated by the rules regulating their activity (issued with Order no. 128/1956/Eü.M.) is to care for and educate young children during the time the mothers are at work. Admission is granted to children when both parents are working and to children of nonworking

TABLE 19.

Total Family Allowance and Coverage, Hungary, 1960–1971

Year	Total Family Allowance (in millions of forints)	Average Number of Families Covered (in thousands)
1960	1,391	570
1965	1,560	600
1969	2,886	721
1970	2,810	713
1971	2,744	704

TABLE 20.

Percentage Distribution of Families Receiving Family Allowance,
Hungary, 1960, 1970, and 1971 (by family structure)

Family Structure	Families of Workers and Employees			Families of Members of Agricultural Cooperatives		
	1960	1970	1971	1960	1970	1971
Single persons						
With 1 child	7.9	13.6	14.4	7.7	5.9	6.1
With 2 children	3.1	4.1	4.1	3.2	2.3	2.4
Families						
With 2 children	56.4	62.8	62.9		67.4	68.4
With 3 children	20.5	13.2	12.6	62.0	17.4	16.5
With 4 children	7.2	3.7	3.4	19.6	4.5	4.3
With 5 children	2.9	1.4	1.4	5.5	1.5	1.4
With 6+ children	2.0	1.2	1.2	2.0	1.0	0.9
Total	100.0	100.0	100.0	100.0	100.0	100.0

mothers if illness prevents them from taking a job. Preference is given to children of single mothers.

Fees for day care in the creche, much lower than the maintenance cost, are regulated by order (Decree no. 1,008/1961/III.28/Korm.) on the basis of the total monthly income of the parents and the number of children in the family. The fee decreases as the number of children in the family increases. Within any one of the nine income categories, the daily fee for families with one child is never more than twice that for families with four children and varies between 2 Ft and 15 Ft depending on the parents' income.

Admission to kindergarten also is regulated (issued with Order no. 155/1966/MM.). If there are more applicants than places, preference is given to children as follows: if their parent is single, if both parents are working, if there is no adult family member to care for the child, if the family has many children, if the child is five years old or ready to go to school the next school year, and if there are other social reasons. Preference is also given to children coming from creches provided their social condition equals that of children not in creches.

Fees for kindergarten and for day-time homes are regulated in the same way as for creches.

The task of the day-time home of primary schools is stipulated (issued with Order no. 123/1964/MM.) to be "to render help in learning, to keep occupied, and to feed people who need it." Preference is given to children of families where there is no adult to take care of them.

In the 1960s, the capacity of the children's institutions increased. In 1970, the number of places had grown by 75 percent in creches, by 30 percent in kindergartens, and by 66 percent in day-time homes of primary schools, compared to ten years earlier (Table 21).

Despite the increase, there are not enough places. At the end of 1970, only 9 percent of children under age three could be placed in creches, 53 percent of eligible children in kindergartens, and 19 percent of eligible students in day-time homes.

Since, in general, only children of working mothers are admitted to creches, it is more useful to examine this institution just for working women. At first sight, it appears that the relative capacity of creches decreased as the number of working women with children grew. For example, in 1960, 21 percent of eligible children of working mothers could be placed in creches. In 1970, this rate fell to 13 percent. The decrease is, however, illusory because the child care allowance introduced in 1967 allows mothers to care for children of creche age at home. Therefore, eliminating mothers on child care leave, we see that, in 1970, 26 percent of children under three of eligible mothers could be placed in creches.

Housing.

Housing rules issued in 1971 have an indirect population policy aim, that of contributing to the improvement of housing conditions for families with children.

The distribution on dwellings (Order no. 1/1971/II.8/Korm.) states that preference for housing is to be given to "claimants having many children."

A reduction in the rent of tenement dwellings in the possession of the local council (Order no. 2/1971/II.8/Korm.) is granted for children and

TABLE 21.

Capacity of Children's Institutions, Hungary, 1960–1971

Year	Creche	Kindergarten	Day-time Home Places of Primary Schools per 100 Children Attending Primary School
	Places per 100 Children of the Corresponding Age (under 3 years and 3–6 years, respectively)		
1960	6.8	29.8	8.1
1965	9.2	46.2	12.7
1969	9.0	52.4	17.3
1970	9.1	52.9	18.8
1971	9.3	54.4	20.5

other dependents as follows: 20 percent for one child, 25 percent per child for additional children, and 20 percent per person for other family members. Young couples under thirty-five years can get a reduction in the rent if they take upon themselves to have one child within three years or two children within six years.

Stipulations (Order no. 7/1971/II.8/Korm.) for buying or building apartments have a similar character in that costs are reduced for the buyer or builder according to the number of children and dependents. Young couples are again given preference.

Birth Control.

In Hungary, birth control methods have been in use for some time. Different traditional contraceptives include: the condom, used at the beginning of the century; the vaginal pessary of synthetic material or rubber, widespread from 1949 on;[4] and jellies or foam, introduced in 1954.

After a long period of control, the oral contraceptive was introduced in 1967 in the form of a Hungarian product called "Infecundin." The dispositions (Order no. 9/1967/Eü.M.) regulating its use allowed the pill to all females, except those under age, by prescription of a specialist in the regional outpatients' National Health Service clinic or of a specialist in a bed-patient health institution. The pill can be taken only after careful examination. Continued use requires additional examinations at six-month intervals.

Social insurance does not cover the cost of oral contraceptives. They are available in pharmacies by prescription, at 31 Ft for a twenty-one-day vial of Infecundin and 24 Ft for Bisecurin. Infecundin was originally available only for three-month periods, a time limit that was extended in 1968 to six months (Order no. 36/1968/Eü.M.) with one further extension for a maximum of two months. The Order (no. 4/1971/Eü.M.) regulating the prescription of Bisecurin, introduced in February 1971, is very similar to that regulating Infecundin.

The intrauterine device (IUD), officially introduced recently, also is regulated (Order no. 40/1971/Eü.M.). Insertion of the Hungarian device called "Intrauterin" can be performed only at the obstetrical/gynecological departments of bed-patient health clinics or in maternity homes directed by a medical specialist. It can be used for women (1) who have already borne a child or (2) who are over eighteen and for whom pregnancy is not desirable because of permanent or temporary disease. It is available to them only on the basis of legitimate professional principles. The timing of the insertion is carefully regulated, as is the nature of the gynecological

[4] Its marketing was permitted by the Decree no. 3, 180/1949/X.9/NM.

examination that precedes it. Although the patient must pay for the device itself (31 Ft), the insertion as well as the related examination are free of charge.

Between 1968 and 1970, a new contraceptive called "C-film" was introduced and then withdrawn from the market because of its lack of effectiveness in preventing pregnancy (Information no. 41,000/1969/Eü.M.).

In Hungary, traditional contraceptives continue to prevail and the use of up-to-date devices is limited (Tables 22 and 23).

The number of women using the oral contraceptive has gradually increased since it was introduced in 1967. According to October 1971 data,

TABLE 22.

Percentage Distribution of Married Women Using Contraception, Hungary, 1965–1966 and 1970 (by major method)

Method	1965–1966	1970
Coitus interruptus	62	53
Condom	15	14
Vaginal douche	5	4
Pessary	5	3
Ogino-Knaus	4	4
Foam and jelly	4	4
Oral contraceptive	0	10
C-film	0	3
Other	5	5
Total	100	100

TABLE 23.

Consumption of Major Contraceptives, Hungary, 1960–1972 (in thousands)

Year	Condom	Pessary	Timidon	
			Foam (15 tablets)	Tube of Jelly
1960	7,489	32	33	86
1965	11,560	42	30	131
1967	10,294	44	58	158
1968	7,103	36	39	148
1969	6,384	34	30	120
1970	8,529	22	24	117
1971	6,733	24	23	103
1972	5,278	29	26	96

209,000 women regularly use the pill. The number increased by one-third in 1970 and by an additional one-fifth in the first ten months of 1971, an increase that is attributed to the introduction of Bisecurin. The increase in the number of women buying oral contraceptives is as follows:

December 1967	16,000
December 1968	57,000
December 1969	127,000
December 1970	175,000
December 1971	222,000
December 1972	247,000

Present data indicate that 8 percent of all women aged 15–49 and 10 percent of married women aged 15–49 use oral contraceptives. Among younger married women, the rate is still higher: Almost 25 percent of 20–24 year olds and 20 percent of 25–29 year olds use the pill.

Induced Abortion.

After several more severe prohibiting orders had been passed, induced abortion was permitted by a Cabinet Decision (no. 1,047/1956/III.3) in 1956 that stated that, "in order to increase women's health protection and to relax procedures relating to the interruption of pregnancy," interruption of pregnancy could be performed in health institutions by authorization from a weekly board meeting at a regional hospital or clinic. The chairman of the board is designated as the chief medical officer of the county or town, and its members are the chief or the referent of the social political group of the executive committee and a woman, possibly recommended by the trade unions. The board can authorize the interruption of pregnancy on grounds of illness as well as personal and family conditions. Its task, beside authorization, is to give information about the harmful effects of abortion as well as to dissuade the applicant when the request seems to be unjustified. If the applicant still insists on the interruption of pregnancy, the board authorizes abortion. If illness is a consideration, the board decides on the basis of the expertise of the hospital staff. If reasons other than illness are under consideration, the applicant or her relatives are obliged to pay the cost of hospital treatment. The decree further stipulates that "the production and the marketing at low prices of convenient contraceptives should be ensured."

The implementing order (no. 2/1956/VI.24/Eü.M.) of the decision outlines detailed measures relating to the procedure for the interruption of pregnancy. After insuring the conditions of the establishment of the authorizing board, it prescribes the kinds of case in which the interruption of pregnancy is justified. These conditions are as follows:

(1) If the abortion is necessary to save the life of the pregnant woman or to protect her from a grave disease or its exacerbation or if the unborn fetus is in probable danger of grave injury.

(2) If personal and family conditions are worthy of appreciation.

Abortion is authorized until the thirteenth week of pregnancy. In the case of single girls under twenty (Information no. 4/880/1961/XXI.14/ Eü.M.), this limit can be extended to the eighteenth week of pregnancy.

The disposition states that the request should be presented personally to the board following an obstetrical and any other necessary examinations on the same day.

Social insurance does not cover the costs of induced abortion when it is obtained for family planning purposes. If the applicant is entitled to the services of social insurance and if pregnancy is interrupted for personal and family reasons, the costs of hospital treatment for the first three days must be covered by the applicant or her husband or by a relative if she is under age and has no income. Sickness benefits and other insurance services are not due to the woman for the first three days that she is unable to work. From the fourth day of inability to work or of hospital treatment, the applicant is entitled to all the services of social insurance.

At the time of admission to the hospital, the woman must pay 210 Ft, comprising the cost of one day of hospital treatment and the operation itself. For additional days, she must pay 70 Ft per day, the regular hospital rate.

The disposition (Law no. 5 of 1961) concerning criminal sanctions of illegal abortion is still valid. The disposition of the criminal code stipulates that a person who brings on a criminal miscarriage should be condemned to prison for three years. The punishment is imprisonment for six months to five years if the person is recidivist, if the crime was committed in a business-like way (that is, for profit), if it was committed without the female's consent, or if it causes gross physical injury. If the abortion caused death, the punishment is imprisonment from two to eight years. A woman who causes her own miscarriage or is responsible for her own abortion performed by another person will be imprisoned for six months.

As a result of the legalization of induced abortion, the number and rate of induced abortions rose gradually from 1956. A maximum of 207,000 induced abortions was reached in 1969 and has been followed by a slow decrease which is probably due to the gradual spread of modern contraceptives (Table 24).

TABLE 24.

Trend in Induced Abortion, Hungary, 1956–1972

	Induced Abortions		
Year	Number (in thousands)	Number per 1,000 Females Aged 15–49	Number per 100 Live Births
1956	82.5	32.7	43
1957	123.4	49.4	74
1958	145.6	58.4	92
1959	152.4	61.0	101
1960	162.2	65.2	111
1961	170.0	68.6	121
1962	163.7	66.1	126
1963	173.8	70.1	131
1964	184.4	74.3	140
1965	180.3	71.6	136
1966	186.8	73.0	135
1967	187.5	72.1	126
1968	201.1	75.9	130
1969	206.8	78.0	134
1970	192.3	72.0	127
1971	187.4	69.5	124
1972[a]	178.4	66.2	117

[a] Preliminary data completed by estimation.

Health Protection of Women.
In order to handle family planning and related questions according to public health principles, the Ministry of Health issued directions (no. 40, 580/1971/Eü.M.) in 1971 concerning the organization and work of consultants for the health protection of women. The task of the consultants is to develop an attitude that takes social and individual interest into account, to educate for family life, and to inculcate the undertaking of parental roles. The fact that childbirth should not occur by chance but should depend on the parents' decision must also be communicated. The consultants for health protection should formally educate young people who are already married or are going to marry, using modern biological and ethical terms. They should also help solve the health problems of childlessness, habitual abortion, or premature birth as well as the problems of couples with many children. In addition to all this, their job is to prevent unwanted pregnancies by means of professional advice, practical instruction, and recommendation of convenient contraceptive methods. At the

consultation, they should give a practical demonstration of contraceptive methods, particularly up-to-date ones. This may contribute to the decrease in the high number of induced abortions and their possible harmful consequences. It is wise to have at the consultation models of all contraceptives and available drugs. The use of mechanical and traditional contraceptives should be demonstrated both in illustrations and on plastic models.

At the same time, the work of the consultant should insure that the population be developed and that an idea of convenient family size be introduced.

RECENT OPINION ON POPULATION

The decreasing birth rate and its all-time low reported for 1962 aroused great interest in Hungary. Not only did demographers study the question in detail but writers, journalists, physicians, and historians investigated the trend of declining births and its causes. An animated discussion developed in published journals among representatives of different views.

In the following, we shall try to group opinion on population policy by positive and negative attitudes. We shall analyze those that call for greater increase in fertility according to those reasons believed to be the cause of the present situation and its solution. Discussion is divided into the press debate, the opinion of demographers, and political attitudes.

¶ PRESS DEBATE

In the middle of 1963, an article appeared in the review *Contemporary* [2] that sounded the alarm because of the low birth rate. Discussion continued in a weekly journal *Life and Literature* [3] in an article about the problems of rapid population growth in developing countries. Although the article did not discuss the Hungarian situation specifically, it created the impression that all populations were increasing except that of Hungary. Such questions arose as: Are we exterminating ourselves? Have we developed a horror of children? And the opposite view—do we want to take upon ourselves the problems of heavy population growth?

The effect of the initial discussion on population could be seen even in 1970 when the *Women's Journal* [4] invited its readers to express their views.

One journalist's [5; 2] opinion on the current situation can be summarized as follows: The low birth rate in Hungary reflects a negative attitude toward life, one of petty bourgeois materialism and selfishness, whereby the emancipation of women leads to an abstention from reproduction in order to gain financial advantages and to an abuse of legalized abortion.

Another journalist stresses that, although the legalization of abortion has reduced unwanted childbearing, it has created a situation in which "we struggle with the specter of depopulation" [6]. In this view, Hungary will become a weak nation if its population is too small.

Another analysis, based on future manpower demand, advocates an increase in reproduction to avoid a situation where there will be "not enough people for the increasing number of machines" [7].

Articles of a more moderate and less literary vein [8; 9] recommend that the childlessness tax be reestablished and that the time limitations imposed on women be recognized: The woman who decides to have several children has to (1) leave her profession, decreasing the income of the family, (2) avail herself of a generous grandmother for child care purposes, or (3) "hurry permanently." Additional references [10] are cited to support the conclusion that the decline in births stems not from attitude but from finances, with present wage conditions allowing only for small families.

The question is raised of how the family allowance system should be organized to equalize the living standards of families with different numbers of children [11]. The fact that the state provides only a limited number of facilities for children and that parents therefore limit their number in order to bring them up "decently" also is discussed [12].

On the other side of the debate are those who consider that increased population growth would be harmful to the country. One journal article [13] expresses the opinion that children, who cause inconvenience and expense, are not needed for old-age support because everyone will receive a pension. Another theory related to this is the "hobby theory"—that enough people will really want to raise children to maintain population growth of the nation [14]. Other views are that women will always want to have children because they represent their only victory over men, in that men cannot bear children themselves [15, p. 297].

Others who oppose further population growth feel that rapid growth per se, as in the case of South America, India, and Africa, presents great problems. Technology can solve any problems created by manpower shortage [16] in this view.

¶ OPINION OF DEMOGRAPHERS

Researchers have investigated different aspects of population increase to elucidate the question from various sides. Professional publications have appeared on such subjects as the future trend of demographic characteristics, the economic effects of a low birth rate, the methodology of reproduction, differential fertility and female cohorts, induced abortion, and the interrelation of population policy and fertility.

In the following, we outline and in some cases discuss the principal points on which Hungarian demographers are agreed.

(1) The present birth rate is very low.

(2) Although the low birth rate will not lead to a national catastrophe, stabilization at the present low level would cause great troubles in the future, particularly with regard to the age structure.

Discussion of this point by demographers [17] emphasizes that continuation of the present fertility level will lead to an age structure by the beginning of the year 2000 that would create a grave socioeconomic situation involving a slow decrease and eventual depopulation. It is also proposed that the slower the growth, the smaller the national income and the slower the economic development of the country [18].

(3) An effective and well-considered population policy is needed. A detailed plan coordinating "many little circumstances of life which still influence population behavior" and not counting on revolutionary changes is advocated [19]. It is urged that special attention be given to increasing the desires of working women to bear children [20]. The experience of other European nations with regard to increasing financial support to families and influencing public opinion in a pronatalist direction is cited as an example for Hungary to follow.

(4) Administrative measures such as the prohibition of induced abortion would not lead to population stability. Instead, at best, they would contribute to a new population wave that is not desirable.

It is stressed by demographers that induced abortion is not the cause of the decline in births but merely a means of birth control [22]. Demographers also emphasize that it would be a mistake to try to force a change in values by abruptly changing administrative measures that have become part of the social fabric, such as the legalization of abortion [23].

(5) The decrease in fertility has social, economic, and population policy causes.

(6) Given that the factors influencing the birth rate are manifold, further studies are needed to determine the extent of their effect.

Specific aspects considered worthy of further research are the relationship between the birth rate and the economy, consumption, and real income [23]; the future trend in fertility of peasants, nonmanual workers, and working women [20]; and the effect on fertility of lengthening the period of education [21]. It is maintained that the spread of marriages that are heterogeneous with regard to occupation structure has increased contraceptive practices in Hungary [24]. Other areas of needed research are outlined as follows: the effect of long-range economic plans on the standard of living, housing conditions, and income; the effect of urbanization, occupational stratification, and rise in the cultural level on fertility;

and the influence on fertility of education, the press, and international events that may develop a social consciousness and through that individual ideals about the family [17].

Future goals of population policy are summarized by Egon Szabady [25] as follows: gradual increase in the number of births in order to ensure reproduction of the population; gradual equalization of the age structure with particular attention to the danger of creating echo effects; development of a positive relationship between income and fertility so that a rise in living standards will create a positive influence on the number of births; a comprehensive and consistent policy that takes into consideration indirect measures such as the child care allowance.

¶ POLITICAL ATTITUDES

The following section summarizes discussion of a number of different political bodies.

The Ninth Congress of the Hungarian Socialist Workers party considered population questions in 1966. "It seems necessary," wrote the referee in his report, "that the competent government organizations deal with the development of population and elaborate measures that satisfy the interest of women, mothers, families, and society, and that take into account the social, ethical, health, and financial aspects of the situation" [26].

The Ninth Congress passed a resolution calling for greater social appreciation for mothers and families of many children and greater attention to questions of family protection, education of children, and "social irresponsibility." It outlined plans for ensuring financial security to large families and mothers who want to work and study and proposed introducing the child care allowance in 1967.

The Tenth Congress of the Hungarian Socialist Workers party, meeting in 1970, also dealt with the position of women and particularly mothers raising children. The president of the National Council of Hungarian Women noted at the congress [27] that the "double duty" of women in work and home required sacrifice and created tension because day care institutions for children did not have enough capacity. The first secretary of the Central Committee of the Hungarian Socialist Workers party [27] pointed out that it was still difficult for women to obtain a high position and that the principle of equal salary for equal work could not be realized everywhere. Noting the need for increased child care facilities, he expressed appreciation to mothers and urged fellow party members to fight against those who spoke ill of pregnant mothers.

In 1970, the Central Committee took the position that the growth of participation of women in the labor force was contributing to favorable changes in the family [28]. Although it considered the ideal family size of two children to be "not reassuring," it stressed that the practice of family planning was not yet widespread enough.

The National Women's Committee of the Patriotic Popular Front recommended in 1970[5] that the women's committees analyze the role of the family in socialist society with a view to both strengthening family planning and developing social opinion in the direction of greater respect for motherhood.

The Central Council of Hungarian Trade Unions [29] urged that trade union committees act more energetically against illegal overtime for women, particularly mothers of small children or many children. It also suggested that society take upon itself to a greater extent than previously the care and costs of raising children—the future labor force—specifically by increasing the family allowance.

FAMILY PLANNING RESEARCH

Since 1958, the Central Statistical Office in Hungary and the Demographic Research Institute have carried out the following surveys (in chronological order) :

(1) *Experimental fertility, family planning and birth control study (TCS-Pilot Study)—1958–1960.*
(2) *Collecting of fertility data of the 1960 population census.*
(3) *Study of women having had an induced abortion, 1960.*
(4) *Fertility and family planning sample survey—1963 (microcensus).*
(5) *Detailed study of females having had an induced abortion—April 1964.*
(6) *Fertility, family planning, and birth control study (TCS. 1966 study)—1965–1966.*
(7) *Sample survey of obstetrical events—1968.*
(8) *Longitudinal marriage study.*
(9) *Detailed fertility and family statistics survey—1970* (25 percent sample of the population census).
(10) *Sample survey on repeated induced abortions—1970 and 1971.*
(11) *Sample survey on women using modern contraceptives*—first survey, 1967–1969; continuous investigation from August 1971.
(12) *Continuous studies of induced abortions—from January 1971 on.*

Research plans for the future include the following:

(1) Investigation of the demographic, social, and economic aspects of fertility.
(2) Study of family planning and birth control.
(3) The evaluation of population policy measures.

---

[5] Recommendations to the working program of women's committees, see [28].

(4) The modification of population policy and the development of alternative population policy concepts.

FUTURE POLICY CONCEPTS

Population concepts for the future are included in the paper "Basic Questions about Population Policy" [1] mentioned above, the main statements of which serve as a basis for long-range planning. They have not yet been adopted officially by the government, but their ideas correspond to the aims of the official population policy.

The objectives of the Hungarian population policy can be summed up as follows:

(1) To contribute to the gradual increase in the number of births to the extent that, at least, replacement of the population be ensured.
(2) To equalize gradually, as far as possible, the age structure of the population.

The considerable drop in the birth rate at the beginning of the 1960s meant that replacement of the population was no longer certain. The number of persons belonging to some cohorts of the younger generation was smaller than the number living in the present adult generation. Although, in the second half of the 1960s, the birth rate increased to some extent, if the present fertility level should continue, the population would gradually decline, starting in the last decade of this century.

This would be deleterious because in a decreasing population the proportion of aged people, which is already very high in Hungary, would continue to grow considerably, and the age structure would become distorted. To prevent this, the recent birth rate of 15 per 1,000 should increase to at least 17 per 1,000.

In developing these objectives, our population policy has three principles:

(1) A great difference in the size of subsequent generations is harmful, creating an irregular age structure.
(2) The present age pyramid of Hungary is very uneven. Thus, for example, the cohort born in 1954 is more than 70 percent larger than that born in 1962. If, in the future, we do not succeed in influencing fertility trends upward, particularly for small cohorts aged 20–29, the dip in births ("wave trough") will repeat itself like an echo and will be accompanied by harmful social and economic effects. Therefore, long-range population policy measures aiming at increasing births should be timed so that they exert the greatest influence from the middle of the 1970s on, when the number of women of reproductive age begins to fall. In this regard, it should be taken into consideration that the impact of pronatalist population policy measures can be felt only some years later.

(3) Although the greatest population policy intervention in the spontaneous processes of reproduction will be needed by the end of the 1970s, some initial measures are required immediately or in the near future. The effect of measures taken to date seems to be to depress fertility below the level necessary for replacement.

In light of the above-mentioned aims and principles, proposals were made regarding different population policy measures, including those already applied that might be used in the future to influence the birth rate in the right direction. Some of the proposed population policy measures are enunciated in the Fourth Five-Year Plan (1970–1975); some will be completely developed by 1985.

(1) The family allowance system should be further developed. Society has to bear an increasing part of the cost of children's education. Thus, according to the concepts, while the present sum of family allowance for the child entitled to it covers 15 percent of the general costs of a child's education in the family, this ratio will increase by 1975 to 20–21 percent and by 1985 to 35–40 percent. In the case of a very favorable rate of economic growth, it can be imagined that it will approach 50 percent. For families with three or more children and for single mothers, the 1972 plan already prescribes the increase in family allowance. Two additional modifications are called for: (a) The progressive allowance should work so that a family with three children receives the highest allowance and the progressive scale decreases with the fourth child, and (b) the family allowance should be paid until the first child is three or even five years old to compensate for higher expenses connected with the first-born and to stimulate the birth of the second child.

(2) It is desirable to maintain and develop the child care allowance system. The sum of the allowance should be increased proportionately to wages. It was suggested that the allowance be given to all working women until the child reaches the age of three, regardless of whether they continued to work, the only condition being that they did not use the creche service.

(3) It is necessary to develop institutions for children, such as creches, kindergartens, and day-time homes, because they contribute to a great extent to the decrease of family burden that, in turn, stimulates women to take maternity upon themselves. We can anticipate a slight development in the Fourth Five-Year Plan. In the long run, we intend to develop kindergartens and day-time homes more rapidly; creches, because of the child care allowance, will be developed more slowly. In 1985, it is possible that 14–15 percent of creche-age children, 60–65 percent of kindergarten children, and 66 percent of primary school pupils can be placed in the appropriate institution.

(4) Young couples and families with many children should have preference in obtaining housing, for example, by delaying repayment or decreasing amortization when children are born to young couples. The long-range plan aims also to increase the floor space of apartments; by 1985, average floor space in new apartments should have increased from 50 m² to 65–68 m², and the number of apartments with three or more rooms should increase from 20 percent to 40 percent of all apartments. According to the plan, all families should have a separate apartment no later than 1985.

(5) Measures for the protection of mothers should be improved because they have to bear the additional expenses associated with larger families. It was suggested that the sum of maternity and pregnancy confinement allowances be increased proportionately to wages and that maternity leave be lengthened by one or two months before the date of expected delivery, which would decrease the danger of premature birth. It was also proposed that the number of part-time jobs for mothers be increased and the period of payment to mothers of sick children be lengthened until the child is two or three years old. Paid leave of mothers with children could also be lengthened.

(6) Social consciousness and public opinion must be influenced in order to change the demographic situation. The forces of mass communication and education, such as the press, the radio, television, literature, and art, should propagate the view that children are a great value for Hungarian society and families with many children deserve respect. It should be made clear that childraising is an important role in society and that the child is a sour of pleasure. Education concerning motherhood and love of children can take place at school also.

(7) Influencing demographic events in the desired direction should not occur through any forced measures. Therefore, it is desirable and necessary to encourage the use of modern contraceptive devices, and it is not desirable to prohibit induced abortion. Because of the harmful effects of many induced abortions on health, however, the number of induced abortions should be reduced. This can be realized, on the one hand, by means of information and sex education of all social strata and ages using all means of communication. On the other hand, a large assortment of modern contraceptive devices of good quality should be made available in the necessary quantity and at a low price.

APPENDIX.   Excerpts from Decision no. 1,040/1973/X.18
of the Council of Ministers
on the Tasks of Population Policy

Late in 1973 the Council of Ministers issued a decision dealing with population policy in Hungary. Excerpts from it are reproduced here as an
appendix to the chapter.

In order to improve the population situation, to increase the pecuniary assistance of
families with children, to protect more efficiently the health of women and of children
to be born, as well as to introduce the organized teaching of knowledge on the health
aspects of family planning, the Council of Ministers adopts the following decision:

I. It is necessary to facilitate the situation of families with children, reduce the costs
of the education of children to be covered by the family, and increase the participation
of society in these costs by money allowance and other facilities, respectively.
    For this purpose the following measures are necessary:
    1. Family allowance to be paid in case of two children should be increased by 100
Ft per month for each child from 1 June 1974 on.
    2. The monthly amount of child care allowance should be increased for the first
child by 150 Ft, for the second child by 250 Ft, and for the third and further children
by 350 Ft from 1 January 1974 on.
    3. . . . [T]he total amount of the present maternity and layette benefit should be
stated uniformly in 2,500 Ft and be paid at the birth of each child. . . .
    4. In case of economically active mother the entitlement to get sick-pay for the
child care should be extended to 60 days at the age of 1–3 years of the child and to
30 days per year at the age of 3–6 years of the child. In case of single father sick-pay
is given to the father at the age of 0–6 years of the child. If the parent is single,
sick-pay for the child care is stated for 60 days per year even at the age of 3–6 years
of the child.
                                    · · · · ·
    6. . . . The prices of products for child care should be controlled to a greater extent
and strictly in the future. . . .
                                    · · · · ·
    8. The payment system for creches and day-time homes introduced in 1961 . . .
should be complemented with higher income (8,000–9,000–10,000 Ft) cateogries and
according to them with growing tariff rates. The number of children in the family
should be considered as a tariff-reducing factor according to the principles taken into
account in this tariff table even up to now.

II. In order to protect the health of the generation to be born already before conception it is necessary to take health policy measures which contribute to family
planning and protect the health of women and descendants.

    A. A great help should be rendered to the population in acquiring knowledge in
family planning. Therefore:
    1. For persons to be married, indicated in the law, it should be compulsory to go
to the physician giving advice on the protection of the family and women, and to
take part in an appropriate consultation and education in family planning. If neces-

sary, the proper method of contraception should be taught to them and they should be provided with contraceptives in a way prescribed by law.

In order to ensure the appearance at the consultation, . . . at the notification of marriage the registrar should advise the persons . . . to go to this consultation; the registrar is obliged to refuse participation in contracting of marriage . . . if the persons to be married do not present a written certificate . . . that they have taken part in the compulsory consultation. . . .

2. Consultation activity for the protection of family and women should be extended to the whole interested population. . . .

    a. . . . The consultation network should be developed as a part of the network of medical treatment and prevention, mother, infant and child protection already in action. . . .

    b. Medical Universities and Institutes for Post-Graduate Medical Training should ensure the acquirement of theoretical and practical knowledge in modern protection of family and women.

    c. Among population living in villages and on detached farms the tasks of advising in respect of the protection of family and women should be performed by the district health service. . . .

3. Medicines for the cessation of sterility, as well as contraceptive medicines and devices should be made available for the population in appropriate quantity, quality and assortment.

B. It is necessary to revise the present system of induced interruption of pregnancy in order to decrease significantly its harmful impact on the health of mother and descendants. . . . non-desired pregnancies should be prevented rather than interrupted. [Abortion is permissible] only in cases indicated by law and only in in-patient health institutions . . . Consistent measures should be taken against persons breaking the legal provisions concerning interruption of pregnancy.

The new regulation regarding interruption of pregnancy should be developed on the basis of the following principles:

1. For the judgement of requests . . . committees of authority should be established. . . . When taking a decision the committees have to keep in view the interest of society, the protection of the health of mothers and children. In case of refusal of the request the petitioner should have the possibility to resort to a legal remedy (to appeal).

    a. The competent committee authorizes induced interruption of pregnancy in the following cases:

        aa. if it is motivated from a medical point of view by health reasons existing with the parents or to be expected with the child to be born;

        ab. if the woman does not live in marriage or lives separately for a long period;

        ac. if pregnancy results from a crime;

        ad. if the pregnant woman or her husband has no flat being her/his property or has no independent tenement-dwelling;

        ae. if she has three or more children or if she had three or more confinements; or if she has two living children and had at least one additional obstetrical event;

        af. if the pregnant woman is 40 years old or older; by the end of 1978, however, this judgment will refer to 35 years old and older women, too.

    b. Besides cases indicated in item a. the law should afford an opportunity to give a permit on the basis of individual considerations in the following cases:

        ba. if the woman has two living children, in case of the third pregnancy, if viability or development of the foetus to be born are probably endangered;

        bb. if the husband is in regular service or special service at the armed forces;

bc. if the pregnant woman or the husband is imprisoned for a longer period;
bd. if it is seriously motivated by social reasons.

2. Interruption of pregnancy might be permitted only during the period fixed by law (expressed in weeks).

. . . . .

6. When submitting the petition concerning interruption of pregnancy the pregnant woman is obliged to present a certificate (certificates) confirming her motives or for lack of such certificates—her declaration which she made being aware of her criminal responsibility.

7. In order to accelerate the procedure an opportunity should be given to the chairman of the first-degree committee to permit interruption of pregnancy without convening the meeting of the committee, in cases indicated in item 1.a. if they are undoubtedly confirmed.

8. The price of induced abortions should be raised in a way to cover completely the actual costs. Tariffs should be stated in a differentiated way, in an amount of 600 and 1,000 Ft, respectively. In cases determined by law the fee might be decreased or even not be paid. . . .

9. In case of each induced abortion the woman in question should be kept on sick-list at least for two days.

10. If interruption of pregnancy is requested by a pregnant female under age, a hearing should be given to her legal representative. . . .

11. It is also prohibited to accept any honorary offered voluntarily for the medical or health activity relating to interruption of pregnancy.

. . . . .

III. Biological, health, ethical, moral knowledge necessary for the establishing of harmonic, desirable human relations and well-balanced family life and for the wide realization of modern family planning has not spread enough in due quantity and quality among population and especially among the youth. Therefore in all forms of public education as well as in health education among population measures should be taken to prepare people for family life.

1. The teaching of knowledge regarding family planning . . . should be built in public education system . . . from primary schools to institutions of third-level education, including all educational—training—plans of armed forces and bodies.

2. A systematic information, training should be ensured for population not included in education, by means of lectures. . . . Cultural institutions . . . too, should play a great part in this matter. It is especially necessary to pay great attention to the enlightment [sic] of parents of children attending primary and secondary schools for the purpose that parents should be properly prepared at the beginning of the training of their children.

3. A written subject matter of instruction of different level, length and form should be ensured in a co-ordinated way . . . both for public education and for the education of population. . . .

4. On the basis of the written subject matter of instruction it is necessary to begin immediately the first-level, then gradually a higher-level training (extension training) of teachers, physicians, skilled health workers . . . acting as instructors in public education, in the education of population and health consultations. . . .

5. From September 1974 on gradually . . . the preparation of pupils for family life and within this their sexual education should begin at the institutions of first-, second- and third-level education, inclusive of educational institutions of armed forces and bodies, and of training of regular soldiers.

6. ... [U]ntil properly prepared teachers in due quantity will be available ... physicans (skilled health workers) should perform this teaching for a payment.

· · · · ·

VI. The Council of Ministers requests the Patriotic People's Front, social organs, trade unions, the heads of wireless, television and other communication organs as well as the organizations of artistic life and the creative artists to contribute continuously with their activity to the carrying out of the purposes indicated in the Decision.

· · · · ·

Jeno FOCK m.p.
President of the Council of
Ministers

REFERENCES

1. "Basic questions about population policy." Manuscript. Budapest, January 1971. (In Hungarian.)

2. Ambrus Bor. "Thirteen per thousand." *Kortars*, no. 5, 1963. (In Hungarian.)

3. Jozsef Palfy. "Humanity asks for bread: Population reproduction and perspectives." *Elet es Irodalom*, no. 47, 1963. (In Hungarian.)

4. "Do we live for ourselves?" Debate and termination of debate by Guyla Fekete. *Nok Lapja*, 1970, in several numbers continuously. (In Hungarian.)

5. Ambrus Bor. "More bread, less children?" *Elet es Irodalom*, no. 50, 1963. (In Hungarian.)

6. Karoly Jobbagy. "Thousand years." *Elet es Irodalom*, no. 6, 1964. (In Hungarian.)

7. Peter Veres. "Planned economy and population policy." *Kortars*, no. 10, 1964. (In Hungarian.)

8. Eva Bozoky. "Contribution to Ambrus Bor's article." *Kortars*, no. 7, 1963. (In Hungarian.)

9. Eva Bozoky. "Is it a private matter or a public care?" *Elet es Irodalom*, no. 2, 1965. (In Hungarian.)

10. Laszlo Velkey. "On account of the future—for the future." *Borsodi Szemle*, no. 3, 1964. (In Hungarian.)

11. Sandor Gyorffy. "Possibilities of increasing family allowance." *Elet es Irodalom*, no. 10, 1964. (In Hungarian.)

12. Laszlo Nemeth. "Closing uteri." *Kortars*, no. 7, 1966. (In Hungarian.)

13. Guyula Fekete. "Fruit on the age pyramid." *Kortars*, no. 1, 1970. (In Hungarian.)

14. Guyula Fekete. "Closing of the debate on the subject 'Do we live for ourselves?' " *Nok Lapja*, 1970. (In Hungarian.)

15. Laszlo Gyurko. "The weaker sex." *Kortars*, 1965. (In Hungarian.)

16. Istavan Lazar. "About ten millions." *Valosag*, no. 4, 1964. (In Hungarian.)

17. Egon Szabady. "Future population perspectives in Hungary." *Demografia*, no. 3–4, 1964. (In Hungarian.)

18. Rudolf Ankorka. "Economic impact of the development of the number of births." *Demografia*, no. 3–4, 1964. (In Hungarian.)

19. Dezso Danyi. "Our population policy and births." *Demografia*, no. 3–4, 1964. (In Hungarian.)

20. Andras Klinger. "Recent tendencies of differential fertility." *Demografia*, no. 3–4, 1964. (In Hungarian.)

21. Egon Szabady. "International and historical aspects of our birth number." *Demografia*, no. 3–4, 1964. (In Hungarian.)

22. Karoly Miltenyi and Egon Szabady. "Abortion situation in Hungary: Demographic and health aspects." *Demografia*, no. 2, 1964. (In Hungarian.)

23. Dezso Danyi. "Our population policy and births." *Demografia*, no. 3–4, 1964. (In Hungarian.)

24. Karoly Miltenyi. "Impact of heterogeneous marriages on birth control." *Demografia*, no. 4, 1962. (In Hungarian.)

25. Egon Szabady. "Economy and population." *Gazdasag*, no. 4, 1970. (In Hungarian.)

26. Ninth Congress of the Hungarian Socialist Workers party, November 18–December 3, 1966. Report of the Central Committee. Referee: Janos Kadar.

27. Proceedings of the Tenth Congress of the Hungarian Socialist Workers party, November 23–28, 1970. Budapest: Kossuth Konyvkiado, 1971.

28. "Political, economic, and social situation of females." Session of the Central Committee of the Hungarian Socialist Workers party, February 18–19, 1970. Budapest: Kossuth Konyvkiado, 1970.

29. "Position and decision of the Central Council of Hungarian Trade Unions on the political, economic situation of females and on the further tasks." Session of the Central Committee of the Hungarian Socialist Workers party, February 18–19, 1970. Budapest: Kossuth Konyvkiado, 1970.

CHAPTER 10

Australia

W. D. Borrie

ABSTRACT

The distinctive feature of Australia's population policy has been its overwhelming concern with immigration. When Australian leaders have urged faster or slower population growth or have advocated the attainment of "optimum" populations, they have almost always placed more emphasis, insofar as they believe growth rates to be subject to policy decision, on immigration rather than on natural increase. Except when the economy has been depressed, the government has been concerned with stimulating and financing an immigration stream to augment the numbers likely to arrive (at least from Europe) above the levels achieved through a laissez-faire approach. Thus, Australian governments and newspapers discuss immigration a great deal—a situation found perhaps in Canada, New Zealand, and Israel but differing, at least in the degree of concern, from most of the world.

For a long time, Europeans were considered to be the only desirable migrants, and in the past, some important governmental actions were taken to preserve this policy. Although Asian immigration has increased lately, the racial question is still a serious concern in regard to immigration.

In terms of volume, immigration over the past quarter of a century has contributed as much as natural increase to national population growth. There has, however, always been some agreement about the desirability of raising the birth rate and some hope that family and social welfare measures would help to achieve this end. But Australia, like other English-speaking countries, has asumed that the state cannot intrude too far into personal lives, and there has been little attempt to make the practice of contraception more difficult. Indeed, any attempt by governments to increase population by making it more difficult for parents to achieve their desired family size would undoubtedly have aroused large-scale opposition in the electorate even from many of those who favor high rates of national growth. Australian governments, however, have been cautious about promoting family planning because of uncertainty about the reaction of the politically important Catholic minority (until recently, largely Irish in origin), but the recent actions of the new federal government suggest that a more positive approach will be followed in the future, both with regard to technical assistance abroad and the provision of family planning services at home.

At present, the population continues its natural growth rate of about 1 percent a year. Whether Australia will soon join the downward trend in fertility now evident in the United States and in many European countries is still a matter of speculation. The achievement of zero levels of natural growth without govenmental intervention may still become a reality, which is, of course, an admission that we know little about people's reactions to their economic, social, and biological environment.

THE DEMOGRAPHIC SETTING

In terms of European settlement, Australia must be considered still a very young country, with a history that covers only 185 years. A vast continent covering almost 2,600,000 square kilometers (3 million square miles), with a great part of it arid and unfit for human settlement, yet possessing great riches in its fertile crescent and great natural resources in much of its arid interior as well as on its continental shelf, Australia may well appear to be one of the world's "undeveloped" countries in terms of the size of its population, which is only 13 million people [1].

¶ IMMIGRATION

Nevertheless, in terms of average annual rates, growth to this number in 185 years implies a very high figure indeed. However, population growth did not receive its first major fillip until the great Gold Rushes of the 1850s into the colony of Victoria. These rushes subsequently spilled new settlers into other colonies through internal migration as the gold fields were worked out, leaving Australia as a whole with some 400,000 inhabitants by 1855. Since then, growth has continued at a high average rate, but the average conceals a number of great waves associated, first, with immigration and, second, with an example of the complete cycle of the

Western type of demographic transition, moving from relatively high fertility of the nineteenth century to the typical "developed" small family of the present day, with completed family size of about 2.5 to 2.8 children for each ever-married woman.

After the Gold Rushes of the 1850s, immigration flowed at a high rate until the 1880s, with assistance of the colonial governments from the revenues from land sales, along essentially Wakefield principles. Passage and settlement assistance was the price Australia had to pay because of its great distances from immigrant markets, if it was to compete with the much cheaper passages from Europe to other immigrant countries, particularly in North America. Immigration ceased after 1890, because of the severe economic recession in all the colonies, and revived in a sudden burst again after 1908, just before World War I. The war stopped the flow, but it revived after 1920, again primed by assisted passages for British settlers, along lines similar to the assisted schemes of the colonies in the nineteenth century. By this stage, immigration was controlled by the federal Commonwealth, which had been established in 1901. A net gain of approximately 312,000 people was attained from this immigration in the 1920s, but the whole process was again brought to an end with the onset of the Great Depression of the 1930s [2]. Immigration was not to revive until after World War II, when Australia entered upon the most intensive program of immigration in its whole history, a program that continued virtually without change of basic principles until the end of the long Liberal-Country party's rule in 1972. The main difference between this postwar scheme and all earlier policies was the degree of passage assistance given to non-British as well as British settlers.

¶ NATURAL INCREASE

With regard to the other element of growth—natural increase—Australia's patterns of fertility and mortality followed directly those of the countries from which most of its people originated, that is, with a completed family size per ever-married woman of about 5.5 children until approximately 1880, accompanied by birth rates that were between about 35 and 38 per 1,000. The first great change in fertility patterns began to occur in the 1880s; since then, fertility has followed a fairly steady downward course until the outbreak of World War II, with a sharp dip (as in many other countries) during the economic depression of the 1930s. According to Australian censuses between 1947 and 1966, the average family size of ever-married women who had reached age 45–49 at the date of each census varied between 2.43 and 2.77 children. There was a sharp lift in fertility immediately after World War II, associated with birth rates of about 22 per 1,000, compared with rates of 17 and 18 per 1,000 before the war. While this increase was associated with some rise in family size of married women, a substantial part of this increase in crude birth rates arose from the remarkable change in marriage patterns that appeared in Australia in the postwar years, as it did in the United States of America and in many northwestern European countries. The proportion of women aged 20–24 who were ever-married rose from an average of about 32 percent in prewar years to about 48 percent by 1947 and 60 percent by 1961. The pattern appears to have remained relatively constant since then, with about 95 percent of women married by the age of forty years [3].

The age composition of Australia since 1947 has been favorable to a

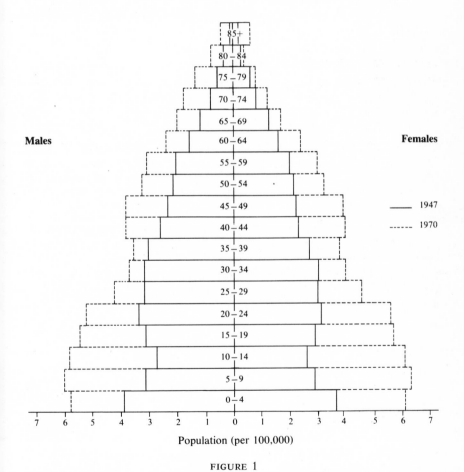

Population (per 100,000)

FIGURE 1

**Population Structure and Increase, Australia, 1947 and 1970
(per 100,000)**

relatively high rate of natural increase, which has averaged between about 1.0 percent and 1.2 percent ever since the end of World War II. Since then, Australia's age composition has consistently shown a relatively large number of young people of marriageable and childbearing age (Figure 1). Whereas many countries of northwestern Europe experienced great deficits in these age groups after 1946 (a direct effect of the decline in birth rates during the 1930s), Australia has supplemented these "deficit cohorts" through its postwar immigration program, which brought in a relatively high proportion of people in the younger working-age groups between about twenty-one and thirty-four years (Figure 2). Since approximately 1960, these young immigrants have been supplemented by the high numbers of children born in the postwar "baby boom," and consequently, Australia is experiencing a birth rate still around 20 per 1,000, even though age-specific birth rates have fallen considerably since 1961. This impetus to growth, therefore, is primarily a function of age composition, although the net reproduction rate of Australia is still relatively high compared with either the United States or most northwestern European countries [4].

Since 1947, the Australian population has grown steadily at a rate of approximately 2 percent a year, from both natural increase and immigration, from a base of 7.6 million in 1947 to approximately 13 million people at the end of 1972. Immigrants and their children born in Australia have accounted for some 54 percent of this growth, with the balance coming from natural increase [5].

The relationship of policy measures in Australia to the demographic patterns may best be considered in three broad time spans: the first until about 1960, which was the year in which postwar growth rates reached their peak; development between 1961 and 1972, a period that closed with traditional policies increasingly subject to critical appraisals; and the changes introduced by the fall of the Liberal-Country party government in December 1972 and the inauguration of the Whitlam Labor government.

POPULATION POLICY TO 1960

¶ ASSISTED PASSAGE SCHEMES
Until 1901, the primary interest of the governments of the separate colonies was with the stimulation of the immigration programs when economic circumstances were favorable and the abandonment of assisted passage schemes when circumstances were unfavorable. On the whole, the pressure for positive action to step up the flow of immigration to supplement the level that might come from natural pull factors was from the employers

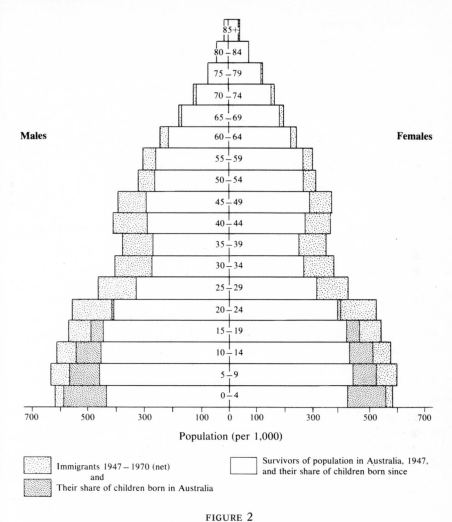

FIGURE 2

Impact of Immigration (1947–1970) on the Age Structure
of the Population, Australia, Mid-1970 (per 1,000)

of labor. In the nineteenth century, the demand for assisted immigration was primarily for rural workers, single men, and female domestics. With the increasing industrialization of Australia since 1901, when the new federal government assumed responsibilities for the recruitment and passage of settlers from overseas, the immigrants covered much more diverse ranges of occupations and were increasingly in demand in industry and manufacturing and particularly in the labor-intensive industries associated with the development of new resources, such as mining, iron and steel development, building and construction, and transportation. Under federation, the central government provided assistance from general revenues collected through taxation. Such assistance was limited before World War II almost wholly to migrants of British origin, but since then, assisted passage schemes have been negotiated with many European governments as well. Passage assistance in recent years has covered about 90 percent of the cost of the fares of transport to Australia. More than half the immigrants, particularly those from the United Kingdom, have come under assisted schemes. It is to be emphasized that this massive scheme of assisted immigration after World War II was initiated by a Labor government, but from then until 1972, the scheme was administered by a Liberal-Country party government, with virtually no change in its basic principles. However, until 1960 and even later, the immigration program had the support of all major political parties in Australia and, in this sense, was nonpolitical.

¶ EARLY CONCERN WITH THE DECLINING BIRTH RATE

Considerable concern had been expressed in Australia from time to time on other aspects of population. The concern was generally with the need to stimulate higher rates of growth and was motivated largely by the desire to give Australia the stature commensurate with its increasing sense of nationalism and, associated with this, its increasing sense of insecurity. A vast country with small concentrations of population around a few centers in the southeastern fertile crescent, it was not unnatural that some sense of insecurity in the face of the rapidly growing nations to the north should be expressed from time to time. The first extensive inquiry into these issues occurred with the establishment in 1903 of a Royal Commission of the Legislative Assembly of the state of New South Wales, which was created to examine the "decline of the birth rate" and "the mortality of infants" in that state. It presented its report in 1904, and this voluminous document stands as the first public inquiry of its kind in any English-speaking country. The report indicated grave concern about the decline in the birth rate since 1881 and also about the relatively slow rate of growth of the Australian population in relation to the vast numbers of peoples lying to its north. As one of the chief architects, Timothy Coghlan, the New South Wales government statist, wrote in 1903:

Large as is the area of the Australian continent, it is impossible that the people will ever become truly great under the conditions affecting population increase which now obtain. . . . The problem of the fall of the birth rate, is, therefore, a national one of overwhelming importance to the Australian people, and on its satisfactory solution will depend whether this country is ever to take its place amongst the great nations of the world [6, p. 69].

The commissioners all took much the same view and considered that the decline of births from rates in the high 30s into the 20s, and a clear indication of a decrease in family size which was associated with this change, were due to undesirable changes in the moral climate of the nation. They assessed the "true" reasons for this decline as:

(1) An unwillingness to submit to the strain and worry of children.
(2) A dislike of the interference with pleasure and comfort involved in child-bearing and childrearing.
(3) A desire to avoid the actual physical discomfort of gestation, parturition, and lactation.
(4) A love of luxury and of social pleasures, which (they considered) was increasing [7].

However, no legislative action of any significance followed the findings of the Royal Commission, and with the recurrence of expanding immigration after 1908, some of the earlier fears seemed to be vanishing. In addition, the war diverted attention after 1914 to other matters.

¶ THE PROMOTION OF IMMIGRATION
The next phase associated with population issues arose from the findings of the Dominions' Royal Commission of the United Kingdom Parliament, which issued its final report in 1917, with recommendations for a program of immigration from the mother country to the outlying dominions with the object of redistributing the "white" population of the empire to give better balance between the location of its peoples and its resources. The report had the enthusiastic support of Winston Churchill and was issued as a clarion call to the dominions for action to implement its proposals. In fact, the only government that entered into any substantial agreement with the United Kingdom in the field of immigration was that of Australia. For the next ten years, governmental concern was primarily with the promotion of immigration and not with the level of natural increase, and on the whole, the population was growing at a rate of about 1.8 percent a year, which seemed to be commensurate with the capacity of the economic organization to absorb growth.

During the 1920s, there was considerable speculation about Australia's ultimate carrying capacity and optimum size. One estimate went as high as 480 million and another as low as 15 million, but the most commonly accepted figures were those put forward by geographers, particularly by T. Griffith Taylor, of about 60 million [8]. The various estimates all claimed to be "scientific" and were based on such factors as rainfall, soil types, and similar comparisons with Europe and the United States. Officially, however, no serious attention was given to the question of the optimum, which, whatever its assessed figure, was felt to be far enough in the future to require no immediate action; and in any case, population growth seemed to be moving along in the 1920s at a sufficient pace without any further policy measures. The completed family size of those women finishing their reproductive lives around the time of the 1921 census still exceeded four children, and immigrants were flowing into the country at levels between 40,000 and 45,000 a year.

An entirely new situation arose as birth rates fell to 17 and below with the onset of the economic depression, and the concern tended to be heightened by popular interpretations of the new "magic index" of the net reproduction rate. When it was shown that this index was falling below unity, increasing concern again was expressed, both officially and unofficially by those who had the welfare of the nation at heart.

¶ CONCERN WITH POPULATION GROWTH

The Australian situation, as seen through the application of the net reproduction rate, was illustrated in two significant publications. S. H. Wolstenholme, a young Sydney economist, published an article in the *Economic Record* in 1936 on the subject of "The Future of the Australian Population." His diagnosis indicated that the population was unlikely ever to reach 8 million. The second publication was the Report of the Eighteenth Session of the National Health and Medical Research Council in 1944, which was based on a comprehensive analysis on trends in marriage, fertility, mortality, and immigration, and which provided a statement on both the aims and possible techniques of a population policy for Australia. This inquiry was perceptive enough to note that a substantial part of the rise in birth rates between 1939 and 1943 was due to the sharp increase in portions of persons marrying and applying age-specific fertility rates to a trend in the fertility of marriage. Nevertheless, it did not predict the revolutionary change in marriage patterns that was to occur after the war. After making reasonable allowance for some further increase in the proportions of persons marrying and applying age-specific fertility rates to a projected population, including a flow of immigration, the report still concluded that the Australian population was not likely to reach 9 million [9].

Although the 1944 report suggested that positive steps should be taken to stimulate fertility, no significant legislative action was taken by the government along the lines recommended. At this time, there was some general interest in the whole field of family policy in terms of social services that would provide a measure of both social and economic justice to the more fertile. Much of the thinking in these directions in Australia had roots in the principle of a fair wage for the average family, which became the foundation of wage adjustment in Australia from the 1920s. In the 1944 report, the National Health and Medical Research Council had suggested that assistance to young couples in establishing homes was desirable because it would, among other things, encourage earlier marriages, thus giving a better prospect for additional births. These discussions were, in fact, reviving many ideas that had been raised in other quarters as far back as the mid-1920s.

Mr. Justice Piddington, writing in 1921 [10], argued against the principle of penalizing the unmarried through high taxation and suggested that marriage endowments would be both expensive and difficult to administer. He argued that it would be preferable to pay both single and married men the same wage for the same work, so that the former should have some opportunity to meet their potential needs and to save for marriage. In the end, the principle of child endowment was adopted in Australia by the federal government in 1942, but this was viewed almost wholly as a matter of social justice and not as a measure to encourage larger families. Quoting Piddington again, he had argued that what was wanted (in 1921) was "not the day of the child" but "strict and even-handed plain justice which would recognize the right of children to be maintained from industry, and which would enable the mother as society's trustee for nature and education to discharge the duties of her trust." Mr. Justice Piddington was pleading for the acceptance of the theory of a living wage "based on the rights of distribution, not on the services in production." Further, he also saw endowments as a means of lowering infant mortality and reviving the downward trend of the birth rate, but this last matter was incidental to the main purpose of his proposals.

The principle of child endowments, which was set in 1946 at 7 shillings, 6 pence[1] per week for each child after the first, has been followed in Australia ever since, with moderate upward adjustments as the value of money has declined and now with a higher rate for third and subsequent births than for first and second births. But the endowments are still a minor part of the total family wage, and the primary choice in the arbitration of wages in Australia is for high basic wages rather than substantial endowments to meet needs according to the size of a family. Indeed, the unions have given very little attention to the matter of endowments.

¶ POLICIES AFTER WORLD WAR II

As World War II drew to a close, the question of the insecurity of Australia, a minute population near a teeming Asia, was again very much in

---

[1] As of January 1, 1973, this sum would be equal to approximately US$1.

the fore. Australia had almost been invaded by an Asian power: Japanese planes had bombed towns in Australia's Northern Territory; Japanese submarines had entered Sydney harbor; and Australians had died in New Guinea in some of the bitterest fighting of the war, holding at bay the aggressive intentions of an Asian power. It was recognized that, but for American support, Australia would almost certainly have been invaded.

In this climate, it was not surprising that there was strong support at the end of the war for measures that would rapidly increase Australia's population. Since the country had barely escaped invasion from an Asian power of great numbers as well as of great industrial strength, it was also hardly surprising that the second objective should be to seek that population increase from non-Asian sources, thereby perpetuating the restrictive aspects of immigration that had effectively prevented any extensive immigration of Asians to Australia for almost a century. Immigration from European sources was seen as the cornerstone of the new policy, but its chief architect, A. A. Calwell, Australia's first Minister of Immigration, also thought that endeavors should be made to sustain natural increase. In the end, the objectives stated by the Labor government aimed at sustaining national growth at the annual level of 2 percent, half of this coming from natural increase and half from immigration. This target remained the basis of policy to the end of the 1960s, and as the postwar baby boom sustained natural increase beyond the 1-percent target, it was not felt necessary to take any action through "pronatalist" legislation. Thus, all efforts were concentrated on the immigration policy, which had two distinct aspects: the restriction of persons of Asian birth and descent; and the vigorous search for new settlers in the United Kingdom and widely throughout Europe with extensive passage assistance to British immigrants and the extension of assisted agreements on a bilateral basis with European governments. The first great flood of immigrants of non-British origin were, however, to be some 200,000 of Europe's displaced persons.

EVENTS SINCE 1960

In 1961, Australia experienced a short economic recession that was associated with a temporary decline in the number of immigrants and also with a sharp fall in birth rates, which dropped from about 22 to approximately 18 per 1,000. This occasioned concern in the federal Parliament among some members, particularly those of the Catholic faith, that the nation might again be on the slope toward decline that had been experienced in the 1930s. There were some proposals for graduating endowments along the lines of the French *code de la famille* in order to stimulate third and later births. However, the arguments prevailed to the effect that the decline in births was really a return to the situation around the mid-1950s and was the end of the baby boom, which had brought on a great crop of first and second births, rather than the decline that had been predicted in the 1930s. Immigration also began to increase from the mid-1960s and rose to the highest peak ever in 1969 and 1970, with a net gain in the latter year of about 129,000 new settlers. At the same time, the birth rate began to climb back from 18 to 20 per 1,000 by 1970 which, although brought about primarily by changes in age structure, tended to allay fears about decline. A new note was, however, introduced around 1968, when it became apparent that major changes were occurring in population structure and when it was also realized that the heavy inflow of immigrants was rapidly changing the annual increment to the nation's work force. Throughout the 1940s and 1950s, the annual increment was about 75,000 a year, giving the work force a growth rate of about 1.8 percent a year, which was still lower than the total growth rate of the population of something over 2 percent [11]. As the baby boom cohorts of the immediate postwar years began to flow into the work force, the annual increment started to catch up with that of total population growth. By the mid-1960s, the annual national growth of the work force was running at about 125,000, and between 1966 and 1970, the increase averaged approximately 148,000, or twice the level of the 1950s. This demographic change was accompanied by some tightening in the economic situation following the relatively depressed state of the wool market, which was still Australia's greatest source of external earnings, and also by some indications that there was increasing competition for jobs in many sectors of the economy. These pressures have become increasingly acute since 1970, and while unemployment is still at a remarkably low figure compared with other countries, the increase from about 1.3 percent of the work force to approximately 1.8 percent at the end of 1971 was sufficient to increase the intensity of concern with the pressure generated in the labor market by the additional inflow of immigrants.

Another aspect of concern expressed since 1968 relates to the popular subject of the environment. In Australia, as elsewhere in industrial countries, there has been growing concern with matters of pollution and environmental deterioration as a result of the development of new urban-based industries. The prospects of Sydney's (2.8 million) and Melbourne's (2.4 million) growing at over 2 percent a year, until they each reach populations of 5 million or more by the end of the century, have tended to encourage the view that immigration should be halted until an adequate policy of urban redevelopment and decentralization has been implemented.

In addition, there was renewed concern about the tendency of some migrant communities to settle in concentrated groups, in particular in the low-income congested areas of some of the major cities. To some extent, this concern was encouraged by a report of the National Institute of Economic and Social Research of the University of Melbourne to the effect that, among Australia's "poor" communities (as measured by a given income level), there was a higher proportion of immigrants than non-immigrants [12]. Certainly, not all immigrants are poor, but there was some evidence that a proportion of the inflow reaching Australia about 1970, particularly from southern and eastern Europe, contained immigrants with relatively low levels of occupational skills and education. There is also evidence that the concentration of these people in certain urban districts has been creating major language problems in education, particularly in the state schools that most of the immigrant children attend. It is also true that about three of every four immigrants have settled in the capital cities of each state, near which a great deal of the nation's industrial strength is located.

In the last two years of office, which ended in December 1972, the Liberal-Country party government had also reacted to these new elements in the population debate by creating inquiries to examine natural growth, urbanization, distribution, and immigration. The first of these inquiries—a longitudinal study of a sample of 10,000 recently arrived migrants—is examining the problems of settlement in Australia, particularly during the first and second years of settlement. This study is being conducted by the Department of Immigration.

The second study, also related directly to immigration, is based on the increasing concern expressed among economists, members of Parliament, and trade union leaders to the effect that the current levels of immigration may have been major factors in sustaining the cost-price inflationary spiral in the Australian economy. Consequently, the government commissioned an inquiry into the costs and benefits of immigration to report the findings through the Immigration Planning Council to the Minister of Immigration.

On the wider aspects of desirable population size, distribution, and growth rates, the federal government has initiated a much more broadly based operation. At the end of 1970, an agreement was concluded between the Minister of Immigration and the Australian National University to permit the university to conduct a major inquiry into all aspects of population in Australia. The task, which is to take a period of three years, is being carried out under the supervision of the director of the Research School of Social Sciences in the Australian National University. Its terms of reference include a study of the situation in countries with which Australia has particularly close associations; the study of contemporary population theories, including the concept of zero population growth; and the economic, sociological, and ecological consequences implicit in the theories. The inquiry is also to examine the national growth potential of the population, the effect of variations in rates and patterns of that growth, the distribution of population with particular reference to the growth of major urban centers, the impact of technological advance on the use of available resources, and the distribution of population.

Finally, almost the last act of the Liberal-Country party government was the creation of a National Urban and Regional Development Authority to examine the nature of metropolitan concentration and to explore ways of containing metropolitan growth through decentralization, through the selection of new urban growth centers and through the encouragement of settlement in a selection of existing "country towns."

This brief historical review emphasizes the point that concern with population growth in Australia traditionally has been primarily with the lack of adequate growth to meet both the economic development and the stature of the country as a new and developing nation. Policies to encourage growth have related primarily to immigration. Twice—at the turn of the century and in the 1940s—there has been official concern with the decline in the rate of natural increase, but this concern has not been followed by policy measures designed to overcome the problems. Nor has immigration always been accepted as desirable. Immigrants have been taken in great gulps, with peaks at the times when economic conditions were good and with long periods of little immigration when economic conditions were bad. Examples of the latter were the periods from 1891 to 1908, and again from 1929 to the end of World War II.

Traditionally, the expansionists have been the employers of labor, and the sections of the population who have tended to be critical of immigration generally have been organized labor. However, the remarkable aspect of the postwar situation was the support over a period of about twenty-five years of both labor and nonlabor for both the postwar immigration program and, in general, population growth. As emphasized above, it has only been since about 1968 that the whole basis of the immigration program has been criticized, and this criticism is still, by no means, universal [13]. The recent critics have tended to be some of the intellectuals, some of the younger sections of the community, and again, representatives of labor at a time when the employment market became increasingly competitive. In general, employers and particularly the employers of labor in minerals, iron and steel, and construction and transportation still wish to see the immigration program carried on, although many would admit that some restraint is desirable at the moment. Few, however, want the program stopped. There is a widespread realization from past history that complete cessation of immigration and a complete scrapping of the whole machinery of the immigration program would create a situation where recovery of immigration would be extremely difficult and require a whole new structuring of policy. Toward the end of the term of office, the Liberal-Country government had reacted to these new trends in public thinking by lowering the official target of settler arrivals from 170,000 a year to 130,000; and since it assumed office at the close of 1972, the new Labor government has reduced that target further to 110,000, with the emphasis on "chain migration" arising from the inflow of immigrants nominated by families, relatives, and employers, rather than a deliberate policy of "search and selection." However, it is to be noted that the emphasis of the Labor party so far is not on the cessation of migration but on lowering the total numbers admitted to the country. The present target of 110,000 new settler arrivals would yield a net gain of some 65,000 to 70,000 after allowing for "permanent departures."

Therefore, in the major political parties, caution and restraint are the order of the day, not an attitude of no migration or zero population growth. The zero populationists are an organized movement, but they are a small minority. They win some support as a result of growing concern with the sprawling urban centers, particularly of Sydney and Melbourne, and with the environmental issues associated with population growth. An examination of age-specific fertility rates in Australia suggests that the actual level of fertility is moving downward, not upward. A continuation of this downward trend would bring fertility in Australia to replacement level within a generation, but the present age structure would make continued population growth inevitable for a considerable period after this. The zero populationists realize this, so again there is little support from their quarter for the notion of halting population growth at the current figure of 13 million: An ultimate stationary figure of 17 or 18 million is probably accepted by most of them.

While political and social pressure groups have been active, it should not be assumed that the populace at large is motivated by sophisticated knowledge and theories. The population problem as a global issue has not received very wide general publicity in Australia. Questions about such matters, administered to a Melbourne sample in a survey recently conducted by the Department of Demography of the Australian National University, suggest that the conceptions of the mass of the people about the population issue are, in fact, fairly rudimentary. This is true of their knowledge of the size and growth rates of populations and of their knowledge about the precise population of Australia, the size of the cities, and the nature and level of the flow of immigration. Major surveys sponsored by a private enterprise organization in the capital cities in 1971 also suggested that, among the people as a whole, the traditional attitude toward immigrants seems to be retained, with a clear first priority in their minds to British and northwest Europeans as desirable settlers and with southern and eastern European settlers lower on their scale of values. In general, Asian immigrants still appear to be the least favorably considered. This conclusion seems to confirm the stereotype that has applied for many years in Australia; yet, there is little doubt that the opinions concerning immigrants have changed a great deal among the more educated classes, particularly within the universities, among the leaders of many of the churches, and in similar circles. The more liberal attitude is especially marked in the advocacy for a more generous attitude toward the admission of Asian settlers. The governmental response to such criticism is that Asians, since 1957, have been able to get naturalization on the same basis as any other settlers and that they are admitted in increasing numbers to settle in Australia, with an annual level over 3,000 at present. However, this does not meet one of the major criticisms to the effect that the government provides passage assistance only to non-Asian immigrants. It is felt by many that this scheme implies a racial bias in the immigration program and that this bias should be removed by giving financial assistance to Asians who are needed for the labor force, in the same manner as it is given to those from European countries.

¶ THE PRACTICE OF BIRTH CONTROL
On the other aspect of population, namely, growth by natural increase, the pattern of fertility in Australia suggests that a very high proportion of couples of whatever occupational status or religion have practiced for a considerable time, and still do practice fairly effectively, some form of birth control. This is apparent in the marked decline in this century in both Catholic and non-Catholic fertility and in the narrowing of the differential between different occupational and educational classes. It appears that the Catholic section of Australia, which comprises about 24 percent of the total population, has moved through the phases of the demographic cycle from high to controlled fertility in much the same fashion and with much the same timing as the non-Catholic majority [14]. Although postwar immigration brought a large flow of European Catholics to Australia, Catholicism still has a substantial Irish base, stemming from nineteenth-century immigration, and as such, is extremely conservative with regard to such matters as birth control. To say that the official attitude of the Catholic church in Australia is almost to the right of Rome is probably no exaggeration. Nevertheless, it is clear here, as in other countries, that a high proportion of those who profess the Catholic faith must, in fact, act in ways other than those dictated by the church. On the other hand, the facts that contraceptive pills can only be purchased with the production of a certificate supplied by a qualified medical doctor and that, until 1973, contraceptives were subject to a very considerable sales tax revealed vestigial remains of the formal position of the Catholic church with regard

to those who wield and exercise the decision-making processes in government.

While contraceptives have long been available through registered pharmacists and could be prescribed by registered medical practitioners, their advertisement has generally been illegal. The matter is usually in the hands of the states of the Commonwealth. West Australia, Victoria, and Tasmania prohibit the sale or distribution of contraceptives in any public place or from house to house, and in the Australian Capital Territory and the Northern Territory, their sale is prohibited by any person other than a registered pharmacist. In Queensland, there is a restriction on selling contraceptives by automatic vending machine. All states and territories except South Australia and Queensland have specific legislative restrictions on the advertising of contraceptives, and in Queensland, the matter is covered by legislation relating to "indecent advertisements." Most of the present legislation of the states was enacted between 1931 and 1946 and arose out of the desire to end the practice of hawking and exhibiting contraceptives and of the gratuitous dissemination of literature advertising birth control methods. In practice, however, there have been very few prosecutions for breaches of these prohibitions, and in indirect ways, there has remained a limited amount of discreet advertising of these articles throughout Australia [15].

Yet, it is surely a matter of very considerable sociological interest that, despite the very conservative views of the Church of Rome, despite the high proportion of the population that recorded itself at censuses as of that faith, and despite the lack of any policy designed to assist family planning and spread contraceptive knowledge, Australian women must be counted as efficient contraceptors. Even in the Great Depression of the 1930s, they managed to bring the birth rate down to 16 per 1,000 and brought the net reproduction rate to replacement level. Undoubtedly, the methods they used were very much those that were reported by the Royal Commission on Population in the United Kingdom in 1949, that is, coitus interruptus and mechanical means, particularly the condom. It is also to be noted that statistics which have been compiled concerning the sale and use of the contraceptive pill between about 1961 and 1968 suggest that the highest users, when measured as a ratio of the population concerned—that is, married women—were to be found in Australia and New Zealand. The Australian ratio exceeded that of the United States and the United Kingdom. On the basis of this evidence, Australian women appear to be among the most efficient contraceptors in the world, yet there is probably no doubt that unwanted pregnancies still form a considerable part of the children born, and if this is as high as 20 percent, as has been suggested for the United States, then a policy of freely available family planning clinics might well reduce the birth rate in Australia to, or even below, replacement level. However, no thorough study has been made of the subject of unwanted pregnancies, although considerable light will be thrown on this by the Australian National University survey recently conducted in Melbourne.

The lack of a public policy to assist family planning—with, indeed, downright opposition to the idea from some lay and religious quarters—might tempt one to draw the conclusion that unwanted pregnancies have been kept in control by illicit methods and, particularly, by abortion. Here again the law has been, and in all but one state still is, extremely conservative. Laws that relate to abortion are state, not federal, matters, except with regard to the territories administered by the federal government. Basically, the laws of the states are in broad conformity with the position in the United Kingdom before the major abortion reform law of 1967. This means, in effect, that abortion is a criminal offense, in all circumstances where it is performed by a person other than a registered medical practitioner and in a registered hospital, and can only be performed by such a medical practitioner where it is deemed necessary "to preserve the life of the mother." These are the crucial words, and while preservation of life has been interpreted to cover situations where the continuance of pregnancy will render the mother physically or mentally disturbed, the grounds for permitting abortion remain very narrowly defined.

¶ ABORTION
The issue of abortion came very much into public attention as a result of a prolonged legal case in Melbourne in 1970 concerning charges against illicit abortionists. This case was concerned with abortion in its moral aspects rather than as a method for population control, and the legal case was concerned with whether or not the rather strict codes of Victoria had been breached. It was not concerned with abortion law reform as such. However, the case did raise interest throughout Australia. Almost simultaneously, the state of South Australia amended its laws relating to abortion in the Criminal Law Consolidation Amendment Act of 1969. By this act, which was modeled on the English act of 1967, "pregnancy may be terminated by a legally qualified medical practitioner in a case where he and one other qualified legal practitioner are of the opinion that the continuance of the pregnancy would involve greater risk to the life of the pregnant woman or greater risk of injury to the physical or mental health of the pregnant woman than if the pregnancy were terminated." Abortion also may be performed on the basis of similar medical opinion where it is deemed that the child to be born "would suffer from such physical or mental abnormalities as to be seriously handicapped." So far no other

state has formally moved toward the position taken by South Australia.[2]

Once the public interest was aroused on the subject of abortion, attention was not unnaturally given to the relationship between abortion and its contraceptive use in preventing unwanted pregnancies. A number of women's movements, and particularly those classified as women's liberationists, did come out in favor of "abortion on request," but this movement does not seem to have brought very active support from women's movements in general. The attitude of women concerning abortion as a method of preventing unwanted pregnancies has not been thoroughly investigated in Australia, but preliminary results from a survey sample of Melbourne women, and also from the pretest of that survey in a country town, do suggest that liberalization of abortion would meet with general approval. Although there might be some opposition to taking liberalization as far as abortion on request, some liberalization of existing laws, along the lines of those now operating in South Australia, would almost certainly receive majority support.

The publicity given to abortion has, however, tended to raise the wider issue of the effectiveness of facilities for planning families and the extent to which such facilities can enable parents to restrict the numbers of children to the levels actually desired. The situation is that family planning information is supplied mainly through a woman's contact with the medical profession, and while the Australian branch of the International Planned Parenthood Federation advocates an extension of family planning clinics to reach the whole population, there was little movement until 1972 to make such a situation a reality.

REACTIONS OF GOVERNMENT

The questioning of the growth syndrome since about 1970 directed increasing attention to the kinds of policy measures required to reduce or prevent growth. In the field of immigration, the answer was obvious: Reduce the level or eliminate altogether the inflow of new settlers. But with regard to

[2] In May 1973, since this article was prepared, a Labor member of the federal House of Representatives introduced a private member's bill proposing an amendment to the laws applying in the Australian Capital Territory to permit abortion on request to the end of the third month of pregnancy and liberalizing the grounds of abortion thereafter until approximately the end of the sixth month. The political parties allowed a "free vote" on the matter. The campaign assumed almost national dimensions and was marked by a vigorous antiabortion stand by the Roman Catholic church and considerable opposition to the bill from many other lay organizations. The bill was defeated in the House of Representatives by a 4 to 1 majority. Despite this defeat, however, there remains little doubt that, among the nation at large, a majority do consider that some reform of existing laws is desirable.

natural increase, the matter was more complex. The zero populationists tended to find a solution by the simple advocacy of "two children per family," but the achievement of this objective was quite another matter.

The whole discussion tended to become linked with the wider social and moral aspects of freedom of choice by couples, incentive systems enforced by governments against children, and particularly, the avoidance of unwanted or unplanned births by liberalizing the abortion laws. It was this last factor that has received the most attention in public discussion, but much of the concern has been motivated by moral issues rather than demographic goals.

The Liberal-Country party government showed little immediate interest in the population debate beyond cutting the immigration targets, but it did foreshadow a wider long-term interest by creating the three inquiries mentioned earlier. Its activities were cut short by defeat in the national elections of December 1972.

In terms of more general social aspects of governmental policy, there was relatively little concern until 1972 with the demographic basis of such policy. For example, there has been considerable concern with the provision of adequate housing for young people, including the provision of loans to enable young married couples to purchase their houses. However, these loans have never been considered against the very great increase in the numbers of young people who marry; both as a result of the demographic bulge factors arising from the postwar baby boom and the tremendous change in the age at marriage and the proportion of young people who marry, which has raised the proportion of ever-married women of ages 20–24 to about 60 percent in recent years compared with only about 31 percent or 32 percent in the years leading to World War II. Family welfare has been dealt with largely by the provision of child allowances in the manner discussed earlier in this chapter. Maternity benefits also have been long established in Australia, being introduced in 1912 in New South Wales and in 1942 for the whole of Australia under the Menzies government; but again, these benefits have never been considered incentives to increase the size of the family so much as the necessary and just part of social service policies in the broader sense. It can be said, therefore, that, by and large, there have been few social policies in Australia that can be called "population" policies.

In the international field, governmental action and policy is the function of the federal government. The state's interests stop strictly at internal matters. It cannot be said that Australia has ever been in the forefront of international policy with regard to population issues; the government has twice served on the Population Commission of the United Nations—first in 1948 and 1949 and on the second occasion between 1965 and 1969.

The government has also joined with other members of the General Assembly of the United Nations in supporting the principle of technical assistance in the field of population on request. The government also supported the establishment of a population division in the ECAFE[3] organization at its conference held in Canberra in 1968. But it was not until 1973 that the Australian government supported these principles with funds. However, the lack of positive action through United Nations channels should not be taken as a sign of complete inactivity. Grants, largely from overseas, have been employed for research in Australian institutions in the field of reproductive behavior and in other aspects of research that relate to methods of reducing population growth through controlled fertility. The Australian government has given technical aid grants in the population field, other than for family planning, and has favored bilateral assistance rather than contributions to general United Nations funds, possibly on the assumption that, by such methods, the funds provided from Australian sources can be directed into regions that are felt to be of particular concern to the Australian government. This is apparent, for example, in the granting of assistance to Malaysia for the preparation and taking of the 1961 census. It is also obvious in the fund set aside through the Department of Foreign Affairs for technical assistance in the field of population in Indonesia, an area now greatly significant in terms of Australia's external policy. So far, the difficulty has been to find the skilled manpower available to assist in the tasks known to be urgent and worthwhile. But it is of some significance that, at last, Australian teachers and research workers have made an appearance at universities in Indonesia, where they are helping with the provision of courses in demography as well as assisting in research projects. Another indication of Australia's growing concern with the problem of population is seen in the government's support in 1967 for the regional conference of the International Union for the Scientific Study of Population, which was held in Sydney in November of that year.

Spasmodic though the interest was, it is, nevertheless, the case that population issues were more alive in the Australian community about 1970 than they had been for a considerable time before. The concern was probably not yet as deep as it was during the Great Depression of the 1930s, but its expression tended to take the opposite form. Whereas the concern of the 1930s was with lack of growth and the prospect of decline, much of the recent concern in Australia has been with the opposite problem of too rapid growth and the danger that, unless growth is curtailed, Australia will be facing the same problems as those facing, for example, the much larger,

[3] Economic Commission for Asia and the Far East.

more congested population of the United States. Much of the recent concern in Australia has appeared, in fact, to have been largely a reflection of the concern expressed in America and many of the congested countries of Europe. Contrasting with this, however, there are many who feel that Australia, still so recently settled, still so vast, must have many decades of development ahead of it. Against that there are those who point out that size should not be mistaken for major resources, particularly in the form of water and a soil that, over vast areas, is a mere topping over desert, which can be destroyed by the winds that blow across the continent. There is an awareness of the dustbowls that have been created by man's mismanagement; there is an awareness that some of the dams that have been built to serve man are tending to silt up and create other problems similar to those that have occurred in other countries. In short, there are those who say that Australia is environmentally a very vulnerable country that requires careful nursing by a limited population if that environment is not to be destroyed.

Precisely where the limits should be put to population in terms of such factors cannot be stated at the moment and may not be capable of statement without, at the same time, knowing the direction technology is to take, but some statement regarding these matters must remain one of the fundamental purposes of the inquiries referred to above.

Finally, there has been a growing awareness in Australia in recent years of the issues of population in Asian countries, although only a minority of people yet have any recognition of the extremely acute situation that has arisen in many of the countries to the north. The cry of "yellow peril" that was so prominent in the nineteenth century is no longer heard, and there is a feeling that numbers now have very little meaning in terms of power politics. In a sense, this may be true, but there is perhaps too great a tendency to feel that numbers have no relevance at all, whereas the truth may lie somewhere in between. With the international recognition of the People's Republic of China, the possible association between population and external relations may, in fact, take on a new meaning in Australia, but the precise impact of that recognition has not been felt by any public expression in policy terms.

Nevertheless, the Labor government is showing a more positive reaction to population issues than did its Liberal-Country party predecessor. One of its first actions was to make a grant of US$300,000 to the United Nations Fund for Population Activities (UNFPA). This was followed by a similar grant to the International Planned Parenthood Federation. In December 1972, it also abolished the sales tax on the contraceptive pill and is now taking steps to permit a prescription supply covering six months, as opposed to one month previously, thus further reducing costs to the consumers. However, pills still have to be prescribed by medical practitioners. The government has also taken steps to initiate a much more vigorous policy in the field of urban development, particularly with reference to major metropolitan areas. The National Urban and Regional Development Authority established in 1972 has been associated with a new Department of Urban and Regional Development. Already the Labor government, acting in coordination with the governments of the states of Victoria and New South Wales, has declared a major country town on the Murray River, on the border of both states, a new development area designed to grow to at least 160,000 persons. These signs all suggest the beginnings of a new and more active policy, both internally and externally, with regard to population, and although the government has also declared its support for adequate family planning services, the measures so far are commensurate with a policy of further development rather than the creation of a stationary state, demographically or economically.

Yet, it must be emphasized that the issues of population, whether Australian or global, still receive only spasmodic treatment in the mass media. News items occur in the press, on the radio, or on television only as some major event draws the population issue to the community's notice. The event may be some announcement from an overseas country, some statement by an official or scholar about immigration or urban congestion, or the report of a threat of famine from inadequate food production in Asia; and occasionally, these events are editorialized in a daily newspaper or commented on in a radio or television broadcast. By far, the most common subject of discussion is immigration. But it cannot be said that the population issue in general receives active and continuous attention and analysis by more than a very small minority of the Australian people. For most, it is extraneous to their daily and weekly affairs. Moreover, within university quarters in Australia, the population issue has not received any major attention by economists, sociologists, or historians, and formal instruction in the field of population has until quite recently been associated with only one of the universities, although now there are signs of considerable development in this regard. On the whole, however, the population issue is still an underdeveloped topic in this highly industrialized, sparsely peopled country.[4]

[4] An aspect of Australian society now of major public concern is the status and economic, social, and cultural situation of the Australian aboriginals, who number about 130,000; but the *population* aspect of the aboriginal "problem" has, so far, received little official attention. This aspect is to form a separate substudy of the present national population inquiry, and in addition, some significant scholarly studies of aboriginal demography have already appeared. See for example [16].

REFERENCES

1. For historical accounts, see P. D. Phillips and G. L. Wood (eds.). *The Peopling of Australia.* 1st series. Melbourne: Macmillan and Melbourne University Press, 1928. And W. D. Forsyth. *The Myth of Open Spaces.* Melbourne: Melbourne University Press, 1942.

2. W. D. Borrie. *Population Trends and Policies.* Sydney: Australian Publishing Company, 1948. And W. D. Borrie. *Immigration: Australia's Problems and Prospects.* Sydney: Angus and Robertson, 1949.

3. Elise F. Jones. "Fertility decline in Australia and New Zealand, 1861–1936." *Population Index*, vol. 37, no. 4 (1971): 301–338.

4. W. D. Borrie. "The recent and potential demographic dynamics of Australasia." In *Contemporary New Zealand* by K. W. Thomson and A. D. Trlin. Wellington: Hicks Smith and Sons, 1973.

5. C. A. Price (ed.). *Australian Immigration: A Bibliography and Digest.* No. 2. Canberra: Department of Demography, Australian National University, 1970.

6. T. A. Coghlan. *The Decline in the Birth Rate of New South Wales.* Sydney: Government Printer, 1903.

7. Legislative Assembly, New South Wales, Royal Commission on the Decline of the Birth Rate and on the Mortality of Infants in New South Wales. *Report*, vol. 1 (1904): 16–17.

8. See W. D. Forsyth [*1*].

9. National Health and Medical Research Council (of Australia). *Report of the Eighteenth Session*, 1944.

10. A. B. Piddington. *The Next Step: A Family Basic Income.* Melbourne: Macmillan, 1921 (reprinted 1925).

11. W. D. Borrie and Geraldine Spencer. *Australia's Population Structure and Growth.* Second edition. Melbourne: Committee for Economic Development of Australia, 1965.

12. R. F. Henderson, et al. *People in Poverty: A Melbourne Survey.* Melbourne: Cheshire, 1970.

13. Australian Institute of Political Science. *How Many Australians? Immigration and Growth*, J. Wilkes (ed.). Sydney: Angus and Robertson, 1971.

14. L. H. Day. "Fertility differentials among Catholics in Australia." *Milbank Memorial Fund Quarterly*, vol. 42, no. 2 (April 1964): part 1.

15. P. Whalley. "Laws Relating to Contraceptives in Australia." Canberra: Department of Demography, Australian National University, 1972. (Unpublished manuscript.)

16. L. Broom and F. Lancaster Jones. *A Blanket a Year.* Canberra: Australian National University Press, 1973.

CHAPTER 11

The Netherlands

Philip van Praag
Louis Lohlé-Tart

ABSTRACT

Until the 1960s, the Netherlands was the demographic anomaly of western Europe: The country, with the largest density in the world, had the highest natality and one of the lowest mortality rates in Europe.

Overcrowding is an important concern in political life. Among the measures being used to fight overpopulation and the unequal density are internal redistribution of population, territorial increase (by reclaiming land from the sea), and subsidized emigration. Nevertheless, during the 1960s, a policy of *immigration* was developed in order to cope with a shortage of unskilled manpower.

Other measures are being taken to help manage the demographic situation in the Netherlands. Contraception has recently been largely liberalized. Abortion, which is officially prohibited, is, in fact, openly practiced; its legal liberalization is expected and may soon occur. Because population problems are a serious concern to the Dutch people, the government in 1972 established a Royal Commission on Population Problems to study the situation and formulate a policy for future development.

INTRODUCTION

More than once, the Netherlands has been called "a demographic anomaly in northwestern Europe." [1] The country passed through the transitional process more rapidly than other industrial countries as far as mortality is concerned, thus achieving and maintaining a low mortality rate. Its transition was much slower with respect to fertility; the people retained highly natalist attitudes into the 1960s. Delayed industrialization and a strong religious and family life may wholly or partially explain these attitudes. The year 1964, when a rapid decrease in fertility began, however, marks a turning point. By then, the Netherlands was a modern industrialized country, with changed sociopsychological and less strong religious attitudes. The pill, although introduced during 1963–1964, is not the only and certainly not the most important factor explaining the changes in the fertility pattern.

Because of the wartime destruction and the postwar "baby boom," the government authorities after World War II were afraid of not being able to provide full employment and, as a safeguard, promoted in every way emigration to other continents. As a supplementary factor, they thought emigration would help to diminish the enormous scarcity of housing. The fear of overpopulation was shared by scholars and expressed in conferences dealing with the population problem. The suitability of the emigration policy was challenged in a report on "Emigration Policy and Employment" of the Center for Political Training in 1961. The ideas expressed in this report were shared by the "Emigration Council," and the government soon changed its policy. Meanwhile, full employment was attained in the mid-1950s; since then, thousands of foreign workers have been recruited.

In the 1960s, public opinion began to favor more deliberate family planning and birth limitation. The rapid increase in the standard of living, infrastructural problems (industrialization, urbanization, roads, spatial planning, secondary residences), better education, and changed ethics and attitudes may be the factors that made overcrowding more visible, particularly in the western parts of the country. Hidden behind an increasing crude birth rate in the late 1950s and early 1960s, the changed fertility and family patterns gradually became clearer. It was, therefore, inevitable that churches, political parties, and professional societies (doctors, family organizations, and others) considered the population problem and changed or even reversed the traditional natalist attitudes (about contraceptives and abortion). The measures resulting from these concerns will be discussed later.

At present, one cannot consider the various measures taken by the government as the outcome of these processes to be a consistent and coherent population policy. But still, we might say that together they are the beginning of such a policy. It is the work of the National Commission on Population Problems, established in 1972, to formulate the basic elements for a future population policy.

¶ MORTALITY RATES

Crude *mortality* decreased very rapidly from 24.3 per 1,000 in 1870 to 15.2 per 1,000 in 1901–1910 and 8.1 per 1,000 in 1965–1969. Since the beginning of the twentieth century, the Netherlands has had the lowest crude mortality rate in western Europe. As the country has a relatively young population, the crude mortality rate may have been influenced by the age structure. But child mortality (that is, deaths under age one year per 1,000 live births) in the period 1965–1969 was only 13.9 per 1,000 in the Netherlands in comparison with 19.2 per 1,000 in the United Kingdom, 20.9 per 1,000 in France, 23.1 per 1,000 in Belgium, and 33 per 1,000 in Italy; and the expectation of life at birth was 71.1 years for males and 75.9 years for females (exceeding almost all other countries). It seems, then, that low mortality is primarily the result of good health care.

¶ NATALITY RATES

Dutch *natality* rates always stood in the first rank in Europe, but recently decreased rapidly from 21.2 per 1,000 in 1958 to 17.2 per 1,000 in 1971 and 16.1 per 1,000 in 1972. The decrease went along with an advancement of both age at first marriage and the mean age of maternity and with a decrease of marital fertility; a general consensus seems to develop toward a number of two or three children. Though the decrease of these unities was highest in the Netherlands, the country still has both the highest marital fertility and the highest mean age at first marriage in comparison with comparable industrial countries.

As a consequence, natural increase fell very slowly from 1.51 percent in the beginning of this century to 1.14 percent in the 1960s, and migration taken into account, population growth never was lower than 1.22 percent (except during the crisis and war period). In absolute figures, the number of inhabitants increased from 5 million in 1897 to 10 million in 1949 and 13 million in 1970, population density increasing during the same period from 158 to 384 inhabitants per square kilometer, and—in the western part of the country—from 322 to 876.

Spatial problems are the very basis of the population problem in this country, whose economy, after 1945, passed rapidly from a mainly agricultural one into a highly industrial one. Besides industry and agriculture, a third area—services—is important economically. If the Netherlands now are highly industrialized, it must be noted that this third sector developed even more rapidly than the industrial one (Table 1). At present (as in the case of Belgium and Great Britain), more than 50 percent of the Dutch working population is occupied in the services sector.

TABLE 1.

Development of the Working Population in the Three Sectors
of the Economy, Netherlands, 1947, 1960, and 1971 (in percents)

Year	Agriculture	Industry	Services
1947	19.3	36.9	42.4
1960	10.7	42.4	44.6
1971	7.0	40.8	52.2

¶ LAND RECLAMATIONS

Dealing with spatial problems, it seems worthwhile to make some remarks on the Dutch land reclamations that began with the closing of the dam in the Zuiderzee (now IJsselmeer) and the draining of some parts of it, mainly for economic reasons. The very recent land reclamations resulting from the *Deltawerken* in the southwestern part (Zeeland), however, began only after the flood disaster on February 1, 1953, and these are predominantly caused by the need for land protection. With regard to the *Deltawerken* land reclamations, better transport communications and more possibilities for use in leisure activities (lakes in the neighborhood of Rotterdam) are secondary but, nevertheless, still of importance. As the first land reclamations (*inpolderingen*) were only finished after 1930 and important works are still being done, these figures give a good idea of present and expected land increase in the Netherlands' overall surface area:

1930: 32,060 km²
1971: 33,686 km²
2000: 34,360 km²

The figure projected for the year 2000 is based on a maximum plan for the Markerwaard (part of the IJsselmeer) and includes another small reclamation in the north of the country (part of the Lauwerszee). The total land increase then would be 7.2 percent of the surface in 1930. The new land is used for capital intensive farming and for leisure activities. In 1971, the total population of the IJsselmeerpolders amounted to 58,823 inhabitants. In 2000, it is projected to be about 400,000.

DISTRIBUTION OF THE POPULATION BY AGE, SEX, AND MARITAL STATUS

Figure 1 shows the population pyramid at five census dates, characteristic of the twentieth century. They are: the latest known situation before World

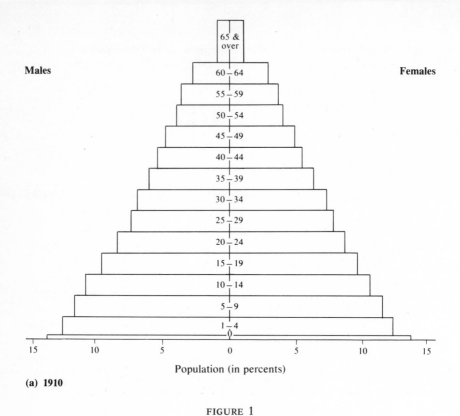

FIGURE 1

Age and Sex Structure of the Netherlands Population in Five Years
(percents calculated separately for each sex):
(a) 1910; (b) 1920; (c) 1930; (d) 1947; (e) 1960

Wars I and II, the situations immediately following the two wars, and finally, the structure of the population at the beginning of the 1960s. The age distribution of 1910 shows the classical young pyramid. The 1920 pyramid reflects a clear recovering from fertility losses during World War I, when there was a shortage of food and most young men were in military service. (As the Netherlands was able to maintain its neutrality, the number of human war losses are practically negligible.)

The 1947 pyramid shows the decreased fertility during the crises' disturbances, particularly severe between 1932 and 1937, and the fertility recuperation after 1945. After the "baby boom," natality remained at a high level (21 per 1,000 during the period 1955–1964) and then declined rapidly.

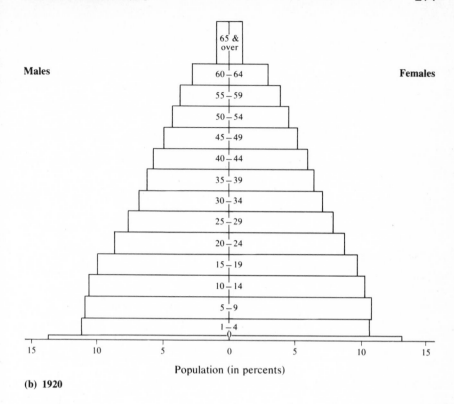

Males   Females

| 65 & over |
| 60 – 64 |
| 55 – 59 |
| 50 – 54 |
| 45 – 49 |
| 40 – 44 |
| 35 – 39 |
| 30 – 34 |
| 25 – 29 |
| 20 – 24 |
| 15 – 19 |
| 10 – 14 |
| 5 – 9 |
| 1 – 4 |
| 0 |

15   10   5   0   5   10   15

Population (in percents)

(b) 1920

At the end of 1970, 49.1 percent of all males (in comparison to 58.2 percent in 1930) and 44.1 percent of all females (56 percent in 1930) were single, the remainder being married, widowed, or divorced. In the age group 45–49 years, 93 percent of males and 91.8 percent of females were ever married, with 90.8 percent of men and 85.5 percent of women being presently married. More important, however, is the age structure and the resulting demographic burden (Table 2).

As a consequence of the aging of the population, the demographic burden of people aged sixty-five and over has increased and will continue to increase until 1980. The demographic burden of the ages 0–19, however, declined and this process too will continue [2]. The decline of the demographic burden is due mainly to its most important component: fertility. Besides the relatively low numbers of people aged 20–64 years in the total population, the participation of the active population in industrial life is low—the lowest in the European Economic Community (EEC)—and this is due mainly to the low participation of married women in the production processes. The low participation rate of these women may be explained by

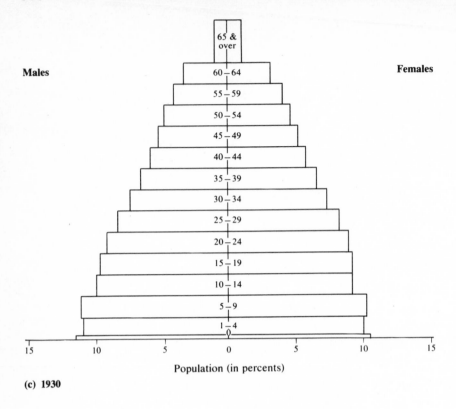

Males   **Females**

Population (in percents)

(c) 1930

TABLE 2.

Age Structure and Demographic Burden, Netherlands,
1960 and 1970 (in percents)

	Age Groups			
Year End	0–19 (1)	20–64 (2)	65+ (3)	Demographic Burden (1) + (3) in percent of (2)
1960	38.0	53.0	9.0	88.0
1970	35.7	54.1	10.2	84.8

religious attitudes and a strong tradition of family life. Important changes,
however, have been registered between 1960 and 1971, when male labor
force increased by 10 percent and the number of female workers by 38
percent. Among them, married female workers increased from 170,000 to
about 480,000.

There has been a similar change with regard to divorces. The divorce
rate increased from 2.2 per 100 couples in 1955–1964 to 3.3 in 1970 and

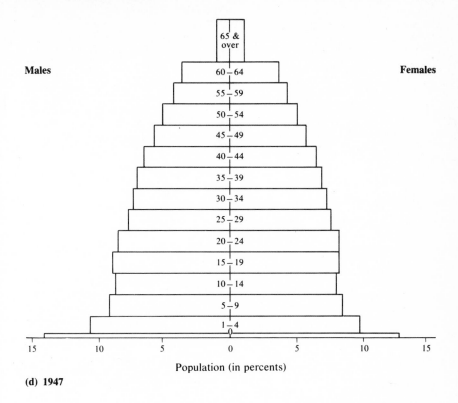

Population (in percents)

(d) 1947

3.6 in 1971; the number of children below twenty-one years of age affected by these divorces has doubled.

On October 1, 1971, marriage legislation was altered; since then, divorce is granted upon the joint request of the marriage partners if the request is based upon their joint conclusion that the marriage is lastingly disrupted. The new legislation, however, cannot have influenced the figures mentioned.

NUPTIALITY AND FERTILITY

The minimum legal age at marriage is sixteen years for females, and eighteen years for males. There are no financial allowances for marriage, nor are there special loans to young people. There were, however, especially between 1945 and 1965, indirect pressures encouraging early marriage. There has been, and in some regions there still exists, a severe shortage of housing, which made it virtually impossible to obtain a dwelling unless one was married and had children; even then, it was necessary to wait for a long time (sometimes for several years). Therefore, many young Dutch shortened their engagements and married quickly in order to have dwellings.

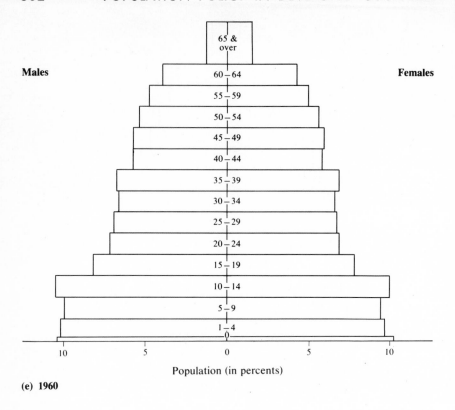

Males

Females

65 & over

60—64

55—59

50—54

45—49

40—44

35—39

30—34

25—29

20—24

15—19

10—14

5—9

1—4

10   5   0   5   10

Population (in percents)

(e) 1960

The government and a variety of administrative bodies made important efforts, and at present, the shortage of housing is no longer a problem except in large towns and some rural regions in western Holland. The solution, however, was reached by increasing the density of inhabitants. It should be noted that steps toward solving the housing problem were taken with the general social welfare in view, and the particular consequences on marriage were not considered.

Full employment and relatively high wages for young workers, together with a change in attitudes, have stimulated marriage at younger ages. The average age at first marriage was 25.6 for females and 28.4 for males in the period 1955–1964. In 1970, these figures were 23.9 and 26.3 [2, p. 18].

Since 1964, a marked turning point, fertility regularly decreased, as is shown in Table 3. The increasing figures shown for the first and second child do not affect this conclusion; they can be explained by the increase in the number of marriages contracted by the generation born after 1945 and by the advanced age at marriage.

The decrease in fertility—with the exception of 1969, when more second

TABLE 3.

Live Births by Birth Order, Netherlands, 1960–1972
(per 1,000 inhabitants)

Year	Total	First Live Birth	Subsequent Live Births			
			Second	Third	Fourth	Fifth+
1960	20.8	6.5	5.6	3.5	2.0	3.2
1961	21.3	6.7	5.8	3.6	2.1	3.1
1962	20.9	6.7	5.7	3.5	2.0	3.0
1963	20.9	6.8	5.8	3.5	2.0	2.8
1964	20.7	6.9	5.8	3.5	1.9	2.6
1965	19.9	7.0	5.7	3.3	1.7	2.2
1966	19.2	7.2	5.6	3.1	1.5	1.8
1967	18.9	7.4	5.7	2.9	1.4	1.5
1968	18.6	7.4	5.8	2.8	1.3	1.3
1969	19.2	7.5	6.2	3.0	1.3	1.2
1970	18.3	7.1	6.1	2.8	2.2	
1971	17.2	7.0	5.9	2.5	1.8	
1972	16.1	6.8	5.8	2.1	1.4	

SOURCE: See [3].

children were born of mothers aged 20–34 years—occurred in all birth orders and for mothers of all ages. Table 4 shows the decrease by the ages of mothers.[1]

When we take into account the big increase in the number of marriages during the 1960s, the rapid fertility decline becomes still more marked. It seems plausible that the interval between marriage and the birth of the first child has widened. However this may be, the extensive marriage cohorts of the postwar years will be replaced by much smaller generations.

The net reproduction rate decreased from 1.5 in 1960–1964 to 1.22 in 1970 and 1.12 in 1971.

Table 5 shows that the general fertility decline was not the same in all provinces. The decline was most rapid in the southern, predominantly Catholic provinces, still characterized by the highest fertility in 1960 (decreases of 23 percent and 25 percent). In the northern, predominantly Protestant provinces, with a relatively low fertility in 1960, the decline was much less than the national average figure (0.3 percent to 8.5 percent; national average 14.5 percent). The result has been an accelerated leveling of provincial differentials in fertility. Changed attitudes of the ecclesiastical authorities, industrialization of the southern provinces, and perhaps most

[1] For live births by birth order, see [3, Table 2 of the 1970 supplement].

TABLE 4.

Legitimate Births by Age of Mother, Netherlands, 1955–1970
(per 1,000 married women in each age)

| | Age (in years) | | | | | | | |
Year	Less than 20	20–24	25–29	30–34	35–39	40–44	45+	Total
1955–1964	531.6	323.1	266.5	178.7	103.5	38.9	3.5	168.7
1968	444.3	285.3	224.8	126.8	60.9	18.5	1.8	141.7
1969	441.9	284.7	229.5	127.3	55.1	17.6	1.5	144.0
1970	411.2	258.4	217.1	119.8	53.7	15.7	1.3	136.3

TABLE 5.

Marital Fertility in Some Provinces, Netherlands, 1959/1961, 1967
(legitimate live births per 1,000 married women under age 45)

Region	1959/1961	1967	Decrease (percent)
Northern provinces			
Groningen	149.2	148.7	0.3
Friesland	182.7	172.8	5.4
Drenthe	164.5	150.5	8.5
Southern provinces			
Noord-Brabant	200.8	154.8	22.9
Limburg	183.2	136.9	25.3
Netherlands	167.8	143.3	14.5

SOURCE: See [4].

important, modern mass media may have caused this rapid and unexpected development; but as long as thorough research has not been finished, there will be much uncertainty about the real underlying factors.

CONTRACEPTIVE METHODS

Only a few surveys have been organized dealing with the use and effectiveness of contraceptive methods. One of them was conducted by Heeren and Moors in 1967 [5]; another was done one year later, sponsored by the woman's magazine *Margriet* [6]. Among the questions asked in the latter survey, one dealt with the objections against purposeful birth limitation and another with the methods ever used or practiced. The results, repro-duced in Table 6, show that the most unreliable method (coitus interruptus) was also the most frequently practiced, followed by the use of the condom; both methods are simple and applicable without medical advice. Not sur-prisingly, a third survey, conducted in 1968 by Kooy and based on the material of the *Margriet* survey, affirmed the low level of knowledge among the Dutch men and women aged 16–20 years about contraceptive methods (for example, 45 percent never heard about coitus interruptus, and 50 percent thought that the condom was a reliable method) [7]. Although 77 percent of the men and 70 percent of the women (*Margriet* survey) accepted the pill from a moral point of view, only 22 percent of the females interviewed had used it. Certainly, the latter percentage has increased after the 1972 change in legislation (discussed later in this chapter).

Attention was also given to regional differences. There seems to be less acceptance of birth limitation in the northern part of the country than in the southern part. In the predominantly Protestant north, the use of coitus interruptus equals the national average, while in the predominantly Catholic south the practice of the rhythm method equals the national average. In the highly urbanized western provinces, the pill and mechanical devices were more frequently used than in other regions [6, pp. 88–90].

From the first results of a recent nation-wide survey on birth patterns (conducted by Heeren), we know the degree to which birth planning was successful. In 55 out of 1,000 marriages, one or more children were born before the planned time. For every size of family, undesired fertility was registered; this increased with the family size up to about 37 percent for families with four or more children. Women who had not had undesired births expected an average of 2.6 children, while they already had families with a mean of 2.2 children [8].

POPULATION CONCERNS AND POPULATION PROBLEMS

¶ PUBLIC OPINION

The past, as well as the present, is characterized by an absence of a popula-tion policy defined as a coherent system of measures aiming at directing or influencing population growth. In the past few years, however, some measures in the field of population policy have been taken or prepared that, correlated, may be considered as a beginning of a consistent population policy.

The process necessary to change the political and sociopsychological attitudes began in the early 1950s, when several universities organized seminars on Dutch population problems. The Royal Academy of Sciences,

TABLE 6.

The *Margriet* Survey on Use of Contraceptive Methods, Netherlands, 1968 (in percents)[a]

Methods	Male Total	Age of Males				Female Total	Age of Females			
		21–24	25–34	35–49	50–64		21–24	25–34	35–49	50–64
In principle no objection to purposeful birth limitation	67	69	74	65	61	60	63	73	62	46
At some time practiced the rhythm method	43	52	43	45	39	38	26	45	41	32
Has practiced coitus interruptus	65	73	66	65	61	55	55	63	57	45
Has used the pill						22	41	37	22	2
Has used the condom	48	79	56	49	36					
Has used pessary or diaphragm						10	4	9	13	6
Has used IUD						1	3	1	1	
Has practiced irrigation						12	6	7	11	20
Has used aerosol						2	6	2	2	
Has used spermicide cream	10	12	13	10	6	8	6	7	9	6

SOURCE: See [6, p. 58].
[a] N = 1,284.

in 1949 and 1966, held conferences on the consequences of a continuing population growth; the latter conference exerted an enormous influence. Almost all churches have paid attention to population problems (contraceptives, abortion, divorce), and traditional points of view often have been adjusted or completely modified. The *Thymgenootschap*, an important Catholic organization, discussed the "Ethics of a Dutch Population Policy" during its annual meeting in 1967. Most political parties gave their opinion on population problems, some of them with great reluctance. The Royal Dutch Society for Promoting Medicine published both a report on the population problem (1970) and "Guidelines on Abortion" for its members. The concern of the widely diffused newspapers and other mass media (radio, television) for population policy has increased enormously. The Foundation on Idealistic Advertisement launched an intensive campaign under the slogan "Too many children will have no life. Birth restriction is a necessity." Women's organizations have joined the action. The Society of Medical Practitioners started, in May 1972, a "contraceptive communication project" for its members. School instruction has been improved and extended.

Children in both primary and secondary schools are taught sexual education on a voluntary basis (that is, with the previous consent of their parents). Toward that end, teachers or instructors received a specialized course, organized and directed by family planning and parenthood organizations. In primary schools, children in advanced classes (age group 10–12 years) are instructed, during three hours a week, on the general biological aspects of human reproduction. Sexual education in secondary schools (age group 13–18 years) takes the form of a discussion, during 3 two-hour sessions a week, on all aspects (biological aspects, sex relations, contraceptive methods) of sexual life.

¶ DISSEMINATION AND AVAILABILITY OF CONTRACEPTIVES

A law of August 28, 1969, replaced the regulation in the penal code prohibiting the display and sale of contraceptives to minors under eighteen years of age. Since then, contraceptive devices have been freely available. Municipalities have the right to issue implementary bylaws but not to prohibit such devices.

A long debate took place about the inclusion of hormonal products (the pill and its derivatives) in the medications delivered free of charge to salaried people insured under the Health Insurance Act. In 1971, the Sick Fund Council declared that it would not allow hormonal contraceptives to be included. Parliament, however, issued a contrary opinion in December 1971, and subsequently, a governmental decree ordered the inclusion of pill, pessary, and IUD under the medical benefits scheme. As of January

1973, all salaried people with an annual income below fl. 20,900² are able to obtain, on medical advice, these contraceptives free of charge. The costs involved are estimated at fl. 20 million, of which 90 percent is for pill prescriptions.

¶ ABORTION

Although induced abortion is prohibited and can be punished rather severely as a criminal offense, the legislation existing at present is not enforced, with the exception of improper and harmful practices.

The number of induced abortions is not known, but some years ago it was estimated at 60,000–70,000 per year. A recent survey indicates that, in 1970, 33,000 women asked their doctors for induced abortions, and 10,000 of them were "legally" treated; these figures deal only with legitimate demands in order to show the gap between registered demand and registered performance.

Today, several abortion clinics, run by a specially created Foundation for Medically Justified Abortion (Stimezo) do, in fact, operate without any interference from the Department of Justice. Doctors now perform more than 30,000 abortions per year. In January 1973, the Central Court of Appeal (*Centrale Raad van Beroep*) stated that the costs of abortion are to be covered under the obligations of the Health Insurance Act. However, as it was the first case of this kind brought before the court, the judgment should not be generalized.

In January 1970, the government appointed a Commission on Abortion, whose interim report was completed three months later. It unanimously recommended a change in the existing legislation, allowing induced abortion.

In June 1970, Messrs. Lamberts and Roethof, members of the Labor Party opposition, introduced a private member's bill to provide free induced abortion under conditions of good medical care. Two years later, the government of the day introduced a compromise bill containing new regulations on induced abortion, which was more conservative than that of Lamberts and Roethof. Under the government's bill, the woman's doctor makes the final decision after consulting a team of experts. Both medical societies and several political parties are opposed to this part of the bill on the grounds that the doctor must be completely free to decide, without any intervention of a third party.

During the November 1972 general election, the abortion issue was a severe concern for all political parties. Advertisements appeared in the press from a dissident Catholic party against the proposed abortion bill. It was

² Approximately US$6,400.

followed by the reply of the Catholic mother party whose minister proposed the bill. The congress of a dissident socialist party voted, against the advice of the executive committee, in favor of a proposed supplementary paragraph, in the election program, on liberalizing abortion. Zero population growth was mentioned in the Liberal party's program. More and better sexual education was favored by the three "progressive parties."

Under the new government appointed in May 1973—a predominantly socialist government with participation of Protestant and Catholic ministers —it is to be expected that the two bills mentioned will be debated as private member's bills, and that the unrestrictive Lamberts-Roethof bill then will be passed.

¶ FAMILY ALLOWANCES

Family allowances were introduced in 1941 for employees only. Until 1946, only the third child and subsequent children were beneficiaries. Family allowances were never considered as part of a demographic policy. On the contrary, they played a role in wage policy, and on these grounds— not to endanger international competition—the introduction in 1946 of child allowances for the first and second child replaced, at least partially, a wage increase. Gradually, the family allowance system has been extended to independent workers with small incomes (income less than US$3,150 per year, an amount that equals the legal minimum wage). In 1970, 90 percent of all children in the 0–19 year age classes benefited from family allowances, the total sum dispensed representing 2.9 percent of the gross national product.

Whether family allowances have encouraged population growth in the Netherlands is, at present, a much-discussed problem. In comparison with the amounts paid to beneficiaries in France and Belgium, the Dutch allowances are relatively low. In agreement with many Dutch authorities, our opinion is that they have not had any stimulating effect on Dutch fertility in general.

Family allowances (per term) from January 1, 1973,[3] onward amount to:

Fl. 164.58 for the first child (US $50)
Fl. 195.78 for the second and third child ($60)
Fl. 261.30 for the fourth and fifth child ($80)
Fl. 289.38 for the sixth and seventh child ($89)
Fl. 318.80 for the eighth and following children ($98)

From January 1, 1973, onward, the amount for the first child has been "frozen," to do away with all future increases, even adjustments to the

[3] On this date, 100 guilders (fl. 100) equaled approximately US$31.50.

cost of living. With regard to the present debate on "zero population growth," one is inclined to consider this measure as part of a population policy. This is, however, not the case. The measure is, in fact, part of a series aimed at revising the whole social security system. The amount saved by the "freeze" will be spent on providing more housing.

¶ EMPLOYMENT OF MARRIED WOMEN

We have mentioned both the low participation rate of married women in the production processes (28 percent of all occupied or working women, compared with over 50 percent in other EEC countries) and the tendency toward an increasing participation. We also alluded to some obstacles. The former progressive tax system was still another obstacle in that the income of a married woman with a salaried job was added to that of her husband, and income tax was levied on the total revenue, with a moderate tax reduction applied. In January 1973, a new tax system was introduced. Under the pressure of public opinion and—possibly—in consideration of the lasting manpower scarcity (discussed later), a completely changed method of tax levying on married women's revenue was part of the revision. Henceforth, an employed married woman will be treated as an independent taxpayer. The tax she has to pay will be calculated from her revenue, reduced by a fixed amount (fl. 1,328 = US$415); no longer will the revenue of both spouses be added together for the purpose of tax calculation.

¶ INTERNAL MIGRATIONS

Because the geographical distribution of the Dutch population is highly unequal, the population density varies in the eleven provinces. Almost half of the population is concentrated in the western part of the country, where the provinces of north and south Holland show the highest population densities (the number of inhabitants in 1970 per square kilometer were, respectively, 842 and 1,050). In the majority of the other regions, population density is below the national average of 385 per square kilometer (see Table 7).

Led by social and economic arguments, the policy of today's government aims at a more equal distribution of the population of the country. The means used are: determining plans, directing investments, industrializing underdeveloped regions, and a gradual transferring of a number of state services from the towns in the western part of the country to towns in other provinces.

The result of this policy, together with the preference of the population to leave overcrowded cities, is already visible. The net migration into the western provinces changed after 1960 into net out-migration. In general,

TABLE 7.

Distribution of the Population, Netherlands, 1957, 1963, 1972
(in percents)

Region	Square Kilometers	1957	1963	1972	Population Density (1972)
Northern part	8,920	11.3	10.9	10.8	174
Eastern part	9,058[a]	17.9	18.3	18.8	284
Western part	7,641	47.8	47.2	46.1	895
Zeeland	2,746	2.5	2.4	2.4	178
Southern part	7,314	20.4	21.1	21.6	406

[a] Excludes *IJsselmeerpolders.*

TABLE 8.

Population Growth in Three Cities, Netherlands, 1930–1970
(in percents)

Years	Amsterdam	Rotterdam	The Hague
1930–1940	7.2	1.1	18.9
1940–1950	5.3	16.2	11.1
1950–1960	2.5	6.6	5.9
1960–1970	−4.0	−5.9	−9.1

there has been, during the past ten years, a departure surplus in the western Netherlands and a settlement surplus in the eastern and southern parts. Particularly in the three largest cities, the trend of the population growth (shown in Table 8) was remarkable.

This development resulted from several factors: natural increase, con-urbanization, commuting, and out-migration. As a considerable number of the foreign workers settled down in these big cities, the figures disguise more or less the real fall of the native population. The trend, however, seems to be clear.

¶ INTERNATIONAL MIGRATION

During the first period after 1945, the governments of the day followed an active emigration policy because of the poor employment situation or for fear of unemployment caused by the rapidly increasing population. The policy consisted of subsidizing emigration, helping to transport emigrants (the Netherlands was one of the founding countries of ICEM, the Inter-governmental Committee for European Migration, in 1951), and promoting a close cooperation between the National Emigration Service (created for this purpose in 1949) and private organizations for emigrants.

Until 1960, the results were not unsatisfactory. In Table 9, the net migration rate is compared with the natural growth rate (both per 1,000 population). The biggest emigration flow took place in 1952, involving

TABLE 9.

Comparison of Emigration and Natural Growth Increase,
Netherlands, 1946–1971

Year	Natural Increase (per 1,000 average population)	Migration Surplus (per 1,000 average population)
1946	21.7	4.3
1947	19.7	−1.2
1948	17.9	−2.1
1949	15.6	−2.2
1950	15.2	2.0
1951	14.7	−2.2
1952	14.9	−4.6
1953	14.0	−3.0
1954	14.0	−1.8
1955	13.7	−0.5
1956	13.5	−1.0
1957	13.7	−1.2
1958	13.6	1.1
1959	13.8	−1.5
1960	13.2	−1.1
1961	13.7	0.5
1962	12.9	1.4
1963	12.9	0.7
1964	13.0	1.1
1965	11.9	1.5
1966	11.1	1.6
1967	11.0	−0.9
1968	10.4	0.1
1969	10.8	0.2
1970	9.9	0.3
1971	8.8	0.3

SOURCE: See [9].

81,000 or nearly 8 per 1,000 of the whole population. The countries of destination were mainly the United States, Canada, Australia, New Zealand, and South Africa. In several years, however, there were strong counterflows; this was the case in 1946 (repatriation of 69,000 people after the war with Japan was over), 1950 (return of 55,000 people after the independence of Indonesia), and 1958 (38,000 repatriations under the influence of political events in Indonesia).

Toward the end of the 1950s, emigration had lost more and more significance, and in 1961, the emigration surplus turned into an immigration surplus. With respect to Dutch migrants only, four emigrants were now counterbalanced by three immigrants, so that emigration appeared costly and not very profitable.

Meanwhile, immigration of foreign workers had begun. It was to last, however, until 1966 when the government decided to change emigration policy. From the initial "active" emigration policy, it changed into a "positive oriented" policy, meaning a favorable appreciation of emigration, on the one hand, in the interest of the demographic development and town and country planning and, on the other hand, in the interest of the emigrants' striving for optimum life conditions.[4]

The increasing scarcity of workers in the late 1950s made it necessary to recruit labor in foreign countries. Though this is a general phenomenon in western Europe, only in the Netherlands was it executed under conditions of an increasing population aged 15–64 years. The most important causes of the labor scarcity were and still are: longer compulsory and voluntary education, better old-age pensions, earlier retirement, better vocational training (with a corresponding decreased supply of laborers for unpleasant and monotonous work), and insufficient geographical mobility of native labor.[5] In view of the recruitment of foreign labor, bilateral agreements were concluded with Italy (1960), Spain (1961), Portugal (1963), Turkey (1964), Greece (1966), Morocco (1968), and Yugoslavia (1969), in addition to the liberalization of the EEC labor market. The number of foreign workers—most of them from Turkey, Spain, Morocco, and Italy—rose from about 25,000 in 1960 to more than 125,000 in 1971. The number of all aliens residing in the Netherlands increased from 117,600 in May 1960 to 204,000 in July 1968 (last known figure); at the end of 1972, the number of aliens could be estimated at about 250,000.

Table 10 shows clearly the change in migration pattern by comparing

---

[4] Comment to *"Wijziging van de Wet op de organen voor de emigratie"* bill proposed [10].

[5] A small advantage was obtained by reducing the number of young men called up for compulsory military service, their part of total manpower subsequently decreasing from 4 percent in 1958 to 3.2 percent in 1971.

TABLE 10.

Migration Patterns, Netherlands, 1946–1960 and 1961–1970

Period	Immigration	Emigration	Surplus
1946–1960	592,767	743,093	− 150,326
1961–1970	689,195	556,884	+ 132,311

fifteen years before 1961 with ten years after 1960. The foreign workers are concentrated especially in industrial and urban regions with a high population density.

The migration pattern of foreign workers, as observed in the period 1960–1970, shows an increased duration of stay and, in connection with this, a decrease of return emigration, to a large extent dependent on cyclical fluctuations. Of the migrant workers from Mediterranean countries (about 80 percent of total immigration) in April 1972, some 63,000 had a labor permit with a period of validity shorter than five years, and 21,000 had a permanent labor permit [11]. A 1968 survey showed that 25 percent of the Mediterranean migrant workers can be considered as long stayers (intending to stay more than five years) [12]. The reemigration of these workers amounted in 1969 to 30 percent, in 1970 to 25 percent, and in 1971 to 33 percent of the immigration from Mediterranean countries in each year. For the period 1970–1975, the Central Bureau of Statistics calculated a total immigration of 188,000 and a return emigration of 71,000 foreign workers from these countries [2]. The resulting net immigration of 117,000, however, seems to be a little too high, considering both the net immigration (46,500) registered for the period 1970–1972 and the now more-restrictive immigration policy.

Compared with the Federal Republic of Germany (8.9 percent), Belgium (7.1 percent), or France (7.6 percent), the number of foreign workers in the Netherlands (1.8 percent of the salaried population) seems to be rather modest. In relation to the population pressure, however, the number seems rather high, and in this connection, the government of the day expressed its concern in a "Note on Foreign Workers," stating: "Finally, one must not forget that the demographic situation in the Netherlands is not such that there are motives present for promoting immigration, as happens to be the case in some other countries. The Netherlands certainly is no immigration country" [13]. One of the most urgent problems is the shortage of good housing (since the war a scarcity of housing exists); another is the forced separation of immigrants from their families.

In March 1972, the Central Planning Office (CPO) published a study on the economic effects for the Netherlands resulting from the recruitment of foreign workers. This study shows, on the basis of a variation model, the favorable and unfavorable consequences that may be expected from the immigration of foreign workers, accompanied by their families or not. One of the conclusions is that the advantages of immigration exceed the disadvantages when the labor demand is temporary and when there is no native supply. As a structural continuance of the need for foreign workers leads to a permanent growth of the Dutch population, the CPO prefers an increase of home labor supply, insofar as the latter is able to fill a migrant worker's job.

The labor shortage could be met partially by a larger participation of married women in the production processes. Although this would mean greater public expenses for children's homes and additional manpower, it may be considered the most profitable solution, since the labor supply would increase without increasing population growth. Also the expenses would be less than those for foreign workers, and the national population alone would benefit from the resulting increase in wage income.

This solution, however, ignores the real causes of the present immigration of foreign workers; the latter perform the jobs local workers are not prepared to assume. In fact, citing the argument of the CPO, the two groups of workers have different vocational qualifications, which explains the country's dependency on migrant workers. Unpleasant and unskilled jobs should be better remunerated, which involves a complete change of the existing wage structure, and this seems impossible with regard to the strong inflationary tendencies and existing attitudes. As the vocational training and general education of women have been improved substantially in the recent past, it is unlikely that, in the present situation, female nationals will replace foreign workers.

The debate on migration policy is still going on. The Royal Commission on Population Problems (inaugurated in 1972) has, moreover, been charged with the study of the effects of immigration of foreign workers on Dutch population problems.

¶ POSITION WITH REGARD TO THE POPULATION PROBLEM
IN DEVELOPING COUNTRIES

On the international level, the Dutch government has signed the world leaders "Declaration on Population" of the United Nations (1967). The Netherlands also adopted the UN Economic and Social Council's Resolution on Population and Development (June 1972) urging all member states "to ensure, in accordance with their national population policies and needs, that information and education about family planning, as well as the means to effectively practice family planning, are made available to all individuals by the end of the Second United Nations Development Decade."

The program of Dutch aid to family planning activities in developing countries began in 1968 with projects for Pakistan and Kenya. The Pakistan project, dealing with research on the motivation of the rural population toward family planning, and assistance to carry out the Pakistan program, ended prematurely with the civil war. In 1972, however, it was decided to continue the project for Bangladesh. The Kenyan program involves the training of local agents in the use of contraceptives and clinical research on the applicability of family planning techniques and the causes and treatment of sterility. This project is still going on. Other comparable bilateral projects are being executed in Tunisia and Indonesia.

The government resolved to pass from bilateral to multilateral aid. In a two-year program, the Dutch aid to the UN Fund for Population Activities is expected to increase from US$1 million to more than $5 million in 1975, amounts that seem modest in comparison to the financial aid of other countries.

INSTITUTIONAL ASPECTS

¶ NETHERLANDS INTERUNIVERSITY DEMOGRAPHIC INSTITUTE

As it has been said, Dutch universities played an important role in the process of raising the alarm about population problems. They also took the initiative for more cooperation and better coordination. And so, as a result of a close collaboration between the Royal Academy of Sciences and the Ministry of Education and Sciences, the Netherlands Interuniversity Demographic Institute (NIDI) was created in 1971. Its task is:

(1) Researching the factors that, directly or indirectly, are involved in population growth.
(2) Promoting and coordinating demographic research.
(3) Promoting demographic teaching and courses in demography.
(4) Collecting documentation and preparing publications to give information and advice on demographic problems.

Almost all universities, the Ministry of Education, and the Central Bureau of Statistics are represented on the board of NIDI. It participates in several surveys organized by the demographic department of the Institute for Sociology of Utrecht University. It also started the publication of a bulletin and a series of monographs.

¶ ROYAL COMMISSION ON POPULATION PROBLEMS

In view of the many problems directly or indirectly linked with population growth—immigration of foreign workers, health protection, spatial problems, different kinds of pollution, abortion—that alarmed both public authorities and public opinion, the government decided to establish a national commission on population growth. This commission was created in the spring of 1972.

It was asked to examine the probable extent of population growth and the future age structure, as well as the factors that have an influence on this development, to check the impact of the demographic development on health care, and to pay attention to the impact of environmental changes such as, for example, population distribution and increasing urbanization. Social and welfare aspects linked with the population growth must be included. The scope of the commission's mandate is to formulate the basic elements for a policy in view of the future development of Dutch society.

The chairman of the commission is Professor P. Muntendam, former Minister of Public Health; there are two secretaries, Dr. D. J. van de Kaa (director of NIDI) and Dr. P. C. J. van Loon (Ministry of Public Health and Environmental Hygiene); the members represent the ministries involved, NIDI, the Central Bureau of Statistics, and private associations (medicine, the sciences, women's organizations, trade unions, employer's organizations). The commission has set up several committees, one of them charged to draft a preliminary report on general outlines for a Dutch population policy. This report is expected to be completed in 1973.

REFERENCES

1. William Petersen. *The Politics of Population.* Garden City, N.Y.: Doubleday, 1964.

2. *Statistical Abstract*, Central Bureau of Statistics. 1972. Also, "Population projections, 1970–2000." *Maandschrift.* Central Bureau of Statistics, April 1971 (In Dutch.)

3. Supplement, 1969 and 1970, *Population and Health Statistics.* Central Bureau of Statistics.

4. "Regional marital fertility, 1959/1961–1967." *Maandschrift.* Central Bureau of Statistics, October 1968. (In Dutch.)

5. H. J. Heeren and H. G. Moors. *Families in Growth* (1967). See also summary in *Journal of Marriage and the Family,* vol. 31, no. 3 (1969).

6. *Sex in the Netherlands.* Utrecht: Spectrum, 1969. (In Dutch.)

7. G. A. Kooy. *Youth and Sexuality toward the Seventies.* Agricultural University Wageningen, 1972. (In Dutch.)

8. "Demografie." *Bulletin*, 1972/1. Netherlands Interuniversity Demographic Institute. (In Dutch.)

9. "Vital statistics and migration statistics of the Netherlands, 1946–1967." *Population and Health Statistics*. Central Bureau of Statistics.

10. *Parliamentary Documents, 1965–1966*, no. 8,727.

11. Ministry of Culture, Recreation, and Social Work. *Foreign Workers' Newsletter*, no. 3, 1972. (In Dutch.)

12. Ministry of Culture, Recreation, and Social Work. *Foreign Workers' Newsletter*, no. 7, 1971. (In Dutch.)

13. Parliamentary Documents, 1969–1970, no. 10,504.

CHAPTER 12

Czechoslovakia

Zdenek Pavlik
Vladimir Wynnyczuk

ABSTRACT

A characteristic feature of population policy in Czechoslovakia prior to 1945 was a number of measures of direct aid to mothers, families, and children. Ever since 1888, mothers have received health insurance benefits for four weeks after confinement; later, this period was extended, and other allowances were added to cover costs in connection with childbirth. There was also significant toleration or even support of migration abroad.

After World War II and during the past twenty-five years, a number of population measures were adopted in Czechoslovakia, which have begun to form a complex set of mutually supplementary and interacting conditions for population growth. Emigration for economic reasons (for example, unemployment) has disappeared. For the first time, attention has been paid to mortality—in particular, maternal and infant mortality—which has been considerably reduced, and life expectancy has increased.

Measures now coming under the heading of population policy were not at first conceived for the purpose of affecting the birth rate; it had been expected that, with rising living standards, the birth rate also would rise. However, its decline in the 1950s led to a differentiated raising of living standards in favor of families with children; these trends have been emphasized particularly since 1968, when Czechoslovakia's fertility reached its lowest point since World War II.

Since 1969, a slight rise in fertility can be noticed. This may be an anticipation of fertility increase caused by measures of population policy. However, no change in the attitude of the population as to family size has occurred. A definite evaluation will not be possible for several years. Until the year 1970, increased fertility was due mainly to the birth of second children. The overall demographic picture of Czechoslovakia in 1971 can be seen in the appendix.

As recently underlined by government spokesmen, Czechoslovak population policy favors natality; it includes not only a wide range of economic and social measures but also parenthood education and attention to the qualitative aspects of population development. From this point of view, population policy is regarded as an integral part of Czechoslovak state policy as a whole.

THE PRESENT SITUATION

At the present time, the Czechoslovak population policy pursues strongly pronatal aims as is apparent in the following quotations from speeches by government representatives.

From Gustav Husak, First Secretary of the Communist party:

As most important, we consider measures to improve population development, increased support to families with children and young married couples. Under the Five-Year Plan, far larger funds than ever before are set aside for this purpose. Their use will have to be effected in a manner which will best serve the aim in mind. (Fourteenth Congress of the Communist party of Czechoslovakia, Svoboda, Prague, 1971.)

From Michal Stancel, Minister of Labor and Social Affairs:

The average is 1.9 children per family. However, for healthy development and our appropriate economic progress, it is necessary to provide conditions so that after the year 1980 the population should not decline; this would happen if the present trend of population development would continue and would further worsen the overall composition of the population. This calls for an increase in the average number of children per family from today's 1.9 to 2.5 [1].

From Matej Lucan, Vice Premier:

Socialist society's present care for population development now mostly centers on ensuring an appropriate birth rate, with the numbers of live-born children corresponding to the long-term requirements of society. A population policy pursued to this end takes into account also significant social aspects, the provision of average living standards for families with numerous children [2].

From Jaroslav Havelka, Vice Minister of Labor and Social Affairs and Secretary of the Government Population Committee:

A basic feature of our contemporary population policy is a complex approach, because we are aware that if population development is to be favorably influenced it does not suffice to take measures of only one kind, e.g., socioeconomic ones. No, within the scope of economic feasibility, one has to proceed consistently and concertedly on all main fronts [3].

Particularly underlined is the need for increased natality (by Husak, Stancel, and Lucan), as well as the need for attending to a wide range of problems that are connected with population development and can affect it (by Havelka) and for using funds to the best effect (Husak). Therefore, not only material measures are involved, but also training for parenthood and all steps ensuring the qualitative aspects of population development, such as health welfare, social measures, and so forth. From this point of view, population policy is conceived of as an indelible part of Czechoslovak state policy, aiming above all at constantly increasing living standards for the entire population, which forms the material basis for the rise of cultural standards; at the same time, it facilitates the further comprehensive development of society and of every individual in it.

Looked upon historically, population policy—whether or not it is called such—emerges on the basis of various individual measures—for example, in the spheres of health, social welfare, judiciary, migration, and so forth —that in some way affect population development. However, such aims may also be clearly defined. In such a sense, one can speak of the existence of a population policy in Czechoslovakia since the year 1945. At that period, aims were first formulated of increasing health welfare and of raising the population's living standards. Infant mortality falls steeply, and life expectancy increases noticeably. Similar developments can be observed in the sphere of general living standards and the social security of the population, where successes are regularly reviewed when analyzing annual or long-term (that is, two- to five-year) economic plans.

As for the birth rate, developments did not bring about the expected automatic rise of natality hand in hand with rising living standards produced by the socialist system. The falling birth rate in the 1950s led to the adoption of various measures, particularly in the sphere of living standards, favoring families with children—for example, family allowances, tax relief, maternity benefits, and so forth. Gradually, such individual measures began to form a comprehensive system of mutually interconnected and interacting moral-political and economic measures of the Czechoslovak population policy.

We shall first examine tangible measures of population policy in context with the population development that has given rise to them. When analyzing the population development of Czechoslovakia, it has to be borne in mind that the country is composed of two populations of distinct historical development, the consequences of which are evident to this day. The importance of the two populations is characterized in Table 1.

Also, a review of contemporarily valid measures of social assistance to families with children is attached; special attention is devoted to parenthood training and to the bodies responsible for population policy.

HISTORY UNTIL 1945

The contemporary population policy is deeply rooted in the historical development of the Czechoslovak population, in particular, during the last 200 years. Two factors appear to be of prime importance: the diverse development of the two components of the Czechoslovak population, that is, the Czech regions and Slovakia; and the position of such development in the overall population development of Europe or, respectively, of the world.

TABLE 1.

Demographic Data, Czechoslovakia, 1970

Item	Czech Regions	Slovakia	Total
Inhabitants:			
Number (average)	9,805,000	4,529,000	14,334,000
Percent	68.4	31.6	100
Live-born children			
Number	147,865	80,666	228,531
Percent	64.7	35.3	100
Marriages			
Number	90,624	35,961	126,585
Percent	71.6	28.4	100
Divorces			
Number	21,516	3,420	24,936
Percent	86.3	13.7	100
Infant mortality (first year)			
Number	2,987	2,072	5,059
Percent	59.0	41.0	100
Reported abortions			
Number	89,509	35,565	125,074
Percent	71.6	28.4	100
Of reported abortions, on application			
Number	71,893	27,873	99,766
Percent	72.1	27.9	100

First, the past development of the Czechoslovak population should be examined in the context of Europe. In the eighteenth and the first half of the nineteenth century, the Czech regions belonged to the relatively developed countries of central Europe, which explains their density of population. A higher density could be found at that time only in Upper Saxonia—a small territory—and on the fringe of central Europe, the Rhineland and Belgium in the west and Lombardy in the south (also comparatively smaller territories). Slovakia, however, as part of Hungary, belonged to the countries with the lowest population density in central Europe, and its economic level ranged it with the countries situated in the east and north of central Europe. This explains also the strong political position of the Czech regions in that part of the world, though it was not emphasized by an independent state. By their geographic position, the Czech regions played the role of a central European center. The end of the eighteenth and the first half of the nineteenth century is a very important period for the population development of Europe, for it saw the beginning process of demographic revolution, an indelible part of the turbulent economic and social development of that time. The situation was reflected in the development of both parts of the Czechoslovak population, as is apparent from Table 2.

TABLE 2.

Approximate Data on Development of Basic Demographic Rates, Czech Regions and Slovakia, 1700–1944

Period	Crude Birth Rate	Crude Death Rate	Crude Rate of Natural Increase	GRR
	Czech Regions			
1700–1784	(42)	(35)	(7)	
1785–1829	42–45	31–35	8–9	
1830–1879	38–40	28–31	10	2.5
1880–1913	30–38	21–29	10	2.0–2.4
1920–1929	20–24	14–16	8	1.0–1.5
1930–1944	15–19	13	4	0.8–1.0
	Slovakia			
1750–1857	(38–40)	(30–40)	(5)	
1858–1900	41–45	29–40	8–10	2.6–2.8
1901–1913	34–39	22–26	12–13	2.4–2.5
1920–1929	31–35	18–20	13–16	1.7–2.4
1930–1944	23–27	14–16	9–11	1.3–1.7

SOURCES: See [4]; for the period prior to 1785 for the Czech regions, the authors have used their own estimates; for Slovakia, see [5].

In the Czech regions, the beginning of the demographic revolution came not far behind that of France, which is considered to be the first country where this process occurred. In the 1830s, a fall in the birth rate can be observed in the Czech regions, which can be explained only in terms of a conscious limiting of the number of children in certain, though not numerous, territories or social groups. It is not important that this process was very slow and lasted almost 100 years; a rapid decline of natality occurs as late as the 1890s, that is, 50 years after the first signs had been registered.

It is not accidental that the Czech regions are compared with France in this respect. They follow the French rather than the English type of demographic revolution, for mortality also remained on a relatively high level throughout the entire nineteenth century. However, this is not the only reason for the comparison. In the 1930s, the Czech regions show strong depopulation trends; the birth rate falls to one of the lowest levels in the world, and again France is in a similar situation.

In Slovakia, the marked decline of the birth rate took place only at the beginning of the twentieth century, and the demographic revolution was concluded after World War II. The difference between natality and mortality is wider and the population increase is larger; its demographic revolution resembles the English type. Population development in the Czech regions and in Slovakia has remained different until now, although leveling-up tendencies can be seen and development will probably even out within one generation.

Speaking of population policy with regard to the above period, one has in mind, above all, various views and later measures concerning migration to other countries or mortality. Measures that would have affected the birth rate were negligible. In Slovakia, they were prevented by the strong position of the Catholic church; but in the Czech regions, where this position was far weaker (though not unimportant), the neo-Malthusian movement did not make any greater inroads.

The Czech regions and Slovakia did not differ from the other European countries in the first stage of capitalist development insofar as there was much emigration at that time. In the eighteenth and nineteenth centuries, Czech and Slovak farmers went east to Russia, south to today's Yugoslavia, and to the majority of countries forming the Austro-Hungarian empire. In particular, much migration took place to both capitals of the empire— Vienna and Budapest—and to other large cities. In the second half of the nineteenth century, migration overseas (mainly to the United States of America) began to gain in volume, climaxing in the Czech lands, in the 1880s, when it reached an annual rate of 3 per 1,000, and in Slovakia, in the first decade of the twentieth century, with a rate of 7.6 per 1,000. At the end of the nineteenth century, Slovak migration to the Czech regions increased, gaining in volume especially after the formation of Czechoslovakia and continuing after World War II. A marked decrease could be noted only in recent years, when Slovakia's economic level approached that of the Czech regions.

Before World War I, migration to other countries developed along natural lines and was not officially discouraged. However, there were certain differences of approach to it in Austria (Czech regions) and in Hungary (Slovakia). In Hungary, though economically less developed, some fears were voiced concerning large-scale migration (it was thought it might lead to national catastrophe); obviously, certain power interests were brought into play here since the living conditions of the population did not form any matter of interest. In the Austrian part of the monarchy, which was economically more developed with higher standards of living (a lower mortality indicated its better public health system, mother and child welfare, a more tolerant attitude to illegitimate children, and so forth), migration was viewed favorably; some economists of that day even voiced fears of excessive density, but these views were by far not generally accepted.

In the sphere of health welfare, the Workers' Health Insurance Act of 1888 already provided sickness benefits to insured women for a period of four weeks after confinement. In 1917, an amendment raised this period to six weeks.

After the foundation of the Czechoslovak Republic in 1918, these influences can be traced, and new ones can be added. The Czech regions belonged to Austria's most highly industrialized countries; the establishment of Czechoslovakia cut them off from their former hinterland. Industry then had to find new markets, which was not easy in a Europe devastated by war. During the first years of the new state, Slovakia's economic position did not change much; only its national position had changed, for the Slovak language finally had won equal rights, even though only as a branch of the then officially professed Czechoslovak language. However, a new and serious fact led to the new immigration policy of many countries which had, to this time, accepted immigrants without restriction.

In the new Czechoslovakia, the Czech—that is, formerly Austrian—part acquired decisive influence and continued in its prewar population policy. Soon after the war, a committee for migration and colonization was set up under the Ministry of Labor and Social Affairs, and the acquisition of some colony (for example, by purchase) was quite seriously considered, in order to provide an outlet for Czechoslovak emigrants to whom some of the traditional immigration countries were now closed. In the official recommendations of that committee (1928), one can read that in Czechoslovakia, and particularly in Slovakia, migration to other countries "is a necessary safety valve which removes the causes of diverse economic and social conflicts." It is necessary to effect emigration, to organize it, and to look for new outlets. There is a fear of overpopulation and social conflicts which sharpened especially during the world economic crisis. Therefore, the official Czech policy can be described as Malthusian, and in accordance with such an approach, the main problem is seen as a shortage of employment, not a shortage of food. In Czechoslovakia, in spite of church opposition, contraception was freely advocated.

On the other hand, in Slovakia (Hungary), optimism persevered, reinforced by the fulfillment of national aspirations and showing all the features of economic and social romanticism typical of the beginnings of capitalist development. The Slovak populationism was supported by religious feeling and was the prevailing opinion among the Slovak intellectuals, the bourgeoisie, and the peasantry alike. The Slovak intelligentsia criticized attempts to justify the advantages of migration as decreasing the number "of superfluous people" and its economic effects for the homeland (rich people returning home, money being sent to relatives, and so forth). All the same, the number of persons leaving Slovakia was very high, which was also a consequence of the large natural increase in the first ten years of the new republic, averaging almost 5 per 1,000 annually, and reaching its peak around 1930 (although it no longer climbed as high as the peak level of the decade prior to the war).

As for the sphere of population measures, in 1920, maternal leave was extended to six weeks before and six weeks after confinement, with sickness benefits paid. This arrangement remained in force practically until 1948, with the exception of certain categories of women workers; in the civil and municipal services and teaching, since 1926, women employees have received 80 percent of their salary for a period of three months, and since 1934, private employees have received—under certain conditions— their full salary for a period of four weeks' maternity leave. Since 1929, some workers have received a marriage grant, and public employees have received family allowances (until 1926, for an unlimited number of children, later practically for two children only). Such allowances were paid also in many private enterprises. In addition, income tax was reduced by 10 percent for families with two children, by 20 percent for those with four children, and so forth.

Such was the situation before the year 1945 and, in particular, before World War II, which had consequences profoundly affecting the living conditions of the population. During the war, a certain increase in fertility can be noticed as compared with its all-time low that, according to the more exact rating of the gross rate of reproduction, was reached in 1935 in the Czech regions and in 1937 in Slovakia.

327

PERIOD OF RELATIVELY HIGH NATALITY AFTER 1945

Immediately after World War II, the birth rate increased in the Czech regions and in Slovakia, as it did in other countries where the process of demographic revolution had ended earlier. (Actually, this increase began during the course of World War II.) The causes lie primarily in the greater number of marriages in the postwar years; however, these reserves are soon exhausted, and the longer duration of the period of increased natality indicates another factor; the reduction of the average age of the mother. This was affected also by the legal adjustment of the coming-of-age, which was reduced from twenty-one to eighteen years; by marriage, the coming-of-age could be effected at sixteen.

As demonstrated in Table 3, this first period lasted in the Czech regions

TABLE 3.

Development of Basic Demographic Rates, Czechoslovakia, after
World War II (during period of relatively high birth rate)

Year	Crude Birth Rate	Crude Death Rate	Crude Rate of Natural Increase	Marriage Rate	GRR
Czech Regions					
1945	18.2	17.3	0.9	7.5	
1946	22.1	14.1	8.0	9.9	
1947	23.6	12.0	11.6	11.2	1.476
1948	22.2	11.4	10.8	10.8	1.392
1949	20.9	11.8	9.1	10.6	1.328
1950	21.1	11.6	9.5	10.7	1.365
1951	20.6	11.4	9.2	10.1	1.350
Slovakia					
1945	23.7	19.5	4.2	7.5	
1946	24.2	14.0	10.2	10.6	
1947	25.8	12.2	13.6	11.1	1.570
1948	26.5	11.9	14.6	10.4	1.591
1949	26.4	12.1	14.3	10.7	1.592
1950	28.8	11.5	17.3	11.3	1.733
1951	28.7	11.5	17.2	10.2	1.747
1952	28.3	10.4	17.9	9.3	1.729
1953	27.5	9.9	17.6	7.9	1.690
1954	26.8	9.5	17.3	8.6	1.665
1955	26.6	8.8	17.8	8.5	1.692
1956	26.3	8.7	17.6	9.3	1.690

SOURCE: See [3].

until 1951, and in Slovakia, for five years longer. The reduction of the mothers' average age began to make an impact toward the end of the first period. It can be characterized by the proportion of children born to mothers under the age of thirty. In the Czech regions, this amounted to 65.6 percent in 1947 and 70.0 percent in 1950, while in Slovakia, the proportion rose from 61.9 percent in 1947 to 67.6 percent in 1956. To round the picture off, Table 4 shows the structure of children born according to rank. In the Czech regions, the proportion of first children declined; the proportion of second and third children remained constant; and the proportion of further children increased slightly, despite a general reduction in the age of the mothers. In Slovakia, a similar development was far more marked. The proportion of first-born children declined more sharply, and all other ranks increased their proportion, except sixth and higher, where there was a slight decrease.

Table 4 also explains the causes of the difference in the birth rate in the Czech regions and in Slovakia. In Slovakia, there exists a far larger pro-

TABLE 4.

Development of Rank Structure of Children, Czechoslovakia, after World War II (born during period of relatively high birth rate)

Year	Total Live Births	Children Born in Rank Order (in percents)[a]					
		1	2	3	4	5	6+
		Czech Regions					
1947	206,745	39.4	29.6	16.3	7.4	3.3	3.9
1948	197,837	29.7	29.2	15.8	7.5	3.5	4.3
1949	185,484	39.6	29.8	15.4	7.4	3.4	4.3
1950	188,341	37.8	30.2	16.1	7.6	3.7	4.7
1951	185,570	37.9	29.7	16.2	7.8	3.8	4.6
		Slovakia					
1947	87,659	34.4	24.3	15.3	9.3	5.8	10.9
1948	91,189	35.0	24.4	15.4	9.3	5.6	10.3
1949	91,053	33.2	26.5	15.6	9.1	5.6	10.0
1950	99,721	31.4	27.0	16.3	9.4	5.7	10.0
1951	100,663	31.2	26.7	16.9	9.8	5.7	9.7
1952	100,824	30.3	26.6	17.5	10.3	5.8	9.5
1953	99,124	29.7	26.2	18.0	10.4	6.1	9.6
1954	98,310	28.6	26.9	18.3	10.7	6.2	9.4
1955	99,305	29.0	26.3	18.3	10.8	6.1	9.5
1956	99,467	29.4	26.1	17.8	10.9	6.2	9.6

SOURCE: See [6].
   [a] In this and other tables, totals may not add to 100.0 because of rounding.

portion of families with several children, and it can be asserted that the demographic revolution ended here as late as immediately after World War II, by its penetrating some groups (territorial and social) of the population.

Soon after 1945, important social measures falling under the heading of population policy were taken, such as the introduction of family allowances for all employed persons alike and covering all children. Allowances were increased for every additional child until the fifth. In 1948, the National Insurance Act no. 99/1948 Sb. stipulated a uniform adjustment of all maternity benefits. This concerned practically all categories of employed women as well as family dependents. Maternity leave was extended to eighteen weeks. For this period, maternity benefit is paid; in Czechoslovakia, benefits are paid according to the wage or salary and the length of employment. There is also the uniform qualification of 270 days of insurance in the two years preceding confinement.

TABLE 5.

Development of Basic Demographic Rates, Czechoslovakia, 1952–1962 (during period of declining birth rate)

Year	Crude Birth Rate	Crude Death Rate	Crude Rate of Natural Increase	Marriage Rate	GRR	Proportion of Abortions to Total Pregnancies
			Czech Regions			
1952	19.7	10.7	9.0	8.6	1.314	
1953	18.7	10.7	8.0	7.6	1.268	
1954	18.1	10.7	7.4	7.6	1.253	
1955	17.7	10.0	7.7	7.6	1.248	
1956	17.2	9.9	7.3	8.5	1.247	
1957	16.3	10.4	5.9	6.6	1.199	
1958	14.8	9.8	5.0	7.2	1.106	32.1
1959	13.4	10.1	3.3	7.4	1.014	37.8
1960	13.3	9.7	3.6	7.7	1.012	39.6
			Slovakia			
1957	25.3	9.3	16.0	7.4	1.631	
1958	23.9	8.2	15.7	8.0	1.574	18.5
1959	22.3	8.6	13.7	8.0	1.480	22.8
1960	22.1	7.9	14.2	8.1	1.489	24.7
1961	20.8	7.5	13.3	7.5	1.444	27.2
1962	19.9	8.1	11.7	7.2	1.375	27.6

SOURCE: See [7].

At the time, although family allowances were raised twice, in 1947 and 1951, the population character of those measures was not emphasized in view of the relatively high rate of natural increase, especially in Slovakia. During the years 1945–1953, food and clothing were rationed, which favored families with children primarily by maintaining low food prices.

DECLINING BIRTH RATE IN THE 1950s

A further reduction in the average age of the mother, which occurred in the Czech regions after the year 1950 and in Slovakia after 1956, no longer sufficed to compensate for the generally lower natality; in fact, the falling birth rate caused it to decline faster. The period is characterized in Tables 5 and 6.

The gross reproduction rate regularly fell in the Czech regions and in Slovakia until 1962. The proportion of children born to mothers under the age of thirty increased during that period in the Czech regions to 83.1

TABLE 6.

Development of Rank Structure of Children, Czechoslovakia,
1952–1962 (born during period of declining birth rate)

Year	Total Live Births	Children Born in Rank Order (in percents)					
		1	2	3	4	5	6+
Czech Regions							
1952	180,143	38.0	29.5	16.1	8.0	3.8	4.5
1953	172,547	36.7	30.1	16.6	8.2	4.0	4.6
1954	168,402	36.0	31.1	16.4	8.0	4.0	4.6
1955	165,874	35.8	31.3	16.6	8.0	3.9	4.6
1956	162,509	36.5	31.2	15.9	7.9	3.9	4.5
1957	155,429	37.4	30.9	15.5	7.6	4.0	4.6
1958	141,762	39.5	32.3	14.9	6.4	3.2	3.8
1959	128,982	43.2	33.4	13.3	5.0	2.2	2.9
1960	128,879	44.6	32.9	12.8	4.7	2.2	2.8
Slovakia							
1957	97,311	29.5	26.2	17.3	10.8	6.4	9.7
1958	93,272	29.4	27.0	17.4	10.4	6.3	9.5
1959	87,991	31.1	27.3	17.4	9.7	5.6	8.8
1960	88,412	31.6	27.3	17.4	9.5	5.3	8.9
1961	87,359	32.5	27.7	17.1	9.3	5.1	8.3
1962	83,899	33.0	28.1	16.6	9.0	5.0	8.3

SOURCE: See [8].

percent and in Slovakia to 72.2 percent. However, the fact remains that in Slovakia in 1962 fertility ends approximately at the same level on which the decline began in the Czech regions ten years earlier.

In the Czech regions, there is a strong trend of decreasing the proportion of children born in higher rank orders, which together with a low marriage rate brings the gross rate close to 1.0. In Slovakia, the decline in the proportion of children born in higher rank order is far less marked; while out of a total number of children born in the Czech regions in 1960, 77.5 percent were first and second children; in Slovakia, these accounted for only 61.1 percent and an important proportion represented children ranking fourth or even higher (22.3 percent in Slovakia, compared with only 9.7 in the Czech regions).

Beginning with 1958, the birth rate was affected also by the new abortion law, permitting the induced interruption of pregnancy on social grounds. In 1958, the first year the act was in force, the proportion of deliberate abortions amounted to 32.1 percent of all pregnancies in the Czech regions; this rose to almost 40 percent in 1960. In Slovakia, the corresponding proportion was far lower. It can be assumed that, as a result of the act, the number of births in the upper ranks, as well as the birth rate as a whole, declined faster, but its adoption meant, at the same time, no marked change in the overall tendency toward a lower natality during that period. It, therefore, proved the prior existence of illegal abortions and the complex social causality of fertility development after the demographic revolution, when the existence or nonexistence of a similar act is of secondary importance for the level of fertility.

In 1953, rationing was abolished and a currency reform carried out. Although family allowances were increased simultaneously, per-head incomes began to rise faster in childless households or one-child families as compared with larger ones.

The declining birth rate of that period, which did not correspond with the theories held at the time, stimulated a more profound study of the objective causes of the demographic process, as well as polls attempting to analyze the subjective approach of the population, especially the females, to the subject of family size. For it is exactly this subjective attitude, though objectively conditioned, that plays the chief role in changing fertility levels.

The first enquiry was organized by the Office of Statistics in 1956 and covered 10,645 women aged 20–39 years. It was conducted by senior nurses of the gynecological departments of public clinics. The selection was not representative, as it included women who, for some reason, came into contact with a medical institution (pregnant women, women after birth, ailing women). All the same, it brought results that can be considered of value. To the question of how many children the woman desired at the time of her marriage, replies yielded an average of 2.10 in the Czech regions and 2.76 in Slovakia. The reply was only negligibly dependent on whether the woman was employed or was a housewife: the first group in the Czech regions wished for 2.08 children, and in Slovakia, 2.73; the second wanted 2.12 children in the Czech regions and 2.80 in Slovakia. A further enquiry organized by the Office of Statistics in 1959 covered 3,191 women aged 15–40 years and brought somewhat higher results. The two enquiries, however, are not comparable.

A comparison of the outcome of the first enquiry with the fertility level in 1956 led to the conclusion that the fertility level would continue to decline. The results are a fairly precise reflection of the difference between the Czech regions and Slovakia, for in 1956, the fertility level in the latter was 35 percent higher, and the number of desired children 31 percent higher. If the first enquiry results should be considered representative, then the corresponding fertility level was reached in the Czech regions by 1958 and in Slovakia by 1962.

Information gathered through statistics and field studies gradually led to an increase in attention to the population situation. Further measures in favor of mothers and larger families were adopted, which were of a population-supporting nature. In 1956, maternity leave was amended. It remains at eighteen weeks, but maternity benefit is now uniform for manual and "white-collar" workers: for employees with less than two years' prior employment, it amounts to 75 percent of their pay; for those with two to five years' employment, 80 percent; for all other employees, 90 percent of their pay. In addition, all women workers and employees as well as dependent women receive a birth grant of 650 crowns[1] (that is, approximately 60 percent of the average woman's wage). Price reductions after the currency reform also acted to help families with children. Moreover, after the price reduction of 1959, children's clothes and shoes were strongly reduced in price; this price subsidy is still in force.

OSCILLATING BIRTH RATE IN THE 1960s

From 1961 till 1968 in the Czech regions and from 1963 till 1968 in Slovakia, the birth rate oscillated slightly, though on differing levels for the two populations, as appears in Table 7. After the low of 1960, fertility rose slightly in the Czech regions until 1964; then it fell again to reach the lowest postwar gross reproduction rate of 0.895 in 1968. Slovak fertility wavered only in the years 1963 and 1964 and to a far lesser degree.

Of course, it is not possible to give the precise causes of that oscillation.

[1] One hundred crowns equaled approximately US$15.40 on January 1, 1973.

TABLE 7.

Development of Basic Demographic Rates, Czechoslovakia,
1961–1968 (during period of oscillating birth rate)

Year	Crude Birth Rate	Crude Death Rate	Crude Rate of Natural Increase	Marriage Rate	GRR	Proportion of Abortions to Total Pregnancies
			Czech Regions			
1961	13.7	9.9	3.8	7.7	1.027	39.8
1962	13.9	10.8	3.1	8.0	1.032	38.3
1963	15.4	10.4	5.0	8.3	1.125	32.3
1964	15.9	10.5	5.4	8.3	1.133	31.3
1965	15.1	10.7	4.4	8.4	1.056	33.9
1966	14.4	10.8	3.6	8.6	0.982	36.9
1967	14.0	11.1	2.9	8.9	0.926	38.4
1968	13.9	11.7	2.2	9.0	0.895	39.2
			Slovakia			
1963	20.4	7.7	12.7	7.2	1.418	24.3
1964	20.1	7.6	12.5	7.0	1.408	24.4
1965	19.3	8.2	11.1	7.0	1.358	25.7
1966	18.5	8.2	10.3	7.0	1.300	28.3
1967	17.4	8.0	9.4	7.3	1.206	30.6
1968	17.0	8.5	8.5	7.5	1.158	31.3

SOURCE: See [9].

The influence of various adopted measures of the population policy cannot be excluded, but on the basis of data contained in Table 8, it can be shown unequivocally that the declining trend of children born fourth or higher in rank continued in the Czech regions as well as in Slovakia. In 1963 and 1964, however, both populations show a slight temporary increase in the proportion of third children, and these are evidently the only gain of the measures mentioned.

Also, in the course of the preceding period, the reduction of the average age of mothers and age at marriage stopped in the Czech regions, and here lie, perhaps, the further reserves of the fertility oscillation of the years 1962–1968. Indeed, beginning with the year 1962, the marriage rate increased markedly, until the end of that period. An analysis of the age structure would show that the larger generations of the war and postwar years entered the reproduction cycle at the time of the climbing birth rate, but they did not affect the decline after 1965. Factors contributing to the

TABLE 8.

Development of Rank Structure of Children, Czechoslovakia,
1961–1968 (born during period of oscillating birth rate)

Year	Total Live Births	Children Born in Rank Order (in percents)					
		1	2	3	4	5	6+
Czech Regions							
1961	131,019	45.6	33.1	12.4	4.4	2.0	2.5
1962	133,557	46.4	33.2	12.5	4.0	1.7	2.2
1963	148,840	45.4	33.7	12.9	4.0	1.8	2.2
1964	154,420	44.9	33.6	13.4	4.2	1.8	2.1
1965	147,438	45.8	33.5	12.5	4.2	1.8	2.2
1966	141,162	47.8	33.3	11.4	3.8	1.6	2.1
1967	138,448	50.2	32.8	10.3	3.3	1.5	1.9
1968	137,437	51.4	32.8	9.7	3.1	1.3	1.7
Slovakia							
1963	87,158	32.3	28.4	17.2	8.9	5.1	8.1
1964	86,878	32.2	28.6	17.4	8.9	4.9	8.0
1965	84,257	32.6	28.9	16.8	8.9	4.8	8.0
1966	81,453	33.9	29.3	16.3	8.4	4.6	7.5
1967	77,537	36.0	29.4	15.6	7.7	4.3	7.0
1968	76,370	37.6	29.3	15.2	7.3	4.1	6.5

SOURCE: See [10].

very low natality in the Czech regions included, no doubt, also greater facilities for traveling abroad, saving to build homes under cooperative schemes, as well as the unstable economic situation prior to 1968.

In Slovakia, the basic feature was the declining trend of fertility throughout the period of 1963–1968, and it almost covered up the small oscillation of 1963 and 1964. It is significant that, at the end of the period, in 1968, Slovak natality was still 30 percent higher than Czech. Children born in the first and second rank in the Czech regions already accounted for 84.2 percent, but in Slovakia, for only 66.9 percent. In Slovakia, 10.6 percent of all children were born in the fifth or higher ranks; in the Czech regions, only 3 percent were in these ranks.

In the middle of the 1960s, the population situation and the system of measures designed to favor families with children became an important political issue, and all party congresses paid attention to them. The Eleventh Congress of the Communist party of Czechoslovakia, held in

1958, called for increasing the personal consumption of families in the lower income brackets, especially families with several children. The Twelfth Party Congress in 1962 dealt with this problem in greater detail. In the resolution on the main lines of development, preschool and out-of-school children's welfare is stressed, as well as school meals and the further establishment of nurseries and kindergartens. The resolutions of the Thirteenth Congress of the Communist party, held in 1966, speak of further support for population development, the erection of nurseries, kindergartens, and dwellings for young couples.

Following from these resolutions, pupils of general educational, trade, and apprentice schools have received, since the school term 1960–1961, all textbooks and teaching aids free of charge. In 1959, family allowances were raised once more, substantially, for the third child and for further children. For higher income groups, family allowances were reduced for the first through third child. In 1964, a differential pensionable age for women was introduced, dependent on the number of children raised. At the same time, a special compensation allowance was introduced to be paid to women during pregnancy or motherhood in case of their transfer to lesser-paying jobs. Since 1964, rent reductions have been granted in state-owned dwellings according to the number of children in a family.

Act 58 of the year 1964 constituted an important increase in welfare during pregnancy and motherhood. Maternity leave was extended to twenty-two weeks. For the first time, a preference was shown to single mothers: their paid maternity leave was extended to twenty-six weeks, provided that they depended on their own earnings. Maternity leave and cash maternity benefits are also accorded to women who take into their care another woman's child for later adoption or in case of the mother's decease. The Increased Mothers' Welfare Act also affords women legal claim to further leave, until the end of the first year of the child's life. The employer is obliged to rehire the mother after this period has elapsed, in the same capacity and under the same financial and legal conditions as prior to her maternity. In 1964, the cooperative farmers' social security scheme was improved: family allowances and birth grants are provided under the same conditions for wage earners.

During that period, several polls were taken to ascertain the subjective attitude of women to family size. In 1963 and 1964, the State Population Committee conducted a poll among couples engaged to be married, where the husband-to-be was not older than thirty years of age. The poll was divided into two parts: In 1963, 1,886 couples were questioned in the cities; in 1964, 1,550 couples were polled in country areas. The data were processed for the whole republic; they showed the planned number of children in the countryside to be 9 percent higher than in the towns. Though these data are not comparable with data given earlier, because they do not differentiate the distinct reproduction conditions in the Czech regions and in Slovakia, they, nevertheless, lead to the conclusion that actual fertility was still higher than that planned by the couples questioned and that its further decrease was, therefore, to be expected.

A further enquiry conducted by the State Population Committee in 1966 and 1967 showed a particularly small number of children wanted among twenty-one-year-old girls. In terms of gross reproduction rate, the result of these girls' wishes would be a GRR of 0.93 in the towns and 1.04 in the countryside. This enquiry, which covered 1,000 girls in towns and 1,000 girls in the countryside, covered the entire republic.

In 1967 and 1968, the natural history faculty of Charles University undertook a study of 2,732 women aged over 15 years in Czech rural settlements. This, however, also has no comparative basis with the preceding enquiries. It showed that women before marriage desired 2.21 children. However, the replies were distinctly influenced by the existing situation of the women. The smallest number of children planned before marriage were by married women aged from 20–24 years (1.91); the largest number, by married women aged 50 and over (2.38). As the fertility level depends on young women, it can be assumed on the basis of this study that the fertility level in the Czech regions about the year 1968 would not rise and might even decline further; in the towns, the situation was probably worse still.

PERIOD AFTER 1968

As is evident from Table 9, after the year 1968, the birth rate somewhat increased in the Czech regions as well as in Slovakia. In the Czech regions, this is the result of the increased marriage rate during the preceding period, with a simultaneous postponement of the birth of first and second children. This fact is borne out by the data in Table 10: it can be seen clearly that in the Czech regions and in Slovakia the proportion of children in third and higher rank order continued to decrease. For 1971, data are not yet available, but if the authors' assumption is correct, then the phenomenon involved is merely an oscillation similar to that of ten years ago, though it is more marked, starting from lower initial values than did the first one.

The development over the period 1961–1970 is described in Table 11. The proportion of families with three or more children declined sharply; on the other hand, the proportion of families with the husband over twenty-five years of age and with three children greatly increased; and finally, though it declined, the proportion of childless couples was still high.

TABLE 9.

Development of Basic Demographic Rates, Czechoslovakia,
after 1968

Year	Crude Birth Rate	Crude Death Rate	Crude Rate of Natural Increase	Marriage Rate	GRR	Proportion of Abortions to Total Pregnancies
			Czech Regions			
1969	14.5	12.2	2.3	9.1	0.908	38.7
1970	15.1	12.6	2.5	9.2	0.94[a]	37.5
1971	15.7	12.4	5.3	9.3	0.98[a]	
			Slovakia			
1969	17.7	9.0	8.7	7.7	1.183	31.0
1970	17.8	9.3	8.5	7.9	1.18[a]	30.4
1971	18.2	9.4	8.8	8.3	1.20[a]	

SOURCE: See [11].
[a] Provisional data.

TABLE 10.

Development of Rank Structure of Children, Czechoslovakia,
since 1968

Year	Total Live Births	Children Born in Rank Order (in percents)					
		1	2	3	4	5	6+
		Czech Regions					
1969	143,165	51.3	33.2	9.6	3.1	1.2	1.6
1970	147,865	50.7	34.8	9.4	2.7	1.1	1.3
		Slovakia					
1969	79,769	38.6	29.8	15.0	7.1	3.6	5.9
1970	80,666	39.3	30.9	14.7	6.7	3.2	5.2

SOURCE: See [11].

Supplementary information on the reproduction of the Czechoslovak population is provided by Table 12, listing the reasons quoted in applications for abortion. A large proportion consists of applications by mothers with a large number of living children, which can be connected also with the woman's older age. Apart from health reasons, which are difficult to

TABLE 11.

Families and Number of Dependent Children, Czechoslovakia,
1961–1970 (in percents)

Age of Husband	Year	Number of Children			
		0	1	2	3+
20–24	1961	42.0	44.6	10.9	2.5
	1970	35.9	52.3	10.7	1.1
25–29	1961	19.7	43.8	27.1	9.4
	1970	14.5	47.9	31.3	6.3
30–34	1961	9.5	29.0	39.7	21.8
	1970	7.0	27.4	47.7	17.9

TABLE 12.

Reasons for Application for Abortion, Czechoslovakia, 1971

Reason Given	Percent
Health	19.60
Advanced age	2.20
Loss or disability of husband	0.20
At least three prior living children	20.60
Marriage failure	4.30
Mother the sole breadwinner	2.90
Unmarried mother	15.80
Financial straits of family	7.20
Unsatisfactory housing conditions	11.20
Rape or other criminal assault	0.01
Failure of IUD	5.60
Other grounds	10.30
Unspecified	0.10
Total	100.00

SOURCE: See [12].

specify precisely, an important group are unmarried women; this is followed by unsatisfactory housing conditions and financial reasons. Though these data should not be overrated, particularly because of the possibility of combined reasons or of their difficult classification, they still may represent an important basis for population policy.

The causes underlying the current increase in fertility may be measures of population policy as well as a certain stabilization of the economic situation. It could hardly be described as a change of a more permanent nature affecting the basic attitude of the population regarding family size. In the Czech regions, second children, who mostly contributed to the fertility rise in 1970, still present a problem for many families. The data for 1971 will show whether the proportion of third children also increased, which would represent a permanent population gain. A significant fact is the further approximation of the fertility levels in the Czech regions to those in Slovakia; all the same, this historically constituted distinction, explained in the introduction, will require at least another ten years in order to even the fertility levels of the two Czechoslovak populations.

The latest enquiry on the subjective attitude of women was conducted by the Federal Statistical Office in 1970 and covered 2,994 women aged 15–24 years. The data show a smaller difference between the Czech regions and Slovakia than did preceding enquiries, but again they do not provide any comparative basis. They could be compared only with the enquiry made by the natural history faculty in 1967–1968: the 1970 enquiry showed that, in the Czech regions, women before marriage desired 2.41 children—14 percent more than women in rural settlements stated in 1967–1968. In Slovakia, they desired 2.68 children. The results demonstrate that, in 1970, the population climate was somewhat more favorable than two years previously, but it is difficult to draw any significant conclusions from this fact that would differ from those stated earlier.

The Czechoslovak population is relatively homogeneous. The only distinctly different ethnic group is the Gypsies-Romanies. The census of 1970 ascertained throughout the territory of the republic a total of 202,885 inhabitants of Gypsy origin, that is, 1.41 percent; 50,542 (0.51 percent) lived in the Czech regions, and 151,743 (3.34 percent), in Slovakia. It is obvious from these figures that the Gypsy population could not affect in any significant measure the reproduction of both Czechoslovak populations, although it is a known fact that its demographic rates distinguish it from the other populations, as long as the Gypsies live relatively isolated in rural settlements. The Gypsies coming to settle in the cities undergo a speedy process of assimilation and integration with the rest of the population. This is confirmed by the census of 1970, listing 24,182 citizens of Gypsy origin, 10.7 percent less than the preceding census in 1968; these citizens no longer stated their origin. The census also brought to light other features of the assimilation process: The proportion of economically active inhabitants of Gypsy origin increased considerably, nearing the national average; the proportion of illiterates sharply declined mainly among the younger generation; and also the equipment of households of the Gypsy population approached national averages.

In the sphere of population policy, the year 1968 brought a further increase in family allowances. At the same time, the social criterion for family allowances, introduced in 1959, was abolished, and allowances were again paid in full according to the number of children, regardless of the recipient's earnings. Maternity leave was extended from twenty-two to twenty-six weeks, and the amended labor code further increased unpaid maternal leave to two years of the child's age, starting January 1, 1970. As of July 1, 1970, a so-called maternity allowance came into force, amounting to 500 crowns per month, to be paid to employed mothers with at least two children who decide to stay home after their paid maternity leave has elapsed in order to look after their children until the end of the first year of life of the youngest child.

The Fourteenth Congress of the Communist party of Czechoslovakia, held in 1971, emphasized new measures designed to improve population development and to support families with young children and young married couples. These resolutions were elaborated on by federal and national governments, who analyzed the population development and its further outlook and proposed new population measures. As of November 1, 1971, the maternal allowance is paid for two years after the birth of the youngest child and applies universally to all mothers, including housewives. The latest measures were adopted as of January 1, 1973. These include the increase of allowances for second, third, and fourth children and credits to young married couples to furnish their households, with gradual depreciation after the birth of children.

REVIEW OF CONTEMPORARY
POPULATION POLICY MEASURES

Contemporary population policy, which constitutes a system of mutually supplementary and interconnected socioeconomic, moral, and educational measures, was formed gradually, hand in hand with the growing awareness and information of demographic processes and the successful development of the economic basis of the country.

At the present time, direct and indirect measures are aimed primarily at improving the socioeconomic situation of families with children, of young people after marriage and at the birth of their first child; solving their housing problems; improving the living conditions of families with young children and of employed women; and improving factors in the sphere of moral and political influence. In a wider sense, atttention is centered also on services rendered to families with children, on the working conditions of women and especially mothers, on mother-and-child welfare, and on the procedure of granting permission for abortion.

In 1970, total expenditures for social aid to families with children amounted to 20 billion crowns, or roughly 8 percent of the national income (see Table 13).

In 1973, total expenditures on assistance to families with children are to be raised to 24.1 billion crowns. With a total of 4 million dependent children in Czechoslovakia, living in 2.2 million households, social assistance to families amounts to roughly 6,000 crowns per child or 10,000 crowns per household, which equals roughly half the average annual wage in Czechoslovakia's national economy in 1972.

¶ FAMILY ALLOWANCES

Among the cash forms of aid to families with children, *family allowances* are the most important. These include health insurance benefits to wage

TABLE 13.

State Expenditure on Various Forms of Social Assistance to Families with Children, Czechoslovakia, 1970

Cash Benefits	Billion Crowns
Cash Benefits: Total	12.6
Family allowances	9.8
Paid maternity leave	0.9
Birth grants	0.75
Maternity allowance	0.65
Benefit for nursing a family member	0.2
Scholarships	0.2
Other benefits	0.1
Subsidies: Total	2.6
To kindergartens	0.7
To school restaurants	0.5
To school clubs	0.2
To infants' homes and nurseries	0.4
To youth and children's homes and social institutions for juveniles	0.4
To students' hostels and canteens	0.2
On textbooks and teaching aids	0.2
Reductions: Total	4.8
On children's clothing	0.9
On income tax	3.3
On fares and transport	0.5
On rent	0.1
Total	20.0

SOURCE: [2].

earners or social security benefits to cooperative farmers. Claim to family allowances is constituted by the breadwinner, working the stipulated time during any given month. Family allowances are paid monthly for dependent children, that is, school children to fifteen years old, for children obtaining professional training to twenty-six years of age (for example, university students), and for children permanently disabled for reasons of physical or mental ill health. Since 1945, when family allowances were first introduced for all children of employed breadwinners, these allowances have been increased seven times. The latest amendment came into force on January 1, 1973 (Act 99/1972 Sb). See Table 14.

The average wage in Czechoslovakia amounts to 2,100 crowns per month. Therefore, today's allowance for the first child amounts to 4.3 percent of the average monthly wage, 20.5 percent for a family with two children, 42.0 percent for a family with three children, 61.0 percent for a family with four children, and for a family with five children, 72.5 percent of the average gross wage. A *reduction of income tax* is granted only for the first child. This means that, with the first child, the family gains not only an allowance of 90 crowns but, in addition, an average tax reduction of 200 crowns per month.

TABLE 14.

Family Allowances per Month, Czechoslovakia, 1973 (in crowns)

Rank Order of Child	Allowance per Child by Rank	
	Until December 31, 1972	From January 1, 1973
1st child	90	90
2nd child	240	240
3rd child	350	450
4th child	350	400
5th child[a]	240	240

Number of Children	Total Family Allowance by Number of Children	
	Until December 31, 1972	From January 1, 1973
1	90	90
2	330	430
3	680	880
4	1,030	1,280
5	1,270	1,520

[a] For each additional child, an additional 240 crowns are paid.

In connection with the new adjustment of family allowances, the limit for the child's own income was raised. Formerly, this was stipulated at 500 crowns per month. As of January 1, 1973, family allowances are paid provided the child's own earnings do not exceed 620 crowns a month. It is expected that the raised income limit will favorably affect an estimated 40,000 children, mostly apprentices in the higher grades of their training.

Also increased on January 1, 1973, was the additional allowance paid for invalid children requiring permanent care. It was raised from 150 to 300 crowns per month.

Up to now, family allowances were paid to the breadwinner, usually the father, provided that during the month for which they were to be received no work shift was missed without due reason. Since their increase on January 1, 1973, stricter conditions have been imposed. Family allowances depend on proper care for the children in the family, as does the maternity allowance. This is an important stipulation, intended to lead to improved family environment for the children's education in the home, improved school attendance, and so forth.

In Czechoslovakia today, the average family allowance amounts to 203 crowns per month. The estimated average costs per child amount to 580 crowns per month, so that average family allowances cover approximately 35 percent of these costs. Costs, of course, differ according to age. At present, it is estimated that the allowance for the second child covers 80 percent of the costs of his upbringing to the age of five years; in the case of the third and fourth child, these costs are covered completely.

¶ ALLOWANCES AND CASH BENEFITS
DURING PREGNANCY AND MATERNITY

During pregnancy, confinement, and maternity, maternity benefits are provided in cash by the health insurance scheme. These include a *reduced earnings compensation allowance* (Trade Union Regulation no. 143/1965), a *maternity cash benefit* (paid maternity leave), and a *birth grant* (Act no. 88/1968 Sb).

The *reduced earnings compensation allowance during pregnancy and maternity* is paid to women workers who, because of their pregnancy and maternity, have to be transferred to lower-paying jobs. This compensation is paid to cover the full difference between present earnings and earnings before the transfer.

The *birth grant* is a lump-sum grant of 2,000 crowns, payable to all women giving birth to a child. In the case of triplets being born and living for at least twenty-eight days, the mother receives an additional grant of

9,000 crowns; 6,000 crowns of this are used for layettes for the children according to the wishes of the parents, and a savings book with 1,000 crowns is given for each of the children.

Maternity cash benefit, which is the official title of paid maternity leave, amounts to 90 percent of the woman's net daily wage. It is paid for a period of twenty-six weeks, provided the woman has been employed for a period of 270 days during the preceding two years and provided she has had health insurance for a period of four weeks prior to her confinement. Further conditions are that the pregnancy should end in birth and that no employment should be entered into during maternity leave.

Lone mothers, that is, widowed, divorced, or unmarried women, and mothers giving birth to more than one child at once are entitled to thirty-five weeks of paid maternity leave. According to the Labor Code Amendment of 1968, all women are entitled, after the end of their paid maternity leave, to a further period of *unpaid maternity leave* to two years after the child's birth. The employer is obliged to grant this unpaid leave upon request and, upon the woman's return to work, has to provide her with a job which corresponds to her working contract or qualifications. Women with two or more dependent children receive, under certain conditions, a maternity allowance for the period of unpaid leave.

The *maternity allowance* is a population measure (Act 154/1969 Sb, Amendment 107/1971 Sb) designed to stimulate the birth of second and third children. Apart from its population character, it aims at improving the family environment and providing proper care for the children. It also takes into account women's rising professional levels and their increasing economic activity; it helps the woman to combine her economic and public role with her function and role as mother.

The maternity allowance of 500 crowns is paid regularly every month to the mother until her youngest child reaches the age of two years, regardless of whether she had been previously employed or not, provided:

(1) The woman has at least one child under the age of two years and at least one child under school-leaving age, that is, fifteen years, or under the age of twenty-six years if the child is disabled and requires permanent care.
(2) The woman provides proper full-time care for the child under the age of two years as well as proper care for the older children; also, her own conduct must not give cause for reproach.
(3) The woman cares for the children herself and is, therefore, not gainfully employed during the period in question.

From these basic rules, some exemptions exist that take into account the particularly difficult situation of some mothers. For instance, a mother with only one child under the age of two years is eligible for the maternity allowance, provided:

(1) She is unmarried, widowed, divorced, or for other reasons alone (for example, basic military service of the husband) and not living with any unmarried husband.
(2) The child is an invalid requiring permanent care.
(3) The woman has taken the child into her permanent care as his foster mother.

With two children under the age of two years, the maternity allowance amounts to 800 crowns per month, and with three children, it amounts to 1,200 crowns.

Proper care for the children is particularly emphasized. For children under the age of two years, full-time care is required. By this the law means direct, personal care corresponding to the age and health of the child and ensuring its healthy development. This condition would not be met, for example, if the child was placed in a nursery or infants' home.

Also, the law requires that the mother care properly for older children of preschool or school age. Proper care is considered lacking if a child regularly misses school or if he or she is placed in a week-nursery or night-and-day kindergarten.

A woman granted a maternity allowance must live in accordance with the principles of socialist morality. Her way of life must not jeopardize the development and education of her child.

To women who, prior to confinement, were economically active and entitled to paid maternity leave, the maternity allowance is paid by the employer; to housewives, it is paid by the appropriate local authority. Local social workers of the national committee check to see that the children are receiving proper care. At the same time, these social workers help children in those cases where the mother was denied maternity allowance on the grounds of immoral behavior or improper care for the children.

In 1972, maternity allowances were paid to 180,000 mothers in Czechoslovakia, or approximately 90 percent of all women who applied for and were entitled to it. Because the allowance is sought mainly by women with lower incomes, the sum of 500 crowns represents one-half to one-third of the net wage of women most frequently applying for it.

In the case of a child's ill health, the employed mother is entitled to *benefit for nursing a family dependent*. This equals the sickness benefit and is paid for three days, or in the case of a lone mother, for twelve days, for every instance of a child's sickness (Regulation of Central Council of Trade Unions no. 143/1965 Sb).

A maintenance benefit is paid to the wife or unmarried cohabitant of a man in the armed forces provided she is not capable of entering gainful employment. One of the grounds on which maintenance benefit is paid is the fact that the woman looks after a child under the age of three years. The maintenance benefit amounts to 500 crowns a month (Act 5/1972 Sb).

¶ OTHER FORMS OF ASSISTANCE TO FAMILIES WITH CHILDREN
Education in all types of schools as well as other professional training (that is, apprenticeships) are free of charge. Also, *textbooks and teaching aids are provided free of charge* to pupils of all primary and secondary schools.

For dependent children, *rent reductions* are granted (Regulation of Central Administration of Local Economy no. 60/1964 Sb). These rent reductions apply to public housing schemes but not to dwellings in private family houses and housing cooperatives and amount to the following percentages of the rent: for one child, 5 percent; two children, 15 percent; three children, 30 percent; four and more children, 50 percent. The number of dwellings covered by such reductions is 1,405,000, or 33.6 percent of the entire housing fund, according to the 1970 census.

Starting with April 1, 1973, *loans for furnishing and equipping households,* which are partially written off after the birth and first year of life of a child, were introduced as assistance to young married couples. The loan is intended to cover costs incurred in setting up a home, in particular the paying of membership fees in cooperative housing schemes, or the building of a private house, or buying a house, or converting other premises into an apartment. It may also serve to buy furniture and other household amenities.

The maximum loan is 30,000 crowns, repayable over ten years. The interest rate for housing construction is 1 percent, for furniture, 2.5 percent. (For general credits, the interest rate is 2.7 percent in the case of housing construction and 5–8 percent for furnishings.) Loans are granted to couples when both partners are under thirty years of age and who married after January 1, 1973, or not more than three years earlier. Their total income must not exceed 5,000 crowns per month. (The average monthly income throughout the national economy is 2,100 crowns.) When the first child is born and reaches the age of one year, 2,000 crowns are written off the debt; for every further child, 4,000 crowns are written off.

In the sphere of social security, the pensionable age of women depends on the number of children raised. Since 1964, women with five children are entitled to their old-age pension at fifty-three years of age, those with three and four children at the age of fifty-four, those with two children at fifty-five, those with one child at fifty-six, and childless women at the age of fifty-seven (Act 101/1964 Sb). In 1948, it was stipulated for the first time that the period of looking after children should be regarded as working activity for the purposes of social security (Act 99/1948). According to regulations now in force, this period covers the time until the child's third year of age.

¶ NURSERIES AND KINDERGARTENS

Nurseries and kindergartens provide an important service for families with small children. Nurseries, which are run by the Ministry of Health, care for children from four months to three years of age. The most current form are day nurseries, but there are also night-and-day nurseries working five- or even seven-day weeks for mothers working alternating shifts. In 1971, there were 66,300 nursery beds, enough for approximately 12 percent of all children of nursery age.

The introduction of the maternity allowance relieved pressure on nursery beds for children to one year of age. The period that children spend in their mothers' care is expected to extend gradually to two years. For children accommodated in nurseries, mothers pay only a contribution toward the meals, which is scaled according to the per-capita income of the family and does not cover the actual costs, which are paid for by the state.

Kindergartens are run by the Ministry of Education. They care for children from three years of age until the time they start school at six or seven years. In 1971, there were 650,000 places in kindergartens, which represents 59 percent of all children of the appropriate age group. As in the nurseries, parents pay only a contribution toward the food, which is scaled according to the per-capita income of the family.

¶ MEASURES CONCERNING ABORTION AND HEALTH
OF PREGNANT WOMEN AND MOTHERS

The conditions for an abortion are stipulated in Act 68/1957. In accordance with that act, beginning from January 1, 1957, abortions are permitted only under the following circumstances:

(1) A pregnancy may be terminated only in agreement with the pregnant woman.
(2) A pregnancy may be terminated artificially only in a stationary medical institution.
(3) The application of the pregnant woman must be submitted to a committee set up for that purpose by district and regional national committees.
(4) The committee may grant permission on the grounds of health or other important considerations.

The other important aspects are listed in a decree on Act 68/1957, which has been amended several times. At present, valid grounds are:

(1) Advanced age.
(2) Having at least three living children.
(3) Loss or disability of husband.
(4) Marriage failure.
(5) Inability to provide normal living standards, in cases where maintenance of family or child depends for the most part on the woman.
(6) Hardship caused by pregnancy of an unmarried woman.
(7) Circumstances indicating that pregnancy is due to rape or criminal assault.

The committee consists of three persons, one of whom must be a physician-gynecologist, with the other members being social workers, elected representatives of the national committee, and so forth.

In Czechoslovakia, medical care is free of charge. This, of course, includes medical attention during pregnancy, birth, and infancy. At present, almost all births take place in medical institutions, that is, in separate maternity homes or maternity wards of hospitals. Expectant mothers visit antenatal clinics which are part of the general health centers. Although attendance at antenatal clinics is not obligatory, 98 percent of all pregnancies are followed up regularly, 91 percent from the first third of pregnancy onward. At the present time, each expectant mother visits the antenatal clinic seven to eight times. After the birth, mothers with young children regularly attend the so-called baby-advice centers for regular medical checkups on the children's state of health.

EDUCATION FOR PARENTHOOD

Recently, all important documents concerning population development and population policy emphasize, in addition to economic and social aspects, also moral and educational measures. These are becoming an indelible part of state population policy.

The constant educational influence of schools, cultural institutions, public organizations, and information media as well as the day-to-day activity of national committees and enterprises endeavor to create a favorable social climate for families with children, to set social values, and to assure that healthy and well-brought-up children should be given top rank in the scale of values of young parents.

A fundamental role is played by the education and training of young people for marriage and parenthood. Upon the initiative of the State Population Committee, government decree no. 71/1966 charged the Ministry of Health, the Ministry of Education, and the State Population Committee with drafting a concept of general training for parenthood. An Advisory

Board for Parenthood Education has been set up, composed of experts of diverse professions and qualifications.

The task contained in government decree no. 71/1966 is being carried out and the measures proposed therein are gradually being implemented. However, the concept is currently being widened and specified according to the latest scientific findings. Recently, the Ministry of Education issued detailed instructions on parenthood education to primary and secondary schools. Their practical application is introduced gradually, as teachers' knowledge and qualifications in this sphere increase. The entire education for parenthood is based along the following lines:

(1) Parenthood education is wider than sex education, which forms a part thereof. The term "parenthood education" includes a whole set of rules and knowledge concerning the relations between man and woman; this also includes intimate relations and instruction on the use of contraceptives.

(2) Education for parenthood should begin in the kindergarten in such a way as to explain the subject matter to the children earlier than they encounter it in life; in the schools, this education should not form a separate subject but should permeate such subjects as biology, literature, the arts, and so forth.

(3) Before such education becomes obligatory in all schools, teachers should prepare for it not only during their university training but also in refresher and postgraduate courses.

(4) Concurrently with information in the schools, where the main agent for imparting parenthood education is the teacher, information also should be given to parents, in order to balance their degree of knowledge with that of the young persons.

(5) Educational welfare for children and juveniles concentrates wherever children concentrate, that is, in schools of all levels, including universities where information on education for parenthood is given in seminars and meetings with experts; a separate problem in this field, therefore, is created by young people who enter industry or trade immediately upon completion of their basic school training or even leave school from a lower form making it difficult to reach them.

(6) The last opportunity for approaching young men in concentrated numbers is during their military service, and therefore, parenthood education gradually is becoming part of educational activities in the army.

(7) In the case of women, such an opportunity is afforded at the time when a woman expects a child and visits an antenatal clinic, where information is given concurrently with gynecological and pediatric care.

As concerns the adult population, the Government Population Committee requested that the press, radio, and television devote greater attention to parenthood education; during its sessions in 1972, it discussed plans for activity in this sphere. Government decree no. 260/1971, which emphasizes the role of the national committees and the information media, including radio and television, in tackling the population situation, places particular stress on the moral-political aspects of population measures and educational activity.

In Czechoslovakia, an important role also is played by *advisory activity*. No laws exist that would impair the diffusion of information or the advocating of contraception. Every woman can go to any gynecologist in a public health establishment and ask him for information on contraceptive devices, which he is obliged to provide. In cases where a pregnancy has been terminated artificially, it is the duty of the gynecologist to instruct the patient regarding suitable contraceptive devices and the harmfulness of possible further operations.

Current contraceptives are freely available. Contraceptive pills are sold by apothecaries on prescription; intrauterine devices are introduced in maternity homes and gynecological wards of general hospitals and clinics. For this type of contraceptive, a small charge is paid; in case contraceptives are required for medical reasons, they are provided free of charge. Czechoslovak contraception research organizations cooperate with the World Health Organization. According to the records of the Ministry of Health, it is estimated that approximately 10 percent of women in the fertile ages use contraceptives regularly, with 20 percent of them using the pill and 80 percent using intrauterine contraception. The authorities support contraceptive research and the use of contraceptives with a view to reducing the abortion rate and to improving the quality of the population.

Advisory activity concerned with family relations already existed in Czechoslovakia prior to 1945; according to its nature, it centered around individual institutes, such as the Sexological Institute in Prague, the Psychiatrics Institute, and some gynecological clinics. Such services still exist today, and in addition, free advice in legal matters is granted by the establishments where people are employed and by national committees (local authorities).

To improve instruction prior to marriage, almost every district national committee introduced during the 1960s so-called premarital discussions, to which young people are invited who have applied for a marriage license and are awaiting their wedding. These discussions are conducted by doctors, lawyers, social workers, and so forth. The weakness of these meetings lies in the fact that they are attended only by those young people who are interested to begin with and are not usually satisfied with the general information that can be given in the short lectures of the invited speakers. At the present time, the Advisory Board for Parenthood Training is working on a new concept of premarital education.

In 1965, the Government Population Committee conducted an inquiry through the pages of Czechoslovakia's largest women's journal in order to obtain information prior to initiating a marital advisory service. It was found that the public is greatly interested in the creation of comprehensive marital advisory bureaus and that the range of problems on which people expect advice by far exceeds the medical and legal spheres (see Table 15).

In 1966, an Experimental Marital Advisory Bureau was set up in Prague as part of a cultural establishment of the national committee. On its permanent staff is a psychologist and a social worker. It cooperates with twelve specialists of various professions who act as consultants on individual cases upon recommendation by the psychologist.

On the basis of the experience of Prague's Experimental Marital Advisory Bureau, the Ministry of Labor and Social Affairs decided to set up a network of marital advisory bureaus of the same type, as institutions of the national committees. The setting up of such advisory bureaus is also in line with government decree no. 260/1971 on the population situation, which requires the vice premiers of the Czechoslovak government to ensure that the governments of the Czech Socialist Republic and the Slovak Socialist Republic will take steps to improve public family welfare and to impel national committees to develop various services for families with children, for marriages threatened by failure, and for lone mothers.

At present, there are nine marital advisory bureaus in the Czech and three in the Slovak Socialist Republic which are of a comprehensive nature, have the same statutes, and inform each other of their results. Further advisory bureaus of a similar kind are to be set up in the near future. The number of consultations given varies according to the size of the bureau and ranges today from 500 to 4,000 consultations annually. For consultation, a small token charge is paid.

TABLE 15.

Kinds of Advice Desired from Marital Advisory Bureaus,
Czechoslovakia, 1965

Subject Area	Percent of Women Interested
Relations between husband and wife	73
Children's education	57
Sexual problems	56
Compatibility	55
Contraception	37
Running a household	31
Adultery	29
Alcoholism	20
Legal advice	17

BODIES RESPONSIBLE FOR POPULATION POLICY

One of the results of the increased interest that party and government bodies took in population problems in the middle of the 1950s was the creation of the State Population Committee as an advisory body of the government. The committee was set up according to government decree no. 918/1957. Its members were nominated by the government and, it was chaired first by the chairman of the State Office of Statistics, then from 1963, by the chairman of the Social Security Office, and since 1968, after the formation of the Ministry of Labor and Social Affairs, by its minister.

The committee consisted of thirty-four members, all of them experts from ministries, research institutes, universities, or medical institutions. As an advisory board of the government, the State Population Committee reviewed population development, gave expert opinion on individual population problems, and tried to coordinate all proposals concerning the population sphere. The committee represented the first link between research and theoretical workers and top-level political authority, who finally decide definite population and social measures in favor of families.

In 1966, a resolution by the Executive of the Central Committee of the Communist party of Czechoslovakia, dated May 5, called for the creation of a working team headed by representatives of the Ministry of Finance to draft a comprehensive socioeconomic program of aid to families with. children. The working team consisted of fifty experts from the Ministry of Labor and Social Affairs, the Ministry of Finance, the State Office of Statistics, the Ministry of Health, the Ministry of Education, the Central Council of Trade Unions, the Czechoslovak Women's Association, and various research institutes. At the beginning of 1969, the working team submitted to the supreme party authorities a document that was later elaborated upon by various government agencies and public organizations.

In 1971, instead of the State Population Committee, a Government Population Committee was created at a higher level (government decree no. 185/1971). A vice premier became its chairman, and its vice chairman was the former chairman of the State Population Committee, the Minister of Labor and Social Affairs. The Government Population Committee has twenty-eight members. It is composed of federal and national vice ministers whose areas of concern include population problems, leading representatives of the trade unions, the Czechoslovak Women's Council, the Socialist Youth Association, as well as representatives of radio and television, in order to ensure direct cooperation with the information media. The scientific sphere is represented by university professors and lecturers and heads of research institutes.

According to its statute, the Government Population Committee is an initiating and coordinating body of the government of Czechoslovakia in the sphere of population policy for the territory of Czechoslovakia. Its activity consists primarily of observing and evaluating the population development of the territory of Czechoslovakia. On the basis of its findings, it submits to the government of Czechoslovakia proposals of measures to be taken in order to achieve present and future aims of population policy; it discusses reports, evaluations, opinions, and suggestions in the sphere of population development.

In 1972, an office of the Government Population Committee was set up and, under the Research Institute of the Federal Ministry of Labor and Social Affairs, also a research department for problems of population policy. It was decided to divide the members of the committee into several working teams for dealing with individual problems and preparing further specified documents.

For the future, it is expected that the committee's activities will not be confined to plenary sessions. The Government Population Committee will itself formulate population policy, organize the study of individual problems, field studies, and enquiries, and upon their basis will propose further action to the Government. According to its statute, it intends also to coordinate the activities of various institutions, give consultations, organize expert opinion on various problems, work with research institutions, information media, and cultural establishments.[2]

[2] Jaroslav Havelka, Vice Minister of Labor and Social Affairs and Secretary of the Government Population Committee, "Government Population Committee Begins Work" [3].

APPENDIX. Demographic Data for Czechoslovakia, 1971

Total population	14.4 million
Population density	113 inhabitants per square kilometer
Rate of natural increase	0.5 per 1,000
Birth rate	16.5 per 1,000
Death rate	11.5 per 1,000
Female life expectancy	73.0 years
Urban population[a]	
Towns of 2,000+ inhabitants	62.4 percent[b]
Cities of 20,000+ inhabitants	30.9 percent[b]
Cities of 100,000+ inhabitants	15.8 percent[b]
Women in labor force	47.2 percent of all economically active

SOURCE: See [11].
[a] Preliminary results, 1970 Census.
[b] Of the total population.

REFERENCES

1. *Population Reports*, 4–5, 1972. (In Czech.)
2. *Children Our Future*. Prague: Vladni populacni komise, 1972. (In Czech.)
3. *Population Reports*, 3, 1972. (In Czech.)
4. *Population Atlas of Czechoslovakia*. Prague: USGK, 1962. (In Czech.)
5. J. Sveton. *Slovak Population under Capitalism*. Bratislava, 1958. (In Czech.)
6. *Population Development*. Prague: SUS, 1947–1956. (In Czech.)
7. *Statistical Yearbooks*. Prague: SUS, 1960–1964. (In Czech.)
8. *Population Development*. Prague: SUS, 1952–1962. (In Czech.)
9. *Statistical Yearbook of Czechoslovakia, 1971*. Prague: SUS. (In Czech.)
10. *Population Development*. Prague: SUS, 1961–1968. (In Czech.)
11. *Statistical Yearbook of Czechoslovakia, 1972*. Prague: SUS. (In Czech.)
12. *Health Statistics of Czechoslovakia: Abortions, 1971*. Prague: Ustav pro zdravotnickou statistiku, 1972. (In Czech.)

BIBLIOGRAPHY

Fajfr, F. "A study of population development." *Demograficky sbornik*, Prague: SUS, 1959. (In Czech.)

Karnikova, L. *Population Development in Czech Regions, 1754–1914*. Prague: NCSAV, 1965. (In Czech.)

Korcak, J. "The contemporary rise in the birth rate of the Czech regions." *Statisticky obzor*, 27, 1947. (In Czech.)

Kucera, M. "Czechoslovakia's population policy." *Demografie*, 4, 1968. (In Czech.)

Pavlik, Z. "Contribution to the study of the contemporary state of the Czechoslovak population." *Demograficky sbornik*, 1961. Prague: SEVT, 1962. (In Czech.)

———. "Nombre désiré et nombre idéal d'enfants chez les femmes rurales en Bohème." *Population*, vol. 5, Paris, 1971.

Population Atlas of Czechoslovakia. Prague: USGK, 1966. (In Czech.)

Prokopec, J. "Young people on the threshold of marriage." *Zpravy Populanci Komise*, 6, 1964; 6, 1965; 2, 1966. (In Czech.)

Srb, V., and M. Kucera. *Research on Parenthood, 1956*. Prague, 1959. (In Czech.)

Srb, V., M. Kucera, and D. Vysusilova. "Une enquète sur la prévention des naissances et le plan familian en Tchécoslovaquie." *Population*, vol. 1, Paris, 1964.

Srb, V., and O. Vomackova. "Research on reproduction of married couples in Czechoslovakia." *Demografie* 3–4, 1971, and 1–2, 1972. (In Czech.)

Vobornik, B. "Demography and policy theory." *Demografie*, 4, 1972. (In Czech.)

Wynnyczuk, V. "Inquiry on Marital Advisory Bureaus." *Czechoslovak Population Problems*. Digest Bulletin of the Czechoslovak State Population Committee, Prague, 1967.

———. "Socioeconomic relations and planned families." *Demografie*, 4, 1969. (In Czech.)

CHAPTER 13

Romania

Petre Muresan
Ioan M. Copil

ABSTRACT

The Romanian state has consistently adopted complex socioeconomic, cultural, and sanitary measures aimed at achieving a reasonable rate of population growth and at ensuring the well-being of the individual. Population programs are means by which the national socioeconomic goals of strengthening the health of the population, reducing and preventing morbidity and mortality, prolonging active life, and promoting harmonious physical and psychological development of the young generations can be implemented.

Starting with this objective of a permanent improvement in health, socioeconomic, and cultural status, and related improvement in general socioeconomic development, demographic policy is based on complex measures with a view toward assuring population growth and progress.

These measures, which are constantly being perfected, include family support, mother and child protection, full use of manpower, social security, social and professional assistance to the disabled, suppression of essential differences between urban and rural life and activity and between physical and intellectual work, and multilateral progress.

The marked industrialization that will take place in coming decades, together with twelve years of compulsory education and the vast socioeconomic programs planned to continue until the end of the century, are all dependent upon proper size and distribution of manpower.

Until 1990, the desired population size of about 24–25 million must be assured by a series of complex demographic measures.

The principal mandate of the National Commission of Demography, an agency of the Council of State in Romania, is to study the evolution of the demographic phenomena within the framework of the socioeconomic development of the country. The commission must submit to the Council of State suggested measures to promote demographic policies necessary to the general development of the country.

In 1973, forty district demographic commissions were established to work in close conjunction with the National Commission of Demography.

THE ROMANIAN POPULATION AND ITS STRUCTURE

¶ SIZE AND DENSITY

Romania is among the nine most populous countries in Europe and is the eleventh largest European country in area. In 1946, the Romanian population was 15,791,000 with a density of 66.5 inhabitants per square kilometer. It grew to 16,311,000 in 1950, to 18,403,000 in 1960, to 20,253,000 in 1970, reaching 20,663,000 by July 1, 1972. The present density is 87.0 inhabitants per square kilometer. Table 1 shows the variations of the growing rate of the Romanian population from 1930 to 1972. Appendix 1 breaks down these data to show the important demographic characteristics over this period.

¶ URBAN, RURAL, AND DISTRICTS' POPULATION

Romania is formed by thirty-nine districts plus Bucharest, the capital.

As of July 1, 1972, the urban population represented 41.6 percent of the whole of Romania, the highest urban concentration ever. By compari-

TABLE 1.

Total Population and Population Density, Romania, 1930–1972

Year	Population	Density (per square kilometer)
1930	14,141,000	60.1
1939	15,751,000	66.3
1946	15,791,000	66.5
1950	16,311,000	69.1
1960	18,403,000	77.5
1970	20,253,000	85.3
1971[a]	20,470,000	86.2
1972	20,663,000	87.0

SOURCE: See [2].
[a] As of July 1.

son, the 1930 census showed that 21.4 percent of the population was urban, and in 1948, the figure was 23.4 percent.

Growth of the urban population during the last decades has been connected to recent trends toward increased industrialization. Industrialization has created new towns, and the people who come to fill them have become the urban population. Census data show that, in 1930, there were only four cities with over 100,000 inhabitants (including Bucharest, the largest city). There are now seventeen cities with over 100,000 inhabitants, a total of forty-seven municipal and urban settlements, and 2,706 communes of which 145 are suburban.

¶ POPULATION BY AGE AND SEX

The two world wars in which Romania was involved had severe and negative consequences on the age structure (see Table 2). By July 1, 1971, the number of persons 50–54 years of age was 29.7 percent smaller than that of group 55–59, and the number of persons 25–29 was 18.5 percent smaller than group 30–34.

During the last two decades, the natality and mortality dynamics have strongly influenced the age structure of the population. This structure is

TABLE 2.

Distribution of the Population by Age Group and by Sex, Romania, July 1, 1970 (figures in thousands)

Age Group (years)	Total		Males		Females	
	Number	Percent	Number	Percent	Number	Percent
0–4	2,039.6	10.1	1,043.0	10.5	996.6	9.7
5–9	1,419.2	7.0	727.8	7.3	691.4	6.7
10–14	1,793.1	8.9	915.9	9.2	877.2	8.5
15–19	1,807.3	8.9	921.8	9.3	885.6	8.6
20–24	1,502.0	7.4	764.9	7.7	737.1	7.2
25–29	1,282.6	6.4	644.7	6.5	637.9	6.2
30–34	1,573.2	7.8	786.1	7.9	787.1	7.6
35–39	1,553.1	7.7	779.3	7.8	773.8	7.5
40–44	1,485.7	7.3	739.8	7.4	745.9	7.2
45–49	1,302.7	6.4	613.6	6.2	689.1	6.7
50–54	749.3	3.7	335.1	3.4	414.2	4.1
55–59	1,065.9	5.3	490.0	4.9	575.9	5.6
60–64	938.5	4.6	439.8	4.4	498.7	4.8
65 and older	1,740.1	8.5	743.1	7.5	937.0	9.6
Total	20,252.5	100.0	9,945.0	100.0	10,307.5	100.0

SOURCE: See [2].

not unusual. It resembles that of other countries with a dominant male-child population up to 25–29 years of age, declining at older ages because of male supermortality. After this age group, males are outnumbered by females (except in age group 35–39 years).

The western part of the country contains a higher percentage of aged population and fewer young people than the eastern districts. This is caused by the lower natality rate prevalent in the west since the beginning of the century.

¶ POPULATION BY MARITAL STATUS

The statistical information issued from the 1966 census showed important changes in comparison with the 1930 census. The married population increased from 40.2 percent to 52.4 percent, and unmarried population decreased from 52.0 percent to 39.5 percent.

¶ POPULATION BY EDUCATIONAL LEVEL

The 1966 census collected data on educational levels attained by the population aged twelve and over, as shown in Table 3. In comparison with census data of just ten years earlier, the 1966 census showed an obvious increase in the population's educational level. In 1966, the number of persons graduating from the lyceum (the equivalent of high school) was 53.6 percent higher than in 1956. Over this same decade, the number of persons graduating from technical, professional, and middle schools was 2.8 percent higher and that from general schools was 1.5 percent higher.

¶ POPULATION BY ECONOMIC SECTOR

A comparison of Romania's 1956 and 1966 censuses reveals that the industrial population experienced strong growth over the period and the size of the agricultural population declined.

The record of Romania's rapid industrialization can be seen clearly by analyzing the growth of the population involved in industry, building, and generally, in production. During the last two decades, the population working in industry and transportation has almost doubled, and that employed in building has more than tripled. In the same period (1950–1970), the percentage of the agricultural laborers diminished from 74.1 to 49.1 percent. Table 4 breaks down the Romanian population by occupational categories in the "productive" and "nonproductive" spheres.

NATALITY, MORTALITY, AND NATURAL GROWTH

¶ NATALITY AND FERTILITY

Natality in Romania, particularly high during the first half of the twentieth century, has, for the last few decades, been on nearly the same level as in

TABLE 3.

Educational Level of the Population, Romania, 1966 (in percents)

Sex	Population Aged Twelve and Over	Superior Schools	Medium and Lyceums	Technical and Special Medium Schools	Vocational and Industrial Schools	General Eight-Year Schools	Primary Schools and Others
				Level of School Attended			
Male	100.0	3.0	3.9	3.3	7.4	11.3	71.0
Female	100.0	1.4	3.4	2.7	2.3	10.9	79.3
Total	100.0	2.2	3.7	3.0	4.8	11.1	75.3

SOURCE: See [1].

TABLE 4.

Distribution of Employed Population by Sphere of the Economy,
Romania, 1950, 1960, and 1970 (in percents)

Sphere	1950	1960	1970
Productive	92.6	91.1	88.1
Industry	12.0	15.1	23.0
Building	2.2	4.9	7.8
Transportation	1.3	1.7	2.9
Goods traffic	2.5	3.4	4.3
Agriculture	74.1	65.4	49.1
Nonproductive	7.4	8.9	11.9
Teaching, culture, art	2.3	2.7	3.7
Science and scientific service	0.2	0.4	0.5
Health, social service, and physical culture	1.1	1.6	2.3
Total	100.0	100.0	100.0

SOURCE: See [2].

other European countries. This close comparison is also true of the levels of industrialization and urbanization and the rise of the cultural aspects of life.

Natality (the crude birth rate) has decreased almost continuously since 1923, reaching 34.1 per 1,000 in 1930 and 28.3 per 1,000 in 1939. After a "compensative" increase following World War II, natality after 1948 again showed a decreasing trend, which became accentuated during 1957–1966, reaching 14.3 per 1,000 in 1966, one of the lowest levels in Europe and in the entire world.

Fertility followed a similar pattern, decreasing from 89.9 per 1,000 in 1956 to 55.7 per 1,000 in 1966 for the female population aged 15–49 years and declining by half for the groups of females over the age of thirty during this decade.

The gross reproduction rate was less than 1 (0.92) in 1966, which means that the population of Romania has not been replacing itself on a one-to-one level. Table 5 shows the measures of population growth from 1930–1972.

The socioeconomic policies adopted by the government have been aimed at increasing the population by encouraging natality, fertility, and natural growth. The indices, after dropping during 1967–1970, rose to levels approaching the higher European ones: in 1972, 18.8 per 1,000 for natality, 72.7 per 1,000 for fertility, and 9.7 per 1,000 for the natural growth rate.

TABLE 5.

Natality, Fertility, and Natural Growth Rates, Romania, 1930–1972

Year	Rate			
	Natality (per 1,000 population)	General Fertility (per 1,000 women)[a]	Gross Reproduction (per woman)	Natural Growth (per 1,000 population)
1930	34.1	124.9		14.8
1939	28.3	103.6		10.1
1946	24.8	90.8		6.0
1950	26.2	95.9		13.8
1955	25.6	93.6		15.9
1960	19.1	73.9	1.15	10.4
1965	14.6	57.3	0.93	6.0
1966	14.3	55.7	0.92	6.1
1967	27.4	105.5	1.80	18.1
1968	26.7	102.9	1.77	17.1
1969	23.3	89.6	1.56	13.2
1970	21.1	81.2	1.45	11.6
1971	19.5	75.3	1.29	10.0
1972	18.8	72.7		9.7

SOURCE: See [3].
[a] Aged 15–49.

The increasing natality during 1967–1968 reflects a change in demographic behavior. Families who, until then, had only one child or none at all were willing to have their first and even their second child. This modified behavior is demonstrated also by the important increase of natality at the beginning of 1967, when the effects of the abortion law could not yet be observed.

We also have to notice that the natality and fertility rates in urban areas have approached the higher rural rates, which in the past were twice the urban rates. This urban increase is due to the migration of the young workers from rural areas, thus enabling natality to be even higher in certain urban zones.

As has already been mentioned, natality is much lower in the western districts than in the eastern part of the country. But the gap is gradually narrowing because of the recent industrialization of eastern districts which, in the past, were primarily agricultural, while in the west, industrialization began many decades ago.

Fertility during 1967–1968 increased most among those aged 30–34 years, followed by those aged 35–39 and 25–29. Table 6 shows the number of live births to women by age groups. The number of third and fourth order live-born children increased threefold in 1967 over 1966, as Table 7 shows.

¶ GENERAL MORTALITY

Mortality (the crude death rate) was especially high between the two world wars (over 18.0 per 1,000) and immediately after 1945, but it decreased sharply and rapidly from 1948 (15.8 per 1,000), reaching less than 10.0 per 1,000 in 1954 and falling to a minimal level of 8.1 per 1,000 in 1964. As in most countries, Romania experiences a male supermortality, which is not obvious for all the causes of death but is evident in all age groups.

By age, mortality is higher among children less than one year old and especially among people over sixty; in 1970, 66 percent of all mortality was among those over age sixty (index of mortality 2,842.3 per 100,000) against 14 percent among those aged 0–14 years (515.3 per 100,000) and 20 percent among those aged 15–59 years (367.9 per 100,000) [4]. In recent decades, mortality has decreased for all age groups. The changes in the structure of general mortality are due to an improved standard of living, medical achievements, and changes in the age structure of the population. Crude mortality rates are higher in the west districts, because the aged population exceeds the young there, although the surplus disappears when mortality is corrected for age.

There has been a decrease in specific mortality by infectious diseases,

TABLE 6.

Live Births by Age Group of Mother, Romania, 1956–1971 (per 1,000)

	Fertility by Age Groups							
Year	15–19	20–24	25–29	30–34	35–39	40–44	45–49	All Ages (15–49)
1956	52.5	180.4	155.9	103.5	58.8	23.8	2.7	89.9
1960	59.1	164.1	121.2	67.6	39.0	14.5	1.4	73.9
1965	52.4	140.7	99.8	53.5	25.1	8.9	0.8	57.3
1966	51.7	143.0	98.2	53.4	25.1	8.3	0.9	55.7
1967	79.8	251.8	198.1	124.1	59.7	16.6	1.2	105.5
1968	82.4	241.4	193.9	126.5	63.9	17.3	1.2	102.9
1969	72.6	215.7	171.7	108.0	54.7	15.0	1.0	89.6
1970	65.7	201.4	151.6	94.9	48.8	13.8	0.9	81.2
1971	62.1	190.9	138.1	82.7	44.3	13.1	0.8	75.3

SOURCE: See [2].

TABLE 7.

Live Births, Romania, 1965–1971 (by birth order)

Rank Order	1965	1966	1967	1968	1969	1970	1971
1	120,276	118,704	180,043	168,396	144,292	134,877	135,328
2	83,967	82,840	167,343	169,307	145,187	127,978	112,720
3	32,777	31,918	97,853	103,114	91,019	81,018	72,232
4	16,307	15,723	43,305	45,765	47,418	45,861	43,078
5	8,965	8,889	17,151	17,342	16,948	16,895	16,416
6+	16,024	15,575	22,033	22,120	20,805	20,317	20,320
Unspecified	46	29	36	47	95	88	52
Total	278,362	273,678	527,764	526,091	465,764	427,034	400,146

SOURCE: See [2].

tuberculosis, the severe conditions of the respiratory and digestive systems, and childhood diseases. Mortality by chronic degenerative conditions of the circulatory system (including vascular lesions of the central nervous system) and malignant neoplasms has increased, but it is lower in Romania than in most European countries.

The structure of general mortality approaches in dynamics that of the developed countries, the main causes of death in recent years being diseases of the cardiovascular system (48 percent of the whole), of the respiratory system (17.4 percent), and neoplasms (8 percent), with an obvious trend of decrease of mortality from diseases of the respiratory system. In 1970, deaths from cardiovascular causes were 458.1 per 100,-000, with 165.9 per 100,000 from respiratory conditions and 123.3 per 100,000 from malignant neoplasms.

The important increases of mortality caused by circulatory diseases were mostly caused by coronary arteriosclerosis, myocardial degeneration, cerebrovascular lesions, and so on. Eighty-five percent of the deaths by circulatory diseases occur to those over age sixty.

Diseases of the respiratory system frequently causing death are virotic pneumonia, in children and the aged population, and chronic pneumonic conditions (chronic bronchitis and scleroemphysema) in old persons.

Most of the neoplastic deaths result from malfunctions of the digestive and respiratory systems in males and of the digestive and genital systems in women. During the last decade, owing to early diagnosis and treatment, neoplastic mortality has remained stable at a relatively low level. As for circulatory conditions, mortality by malignant neoplasms is higher for the aged; 84.1 percent of the 1970 deaths registered occurred among those aged fifty years and over.

The three classes of diseases discussed account for 75 percent of all deaths in Romania.

The Ministry of Health has developed long-term programs of preventive measures and treatment of chronic and degenerative diseases, aimed at preventing and reducing morbidity, resumptions, mortality by circulatory system diseases, malignant neoplasms, rheumatism, neuropsychic diseases, and so on, which are responsible for a large part of the total morbidity and mortality. These programs are part of a technical and organizational plan that also projects needed equipment (units or services, sanitary staff, drugs, apparatus, and so forth) and establishes priorities.

¶ NATURAL GROWTH RATE OF THE POPULATION

The variations in the natural growth rate of the Romanian population were caused, during the 1930s, especially by the decrease of the natality; during the 1940s, by the sharp decrease of general mortality; and during the 1960s, again by the decrease of natality. The natural growth rate declined from 14.8 per 1,000 per year in 1930 to 10.1 per 1,000 in 1939. During the period 1946–1955, natural growth rose to 15.9 per 1,000 in 1955. Following this rise, however, it declined again to 6.0 per 1,000 in 1965. After an important rise in the years with a higher natality level (1967–1968), the natural growth rate has settled at a level of 9.7 per 1,000 (1972).

Because natality and mortality levels are different in the eastern and western districts of the country, the natural growth rate differs, too; it is higher in the districts of the east than in those of the west.

¶ INFANT AND NEONATAL MORTALITY

Infant mortality was very high until 1948, then began to decline to its present rate, which is less than 25 percent of its 1930s level. The infant mortality rate increased during 1968–1969 because the natality rate rose and the proportion of premature births (children weighing less than 2,500 grams, or 5.5 pounds, at birth) almost doubled compared to the previous years.

Recently, infant mortality has shown a continuous decreasing trend, which should soon permit its indices to reach the low levels of the other European countries. Table 8 depicts this trend.

Precocious mortality (mortality during the first six days of life) is continuously dropping (except during 1968–1969) reaching 9.1 per 1,000 live births in 1971, one of lowest figures in Europe (see Table 8). Neonatal mortality (during the first month) has also been in a phase of marked lowering, from 65.6 per 1,000 in 1948 to 15.7 per 1,000 in 1971 (see Table 8).

The main causes of infant deaths are the acute respiratory diseases, which account for about half of the deaths below the age of one year

TABLE 8.

Infant, Precocious, and Neonatal Mortality Rates and Stillborn Rates,
Romania, 1930–1972 (per 1,000 live births)

Year	Rate per 1,000 Live Births			
	Infant Mortality	Precocious Mortality	Neonatal Mortality	Stillbirths
1930	175.6			
1938	179.0	34.7	70.4	24.8
1939	170.2			
1948	142.7	33.3	65.6	26.9
1950	116.7			25.2
1955	78.2	14.4	30.7	18.4
1960	74.6	8.8	21.2	16.2
1965	44.1	6.2	14.1	14.5
1970	49.4	11.1	18.7	13.4
1971	42.5	9.1	15.7	12.1
1972	39.9			11.0

SOURCE: See [2].

(22.1 per 1,000 in 1970). This cause is followed by a much lower percentage of infectious diseases (6.1 per 1,000) and then by congenital anomalies (3.8 per 1,000).

There is a direct correlation between the natality level and postneonatal infant mortality; the latter is higher in the districts with higher natality.

A direct correlation can also be observed between infant mortality—especially neonatal mortality—and the mother's age. This is also the case for perinatal mortality.

Stillbirth rates have followed a pattern similar to that of infant mortality, falling in 1972 to 11.0 per 1,000, almost half the level of the years previous to World War II.

Conditions of anoxia and hypoxia are the greatest causes of stillbirths, 28.4 percent of the total in 1970, followed by the diseases or anomalies of the placenta or umbilical cord (24.6 percent), distocia without obstetric lesions, asphyxia, anoxia, or hypoxia (3.5 percent), and so on.

NUPTIALITY AND DIVORCE

During the 1930s, nuptiality declined. In the postwar period, it rose rapidly, peaking in 1954 at 12.1 per 1,000. It declined thereafter, falling to 7.6 per 1,000 in 1972.

The rise and subsequent fall in nuptiality were caused primarily by the evolution of marital patterns, with the lowering of fertile cohorts, urbanization, and the dynamics of divorce exerting less influence. The number of divorces, after increasing during the 1950s and the beginning of the 1960s, fell, especially after 1966, because of amendments in the divorce legislation. Since 25 percent of nuptiality was due to remarriage before the amendment, the decrease in divorces certainly contributed to lowering nuptiality, as can be seen from the dynamic comparison of the indices in Table 9.

The phenomenon of the "crossing" levels of urban and rural nuptiality has been important also. Urban nuptiality was lower before World War II but exceeded rural nuptiality after 1950 with the increasing migration of young adults from rural to urban areas.

Another factor in the nuptiality patterns, also noted by other European countries, has been a lowering of the average age at marriage.

LEGAL ABORTION

In 1957, Decree no. 463 made abortion legal upon request for all indications. Abortion could be legally performed at the simple request of the patient in any special health service in the country to the third month of pregnancy without regard to the name, residence, age, or legal status of the mother upon payment of the slight sum of 30 lei (less than US\$2).

TABLE 9.

Nuptiality and Divorce Rates, Romania, 1930–1972

Year	Nuptiality (marriages per 1,000 inhabitants)	Divorces (per 1,000 inhabitants)
1930	9.4	0.45
1950	11.7	1.47
1955	11.4	1.80
1960	10.7	2.01
1965	8.6	1.94
1966	8.9	1.35
1967	8.0	a
1968	7.5	0.20
1969	7.0	0.35
1970	7.2	0.39
1971	7.3	0.47
1972	7.6	0.54

SOURCE: See [2].
a Below 0.01.

The number of abortions increased steadily thereafter, reaching 1,115,-000 in 1965, or four abortions for every live birth. The great number of abortions made heavy demands on health services and increased gynecological morbidity and sterility. In spite of the possible medical complications of abortion, the availability and low cost of this caused most couples to omit any other contraceptive procedure. Although excessive freedom to obtain abortions was not the only significant reason for the rapid decrease in natality rates, it was an important factor.

Considering the structure and dynamic development of demographic aspects in the light of the rapid industrialization of the country and of the necessity to assure sufficient proper manpower in the future, the government adopted new complex socioeconomic measures designed to alleviate the overdependence on abortion. These measures, which affect the demographic behavior of the population, aim to protect the family, mother, children, and youth and to stimulate the natality to reach 18–19 per 1,000, a rate corresponding to the economic progress of the population.

Although we shall focus here on the most important legislation, numerous programs and proceedings have been adopted to influence couples to adopt a certain family size, and as a matter of fact, fertility studies confirm that Romanian families are eager to have children so as to assure a rate of natural increase concomitant with the socioeconomic growth. Past as well as present policies tend to support this behavior.

The principal task of the National Commission of Demography is the study of the interrelationships of changes in the economic and social structure and the evolution of demographic phenomena. The commission must submit to the Council of State proposals of socioeconomic, educative, sanitary, legislative, and other policies intended to encourage demographic behavior adequate to the general development of the country.

Among these measures is Decree no. 770 of 1966, regulating abortion in order to avoid its abuse. The law limits the grounds for abortion to cases where pregnancy endangers life, where there is risk of congenital deformity, after rape, for women over age forty-five, and for other physical, psychological, and emotional grounds. Instructions, no. 8.9 of 19.X.1966, specify grounds in detail. Each application for abortion is reviewed by a medical commission.

Further modifications in the law occurred in 1971. Abortion was allowed for women aged forty and older instead of age forty-five, for mothers caring for four or more children, and for teenagers under age fourteen (and sometimes from 14–16). The 1971 amendment also listed other diseases that are considered grounds for abortion.

As for contraceptives, the usual mechanical methods are available for sale in sufficient quantities to enable couples to practice birth control. Pills and other contraceptive devices (IUDs), although they are not forbidden legally, are used only on medical indication and under the supervision of a gynecologist. Possible immediate and future complications (for the woman and her offspring) must be considered as there is not yet sufficient knowledge available concerning these contraceptives. After the 1966 legislation, the number of abortions decreased dramatically and then, in the late 1960s, rose slightly because of the numerous cohorts of women reaching the fertile age. In 1971, 330,000 abortions were performed.

The aim of the demographic policy is to eliminate abortion as a form of birth control, assuring, at the same time, family sizes commensurate with the national purposes. The national socioeconomic plan of development desires a population of about 24–25 million inhabitants by 1990, and the National Commission of Demography must propose complex measures to attain this level. The measures that will be taken in the future must be based on thorough studies of demographic behavior. Appendix 2 presents excerpts from the decree for the regulation of legal abortion.

LEGISLATION AFFECTING DEMOGRAPHIC BEHAVIOR

The family, as the basic nucleus of society, ranks foremost in the attention of Romania. The fundamental statute of the state, the Constitution, proclaims as a basic normative principle the establishment of the family, the protection of marriage, and the interests of mother and child. Based on this juridical guarantee, matters of matrimony, maternity, and child protection are dealt with in any normative deed adopted or issued by the bodies of the executive branch and of the administration.

The special care granted by the state to the family—to its creation and expansion and to its harmonious development—is rooted in the esteem which the Romanian woman enjoys. Being on equal terms with the Romanian man, the woman's rights are ensured and warranted by law, since her accomplishments are viewed as a double task: She is a producer of material goods and a guardian of the state's spiritual assets. And as a mother, she is the foremost factor in population reproduction.

With these considerations in view, the state has assumed a decisive quota of the expenses for the care and upbringing of children. The state's investment in its children forms and improves its future manpower.

In 1970, roughly 22 million lei (approximately US$4 million) from the state budget was dedicated to maternity and child protection, to the care, upbringing, and formation of the young generation. This expense amounted to more than 60 percent of the total social-cultural expenses of that year.

The main aspects of the socioeconomic activity supported by the state that are included in the legislation protecting maternity and child welfare are as follows:

(1) Services ensuring proper conditions for the completion of a pregnancy as well as for the growth and upbringing of the child.
(2) Guarantees referring to the working place of the pregnant woman and of the working mother.
(3) Granting of maternity leave and the right to a pension for the pregnant woman and the working mother.
(4) Family allowances.
(5) Moral recognition for mothers who have given birth and have raised several children.

Each of these aspects is discussed below.

¶ SERVICES ENSURING PROPER CONDITIONS FOR THE COMPLETION OF A PREGNANCY AS WELL AS FOR THE GROWTH AND UPBRINGING OF THE CHILD

In order to protect the mother and the child, the state grants free medical assistance and medicines to all pregnant women, working mothers, and children to the age of sixteen. The state provides gratuitous legal abortions under the terms of the law. Regarding child development, the state ensures gratuitous education to any degree, free schoolbooks, places in baby- and child-care centers, kindergartens, student hostels, boarding schools and semiboarding schools, and boarding houses for meals. The extent of this protection also includes granting to parents priority in the allotment of lodgings, granting of credits for building personally owned lodgings, and the allotment of places in summer encampments and children's camps.

The Romanian Constitution protects marriage and the family and the interests of mother and child. Two persons marry and their marriage, concluded by free will of the spouses, becomes the basis for family growth. Husband and wife have equal rights in their own relations as well as in the exercise of rights toward their children. A legal "code of the family" ensures that parental rights are exercised in the child's interest.

¶ GUARANTEES REFERRING TO THE WORKING PLACE OF THE PREGNANT WOMAN AND OF THE WORKING MOTHER

The pregnant woman and the working mother enjoy special attention from the management in all working units. They are protected against hard work or work injurious to health, and they are not asked to work after regular working hours. From the fifth month of pregnancy through nursing, women are granted adequate working conditions, sheltered from great exertions or from working places that might expose them to injurious effects, and exempted from night work and overtime.

Pregnant women employed at hard labor are assigned to other, lighter, work without any reduction in wages. After the sixth month of pregnancy, a working woman may not be sent on assignments to other towns without her consent.

The leaves of absence for pregnancy, for maternity, or for caring for sick children under age two are counted against the yearly vacation time. Employed women with sick young children are granted this leave, with pay, upon the recommendation of a physician, in order to look after the children. In addition to the normal work break for rest and for meals, a break for the suckling of children is granted to nursing women at each three hours, not to exceed one-half hour and two hours daily. The length of this break is included in the normal working time [5].

Youths below fourteen years of age may not be hired for work. Youths from 14–16 years of age may work only with the approval of their legal guardians and with a physician's consent, but they cannot be assigned to hard labor or to work injurious to health. The working time allowed in such cases amounts to six hours daily.

¶ GRANTING OF MATERNITY LEAVE AND THE RIGHT TO A PENSION
FOR THE PREGNANT WOMAN AND THE WORKING MOTHER

Employed women in all branches of paid labor are entitled to paid maternity leave, both before and after childbirth. If the child is born dead or dies after birth, the length of the childbed leave is shorter than usual. The length of the paid maternity and childbed leave is also shorter for women who are members of agricultural-producing cooperatives.

Paid maternity leave extends for 112 days, 52 days before childbirth and 60 days after. Shorter or longer leave for pregnancy or childbed may be granted in individual circumstances.

If the child is born dead or dies after birth, childbed leave amounts to forty-two days. If the death of the child occurs after forty-two days from childbirth, the childbed leave ceases (Decision of the Council of Ministers no. 880, August 21, 1965). Women with children under age six are permitted to cease completely any activity that endangers the care and upbringing of their children. This length of time is taken into account as uninterrupted service in the same work.

Employed women are entitled to maternity aid for pregnancy and childbirth and are also entitled to aid for caring for a sick child. The following amounts of pregnancy and childbirth aid are provided:

(1) Eighty-five percent of the monthly wage rate for employed women with an uninterrupted length of service of more than twelve months.
(2) Sixty-five percent of the monthly wage rate for those with a length of service from 6–12 months.

(3) Fifty percent of the monthly wage rate for those with a length of service to six months.

(4) Ninety-four percent of the monthly wage rate, regardless of the length of uninterrupted service, for those giving birth to the third child and all subsequent children.

The labor contracts of employed women on maternity leave may not be canceled at the employer's initiative (Decision of the Council of Ministers no. 880, August 21, 1965).

Employed women with children younger than two years of age are entitled to aid for caring for them when they are sick. The amount of aid for the care of a sick child is assessed in accordance with the uninterrupted length of service of the mother, based on wages, in the following manner: to two years of service, 50 percent of full salary; two to five years, 65 percent; five to eight years, 75 percent; and over eight years, 85 percent (Decision of the Council of Ministers no. 880, August 21, 1965).

There is a provision to lower the retirement age for women depending on the number of children they have borne. In these cases, the mothers must have raised their children to the age of ten years.

Children of employed people or of pensioners are entitled to an inheritor pension to the age of sixteen. If they continue their education, this pension is paid to the end of their studies but not beyond age twenty-five. Children who are disabled in any way receive the inheritor pension for the whole period of their disability, irrespective of age. In case of the death of one parent, a child is entitled to receive the inheritor pension even if the living parent is working (Law no. 27, December 28, 1966).

As mentioned above, women employed full time who have children under age six may, at their request and with the approval of the management, work only half time for half pay if the job activity allows for the use of part-time employees. In this case, their length of service is counted as if they had worked full time. An appointment to half-time work is made where positions correspond with the woman's qualifications, without exceeding the indicators established by the labor and wages plan.

The vacant positions in units where half-time work is available will be allotted with priority to women with children under the age of seven who request half-time work (Decision of the Council of Ministers no. 54, February 1, 1967).

¶ FAMILY ALLOWANCES

The family allowances in Romania extend into several areas. *A childbirth compensation*, paid at birth, is granted to all women who have given birth to three or more live children, regardless of their social position (employed or nonemployed) or their professional position. *Monthly allowances* are granted *to the children* of wage earners or of members of agricultural-producing cooperatives, in varying amounts, until each child reaches age sixteen. The amount of the allowances differs for wage earners depending on their place of residence, the level of income realized, and certain behavior at their place of work (that is, absence without leave, specified initial length of service, and so forth). *Monthly aid* is provided *to wives of men in military service* who are unable to work or are pregnant, irrespective of their social or professional position. A *state family allowance* is granted monthly to families with four or more children, regardless of their social or professional position. The amount depends on the recipient's place of residence—rural or urban areas. The family allowance is granted only to those families of wage earners or of unemployed people who do not receive other monthly aids from the state such as scholarships or state allowances for children. *Monthly pecuniary supports* are granted *by agricultural-producing cooperatives* to their members, starting from the birth of a couple's first child until that child reaches the age of sixteen years. Another form of family allowance is a *reduction of income taxes* for families with several children. In addition, the state grants *special care to children* whose parents are deceased, unknown, deficient, and so on. All of these family allowances are elaborated below.

Childbirth Compensation, Paid at Birth.

For each child born, starting with the third, a childbirth compensation of 1,000 lei (US$181) is granted to the mother. The compensation is not taxable and is supported by the state budget. It can be applied for within three years of the child's birth. Payment of childbirth compensation is arranged by the People's Councils and is given directly to the mother or, in case of the death or legal confinement of the mother, to the father (Decree no. 954, December 5, 1966).

State Allowance for Children.

The state allowance for children is granted to families with children if one or both of the parents are wage earners, students, writers, artists, invalids, pensioners, military men, and so forth. It is granted in accordance with the amount of the tax rate, the average income, the pension, the social aid, the scholarship, and so forth, depending on the number of children and the subsistence of the family and on the place of residence of the parents (that is, urban or rural areas). The amount of the grant is determined by the schedule shown in Table 10.

The allowance is not granted for children who are being cared for by the state subsistence or by a public body. Furthermore, the allowance for children cannot be granted cumulatively with the grant or subsistence allow-

TABLE 10.

Rates for State Allowances for Children, Romania, 1972

Rank of Children in the Family	Area	Income Ceilings (monthly)				
		To 1,500 Lei	1,501– 2,000 Lei	2,001– 2,500 Lei	2501– 3,000 Lei	3,001– 4,000 Lei[a]
Rank 1	urban	150	120	100		
	rural	100	70	50		
Rank 2	urban	160	130	110	100	
	rural	110	80	60	50	
Rank 3–5	urban	180	150	130	110	100
	rural	130	100	80	60	50
Rank 6	urban	200	170	150	130	120
	rural	150	120	100	80	70
Rank 7	urban	210	180	160	140	130
	rural	160	130	110	90	80
Rank 8	urban	220	190	170	150	140
	rural	170	140	120	100	90
Rank 9 and following	urban	230	200	180	160	150
	rural	180	150	130	110	100

[a] The state allowance for children is not available for the monthly income over 4,000 lei (US$724).

ance. Those who have children in their care must choose the provision that is most to their advantage; should they choose the grant, the allowance will be granted during the summer school holidays.

The following groups of children are entitled to the state allowance, under the same terms as the children born from marriage of the parents:

(1) Adopted children.
(2) Children outside wedlock of the mother or the father if they are claimed by either parent or if their filiation has been determined by decision of a law court.
(3) Children born from a previous marriage of one of the spouses who are in his (her) care.
(4) Adopted children in the categories provided by Article 1 of the present decree if they have been entrusted to a family by the appropriate judicial bodies according to the legal provisions.

The families of wage earners and of the other classes enjoy the state allowance for children for a period of sixteen years. For children who are or become invalids of the first or the second degree[1] prior to reaching this age, the allowance is paid during the entire length of the disability to the age of eighteen.

The recipient of the state allowance for children is one of the parents; the child receives it only if both parents are deceased and if he is eligible for an inheritor pension.

Receipt of the state allowance for children is dependent on the behavior of the parent at his place of work. An employee absent without leave from his working place for more than three working days per month does not receive the state allowance for children in that month. Likewise, the parent does not receive this allowance if he or she is on a holiday without pay, with the exception of the first holiday without pay lasting to fifteen working days inclusively. Leaves with permission to three consecutive working days, granted during the course of a calendar month, as well as longer leaves with permission based on certain normative deeds are not considered absences without leave.

Those citizens entitled to the state allowance for children may not enjoy at the same time state family aid granted to families of four or more children. The wives of men in military service who receive aid may not simultaneously receive the state allowance for children. They are, however, entitled to choose the form of assistance that is to their best advantage (Decree no. 285, 1960, with subsequent alterations).

Monthly State Aid.

Since November 1, 1972, the state pays a monthly aid of 200 lei (US$36.20) to mothers who gave birth to eight or nine children and 300 lei (US$54.30) to those who gave birth to ten or more (Decree no. 411, October, 1972).

Monthly Aid to Nonworking Wives of Servicemen.

The wives of men in military service who are unable to work because of a disability of the first or second degree, those who are pregnant, and those with children under age eight receive an aid of 150 lei (US$27.15) monthly if they live in an urban area and an aid of 100 lei (US$18.10) in a rural area. This aid begins at the fifth month of pregnancy and continues after childbirth until the child reaches age eight. This aid also is granted to persons looking after children because of the death of a military man's wife (Decree no. 258, June 1, 1956).

State Family Aid.

State family support is granted to families with four or more children if one or both spouses earn a living as wage earners, members of handicraft

[1] First-degree invalids are not capable of self-care; second-degree invalids are unable to work but are capable of self-care.

cooperatives, or members of small individual agricultural farms exempted from the agricultural tax. Mothers without husbands are eligible if they belong to one of these classes.

Support is given for each child separately to five years of age and progressively with respect to the number of children in the family beginning with the fourth child. Mothers without husbands receive family support starting with the first child. The mother without a husband is eligible for support for each child under age twelve years.

Children are considered to be in the family's care to age fifteen years in rural areas and age eighteen in urban areas.

The basic amount of family support for each child is 40–60 lei (approximately US$9.05) monthly for people from urban areas and 30–50 (approximately US$7.24) lei for those from rural areas.

The basic amount increases with the number of children in the family (Decree no. 106, April 29, 1950, and no. 339, August 27, 1953).

Monthly Support in Agricultural Cooperatives.

To families who are members of agricultural cooperatives in which at least one of the spouses is working, a monthly state aid of 50 lei (US$9.05) is granted since January 1, 1972, for each child in the family to sixteen years of age. The aid is given in any month in which one of the spouses worked at least fifteen days at the agricultural cooperative and accomplished the production tasks in accordance with the quotas established by the general assembly. The aid continues to be granted during any period in which the cooperative member receives an allowance for temporary disability (Decision UNCAP, October, 1971).

Payment of the state allowance for children and of the aid for children of members of agricultural cooperatives is effected through the state or through public organizations that designate recipients. State allowances and aid for children of members of agricultural cooperatives are not granted when children are cared for by the state or by a public organization. Likewise, neither type of allowance can be granted cumulatively in conjunction with a scholarship or with the subsistence allowance provided by the regulation for the protection of certain classes of infants.

Reduction on Income Taxes.

The tax normally owed by the worker or employee is reduced by 30 percent if that individual supports more than three persons (Decree no. 153, 1954).

The taxes on individual income and on agricultural income are increased by 10–20 percent for persons without children. This increase is applied both to men and women without children, beginning at age twenty-five, regardless of whether or not they are married. Exempt are persons whose children have died, invalids of the first and second degree, and persons whose spouses have children (Decree no. 1086, 1966).

Infant Protection.

Infant protection is granted to those infants or young children whose parents have died or are unknown, to infants or young children who are deficient and whose physical, moral, or intellectual development or health is endangered in their family, or to young children who have committed illegal deeds without penal responsibility or who are exposed to committing such deeds or who partake in the diffusion of vices or immoral practices among other children.

Children whose parents have died, are unknown, or are in any status that could lead to the creation of guardianship may be given in family disposal, with the consent of the parents, or be entrusted to a family or to a person, when the consent of the parents is not required but with the agreement of the entrusted persons. Infants with certain disabilities or illnesses, those without parents, and those whose development or health is endangered in the family may be entrusted to nurseries until they reach the age of three years; after that, they may be sent to preschool and school homes; to kindergartens; to common schools and secondary schools of general education for recoverable disabilities; to vocational schools and to specialty high schools for recoverable disabilities; to school hostels and to workshop hostels for partly recoverable disabilities; or to homes for unrecoverable disabilities.

The subsistence allowance for infants given in family disposal or entrusted to a family or to a person amounts to 400 lei (US$72.40) monthly (Law no. 3, 1970).

¶ MORAL INCENTIVES FOR MOTHERS WHO HAVE GIVEN BIRTH
AND HAVE BROUGHT UP SEVERAL CHILDREN

Honoring women and at the same time encouraging them to give birth to as many children as possible has been an important goal of the state. The honorary title of "Heroine Mother," the order of "Heroine Mother," the order "Maternal Glory," and the "Maternity Medal" have been created. These honors are bestowed upon mothers who have given birth to and raised more than five children, when the last-born child has reached the age of one year and if the other children are alive.

The honorary title and order of "Heroine Mother" are bestowed upon mothers who have given birth to and brought up ten or more children. The order of "Maternal Glory," which has three classes, is bestowed upon mothers who have given birth to and brought up nine children (the order of the first class), eight children (the second class), and seven children (the third class). Likewise the "Maternity Medal" is granted to mothers who have borne and brought up six children (class one) and five children (class two). The title, order, and medal are bestowed when the youngest child has reached the age of one year providing that the other children are alive.

A mother can also be honored if any of her children lost their lives or disappeared during World War II (Decree no. 195, November 8, 1951).

ORGANIZATION AND TASKS OF THE NATIONAL COMMISSION OF DEMOGRAPHY

As part of the complex process of economic growth, an important place among the socioeconomic measures is reserved by the state to care for the harmonious development of its younger generations, strengthening of the family, and the many-sided flourishing of the human personality.

The evolution of demographic phenomena has been strongly influenced by the deep political and economic transformations during the years of socialist construction. Fundamental changes have occurred in the number and structure of the population. There has been a high rate of growth in the population occupied in industry and in the other nonagricultural branches of the national economy, which represent at present more than 50 percent of the entire employed population. This increase has occurred concurrently with the natural annual population growth and the gradual reduction of the population employed in agriculture.

Following the quantitative and qualitative intensity of the urbanization process in the last two decades, the population structure has changed fundamentally. Inhabitants of towns, cities, and suburban parishes in 1950 constituted 21.1 percent of the population; in 1971, they constituted 41 percent of the population.

The extensive process of socialist economic development has engendered essential changes in the structure and mobility of the population, from both a social and a territorial point of view. In the last two decades, with an overall population increase of 124 percent from 1950–1970, the active population has increased by 118 percent, the wage earners by 241 percent, and the workers by 314 percent. More than half of the employed population carries on its activities in nonagricultural endeavors.

The continuous rise of the living standard, expressed as growth equaling six times the national income during the last twenty years, has stimulated an extensive program of health protection and of raising the population's educational and health levels. The improvement of the network of free sanitary services has had a favorable influence on the demographic trends. Thus, the overall death rate has decreased markedly, from 19.4 per 1,000 inhabitants per year before World War II to only 9 per 1,000 during 1960–1970. Currently, Romania is among the countries with the lowest death rate indices.

The complexity of socioeconomic measures operating in the field of maternity and child protection—childbirth allowance, paid maternity and childbed leaves, allowances for children, the network of nurseries and kindergartens, various other material aids and moral incentives—and the continuous improvement of this system guarantee a pronatal state demographic policy. In 1971, the birth rate was 19.5 live births per 1,000. Almost half of the population of Romania was born during the last 2.5 decades.

Thus, the evolution of demographic phenomena in Romania—the birth rate, fecundity, the death rate, the natural growth of the population, the rate of marriages and of divorces—is powerfully and directly affected by a number of social, economic, psychological, educational, and legislative factors. These factors are affected, in turn, by the structural changes of the demographic phenomena.

The study of the complex processes of mutual dependence between the socioeconomic and the demographic phenomena requires a general survey, a many-sided knowledge, and a concentration of analyses and of resolution. The fragmentary, sporadic, and independent analyses generally undertaken are insufficient to explore such problems as: the increase of the birthrate and its prospective implications; feminine fecundity and the behavior of couples in relation to the optimal number of children necessary to a family; the fundamental aspects of the family as a basic nucleus of society; the securing of a fair distribution of the active population in respect to branches of activity and to territorial-specific features; the socioeconomic and demographic aspects of urbanization and territorial systematization; and the optimal relationship between demographic investments, economic investments, and other investments.

The settlement of these complex problems calls for the creation of a body to coordinate, follow up, and check the manner in which the measures of demographic policy of the state are implemented, a body to study the implications and to assess the efficiency of these measures and their consequences upon the economic, social, and cultural activity of the state. Bearing in mind the many-sided importance of demographic phenomena, their decisive role in the past and future development of the country, and the complexity of implementing the measures involved through central and local state organs and cooperative as well as public organizations, it appears that the body or institution required to settle the problems can only be part of the highest form of the state power, the Council of State.

The important role assigned by the Romanian Communist party to demographic policy is reflected essentially in the fact that at one of its plenary sessions, in which the improvement of the medical assistance of the population was being analyzed, special attention was paid to demographic phenomena, and it was decided to create a National Commission of Demography.

The law providing for the creation, organization, and operation of the National Commission of Demography states that this "is a body of the Council of State having the basic task to study the demographic phenomena, to draw up proposals to be submitted to the Council with regard to matters concerned with the demographic policy of the Party and the State."

Among the main tasks devolving upon the National Commission of Demography are:

(1) To prepare studies referring to the evolution of demographic phenomena and processes as part of the economic and social development of the country by:
   Analyzing the changes occurring in the economic and social structure and the bearing of these changes on the evolution of the demographic phenomena and processes;
   Studying the prospective dynamics of the population and its implications for the requirements for educational development, for the full and rational use of manpower and the production of consumer goods, for transports, pleasure and sports resorts, as well as for other matters connected to the living standard of the population;
   Studying the systematization and urbanization processes and their demographic consequences.

(2) Studying the demographic effects of pollution of the environment. To present to the Council of State proposals of socioeconomic, cultural, health, legislative, and other similar measures in view of the promotion of a demographic policy complying with the general development of the country.

(3) To follow up the application of the measures laid down in the sphere of its activity and to maintain their efficient functioning, informing the Council of State of the results attained.

(4) To collaborate with ministries and other central administrative organs to elaborate normative deeds projects and demographic measures.

(5) To coordinate on a national level the research activity in the field of demography in cooperation with the academies of sciences and other central bodies.

(6) To maintain in its sphere of activity, within the law, cooperative relations with similar organizations of other countries and with international organizations of which the Romanian republic forms a part.

(7) To carry out other tasks provided by the law.

In carrying out its tasks, the National Commission of Demography will be closely assisted by the ministries and by other central synthesizing bodies, by the executive committees of People's Councils, and by the organizations under the commission. The papers, the data, and the information the commission requires will be supplied to it by these groups.

In recognition of the complex mutual dependence between the demographic and the socioeconomic phenomena, the National Commission of Demography will call upon and ask the following persons and organizations to contribute to its aims: scientists; members of the professorial staffs and other highly qualified specialists whose activity is connected with demographic matters; representatives of the State Committee for Planning, the Ministry of Health, the Ministry of Labor, the Ministry of Finance, the Ministry of Education, the Council for Socialist Culture and Education, the Ministry of Justice, the Ministry of National Defense, the Ministry of Internal Affairs, the State Committee for Local Economy and Administration, and Central Direction of Statistics, the Academy of Social and Political Sciences, the Academy of Medical Sciences, the Central Council of Trade Unions, the Women's National Council, the Union of the Communist Youth, and the National Union of the Agricultural Production Cooperatives.

As an expression of the important role assigned to demographic policy and in carrying out the tasks established by the National Conference of the Party concerning the further development of the country until 1990, forty district demographic commissions were created in 1973. The tasks of the district commissions are similar to those of the National Commission of Demography, in broadening studies and analyses with emphasis on local features. The presidents of the district commissions are also members of the National Commission.

Representatives and specialists of other state or public bodies and of organizations concerned with these matters may take part in sessions. These include research or educational institutes concerned with the investigation of problems that form the object of debates within the National Commission of Demography.

The fact that the National Commission of Demography has to appeal to a large extent to specialists in its efforts to settle the problems arising in the field of demography also follows from the provision that, in order to conduct studies, research, analyses, and other work, the commission "will set up collective groups of workers consisting of members of the National Commission of Demography as well as of specialists from various fields of activity having connection with demographic matters." Furthermore, after debate in its plenum of the studies, researches, and other papers, the National Commission of Demography will present its conclusions and its proposals to be approved by the Council of State. The practical application of the socioeconomic measures adopted, consequently, then forms one of the main tasks of the National Commission of Demography.

The National Commission of Demography since its formation has already approached a series of problems concerning the coordination of studies referring to the evolution of demographic phenomena and processes (birth rate, fecundity, natural growth, rate of marriages, of interrupted pregnancies, and so forth) in order to assess the manner and degree of their bearing on the economic and social development of the country. It pursues, through its activity, studies referring to population structure—its classification of sexes, ages, residences, occupations, and so forth—and the prospective change of this structure. It maintains the close mutual dependence between the demographic structure and the well-balanced development of the national economy in order to proceed with an elaborate study of the phenomena and to formulate proposals referring to the implementation of demographic policy as part of the present and prospective economic and social policy of the state.

APPENDIX 1. Demographic Trends of the Population, Romania, 1930–1972

Year	Population on July 1 (in thousands)	Live Births	Deaths	Natural Growth (per 1,000)	Marriage	Divorce	Stillbirths (per 1,000 live births)	Deaths below One Year
1930	14,141	34.1	19.3	14.8	9.4	0.45	16.1	175.6
1935	15,069	30.1	20.1	10.0	8.9	0.56	23.6	181.0
1940	15,907	26.0	18.9	7.1	8.7	0.50	25.0	
1946	15,791	24.8	18.8	6.0	11.8	1.36	26.3	164.1
1950	16,311	26.2	12.4	13.8	11.7	1.47	25.2	116.7
1955	17,325	25.6	9.7	15.9	11.4	1.80	18.4	78.2
1960	18,403	19.1	8.7	10.4	10.7	2.01	16.2	74.6
1965	19,027	14.6	8.6	6.0	8.6	1.94	14.5	44.1
1966	19,141	14.3	8.2	6.1	8.9	a	14.9	46.6
1967	19,285	27.4	9.3	18.1	8.0	0.20	18.3	46.6
1968	19,721	26.7	9.6	17.1	7.5	0.35	16.4	59.5
1969	20,010	23.3	10.1	13.2	7.0	0.39	15.0	54.9
1970	20,253	21.1	9.5	11.6	7.2	0.47	13.4	49.4
1971	20,470	19.5	9.5	10.0	7.3	0.54	12.1	42.4
1972	20,663	18.8	9.1	9.7	7.6		11.0	39.9

SOURCE: See [2].
a Below 0.01.

APPENDIX 2. Instructions no. 8.9/19.X.1966 Regarding Application of Decree 770/1966 for the Regulation of Legal Abortion (excerpts)

The Ministry of Health

According to the dispositions of Article 8 of Decree 770/1966 regarding regulation of legal abortion and Article 28 of the Law no. 6/1957 issues the following.

Instructions

1. The day that Decree no. 770 of 1966 regarding regulation of legal abortion comes into force, the activity of all special services must cease.

The same day, interruption of the course of pregnancy is prohibited.

2. The interruption of pregnancy will be permitted only for exceptional cases, such as:

(a) The pregnancy endangers the mother's life and there is no other means of eliminating this danger.

(b) One of the parents is subject to a serious disease of a hereditary nature or liable to cause severe congenital malformations.

(c) The pregnant woman is subject to a serious physical, psychical, or sensory disorder.

(d) The woman is over age forty-five years.[2]

(e) The woman has already borne four children who are in her care.

(f) Pregnancy is the consequence of rape or incest.

The medical and forensic indications under which legal abortion will be allowed are stated in Annex 1 of the present instructions.

3. In case of demand for abortion, the general practictioner, the specialist, or the physician of specialized services, if the patient is hospitalized, shall fill a "File for abortion on demand" according to the model in Annex 2.

4. For the cases stated in Article 2, items d, e, and f, Decree no. 770/1966, the pregnant woman must present the following justificative documents: her own birth certificate and those of the children she has in her care, her identity card, and if applicable, an attestation of rape or incest issued by a proper authority.

5. Legal abortion will be authorized by medical commissions, especially designated.

The applicant must present to the medical commission the "File for abortion on demand" in which diagnosis of pregnancy and the grounds for its interruption are indicated.

For the cases specified in point 4 above, the specified justificative documents will be annexed.

6. The medical commissions authorizing abortion are assigned in districts, in republican, regional, and district towns possessing medical staff, and special obstetrics and gynecology units.

In districts where there are no hospitals or specialized units, the applicants will be sent to neighboring districts able to provide medical care.

Medical commissions will be appointed by decisions of the Regional Executive Committee of the People's Council or by the municipalities of Bucharest and Constanta.

The medical commissions will be reconfirmed yearly and brought to full strength as often as necessary.

7. Each medical commission will consist of:

(a) A head physician or a specialist in gynecology or, if need be, a surgeon, as chairman.

[2] Modified in 1971 to age forty.

(b) A head physician or an internal medicine specialist as member.

A medical assistant or a registering clerk of the hospital or of the gynecology service in which the commission is working will be assigned as secretary of the commission.

The decision by which the commission is assigned, must provide a deputy for each occupant member.

· · · · ·

10. In case of need, in order to make a decision, the commission will take counsel with other specialists (between one and three others). For medical indications difficult to diagnose and requiring complementary functional explorations, the commission is empowered to hospitalize the patient in a specialized service.

The specialized physicians are obliged to solve the respective cases promptly.

11. If authorization is granted, the medical commission will send the "File for abortion on demand" to the obstetrics and gynecology service of the hospital where the applicant will be hospitalized to undergo the operation. If the application is declined, the file will be officially forwarded to the district or local clinic which the pregnant woman uses or, if there is no specialist gynecologist in the clinic, to the sanitary circumscription she uses in order to be registered.

If subsequent course of the pregnancy of a patient refused abortion necessitates its interruption, necessary measures will be taken to assure proper medical assistance or send her again to the medical commission.

12. An abortion authorized by the medical commission under circumstances stated in Article 2 of the Decree no. 770/1966 may be performed during the first three months of pregnancy, provided the woman is an in-patient in specialized services or hospitals.

In exceptional cases, if a severe pathological state is considered to imperil the woman's life, abortion may be performed up to six months. In these cases, it will be performed only in regional hospitals and in specialized services.

Abortion shall be performed as soon as possible.

· · · · ·

15. In cases of extreme medical emergency, if miscarriage or criminal abortion (abortion in progress, incomplete) is endangering the woman's life, any kind of sanitary unit (that is, sanitary points, clinics, hospitals, sanatoria) shall act as in all emergency cases (medical examination, emergency medical care, and if necessary, emergency transportation to the nearest service, or hospital of obstetrics and gynecology or of surgical services).

In a district with no hospitals or obstetrics and gynecology units, in cases of extreme emergency, the patients will be hospitalized and the cases solved in the respective surgical services, properly equipped and able to solve emergencies.

REFERENCES

1. *Population and Dwellings Census.* Bucharest: Romanian Statistics Central Bureau, March 15, 1966. (In Romanian.)

2. *Statistical Yearbook of the Romanian Socialist Republic, 1971.* Bucharest: Romanian Statistics Central Bureau, 1971. (In Romanian.)

3. *Demographic Yearbook, 1968.* New York: United Nations, 1971.

4. *World Health Statistics Annual, 1968.* Geneva: World Health Organization, 1971.

5. Labor code, Articles 151–158. (In Romanian.)

CHAPTER 14

South Africa

L. T. Badenhorst

ABSTRACT

South Africa's population problems and policy must be seen against the background of its highly heterogeneous population—its diverse ethnic and cultural composition, its differential rates of growth and demographic structure, and its various stages of economic and political development. The politically and economically dominant, highly urbanized, high-income white population has a low mortality rate and a relatively low and still declining birth rate. This group is less concerned that it will be increasingly outnumbered by the more numerous Bantu, colored, and Asian populations than that it will not be able to provide enough jobs for the growing population and thus avoid dissatisfaction and social unrest, which could lead to political revolt. Hence, the policy is one of highly selective immigration in order to provide managerial and entrepreneurial ability. The native peoples also have become increasingly concerned about their rapidly growing numbers and earnestly solicit the government's aid in implementing population control among their emerging independent national units.

The government, as an inherent part of its separate development policy, prevents an uncontrolled influx of domestic and foreign Bantu into the metropolitan areas, where millions have been spent on low-income housing, schools, recreational facilities, and other amenities for the existing urban Bantu population. In addition, large subsidies have been instituted to induce industrialists to locate their factories in the border areas, thus promoting the government policy of industrial decentralization and, at the same time, enabling Bantu workers to live in their own "home lands" and work across the border in South Africa. The home lands are being developed at a rapid pace simultaneously by the government and private enterprise on an agency basis.

The Department of Health has launched an extensive family planning program throughout the country for all ethnic groups alike. These activities include education, motivation, and information on all methods of contraception.

DEMOGRAPHIC BACKGROUND

South Africa is a state of tremendous demographic and cultural diversity. Partly because of this fact and closely related thereto, it is both a developed and a developing country—depending on which geographical areas, emergent states, and population groups are being considered. Population policy, insofar as it exists in unarticulated and latent form, and the measures that reflect it are closely related to the facts of the kaleidoscopic population situation. "Policy," or rather, action, in the population field, often unintentional offshoots of political and general welfare measures, must be seen against the demographic, social, and political realities of the situation to be understood fully.

¶ ETHNIC AND CULTURAL COMPOSITION OF THE POPULATION
South Africa's population is highly heterogeneous in its ethnic, linguistic, and cultural composition. The Bantu (pure-blooded aborigines of African origin), constituting 70.3 percent of the total population, is numerically the most important ethnic group in the country. Second in numerical strength is the white group (of European-Caucasian ancestry), which accounts for 17.4 percent of the total population. The other two major ethnic groups are the colored (9.4 percent) [1] and Asians (mainly Indians), who constitute 2.9 percent. Each of these cultural groups is, in turn, fragmented into subcultures largely determined by language, ethnic origin, religion, and tribal origin. Thus, we have the dominant minority white population, speaking either of the two official languages (Afrikaans and English), consisting largely of Protestants, with a distinctly western European culture; the colored group, using largely the same two languages,

---

[1] The colored population may be defined as the result of an admixture over approximately three centuries of many different groups from Hottentots, Bushmen, and other indigenous peoples to Asian and African slaves and their descendants and, more recently, of European peoples.

highly urbanized and concentrated in the Cape Province, and having great cultural affinity with the whites; the Asians, speaking largely Hindi and Tamil, urbanized to the same extent as whites and colored, belonging to the Hindu and Moslem faiths, and concentrated in the province of Natal; and finally, the large Bantu majority, speaking mainly seven different Bantu languages (the symbols of their tribal origin and closely related but clearly differentiated cultural groupings), about one-third of them urbanized (mainly during recent decades) while another third still live in their traditional home lands under conditions of subsistence farming.

The cultural heterogeneity of the population results in diverse attitudes toward ideal family size, population growth, contraception, abortion, polygamy, and so on.

¶ DEMOGRAPHIC DEVELOPMENT OF THE POPULATION
The various ethnic groups are in different stages of demographic development. Whites are the most advanced, with a relatively low growth rate as a result of low mortality and fertility rates. Second in demographic development is the Asian group, which made a demographic transition toward the middle of this century. Their death rate is the lowest of all ethnic groups (6.9 per 1,000 in 1970), mainly as a result of their relatively low median age and their declining birth rate. The colored population has recently reached a stage of extremely rapid growth through a sudden decline in their death rate accompanied by high birth rates; in fact, their birth rate, until recently, was one of the highest recorded rates in the world. The Bantu population has a growth rate of 2.8 percent per year, which may accelerate further as tribal control relaxes and death rates decline as a result of urbanization. They are likely to remain in this phase of demographic development for some time until social pressures cause the birth rate to decline along with the death rate.

¶ POPULATION SIZE AND DISTRIBUTION
According to the 1970 census, the total population of the republic was 21.5 million, of which 15.1 million were Bantu, 3.8 million whites, 2 million colored, and 0.6 million Asians. South Africa, being a vast country, has a relatively low population density—approximately 18 persons per square kilometer in 1970. The white population is largely urbanized, with nearly 87 percent living in cities and towns of more than 500 persons. Asians are urbanized to a similar degree, while the comparable figures for colored and Bantu are 74 percent and 33 percent, respectively. All four population groups are still to a greater or lesser extent in the process of urbanization. During the period 1960–1970, both the white and Asian urban populations increased to the same extent—from 83 to 86 percent.

During this period, the proportion of the colored population living in urban areas increased from 68 to 74 percent and, in the case of the Bantu, from 32 to 33 percent. Urban migration by the Bantu is restricted by the government and is influenced also by the government's policy of decentralization of industry and the economic development of Bantu home lands (Bantu areas having or in the process of gaining self-government).

Approximately one-third of the population is concentrated in five major metropolitan complexes: the Johannesburg/Witwatersrand area, Pretoria, Cape Town, Durban, and Port Elizabeth. Each of these metropolitan areas has a different ethnic composition. In the Witwatersrand metropolitan area, the Bantu population outnumbers the white by about 1.7 to 1, while together the colored and Asian groups form little more than 5 percent of the population. In the metropolitan area of Pretoria, whites and Bantu are almost equally represented and together constitute more than 96 percent of the total population. The Cape Town metropolitan area is characterized by a concentration of colored, who outnumber whites by about 1.4 to 1. In the Durban population, whites, Asians, and Bantu are almost equally represented. In the Port Elizabeth metropolitan area, whites and colored are outnumbered by Bantu, 1.3 to 1 and 1.8 to 1, respectively.

¶ POPULATION GROWTH AND AGE STRUCTURE

The total population of the republic increased at an average rate of 2.35 percent per year during the decade 1950–1960 and 2.66 percent during the most recent intercensal period. The latter rate implies a doubling of population in twenty-seven years. The main source of this population growth is natural increase, although in the case of the white and Bantu groups, immigration is an important factor. It is extremely difficult to estimate accurately birth and death rates for the population as a whole since these events are only partially registered in the case of the Bantu majority. For this reason, and in view of the considerable differences in the vital statistics of the four groups, they are discussed separately.

The white population increased at an average rate of 1.69 percent per year during 1950–1960 and 2.04 percent per year during the period 1960–1970. The latter growth rate implies a doubling of size in thirty-four years. This growth is, to a large extent, the result of a fairly constant gain through immigration. Without immigration, the average growth rate for the 1960–1970 period would have been only 1.4 percent per year. The average annual net migration gain for whites averaged about 23,000 per year during this period (an average net gain of about 15,000 per year during the first five years of the decade compared to more than 30,000 during the second half). The 1970 birth and death rates for the white population were 23.5 and 9.1 per 1,000, respectively, giving a net natural growth rate of 14.4, compared to the 1960 figure of 16.1. Infant mortality rates among whites have decreased considerably, from 29.6 per 1,000 births in 1960 to 19.4 per 1,000 births in 1970.

Of the four main ethnic groups, whites have the highest median age (twenty-six years) and the lowest dependency ratio (60 per 1,000 in 1970).

The colored population increased at an average annual rate of 3.07 percent during 1960–1970, which is considerably lower than their average growth rate during the previous decade (3.43 percent) but still much higher than that of any of the other groups. The rapid growth of this population group (doubling time, twenty-three years) is almost wholly attributable to their high rate of natural increase. Although their birth rate dropped by 7.6 points between 1960 and 1970, the 1970 figure is still phenomenally high (estimated at 39 per 1,000). Their death rate has declined steadily over the past decades and the crude death rate reached 14.1 per 1,000 in 1970. The same applies to their infant mortality rate, although this figure was still 121 per 1,000 births in 1970.

As a result of their high birth rate and relatively high death rate, their median age and life expectancy is much lower than that of the white group. In 1970, 45.5 percent of the colored were fourteen years and under, while only 3.1 percent were sixty-five years and over, giving a dependency ratio of 95 per 1,000. The median age in 1970 was 17.1 years.

The Asian population increased at an average rate of 2.72 percent per year during 1960–1970, compared to 2.87 percent per year during 1950–1960. This growth is the result of a declining, though still relatively high, birth rate (34 in 1970) and a crude death rate of only 6.9—lower than that of any of the other population groups. The Asian infant mortality rate, however, is still much higher than that of the whites, namely 38.3 per 1,000 births in 1970. The latter statistic shows a sharp decline; in 1960, it was 59.6.

Of the four ethnic groups, Asians have the second highest median age (19.1 years in 1970), which has steadily risen during the period 1960–1970. Their dependency ratio dropped from 86 per 1,000 in 1960 to 73 in 1970, mainly as a result of a decreasing percentage of children (0–14 years) in the total population. In 1960, this age group constituted 44.6 percent of the Asian population compared to 41.2 percent in 1970. The median age of Asians was 19.1 at the 1970 census.

The Bantu population increased at an average rate of 2.37 percent per year during 1950–1960 and 2.73 percent per year during 1960–1970. Although the main source of their population growth is natural increase, the rate is influenced by migration, especially illegal and unrecorded immigration from African countries to the north. These illegal Bantu immigrants, who are largely unenumerated during censuses, have been estimated at between 0.5 million and 1 million at various times. Foreign Bantu laborers, mostly in mining activities under the traditional migratory labor system, also amount to about 0.5 million on the average. Accurate vital statistics for the Bantu population as a whole are not available, but fairly reliable estimates have been made from time to time from census statistics on age and sample data on age, births, family size, and so forth. Over the last decade, the Bantu birth rate remained fairly constant at approximately 42 per 1,000 per year, while the crude death rate decreased from approximately 18 to 15 per 1,000 per year.

REASONS FOR CONCERN AND THE ROOTS OF ACTION

South Africa, for most of its history, has been predominantly rural. Large-scale urbanization and industrialization only started about half a century ago and then did not, until recently, affect the tribal Bantu population, who largely practiced extensive agriculture on native reserves and worked on white farms. Mining and agriculture long constituted the main sources of national income. It was only shortly before and during World War II that South Africa was transformed by rapid industrial and urban growth to a modern "developed" state. With an area of almost 1.25 million square kilometers and a rural and pastoral philosophy of life prevailing among whites and Bantus alike, there was, until recently, little concern about the size, density, or growth of the total population. In the case of whites, the Biblical injunction of "multiply and fill the earth" correctly reflected the fertility outlook of this group during most of its history. With regard to the Bantus, a large family was easily accommodated in the extended-family system, and children traditionally were considered part of a man's wealth. Childlessness was considered a personal tragedy and was felt to reflect on a man's virility.

With rapid urbanization and the resulting inadequacy of housing and other living conditions and the gradual dissemination of modern aspirations pertaining to the welfare of children, a gradual change in outlook if not in behavior came about among all groups of the population. Sample surveys have shown that the usual proportion of about 75 percent accept and approve of family planning, while a mere 10 percent practice it.

Among the politically dominant white population, the ratio of white to Bantu was no doubt a matter of concern under the surface but never strong enough to induce successive governments to change their policy of selective white immigration (mostly from Europe) to one of indiscriminate highly subsidized white immigration (as, for example, in other countries of rapid immigration such as Australia and Israel). Limiting immigration to whites with specified skills has always been justified on the grounds that their know-how, managerial ability, and entrepreneurial qualities are required to create work opportunities for the increasing numbers of Bantu entrants in the labor market. It has always been considered that one of the greatest threats to the white population's political and social dominance would be their inability to afford the Bantu majority a living or gradually improving living standards. For some, part of the solution is to reduce the growth rate of the Bantu population:

> In some urban areas . . . many [Bantu] leaders appear to hold the view that in proliferating numbers the Bantu peoples have a potent political weapon which can be used to good effect. This is, of course, a delusion. They are already a majority group in a 7 to 3 ratio. They cannot lose their majority status. Insofar as political power is related to numbers, a rise in the ratio to 8 to 3 or 10 to 3 cannot add anything to it. Any marginal significance it may have will be wiped out by the erosion of their economic status. It will be greatly to their advantage to improve their bargaining power by way of economic progress, [partly] achieved through the reduction of the annual increments in population [1].

That the Bantu masses are aware of these sentiments or that they influence the reproductive behavior of the Bantu is highly doubtful.

The above argument, in reverse, probably has been tacitly accepted by white leaders, namely, whites cannot change their minority status by massive immigration or in any other conceivable way. As a result, there is very wide acceptance among whites of the policy of "separate development," or "separate freedoms," that is, developing the home lands of the Bantu peoples physically, economically, and politically until self-government, economic independence, and ultimately, in the not-too-distant future, full national independent status is achieved. (Thus far, the Transkei, Ciskei, KwaZulu, Bophuthaswana, Gazankulu, Venda, and Lebowa have received full self-government and are well advanced on the road to independent national status. Together the above-mentioned home lands had a population of 6.5 million people in 1970.)

These considerations were, at least in part, responsible for the following tenets being accepted and propagated by persons interested in population control—private individuals, government officials, and politicians alike. First, it is felt that any population control program should be nondiscriminatory on ethnic or any other lines. A contributing consideration here was almost certainly that any discriminatory scheme or program, in spite of any justification offered by the differential nature of demographic realities among the various ethnic groups, would leave the white propagandists open to cries of selfish discrimination and racial superiority, if not deliberate genocide. Then, too, any scheme that was not nondiscriminatory would constitute a poor strategy and be doomed to failure from the start. In fact, it was soon realized by demographers and others that there would be no advantage for the white group in a discriminatory program anyway—their already relatively low birth rate was expected to decline further in any case (with or without the availability of family planning means and motivation), while there was so much more scope to reduce the extremely high birth rates of the other ethnic groups. Another principle that was often mentioned in connection with population control programs was that they should be aimed at the welfare of the individual, the family, and the group, that is, be part of a wider program to raise the welfare and standards of living of all members of the community. This belief was expressed in a personal interview by Dr. J. P. Roux, Director of Health Services in the Department of Health:

> It is considered a basic human right that parents can decide for themselves the size of their families and their spacing. Equally, however, it is regarded as a human right that all parents should be entitled to information and facilities for family planning. . . .
> [We] regard a high birth rate and rapid population growth as the greatest single handicap to economic and social development in developing countries. An effective policy to control population increase is considered an essential element in any development plan and family planning is therefore one of the most important instruments in the implementation of such a policy. Justification for such a policy is not limited to the demographic situation. Of equal importance are the welfare considerations, the health aspect and the need for an improved quality of life.

The above approaches to and principles underlying that which is considered a sound population program for South Africa were enumerated by Professor S. P. Cilliers of the University of Stellenbosch in a public address some years ago:

(1) In heterogeneous societies such as ours a population programme should be directed equally at all sectors of the population without distinction.
(2) Equal emphasis should be put on bringing knowledge, understanding, and motivation to people, on the one hand, as well as means and facilities, on the other hand.
(3) Such a programme must be a public programme in which all sectors of the community must be involved.
(4) A programme for the reduction of population growth rates must form but part of a broader programme for social, economic, cultural, moral, and political advancement.

As reflected in the statement, there is a distinct element of concern for the health and welfare of all members of the population when population policy is considered. Sometimes, as here, the general, positive, welfare aspects are stressed, while in other instances the cost, wastefulness, suffering, and obstacles to development that occur in the absence of an integrated, scientific, preventative population policy are emphasized. So, for example, the Abortion Reform League has often appealed for the liberalization of South Africa's abortion laws, largely on the grounds of the waste and many undesirable consequences of illegal abortion (for example, death, sterility, chronic ill health, psychological disturbances, unnecessary medical costs). This is, by no means, a problem of minor magnitude since "back-street" abortions are estimated at about 220,000 per year in South Africa. This figure, if correct, means that, without abortion, the crude birth rate would be raised by about 10 births per 1,000 population per year. More and more attention is now being focused on the most crucial problem that results from a population whose reproductive behavior still largely conforms to circumstances no longer true (that is, high infant and child mortality)—the problem of unwanted children. As Dr. Sharratt of the Abortion Reform League has said:

> If, for argument's sake, laws could be devised that were so strict that they did wipe out "back-street" abortion, such a solution would not be effective, for the malaise—the unwanted nature of many pregnancies—would simply transform into a new problem of comparable gravity: the birth of many unwanted babies [2].

Whereas there has been limited concern with the absolute size and the growth rate of the population as a whole, there has been rather more concern among whites with the ratio of whites to Bantus in the country as a whole and in certain parts in particular—rapidly growing metropolitan areas such as Johannesburg and the Witwatersrand, Durban, Cape Town, Port Elizabeth, and Pretoria. A system of "influx control" was instituted to prevent the rapid migration of Bantus to these cities—both from the agrarian South African Bantu areas and from other African states as far as 3,000 kilometers away. (There has always been a steady flow of loosely controlled, illegal labor southward to areas of industrialization and development.) It was felt that the benefits resulting from huge expenditures for public housing and services for the poor would be lost through hopeless overcrowding and the development of shanty towns and other slum conditions. As a result, the government has developed an active industrial decentralization policy as a desirable goal in itself but also as a concomitant of the population distribution policy in general.

Closely related to the fear of overcrowding and the deleterious effects of overconcentration in large cities is concern for the political future of the different ethnic groups in a harmonious whole of national and self-governing units. Both the policies of industrial development on the borders of the home lands and of active home land development are related to the concern with and the overall regulation of current and future peaceful coexistence of the races.

What do the Bantu leaders in the emerging home lands feel about population control and family planning programs for their people? Several have made public pronouncements on the subject, and all have had extensive discussions and correspondence on the matter with the Department of Bantu Administration and Development and the Department of Health. Chief Lucas Mangope, Chief Minister of the Bophuthatswana government, recently stated in a public address:

The problem of uncontrolled population growth is a problem of such immense seriousness that its solution must enjoy the highest priority. Otherwise, all our attempts to sort out a pattern for peaceful and prosperous coexistence in the future will be rendered utterly futile and meaningless. The longer population control is retarded, the more our land hunger will increase.

On another occasion, he appealed to the South African government to immediately formulate and implement a population policy for all communities:

We have reached the time when we can no longer run away from this hard and uncomfortable fact: If our numbers increase more rapidly than our pace of development, and beyond our resources, the standard of our existence will inevitably fall, and all our dreams of a better life will be dashed to pieces.

The Chief Minister of the Transkei, the oldest self-governing territory in the republic, has often referred to the need for population control and for giving it high priority in development and the role that family planning can play in raising living standards:

I should like to conclude by registering awareness that my people have a very large part to play in ensuring that they and those who come after them have the benefit of even better health care in the future. Put bluntly, the indiscriminate giving of life to children by parents without a thought of their ability to house, feed, clothe, and educate them is a primary factor in malnutrition and disease, the overloading of schools and hospitals, and the consequential lowering of standards. In short, the population explosion makes difficult, if not impossible, the raising of standards in any field, not the least of which is health care which, if nevertheless somehow improved, paradoxically aggravates the situation by increasing life expectancy.

It is evident from these few quotations that the Bantu leaders are fully aware of the role high growth rates play in retarding or rendering impossible the raising of living standards and the quality of life in their nations.

POPULATION POLICY AS REVEALED IN ACTION

South Africa's population policy is not explicitly formulated, but government thinking and intentions with regard to family planning, population control, and demographic development are reflected in the following policies, programs, laws, and actions:

(1) The National Family Planning Program of the Department of Health.
(2) Family planning services rendered by various private and public institutions.
(3) Laws regarding the availability and use of contraceptive methods, sterilization, and induced abortion.
(4) Family assistance programs.
(5) Immigration policy.
(6) Measures designed to control and influence the geographical distribution of the population.

¶ THE NATIONAL FAMILY PLANNING ASSOCIATION

The government National Family Planning Program aims at coordinating all activities of the numerous institutions concerned with family planning, welfare, and related services throughout the country. The program, which is administered by the Department of Health, is intended to ensure the effective mobilization of all available facilities (hospitals, district surgeons, nurses, clinics, welfare organizations, research, and so forth) toward a common end. The primary goal of the program is to supply contraceptive services free of charge to all who desire such means, regardless of race, creed, marital status, or socioeconomic circumstances. Secondly, the program actively promotes the idea of family planning and seeks to motivate the population to practice family planning by educating them to the benefits of population control and smaller families.

A large number of prenatal, postnatal, and family planning clinics spread throughout the country are operated by various government departments, provincial administrations, local authorities, and welfare organizations. The activities of these clinics are coordinated and, in many cases, subsidized by the Department of Health. They render services to all population groups, even in the most remote rural areas. These services include medical consultation and treatment, prescription and free supply of contraceptives, treatment of side-effects arising from the use of contraceptives, cytological examinations and treatment, general medical attention to prenatal and postnatal ailments, and the dissemination of information and motivational material on family planning.

Total figures for all the clinics in the country are not readily available, but figures describing the activities of the clinics in one city are presented here. According to the statistics supplied by the maternal and child welfare officer of the municipality of Cape Town (population 750,000), 26,842 persons attended the local clinics during 1972. More than 20,000 of these were colored women and approximately 5,000 were Bantu. Of the 90,000 clinic visits, 72,000 were by colored and 13,500 by Bantu women. Of the colored women attending the clinics, 7 percent were in the age group 15–19 years, 27 percent were 20–24 years, 27 percent were 25–29 years, 20 percent were 30–34 years, 12 percent were 35–40 years, and 7 percent were 40 years or over. Also of interest is the fact that almost two-thirds of the colored clinic attenders had three or fewer children (2 percent, no children; 19 percent, one child; 24 percent, two children; and 19 percent, three children). An analysis of all contraceptives supplied by the clinic shows that, with all population groups, the pill was the most popular method. In the case of whites and colored, almost 80 percent used the pill, while in the case of Asians and Bantu, approximately 60 percent did (more than a third of Bantu women used *Depo provera*). An analysis of requested changes of contraceptive means indicates a trend away from the IUD and especially toward the pill. Unfortunately, no figures are available for the failure rate of the IUD. Since 1947, postnatal clinics have been held fortnightly in cooperation with the South African Council for Maternal and Family Welfare (now the National Family Planning Association). At these clinics, each woman receives a routine postnatal examination and any case requiring further treatment is referred to the gynecological department of a hospital. Instruction in family spacing and fertility control is also given. These figures for the municipality of Cape Town clinics must be measured against the following population figures: colored 412,340 and Bantu 91,150 in 1972. In addition, there were two large clinics run by the Family Planning Association in this municipal area.

¶ THE NATIONAL FAMILY PLANNING ASSOCIATION
The association (originally the South African Council for Maternal and Family Welfare) was founded in 1932 in Cape Town and is affiliated with the International Planned Parenthood Federation. Its main objective is to provide free prenatal and postnatal medical and welfare services to mothers of all population groups. Since 1938, the council has been subsidized by the government. In 1962, it was divided into five branches or constituent associations—Eastern Cape, Western Cape, Natal, Orange Free State, and Transvaal—and the activities of these branches were coordinated from Johannesburg.

In 1967, some of the clinics of the South African Council for Maternal and Family Welfare were taken over by the health departments of municipalities and other local authorities, and the South African Council for

Maternal and Child Welfare began to focus their activities more and more on the promotion of family planning. In 1969, the council changed its name to the National Family Planning Association. At that stage, they were still responsible for running 166 clinics in all parts of the country. At present, the association is concerned largely with the training of nurses and social workers in fertility control and promoting the advantages of family planning. To this purpose, they employ various promotional methods such as newspaper and magazine articles and advertisements, educational films, brochures, sex education pamphlets, and seminars (on their own or in conjunction with welfare organizations). The association is a registered welfare organization and heavily subsidized by the Department of Health.

¶ CONTRACEPTION AND THE LAW
There is no legal restriction on the practice of contraception in South Africa. The availability of certain means of contraception (for example, the pill and IUD) is, however, subject to medical prescription and/or supervision. Paradoxically, however, the law does not permit commercial advertising, promotion, or display of any contraceptives. This is probably, as in many other countries, a hang-over from the pronatalist past and the influence of the churches.

Commercially, most modern contraceptives are freely available at retail chemist shops throughout the country. All district surgeons, family planning clinics, and many mines and factories are issued contraceptives by the Department of Health, and they are freely available through these channels.

In May of 1973, the government accepted a scheme proposed by the Pharmaceutical Society of South Africa for free distribution of the pill to all women, irrespective of race, marital status, or age (except that females under sixteen need their parents' consent). The distribution will eventually be done through a countrywide network of 2,342 retail pharmacists who will issue the pill to all women on presentation of a medical certificate issued by a family planning clinic, district surgeon, or private doctor. This step clearly demonstrates the government's sincere concern with excessive population growth and its firm intention to deal with the problem on an extensive scale. Previously, the government has tended to approach the problem by indirect and rather unobtrusive means. They were reluctant to act openly for fear that Bantu leaders would oppose family planning for their people on the ground that whites were only interested in reducing their numbers for political reasons. Also, as mentioned earlier, many Bantu males are traditionally opposed to family planning because they regard small families as a serious reflection on their virility.

¶ ABORTION AND STERILIZATION LAWS

Induced abortion is not legally permitted in South Africa. A medical doctor who has performed an abortion is not protected by the law against any legal claims resulting from the operation. The abortion law does, however, provide for induced abortion by a qualified surgeon in a public hospital in a case of rape. A woman who wants an abortion on these grounds first has to make a sworn statement to the police and a magistrate and then has to be examined by two qualified doctors with at least five years' experience. Briefly, these points summarize the most salient points in the February 1973 bill on abortion.

Abortion was always prohibited by law in South Africa; this latest legislation was aimed at consolidating and strengthening previous legislation in this regard. Public reaction to this law has been diverse in nature as may be expected in a heterogeneous society. Spokesmen of various churches generally welcomed the bill, some with certain reservations. On the other hand, spokesmen from a number of welfare committees and councils have expressed total opposition to the bill, for example, the Abortion Reform League and the National Family Planning Association. The important point is that legally induced abortion, as a result of its strict provisions, plays a very minor role in population control. The chances for a liberalized abortion bill in the foreseeable future are extremely slight.

Sterilization by qualified medical doctors in approved hospitals is legally permitted and available to all persons on request. In the case of a married person, the consent of the spouse is required. A vasectomy can be performed in special circumstances, for example, where childbirth would endanger the life of the mother or where one of the parents suffers from an hereditary physical or mental disease, certain disabilities, or mental derangements.

Sterilization contributes very little toward fertility control, especially among the lower socioeconomic strata of the population. Many Bantu and colored males would not consent to the sterilization of their wives for various reasons stemming from their tribal and cultural traditions, beliefs, and mores or out of fear that promiscuity of their women would result.

¶ CONTRACEPTION: ATTITUDES AND PRACTICE

Having briefly outlined certain steps taken with regard to family planning and contraception and the legal position with regard to the availability of contraceptives, the question arises as to what extent contraceptives are used by various groups of the population and to what effect.

Since 1950, a number of sample surveys have been conducted among different population groups in certain metropolitan areas. Although not representative of the total population, these studies give valuable information on attitudes toward family planning and contraception and the use of various forms of contraception among some important groups. For example, a recent survey by the Human Sciences Research Council of married colored women aged 15–44 in the Cape Town metropolitan area indicated that contraception was practiced in relatively few cases. Fifty-five percent of the married couples had never used any of the eight contraceptives on which information was elicited, and two percent had never heard of any of them. Among the chemical or appliance methods, the pill (31 percent) and the IUD (11 percent) were used in most cases. Of the nonappliance methods, coitus interruptus (14 percent) and rhythm (4 percent) were most commonly used. The survey results showed that contraception is practiced as a means of birth control rather than as a means of spacing births; in the majority of cases, it is practiced for the first time after a number of children have already been born in order to prevent further conceptions. A further reason why the use of contraceptive devices and techniques has not as yet made any significant change in the colored birth rate is the ineffective application of contraception through, for example, an inadequate knowledge of the biological processes of reproduction. Only 5 percent of the sample knew when the "danger period" in the monthly cycle occurred.

The study revealed almost no serious opposition toward the idea of contraception among both the male and female colored population. A large proportion of respondents, especially among the young ones, expressed a desire to know more about the subject. This finding is encouraging in view of the government's attitude that family planning should be entirely optional and that the need for it should arise from each individual family's own realization of its benefits. However, the survey clearly showed that, on the whole, reproduction among the colored population is still taking place at a rapid rate—in only 3.3 percent of the case, conception had never taken place; 10.2 percent of respondents had experienced ten or more conceptions (in some cases as many as 18); premarital pregnancy occurred in 38.5 percent of the cases.

¶ FAMILY ASSISTANCE PROGRAMS

Family assistance in financial and other forms is given by the government and various private welfare organizations. Government assistance to families mainly takes the form of income tax allowances and payments of subsistence allowances to needy families. Married persons are taxed at a lower rate than unmarried persons (approximately 25 percent less). Apart from the lower tax rate, a person's taxable income is reduced by 1,000 rands[2] (R1,000) for being married, R450 per child for the first two chil-

---

[2] Approximately US$1,274. As of January 1, 1973, R1 equaled US$1.274.

dren, R550 per child for the third and each additional child, plus an additional R100 per child born in that particular tax year. Other forms of family assistance include the following:

(1) Low-income housing.
(2) Family allowances to low-income families (for example, in the case of a family consisting of both parents and three children with an income of less than approximately R2,000 per year, the allowance amounts to the difference between their income and R2,000).
(3) Children's allowances payable to widows or deserted women with very low incomes.

Although these measures seem pronatalist in nature, they can have little influence on population growth; their primary purpose is to provide a certain minimal standard of living for all.

¶ IMMIGRATION POLICY

The South African government's policy on immigration is aimed mainly at alleviating the country's acute shortage of skilled and professional manpower. Prospective immigrants are selected strictly on the basis of their skills and potential entrepreneurial abilities. The Department of Immigration must be satisfied that the prospective immigrant already has acquired a post or job or that the demand for his skill or professional qualifications is sufficiently high to ensure immediate employment.

The government's immigration policy has certain other important economic advantages for the country, such as savings in the cost of training workers in a skill or profession, benefits arising from imported (and often superior) skills and know-how, and the generation of job opportunities for the increasing numbers of unskilled black workers entering the economy.

In view of the dualistic nature of the white population (those of Anglo-Saxon as against those of continental European descent), the government must avoid disturbing the *status quo* by their selection of immigrants. Also, there are strong sentiments in favor of Protestant rather than Catholic immigrants.

Strenuous efforts are being made to prevent black foreigners from entering and settling in the country. In spite of the large annual number being deported and repatriated, the number of illegal black immigrants is estimated variously as between 0.5 million and 1 million. As may be expected in the prosperous tip of a poverty-stricken continent, this problem is likely to remain with us for a long time in spite of strict control. At the same time, there is hardly any discernible migration of Bantus out of South Africa, although such movement is, in practice, easily affected without the knowledge of the authorities across a long and largely unguarded border.

While a passport or exit permit is formally required by law for international movement, such emigration is not at all inhibited by these measures.

¶ MEASURES TO GEOGRAPHICALLY REDISTRIBUTE THE POPULATION
According to the government's policy of separate or multinational development, each Bantu nation should have its own territory in which it can
develop toward full national independence. The ultimate aim is a South
Africa consisting of a commonwealth of sovereign states, each with its own
national identity, living in peaceful coexistence and linked together by
mutually beneficial economic ties.

One of the most important implications of the policy of multinational
development is that its execution involves eventual geographical redistribution of the population along ethnic and cultural lines and the resettlement of large numbers of Bantu in their own national areas. The complete
geographical separation of ethnic groups will probably never be realized,
but government policy is aimed at reducing both the push of the agrarian
and underdeveloped home lands and the pull of the industrialized metropolitan areas. Hopefully, the stream in the direction of the cities will be
stopped or stemmed and ultimately, perhaps, be reversed.

Measures to achieve the aims outlined above consist mainly of steps
taken to:

(1) Exercise control over and discourage the entry of Bantu workers into
    certain industrial areas.
(2) Support border industries near the emergent Bantu states.
(3) Promote the economic development of the Bantu home lands.

The entry of home-land Bantus into metropolitan areas is controlled by
means of a permit, or internal "passport," system. These permits allow
Bantu workers to enter and reside in a prescribed area for a specified
period, after which they must return to their home lands or apply for
renewal. Apart from the fact that influx control is a logical consequence
of the government's multinational development program and industrial
decentralization policy, the measure is justified on the ground that it helps
to prevent overcrowding and urban deterioration, the depression of
(Bantu) wages and salaries, the destruction of the carefully constructed
and costly infrastructure, and the detribalization of national units that
should form the building blocks of the emergent Bantu national states.

Under the Physical Planning and Utilization of Resources Act, which
was designed, *inter alia*, to promote the decentralization of industries and
discourage the flow of Bantus to the metropolitan areas, the Department
of Planning was given control over the zoning and subdivision of indus-

trial land, the establishment of industrial townships, and the number of Bantus employed in a given factory or extension thereof in certain prescribed areas. Implementation of this act, together with other influx-control measures, contributed substantially to slowing the relative growth of the metropolitan centers.

¶ HOME LAND DEVELOPMENT

Large sums have recently been made available by the central government through the Bantu Development Corporation and other similar organizations to speed economic growth, industrialization, and urban development in the home lands. This means of stemming the flow of the Bantu population to the rapidly growing urban centers through building the infrastructure and improving the living conditions and employment opportunities in the home lands is gathering momentum and probably will contribute largely to the ultimate patterns of population distribution. Lately, the effects of this policy have been enhanced by allowing white entrepeneurs to locate factories in the home lands on an agency basis. National leaders are actively engaged in obtaining more aid from national and international bodies for the development of their national units. If the joint efforts of the home land governments and the Department of Health in their population-control endeavors are only mildly successful, they should help considerably in getting the home-land development program off the ground.

¶ THE DEVELOPMENT OF BORDER INDUSTRIES

The development of industries near home-land borders is encouraged by the government through attractive direct subsidizations and income tax allowances to private enterprises. This policy is aimed at industrial decentralization in such a way that the Bantu worker can reside in his own home land but work across the border in South Africa during the day. Recent studies by the Institute of Manpower Research of the Human Sciences Research Council revealed that more than 104,000 employment opportunities have been created in border areas as of 1971. It was also established that employment opportunities have increased at a rate of 18 percent per year in border areas as compared to 6 percent per year in the country as a whole.

REFERENCES

1. J. L. Sadie, "The costs of population growth in South Africa." *South African Journal of Economics*, vol. 40, no. 2 (June 1972): 117–118.
2. Brian Rudden. "Shock abortion death toll in South Africa." *Sunday Times*, March 11, 1973, p. 15.

CHAPTER 15

Canada

Jacques Henripin
Hervé Gauthier

ABSTRACT

Two aspects of the Canadian population can be stressed as the object of intentional population policies: immigration and the preservation of the French-speaking minority. Governmental action on the first issue can be traced back to the nineteenth century and has been centered on the general conviction that immigration was desirable. The main criterion on which immigration policy was based switched from the rather discriminatory basis of country of origin to a definitely labor-market-oriented policy.

Concern for the survival of French-speaking communities throughout the country is of more recent origin. Policies in that domain may be seen as a way to counteract the English-oriented immigration and the assimilation of scattered French communities among the English.

There is no longer any legal barrier to birth control propaganda, and problems in this area are related to the organization of clinics that can reach all social strata. Abortion has been liberalized recently but is still far from "abortion on demand." But none of the issues are related to any intention to control the population. That is also the case for a certain number of social programs (family allowances, for instance) that might have an effect on population increase.

Concern with population increase, scarcity of resources, and urban concentration has increased recently, with some Malthusian flavor, and it might attenuate the traditional ideology of growth.

INTRODUCTION

With 22 million inhabitants (January 1973) and a land area of 9.2 million square kilometers, Canada has a very low density: 2.4 per square kilometer. But the largest part of the territory is almost uninhabited. About 80 percent of the total population live within a range of 200 kilometers from the United States border. Such a low density surely plays a role in the widespread idea that Canada is an almost empty land and that its population could or should be multiplied by at least three or four times. But it must be considered that, although at comparable latitudes, Canada is much colder than Europe; except for Eskimos and Indians, few persons would consider living permanently north of the presently settled part of the country.

Not only is the Canadian population concentrated in the southern part of the territory, it has also achieved—relatively recently—a high degree of urbanization. Thirty percent live in the three largest cities and 47 percent live in cities of 100,000 or over. A mere 6.6 percent still live on farms.

Until recently, a relatively high birth rate has been maintained that accounts for an age distribution which is relatively young compared to other industrialized populations. The fact that only 8.1 percent of the population is sixty-five or over certainly has facilitated the establishment and the improvement of a universal security system for the aged, which is now relatively generous. But with the recent sharp decrease of the birth rate (27.4 per 1,000 in 1959 and 15.7 per 1,000 in 1972) and the probable stabilization of about that level, Canada probably will have to face more and more difficulties in improving the share of older people.

The general level of mortality is low. The gross death rate varied between 7.3 and 7.5 per 1,000 since 1966, and the life expectancy at birth was 72 years (1966). But Canada has a better female life expectancy (75.2 years) than male life expectancy (68.8 years). The birth and death rates account for a rate of natural increase of about 1.0 percent per year for the last five years. Average net immigration added about 0.4 percent per year.

It has been estimated [1] that, by 1984, the population of Canada would total between 25.2 and 28.5 million inhabitants. In an unpublished paper, Frejka has estimated that, without migration, the Canadian population would stabilize at a level of 29.4 million about 2050, if a net reproduction rate of 1.0 was reached now and maintained. That level was reached, in fact, in 1971, but it might increase in the near future. If the level of 1.0 was reached only in 2000, the population would stabilize at 33 million about 2050.

The particular features of the Canadian population are not revealed by vital rates. Probably the most uncommon feature is in the cultural diversity of the elements. In terms of ethnic origin, the diversity is increasing: A century ago, 91 percent of the population were of British or French origin; in 1971, that proportion was only 73 percent. The British stock has been reduced from 60 percent to 45 percent, to the benefit of other origins. The percentage of the total population represented by the most important of them (1971) is as follows:

British:	44.6
French:	28.7
German:	6.1
Italian:	3.4
Ukrainian:	2.7
Netherlands:	2.0
Scandinavian:	2.0
Polish	1.5
Jewish:	1.4
Indian:	1.4

Many of the groups (particularly in the Prairie Provinces, where they constitute the majority of the population) wish to retain some of their cultural traits. But the great majority learn English, and the children are raised in that language. So this ethnic diversity is associated with a tendency for the population to separate into two linguistic groups: English and French. Because of the adoption of English by the "other" groups, Canadians of English mother tongue are 60.2 percent of the total population (1971), whereas those of French mother tongue are 26.9 percent; most of the remaining 12.9 percent still use the language that corresponds to their country of birth,[1] and about 90 percent of these finally will adopt English (or their children will).

The most conscious population problems and policies in Canada are linked with immigration and linguistic dualism. We shall examine them later. Beside these, attention has been attracted recently by the concentration of population in a few large cities, but policy in this domain still is at the stage of intention to have one.

Of course, many laws and government programs have some effect on population, but they are not intended to have any demographic effect. That is the case for the legislation on divorce and age at marriage, family allowances, income tax exemptions, contraception, abortion, and the

---

[1] In 1971, 3.3 million people living in Canada (15.3 percent of the total population) were born in another country.

status of women. Abortion, in particular, is presently a widely debated question. We shall review these questions briefly.

INTERNATIONAL MIGRATION

It is estimated that, since confederation (1867), Canada has received more than 8 million immigrants. Even though many foreign born and Canadian born emigrated to the United States, positive net migration played an important role in the growth of the Canadian population. Emigration to the United States has been an important concern during the second part of the nineteenth century.

Although favorable to immigration, Canada never had a clear immigration policy with long-term objectives and a program of implementation. Immigration policy has never been a high-priority area for political leaders or a major subject of concern for the general public.

With the 1962 and 1967 regulations, education and training replaced racial discrimination as the major criterion in the selection and control of immigration to Canada. Under the responsibility of the Department of Manpower and Immigration since 1966, immigration has become more and more related to manpower policy.

The limited public discussion has centered on the issues of admission and, before 1962, on racial discrimination. Public concern over immigration usually is related to unemployment levels.

¶ BEFORE 1945

How to stop the emigration of Canadians to the United States and how to attract more European immigrants were two important concerns of the governments in the second part of the nineteenth century.

The 1851–1861 decade was the last decade of that century during which the gain through immigration exceeded the losses through emigration. Emigration was caused by the more rapid development of the United States [2]. It is estimated that, in the century before 1930, Canada lost almost 3 million inhabitants, not including European immigrants who went to the United States after a short stay in the country [3].

In 1849 and 1857, special committees were formed to study the causes and the consequences of Canadian emigration. Although these committees were concerned mainly with the situation in Quebec (Lower Canada), emigration affected all the country. Special repatriation programs were launched by the Quebec government (1870) and by the federal government (1890).

Canada was more active in promoting European immigration to Canada than in trying to repatriate Canadians settled in the United States. In 1859, three special committees were formed to study immigration and to propose recommendations to increase the number of immigrants. From 1856 to 1930, immigration to Canada was promoted by advertising in the northern countries of Europe. From 1872 to the beginning of the twentieth century, subsidies were given to maritime and railway companies for transportation of immigrants. Free lands were given to settlers under the Free Grants and Homesteads Act (1868) [4]. These programs were not successful in attracting more immigrants than emigrants. For three years only (about 1883) between 1867 and 1902, Canada did receive more than 100,000 immigrants.

Economic development was, in fact, the most effective factor in attracting immigrants. With the opening of the west and the beginning of industrialization, Canada experienced great waves of immigrants that ceased only with World War I. (Between 1903 and 1915, almost 2.8 million immigrants came into the country.)

In general, employers favored large-scale immigration. The encouragement of immigration by the railway companies has taken many forms: irrigation of lands, establishment of experimental farms, assistance to private organizations.

On the other hand, without being categorically opposed to immigration, labor unions were more critical. During the first decade of the century, when Canada received a great number of immigrants, labor unions asked to stop the misrepresentation of Canadian opportunities. Labor's efforts were to counteract the campaigns of promises and propaganda launched in countries of emigration by the Canadian Manufacturers Association and others. But during the Great Depression of the 1930s, labor's campaign was simply to stop immigration because of high unemployment. It was a campaign in which virtually the whole Canadian community joined.

The government responded to the pressures, and during the Great Depression, the number of immigrants was limited severely. In 1935, only slightly more than 11,000 immigrants were admitted into Canada. After 1901, the decade of the Great Depression (1931–1941) was the only decade during which net migration was negative.

Most legislative measures concerning immigration that were adopted between 1868 and 1945 (and we should say, until 1962) were restrictive measures. Their aims were (1) to prevent the entry of undesirables (indigents, insane, and so forth) and (2) to limit considerably the number of non-European immigrants. From 1885, a tax was required from each Chinese immigrant. That tax was increased in 1900 and again in 1903. Measures also were taken to limit the Japanese (1908, 1928) and the Indian (1910) immigration [5]. Preferred classes of immigrants were defined: British subjects, United States citizens (1923).

¶ POSTWAR PERIOD (1945–1961)

During the first half of the postwar period, measures were taken by the government to open Canada to immigrants. Admissible categories of immigrants, confined mainly since 1923 to British subjects and citizens of the United States, were expanded to include citizens of France (1948) and citizens of other western European countries (1956). Special efforts were made to receive the refugees or displaced persons of various origins. The Assisted Passage Loan Scheme was put into effect in 1951 to provide loans to immigrants needing financial aid. In 1970, this program was extended on a worldwide basis.

From 1946, immigration recovered rapidly. The decade 1951–1961 can be compared to the 1901–1911 decade (about 1.5 million immigrants came into Canada during each decade).

At the beginning of the postwar period, an important statement of the Prime Minister (1947), the creation of the Department of Citizenship and Immigration (1950), and the adoption of a new Immigration Act (1952) are proofs of a renewed interest in immigration. In the last year, there were more and more criticisms of the discrimination of the immigration policy against non-Europeans and of the high proportion of unskilled workers among immigrant workers.

Prime Minister Mackenzie King's statement of May 1947 on immigration policy served as the official formulation of Canadian immigration policy until 1962. Here are some extracts of what the Prime Minister said.

The policy of the government is to foster the growth of the population of Canada, by the encouragement of immigration. The government will seek . . . to ensure the careful selection and permanent settlement of such number of immigrants as can be advantageously absorbed in our national economy. . . .

[Canada] should take account of the urgent problem of the resettlement of persons who are displaced and homeless, as an aftermath of the world conflict [6].

However, the government did not indicate how it would apply the general principles outlined by the Prime Minister.

The Department of Citizenship and Immigration replaced, in 1950, the Immigration Branch of the Department of Mines and Resources. The department was convinced that immigration was beneficial on all counts.

Despite some criticism, the Department of Citizenship and Immigration tried to manage immigration in relationship with the economic situation; the number of immigrants declined between 1958 and 1963, a period during which Canada experienced economic difficulties. But it is true that an appreciable proportion of immigrants were difficult to control, especially among the so-called sponsored immigrants, that is, immigrants for which a relative already established in Canada was prepared to give support. Requirements for sponsored immigrants were much lower than for independent immigrants. The government of that time prepared new regulations to control the growing sponsored movement, which consisted largely of unskilled labor. But opposition in Parliament and protests from the press and from some ethnic organizations forced the government to withdraw the new regulations.

¶ RECENT YEARS (1962–1973)

Emigration, as in the postwar period, did not receive much attention, with the exception of the loss of professional and skilled manpower to the United States. The Department of Manpower and Immigration initiated a program to incite Canadian students in foreign universities to return to Canada, by providing them with information about opportunities of employment and the labor market in Canada. However, the problem was not a very important concern for various reasons: Emigration of Canadians to the United States is seen as inevitable; the return flow from the United States of Canadian-born emigrants has been substantial in recent years; and emigration of highly qualified people from Canada to the United States is more than compensated by the immigration of professional and skilled persons.

Canada received a large number of immigrants from the United States. In 1971, that country became the first major source country for Canadian immigration, with 24,366 immigrants. A particular aspect of the movement should be mentioned: the great increase of the proportion of non-Canadian teachers in universities, in which American teachers formed a large part, has become a sensitive issue because it is considered by some Canadians as another element of the "Americanization of Canada" [7].

Since 1962, Canadian immigration policy has undergone two major changes: Racial discrimination was removed almost completely from the regulations and was replaced by education and training as the most important criteria for the selection of immigrants, and immigration was given a clear manpower orientation.

According to the 1962 regulations, a person was admissible "by reason of his education, training, skills, or other special qualifications." Previous regulations (1956) spelled out the classes of admissible persons by country or area of origin.

In fact, the occupational structure of Canadian immigration did begin to change before 1962. This can be shown by examining the intended occupations of immigrants admitted between 1946 and 1962. The percentage of farmers declined sharply from 21.7 percent in the period 1951–1956 to 7.8 percent in the period 1956–1962; migrant workers in managerial and professional occupations increased from 7.6 percent to 14.3 percent; those in the service occupations increased from 10.9 percent to 15.3 percent [8]. The changes in the occupational structure of immigrants can be explained partly by the fact that, as early as in the mid-1950s, instructions were given to immigration officers to take account of occupational suitability when assessing a nonsponsored immigrant.

By 1971, however, there were further changes in the occupational composition of the immigration movement. There were other increases in the professional and managerial categories. (In 1971, 32.3 percent of all the workers who came to Canada were classed in that group.) On the other hand, the proportion of immigrant workers classed as laborers showed a striking decline. (In 1971, they represented only 2.2 percent of all migrant workers, as compared with 13.4 percent for the period 1956–1962). These changes in the composition of immigrant workers reflected the new emphasis given to manpower requirements by the 1962 and 1967 regulations.

The 1962 regulations, which represented an improvement over the previous regulations, did not solve the problem of the sponsored movement. A clause still permitted Europeans, Egyptians, and West Indians to sponsor distant relatives. (This was the only discriminating clause of the new regulations.) Between 1946 and 1967, of the 2.5 million immigrants admitted in Canada, 900,000 were sponsored.

In 1966, the government created the Department of Manpower and Immigration. Since then, immigration policy had a strong manpower orientation, and planning was done on a five-year basis. On this occasion, the Prime Minister said:

Immigration policy obviously must be administered in the interest of the country and of the immigrants themselves in a context that takes into account the entire position of employment, training, and placement in Canada. The association of the various aspects of manpower policies under the same minister should make it easier to implement programs and to implement them more effectively [9].

Before presenting the main features of the new regulations adopted in 1967, it is worth mentioning that, as in 1962, a major change in immigration policy was accomplished by changing the regulations and not the Immigration Act. In fact, although the Minister of Manpower and Immigration is still reviewing the whole field of immigration policy in anticipation of preparing a new Immigration Act (the present Immigration Act dates to 1952), the government always has assumed political difficulties concerning major changes in immigration law.

With the 1967 regulations, a point system for the selection of immigrants was created. Three basic admission categories were defined: independent applicants, sponsored dependents, nominated relatives (or nondependent relatives). The assessment system for potential independent immigrants is now based on the following factors: education and training, personal assessment (motivation, initiative, and so forth), occupational demand, occupational skill, age, arranged employment, knowledge of English and French, relative already in Canada, and employment opportunities in the area of destination [10]. The nondependent relative does not enter automatically. He is assessed on the first five factors. This last clause permits a control over the more distant relatives, which was not possible with the 1962 regulations.

Concerning this aspect, Canadian immigration policy differs considerably from policies of western European countries that tend to attract immigrants of low economic qualifications. The emphasis on a quality immigration has been related to the shortage of highly skilled manpower in Canada. The question is whether or not this characteristic of immigration policy will be maintained for a long time, considering the improvement of the quality of the national labor force through great efforts of education and training, particularly since the beginning of the 1960s. But the impact of the recent low birth rates on the future labor force may bring Canada to accept again a large number of immigrants, irrespective of their qualifications.[2]

The 1967 regulations are applied universally, and no discriminating clause based on ethnic origin or area of origin exists anymore. There are offices of the Immigration Division in thirty-one foreign countries, including three countries in South America and the Caribbean, seven countries in Asia, but only one in Africa. By comparison, in 1955, only two offices among the twenty offices abroad were not in Europe (New Delhi and Hong Kong).

The nondiscriminating policy increased the number of professional and skilled immigrants from developing countries. The proportion of immigrants who came from Asian countries showed significant increases, from 4.2 percent of all immigrants in 1963 to 18.2 percent in 1971. However, immigration policy in Canada has been separated completely from the policy of aid to developing countries.[3]

The major public concern in the immigration area in the last few years has been the problem of the visitors who apply in Canada for permanent

[2] The need for seasonal workers already is felt in the agricultural industry. Each summer since 1966, workers are admitted from the West Indies to work on Ontario farms (1,500 came in 1969).

[3] It should be noted that foreign students admitted into Canada must return to their country before applying for permanent residence.

residence. It emerged as a sensitive issue during the 1972 federal election campaign. The 1967 regulations gave to visitors the right to apply in Canada for permanent residence. The large numbers involved soon revealed the source of major problems. (In 1969, 42,000 visitors asked for permanent residence.) In addition, the number of cases waiting to be heard before the Immigration Appeal Board[4] inflated dramatically, because the visitors had a right of appeal if they were refused immigrant status. (At the end of 1972, the board had a backlog of 11,875 cases.) The main problems created by this situation were the delay of appeals presented by landed immigrants and refugees and the undermining of immigration policy to control the volume of immigration and select immigrants. The public reaction against "short-cut" immigration, as it was called, is explained partly by high unemployment rates in recent years.

The government has taken measures to solve the problem. In November 1972, visitors were no longer permitted to apply for permanent residence. In January 1973, regulations were introduced requiring registration of visitors who stay in Canada more than three months as well as employment visas for visitors who wish to take jobs. In June 1973, the Immigration Appeal Board Act was amended so that the right of appeal is limited to persons who have been issued an immigrant or nonimmigrant visa abroad, to landed immigrants, and to refugees.

Throughout the history of Canadian immigration, public support depended in large part on the economic conditions in the country. Even if the immigration volume was slowed between 1967, when a peak of 222,876 was reached, and 1972, when only 122,009 immigrants were admitted, the government sometimes is strongly criticized because of the high level of unemployment.

However, irrespective of economic conditions, French Canadians traditionally were more opposed to immigration than were English Canadians. In the postwar period and until the mid-1960s, Quebec political parties were indifferent or even hostile to immigration. This reaction was caused partly by the fact that a great proportion of immigrants of other origin integrated with the English-speaking group. However, in the 1960s, the government of Quebec adopted a positive policy toward immigration and a provincial Department of Immigration was created in 1968. The main activities of the department are to provide information to potential and actual immigrants and to offer French and English courses. (The courses are financed by the federal government.)

---

[4] The Immigration Appeal Board was created in 1956; its powers were enlarged in 1967. Before 1967, the board was subject to many criticisms because its decisions could be reversed by the minister.

Even though provincial initiatives[5] indicate greater concern with the adaptation of the immigrants, this area of immigration has always been neglected. Because of the federal constitution of Canada, the responsibilities for many programs that affect immigration are shared between different levels of government. The prime concern of the federal government has always been with the control of the immigration movement. Adaptation of immigrants to Canadian life has received little attention, but some action has been initiated. On the other hand, the provinces have limited resources.

Since 1966, the federal responsibilities for the immigrants who are admitted have been within two departments. The Department of Manpower and Immigration is responsible for the settlement of the individual immigrant worker, and it has established five Immigrant Centers in the main receiving cities. A study of the economic and social adaptation of immigrants was started in 1969 and will continue until 1974. It is hoped that the emphasis on the admission of well-qualified immigrants will facilitate adaptation in Canadian society. In 1967, the Canadian Manpower and Immigration Council was created. The primary function of the council is to advise the minister, in particular, "on all matters pertaining to the effective utilization and development of manpower resources in Canada, including immigrants to Canada and their adjustment to Canadian life."

The other department that is responsible for the integration of the immigrants is the Secretary of State. While the Department of Manpower and Immigration is responsible for the economic integration of the immigrant worker, the Secretary of State is responsible for the social, political, and cultural adaptation of the immigrant.

POLICIES RELATED TO LINGUISTIC AND ETHNIC GROUPS

In Canada, two languages—English and French—benefit from constitutional guarantees, mostly in matters pertaining to federal jurisdiction or to the Legislature and the Judiciary in the Province of Quebec. English- and French-speaking persons are also the two most important linguistic

[5] Ontario was the first province to take an active part in immigration. It had a recruitment program just after the war. The present activities in immigration consist in providing a specialized personnel service for employers and prospective immigrants. There is also a Citizenship Branch whose main activities are to provide language courses.

The three Prairie Provinces created Immigration Bureaus in the 1960s. Manitoba and Saskatchewan have established their own assisted passages programs to increase their share of the immigration movement to Canada.

groups. According to the 1971 census, 60.2 percent of the Canadian population used the English mother tongue and 26.9 percent used the French mother tongue, the remainder being distributed among the original languages of immigrants.[6] About 90 percent of the latter choose English as their language of adoption, and their children learn English.

It is clear from the figures that English has a clearly dominant position from a demographic point of view. This demographic dominance is reinforced by a still stronger predominance in the management of the affairs of the nation, whether in the private or the public sector.

The strength of the French group resides in its geographical concentration in the Province of Quebec: 84 percent of French mother-tongue Canadians live in that province, where they constitute 81 percent of the population. Although they do not have great economic power, at least they can use their political majority to preserve the survival of their community. They are beginning to use it.

The political implications of this situation—particularly from a demographic point of view—cannot be understood without some glance at the history of the demographic race between the two main linguistic groups. Considering the present territory of Canada, it took about half a century after the conquest of New France by England (1760) for the British population to balance the number of French Canadians. From 1815 to 1871 (when most provinces were part of the Canadian Confederation), waves of British migrants brought the English majority to 70 percent. From that time until 1951, the French succeeded in maintaining their relative importance (30 percent of the total population).

That was a fragile equilibrium that could be maintained by means of compensating factors. On the one hand, a great number of immigrants continued to settle in Canada and add to the English-speaking population. On the other hand, the French—who were losing emigrants to the United States, as did the English—nevertheless succeeded in maintaining percentages with the immigrants because of their exceptionally high level of fertility.

It is not clear that we can speak of explicit policies with regard to demographic behavior of the two "opponents." That the French Canadians maintained a very high fertility for so long a time most probably is explained more in terms of religious obedience and traditional values than in terms of a conscious strategy to maintain a relative importance, although

---

[6] Indians and Eskimos are a special case from many points of view. They are entitled to special rights or to special help granted by the federal government. Indians number 297,000 (1.4 percent of the total population) and Eskimos are about 15,000.

French Canadian leaders were prone to acclaim the behavior and to encourage it. There is even a widespread expression to designate it: "cradle revenge." A policy often is a law without efficient action. Cradle revenge was not a policy in the strict sense; it was efficient action without law! Even now, a few nationalist French Canadian leaders cannot help regretting the past "natural" fertility, and most of them would applaud some measure of recovery from the present "miserable" level of fertility.

As for the English-speaking group, it would be an exaggeration to say that the huge number of immigrants to Canada was a pure Machiavellian plot to swamp the French Canadians. But such an attitude has its official "blueprint" and goes back to the middle of the nineteenth century. In 1839, Lord Durham came to Canada and wrote an important "Report" in which he straightforwardly proposed to assimilate the French Canadians to English [11]. One of the means he proposed, in addition to promoting the simple attractiveness and effectiveness of English laws, customs, and culture, was to pour English-speaking people into the Province of Quebec (then Lower Canada). The proposal was made with great ingenuity and without hostility; in Lord Durham's mind, it was simply the most desirable thing that could happen to the French Canadians.

Since World War II, the condition of equilibrium between the English and the French has changed. Immigrants still settle in Canada and predominantly continue to adopt English. But the overfertility of French Canadians has progressively been reduced and is now quite negligible. Moreover, another phenomenon has gained momentum: communities of French origin who settle outside the Province of Quebec and abandon French. The proportion of persons of French origin who adopt English as their mother tongue increases according to a geometric progression. In 1971, of 1.4 million French Canadians who live outside the Province of Quebec, about 40 percent have English as their mother tongue and another 12 percent do not speak it regularly at home. According to Robert Maheu [12], these proportions will be about 50 percent and 15 percent in 1990.

The main result of these trends is that the relative importance of French-speaking people is declining steadily: It was 29 percent in 1951, 28.1 percent in 1961, and 26.9 percent in 1971.

That situation, combined with the relatively low economic power of French Canadians and the fact that the federal administration functions mostly in English, has led many French Canadians to the following conclusion: If there is room for a French-speaking community in Canada, it can only be in the Province of Quebec, and the simplest and most efficient way to ensure its progress is the separation of that province from the rest of Canada.

To prevent such an outcome, the federal government established the Royal Commission on Bilingualism and Biculturalism in 1963. Its terms of reference included:

To enquire and report upon the existing state of bilingualism and biculturalism in Canada . . . on the basis of an equal partnership between the two founding races, taking into account the contribution made by the other ethnic groups . . . and in particular:
1. To report upon the situation and practice of bilingualism within all branches and agencies of the federal administration . . . and in their communication with the public. . . .

The commission worked for seven years, collecting opinions and suggestions and requesting a great number of studies. Its *Report* was published in six volumes and included about 130 recommendations [13].

Among the recommendations more directly related to the survival of the French-language communities across Canada were:

(1) That the two provinces other than Quebec where there is a substantial minority of French-speaking people (New Brunswick and Ontario) declare that they recognize English and French as official languages.
(2) That the other provinces provide appropriate services in French for their French minorities.
(3) That bilingual districts be established throughout Canada (where the official language minority attains or surpasses 10 percent) and that, in these districts, the provinces establish elementary and secondary schools in both official languages.
(4) That the federal government appoint a Commissioner of Official Languages charged with ensuring respect for the status of French and English in Canada.
(5) That the federal government create French language units within its administration.
(6) That in the private sector of Quebec economy, French be the principal language of work at all levels, and that the government of Quebec establish a task force to implement that recommendation.
(7) That the teaching of languages other than English and French, together with courses related to corresponding cultural groups, be incorporated in the programs of schools and universities, when there is sufficient demand for such classes.
(8) That federal agencies with responsibilities in matters of radio, television, and films try to determine the best means by which they can contribute to the maintenance of languages and cultures other than English and French.

The federal government has initiated a series of measures to implement most of these recommendations: A commissioner has been nominated; French-language units have been created within the federal administration;

and the Secretary of State is responsible for a series of programs aimed at ensuring an equal status for both official languages within the federal administration and encouraging their use in the whole Canadian society. The most important programs include:

(1) Establishment within the federal administration of a list of positions that must be filled by bilingual persons.
(2) Language courses offered to public servants.
(3) Financial assistance to provinces for their educational programs in the language of the minority.
(4) Financial assistance to voluntary associations that represent official language minorities.
(5) Scholarships to teachers and university students who wish to get training in the "other" official language.
(6) Technical or financial assistance in the fields of translation and linguistic research.

Of course, most of the programs, although spelled out as directed to both official languages, in fact, serve essentially the promotion of the French language. Whatever their effectiveness might be, they are readily accepted by the French-speaking population. But there is some resistance on the part of a certain proportion of English-speaking persons and, particularly, from some unilingual English civil servants whose positions or promotions might be threatened by the bilingual obligation. And this resistance is not solely verbal: The Liberal party, which had been the promoter of the policy, lost its majority at the last federal election (October 1972), and it has been suggested by many politicians and commentators that the loss of many seats in English-speaking constituencies might be explained—at least partially—by resistance to the bilingual programs and to "French power," an expression used to designate the influential French-speaking ministers (including the Prime Minister) in the federal cabinet.

One aspect of the policy may be underlined: Contrary to the rule in other countries who have many official languages (such as Belgium and Switzerland), the policy of bilingualism in Canada aims at maintaining the use of both languages throughout the territory of Canada. This is no great problem as far as English is concerned. But the success of such a policy, as far as French is concerned, depends upon the existence of substantial French-speaking communities outside the Province of Quebec. Given the tendency to adopt English as the mother tongue, that condition might not be realized.

To some degree, the same challenge exists for the Quebec French community. Its very comfortable majority (81 percent) is eroded by the adoption of English by the majority of immigrants who settle in that province.

Moreover, the private business world very predominantly functions in English, which is probably the main reason for the adoption of English on the part of the immigrants. The Royal Commission on Bilingualism and Biculturalism recommended that the Quebec government establish a task force to find the best means by which French could become the principal language of the work world in the province. The Quebec government created the Commission of Inquiry on the Status of the French Language and on Linguistic Rights in Quebec in 1968. The first volume of its *Report* was published at the beginning of 1973 [*14*]. There are forty-eight recommendations in the part related to the situation of French in the work world. They aim at making French the principal language of communication, but almost all measures proposed are on a voluntary basis. But there is one exception: The commission recommended that the legislation governing professional corporations be amended so that a working knowledge of French would be necessary to secure the right to practice.

The preponderance of French in the Province of Quebec is a widely debated subject. A substantial part of opinion in the province would favor the obligation on immigrants to send their children to French schools, leaving the English system accessible only to children whose parents are already established in the province. But neither the commission nor the government have agreed to that type of action.

Before ending this section, a remark should be made on the scope of the issue. The survival of a French-speaking population within Canada probably encompasses the existence of Canada itself. If the majority of French Canadians are led to the conclusion that the best way to ensure their survival is to separate from the rest of Canada, the remaining part of the country would be divided into two separate geographical areas, and it is doubtful whether, in the long run, either country would be viable.

CONTRACEPTION AND ABORTION

We know little about the development of contraception in Canada. However, from fertility data, we may assume that birth control methods have been used for a long time by a significant number of women.

During the eighteenth century, married women of forty-five had an average of 8.4 live births. For women who reached forty-five in 1910, the number had been reduced to 4.8. This provides evidence that birth control was practiced to a significant degree before the end of the nineteenth century. Women married during recent years have no more than 2.2 live births, on the average, during their reproductive age. This indicates the extent to which birth control is practiced: nearly 75 percent of potential births are avoided. According to some partial surveys, the method most used is the pill, followed by the condom and rhythm methods.

The evolution toward small families took place without governmental help. The advertisement or sale or disposal of contraceptives has been prohibited by the criminal code since 1892. But few attempts were made to enforce the law. Birth control drugs and devices have been available at pharmacies for years.

In 1969, the sale and use of contraceptives were authorized, but all commercial advertisement was banned. It was only following pressure from various concerned people that commercial advertisement was permitted (1970), except for the pill and the intrauterine device, which are treated as prescribed drugs or products. Nevertheless, some groups are pressing the government to remove the restrictions on these two methods, since they are two of the most effective.

Governmental activities in contraceptive information and services are neither widespread nor uniform. According to a recent estimate [15], there were only about forty-eight family planning clinics operated by the governments[7] in Canada (1972). Information and services are provided by other health units, voluntary organizations, and private doctors. The role of the small Family Planning Division of the federal government is mainly to provide information. The federal Department of National Health and Welfare convened in 1972 a conference on family planning to consider how the public and voluntary organizations could cooperate to improve services. The costs of family planning consultations with physicians and out-patient clinic care are publicly financed under provincial medical insurance plans. The cost of contraceptives is not covered by public insurance except for public assistance recipients.

One reason for the scarcity of contraceptive information and services provided by the governments is, of course, the fact that contraception has been authorized only since 1969. But the local or regional demographic situation may have had a certain influence. Indeed, according to the paper already cited, several provinces and municipal governments state that they have not formulated a policy on family planning because of a low birth rate or population decline.

The role of voluntary organizations in disseminating birth control information should be underlined because of their pioneering efforts. The first organized activities in this field were under the auspices of voluntary agencies.

Even though the expressions "family planning policies" and "family planning services" are used by the government and by family planning associations, it is birth control (information, education, and services) that is indicated. Little attention is paid to the problem of comprehensive services and financial help for the couples with children. The Malthusian ori-

---

[7] At provincial or municipal levels.

entation of the important Family Planning Federation of Canada[8] is accentuated by their recent concern for the problems created by over-population:

> The dual thrust of the Family Planning Federation of Canada has two main areas of concern. One area of concern is for the individual and his needs, and the other concern for the mass implications of unrestrained fertility.
> The present challenge family planners face is to make birth control readily available to all individuals so that the control of fertility will always remain with the individual. However, we must keep in mind that continuing to over-populate the world will lead to disaster [16].

The main demands of those interested in "family planning" are that information and services on birth control methods should be made available to any individual in the country and should become an integral part of public health programs.

The movement toward the liberalization of birth control methods has now reached the question of sterilization and abortion.

There is no law in Canada that expressly prohibits a physician from sterilizing an individual on request for contraceptive purposes only, and there is no case law to that effect in Canada. In fact, sterilizations are performed for contraceptive purposes by many doctors, but it is far from being accepted on request by all of them. The position of the Canadian Medical Association changed in 1971, when it recommended to doctors to be more liberal concerning sterilization and abortion. But many groups and persons demand that the government clarify the criminal code. Indeed, the criminal code is not clear in the sense that the physician could be found criminally liable if a court of law were to rule that sterilization entails bodily harm or maiming. In a recent debate in the House of Commons, the government revealed that reform of the law is not necessary, since sterilization is solely a medical question [17].

The government is not likely to move in the direction of those who wish to have a complete liberalization of abortion law. A recent statement by a cabinet minister in the House of Commons indicates that the government is satisfied with the present situation. The government is supported fully by an important part of the population and by influential bodies such as the Catholic church, which is a prominent group. Furthermore, some people believe that the existing abortion law is too liberal.

Under the amendments of the criminal code passed in 1969, a qualified physician in an accredited or approved hospital may procure a miscarriage if the hospital's therapeutic abortion committee, by a majority of its members, has certified in writing that the "continuation of the pregnancy . . .

---

[8] The federation has seventeen member associations.

---

would or would be likely to endanger the life or health of the woman."

As a result of the free interpretation of the law, abortions are performed in many Canadian hospitals. In 1971, there were 30,923 abortions in Canadian hospitals (8.3 per 100 live births). But the number was far from including all abortions performed on Canadian women. It seems that the total number of induced abortions—legal and illegal—must fall within a range of 50,000 to 100,000 annually. In 1972, close to 6,000 Canadian women had abortions in New York State hospitals.

Apart from the argument that a woman should have control of her own body, important criticisms of the actual law are, in fact, related to the application of the law by the hospitals. Therapeutic abortion committees have not been established in all hospitals. In addition, various interpretations are given by existing committees of the word "health" that are not defined by the legislation [18].

How long the government will retain its negative attitude to any new change in the abortion law is difficult to predict. Some surveys indicate that a large part of the population favors abortion on request. Many groups have recommended a change in the abortion law. On the other hand, the government has its own supporters and will probably delay any major change for the time being.

OTHER MEASURES THAT MIGHT AFFECT POPULATION

¶ HEALTH

We mentioned in the introduction that life expectancy at birth was 72 years in 1966. There are no great variations among provinces, and it is clear that, from that point of view, the health situation compares favorably with most advanced countries. It is probable that all social classes do not benefit equally from health services, but there is no serious financial barrier; all provinces have universal health insurance plans that cover, at least, hospitalization and physician costs. The plans are administered by the provinces, but half of the costs are paid by the federal government. Legal abortions and medical advice on contraception are covered.

But two groups, Indians and Eskimos, are still far from the same level of health. Particular federal programs have been created to tackle the problem, as well as to improve general life conditions.

Although many health costs are still not covered (drugs and dental care, for instance), the greatest attention is now given by governmental authorities to rapidly increasing costs of the present system and to the organization of health care, as evidenced by many speeches given by the federal Minister of National Health and Welfare.

¶ MARRIAGE AND DIVORCE

There is no demographic intent in the present legislation concerning minimum age at marriage. According to the Constitution, the validity of marriage is a matter of federal jurisdiction, but the Canadian Parliament never discussed a law concerning marriage age. It is through the power given to the provinces that minimum age at marriage comes under legislation. And it varies from province to province: without parental consent, from eighteen to twenty-one years for both sexes; and with parental consent, from twelve to sixteen years for women and from fourteen to sixteen for males.

In 1970, the Royal Commission on the Status of Women in Canada [19] recommended that the minimum age at marriage be eighteen years for both sexes and without parental consent.

Divorce has been a matter of greater concern. Before the present law was passed by Parliament in 1968, divorce could be granted in eight provinces on the ground of matrimonial offense or fault. In 1966, a Joint Committee of the Senate and the House of Commons was formed to study the question. Its report was published in 1967 [20], and it was the basis for the new legislation of 1968. The major innovation of the new law, now applicable everywhere in Canada, was the introduction of the concept of marriage failure or breakdown as a basis for granting divorce. To the old grounds (adultery, sodomy, bestiality, rape), it adds homosexuality, physical and mental cruelty, and marriage breakdown as evidenced by imprisonment, drug addiction, alcoholism, three-year separation, desertion, and nonconsumation.

The Royal Commission on the Status of Women in Canada [19] recommended that the three-year separation as evidence for marriage breakdown be reduced to one year.

¶ FAMILY ALLOWANCES AND INCOME TAX EXEMPTIONS

The federal government instituted a universal noncontributory system of family allowances in 1945. Since that date, the modalities have changed somewhat, but on the whole, the system has shown a remarkable stability, simplicity, and modesty. The average monthly allowance per child under age sixteen has varied from about US$6.00 in 1946–1947 to about US$7.00 in 1970–1971.[9] Until recently, family allowances received very little attention; the purchasing power of the allowances has been reduced almost by half without raising any significant protest.

The system—despite its obvious lack of generosity—was envisaged as a relief for families. Never was it intended as an encouragement to fer-

---

[9] US and Canadian dollars are approximately equal.

tility, except by some marginal segments of the public (particularly in French Canada, recently).

In 1964, another federal program extended allowances ($10 a month) to children aged 16–17. Only one province (Quebec) has its own supplementary family allowances, but the average monthly allowance is minimal: about $3.25. It contains a natalist feature: The allowance varies according to the rank of the child in the family, about $30 a year for the first to about $70 for the sixth and over.

These family allowances are not taxable. They even are complemented by an exemption on taxable personal income: about $300 per child if the child receives family allowances and about $550 if the dependent child is over sixteen years of age. These exemptions exist also for the provincial income taxes, except that, in the Province of Quebec, they were eliminated when the province established its own system.

A renewal of interest in family allowances has appeared since 1969. First, the Canadian Welfare Council, in a statement published at the beginning of that year [21], proposed a reduction of the income tax exemption (because it represents a greater advantage to higher-income families) and a substantial increase of family allowances, including "student allowances graded upward according to level of educational attainment." The council (a private organization) also proposed that all the allowances be subject to income tax.

In 1970, the Royal Commission on the Status of Women in Canada proposed an annual allowance of about $500 per child with the abolition of tax exemptions. Allowances were to be taxable.

In 1971, both the federal and the Quebec governments presented new legislation in this field, on which both claim jurisdiction. There was much similarity between the two projects; for instance, both proposed a reduction of benefits with increasing income, with complete elimination when income reached a certain level, depending on the number of children. Both projects seem to have been abandoned, and recently (spring 1973), the federal governments presented a new proposal. The average monthly allowance would be about $20 per child, but the provinces would be allowed to choose how they wish to distribute it, according to the age or rank of children, and provided they respect certain minimum requirements that would be set by agreement between the provinces and the federal government. The allowance would be taxable. No formal discussion has taken place, but it seems that the proposal is acceptable. Under the proposed system, the annual total cost would rise from about $650 million to about $1,500 million.

Here again, there was no intention to pursue a natalist policy. Moreover, all recent proposals or statements imply a clear objective: to help families with low incomes.

¶ THE STATUS OF WOMEN

Problems related to the status of women in Canada are not different fundamentally from those in most industrialized countries. Although important changes have occurred regarding their participation in the labor force and their role in society, women still have the main responsibility for the care of children, and there are few women in high-level occupations, either in the private or the public sector.

In February 1967, the federal government created a Royal Commission on the Status of Women in Canada, which published its report in 1970. Of the 167 recommendations, some are more or less directly related to population policies. We mentioned the recommendations concerning age at marriage, family allowances, contraception, and abortion. A few other points should be noted that relate to childbearing and labor-force participation.

In accordance with a proposal of the commission, the new Unemployment Insurance Act (effective since June 1971) provides unemployment benefits for maternity leave for a period of fifteen weeks, of which eight weeks must be before the confinement. One of the guiding principles of the commission was that women—and particularly, married women—should have a true choice between child rearing and labor-force participation and that conditions be such as to permit them to combine both if they so wish. As the present balance is in favor of the traditional role of women, numerous recommendations lean toward facilitating entry and promotion in the labor force, economic independence, and equal opportunity in all walks of life. The urgent and widely spread need for day-care centers was stressed, and many recommendations aimed at increasing these facilities.

Most of the recommendations directed to the federal government already are implemented or under active examination by responsible departments. In March 1971, the Prime Minister pledged the full support of the government for the commission's recommendations. Among measures of general interest, we should mention the creation of the Office of the Coordinator, Status of Women; the establishment of an Interdepartmental Committee; the designation of a Cabinet Minister for the Status of Women; and in May 1973, the creation of a Status of Women Council, composed of twenty-eight members, whose mandate is to advise the responsible minister on matters relating to the status of women.

It is impossible to predict the future influence of such measures. They cannot but reinforce the trend, which has been observed for many decades, to increasing labor-force participation of women. From 1960 to 1970, the participation rate of women aged fourteen years and over has increased from 27.9 percent to 35.5 percent. For the latter year, 57 percent were married. It is probable that this trend reflects an important change in the role of women and has an influence on the fertility of married women. Data from the 1961 census indicate that married women who work outside the home have a much lower fertility than do women who stay home.

CONCLUSION

It is impossible to cover all policies that might have an effect on population. We have focused on governmental measures that are clearly related to demographic phenomena, although some of them were not intended to influence population. Policies concerning marriage, divorce, contraception, and abortion, for instance, imply no objective to influence population trends. On the contrary, there is a clear intention to affect population trends in the immigration regulations and in the programs designed to contribute to the survival of French-speaking communities throughout the country.

More recently, two issues have retained the attention of public opinion, scholars, and governments, and they are sometimes confused. First, there is wide recognition that the trend toward the concentration of the Canadian population in the three largest cities should be controlled. No policy has been presented, but recently, the Prime Minister declared that the present government was determined to act against these tendencies. Second, there is the desirability of stabilizing the total population. As in other countries, partisans of zero population growth are prone to associate population increase with pollution, scarcity of resources, and urban problems. A group of experts convened by the federal government in 1972 endorsed such an attitude. But it has been an easy task for some opponents to stress the fact that, in an almost empty country, population problems are more related to the distribution of population than to its total size.

These new issues have led many groups to suggest—sometimes very naïvely—that the Canadian government should have a population policy. Nobody would deny that it would be a desirable thing. But it is easier to request it than it is to spell it out.

REFERENCES

1. Ottawa Dominion Bureau of Statistics, Census Division. *Population Projections for Canada, 1969–1984.* Analytical and Technical Memorandum No. 4. 1970.

2. A. Faucher. *Economic History and Canadian Unity.* Montreal: Fides, 1970. (In French.)

3. Y. Lavoie. *The Emigration of Canadians to the United States before 1930.* Montreal: Presses de l'Université de Montréal, 1972. (In French.)

4. N. MacDonald. *Canada: Immigration and Colonization, 1841–1903.* Toronto: Macmillan of Canada, 1966.

5. W. E. Kalbach. *The Impact of Immigration on Canada's Population.* Dominion Bureau of Statistics, Census Division, 1961, Census Monograph. Ottawa: Queen's Printer, 1970.

6. D. C. Corbett. *Canada's Immigration Policy: A Critique.* Toronto: University of Toronto Press, 1957.

7. J. Steele, and R. Mathews. "The universities: Take-over of the mind." In *Population Issues in Canada,* edited by C. F. Grindstoff, C. L. Boydell, and P. C. Whitehead. Toronto and Montreal: Holt, Rinehart and Winston of Canada, 1971.

8. *Immigration Statistics, 1965.* Ottawa: Department of Citizenship and Immigration, Immigration Branch, 1966. *Immigration Statistics, 1971.* Department of Manpower and Immigration, Canada Immigration Division, 1972.

9. F. Hawkins. *Canada and Immigration: Public Policy and Public Concern.* Montreal and London: McGill-Queen's University Press, Institute of Public Administration of Canada, 1972.

10. *The Immigration Act: Immigration Regulations Part I, Immigration Inquiries Regulations.* Ottawa: Queen's Printer, 1968.

11. *The Report and Despatches of the Earl of Durham, Her Majesty's High Commissioner and Governor General of British North America.* London: Ridgways, Piccadilly, 1839.

12. Robert Maheu. *The French-speaking Canadians, 1941–1991.* Montreal: Editions Parti Pris, 1970. (In French.)

13. *Report of the Royal Commission of Bilingualism and Biculturalism.* Six volumes. Ottawa: Queen's Printer, 1967–1970.

14. *Report of the Commission of Inquiry on the Position of the French Language and and on Language Rights in Quebec.* Book I: *The Position of the French Language in Quebec.* Quebec: l'Editeur officiel du Québec, 1972. (In French and English.)

15. *Family Planning Services in Canada, 1972.* Ottawa: Department of Health and Welfare, Health Research Division, 1972.

16. Dr. Marion Powell. "Editorial." *Family Planning and Population,* Quarterly Newsletter published by the Family Planning Federation of Canada, vol. 1, Spring 1973.

17. House of Commons Debates, April 2, 1973.

18. J. E. Veevers. "Liberalization of the Canadian abortion laws." In *Population Issues in Canada,* edited by C. F. Grindstoff, C. L. Boydell, and P. C. Whitehead. Toronto and Montreal: Holt, Rinehart and Winston of Canada, 1971.

19. *Report of the Royal Commission on the Status of Women in Canada.* Ottawa: Information Canada, 1970.

20. *Report of the Special Joint Committee of the Senate and House of Commons on Divorce.* Ottawa: Queen's Printer, 1967.

21. *Social Policies for Canada, Part I.* Ottawa: Canadian Welfare Council, 1969.

CHAPTER 16

Argentina

Horacio D. Gregoratti
Carlos Luzzetti

ABSTRACT

The quantitative and qualitative aspects of the Argentine population have been two ever-present problems since Argentina became a nation in the nineteenth century and recently have become even more pressing because of new external and internal factors in the national life.

The "external" factor refers to the fact that, while today's population in the country is increasing moderately—and chances are that this trend will continue for the next twenty or thirty years—Argentina's neighbors, with the exception of Uruguay, are undergoing an explosive population expansion. This expansion evidently worries both those who rule Argentina and a wide range of people within the country.

The "internal" factor that has contributed greatly in focusing the attention of the inhabitants on population is the geographical distribution of the population and the persistent tendency toward concentration of the inhabitants of the country in a few large urban areas.

It is likely that the Argentine government will take some action to counteract the low rate of births by enacting new laws and regulations to (1) limit, deter, and even prohibit some family limitation practices and (2) foster the formation of larger families.

It appears as very probable that among the measures to be adopted to promote births will be an action to substantially increase the payments made to couples according to the numbers of their children. It is also quite possible that large families will be given first priority in the renting or buying of new apartments or houses built by the state or with the financial help of the state.

In the "struggle" for quantity, the national and provincial governments are determined to achieve new targets in the reduction of mortality rates, particularly by reducing the stillbirth rate and the infant mortality rate. With these and other purposes in view, the government is considering reorganizing the office of the Under Secretary of Public Health and elevating it to a ministerial rank. The National Ministry of Public Health, should it come into being, is certain to play a very important role in the fight for the reduction of mortality.

Concerning immigration as a means of increasing the population, it should be pointed out that today the flow of immigrants from overseas practically is nonexistent, and this situation presumably will continue in the foreseeable future. Immigration from neighboring countries creates political and social problems. The Argentine government will need new legislation in order to regulate and analyze this type of immigration.

Regarding the unequal distribution of the population within the country, the new law regulating industrial promotions is supposed to be only a first step in a more ample policy aimed at discouraging future urban growth. However, the outlook is not very promising in the effort for dispersion, and it is highly probable that the present prevailing trend toward greater urbanization will continue.

With respect to the problem of the population's quality of life, the outlook seems brighter. The quest for quality means continued action in several directions such as improving children's diet, improving health care for children and young persons, and creating more facilities for education. In this area, governmental and private actions have always received the support of the immense majority of the inhabitants of the country.

DEMOGRAPHIC AND ENVIRONMENTAL FACTORS IN POPULATION GROWTH

Argentina, located in the extreme south of the American continent, has a total area of 4,024,691 square kilometers (km²), including 2,776,888 km² in continental South America and 1,247,803 km² of the Antarctic continent and South Atlantic islands.

The average density of the mainland population, according to 1970 national census data, is 8 inhabitants per km², which is very low compared to the average of 22 inhabitants per km² in the United States and 11 inhabitants per km² in the Soviet Union.

The vast extension of the Argentine continental sector, located between the 53°39' and the 73°30' meridian lines of western longitude and the

21°46′ and the 55°3′ parallels of southern latitude, has a great variety of climates. Most of the productive area is in the humid pampa, which covers the central zone, where the climate is ideal for agriculture and raising cattle. And it is here that most of the population is settled, nearly 8 million people—not including the inhabitants of the Gran Buenos Aires, the largest built-up area in the country and also located in the central zone. Gran Buenos Aires, which is composed of the federal capital and several bordering districts of the province of Buenos Aires, covers 0.1 percent of the total land area of continental Argentina and contains 35.7 percent of the total continental population.

Patagonia, formed by the provinces of Rio Negro, Neuquen, Chubut, and Santa Cruz and the Gobernacion of Tierra del Fuego, covers almost a quarter of the continental territory, about 786,000 km², in the southern zone. Its inhabitants number 705,000, about 3 percent of the country's total population. The inhabitants of this dry, windy, semidesert area raise sheep and mine petroleum.

The Littoral and Mesopotamian areas are formed by the provinces of Entre Rios, Corrientes, Misiones, Chaco, and Formosa. They cover an area of 365,915 km², which is 13.17 percent of the total continental area. They have a population of 2,619,546, or 11.2 percent of the country's total. The land is mainly used for raising cattle, growing citrus plants, silviculture, and growing tea, rice, tung trees, and cotton.

In the west is the Cuyo region, formed by the provinces of Mendoza, San Juan, and San Luis. The total area is 313,724 km², with a population of 1,540,819 inhabitants who are fundamentally involved in cattle raising, agriculture, viticulture, and mining minerals and petroleum.

There is a vast northwestern region, formed by the Tucuman, La Rioja, Catamarca, Santiago del Estero, Salta, and Jujuy provinces, that covers 557,921 km² and has a total of 2,382,180 inhabitants. It is an arid or semiarid region with important natural and artificially watered oases.

Until the late 1930s, agriculture and cattle raising were the country's most important occupations. During World War II, when it was difficult to import merchandise, industry expanded rapidly and production was intensive in the areas of textiles, foods, and light metallurgy. More recently, automobile, petrochemical, and heavy metallurgical industries were developed.

¶ POPULATION SIZE
According to estimates of the Instituto Nacional de Estadisticas y Censos de la Nacion (INDEC) (National Institute of Statistics and the Nation's Census), on September 30, 1970, the total population of Argentina was 23,364,431. Ten years earlier, in 1960, national general census data esti-

mated the total population at 20,013,793. In preceding censuses over the last century, Argentina's population was estimated as follows:

Year	Size
1869	1,737,076
1895	3,954,411
1914	7,885,237
1947	15,893,827

For the year 2000, the most probable projection is 35 million, the most optimistic figure is 37,515,000, and the most pessimistic, 31 million, according to an INDEC study.

¶ POPULATION GROWTH TRENDS

Until 1914, population growth had been rapid. Many immigrants, mostly of European origin, settled in the republic between 1869 and 1914. During that period, the death rate diminished considerably. These two factors, plus a high birth rate, made the population's doubling time quite short— about every twenty years—between 1869 and 1914. The time it took for the population to double increased to thirty-three years between 1914 and 1947, and results of the 1970 census suggest a greater lengthening of the duplication cycle. Since 1914, net migration has diminished, except in a very few exceptional years, and birth rates have decreased; these two factors are responsible for the present low population growth rate. According to INDEC, the average population growth rate from 1947 to 1960 was 1.72 percent; from 1967 to 1969, it was about 1.5 percent.

Figure 1 depicts the growth trend in Argentina since 1914, together with the steady reduction in both the birth and death rates during the last two decades and the generally steady decrease in migration. Note that the two exceptions in the migration trend both occurred in postwar periods— 1920–1930 and 1947–1953—when higher rates were observed. A clearer picture of the Argentine population's relatively slow evolution is given in Table 1, which transcribes the vital rates for 1914–1970 from Figure 1. Birth and death rate reductions have not been even across the country. Today, some underdeveloped provinces show high birth and death rates, as shown in Table 2.

¶ GENERAL FERTILITY RATE REDUCTION

In 1914, there were 1,705,000 women of reproductive age, and about 287,000 births. Thus, in that year, 167.6 children were born per 1,000 fertile women. By 1960, the general fertility rate was only 92.58. Since

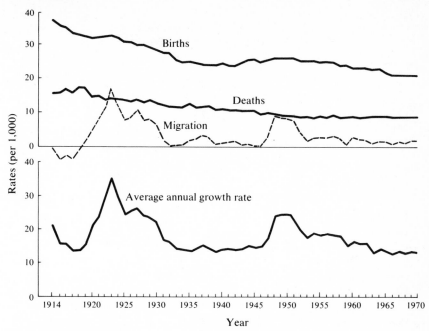

SOURCE: Courtesy of INDEC

FIGURE 1
Selected Measures of Demographic Change, Argentina, 1914–1970
(per 1,000)

then, the rate has only varied slightly from this level; for example, in 1968, it was 90.41, and in 1970, there was a slight improvement, probably in part because of a greater proportion of young people (15–24 years) and in part because of a higher fertility rate among the women aged 15–34. (See Table 3 for age-specific fertility rates in 1950, 1960, and 1968.)

Age Structure.
According to the 1914 national census, 39 percent of the population was under age fourteen years. In 1970, only 29.30 percent of the population was under age fourteen years.

Migration Reduction.
With the exception of a few years after each of the two world wars, recorded migration to Argentina after 1914 has been very small, with overseas migration to Argentina almost nonexistent. During the last ten years, emigration of professionals and of qualified technicians has in-

TABLE 1.

Total Demographic Rates, Argentina, 1914–1970
(per 1,000 population)

Years	Birth Rate	Death Rate	Migration	Annual Average Growth Rate
1914	36.4	15.2	0.3	20.9
1915	35.1	15.5	3.8	15.8
1916	34.9	16.8	2.4	15.7
1917	33.1	15.5	3.7	13.9
1918	32.4	17.4	1.0	14.0
1919	32.0	17.4	1.4	16.0
1920	31.5	14.7	4.5	21.3
1921	31.9	15.0	7.3	24.2
1922	32.1	13.3	11.1	29.9
1923	32.5	13.8	16.6	35.3
1924	31.7	13.6	11.3	29.4
1925	30.7	13.3	7.3	24.7
1926	30.1	12.8	8.5	25.8
1927	29.8	13.4	10.3	26.7
1928	29.8	12.6	7.7	24.9
1929	29.3	13.1	7.8	24.0
1930	28.7	12.2	6.3	22.8
1931	27.8	11.9	1.4	17.3
1932	27.4	11.4	0.2	16.2
1933	25.5	11.3	0.3	14.5
1934	24.9	11.1	0.5	14.3
1935	24.7	12.5	1.6	13.8
1936	24.1	11.3	2.1	14.9
1937	23.8	11.5	3.3	15.6
1938	23.7	11.8	2.9	14.8
1939	23.6	10.7	0.4	13.3
1940	24.0	10.7	1.0	14.3
1941	23.7	10.4	1.2	14.5
1942	23.3	10.3	1.3	14.3

creased, with most of these Argentines resettling in the United States. Nevertheless, considerable unrecorded migration to Argentina occurs. Those South Americans who cross Paraguay, Bolivia, Chile, and Uruguay frontiers are not duly registered in the national migratory registers.

¶ URBAN/RURAL DISTRIBUTION
Another factor that undoubtedly has contributed to a decreasing birth rate has been the prolonged urbanization process. Although this process

TABLE 1. (*continued*)

Years	Birth Rate	Death Rate	Migration	Annual Average Growth Rate
1943	24.2	10.1	0.5	14.6
1944	25.2	10.2	0.5	15.5
1945	25.2	10.3	0.2	15.1
1946	24.7	9.6	0.2	15.3
1947	25.0	9.9	2.9	18.0
1948	25.3	9.4	8.5	24.4
1949	25.1	9.0	9.4	25.5
1950	25.5	9.0	9.3	25.8
1951	25.2	8.9	7.3	23.6
1952	24.6	8.5	3.7	19.8
1953	24.6	8.7	1.6	17.5
1954	24.7	8.4	2.6	18.9
1955	24.4	8.9	2.9	18.4
1956	24.6	8.4	2.7	18.9
1957	24.3	9.1	3.3	18.5
1958	23.5	8.3	2.8	18.0
1959	23.3	8.5	0.4	15.2
1960	22.7	8.6	2.7	16.8
1961	22.5	8.3	2.0	16.2
1962	22.8	8.5	1.9	16.2
1963	22.5	8.6	0.8	13.1
1964	22.4	8.7	1.2	14.9
1965	21.4	8.7	1.2	13.9
1966	20.9	8.4	0.4	12.9
1967	20.9[a]	8.4[a]	1.2	13.7
1968	20.9	8.4	0.9	13.4
1969	20.9	8.4	1.4	13.9
1970[a]	20.9	8.4	1.2	13.7

SOURCE: Courtesy of INDEC.
[a] Estimated values according to the historic trend.

has been most marked since 1945 (and already is evident in the 1947 general census), it started as early as 1914 (see Table 4). At the present time, in addition to a "megalopolis," the so-called Gran Buenos Aires, there are three other urban areas of more than 500,000 inhabitants each: the Gran Rosaria, the Gran Cordoba, and the capital of the Buenos Aires province, La Plata, and its outskirts. In 1947, Gran Buenos Aires contained 4,722,381 inhabitants and Gran Rosario 529,801. At that time, these were the only urban centers in the country with more than 0.5 million people. In 1970, Gran Buenos Aires, together with the three other

TABLE 2.

Crude Birth and Death Rates by District, Argentina, 1968
(per 1,000 population)

District	Birth Rate	Death Rate
Federal capital[a]	27.1	14.5
Buenos Aires province	15.8	7.9
Catamarca	27.9	9.1
Cordoba	23.2	9.7
Corrientes	29.4	9.9
Chaco	35.8	9.7
Chubut	29.3	9.2
Entre Rios	21.6	8.4
Formosa	31.2	7.1
Jujuy	37.4	15.0
La Pampa	22.4	7.9
La Rioja	24.3	7.8
Mendoza	22.4	8.3
Misiones	42.0	9.1
Neuquen	36.6	11.9
Rio Negro	31.7	11.5
Salta	33.7	12.2
San Juan	29.1	8.8
San Luis	21.2	8.3
Santa Cruz	22.5	7.6
Santa Fe	20.0	8.9
Santiago del Estero	30.6	7.7
Tierra del Fuego	22.1	8.2
Tucuman	28.3	9.2
All districts	22.6	9.5

SOURCE: Courtesy of INDEC.
  [a] People come to the federal capital to give birth and to die because it has more and better facilities.

TABLE 3.

Age-Specific Fertility Rates, Argentina, 1950, 1960, and 1968
(per 1,000 women)

Age Group of Mothers	1950	1960	1968
15–19	55.31	58.22	60.77
20–24	147.46	163.66	156.17
25–29	176.20	170.12	167.92
30–34	128.61	117.82	124.65
35–39	78.46	70.36	73.65
40–44	31.09	28.07	24.94
45–49	10.26	6.99	6.31

SOURCE: Courtesy of INDEC.

TABLE 4.

Percentage Change in Urban Growth and Industrial Employment,
Argentina, 1914–1960

	Percentage Change Registered in:			
	Urban Population		Industrial Population	
	1947	1960	1948	1960
District	1914	1947	1914	1948
Federal capital	89.2	−4.3	222.4	−17.3
Buenos Aires province	171.3	88.8	274.9	132.7
Catamarca	191.4	49.2	−11.1	115.3
Cordoba	161.1	54.0	177.0	137.3
Corrientes	63.9	33.3	−48.8	139.0
Chaco	21.5	58.5	181.2	122.9
Chubut	852.7	62.8	3,451.4	−37.4
Entre Rios	163.5	−19.7	9.1	112.3
Formosa	504.7	130.8	178.3	233.7
Jujuy	318.8	93.7	20.8	165.9
La Pampa	198.5	38.8	257.9	54.0
La Rioja	235.2	57.2	−28.6	91.7
Mendoza	233.4	77.8	109.2	66.0
Misiones	352.2	168.5	137.7	268.7
Neuquen	841.6	167.9	785.5	44.7
Rio Negro	1,041.3	239.6	822.4	93.3
Salta	278.7	96.8	113.8	98.7
San Juan	411.2	59.3	63.0	119.2
San Luis	94.1	39.5	42.5	113.3
Santa Cruz	323.2	217.5	863.0	52.0
Santa Fe	131.4	47.2	144.9	55.0
Santiago del Estero	238.0	36.0	81.3	118.2
Tierra del Fuego	–	–	–	–
Tucuman	97.2	40.6	77.0	81.7
All districts	138.9	45.3	191.9	57.9

SOURCE: See [1].
NOTE: The activities of the 1914 and 1947 censuses are not strictly comparable.

congested areas previously mentioned, contained 47 percent of the country's total population.

The migration of population from high-fertility rural and semirural areas to urban centers of all sizes is creating an unprecedented housing problem. It is difficult today for a family of limited means, in either a big city or a small town, to find a house they can afford. In spite of all the official plans to solve construction problems and to finance low-income housing, there is considerable overcrowding in the big Argentine cities today. These conditions naturally have an adverse affect on family relations and on procreation; city dwellers are not inclined to have large families.

Beyond the purely demographic explanations for the decline in family size are the motivational reasons within individual families. This process is difficult to evaluate. For example, there are no statistics to support the assertion that the improved nutritional conditions that prevail in a large part of the Argentine rural areas, and particularly in the cities, have lowered fertility levels. The reasons for a reduced birth rate are not physiological but the result of personal decisions people have made voluntarily. Those factors that influence the reproductive behavior of couples could be grouped into psychological reasons and economic reasons. These reasons interact.

¶ PSYCHOLOGICAL FACTORS INFLUENCING FERTILITY

People in Argentina today tend to have fewer children and provide them with better educational and living conditions, particularly in the urban areas. Although the average Argentine believes emotionally and intellectually in family life, the environmental conditions he lives with have made a large family less feasible. In the past, the extended family was a common living unit. Now the nuclear family predominates in the urban areas. In the urban environment, customs, life styles, and the constant influence of the mass media act either directly or indirectly to limit family size. In a poll conducted in Buenos Aires by Raul Castor Olivera [2], of 700 respondents in greater Buenos Aires, 69 percent answered the question, "Why do you get married?" with, "To have children," reaffirming the average Argentine's family vocation. In the same poll, 74 percent answered that the number of children must be determined by each couple. To a question about the "ideal" number of children they would like, the respondents answered as follows:

Number of Children	Response (in percents)	
	Women	Men
1	1	1
2	26	42
3	32	30
4	25	14
5	6	0

¶ WOMEN'S ROLES

Concurrent with urbanization has been a change in the traditional roles of women toward increased employment and higher levels of education. Women are increasingly being employed in more technical and professional fields, and they have greater access to higher education and universities.

According to the 1960 census, the latest data tabulated by INDEC, the number of women in industry, commerce, and services was 1,645,415. This figure represented 21.86 percent of all workers in these sectors. It also represented 23.2 percent of all women over fifteen years of age.

Single women who hold professional, industrial, or commercial jobs become accustomed to a standard of living that they can only maintain if they continue to work after marirage. To support and care for many children involves time and expense, which infringe on employment and reduce the standard of living. All of this works against large families, in spite of some legal measures designed to economically protect and assist motherhood and large families.

¶ ECONOMIC IMPEDIMENTS TO LARGE FAMILIES

Table 5 shows per-capita income, in dollars in constant value prices until 1964. Since 1964, per-capita income has varied favorably but very slightly. At present, it is fairly high. The growing middle classes here, as in other countries, tend to practice voluntary family planning.

¶ HOUSING

Rising construction costs have discouraged people from building housing. At the same time, the rent freeze laws have discouraged people from building new housing and renting what little housing there is available. These two factors, added to the influx of people into urban areas, have produced a considerable shortage of housing. Many young married couples live with one set of parents, and if they obtain their own house later, it is generally small and expensive. Dwellers in poorer sections outside the cities settle

TABLE 5.

Per-Capita Income, Argentina, 1916–1964

Year	US$
1916	608
1928	719
1929	743
1935	721
1938	745
1950	928
1957	922
1960	970
1963	911
1964	978

SOURCE: *TECHINT Information Bulletin*, no. 154. Buenos Aires, September, 1966.

in slums or "emergency villas." These slum areas keep increasing despite government attempts to remove them, because there is a constant migration to them from the interior and from neighboring countries.

¶ EDUCATION

Since the time of President Sarmiento (1869–1874), a great Argentine educator, public education has been a constant concern of the government and the people. During Sarmiento's presidency, a free and compulsory elementary educational system was established. Toward the end of the nineteenth century, literacy was quite widespread. Gradually secondary and high schools, both public and private, began to appear. According to the 1960 Argentine census, of a total of 14,232,200 inhabitants over age fourteen years, 12,950,262 knew how to read and write.

Although public education practically is free, it is still expensive for a couple of average income to support a child from kindergarten through the university, paying for books and other school supplies, clothing, transportation, and social activities. Many high school and university students must work and study at the same time to finish their education. In addition, National Education Law, requiring that children finish their elementary education, often places a burden on poor parents. Even though education is free, its compulsory character hinders children from working and makes it hard for parents of low income to support them. The well-to-do and large sectors of the middle class prefer to send their children to private schools and universities. This type of education is costly but very sought after for status reasons. Thus, this circumstance also works against larger families in the higher-income groups of the population.

These and other factors have weakened the traditional ways of living. The presence of growing populations in large cities and towns has also changed the life style of the current and future generations.

VOLUNTARY REDUCTION IN FAMILY SIZE AMONG THE URBAN POPULATION

A reduction in the birth rate began in Argentina in 1914. In that year, the birth rate was 36.4 per 1,000. As of 1970, it had decreased to 20.9 per 1,000. This decline can be explained largely by the social and economic changes that have taken place in the country during the last fifty years (urbanization, industrialization, education, the movement of women into the labor force, housing shortages, and so on).

The typical Argentine family of the past was large. The average family size today, as attested to by official public documents on the costs of living and housing, is four (two parents and two children). The great decrease in family size over the last fifty years seems to have been caused primarily by a voluntary reduction of births.

Sudden variations in marriage rates do not seem to explain the population's expansions or contractions and the changes in family size. The statistics on marriage do not represent the actual rate, because there are "unregistered unions" throughout the country. (In 1914, 5.9 percent of unions were "unregistered"; in 1947, 8.7 percent; in 1960, 7.3 percent; and in 1966, 6.9 percent.) However, the statistics do show that thirty or forty years ago those who married did so generally at an older age than is true today. At all social levels, engagements were very long when the engaged couple was young. This was because many men wanted to have a minimum income before being married. Quite a few years ago, engagements became short, and people began to marry at younger ages without waiting to establish financial security.

BRINGING ABOUT VOLUNTARY REDUCTION OF THE BIRTH RATE

In the Argentine Republic as well as in other countries where birth rates have decreased, the methods or means of birth control used by married couples and couples with unregistered unions include the following:

(1) Coitus interruptus. It is practically impossible to determine the number of persons practicing this method because its intimate nature makes sampling difficult. Many professionals who deal with conjugal life believe that this method does contribute to the limitation of births, although not in a very large degree.

(2) Rhythm method. Since this is the only method accepted by the Roman Catholic church and most Argentinians are Catholic, it seems reasonable to assume, after having studied the results of surveys of Latin American capitals, that this method is used by many couples in legal or otherwise stable relationships.

(3) Abortion. Voluntarily induced abortion, unless medically authorized for major medical reasons, is penalized by law as a serious crime. It is impossible to estimate the number of illegal abortions, but sociologists and gynecologists estimate that it is of significant magnitude.

(4) Contraceptives. Although there are no conclusive studies on the variety and numbers of contraceptives distributed in the country over a fixed time span, investigations and approximate data show that several contraceptive devices are being used. They can be divided into three groups: (a) preservatives (also called "prophylactics"); (b) intrauterine devices and diaphragms, and (c) oral contraceptives.

Preservatives are available throughout the country in drugstores. They cost about US$0.20 each.[1] Although their use is permitted and even

[1] US$1 equaled 5 Argentine new pesos as of January 1, 1972, but many imports were "penalized" having to pay the basic import dollar-peso rate plus a tax.

encouraged to prevent venereal disease, consumption seems to be diminishing, according to data from the no. 4 *Bulletins de Demographie et de Planning Familial*. As of March 1971, about 14 million units were distributed per year.

Intrauterine devices, generally plastic, are sold at certain drugstores and distributed and inserted free at some centers by family planning organizations. It is hard to estimate the extent of their use because of lack of complete information.

Oral contraceptives are sold at drugstores. The raw material is imported, and the pills are manufactured in Argentine medical laboratories. They are sold on prescription only, but the prescription does not need to be turned in, as is the case for other prescribed medicines, and this means, in effect, that they can be bought without a prescription. The cost per cycle is about US$1.50. In the last three years, the consumption of oral contraceptives has increased; the estimate for 1967 and 1968 was about 334,000 to 420,000. Among the female population aged 15–44, this would represent 8.2 cycles per 100 women (*Bulletin*, no. 4, March 1971). In a survey in Buenos Aires City, Carmen Miro [3] reported that 77.6 percent of the respondents (women of reproductive age) had used contraceptives.

Although there is no reliable information, it is apparent that an increasing proportion of urban couples use contraceptive methods other than coitus interruptus and the rhythm method.

The standing laws and regulations of Argentina do not forbid the use of contraceptives, although public advertising of contraceptive methods practically is prohibited.

Several organizations concerned about "responsible paternity" advocate family planning. For example, the Argentine Association for Family Planning, founded in 1966, held the first national meeting of the Family Planning Centers of the City of Buenos Aires, in October 1970. This organization is creating member groups throughout the country and operates in several health centers in the republic.

THE POSITION OF THE GOVERNMENT ON POPULATION GROWTH

Although Argentine statesmen advocate rapid growth of the population, few measures have been taken to effect growth. One of the major areas of pronatalist legislation has been the constant revision of the tax laws to provide tax exemptions for large families. Social security organizations provide higher subsidies to workers who have many children. The impact of these subsidies is greatest in the country's inland areas; in major urban areas, the two-child family tends to predominate. The Fund for Family Allowances, in operation for about twenty years, provides allowances for the wife, the children, schooling, marriages, and births. The fund pays US$80 per birth and US$100 per marriage. In addition, there are special funds for industrial personnel, dock workers, state workers, and commerce employees. There also are sectional maternity benefits and a national law on maternity leave.

Another law that has solidified the family is the Family Property Act, which provides that the house a family owns and uses can be entered in a special registry that lists each province and the federal capital. Such registration transforms the property to a certain amount into an estate that cannot be taken from the family group.

The Argentine government's philosophy of population expansion received formal expression in a lecture given at Geneva to the Intergovernmental Committee of European Migrations (CIME) by the Argentine Chancellor Dr. Luis Maria del Pablo Pardo, who on November 30, 1971, said: "The Argentine Republic cannot share with those who indiscriminately sustain the necessity of restraining the demographic growth. This position is not only based on scepticism in view of history's causal laws but also on concrete data of our own reality. The actual Argentine population is *insufficient* to exploit adequately its resources and its material possibilities."

These official statements are in agreement with the policies of the founders of the country who repeatedly stated in the past "to govern properly is to populate." This continues to be the official Argentine position.

In October 1971, the Ministry of the Interior created the Demographic Policies Work Group, whose duty it will be to recommend to the government a concrete, detailed policy on population growth and the pertinent measures to be adopted to implement it. More specifically, the work group will be responsible for formulating long-range plans and programs, laws, decrees, and other directives that would define and put into action a national demographic policy, particularly in regard to the following areas: (1) the natural growth of the population, (2) immigration, (3) regional distribution of the population and internal migration, and (4) social mobility of the population. The National Director of the Development of Human Resources is coordinator of the work group, which consists of representatives of relevant public and private organizations. This office has produced a "working paper" on a "demographic policy for Argentina" [4].

OPINION OF INFLUENTIAL GROUPS
ON POPULATION GROWTH

Few private groups have conducted investigations of public opinion on population growth. Political parties have not been active since 1963.

Congress has not been convened, and so there has been no way to ascertain political positions on the subject. Public statements by leaders of various factions enable us to draw the following conclusions: (1) The socialists and leftists in general are against any kind of family planning because they see in it the "American imperialistic" influence, which only helps to create demographic weakness in underdeveloped nations. This opinion is expressed in a recent article by Leopoldo Halperin [5]. (2) The neoliberal groups, who believe in the free market economy, are also against state support of family planning, for they consider state interference an infringement on human liberty. (3) The nationalist groups of left and right, like the socialists and communists, oppose family planning as a manifestation of American imperialistic influence in developing countries. They believe Argentina needs a larger population in order to compete with neighboring countries, especially Brazil. The Argentine Roman Catholic church supports Pope Paul VI's opposition to the use of any contraceptive devices. The only family planning method the Catholic church condones is the rhythm method. Well-known lay Catholics' opinions usually agree with the ecclesiastic hierarchy.[2]

The Family Parent League, a Catholic organization, is actively working against birth control. The organization's ex-president, Dr. Pedro Shang, of the Academia Nacional de Medicina, published several articles on the subject [9].

The largest non-Catholic religious groups are the Protestants of various denominations, who total about 0.5 million people. Although their attitudes toward birth control vary, they do not publicize their positions. The Orthodox Jews, numbering about 300,000, are against any kind of birth control.

As far back as 1941, the authorities of the Museo Social Argentino, a lay group, organized and successfully carried out the First Argentine Population Congress. The congress concluded by recommending population increase. Their conclusions were later published under the direction of the congress' executives, Drs. Tomas Amadeo and Giullermo Garbarini Islas.

The consensus of the various groups is that Argentina needs to increase its population. How widespread and strong is this belief is evident from the impact of a newspaper article originally published in the Buenos Aires *Herald* and later in the influential *Semanario Economico* (*Economic Survey*) written by the well-known reporter Clive Petersen, titled "Can Argentina Survive in the Year 2000?" This article informed the public of Argentina's slow population growth and of the resulting danger to Argentina's

---

[2] See, for example, Ingeniero Nestor Ottonello's recent publications [6, 7, and 8].

survival as an independent nation. The article warned: "Unless 23 million Argentines prove that they are capable of using their land adequately, others will be tempted and compelled to do it."

In recent years, in addition to the expression of concern over slow population growth, many groups are becoming aware of the enormous urban concentration and are speculating on the social and economic consequences of this trend. The Gran Buenos Aires metropolis suffers from many problems in transportation, water, electrical power, sewers, pollution, and so on. Here almost 8.5 million people live on 0.1 percent of the country's total continental land. Many public statesmen have proposed the radical measure of moving the federal capital to another part of the country in order to spread out the governmental apparatus that is now concentrated in the present federal capital.

Articles by the following individuals were published on this matter: Adolfo Dago Holmberg [10]; engineer Julio Broner, Director of the Patronal Entity, General Economic Federation of the Argentine Republic [11]; and Dr. Alejandro Von Der Hayde, contributor to the well-known newspaper La Prensa [12]. In one recent lecture, he discussed ways to balance Argentina demographically and economically. In these and other similar statements, the capital's transfer is proposed as a means of relieving urban crowding to improve the territorial distribution of population.

Also very recently, the government has announced the promulgation of a special law to promote the future decentralization of industries in order to achieve a better distribution of the population in the country.

The army, the navy, the air force, and some intellectual groups are becoming increasingly concerned over the relative decrease of the Argentine population in the frontier areas and in Patagonia, which is gradually becoming populated by foreigners, mostly Chileans. The army and especially the air force, with the purpose of "Argentinizing" those areas, are operating a sort of official commercial nonprofit airline to these areas at very cheap rates, to stimulate Argentines to populate this large section, which represents almost a quarter of the total continental national territory.

REFERENCES

1. "Argentine Financing & Economy." Fiat Concord. Buenos Aires, 1966. (In Spanish.)

2. Raul Castro Olivera. "Family and Youth." Lecture given at the Primera Reunion Nacional de Centros de Proteccion Familiar. Buenos Aires, October 30, 1970. (In Spanish.)

3. Carmen Miro. "A program of comparative studies of fertility in Latin America." CELADE, series A, no. 49. (In Spanish.)

4. Ministry of the Interior. Buenos Aires, 1972. (In Spanish.)

5. Leopoldo Halperin. "Birth control and world's population." *Revista Transformaciones*, no. 5. Centro Editor de Americana Latina. (In Spanish.)

6. Ingeniero Nester Ottonello. "An x-ray of the demographic explosion." *La Nacion*, February 3, 1969. (In Spanish.)

7. Ingeniero Nester Ottonello. "Colin Clark refutes Malthus." *La Nacion*, September 29, 1968. (In Spanish.)

8. Ingeniero Nester Ottonello. "Man and hunger." Vincente Lopez Rotary Club, January, February, and March 1970. (In Spanish.)

9. Pedro Shang. "To govern properly is to populate with Argentines: Should we limit the birth rate?" In *Science and Doctrine*, vol. 2, Buenos Aires: University of Buenos Aires. (In Spanish.)

10. Adolfo Dago Holmberg. "Move the capital? Where to?" *Revista del Centro Naval*, December 1971. (In Spanish.)

11. Julio Broner. *The Nation and the Provinces.* 1971. (In Spanish.)

12. Alejandro Von Der Hayde. "First priority—to balance Argentina demographically and economically." Lecture at the Instituto Popular de Conferencia, August 30, 1971. (In Spanish.)

CHAPTER 17

Poland

Janusz A. Ziolkowski

Acknowledgments: The author thanks Drs. L. Lukaszewicz,
H. Przeslawska, and J. Pieprzyk for assistance in data collection.

ABSTRACT

In the evolution of postwar population policy in Poland, three periods could be distinguished.

The period *from 1945 to the early 1950s* is characterized by rapid population growth and a pronatalist policy of the state. Population policy was determined by the necessity to compensate for the drastic population decrease caused by the war and Nazi persecutions; the necessity to populate the western territories acquired in the Potsdam Agreement (1945); and the anti-Malthusian attitude of the socialist state based on Marxist ideology. The pronatalist policy was expressed in legislation and in social policy measures. The result was a live birth rate of 29–31 per 1,000 by 1955.

The period *from the late 1950s to the late 1960s* is characterized by the introduction of birth control measures to curb the "baby boom," considered to be the main cause of the economic difficulties in the mid-1950s. An intensive campaign for family planning and contraception was conducted through mass media, hospitals, and clinics. However, in view of the still imperfect methods of contraception, the need for legitimized, free, and widely accessible abortion became an obvious solution, and this resulted in the Abortion Act (1956). In 1967, there was one abortion for every two live births. Legal abortions and the decreasing number of women of childbearing age caused a marked drop in the fertility rate, particularly in urban areas. The birth rate decreased to 6.3 per 1,000 in 1965. Birth control was accepted as part of the modernization process, and the small family became a pattern.

Another preoccupation was that of adjusting internal migration to assure a better distribution of investment and a more adequate pattern of human settlement. Intensive urbanization resulted in the increase of population employed outside agriculture from 26.8 per 1,000 in 1950 to 57.2 in 1970 and in the emergence of large urban-industrial agglomerations, containing 40 percent of the total urban population.

The period *from the late 1960s to the present* is characterized by heated discussions on population problems and adoption of a moderately pronatalist policy. Declining fertility, resulting in a much lower reproduction rate (one likely to drop below net replacement level), has caused much concern. It is generally agreed that a net reproduction rate just above replacement (an annual natural increase of 5 per 1,000) is indispensable for the demographic future. Discussion, therefore, is centering around the fertility model, the economic and sociocultural factors that may bring it down, and measures to overcome demographic decline:

(1) Economic conditions more conducive to childbearing.
(2) Better housing conditions, particularly for young couples.
(3) Improvement of women's emerging dual career role through expanded part-time employment; better maternity and child care, particularly for working women; and elevation of the social status of motherhood.
(4) Reduction of infant mortality, which would have far-reaching consequences for population growth and quality of life.

It has been suggested that in order to carry out a "manifest" population policy, the government should create a State Population Commission with broad powers to formulate and implement this policy.

INTRODUCTION

In this review of population policy in Poland, our concern is primarily with the official government policies in the field of population. We are interested not so much in general principles as in what may be described as the strategy of action—the choice of means that would best fulfill the desired ends—and the sequence of steps. Thus, a basic document of the state, such as the Constitution, cannot be treated as the policy itself. It is only when these broad directive principles of the conduct of state affairs are translated into specific legislation, institution building, and national plans that we can speak of the policy proper. The plans are particularly important in Poland, a country whose whole social, economic, and cultural life is based on the principle of planning.

By the term "population policy" we mean those governmental measures that affect demographic phenomena and processes: population growth and replacement, internal distribution, and migration. It is clear that population policy is not autonomous in character but is an integral part of a wider strategy of action—"social policy." The latter, in Poland and probably elsewhere, denotes not only social and welfare services but also a wide range of socioeconomic and cultural actions.

How does the population policy express itself? The study of social policy in this important field is beset by many difficulties. Contrary to expectations, there is no comprehensive statement or resolution that sets the guidelines for population policy in Poland. One has, therefore, to decipher the contours of population policy from various documents, published statements, legislative actions, resolutions of public bodies and state-run associations, and administrative and welfare measures that may have a bearing on demographic events.

Some of these actions will have a direct and some an indirect influence on demographic behavior. A typical example of an action with direct influence on demographic trends would be the Abortion Act of 1956.[1] Examples of actions with indirect influence are the housing and social welfare policies that may not have been implemented explicitly to alter demographic behavior but, nonetheless, influence it very deeply. In other words, we must deal with both "manifest" and "latent" population policies [1].

In defining the scope of this review, we should mention the following considerations:

First, although the main subject of inquiry is the population policy as formulated and adopted by the state, we also shall deal with views expressed by various social groups of the national community—both formal and informal. These popular views may have two effects: (1) They influence the policy itself; (2) they influence the demographic behavior, which, in turn, may have a bearing on the course of action adopted by the state.

Second, since population policy is related to concrete demographic events, an attempt will be made to strike a balance between these two spheres—not overburdening the study with demographic data but, at the same time, not making it statistically barren.

Then, there is a problem of values. Population policy formulates goals and the means to achieve them that are unavoidably value-loaded. The value premises of the population policy are embedded in the total social system. In other words, population policy, like every form of intellectual activity, is determined by social conditions. The policy makers are, them-

---

[1] We cannot, of course, discuss the extent to which legal norms are convergent with social norms of the society at large or the extent to which legal norms that are prohibitive in nature are really effective. These interesting and important problems are beyond the scope of our study.

selves, part of the society; they share much of its emotional and intellectual climate and have their own preferences and prejudices.[2]

Equally important are value judgments on population problems expressed by various segments of the national community. The problems of procreation, sex, and contraception reach the deepest layers of human nature. When combined with attitudes toward population growth as a positive or negative factor in national development and as a means of achieving national—and sometimes nationalistic—goals, they give rise to highly emotional, biased, or prejudiced opinions. These will also be of great interest to us.

The approach adopted in the organization of this study is historical, covering demographic trends and policies from the post-World War II period to the present. The demographic events at a given point in time have consequences reaching far beyond the period in which they occur. This can be seen in the phenomenon of the "demographic echo"—in fluctuations over time in total growth, and sex, age, and dependency composition. The impact of the past is particularly pertinent to Poland's population problems. The watershed in her demographic history in this century is, of course, World War II. The war and its aftermath have had a profound influence. Postwar Poland has been a scene of tremendous territorial, sociopolitical, and economic changes, which, in turn, have influenced the demographic events.

Accordingly, the postwar demographic history and population policy of Poland can be roughly divided into three periods:

(1) From 1945 to mid-1950s, characterized by the rapid population growth and a pronatalist policy of the state.
(2) From mid-1950s to late 1960s, characterized by the introduction of various birth control measures aimed at curbing the "baby boom."
(3) From late 1960s to the present, characterized by heated discussion on population problems and adoption of a moderately pronatalist policy.

POLICY FROM 1945 TO MID-1950s

¶ POLICIES WITH REGARD TO POPULATION GROWTH
In the first decade after World War II, the population policy was determined by the following main factors:

[2] To discover the social conditions that have formed the valuations of the policy makers, to trace back the social roots of their "population ideology," and to discover how it finds its expression in actual policy are important but, unfortunately, much neglected areas of study. Although we are not able to present a methodical investigation of these complex problems, nonetheless some impressionistic guesses will be ventured in this respect.

(1) The need to compensate for the drastic decrease in population caused by the war and the Nazi occupation. The population of Poland in 1938 (in her former frontiers—388,000 square kilometers) amounted to 34.8 million people. In 1946 (in her new frontiers—312,000 square kilometers), it dropped to 23.9 million. In 1950, it was 25 million.[3] The biggest share in the decline must be attributed to the Nazi extermination policy, which cost the lives of some 6 million people (of whom about half were of Jewish origin), that is, one-sixth of the prewar population. Although it is impossible to give here a detailed analysis of the political, territorial, and demographic changes brought about by World War II, it is worth mentioning that Poland emerged from the war as an ethnically homogeneous country, whereas before 1939, minority groups represented not less than 32 percent of the total population.

(2) The need to populate the western territories (100,000 square kilometers, about one-third of the country's territory) which were acquired under the Potsdam Agreement of August 2, 1945, and from which the transfer of the remaining German population was gradually being carried out.[4] We will discuss the settlement of the western territories later on.

(3) The anti-Malthusian attitude of the socialist state based on Marxist ideology. It was maintained that the pressure of population on the means of subsistence arose from inadequate socioeconomic structures in the fields of production and income distribution. The crux of the matter, therefore, lay not in checking population growth but in introducing profound changes in the total socioeconomic structure of the society.

Postwar Poland experienced an extremely rapid population growth due mainly to the very high birth rate, as seen in Table 1. The high birth rate was a product of the following factors:

[3] The figures for the year 1950 rather than those for 1946 (the date of the first postwar provisional census) should be taken as a basis for comparison; it was only at that time that the large-scale migratory movements came to a close. Such operations as the removal of Germans from the former eastern provinces of the German Reich according to the Potsdam Agreement, the repatriation of Poles from the former Polish provinces east of the rivers Bug and San taken over by the Soviet Union, and the remigration of Polish people from other European countries (Germany, France, Belgium, Romania, Yugoslavia) had largely been completed.

[4] The "transfer of the entire German population, or elements thereof, remaining in Poland" (Article 13 of the Potsdam Resolutions) was initiated February 20, 1946; the repatriation was closed in 1948. The number of Germans who left Poland under the Potsdam Agreement totaled 2,213,000. In the subsequent years, only small groups of Germans left Poland under the Family Link Campaign and so forth. In the western territories, only slightly over 50,000 Germans remained (in the whole country—according to the data issued by the Polish Parliamentary Commission for Internal Affairs—there were 65,000 Germans in 1957).

There were 7.6 million Germans living in these lands in 1939 (the total population of these territories was 8.8 million, including 1.2 million people of Polish origin); however, some 5 million Germans living in these territories left before the conclusion of war operations. See [2].

(1) The compensative character of postwar fertility. There was a surge of births that had been postponed during the war either because of the separation of couples, the hard conditions of war existence, or sheer inability to get married under existing rules. (Marriages were prohibited in many parts of occupied Poland as part of the Nazi extermination policy.)
(2) The prolonged demographic "echo" of the large numbers of young people born in the 1920s, who reached childbearing ages in the postwar period.
(3) The relative ease with which one could get married after the war (the marriage rate was 11.9 per 1,000 in 1946) as a result of an increased social and geographic mobility; an abundance of employment; changes in sociocultural norms related to marriage (for example, the decline of the institution of the dowry, less interference of elders); minimal standards after the war hardships with regard to housing, furniture, and so forth; and the general atmosphere of enthusiasm of the postwar reconstruction.

This dynamic population growth enjoyed the full support of the state. The policy makers were both influencing and being influenced by the course of events. They were independent actors grasping an initiative; at the same time, they were sensitive to and supportive of the nation's attitudes.

The pronatalist attitude of the state was evident in its legislation. The new family code, undertaken immediately after the war and completed in 1950, was drawn with the interests of child and family in view. Its main theses were introduced into the new Constitution promulgated in 1952: "Marriage and the family are under the care and protection of the Polish People's

TABLE 1.

Live Births, Poland, 1946–1955

Year	Number (in thousands)	Per 1,000 Population
1946	622	26.2
1947	681	28.7
1948	704	29.4
1949	725	29.7
1950	763	30.7
1951	783	31.0
1952	779	30.2
1953	779	29.7
1954	778	29.1
1955	793	29.1

SOURCE: See [3].

Republic. The State gives particular care to families with many children" (Article 67, paragraph 1). "Birth out of wedlock is not to impair child's rights" (Article 67, paragraph 2). "Polish People's Republic takes particular care of the education of the youth and assures to them the broadest opportunities for growth" (Article 68). The social services legislation put particular emphasis on the welfare of mother and child, as is evident from provisions for twelve-week paid maternity leaves, free medical services for mother and child, birth grants, free baby clothing, progressive family allowances, free nurseries and kindergartens for working mothers, and special taxes on unmarried persons. These provisions acted as a definite economic incentive to fertility and, at the same time, created an atmosphere of social recognition for large families. The net result was a rapid population growth until 1955, as shown in Table 2.

¶ POLICIES WITH REGARD TO MIGRATION

Settlement of the Western Territories.

The campaign, undertaken by Poland in 1945, for settlement of the western territories that covered an area of 100,000 square kilometers and in which 54 percent of urban edifices and 27.5 percent of rural edifices were destroyed, was an ambitious enterprise. In order for these regions to develop, several million people would have to be settled in them. This seemed impracticable in view of the heavy losses in population of the Polish nation during the war. Yet, the settlement scheme developed from the initial months onward on a large scale, and in the course of three years, some 4.5 million settlers arrived in the western territories. In 1948, the population of these lands, including about 1 million indigenous inhabitants

TABLE 2.

Population Growth, Poland, 1950–1955

Year	Population (in millions)	Annual Growth (in thousands)	Natural Increase (per 1,000 population)
1950	25.0	474.4	19.1
1951	25.5	471.3	18.6
1952	26.0	492.3	19.1
1953	26.5	572.5	19.5
1954	27.0	501.7	18.8
1955	27.6	532.2	19.7

SOURCE: See [3].

of Polish origin,[5] totaled 5.5 million; this amounted to 65 percent of the prewar population. Considering the damages in economic productivity and housing facilities, this number was the maximum that could be absorbed by these lands at that time.

There were two major sources of settlers for the western territories. The first was the Polish population repatriated from the former Polish eastern provinces; it was intended that these people should find here an equivalent for their homes and trades abandoned in the east. These people, however, by no means constituted the most numerous group of settlers. Almost two-thirds of all settlers came from the central provinces; these were called resettlers to distinguish them from repatriates. Their migration was occasioned by the problem, still existing despite the effects of the war and the land reform, of overpopulation in the central regions of Poland. A natural outlet was the movement toward the western territories. In addition to the two groups, some settlers arrived as emigrants from other European countries.

As early as the spring of 1945, a State Repatriation Board (SRB) was set up to direct the settlement scheme. Repatriation committees cooperating with the central office also were established for the districts and provinces. Thanks to the efforts of the most outstanding Polish demographers, economists, sociologists, and geographers, a Bureau for the Study of Settlement Problems was created, together with a Scientific Council for Problems Connected with the Recovered Territories, which cooperated closely with the bureau. On the basis of exhaustive research, these two bodies worked out the principles and directives for the settlement campaign. According to the program, settlers were to be directed to those areas of the western territories that had a climate, type of soil, and manner of farming similar to those in their places of origin. In addition to geographical and economic premises, sociocultural factors were also to be taken into consideration; there was a tendency to settle people in unified groups so that they could maintain the old social ties and, thus, adapt more readily to the new conditions and strike roots in the new environment. These principles were implemented with varying degrees of success. They were observed very strictly in the case of repatriates who migrated and settled in unified groups in climates similar to those from which they came. The guidelines were not adhered to as strictly in the case of resettlers who chose their sites of settlement for themselves and, in most cases, moved individually or in nuclear family groups.

[5] In order to determine actual nationality of that group, a special verification was carried out, following the provisions of the act of April 28, 1946, "concerning Polish citizenship of persons of Polish nationality inhabiting the Recovered Territories"[4].

A picture of the migratory movements toward the recovered territories was presented by the returns of the national census of December 3, 1950. On that day, the western territories had a population of 5,602,000 persons, of whom 4,498,000 were new settlers.[6] Classification by place of origin (residence as of August 1939) was as follows:

Total of new arrivals: 4,497,984

   Of these, people from Polish lands
      within the present boundaries: 2,792,714
                                     (62 percent of all newcomers)

Repatriates (total):   1,705,270
                                     (38 percent of all newcomers)
   Of these:
      from the USSR (mostly from
         former Polish lands):   1,553,512
      from France: 54,576
      from Germany: 44,170
      from other countries: 53,012[7]

SOURCE: National census of December 3, 1950.

Urban Migration.

After the period of postwar reconstruction and stabilization of migratory movements, population policy became concerned with the processes of internal migration. Measures concerning migration were connected closely with the planned transformation of the socioeconomic structure of the society. Toward this end, an intense industrialization campaign was embarked upon in 1949–1950 and continued vigorously during the First Six-Year Plan (1950–1956). The rationale behind it was both economic (to absorb the excess labor force, to improve economic standards in the most backward parts of the country by a more equitable distribution of the productive forces, and to increase the national income) and politico-ideological (to increase the members of the working class). Since industries were located in urban areas, the result was a large-scale and officially encouraged urban migration (see Table 3). Between 1946 and 1960, as many as 2.5 million people left rural areas and went to live in urban areas

[6] The remaining population—1,104,134—were Polish autochthons, that is, persons who inhabited the present western territories in August 1939 together with children born between 1939 and 1950.

[7] Excludes 59,915 persons in the western territories whose domicile immediately before the war could not be established.

TABLE 3.

Urban/Rural Distribution of Population, Poland, 1950–1970

Year	Population (in thousands)	Towns and Cities	Rural Areas	Urban Population as Percent of Total Population
1950	25,035	9,244	15,791	36.9
1955	27,550	12,067	15,483	43.8
1960	29,795	14,401	15,394	48.3
1965	31,551	15,681	15,870	49.7
1970	32,605	17,031	15,574	52.2

SOURCE: See [3].

and towns. It has been estimated that some 8 million urban dwellers were members of families in which one or both parents had come from rural areas during those fifteen years. The percentage of the urban population increased steadily and absorbed practically the whole natural increase over the period. The size of the rural population has remained unchanged during the whole postwar period, oscillating between 15.4 and 15.9 million.

The migration was highly selective, embracing mainly young people aged 20–29. This had serious consequences for the geographic distribution of fertility patterns between urban and rural areas. The countryside was deprived of the most fertile age groups. At the same time, those young people in the childbearing age, in migrating to urban areas, brought with them rural fertility patterns, producing a soaring urban birth rate. This phenomenon was called the "demographic ruralization of towns." During 1951–1955, the urban live birth rate was almost on a par with that of the countryside and sometimes even surpassed it.

These processes exerted heavy pressure—particularly in centers undergoing the most vigorous industrialization—on housing, transportation, health, education, and other social welfare services. (It must be remembered that to provide these social amenities was considered a responsibility of the socialist state.) The process of industrialization accompanied by increasing employment of women aggravated the situation by increasing the demand for child care services. (Thirty-five percent of the female population of working age were employed by 1962, and the rate of increase of the female labor force was higher than that of the male labor force, the indices for the years 1946–1960 being 175 and 135, respectively.) The children of the postwar baby boom passed through the nurseries and kindergartens and quickly reached the schools: Whereas in 1950, there were 5.0 million children aged 0–9; in 1955, there were already 6.6 million. The concentration of investment on capital-intensive industrial growth put a very heavy strain on the national economy and left very small resources for the development of the whole social infrastructure, which lagged increasingly far behind. Simultaneously, the one-sided development of heavy industry and the neglect of the consumption industries, combined with a campaign against small private commercial, business, and handicraft enterprises, created great shortages of goods and services for consumption.

FROM THE MID-1950s TO THE LATE 1960s

¶ THE RATIONALE BEHIND THE BIRTH CONTROL POLICY

In this situation, the high birth rate that added about 500,000 people to the country annually (for a 2 percent annual growth rate) came to be considered a liability if not the main cause of economic difficulties both present and projected. The strategy of national development was heavily influenced by what might be called excessive "econocentrism"; development was mainly centered upon investment in physical things, with an expected result of an increased total output. Social development was completely subordinated to economic development. Population growth became a scapegoat to be blamed for all the inadequacies of national development.

Hence, the 1960s saw a reversal of the population policy that dominated the 1950s. An intensive campaign was launched by mass media (which in Poland as elsewhere in eastern Europe are run by the state) advocating birth control and upholding the model of the emancipated, working woman freed from the burden of a large progeny. In a growing climate of social disapproval, families with many children were not only held responsible for the socioeconomic predicament of the country but also ridiculed as backward in outlook and way of life.

¶ LEGISLATIVE ACTION AND INSTITUTION BUILDING
FOR FAMILY PLANNING AND BIRTH CONTROL

The turning point was the act of April 27, 1956, allowing abortion on medical or socioeconomic grounds (including pregnancy resulting from criminal assault). Abortion on demand was, of course, confidential and left to the discretion of the woman. This was further liberalized by the decree of the Minister of Health of December 19, 1959, which made it possible for a woman to appeal a medical verdict not permitting abortion. Abortion was to be performed by the state health centers free of charge as part of the national health insurance system. At the same time, the act treated abortion as a "necessary evil" that was to protect women against the danger of clandestine operations. The act stressed the need for widespread dissemination of information about means to prevent unwanted pregnancies and assigned to physicians (most of whom were state employees) the responsibility for instructing women about preventive measures. Thus, gynecologic hospitals and clinics and health advice centers for women became the main institutions enforcing the new population policy.

Another important agency in the family planning movement was the Society for Conscious Motherhood (since 1970, named the "Society for Family Planning," or SFP), founded under state auspices on November 13, 1957. This agency included in its membership prewar family planning workers. (Their leader was a renowned writer, T. Boy-Zelenski, who coined and popularized the term "conscious motherhood.") The society set up branches and advice centers in all *voivodships* (provinces) and *powiats* (counties) as well as "local circles" at bigger industrial enterprises and in rural areas. Starting in September 1961, the society published a bimonthly journal *Family Problems*. The main aims of the society were: to combat the widespread practice of abortion as the main means of birth control; to spread knowledge about contraceptive methods; and to propagate rational family planning and sexual culture, particularly among adolescents. The society's activity was linked closely to the national health scheme.

Besides the mass media and the aforementioned organizations, many other state-run institutions and associations, such as the Women's League (a mass political association of women), Society for Fostering Secular Culture, Society for Popular Knowledge, social and political youth organizations (of students, boy scouts, urban working-class youth, and rural youth), and schools, mainly at the middle level, joined in the movement to promote "conscious motherhood."

We can summarize the goals and programs of all the institutions carrying out the population policy as follows: (1) prevention of unwanted pregnancies;[8] (2) therapy for infertility; (3) therapy for sexual disturbances; (4) premarital and family advice; (5) sex education of the youth in order to prepare them for their marital and parental responsibilities.

The activities of these institutions assumed a variety of forms. In terms of *counseling services*: (1) Telephone services provided advice on sexual matters, family planning, contraceptive methods, legal matters related to childbearing and family problems; (2) premarital and familial counseling centers were created; (3) courses were held for the betrothed; (4) courses in sexual culture were held for teenagers; and (5) correspondence centers offered advice on family planning;

---

[8] In the first period, the activities concentrated on information and medical and legal advice concerning abortion; this activity is much less accentuated now. At present, the main preoccupations are the problems of contraception and sexuality.

In the realm of *information and training*: (1) A so-called Parents University was formed; (2) special lessons on reproduction and sexual problems were introduced in primary and secondary schools; (3) special courses on family planning and sexual problems were held at teachers' colleges, for the military service, at students' clubs, and among groups of rural housewives; (4) seminars and conferences were given for family planning personnel led by physicians, sociologists, psychologists, adult educators, and so on; (5) information on family planning and sexual matters was disseminated through publications and audiovisual aids.

Medical services offered included premarital examinations, periodic check-ups for young couples, special treatment for fertility and infertility, medical advice on contraceptive methods, provision of contraceptives, and safe termination of unwanted pregnancy if advisable on medical or socioeconomic grounds.

A subsequent legislative measure that has had a definite bearing on birth reduction increased the legal age of marriage for men from eighteen to twenty-one years in the new family and social care code introduced on January 1, 1965.

¶ THE VIEW OF THE CATHOLIC CHURCH

The most basic family planning measure was the Abortion Act of 1956. Clearly, the act was highly controversial from the very beginning; the legislators themselves considered it a necessary evil. Nevertheless, the implications of the legalization of abortion, and particularly the liberal amendment of 1959, were understood unmistakably by all parties involved. Spoken opposition to the act was concentrated in the Roman Catholic church (it should be noted that the majority of Poles are Catholics). The Catholic members of the Seym (Parliament) voted against the Abortion Act; the Catholic press criticized it bitterly; priests denounced it as an encouragement to commit infanticide. Nevertheless, in the prevailing circumstances, the least the church could do was to relax its attitude toward family planning. The church openly permitted family planning, citing health reasons and general living conditions as the grounds for regulating the number and spacing of children. Moreover, in order to help Catholic couples to practice contraception, counseling services were established at parish churches. The only contraceptive method acceptable to the church was periodic abstinence, or the rhythm method. Simultaneously with its advocation of this method, the church launched a wide information campaign aimed at preparing youth for marital and family life in accordance with Catholic principles. Here a characteristic new accent was introduced, which was gradually becoming more and more dominant, namely, the view that, along with the procreative function, equally important aspects of marriage were physical love, affection, and companionship.

¶ ATTITUDES AND PRACTICES WITH REGARD TO CONTRACEPTION

The results of the birth control campaign were dependent to a large extent on the supply of contraceptive devices, a situation that was at first far from satisfactory. There were shortages of contraceptives; the ease with which they could be used and their efficacy were very inadequate. But the situation was gradually improving. Production of oral contraceptives was started on a larger scale in 1968, and that of IUDs, in 1969. Out of 30 million contraceptive items sold in 1968, 22 million were condoms (which were rather rarely used in marital intercourse).

As important as the ready supply of contraceptives was the adoption of new practices by the population. The idea of planned fertility was rather widely accepted. The research carried out by the Center for Investigation of Public Opinion in the late 1950s revealed, among a sample of 2,800, that 48 percent were of the opinion that the high birth rate was responsible for deteriorated living conditions and difficulties in the labor market; 66 percent were in favor of curbing population growth through birth control (87 percent of nonbelievers and 65 percent of Catholics); and 55 percent stated that they used contraceptives (53 percent of Catholics). In practice, however, use of contraceptives was rather limited until the late 1960s.

Investigations conducted during 1966–1968 revealed a negligible incidence of contraceptive use both among men and women, particularly in marital intercourse, and a great deal of prejudice against various methods, coupled with lack of skill on the part of women.

The analysis of contraceptive practices among 3,656 married women coming to the medical clinic of the Society for Family Planning in Warsaw gave the following findings:

(1) 25.5 percent practiced coitus interruptus.
(2) 22.7 percent practiced rhythm (thermic method).
(3) 9.1 percent of couples made use of condoms.
(4) 5.1 percent made use of chemical devices.
(5) 1.4 percent practiced other methods.

It should be added that 31.9 percent of investigated couples were using two methods, that is, mechanical (condoms) and chemical contraceptives.

Another study on the practice of 500 urban women aged 18–62 produced the following results:

(1) 47.2 percent did not practice contraception at all.
(2) 25.0 percent practiced either withdrawal (19.2) or rhythm (5.0) or both (0.8).
(3) 19.0 percent used chemical and mechanical contraceptives.
(4) 8.8 percent used various other methods.

The age groups of women in which practice of contraception was lowest were to age twenty (76.3 percent not practicing) and over age fifty (47.7 percent not practicing in the past). It can be assumed that, in the first case, it was caused by thoughtlessness and lack of experience; in the other, it was caused by a limited acquaintance with contraceptive methods dating back to the childbearing ages.

It was also observed that there was a relationship between the method of contraception and level of education. Among those women who used rhythm or withdrawal rather than chemical or mechanical contraceptive devices, there were:

(1) 36.5 percent with unfinished primary education.
(2) 33.0 percent with completed primary education.
(3) 16.7 percent with secondary (high school) education.
(4) 11.0 percent with higher education.

It should be mentioned that in the sample, among women practicing some form of contraception, 76 percent became pregnant. This, of course, reflects the poor quality of contraceptives and inconsistency in use, not to mention the repercussions for the entire birth control campaign.

Until recently relatively little was known about contraceptive practices of rural women. It was only in 1972 that this gap was filled. Investigation carried out since 1958 among 13.7 percent of married women in the Lublin province revealed that 52.8 percent did not practice contraception at all. Out of the remaining 47.2 percent:

(1) 65.8 percent practiced coitus interruptus.
(2) 14.0 percent of couples made use of condoms.
(3) 9.3 percent made use of chemical devices.
(4) 4.8 percent were applying the rhythm method.
(5) 3.9 percent were using douche.
(6) 2.9 percent were using chemical and mechanical devices.

Comparison of contraceptive practices between the urban and rural women stresses that among the first category most frequently used were coitus interruptus and the thermic method; among the other, coitus interruptus and condoms.

¶ ATTITUDES AND PRACTICES WITH REGARD TO ABORTION
None of these surveys based on relatively small samples could claim to be fully representative of the whole Polish population. Their results, reflecting different social and ecological environments, differed considerably. However, one fact came clearly to the fore, namely, the relatively weak impact of efforts to limit births through contraception because of inade-

TABLE 4.

Numbers of Abortions Performed, Poland, 1957–1970

Year	Number of Abortions
1957	122,000
1958	126,000
1959	162,000
1960	233,000
1961	230,000
1962	272,000
1963	260,000
1964	247,000
1965	235,000
1966	226,000
1967	221,000
1968	219,000
1969	212,000
1970	214,000

SOURCE: See [5].

quate diffusion of new ideas among the masses of the population and the poor efficiency of adopted methods. These limitations help to explain the high number of abortions performed in state hospitals and other health institutions from the moment the new act was declared, as shown in Table 4.

It should be mentioned that statistical sources do not include abortions performed in private physicians' consultation rooms, and—as assessed by all students of the problem—the figures most probably are much below the actual numbers.[9]

Nonetheless, the data show a sharp rise in the number of performed abortions almost immediately after the Abortion Act was introduced. The index of abortions for 100 women aged between 15–49 in 1957 was 1.7, whereas in 1962, it increased to 3.8. Most of the abortions were performed in urban and industrialized areas (among big cities, Warsaw took the lead). Since the latter were characterized also by a low fertility rate, there seems to be a correlation between a tendency to limit the number of children through abortion and the decreased birth rate. Even according to the official statistics, the number of abortions as compared with that of live

[9] Although abortion is a confidential matter, it cannot remain unreported when performed in a hospital. Therefore, many women prefer "private" abortions and pay fees, rather than submit to the state-run hospitals, which are free of charge. "Private" fees have been lowered considerably in the last few years, however.

births assumes considerable proportions: In 1967, there was one abortion for every two live births. Of 500 urban women mentioned above, 488 were involved in abortion practices in one way or another. With regard to the reasons, most often given were bad material conditions (36.3 percent) and high number of children (34.3 percent).

It stands to reason that the Abortion Act did not create a phenomenon; clandestine abortions were practiced widely before 1956. The number of cases of postoperative complications was 73,000 in 1951 and 103,000 in 1955.[10] In 1960, according to authorities, the cases of postoperative complications registered by the hospitals were only 40 percent of the total. The avowed goal of the act was precisely to combat the plague of clandestine abortions. As advocates of the act indicated, the increase of legalized abortions was bound to be accompanied by a decrease in illicit abortions and would also bring down the total number of abortions, if accompanied by a contraception campaign. On the other hand, while the idea of birth control was gaining ground steadily among all strata of society and methods and devices of contraception were imperfect, legalized abortion, which was free and widely accessible, became the obvious solution to unwanted pregnancy.

Religious opposition to abortion, although undoubtedly an inhibiting factor, played a much weaker role than expected. Research of the Center for Investigation of Public Opinion found that 50 percent of Catholic women admitted to having had an abortion. It seems that among Catholic women the following syndrome operated: Practice of the rhythm method (the only method permitted by the Catholic Church) led to unexpected and unwanted pregnancy, which in turn led to abortion with a guilty conscience.

¶ RESULTS OF THE ANTINATALIST POLICY

The years after 1956 were characterized by a steady decline in the birth rate. Although the birth rate had begun to decrease in the early 1950s, the drop was relatively slight. It was only from 1956 that the tempo accelerated noticeably, from 793,000 live births in 1955 (the highest figure ever in the postwar period) to 520,000 in 1967 (the lowest figure since the war), as shown in Table 5.

Undoubtedly, a considerable portion of this decrease arose because the smaller birth cohorts were reaching their childbearing age in 1960–1965. Whereas, in 1955, the category of women aged 20–34 years constituted 48.5 percent of the total number of potential mothers, in 1965, they accounted only for 41.5 percent. But this deflation of the birth rate was compensated for to some extent in the last years by the reproductive activ-

---

[10] According to unpublished data at the SFP.

TABLE 5.

Live Births, Poland, 1956–1971 (by area)

Year	Total		Rural		Urban	
	Number (in thousands)	Per 1,000 Population	Number (in thousands)	Per 1,000 Population	Number (in thousands)	Per 1,000 Population
1956	779	28.1	331	26.8	447	29.1
1957	782	27.6	333	26.0	448	29.6
1958	755	26.3	325	24.5	430	27.8
1959	722	24.7	306	22.4	416	26.8
1960	669	22.6	280	19.9	389	24.9
1961	627	20.9	261	18.1	365	23.6
1962	599	19.8	250	16.9	349	22.4
1963	588	19.2	245	16.3	343	21.9
1964	562	18.1	238	15.5	324	20.5
1965	546	17.4	233	14.9	313	19.7
1966	530	16.7	227	14.4	303	19.1
1967	520	16.3	223	14.0	296	18.6
1968	524	16.2	228	13.8	296	18.7
1969	531	16.3	235	14.1	296	18.7
1970	546	16.6	248	14.7	297	18.8
1971	562	17.2	258	15.0	304	19.5

Source: See [6].

ity of the larger cohorts born just after the war, visible in the slightly growing number of live births (562,000, that is, 17.2 per 1,000 population in 1971). These two phenomena account for the fluctuation of the marriage rate (see Table 6). The year 1965 recorded the smallest number of marriages, 199,000, that is, 6.3 per 1,000 population—a consequence of less numerous age groups born during the war who were of marriageable age of 20–24. (The average age in 1970 among men was 24.1; among women, 21.6.) As a result of the baby boom after the war, the number of marriages has been growing steadily and is expected to reach a record high of 400,000 in 1980. Needless to say, this phenomenon, though accounting for an increase in the birth rate, is unlikely to be translated into fertility rates equal to those of the 1950s.

The most striking evidence of the effectiveness of birth control (and abortion) as a factor in the decline of births in Poland can be found in the marked decrease of the fertility rate (see Table 7).

Apart from the general declining trend, two other phenomena deserve attention. The first is the shortening of the reproductive period, which now mainly embraces age groups between fifteen and thirty-four. The most noticeable decline of fertility has occurred in the oldest age groups (35–39, 40–44, 45–49). The second is that the difference between the urban and rural fertility is still rather pronounced and actually widening. The rural fertility rate in 1960 was 40 percent higher than the urban one; at the end of the decade, the difference was 60 percent. Since the urban population now includes more than 50 percent of the total, the consequences of the urban "demographic decline" for the population growth and replacement

TABLE 6.

Marriages, Poland, 1950–1971

Year	Number (in thousands)	Per 1,000 Population
1950	267	10.8
1955	258	9.5
1960	244	8.2
1965	199	6.3
1966	225	7.1
1967	238	7.5
1968	257	8.0
1969	270	8.3
1970	280	8.5
1971	291	8.9

SOURCE: See [6].

TABLE 7.

Live Births for the Total Population and for Urban and Rural Areas,
Poland, 1950–1970 (per 100 women by age groups)

	Live Births by Age of Woman							
Year	15–19	20–24	25–29	30–34	35–39	40–44	45–49	All, 15–49
	All Areas							
1950	3.9	19.4	20.9	15.7	10.0	3.8	0.4	10.9
1955	4.2	20.8	20.3	14.4	8.9	3.2	0.3	11.0
1960	4.5	19.9	16.5	10.3	6.0	2.2	0.2	9.3
1965	3.2	18.4	14.4	8.4	4.3	1.5	0.2	7.2
1970	3.0	16.5	12.6	7.1	3.6	1.1	0.1	6.4
	Urban							
1950	4.1	18.9	18.7	12.9	7.5	2.4	0.2	9.9
1955	4.6	19.8	18.3	11.7	6.7	2.2	0.2	10.1
1960	4.5	18.2	13.3	7.3	3.9	1.3	0.1	7.7
1965	2.9	14.8	11.2	5.9	2.6	0.8	0.1	5.7
1970	2.6	13.4	10.2	5.2	2.2	0.6	0.0	5.1
	Rural							
1950	3.8	19.7	22.6	17.7	11.6	4.7	0.5	11.6
1955	3.9	21.8	22.2	16.9	10.9	4.2	0.5	11.8
1960	4.5	21.7	20.2	13.7	8.2	3.2	0.3	10.9
1965	3.4	23.1	18.6	11.7	6.4	2.2	0.3	8.8
1970	3.4	20.8	16.1	9.9	5.5	1.8	0.2	7.9

SOURCE: See [3].

in general are obvious. The latter is due mainly to the rural natural increase.

This rural-urban differentiation with regard to natural increase should, however, be put into proper perspective. It is not only the urban environment that undergoes the demographic transformation. This is true also of the rural environment. The only difference is the pace of change—much quicker in towns (particularly the big cities) and slower in the rural areas. We are witnessing the sociocultural urbanization of the country as a whole, as the urban way of life spreads irrespective of place of residence. Deliberate restriction of the number of children is one of its most characteristic features. This could first be seen in urban areas where, after the initial wave of the "demographic ruralization," a low fertility pattern reemerged as a result of the rapid sociocultural urbanization of rural newcomers; now it is seen in the gradual adoption of the urban way of life with regard to fertility patterns in the rural areas.

It is not easy to determine how far the birth rate was affected by biological factors—that is, the changing age structure of the population—or by social factors in the wide sense of the word, including the economic conditions, the intervention of the state in the demographic processes, human aspirations and preferences, and values with regard to childbearing. One may, however, risk the statement that the birth rate in Poland seems to be more and more influenced by social factors, which means the acceptance of birth control and small family size as a pattern. Poland, thus, has achieved, on a large scale, psychosocial modernization in the field of demographic behavior, a process that was largely a repetition of the great structural and behavioral changes that occurred in the most developed countries by and large in the nineteenth century.

In fact, this process of demographic modernization began in Poland in the early twentieth century together with the spread of industrial civilization. Whereas, until the end of the nineteenth century, the live birth rate was 40–45 per 1,000, just before the outbreak of World War II, it was 24.6 per 1,000. But it was only after 1960 that this process has reemerged and has accelerated considerably.

Another way of looking at the demographic transformations that have taken place in Poland is to consider them as a process of social democratization both by class, since those which before 1939 were characteristics of the urban middle class have become features of the working and farming classes, and by sex, since the emancipation of women was characterized by a movement away from "natural," unrestricted fertility toward "conscious motherhood."

The net result was a much lower natural increase, as shown in Table 8. Whereas, in the 1950s, natural increase was on the average 500,000 per annum, in the first half of the 1960s, it was 350,000 and, in the second half of the decade, 280,000. The rate of natural increase dropped from 19.5 per 1,000 in 1955 to 8.5 in 1970 (the lowest rate, 8.2 per 1,000, was in 1969). Here it should be added that the tempo of the decline was cushioned by the low mortality rate.[11]

---

[11] A low mortality rate was caused mainly by decreases in infant mortality, which fell from 118 per 1,000 live births in 1951 to 33.4 in 1970, as well as increases in life expectancy at birth (for men from 48.2 years before 1939 to 66.8 in 1965; for women from 51.4 years to 72.8 in these same years). Low mortality rates were maintained by the additional historical factor, caused by the Nazi extermination practice, of a small surviving population in age groups above sixty. This age group gradually increased in size, and by 1966, there appeared a slight increase in the mortality rate for the group.

TABLE 8.

Population Growth, Poland, 1950–1971

Year	Population (in millions)	Natural Increase (in thousands)	Natural Increase (per 1,000 population)	Births (per 1,000 population)	Deaths (per 1,000 population)
1950	25.0	474.4	19.1	30.7	11.6
1955	27.5	532.2	19.5	29.1	9.6
1960	29.8	441.7	15.0	22.6	7.6
1965	31.6	313.9	10.0	17.4	7.4
1970	32.6	279.2	8.5	16.6	8.1
1971	32.8	278.6	8.5	17.2	8.7

SOURCE: See [6].

The natural increase was by no means evenly distributed about the country. Apart from the basic dichotomy between urban and rural areas, those "natural areas" of low and high increase, there was also a regional differentiation at play. The western territories differed markedly from the rest of the country. Settled mostly by the young people (in 1950, the number of those aged 15–34 was 5.6 percent higher than in the old lands; the number of married women aged 15–29 was 16 percent higher than in other parts of the country), these territories were characterized by an extremely high natural increase. In 1950, their rate of natural increase was 29.2 per 1,000 as compared with 16.1 percent in the rest of the country, and although it decreased gradually (20.0 percent in 1960 as against 14.9 percent in other parts of the country), it was still an unprecedented phenomenon by European standards. It was estimated that about 3 million children were born between 1945–1960, increasing the population of these lands to 8 million (almost on a par with the prewar population).

The drop in the natural increase that occurred in Poland in the late 1950s and the 1960s was most marked in the western provinces. The main reason was changes in the age structure; women born before and during World War II were less numerous in the western territories than in the rest of the country, which resulted in a sharp decline in the natural increase. It is only since 1965, when the extremely numerous age groups born after 1945 entered the reproductive age, that the western territories, which have drawn the most vital part of the nation, have been experiencing a second wave of relatively high—though much lower than before—natural increase. The natural increase in the western provinces was 11.1 percent in 1970 compared with 8.5 percent for the country as a whole—a difference of 2.6 percentage points. (This difference was 13.1 in 1950.)

The drop in the natural increase to an average European standard was greeted, on the whole, as a highly positive phenomenon. This was true particularly with the state authorities for whom it gave a necessary "breathing space" in coping with many difficult economic problems in the 1960s connected with the postwar baby boom (requiring expansion of education, employment, and housing for about 2 million young people).

¶ POLICY TOWARD INTERNAL MIGRATION
AND HUMAN SETTLEMENT PATTERNS

In the 1960s, attention was focused also on the problems of internal migration and distribution of population. One of the most typical features of Poland's recent social history has been the movements of population. Apart from migrations just after the war, which were precipitated by the shifting of the country's frontiers, the main impetus came from the process of industrialization and general economic development. In the twenty years from 1951 to 1970, approximately 23 million (that is, 80 percent) of all the country's inhabitants, have relocated.

There have been four major types of migration.

First, migration from village to town was the most typical characteristic of the population movements of the 1950s and 1960s. Between 1951 and 1970, a total of 6 million people migrated to the towns.

Second, there has been heavy intervillage migration, which accounted for 7.7 million moves. Two factors were at play here: (1) New agricultural policy after October 1956 reversed the trend toward collectivization and made farming a much more attractive proposition, resulting in more numerous transfers of land, farming of new holdings, and redistribution of labor between the areas characterized by either a surplus or a shortage of manpower; (2) rural "matrimonial tradition" was characterized by the fact that farmers' sons usually found brides in other villages.

Third, there have been interurban transfers—in spite of housing shortages and administrative restrictions on change of residence (we will come to this later)—that accounted for 5.5 million changes in the last twenty years. The main impulse was the pull of new jobs in the fastest-growing centers. The drift, in other words, was mainly from small towns to bigger ones.

Fourth, there also have been movements from town to village embracing 3.8 million people in the last twenty years. Migration to big cities was viewed with apprehension, because the tremendous influx of newcomers put an intolerable strain on the urban economy. The big cities responded by a policy of closing their gates, and relaxing the policy only after December 1970. The policy resulted in an influx to suburban areas, which, although rural, were almost completely urbanized from the economic, physical, and sociocultural point of view.[12] Migration from town to village was, therefore, often part of the process of metropolitanization.

The socioeconomic and demographic consequences of population movements were manifold. We will dwell on two of these which seem to be the most important ones for the problem under review.

One is the change in the size and balance of the urban and rural population. Poland has become in the last quarter century a predominantly urban-industrial country. As far as the distribution of the urban migratory population movements is concerned, the preference was clearly for big cities. Of the permanent migrants, 57 percent settled in cities of 100,000 or more population (permanent migrants in 1967 accounted for 43 percent of the total urban population), 20 percent settled in medium towns (20,000–100,000), and 23 percent in small towns (under 20,000).

The other main consequence of urban migration was the aging of the farming population. Migrants were mostly young people who were escaping from the relentless drudgery of farming, the rigid social control of small communities, the monotony of rural life, and cultural backwardness. It was not the economic motivation that prevailed among young migrants since their native villages quite often ensured them a more prosperous life than the towns to which they went (about 80 percent of the land is privately owned) but rather the desire for freedom in the city. The result was that the peasant farms were primarily worked by old people; the average age of a farmer in the 1960s was fifty.

The problems of internal migration should be viewed in a wider context, that is, the policy of assuring a better distribution of investment and a more adequate pattern of human settlement.

In the first period (1950s and early 1960s), the policy of a more equitable distribution of productive forces prevailed. Efforts were made through national and regional plans to arrive at a more balanced development of particular regions and to reduce the economic and social interregional disparities. Typical were attempts to "deglomerate" the Silesian industrial district where about 25 percent of the country's total industrial production and industrial employment were concentrated. One approach to this task was establishing branches of big industrial enterprises in large

---

[12] We are not able to consider some other problems such as the overburdened metropolitan infrastructure and its increasing maintenance cost, transportation difficulties, social and economic costs of commuting, and the deterioration of health standards and environmental conditions, particularly in the areas of heavy industrial concentration (Upper Silesia).

and congested cities outside the region. This was accompanied by locating new industrial works and related investments in the less active regions. Although a complete reduction of disparities in distribution of industrial production and of population could not be achieved, the "policy of deglomeration" resulted in the growing equalization of living standards throughout the country, particularly with regard to consumer goods and services. Per-capita indices of Poland's individual consumption by region differed relatively slightly in 1961—from 78.7 in Kielce province to 119.5 in Katowice region (the average for the whole country being 100).

In the second period (late 1960s and early 1970s), more and more consideration was given to the economic aspects aimed at the fuller utilization of the existing technical infrastructure. The net outcome has been the emergence of a number of large urban-industrial agglomerations occupying 8.6 percent of the country's area. They contain 40 percent of its total population and produce 67.5 percent of its industrial output. In other words, even in a centrally planned economy, freedom of movement is limited by the inexorable rules of growth leading to the expansion of the existing urban centers in direct proportion to their size.

Recently, among leading economists and regional planners, two models of the settlement network have been advocated that might shape the policy of the location of the increasing urban population in the years to come. (It is expected to almost double by the year 2000—from 17 to 30 million.) One model is the design of the settlement network according to "urbanized regions" characterized by specialized functions. Thirty such regions, each with a radius of some 50–60 kilometers from their core, would cover the area of the country almost entirely. The second model utilizes the linear-nodal system as a pattern for the settlement network. Its aim is not so much to arrest agglomeration but rather to guide it along the technical infrastructure lines that form a development axis.

In order to check the rural exodus, various actions were undertaken to improve the standard of living as well as the economic and sociocultural attractiveness. Thus, higher priority was accorded to this sector of the national economy, and investments in agriculture and supporting services were increased correspondingly. Agricultural processing, household industries, local retail outlets, private handicraft, and services were developed; tourism and leisure facilities were developed. The physical environment was improved by the introduction of basic infrastructure amenities (drinking water, sewage, electricity, and access roads). Intensive development of bus transportation made accessible even the remotest rural pocket. Social welfare and recreation programs were developed, including intensive construction of rural primary and secondary schools (within a campaign "thousand schools for the millennium"),[13] introduction of health centers, "café-clubs," newspaper kiosks, cinemas, and so on.

All this partially removed the major causes of the "inferiority complex" of the rural people, particularly the younger ones, thus inducing them to some extent to remain in the countryside. More significantly, it effected proliferation and increase of the nonagricultural occupations in the countryside—perhaps the most telling illustration of the extent to which sociocultural homogenization and modernization have gone in Poland (see Table 9). The implications of these processes for fertility behavior cannot be overemphasized here.

The intensive occupational urbanization of the rural areas accounts also for the marked difference between the demographic and economic indices of urbanization in the country as a whole—the latter have been much ahead of the former particularly in the last decade (see Table 10).

The stabilization of the farmer population also was promoted by the Rural Heritage Act of 1968, which stated that a farm could be inherited only by a child who remained and worked on the farm. (It also rendered invalid the ruling that the inheritor must make proportionate payments to migrating members of the family.) Another essential measure in the process of equalizing the standard of living between the urban and rural pop-

[13] In 1966, Poland celebrated 1,000 years of statehood (coinciding with the introduction of Christianity).

TABLE 9.

Rural Population According to Main Source of Livelihood,
Poland, 1950–1970

Year	Total (in thousands)	In Agriculture (in thousands)	(percent)	Outside Agriculture (in thousands)	(percent)
1950	15,009	10,981	73.2	4,028	26.8
1960	15,187	10,458	68.9	4,729	31.1
1970	15,582	8,904	57.2	6,678	42.8[a]

SOURCE: See [3].

[a] A complete picture of the changes in the sociooccupational structure of the rural areas should mention the "peasant-workers" who, although living in the country, have permanent nonagricultural jobs and are only loosely connected with farming. (In the first half of the 1960s, they numbered 1.7 million.) To this should be added a category of people who, although living in "villages," have nothing to do with farming—in either the legal or the occupational sense—and commute daily to urban centers. Moreover, it was estimated that, in half the households that declared themselves dependent on agriculture for a living, at least one person was employed outside agriculture.

TABLE 10.

Population by Demographic (Urban) and Economic (Nonagricultural)
Indices, Poland, 1950–1970

Year	Total (in thousands)	Urban (in thousands)	Urban (percent)	Nonagricultural (in thousands)	Nonagricultural (percent)
1950	25,008	9,244	36.9	13,106	52.9
1960	29,776	14,401	48.3	18,125	61.6
1970	32,589	17,031	52.2	22,966	70.5

SOURCE: See [3].

ulations was the recent inclusion of the farm population in the national
health insurance scheme (1971).

FROM THE 1960s TO THE PRESENT

The fall in the natural increase of the Polish population met with wide
social approval. It was in accord with the official population policy of the
state as well as with the strong desire on the part of individual families to
restrict the number of children. Under the surface of public approval, however, some doubts have arisen about the advisability of the course of population growth. These doubts, which have been voiced in various quarters,
differ in their nature and intensity.

(1) Most outspoken, unwavering, and incessant has been the criticism
of the *church*. It was directed, first of all, against all forms of contraception
except periodic abstinence and, in particular, against abortion. Opposition to the adopted policy stemmed from moral grounds, but the church
was equally concerned about the rapid decline in the natural increase,
which it felt jeopardized the nation's future.

(2) The *physicians*, divided from the start on the legalization of abortion,
have been concerned about the mass character of abortions and the
consequences for the individual woman's health and for fecundity.

(3) The *demographers*, gathered in the Central Statistical Office and in
the Committee for Demography of the Polish Academy of Sciences, were
first to point out on the basis of the long-term population projection (1970–
2000) that because of the declining fertility the net reproduction rate was
approximating unity and was likely to drop below the replacement level
at the start of the twenty-first century (see Table 11).

The demographers fell into two groups in terms of their conclusions and
proposals. One group favored an immediate pronatalist policy. Advocates

TABLE 11.

Gross and Net Reproduction Rates and Population Projections,
Poland, 1950–2000

Year	Total		Urban		Rural	
	Gross	Net	Gross	Net	Gross	Net
1950	1.790	1.491	1.558	1.300	1.936	1.160
1955	1.742	1.519	1.546	1.366	1.941	1.675
1960	1.438	1.339	1.168	1.098	1.731	1.601
1965	1.217	1.149	0.925	0.879	1.582	1.487
1966	1.174	1.128	0.891	0.847	1.548	1.459
1967	1.127	1.071	0.856	0.818	1.493	1.421
1968	1.084	1.044	0.828	0.791	1.424	1.347
1969	1.065	1.013	0.820	0.783	1.403	1.389
1970	1.064	1.011	0.832	0.794	1.328	1.315
2000 (projection)						
Version 1		0.890				
Version 2		0.805				

SOURCE: See [3].

of this stance warned that the tempo of the decrease of women's fertility was unprecedented in Europe and the rate was lower than in such highly modernized and secularized countries as France, Great Britain, and Germany. The other concern was for the ongoing process of the population. The postproductive age group was expected to increase from 15.5 percent of the population in 1970 to 20.5 percent in 2000. The second group of demographers was somewhat more optimistic, pointing out that individuals born after 1945 were just about to enter the age of reproductive activity, which might result in a new wave of the baby boom—surely not as large as the earlier one but sufficiently high to alleviate any fears about Poland's future.

(4) The *economists and economic planners* have been concerned about the implications of demographic processes for economic growth in general and for reproduction of the work force in particular. From the point of view of supply, there was no immediate cause for concern. In 1970, there were 18.5 million people of working age, which represented 56 percent of the total population. From 1970 onward, the working-age population will continue to rise until the end of the century. It is rather from the point of view of demographic demand that economic policy is facing serious problems. A considerably higher number of young people, born during the postwar baby boom, are now coming of age and entering the labor market. During the current five-year period it will be necessary, as a result, to find

jobs for some 3.5 million persons. If persons leaving the labor market (due to retirement, death, and so forth) are taken into account, the net increase in employment will come to almost 2 million persons. Though economic planning is not haunted by the specter of demographic pressure as the main obstacle that impedes economic development, it must reconcile the "intensification phase" of economic growth (when the increase in net output is due more to the rise of labor productivity than to a maximum growth of employment) with securing jobs for huge masses of skilled newcomers (whose educational standards are much higher than those of the age group on the verge of retirement) and satisfying steadily growing appetites for social amenities, consumption goods, and services.

(5) The *social policy specialists* have been rather reluctant to opt for a pronatalist policy. In their opinion, the alarms about a nongrowing or diminishing nation are ill-founded. Social policy of today is less concerned about quantitative aspects than qualitative aspects of the demographic processes, meaning the well-being of the whole population, or the quality of Polish society (physical and mental welfare, levels of education and general welfare, equitable participation in the national income). "What it stresses is the need to pay greater attention to the conditions of life of the population already present and so the way it provides for the welfare of succeeding generations whose numbers are best decided by its sense of responsibility for, and joy in, the children brought into the world" [7]. As a result, the establishing of much closer interactions between social and population policies is advocated.

(6) The *sociologists and social psychologists* have been unhappy that population policy has been considered a purely demographic domain. The demographic phenomena, and particularly the fertility pattern, are interlocked with social and moral values, motivations, social stratification (the model of fertility and subsequent childrearing is different in families belonging to different social groups), the structure and living conditions of families as well as changing social roles of family members, and so forth. Very little was known about social and psychological factors influencing both the decrease in fertility rates and pronatalist attitudes of individuals and social groups. These social scientists called attention to the grave social consequences of a rhythmical demographic growth and disproportions between the basic age groups of the population. Finally, they voiced a word of warning against population policy trying to steer demographic processes directly. Demographic processes, they feel, are far too complex, too much a part of the intimate and emotional sphere of life, of the internal dynamics and circumstances of each family. For these reasons they cannot agree that demographic processes can be planned and controlled by a policy.

A public signal of the change in the state's stand with respect to the population policy was its very act of submitting the policy to public discussion. The first critical comment on the systematic decrease of birth and its adverse effects for the nation's future appeared in Poland's leading daily newspaper *Zycie Warszawy* in November 1968[14] in the column "free opinions." Since 1969, the discussion in the press has assumed a "snowball" character. Journalists, demographers, economists, sociologists (particularly those working in the field of family sociology—a well-established and productive branch of social science in Poland), psychologists, educationists, physicians, social workers, state officials, and ordinary citizens have voiced opinions on the matter. Extremely thorough and widely publicized preparations for the national census in December 1970 (which included a study of fertility trends based on a 5-percent sample of women aged 15–70 who were or had been married) and ensuing publication and interpretation of the results kept the discussion alive, as did the establishment of a special committee in the Polish Academy of Sciences, "Poland 2000," for which demographic data constituted a natural basis.

Despite opinions that the world-wide trend for the next decades is toward population stabilization, consensus among all interested parties is that the most favorable course for Poland's future is a reproduction rate just above replacement. Nobody advocates a return to the extremely high reproduction rate of the early 1950s, but the present net reproduction rate (1.01 in 1970) is considered too low and unacceptable in the long run. It is indicated that the rate is much lower in towns (0.8 on the average) and in the big cities (0.6). Thus, the heated discussion on population problems, so characteristic of the last few years, centers around the ideal fertility model, the economic and sociocultural factors that tend to depress fertility, and the measures—either undertaken or suggested—to overcome the present "demographic decline."[15]

¶ ECONOMIC CONDITIONS

The following considerations have come to the fore:

(1) The standard of living is inversely proportionate to the number of children. According to an investigation carried out by the Central

---

[14] Actually, the problem had been raised in 1967 during a conference organized at Tard by the Polish Academy of Sciences.

[15] It would be interesting to look—in terms of the sociology of knowledge—for social roots of this state of disquietude. It is rather beyond doubt that, even in the light of the drastic decrease of births in recent years, Poland is not really facing a "demographic decline" in the foreseeable future. The uneasiness about the population growth reflects, perhaps, the nation's bitter war experience, when the very existence of the Polish nation was threatened.

Statistical Office, per-capita income in two-person households (that is, couples without children) was 31 percent higher than the national average; in five-person households (that is, couples with three children), it was 23 percent lower; in six-person households (that is, couples with four children), it was 41 percent lower than the national average. In families with four children, per-capita income was 55 percent lower than among childless couples [3].

(2) Having many children restricts the mother's opportunities for gainful occupation, an economic necessity for most families.

(3) The increasing standard of living and growing socioeconomic aspirations are elevating the socially recognized minimum level of basic human needs. Elementary biological needs are taken for granted by now, and social needs are considered necessary from the point of view of group standards and individual aspirations (life style).

(4) At the same time, the required level of education for children has been growing steadily since 1945, particularly among urban families (laborers' families included), and is now penetrating the countryside.[16] As the costs of childraising increased, a definite competition arose between more sophisticated social needs and childbearing ("either a car or a child"). This also accounted for the fact—in accordance with evidence from other countries—that, the better off a social group was, the less willing its members were to have the second or third child. This attitude prevailed especially among the urban intelligentsia.

To alleviate the costs of childraising, a decree was issued in December 1970 increasing family allowances by 40 percent, as shown in Table 12. Although this is hardly a major stimulus to greater fertility, it is undoubtedly a relief for families with many children.[17]

TABLE 12.

Monthly Family Allowances, Poland, 1970 (in US$)[a]

Child	Before December 1970	After December 1970
First	$17.50	$27.50
Second	26.25	37.50
Third	33.75	47.50
Fourth +	38.75	52.50

[a] As of January 1, 1973, 4 zlotys equaled approximately US$1.

[16] Although education is free to the highest grade, the time period of education has been lengthened. In families where higher education aspirations are aroused, children are economically dependent almost until they are twenty-five.

[17] It was estimated that, whereas family allowances constituted 17 percent of an average net wage in 1955, before the increase in 1970 such allowances amounted to only 9.3 percent.

¶ HOUSING CONDITIONS

There are two basic problems connected with housing: shortage and structure.

(1) Shortage of housing. The number of persons on the waiting list in housing cooperatives (54.6 percent of all dwellings) was more than 1 million in 1970. To this should be added 250,000 applications for new apartments addressed to state authorities from those social groups whose housing conditions are very bad.[18] To be sure, construction during 1960–1970 increased the number of dwellings by 15.3 percent and the number of rooms by 35.0 percent (against a 9.4 percent population increase) and lowered the average density from 4.08 person per dwelling to 3.93 and from 1.66 person per room to 1.37. But the beneficiaries were mainly those persons (families) who had been employed a long time and/or had some savings. That means that by the time most couples attained acceptable dwellings, they were already middle-aged and beyond the fertile years. (Among urban women, the reproductive period was practically over by age thirty-nine.) A working principle when the apartments were allotted was: "The young may wait." And because the average waiting period is five to seven years, young people at last occupying their own cooperative dwelling are, as a rule, beyond the age that accounts for the greatest number of births (20–24 years). Some students of the problem have warned that couples who postpone the birth of their first child until the allotment of a dwelling grow accustomed to living without children and that a "postponed" child in most cases will never be born.

(2) The structure of housing is not conducive to childbearing. A childless couple in the reproductive age group is allotted a dwelling for three persons. The apartments are very small, being subject to rigid and scanty "allotment norms" (see Table 13). The couple is likely to remain in their dwelling for years to come even if more than one child is born. The exchange of apartments, though theoretically possible, in practice is an extremely cumbersome and lengthy process and requires an additional expenditure which, in turn, is more difficult for large families.

In December 1970, an energetic action was launched by the government and the ruling Polish United Workers party (PUW) aiming at a considerable increase in housing space, particularly for young couples. It remains to be seen to what extent it can act as an incentive to have more children. So far, the "negative effect" could be seen. Improvement of housing con-

---

[18] There are three basic housing schemes: (1) those subsidized by the state (45,100 constructed dwellings in 1970, 17.8 percent of the total); (2) cooperatives (95,000 dwellings, 54.6 percent of the total), where private resources are combined with the state contribution; (3) private, mostly individual, houses (53,600 dwellings, 27.6 percent of the total).

TABLE 13.

Housing Standards, Poland, 1970

Average per Dwelling	Total	Urban	Rural
Number of rooms	2.88	2.77	3.01
Space (in square meters)	50.5	46.6	55.5
Number of persons	3.93	3.62	4.31
Persons per room	1.37	1.31	1.43
Living space per person (in square meters)	12.9	12.9	12.9
Number of households per 100 dwellings	113.9	116.6	110.4

SOURCE: See [3].

ditions is clearly a necessary but not a sufficient condition for increased fertility. It depends in the last analysis on the broader psychosocial context, in particular on the prevalence of either pronatalist or antinatalist attitudes among the masses of populace.

¶ NEW IMAGE OF WOMEN'S SOCIAL AND ECONOMIC ROLE
Considered a storm center of the recent discussion on population problems is the apparent conflict between "women's two worlds"—the home and gainful employment. The tremendous demand for labor, characteristic of intensive industrialization, has given women an increasingly strong position in the labor market (Table 14). Women's professional activities have become one of the prerequisites of the functioning of the industrial-urban type of society prevailing in Poland. This is even more pronounced now in view of the transition to the "intensive phase" of economic development, which implies, among other things, a steady reduction of industry's share in total employment and a corresponding increase in employment in services.

To date, the prevailing motivation for working women has been economic: Women have taken jobs to improve the family budget. But, increasingly, a Polish woman works not because she has to but because she wants to work. Her professional activity is a vehicle of emancipation. Under Polish conditions (inadequate dwelling space, high costs of bringing up children, limited possibilities to increase income, inadequate service institutions, and aroused aspirations with regard to herself and children), she is also more and more often confronted with a dilemma of whether to work or have children. Her choice today seems primarily to be work. The more educated she is, the more likely she is to work. It should be mentioned that today, in workers' families, this is true of every second woman.

TABLE 14.

Women in the Labor Force, Poland, 1950–1970 (public sector)

Year	Percent
1950	30.6
1955	32.0
1960	32.9
1965	36.1
1970[a]	39.5

SOURCE: See [3].
[a] The end of the 1970s is forecast at 45 percent.

TABLE 15.

Women by Social Group and Education, Poland, 1970
(and average number of live births)[a]

	Percentage of Women by Number of Children					Average Live Births per Woman
	0	1	2	3	4+	
Social group						
Manual workers	9	21	29	19	22	2.54
White-collar workers	13	32	34	13	8	1.74
Housewives	5	10	21	22	42	3.44
Others	9	20	31	20	20	2.44
Education						
Higher	19	41	32	6	2	1.29
Postsecondary or incomplete higher	17	39	32	9	3	1.45
Secondary	14	36	34	11	5	1.58
Basic vocational and incomplete secondary	12	33	33	13	9	1.77
Elementary	7	18	29	21	25	2.60
Other and unidentified	6	10	19	21	44	3.52

SOURCE: See [3].
[a] National average 2.65 (in urban areas, 2.18; in rural areas, 3.17).

Table 15 is a telling testimony to a positive correlation between social status, education, and fertility: the higher the social stratum and the higher the educational level, the smaller the number of children.

In this situation, the increasing level of education of Polish women is becoming another essential factor in lowering the fertility level. Table 16

TABLE 16.

Women Employed in the National Economy, Poland, 1958 and 1970 (according to education)

Educational Level	1958				1970			
	Number of Persons (in thousands)	Percent of Persons	Number of Women (in thousands)	Percent of Women	Number of Persons (in thousands)	Percent of Persons	Number of Women (in thousands)	Percent of Women
Total (all levels)	6350.8	100	2091.6	100	9312.0	100	3693.0	100
More than primary	1476.2	23.2	526.8	25.1	3839.0	41.7	1662.6	45.0
Primary and vocational training	522.0	8.2	99.1	4.7	1589.3	17.1	472.3	12.7
High general education	275.6	4.3	135.7	6.5	526.1	5.6	344.1	9.3
High vocational training	438.7	6.9	225.0	10.7	1273.9	13.6	662.3	18.0
Higher education	239.9	3.8	67.0	3.2	501.6	5.4	183.9	5.0

SOURCE: See [3].

shows the changes in the levels of education of the female labor force (employed in the public sector). It should be noted that women's educational levels are rising more rapidly than men's because men are taking jobs at earlier ages, at the price of giving up their further education.

Since women's employment is considered an irrevocable process, the crux of the matter is how to reconcile women's two social roles—that of mother and that of employee. A result of the social-welfare-oriented approach of the state and party authorities after December 1970 was the new act of January 14, 1972, which prolonged the unpaid leave for a mother to thirty-six months (previously twelve months) to take care of a newly born child and secured full payment during sixty days a year to look after a sick child. It is hard to say whether the act was formulated to influence fertility, but its bearing on the problem under review is unquestionable.

Following is the up-to-date list of various benefits for working women in Poland with regard to maternity and childrearing:

(1) Twelve weeks paid maternity leave.
(2) Two paid, nondeductible, half-hour breaks in the course of the working day for feeding an infant (in effect, a one-hour shorter working day).
(3) A potential thirty-six months of unpaid leave of absence in the case of a mother with a child or children under two years of age in her charge. During this period the mother and her family retain the right to free medical attention and to the children's allowances drawn previously. Throughout the duration of this leave of absence, her employer is forbidden to sever her contract and must restore her to her old job when she returns from her leave of absence.
(4) A guaranteed right to special paid periods (sixty days a year) of release to attend to a sick child.
(5) A guaranteed right to periods of release in other special circumstances connected with the care of a child.
(6) A prohibition against dismissal or notice of dismissal at any time during the period of pregnancy and maternity leave.
(7) The obligation of the employer to provide suitable working conditions during the period of pregnancy (transfer to a lighter job without any loss of earning if the present one is adjudged by a doctor to be too onerous) and even for a year after the birth of the child. Also prohibited is overtime, night shifts, or detailing the woman to a job outside her regular work place.

A further factor that enables mothers to take full advantage of their right to work is the development of welfare amenities such as infant and nursery schools for children under school age and day hostels for older children. These make it possible for mothers who have no other opportunities to arrange supervision for their children while they are at work. The number of nursery schools totaled 8,757 in 1969—4,066 in urban and

4,691 in rural areas. They were attended by 512,000 children (39.7 percent of all children aged 3–6 in urban areas). The number of infant schools was 1,018 in 1969, with 63,300 places.

Present social policy is aiming at solving the problem of women's employment while at the same time making it easier for women to perform the childrearing duties that are considered of crucial importance. This is coupled with re-evaluation of the status of a woman who stays at home and devotes herself to bringing up children. The latter now is ranked among the public services essential to the welfare of the community.

¶ A NEW MODEL OF MARRIAGE AND FERTILITY AMONG THE YOUNG
A conflict between woman's two roles lies not only on the economic but also on the sociocultural plane, visible in the increasing frequency of marriage among persons of the same age contracted before their professional and economic stabilization. The youth subculture in Poland as elsewhere, with its ideal of leisure and separation of sexual pleasure from procreation, is not conducive to high fertility patterns. To the young people, the function of marriage is companionship, not procreation. There is equality between the two sexes with regard to expectations and actual social roles, which acts as a fertility-inhibiting factor for women who do not want to be handicapped by motherhood in performing various social roles in the "outside world."

In Poland it seems the image of the girl "waiting for a husband" and considering marriage and motherhood as her exclusive role is on the wane. The first duty of a young woman now is to have a profession. The prevailing pattern is more and more a "double-career" marriage. Her gainful employment is necessary—as much as that of a man—when a family is established. It gives her material security during old age or in case of invalidism; it is a guarantee of independence if a marriage is broken. The latter reason is not without validity considering the constant increase of divorces (see Table 17).

It should be added that, according to research carried out in the late 1960s, about 87 percent of women and 79 percent of men applying for a divorce were under age thirty. This contributes to a low fertility pattern. The high divorce rate exists not only among young women from the "higher" social strata but also among women from the working class.

Research conducted among older working-class women in Poznan in the early 1960s revealed the attitude that "it is best to have two children; but because one may die, it is better to have three." Younger women, free of this fear because of the dramatic drop of infant mortality (a result of health services and new potent medicines) were in favor of the two-child pattern without the one-child safety valve. However, more recent research

TABLE 17.

Rates of Marriage and Divorce, Poland, 1950–1970
(per 1,000 population)

| Year | Marriage | Divorce | Areas | |
			Urban	Rural
1950	10.8	0.44	0.88	0.16
1955	9.5	0.49	0.92	0.15
1960	8.2	0.05	0.88	0.15
1965	6.3	0.75	1.27	0.23
1970	8.5	1.05	1.75	0.31

SOURCE: See [3].

conducted in Silesia showed that the fertility model among older women was two children; among younger ones, one child.

The same attitudes were revealed by an investigation conducted during the 1970 census on a rather large 5-percent sample of urban women to age seventy who were or had been married (representative of 13.8 million, that is, 82 percent, of urban population). Their husbands were also requested to answer the questionnaire. The first question put to them was: "Would you like to have more children beyond those you already have? If yes, indicate how many more." The question was answered in the negative by 66.3 percent of women and 67.2 percent of men.

On the average, 16.7 percent of men whose wives had not given birth to a child did not want to have more children. The same was true of 19.0 percent of manual workers' wives and of 15.0 percent of white-collar workers' wives. In the case of couples with one child, the negative answer was given by 40.0 percent of men and 45.0 percent of women. These negative statements are, of course, more frequent in the case of couples with two or more children. Only 1.5 percent of female respondents wanted to have three or more children. This was true mainly of young couples—women to age twenty-five and men to twenty-nine. It was very characteristic that among those who declared their willingness to have more children were couples living in the worst dwelling conditions. It seems, therefore, that an improvement in this respect might bring about an increase in the number of children.

What were the conditions conducive to having more children? Of the men, 38.7 percent and 37.9 percent of women did not want to have more children under any conditions. With regard to the rest of respondents, the most frequently stated condition was that of higher income. This was true both of manual workers and white-collar workers. The higher the age of respondents, the weaker was the influence of this factor. The next condition most frequently cited was a better dwelling. Family allowances were considered to play a negligible role in this regard.

The most general results of this investigation could be formulated as follows: (1) Among young urban couples, the prevailing tendency is to have one to two children. (2) This tendency is equally strong among more as well as less educated persons; this means that, in urban conditions characterized by a low fertility pattern, the level of education—and more generally, the level of culture—is not a crucial differentiating variable.

Another question put to the respondents was the following: "How many children do you think ought to be in a family?" The answers to this question, dealing with a normative model rather than actual behavior, should, of course, not be taken too literally. Nevertheless, the investigation corroborated the previous research results. It was revealed that those persons who had more children, that is, the older ones, born in the rural areas, of lower level of education, and belonging to the manual workers' stratum (among women, mainly nonworking ones), were evaluating an "ideal" fertility that was higher than that evaluated by those persons who had fewer children, were younger, born in urban areas, more educated, and belonging to the white-collar workers' stratum. What was most characteristic—and of crucial importance for fertility patterns in the future—was that, among young respondents below age thirty (both childless couples as well as those with two or three children), two children were considered an "ideal" situation.

¶ ABORTION AS A BIRTH CONTROL METHOD
Abortion has been, of course, a major topic. (That this problem is debated openly is a novelty; for many years, it was taboo.) Both the legalization of abortion and the impact of legalized abortion on fertility have been subjects of repeated studies. But critics and protagonists agree that abortion is an ultimate birth control device bringing about deep and many-sided repercussions in the biological, social, and psychological fields. It is stressed that the incidence of abortion would be minimal if contraceptive devices were more widespread and effective and sexual education was more widely introduced.

¶ INFANT MORTALITY
The problem of infant mortality has received much attention in the last few years. It has been viewed both as an autonomous subject (infant mortality is rightly considered as one of the most sensitive yardsticks of modernization) and in relation to population growth. In spite of considerable progress made in this respect in the postwar period (a decrease from 139.2 per 1,000 live births in 1938 to 29.7 per 1,000 in 1971), there is a

widespread feeling that the situation in Poland is far from satisfactory. Poland occupies one of the last places in Europe's vital statistics with regard to this demographic phenomenon. It is estimated that, if all factors causing infant mortality had been considered properly, it would have been possible to reduce the number of infant deaths in 1951–1970 by 400–460, that is, half of the actual number.

Of the many factors responsible for infant mortality in Poland, the most heatedly discussed is that of inadequate health services for mother and child, particularly in the rural areas. Whereas, in the big cities, almost 100 percent of women are benefiting from health care prior to childbirth, in the rural areas the index is only 30 percent. Out of 45,000 physicians in Poland, there are only 2,970 specialists in gynecology and pediatrics. Moreover, they are located mainly in big towns. There are districts where there is not a single pediatrician.

However, there are unmistakable signs of improvement. Mention should be made of the following: (1) More energetic measures have been taken aimed at guaranteeing working mothers a much fuller and effective range of health services and more suitable working conditions during the period of pregnancy and after the birth of a child. (2) Legal and administrative measures made available in 1971–1972 free medical services to 6.5 million private farm owners. In this way, the constitutionally guaranteed right to health protection has become a reality in the rural areas. Measures are also being taken to encourage doctors to practice in villages and small localities (for example, extra—and appreciable—payment allowances, free accommodations, refund of car expenses).

In general, in the comprehensive program for a marked improvement in living standards, which has been implemented since December 1970, health is on the top-priority list: Between 1971 and 1975, the total expenditure on health services will grow by 80 percent.

Poland now seems to have a good chance not only to reduce infant mortality, with its far-reaching consequences for population growth, but also to improve the quality of life.

CONCLUSION

Although population policy in Poland has not been formulated explicitly and/or in such a comprehensive way as to make critical and detailed examination feasible, nonetheless it is implied in a number of measures aimed at improving the socioeconomic conditions of people in general (higher real wages, housing construction, an emphasis on consumption rather than on growth per se) and of women, both working and nonworking, in particular. For the first time since the war, both long- and short-term development plans may be called "socioeconomic" rather than simply economic in nature.

So much for a "latent" population policy. It seems, however, that a "manifest" population policy is also in the making. Its most general objectives were formulated by the First Secretary of the Polish United Workers party, Edward Gierek, at the Seventh Trade Union Congress:

> I think that in a not too distant future it will be possible for us to prepare and to submit to wide consultation a comprehensive program of actions for the benefit of a family, for the benefit of working women and multi-child families, and also of lone women bringing up children. We should create in our country such socioeconomic conditions, and also such psychological and moral climate, which will foster the development and the optimal shaping of the family size. This is our duty toward the future [8].

Among the demographers, who undoubtedly will play a leading role in working out a detailed program with regard to population matters, the following elements of population policy are discerned:

First, the immediate checking of what is considered an excessive birth rate decline in urban areas or—to use social stratification as terms of reference—among working class and urban intelligentsia (predominantly of working-class origin). What, in fact, is propounded is a moderately pronatalist policy. The concern is with maintaining the reproduction of the population for the next two generations at a minimum rate of 5 per 1,000 yearly. In other words, the battle is being fought for the third child in an urban family.

Measures necessary for bringing about what is called "small" population policy are: (1) adequate housing for young couples; (2) extension of part-time employment for women; (3) proper maternity and child care, particularly for working women; (4) an appreciable increase in the family allowance for those who have more than two children; and (5) elevation of the social status of motherhood.

Second, efforts are being made to frame the long-term aims of population policy. Fortunately, the current period from 1971 to 1980, characterized by a slightly higher birth rate than in the previous decade, gives the needed respite for laying the foundation for the scientifically sound and socially desirable population policy in the decades to come.[19]

---

[19] It is proposed that a State Population Commission be established, endowed with broad powers in respect to both formulation and implementation of this policy.

REFERENCES

1. R. Merton. *Social Theory and Social Structure.* Revised edition. New York: Free Press, 1957.

2. E. Wiskemann. *Germany's Eastern Neighbours: Problems Relating to the Oder-Neisse Line and the Czech Frontier Regions.* London-New York-Toronto: Oxford University Press, 1956, pp. 87–92. (Based on Bundesrepublik Deutschland, Bundesministerium für Vertriebene, *Dokumentation der Vertreibung der Deutschen aus Ostmitteleuropa,* Bonn, 1953, I/I, 23–24E.)

3. *Statistical Yearbook, 1971.* Warsaw: Central Statistical Office, 1972. (In Polish.)

4. *Dziennik Ustaw (Journal of Laws)*, no. 15 (May 10, 1946): item 106.

5. *Statistical Yearbook of Health Care, 1971.* Warsaw: Central Statistical Office, 1972. (In Polish.)

6. *Statistical Yearbook, 1972.* Warsaw: Central Statistical Office, 1973. (In Polish.)

7. A. Rajkiewicz. "Social policy and tomorrow," *Polish Perspectives,* June 1972.

8. *Trybuna Luda* (November 14, 1972). (In Polish.)

BIBLIOGRAPHY

Adamski, F. *Marriage and Family Models and Mass Culture.* Warsaw: State Scientific Publishers, 1970. (In Polish.)

Bednarski, B. "Brief balance sheet and perspectives of the activity of the Society for Conscious Motherhood." *Problemy Rodziny,* 1, 1961. (In Polish.)

Borowski, S. "Migrations in western and northern territories in 1945–1966." In *Problemy demograficzne Ziem Zachodnich.* Warsaw: Central Statistical Office, 1969. (In Polish.)

Chadzynski, H. "Demographic probe of the Central Statistical Office: Family questionnaire 1970." *Problemy Rodziny,* 4, 1972. (In Polish.)

Dodziuk-Kitynska, A., and D. Markowska. *Polish Urban Family: A Review of Social Surveys in 1945–1968.* Wroclaw: Ossolineum, 1971. (In Polish.)

Dzienio, K. "Changes in fertility level of women in Poland." *Studia Demograficzne,* 7, 1965. (In Polish.)

———. "Trends and means of natalist policy as experienced by some Socialist countries." *Studia Demograficzne,* 17, 1968. (In Polish.)

Dzieciolowski, J. "Can we build more houses?" *Polish Perspectives,* 11, 1971.

Dziewonski, K. "Urbanization in contemporary Poland." *Geographia Polonica,* vol. 3, 1964.

Fisher, J. C. (ed.). *City and Regional Planning in Poland.* Ithaca, N.Y.: Cornell University Press, 1966.

Gorecki, J. "Divorce in Poland—a socio-legal study." *Acta Sociologica,* vol. 10 (1966).

Gorynski, J. "Housing policy in Poland." In *Social and Political Transformations in Poland.* Edited by S. Ehrich. Warsaw: State Scientific Publishers, 1964.

Grabowiecka, L. "Analysis of the implementation of the act on admissibility of abortion." *Problemy Rodziny,* 4, 1962. (In Polish.)

———. "Causes and consequences of the slow development of contraception in Poland." *Problemy Rodziny,* 3, 1967. (In Polish.)

Holzer, J. "Problems of population reproduction of Poland in the seventies." *Problemy Rodziny,* 4, 1970. (In Polish.)

————. *Births and Deaths and Poland's Population Structure.* Warsaw: Polish Economic Publishers, 1964. (In Polish.)

Jozefowicz, A. "Socioeconomic consequences of changes in the age-structure of the population till 2000." In *Prognozy rozwoju demograficznego Polski.* Warsaw: Polskiej Akademii Nauk, 1971. (In Polish.)

Kasprzak, M. "This has been only ten years!" *Problemy Rodziny,* 6, 1967. (In Polish.)

Kawalec, W. "An outline of the research program on demographic forecasts." In *Prognozy rozwoju demograficznego Polski.* Warsaw: Polskiej Akademii Nauk, 1971. (In Polish.)

Kloskowska, A. "Family in people's Poland." In *Przemiany spoleczne w Polsce Ludowej.* Edited by A. Sarapata. Warsaw: State Scientific Publishers, 1965. (In Polish.)

Kozakiewicz, M. "Young Poles A.D. 1970." *Polish Perspectives,* 7–8, 1970.

Krysztofowicz, I. "Present problems of infant mortality." *Problemy Rodziny,* 3, 1966. (In Polish.)

Kuklinski, A. "Regional differentiation of the Polish national economy." In *Proceedings of the First Scandinavian-Polish Regional Science Seminar.* Committee for Space Economy and Regional Planning of the Polish Academy of Sciences. Studies, vol. 17. Warsaw, 1967.

Labudzka, I. "Social causes of abortion in the light of preliminary sociological research." *Problemy Rodziny,* 3, 1966. (In Polish.)

Latuch, M. "Problems of population policy." *Studia Demograficzne,* 21, 1970. (In Polish.)

————. "The impact of internal migrations on the reproduction process of the urban population in Poland in 1950–1960." *Biuletyn IGS,* 1, 1969. (In Polish.)

Leszcxycki, S. "Patterns of industrialization." *Polish Perspectives,* 7–8, 1964.

Malanowski, J. *The Attitude of Society toward Natural Increase.* Warsaw: Center for Investigation of Public Opinion, 1966.

Malewska, H. *Cultural and Psycho-Social Determinants of Sexual Behavior.* Warsaw: State Scientific Publishers, 1969. (In Polish.)

Musialowa, A. "Premarital and family counseling." *Problemy Rodziny,* 2, 1972. (In Polish.)

Peterson, W. *Planned Migration: The Social Determinants of the Dutch-Canadian Movement.* Berkeley and Los Angeles: University of California Press, 1955.

Piotrowski, J. *Women's Gainful Employment and the Family.* Warsaw: Ksiazka i Wiedza, 1963. (In Polish.)

Rajkiewicz, A. "Problems of social policy." *Polish Perspectives,* 12, 1970.

————. "Social policy and tomorrow." *Polish Perspectives,* 6, 1972.

Romaniuk, K. "Economic consequences of the demographic 'high tide.'" In *Problemy demograficzne Polski Ludowej.* Warsaw: Central Statistical Office, 1967. (In Polish.)

Rosner, J. (ed.) *Social Policy and Social Services in the Polish People's Republic.* Warsaw: Polish Economic Publishers, 1972. (In Polish.)

Rosset, E. *Demographic Transformations in Poland.* Gdansk, 1970. (In Polish.)

————. "Fertility of urban and rural women in Poland." In *Zeszyty Naukowe WSE w Lodzi,* 15, 1, 1961. (In Polish.)

————. "Principles of the long-term population policy in Poland." In *Prognozy rozwoju demograficznego Polski.* Warsaw: Polskiej Akademii Nauk, 1971. (In Polish.)

————. "Changes in the birth structure as a consequence of evolution in the 'family model.'" *Studia Demograficzne,* 17, 1968. (In Polish.)

Rozewicki, S., et al. "Some problems connected with contraception and abortion." *Problemy Rodziny*, 2, 1971. (In Polish.)

Secomski, K. "Demography and planning of socioeconomic development." In *Problemy demograficzne Polski Ludowej*. Warsaw: Central Statistical Office, 1967. (In Polish.)

———. *Elements of Economic Policy*. Warsaw: Polish Economic Publishers, 1970. (In Polish.)

Sikorski, R., and B. Trebicka-Kwiatkowska. "Research results on sexual behavior of rural women." *Problemy Rodziny*, 5, 1972. (In Polish.)

Smolinski, Z. "Evaluation and postulates of population policy in Poland." *Problemy Rodziny*, 2, 1970. (In Polish.)

———. "Female fertility in large towns." *Wiadomosci Statystyczne*, 1, 1969. (In Polish.)

———. *Fertility in 1945–2000*. Warsaw: Central Statistical Office, 1971. (In Polish.)

———. "New population forecast of Poland." *Problemy Rodziny*, 3, 1972. (In Polish.)

Sokolowska, M., and B. Lobodzinska. "Contraceptives and abortion." *Problemy Rodziny*, 1, 1971. (In Polish.)

Strzelecki, E. "Population growth of Poland in 1944–1964." In *Przemiany spoleczne w Polsce Ludowej*. Edited by A. Sarapata. Warsaw: State Scientific Publishers, 1965. (In Polish.)

Strzeminska, H. *Social Progress in Poland*. Warsaw: Interpress Publishers, 1971.

Szczepanski, J. "Some characteristics of contemporary Polish society." *The Polish Sociological Bulletin*, no. 2, 1964.

Szeliga, Z., and T. Stpiczynski. "Internal migrations." *Polish Perspectives*, 12, 1971.

Szturm de Sztrem, E. "Fertility in Poland and its biological and sociocultural context." *Biuletyn IGS*, 1–2, 1962. (In Polish.)

Trawinska, M. "How Warsaw couples perceive family planning." *Problemy Rodziny*, 2, 1972. (In Polish.)

Trepczynski, S., and M. Sadowski. *Socialism and National Development*. Warsaw: Interpress Publishers, 1971.

Turski, R. (ed.) *Changes in Rural Poland*. Wroclaw: Ossolineum, 1970. (In French.)

UNESCO. *The Cultural Integration of Immigrants*. Paris, 1959.

Vielrose, E. *Research Results on Female Fertility in Poland*. Warsaw: State Scientific Publishers, 1967. (In Polish.)

———. "Some remarks on correlation between GNP and fertility." *Studia Demograficzne*, 15, 1968. (In Polish.)

Waszak, S. "Demographic development of Poland in long-term planning." *Ruch Prawniczy i Ekonomiczny*, 2, 1960. (In Polish.)

Winiarski, B. "The programming and development policy of backward areas in national economic planning in Poland." In *Backward Areas in Advanced Countries*. Edited by E. A. G. Robinson. London: Macmillan, 1969.

Wrochno, K. "The dual career family." *Problemy Rodziny*, 2, 1972. (In Polish.)

Ziolkowski, J. A. "Demographic and social changes in Polish recovered territories." *The Review of the Polish Academy of Sciences*, 3–4, 1958.

CHAPTER 18

Spain

Salustiano del Campo

ABSTRACT

This study proposes to collect and analyze the major legal measures that affect the demographic variables of birth, death, and migration in Spain. It opens with a short presentation of the present demographic situation, using data from the 1970 census. Following this, the attitudes maintained since the eighteenth and nineteenth centuries concerning the depopulation of the country and emigration are described. Finally, the principal areas of implicit demographic policy are discussed in considerable detail: (1) family and birth; (2) mortality and health; (3) labor and emigration; and (4) redistribution of the population and regional policies.

THE PRESENT DEMOGRAPHIC SITUATION[1]

¶ TOTAL POPULATION

The census carried out by the National Statistical Institute set the population of Spain at 34 million inhabitants on December 31, 1970, including the inhabitants of its African territories.

In 1900, the population of Spain numbered 18.6 million. The increase of over 15 million inhabitants between 1900 and 1970 represents, nevertheless, a rather moderate growth rate; only during the decades 1920–1930, with a 1.07 percent increase, and 1960–1970 has the intercensal growth

---

[1] The summary in this section is based upon [1].

489

rate exceeded 1 percent. At the same time, the density of Spain continues to be lower than that in the rest of Europe. In 1970, there were only 62.27 inhabitants per square kilometer. The Basque provinces, with 259 inhabitants per square kilometer, had the highest density in the country. In general, it can be said that the two insular regions of Spain plus the industrialized regions in the periphery showed the highest densities, whereas the central plateau and the provinces of Aragon, Old Castile, Extremadura, and León registered the lowest densities. The division between the industrialized periphery and the impoverished agricultural interior has been longstanding in the history of Spain.

¶ URBAN/RURAL DISTRIBUTION
Together with this increase in the density of the periphery, a concentration in urban centers has also occurred in Spain in the last seventy years. The portion of population living in rural municipalities—that is, those of 2,000 inhabitants or less—declined from 27.5 percent in 1900 to 11 percent in 1970. On the other hand, the urban population—that is, those in towns with more than 10,000 inhabitants—increased from 32.2 percent of the total population at the beginning of this century to 66.5 percent in 1970. Since the census classifies the urban population by municipalities and not by population clusters, it is likely that the level of urbanization in Spain is overestimated; but in any case, in 1970, the population of municipalities of more than 20,000 inhabitants represented 55 percent of the total population.

Because of the intense internal migration that occurred in Spain between 1960 and 1970, the number of Spanish municipalities of 10,000 inhabitants or more increased from 423 in 1960 to 488 in 1970; the municipalities with less than 10,000 inhabitants decreased by 612 over this same period. Also, the number of municipalities with more than 100,000 inhabitants rose to 38 in 1970, representing almost 37 percent of the total population of the country; at that time, the four municipalities with more than 500,000 inhabitants—Madrid, Barcelona, Valencia, and Seville—contained 6,093,000 inhabitants, an increase of 1,770,000 persons over the population of the three centers of this size in 1960.

The population of the 451 municipalities with fewer than 100 inhabitants in 1970 included some 31,000 inhabitants, which gives an idea of the intensity of the rural exodus during this period. On the other hand, among the 38 municipalities of more than 100,000 inhabitants, some registered gigantic growth figures between 1940 and 1970; examples are some towns outside of Barcelona such as Santa Coloma de Gramanet, Tarrasa, Sabadell, Badalona, and Hospitalet. Baracaldo near Bilbao exceeded a 200-percent growth rate between 1940 and 1970.

The phenomenon of internal migration is not new in Spain; a series of observations from the nineteenth century comment on the unusual growth of some cities [2, pp. 50–53]. However, in'this century, the rural exodus has been most marked in two periods: between 1920 and 1930 and between 1960 and 1970. Data on internal migration were not gathered systematically in Spain until 1962, but according to the most reliable calculations, at least 3,519,000 Spaniards changed residence during 1920–1930. Internal migration was at its highest in 1964 and 1965 and lowest in 1966.

Internal migration in Spain has meant a movement of people from the center to the periphery and a concentration of population in urban centers. It is estimated that the rural municipalities of less than 10,000 inhabitants registered a loss between 1961 and August 1969 of 979,976 inhabitants, whereas the municipalities of more than 100,000 inhabitants showed an increase of 717,895.

¶ BIRTH, DEATH, AND NATURAL GROWTH

Table 1 shows that the crude birth rate has declined from 34.5 per 1,000 in the first decade of this century to 20 in the five-year period 1966–1970. The regional variations in the rate are not necessarily related to the level of economic development. The regions of Aragon, Asturias, the Balearic Islands, Old Castille, Catalonia, Galicia, León, Navarra, and Valencia have lower birth rates than the country average.

TABLE 1.

Vital Demographic Rates, Spain, 1901–1970 (per 1,000)

Period	Marriage Rate	Crude Birth Rate	Crude Death Rate	Infant Death Rate[a]	Natural Increase
1901–1910	7.4	34.5	24.4	186.0	10.1
1911–1920	7.1	29.8	23.5	162.0	6.3
1921–1930	7.3	29.2	19.0	147.0	10.2
1931–1935	6.4	27.0	16.3	116.0	10.7
1936–1940	6.0	21.6	17.9	130.0	3.7
1941–1945	7.1	21.6	14.3	143.0	7.3
1946–1950	7.6	21.4	11.6	71.0	9.9
1951–1955	7.8	20.3	9.8	62.6	10.5
1956–1960	8.3	21.4	9.1	46.4	12.3
1961–1965	7.5	21.3	8.6	37.4	12.7
1966–1970	7.1	20.0	8.5	32.3	11.5

SOURCES: See [1, pp. 34, 42, 55, 61, 81; 3, table 7].
[a] Rate in the first year of each period.

The crude death rate in Spain has fallen from 24.4 per 1,000 in 1901–1910 to 8.5 in 1966–1970. This reveals that the demographic transition has already taken place and, with regard to standards of mortality, Spain is completely modernized, although the infant death rate continues to be high for a European country. In 1901–1904, the infant death rate was 175 for every 1,000 live births, and in 1966–1970, it was 24. Nevertheless, the proportion that endogenous infant death represents in the total infant death rate has increased from less than 15 percent in 1948 to 50 percent in 1967.

The average life expectancy has increased from 33.8 years for men and 33.7 for women in 1900 to 69.24 years for males and 74.6 for females in 1967. Although the Spanish data are not exact enough to give a clear picture of the incidence of certain causes of death, the causes of death follow modern standards, that is, a decrease in infectious and parasitic illnesses and an increase in accidents, cardiovascular diseases, and cancer.

Since 1956, the rate of natural increase has surpassed 1.2 percent. This is undoubtedly related to an improvement in living conditions, although the stabilization of the birth rate must be interpreted with certain reservations, since it may be due to a variation in the spacing of children. Therefore, it can be said that Spain has fully experienced the demographic transition.

¶ MARRIAGE RATE

The marriage rate in Spain has remained constant in the last seventy years. Nevertheless, the proportion of single persons (50.7 percent in 1965) is higher than in the majority of Western countries, and the average age at marriage continues to be high, as the following figures show:

| | Average Age at Marriage | |
Years	Males	Females
1901–1905	27.75	24.73
1941–1945	29.70	26.03
1969	27.56	24.66

¶ ECONOMICALLY ACTIVE POPULATION

The most outstanding characteristic of the economically active population in Spain is the low employment rate of women. In 1970, only 18.1 percent of the economically active female population was working or seeking work. This proportion is expected to increase, since almost all males who are of working age are employed and there is still a demand for labor. The massive incorporation of the women into the working force is occurring rapidly; of the 1.2 million positions created between 1960 and 1970, 1.02

million were filled by women. Because of their lower level of education, they are employed in subordinate positions within the labor force.

The second important development in the economically active Spanish population is the change in the sectorial composition reflected in the following percentages:

Years	Primary (agriculture)	Secondary (industry)	Tertiary (services)
1900	69.6	15.2	15.2
1930	54.0	24.3	21.7
1969	31.0	35.7	33.0

¶ EMIGRATION

Spain is a country of emigrants. Since the discovery of America and the age of the Spanish empire, millions of persons have left for overseas territories. The "enlightened men" of the eighteenth century, among them José del Campillo, pointed out that, because of emigration, Spain lacked the manpower for the task of making the peninsula prosper. In this century, in 1908, 1910, and 1911, over 150,000 persons per year emigrated, and in 1910, the figure is known to have reached a maximum of 191,000. Emigration decreased after 1914, the only exception being 1920, when 150,000 people emigrated.

During the second half of the nineteenth century, an important part of the Spanish emigrant population went mainly to the Philippines and Cuba. They usually were public employees and military personnel bound for colonial service. The destinations of the emigrants in the early part of this century were the old Spanish colonies, the European continent, North Africa, and America. Emigration to North Africa was concentrated in Tunisia and Algiers at the end of the last century and in Algiers to 1936. Until 1950, the favorite countries of the Spanish emigrants were Argentina, Cuba, Brazil, and Venezuela.

In the 1930s, the traditional currents of Spanish emigration were interrupted, primarily because of the restrictive measures imposed by the overseas countries, the economic crisis of those years, the Spanish Civil War, and finally, World War II and the international isolation of Spain that followed. The flow did not resume consistently until 1946; in that year, the Spanish government reversed its former policies and allowed emigrants to leave the country freely. After 1946, therefore, the overseas emigration resumed with considerable growth, only later to slow down and decrease once more.

From 1946 to 1959, Spanish emigration was channeled almost exclusively toward America. After 1960, with the need for manual labor in the European countries coinciding with an increase in unemployment in Spain caused by the Economic Stabilization Plan, continental emigration began and then was converted into a demographic, economic, social, and political phenomenon of great consequence, which characterized the decade of 1960–1970 and continues at the present time.

The number of emigrants to Europe is very difficult to calculate, for the official figures in Spain generally do not coincide with the figures given by the countries of destination. Nevertheless, it is estimated that, between 1959 and 1970, 1.74 million Spaniards left their homeland and established themselves in other European countries. Some surveys show that at least 80 percent of these Spaniards returned to Spain within three years.

Those emigrating to European countries came almost exclusively from the active male population: 86.5 percent are males and 99.3 percent of them between the ages of fifteen and fifty-five years. In contrast, overseas emigrants are characterized by greater proportions of females (43.5 percent) and children and older citizens (22.9 percent).

Research to date shows that the emigration is of an exclusively economic nature. It is calculated that, in 1970, some 3.36 million Spaniards were distributed throughout the world. In this same year, the Third Economic and Social Development Plan estimated the working population at 12,855,000 persons.

One of the most important factors of emigration is the influx of foreign currency to the Spanish economy. In 1970, Spanish emigrants contributed US$469 million, and it is estimated that, between 1959 and 1969, the net income derived from emigration exceeded the total amount of foreign capital investment.

¶ POPULATION PROJECTIONS

The figure of 37,429,000 inhabitants estimated by the Third Economic and Social Development Plan for the country in 1980 represents a midpoint between two estimates but reflects the fact that the Spanish population will not increase extraordinarily in size, although it will contain a greater number of senior citizens. The same source estimated the following change in the percentage distribution of the three age groups [4, p. 104]:

Age	1970	1980
0–14	28.02	25.67
15–64	63.54	63.37
65+	9.44	10.96

The population projections also indicate an accelerated concentration of population in the large cities. The province of Madrid will increase by more than 1.2 million inhabitants by 1980, and the province of Barcelona will reach 4,508,000 (from its present size of 3,750,000 inhabitants). If we consider that a growth of 3.6 million inhabitants is foreseen in the decade 1970–1980, it is clear that during those ten years one-third of the population increase to be produced in the country will be concentrated in Madrid.

Mortality is expected to continue current trends with provincial mortality levels falling and approaching urban levels. Fertility is expected to continue decreasing; given its general trend and its relatively high level, such an expectation seems reasonable [5, pp. 133, 136].

TOWARD A DEMOGRAPHIC POLICY

¶ CENSUSES AND VITAL STATISTICS RECORDS

The historian Jorge Nadal, in his recent "History of the Population of Spain" [6], collected data about population size prior to the censuses to complement the censuses taken between 1900 and 1970,[2] as shown in Table 2. In his work, there is a detailed analysis of the various sources for these data, which were not compiled for all of Spain until 1717.

In 1717, the Bourbon dynasty imposed an administrative unification that helped create national censuses. The Aranda census of 1760–1769 was the first survey to cover individuals rather than households. In 1857, the first census by direct registration of the National Statistics Council was taken. This marked the beginning of a task continued in 1860, 1877, and 1887 and performed regularly after 1900 by the population censuses every ten years. Census day in Spain is December 31, and the series is complete to 1970.

The antecedents to the Spanish Civil Registry can be found in an 1801 circular, which stated: "Being of the utmost importance to know at any given time the state of the population and to impede the causes which may contribute to its decline . . . I resolve that in all my kingdoms of Spain any births, deaths and marriages will be recorded, and the circumstances under which they occur will be specified" [6, p. 651].[3] The provisional law of the Civil Registry was passed in June 1870 and allowed for information on a regular basis as to natural movement of the population after 1878. It is estimated that, in 1900, only 89 percent of the births were recorded [7. p. 271, n. 1].

---

[2] Nadel's work is unique in Spanish demographic literature and very useful for the purposes of this study.

[3] The author expresses his doubts that this circular really proposed to institute an authentic civil register separate from the ecclesiastic authorities.

TABLE 2.

Total Population and Intercensal Growth, Spain, 1541–1970

Year	Inhabitants (in thousands)	Percentage of Intercensal Growth
1541	7,414	
1591–1594	8,485	
1717	7,500	
1768–1769	9,300	
1787	10,409	
1797	10,541	
1857	15,455	
1877	16,622	0.76
1887	17,534	0.55
1900	18,616	0.47
1910	19,990	0.74
1920	21,388	0.70
1930	23,677	1.07
1940	26,014	0.99
1950	28,117	0.81
1960	30,528	0.86
1970	33,956	1.12

SOURCES: See [1, p. 12; 6, p. 569].

¶ ANTECEDENTS TO A DEMOGRAPHIC POLICY

The earliest population-related policies and programs in Spain were created to combat depopulation. Mounier states that the population of Spain, which had declined considerably in the sixteenth century, decreased much less rapidly in the seventeenth century, except for the sudden drop that occurred when the Moors were expelled in 1610 [8]. Colmeiro, in his *Political History of the Economy,* estimated that, after the expulsion of the Moors, the total population of Spain was 7.5 million. Since then, it must have continued decreasing. The progressive writers of the eighteenth century, such as Uztariz in his *Theory and Practice of Trade and Merchant Marine,* cite some of the main causes of the depopulation of Spain: the continuous wars during seven centuries of fighting against the Moors; emigration to the West Indies; the overabundance of Catholic clergy somewhat later; the poor distribution of land; and the large-scale decline of industry.

Populationist sentiment and policy in Spain were manifested clearly in the eighteenth century. Already in the seventeenth century, planners cried out against depopulation, but in the eighteenth century, they struggled to decrease the mortality rate and reduce celibacy [6, p. 647].[4] "As depopula-

---

[4] The number of clerics in 1797 was estimated at 148,409. See [9].

tion grows the State rides to its ruin; and the country which increases its population, even though it may be the poorest country, is certainly the best governed." This statement, made by Capmany in 1792, epitomizes the demographic thought of the age [6, p. 647].

In 1720, a Supreme Health Commission was named, "the first directive or administrative institution, regular and methodical, which records our health history." Its purpose was to decrease the mortality rate. It lasted until 1847, when it was replaced by the Health Council of the Kingdom [6, p. 649]. During the eighteenth century, efforts were recorded in the field of hygiene-health policies resulting in a decline in the mortality rate.

Mercader pointed out the most salient pronatalist measures in the eighteenth century:

> Prizes for child-bearing were offered, mainly by promoting young marriages, and those families with six male children were awarded prizes (according to the *Novisima Recopilación*),* and in some cases personal taxes were rescinded; for example, to heads of households with a large family (twelve or more children and grandchildren). Aid was also given to foreigners so that they could establish themselves in Spain and become naturalized, the only stipulation being that they profess to the Catholic religion [*10*, p. 15; quoted in *6*, pp. 651–652].

According to Nadal, the pronatalist ideas of the eighteenth century carried over into the nineteenth century, as measures for increasing the Spanish population either by natural growth or by repopulation were adopted. Among a series of measures taken between 1767 and 1855 for the purpose of attaining rural repopulation directly or indirectly were the following [6, pp. 678–679]:

(1) The Royal Order of July 5, 1787 (third law, book 7, title 22 of the *Novisima Recopilación*), for the new populations of Sierra Morena, conceded to German and Flemish colonists a two-year exemption from rent and a four-year exemption from tithes, with other advantages of disembarkation and establishment. The fourth law of the same book and title admitted Greek colonists from Corsica with the same advantages.

(2) The Royal Order of July 22, 1819, ordered the selling of uncultivated lands to town laborers.

(3) The Royal Order of March 23, 1865, conceded to Francisco Sánchez Gadeo exemption from taxes and municipal charges and the right to collect tithes for fifteen years, on the condition that he build five towns of sixty citizens each in the unpopulated areas of his property near Hornachos and Espiel in the province of Córdoba. Along these lines, several concessions were made in Sevilla, Toledo, and other provinces until 1836.

(4) The Law of Parliament of November 18, 1855, established farming com-

---

* Note from translator: Literally translated "Newest Compendium," this is a revised code of laws passed in Spain on July 15, 1805.

munities for which purpose uncultivated and state lands were allocated and granted exemption from taxes for ten years to the naturalized citizens of these kingdoms, with the addition of exemption from military service for foreigners.

Apparently, these measures were effective and were followed, in the period beginning in 1853 and ending in 1903, by more lenient policies toward emigration from Spain.[5] Along these lines, according to Nadal, the most significant steps were the following [quoted from 6, pp. 680–681]:

(1) The Royal Order of September 16, 1855, repealed, with many reservations, the law which prohibited the inhabitants of the Canary Islands in particular and the inhabitants of the Peninsula in general to emigrate to South America. . . .

(2) The Royal Order of January 12, 1855, proclaimed the rights of the State in matters pertaining to migration, although "it must respect the ability of all Spaniards to emigrate."

(3) The Royal Order of January 30, 1873, decreed the recision of the surety of 32 *reales* per emigrant which was imposed by the Royal Order of 1853 on the shipowners in charge of expeditionary embarkations.

(4) The Royal Order of May 6, 1882, created a Bureau of Emigration in the Geographic Institute and a section in charge of questions pertaining to emigration in the Office of Agriculture. . . . Among its objectives were "to seek understandings with railroad companies in order to facilitate the transportation of workers," which was one of the first official acts relative to internal migration.

(5) The Royal Order of July 11, 1891, was intended for the diplomatic and consular corps in Africa and America and directed toward "knowing the present situation of Spanish emigrants in the various foreign countries. . . . The role of the Government must be limited to studying the true working conditions of those places where the current is flowing and seeing whether it can channel this current within the limits of its own territory or direct it to our overseas possessions."

(6) The Circular of December 22, 1896, of the General Office of the Geographic and Statistics Institute asserted that "one of the main causes of emigration is the lack of articles of primary need and the meager possessions of the workers," and as a consequence, obtained from the City Councils "the average prices of the major articles of consumption and typical wages."

(7) The Royal Order of April 8, 1903, rescinded the need for a passport or special permission from the authorities and permitted the dispatching of ship passages with only personal identification papers.

Two trends were noteworthy between 1903 and 1940: first, the very heavy emigration to Spanish American countries, which peaked immedi-

---

[5] In the period of change from repopulation interest to liberalizing emigration laws, Malthus' *Essay* was translated and published in Spain in 1846 [*11*].

ately preceding World War I; and second, the rural exodus, which was intensive during 1920–1930 and which was interrupted in the decade 1930–1940 during the Great Depression and the Spanish Civil War.

After 1939, the policies of nationalism and pronatalism reappeared and partially characterized, as we will see later, the demographic policy of the new regime. The demographer Ros Jimeno expressed the problem in this way: "We are facing a dilemma: either Spain increases its birth rate or it will stop its ascension to the rank of a great power" [12, p. 86].

As the years passed, it became apparent that the awaited increase in the birth rate was not forthcoming. Ros Jimeno stated in 1943:

The decrease in the birth rate in Spain has already arrived at a critical point, as we have seen. The belief in the supreme reality of Spain and the intention to exalt, elevate and fortify it constitutes the principal basis of the New State. It is therefore possible to rely on future generations to bear many children to fortify, elevate and exalt their country with happiness in their hearts and pride in their country. Meanwhile, we must put an end to the decrease in the birth rate and initiate the road to its ascent [13, p. 60].

Jimeno wrote in 1959:

At any rate, the instinct which impelled procreation without limits seems in our days to be dominated by the power of reason. Fertility does not depend upon blind will, but on a rational act. . . . The tendency toward conscious procreation, even if seen from different views, can scarcely be considered by everyone as the ideal human procreation under present circumstances [14, p. 424].

After the new regime was constituted, the goal of a population of 40 million in Spain was mentioned frequently. Francisco Franco, head of the state of Spain, said in 1938: "The day will come when our country will reach 40 million inhabitants who will live with complete dignity, thanks to our great resources [15, pp. 305–306].

It appears that measures will be adopted to reach this national desire. As Ros Jimeno said: "But Spain today aspires to have 40 million inhabitants. Therefore, it needs to develop a policy to radically modify those tendencies and for this, to know in the greatest possible detail the natural movement of the population and the least or most effective measures to be taken to direct it in a certain way" [13, p. 57]. At the present time, some measures for protecting the family have been formulated, which we will discuss later.

Since 1945, the defeat of the Axis powers, the international isolation of Spain, and the loss of imperial aspirations of the regime have brought an almost absolute neglect of the Spanish demographic problem. Around 1945, the rate of Spanish emigration to America had decreased to almost nothing, and the current Spanish emigration to the rest of Europe had not begun. After 1959, however, the interest in demographic studies was revived and advanced considerably to the present day.

The First Economic and Social Development Plan (1964–1967) expressed no form of demographic policy beyond a desire to promote the welfare of the Spaniards and to decrease the need for emigrating abroad. (The great Spanish emigration to Europe had begun.) Nevertheless, it is not widely known that, on the occasion of the Second Economic and Social Development Plan (1968–1971), a demographic and family policy plan circulated among the provisional documents; this was probably the first attempt to formulate a demographic policy for the country. Since this provisional plan reveals a great deal concerning the orientation of Spanish demographic policy implicit in political planning, it is reproduced on the pages that follow.

DEMOGRAPHIC AND FAMILY POLICY
(provisional plan)

A. Introduction

"Demographic and Family Policy" will refer to two important themes in particular: the spatial and geographic distribution of the population, which has been seriously affected by the strong current of internal migration in the last few years, and demographic growth. With regard to the former, there is a strong and well-defined tendency of the population to become concentrated in three areas of the Spanish geography (Madrid, Barcelona, and Bilbao). In order to overcome this problem, it would be necessary to stimulate the growth of a selected number of suitably urbanized cities and convert them into places that would attract people without taking away from them freedom to choose their places of residence.

In Spain it would be advantageous to increase the rate of demographic growth. It obliges us to create the economic and social conditions that favor an increase in the birth rate. At the same time, it is necessary to update systems for protecting families.

B. Objectives

(1) To attain a spatial and geographic distribution of the Spanish population more in accord with the natural and potential resources of each zone.

(2) To slow the growth of the demographically congested cities.

(3) To facilitate the urbanization process of the Spanish population

and, in particular, to promote urbanization and services in those cities within regions capable of absorbing growth.

(4) To attain population growth at a rate higher than the present one.

C. *Guidelines*

(1) To adapt the regional and territorial divisions of the country to the needs of the people for the purpose of avoiding excessive tension in migratory movements.

(2) To adopt suitable measures for converting large regional cities into places that would attract the people.

(3) To stimulate demographic growth in major cities of each natural region so that it would be possible to establish in them the necessary urban services.

(4) To orient and channel internal migrations by trying to reduce the number of isolated areas as much as possible.

(5) To create social and economic conditions that would permit the most flexibility possible in the family composition.

D. *Measures*

(1) To create new jobs in industry and services in the centers to be expanded through appropriate economic and administrative policies.

(2) To establish in certain urban centers public and administrative services necessary to convert these centers into true places of demographic attraction.

(3) To improve and expand urban services in the most dynamic centers in order to avoid excessive differential situations.

(4) To establish enough incentives so that public employees effectively reside in the regional centers.

(5) To update the existing norms on protection of large families (education; legal rights; air, sea, and land transportation; and so forth).

(6) To lower inheritance taxes at the time of death of a head of household of a large family. Also, to lower inheritance taxes corresponding to abnormal children.

(7) To update the figures for the number of children needed to qualify as a "large family" and count as double those abnormal children with an IQ equal to or less than 50 as well as invalids, maimed, or obviously less than normal family members.

(8) To make family assistance systems more effective by adapting them to new realities and in accordance with available resources.

(9) To extend social security benefits on a voluntary basis to large fam-

ilies through the heads of household by means of payments of employer and worker shares.

(10) To reconsider minimal housing and social standards and initiate the construction of those with at least two or more bedrooms in addition to the master bedroom.

July 1, 1967

This plan was never incorporated in the Second Economic and Social Development Plan; however, an institutional-level decree (no. 246, 1968) concerning the organization of the Department of the Interior, provided for a general sub-office of population within the Central Health Commission, composed of the Sections of Industry and Classified Activities, Population Health and Security, and General Affairs [*16*].

In the Third Economic and Social Development Plan (1972–1975), there is a new preoccupation with the environment. The plan specifies four concrete projects on environmental improvement and defense against air and water pollution [*4*, p. 318]:

(1) Desulfurization of fuel oil gases and purification of residual gases containing sulfuric anhydride.
(2) Fight against water pollution.
(3) Noise-pollution control.
(4) Conservation of natural parks, green areas, and recreation sites within the large cities.

The plan does not outline policy guidelines for the development of these four programs, although the section includes housing, transportation and communications, regional development, urbanism, and the protection of nature in "environment." In December 1972, a law against air pollution was approved in Parliament. The law, although limited, represents the first step of the Third Economic and Social Development Plan toward alleviating these problems. This law states that its objective is to prevent, watch over, and correct situations where air pollution occurs, whatever may be the causes that produces it. The law is limited to fighting air pollution, leaving the struggle against other forms of environmental pollution to other legal measures.

In summary, the Third Economic and Social Development Plan did not use the opportunity to formulate a coherent demographic policy. For this reason, the remaining pages of this study are dedicated to describing in a general context the main decisions and norms regarding demographic policy that are scattered and isolated throughout various legal documents.

PRINCIPAL AREAS OF DEMOGRAPHIC POLICY

¶ FAMILY AND BIRTH

Kinds of Marriage.

The law of June 18, 1870, made civil marriage obligatory in Spain, deny-
ing to canon marriage the civil effects it enjoyed in previous laws. After the
restoration of the monarchy, the Royal Decree of February 9, 1875, repealed
the 1870 law and again gave validity to canon marriage for Catholics, while
the previous law was left effective for non-Catholics. The civil code of 1888
and the order of April 23, 1889, established the present system of regulations, according to which canon marriage must be confirmed by the state
and inscribed in its registers in order to obtain the desired civil effects.
Except for a brief period during which the second republic established the
possibility of divorce by a law of June 28, 1932, which was repealed by
another law on March 12, 1938, marriage is subject to canon law, in which
divorce does not exist.[6]

The Law of Principles of the National Movement of May 17, 1958, in
its second article states: "The Spanish nation considers as a sign of honor
the obedience to and respect for the Law of God according to the doctrine
of the Holy Catholic Church." This article reiterates article 6 of the Rights
and Privileges of the Spanish People (July 17, 1945), which identified the
Catholic religion as the official religion of the Spanish state. This 1945 law
was modified as the Law of Principles of the National Movement by the
Organic Law of the State of January 10, 1967 [19].

In accordance with articles 42 and 75 of the civil code, revised by the
law of April 24, 1958, "The Law recognizes two kinds of marriage: canon
and civil. Marriage will be contracted canonically when at least one of the
partners professes the Catholic religion. Civil marriage is authorized when
it is proven that neither of the partners professes the Catholic religion."
And in accordance with article 75 of the same law: "Canon marriage as
regards its constitution and validity and in general its legal regulations,
will be governed by the orders of the Catholic Church."

The sacred character of the Spanish family is, therefore, clearly expressed
in the laws. From this, one can deduce the impossibility of the dissolution
of marriage by means of divorce. There are now only four countries in the
world where, in some way, marriage is a form of religious celebration of an
indissoluble nature: Colombia, Vatican City, Lichtenstein, and Spain. Also,

---

[6] Available data suggest that the number of divorces in Spain was low after the
approval of the republican law. Between 1932 and 1933, 7,059 cases were registered [17]. In Madrid, only about 750 cases of annulment and separation were initiated in 1971 [18].

examination of the laws of 101 countries shows that only eight do not presently admit divorce, and one of these is Spain.

Some critics have suggested the need for a reassessment of marriage in the modern world:

Marriage presently is full of problems. Among other reasons because in the 17th century, for example, the average number of years for a marriage union did not exceed 17, whereas today it exceeds 45 years. And [the problems are] logical, living as we are, ... with the same identical laws as those which governed the institution of marriage in times past; with the pre-eminence of some lack of values—all of these seem to demand a very responsible restatement of the problem, benefiting both the idea itself and society, a restatement that would naturally include a greater integral formation of the protagonists of the marriage union [20].

The church has responded to such questionings. In a recent declaration, the bishops of Madrid stated:

Permit us ... to take advantage of the family atmosphere before us during the Christmas holidays and to call your attention to the institution of the family and Christian marriage, which is its beginning. Voices are being raised, each day more intense, even among us, regarding the unity and indissolubility of marriage, and regarding the sacred character of human life, even before birth, voices that differ from the doctrine taught by the Church. And it is necessary that we all agree to repress this movement which could be most dangerous, not only for Christianity but also for nature itself [21].

Marriage Age.

Article 83, part 1, of the civil code prohibits males under age fourteen years and female under age twelve to marry. The average age at marriage in Spain, however, continues to be extraordinarily high. Furthermore, the percentage of single women over age fourteen years in 1960 (31.5 percent) is only exceeded in Europe by Italy (32.2 percent), Portugal (32.4 percent), Iceland (34.8 percent), and Ireland (38.9 percent). The high marriage age and the low percentage of married couples have been shown to represent indirect means of birth control.

The modal frequencies in the percentages of marriages, according to the age of the contracting parties in the five-year period 1961–1965, are 25–29 years of age among males and 20–24 among females. Specifically, about 26 percent of all marriages take place between persons within these two age groups. In that same five-year period, 44.8 percent of all females who married were in the age group 20–24, and 50.33 percent of males were in the age group 25–29. The proportion of marrying parties under twenty-five years of age has varied since the beginning of this century [22, p. 13].

It is interesting to note that the proportion of marrying males of less than twenty-five years of age increased in 1966–1969 to 27.9 percent and that of marrying females increased to 61.7 percent. A definite tendency toward a decrease in the marriage age seems confirmed, the social consequences of which should not be overlooked.

The Family.

It is curious that, given the importance of the family in the planning of the state after the Civil War in 1939, it has not been possible to calculate the average size of the Spanish family; rather, it is only possible to divide the total population by the number of census sheets. Naturally, if both family and collective census sheets are included in the denominator, the quotient suffers a great distortion. Since the beginning of the century, the average size of the census family, that is, the number of persons who live together occupying the total area of one dwelling house, has varied as follows:

Year	Average Family Size
1900	3.87
1910	3.98
1920	4.08
1930	4.09
1940	4.22
1950	3.74
1960	4.00
1970	3.84

The number of census families in Spain, in accordance with the results of the 1970 census, is 8,850,480. The average size varied according to Table 3 for the national total, the provincial capitals, and municipalities of more than 200,000 inhabitants.[7]

The 1970 population census registers an important innovation by defining what it calls "family nuclei." These are equivalent to conjugal families, which sociologists describe as families composed of both parents and their children. It is possible, naturally, that these families may be incomplete, since one of the parents could be lacking. According to the census data, of the 8,430,980 family nuclei in the country in 1970, 90.2 percent were complete. On the other hand, 672,183 individuals composed one-person census families, a fact that concurs with the high proportion of single persons in the population.

The data, then, give a reliable idea of the number of large families in

[7] Calculated from data furnished by the National Statistical Institute.

TABLE 3.

Average Family Size, Spain, 1970

Country and Municipalities	Average Family Size
Total of nation	3.84
Total of capitals	3.89
Madrid	3.85
Barcelona	3.65
Baleares (Balearic Islands)	3.67
Córdoba	4.22
Malaga	4.18
Murcia	3.87
Las Palmas	4.34
Sevilla	4.07
Valencia	3.70
Valladolid	3.96
Bilbao	4.00
Zaragoza	3.78
Hospitalet	3.94

SOURCE: Based on data from the National Statistical Institute.

Spain. Considering only the family nuclei, there are 1,097,346 with four or more children—13.01 percent of the total family nuclei.

Actually, the Survey of Family Budgets, 1964–1965, cited a figure of 18.3 percent of Spanish households as containing families with four or more children. Among households with an annual income of over 60,000 pesetas (approximately US$1,050),[8] more than 18.3 percent had large families (four or more children). The modal frequencies of the percentages of households according to their size were distributed in the following manner:

Persons	Percentages of Households
1,2	22.9
3–5	58.2
6+	18.9

Legislation for the Family.

In accordance with the ideological guidelines of the present regime in Spain, the family has always been the object of special attention on the

[8] As of January 1, 1973, 1,000 pesetas equaled approximately US $17.50.

part of the state. The law of August 1, 1941, began with a formal statement
of protection of large families; it was superseded subsequently by the law
of December 13, 1943, with its bylaw of March 31, 1944. A law approved
on June 19, 1971, and a bylaw of December 23, 1971, offered new benefits
to large families and to those with abnormal children. This new law and its
bylaw offered family subsidies in matters of employment, education, credit,
living quarters, and others to families with three children and some incapacitated member or those with four or more children. Apart from the
bylaw of December 23, 1971, previously mentioned, a series of orders
developing various aspects of the law have been written [23].

The press has discussed the fact that school subsidies do not form a part
of the benefits applicable to large families. One writer has claimed that the
Law of Protection to Large Families is not very protective, since in centers
not run by the state, in spite of the subsidies which the law in principle
recognizes, the students have to pay the entire tuition cost [24].

The state establishes other standards of protection for the family. The
decree of December 3, 1970, which convokes the national and provincial
prizes of the Department of Welfare for birth and family promotion,
increases the number and scope of these prizes, which are becoming traditional. Prizes are awarded to those families who have done the most in
promoting their members in the areas of formation and culture as a stimulus to responsible parenthood and not only to those families with the
greatest numbers of children. There is, therefore, a new trend in the law,
which is of special importance in the present study.

Independent of salary levels, some benefits of family assistance are established that affect family income. Under an updating of the decree of January 9, 1971, subsidies to the wife at the time of marriage and at the time
of birth of each child are as follows [25, p. 393]:

(1) 250 pesetas per month for each child.
(2) 375 pesetas per month for the wife.
(3) 6,000 pesetas at marriage.
(4) 3,000 pesetas at the birth of each child.

It is opportune to quote from a speech given by the Minister of Labor
in the official closing of the General Assembly of Large Families, which
took place in Valencia on November 4, 1972:

When the draft of the Law of Large Families was sent to the Parliament,
only 286,000 large families had requested this status, and today the number
approaches 500,000, which indicates that an interest exists which did not exist
before. In 1970, only 43,000 new licenses were transacted; in 1971, while the
law was being discussed in Parliament, 86,000 were presented, and this year
there are 120,000 more. The beneficiaries have surpassed the figure of
1,800,000 to nearly 3 million Spaniards.

At the end of November 1972, for the first time, the balance of income and expenditures of the Department of Social Security was presented to the public. Of a total expenditure of 208.2 million pesetas, 52.2 million were invested in family protection, that is, approximately 25 percent of the total, as compared with 20.8 percent of the total in 1971 [26; 27].

The Twentieth Assembly of the National Catholic Confederation of Parents of Families and Parents of Students, held in Madrid in October 1972, requested in their first proposal the "updating of the permanent values of the family"; "the family policy of the State should be improved in organization and structured by the creation of a specialized department dependent on the families themselves by means of promoting the exercise of the right of family association and dependent on the healthiest part of public opinion in the country" [28]. This petition for the creation of a ministry of the family would mean the elevation of the department that exists within the office of the Secretary General of the Movement, created by decree 15/1970, by which the standards for the structure of the Secretary General of the Movement are sanctioned.[9]

It is appropriate to say some final words regarding the history of the family movement in Spain [29, pp. 70–71; 30, chaps. 3 and 4]. The antecedent to this movement was the Catholic Confederation of Parents of Families, which began in 1930 for the promotion of a completely Christian education. Nevertheless, the National Delegation of Association of the Movement was not created until 1957. In 1966, the National Union of Family Association (NUFA) appeared, with the purpose of giving authority to the different family associations. It is estimated that nearly 1 million families participate in the associations of family heads. On December 4, 1968, the Statute of Organization of the Movement was approved, which provided the constitution for the associations for developing family participation. The heads of family elect two provincial representatives to the Spanish Parliament.

Birth Control.

In the Rights and Privileges of the Spanish People of July 17, 1945, the intention of the new state to protect the family can clearly be seen. Thus, article 22 says: "The State recognizes and protects the family as a natural institution and foundation of society, with rights and duties before and above all positive human law. Marriage will be one and indissoluble. The State will especially protect large families." It is appropriate to cite parallel

---

[9] See also decree 2485/1970 of August 21, on the publication of standards of organization and development of the agencies of the Secretary General of the Movement, especially articles 21–27.

to this declaration part 12.3 of the Rights and Privileges of Employment of March 9, 1938: The state "recognizes the family as the primary natural cell and foundation of society and at the same time as a moral institution, bestowed with inalienable rights and superior to all positive law. For a greater guarantee of its preservation and continuation the indestructibility of family patrimony will be recognized."

This inclination to favor families and especially large ones has caused the state to establish a series of incentives for the establishment and maintenance of families. We previously referred to the legal protection of large families, and the position of critics that this protection does not extend to educational benefits [31]. We also mentioned the annual awards of the National Birth and Family Promotion Prizes [32; 33].

These benefits that the law awards for births are a source of controversy in the Spanish press. The Law of Maternal Relief of July 12, 1922, establishes a period of absence from work of six weeks (voluntary, except when a physician so orders) before giving birth and six weeks after birth. There are those who feel that it is an excessive amount of time since, at the present time, a normal life can be carried on until a few days before and beginning a few days after giving birth; however, because of this benefit, many companies are inclined to reject qualified women who seek employment. The opposing view maintains that this benefit not only protects the woman but also the child and that a good solution would be to deal with it in the context of an economic contribution from the Department of Social Security, making it their duty to remunerate the person during the time of pregnancy [34].

We can now undertake, with some initial preparation, the subject of birth control in Spain and, above all, examine the attitudes that are manifested in the light of it. On April 5, 1973, the press published some questions that a member of Parliament asked of the government about abortion and contraceptives in Spain. The last three questions were:

Is the Government able to state whether the consumption or use of contraceptives is increasing in Spain, and what are the figures of those sold on the market under medical control and those used without any control?

Does the Government understand that the time to confront this delicate problem by sociopolitical action has arrived? If the answer is yes, what measures does the Government propose to adopt and by what course does it plan to carry them out?

Granting the natural limits of all due respect to the Catholic morals, is the Government able to start creating in our country family orientation centers to deal with these delicate matters for persons, single or married, who may need your assistance? [35][10]

[10] For the government's reply, see [36].

The three questions epitomize a deep social preoccupation and also recognize the existence of efforts to limit fertility. The existing centers of psychopedagogic orientation for the family do not give any information pertaining to contraception or sex life. The programs of the Second Seminar of Family and Psychosexual Education and of the School of Parents of the National Family Delegation omit all information concerning family planning.

The mass media in Spain generally have a very negative attitude toward the use of contraceptives. A good example is a recent newspaper article in which the conclusions of the roundtable on contraception, held at the Official College of Physicians of Murcia, were stated:

This roundtable does not enter specifically or nonspecifically into the subject of abortion, because we consider that in Spain it is clear in the minds of everyone that interrupting life from the time of conception is a crime, nor do we enter into the subject of birth control. This table adopts as their own the following conclusions:
(1) Oral or injectable contraceptives are not correctly called anovulators, ovulation regulators, and so forth, because this is not its only effect; in fact, modern contraceptives have an antipregnancy effect without stopping ovulation or with an abortive effect (morning-after pills).
(2) Presently, there exists no alteration which can be correctly treated by the need to resort to contraceptives.
(3) The general techniques of administering this medicine pretend to obtain a contraceptive effect by simulating a normal cycle. For this reason, in these cases they should not be considered as medication but as contraceptives.
(4) The influence on endocrine and metabolic processes demonstrates that administering these medicines produces a situation analogous to gestation (an increase in the secretion of adrenaline and of the growth hormone, alteration in the concentration of certain fats in the blood, and so forth), with the clinical repercussions implicit in it.
(5) The magistery of the Church does not enter into the discussions on proper medical use of these medicines. But its use for contraceptive purposes is not legal.
(6) Our Penal Code not only punishes any type of sterilization-ligatures of tubes in the women and vasectomy in the male but all means or procedures capable of impeding procreation as well as the mere indication of contraceptives. The execution of the Law in matters of protection against the use of contraceptives will have to be obtained, among other procedures, by increasing the vigilence of its use and persecuting implacably those unequivocally indicating contraception [37].

Another very significant example is the letter written to the newspaper *Ya* by Dr. Antonio de Soroa y Pineda, ex-president of the Academy of Medical Deontology and recipient of the National Award of Deontology of the Royal Academy of Medicine, in which he states:

We have read that in the House of Lords a proposal presented by' one of its female members, the Baroness Llewelin Dabies of the Labor Party, has triumphed, a proposal that proclaimed nothing less than another audacious social advance in the sense that "the National Health Service should provide free of charge contraceptives to those who want them, as well as instructions, also free of charge, for birth control to all citizens in the country."

These sexual aberrations, which serve to materialize humanity, propagate and exalt the practice of abortion and extol contraceptives; they interpret a psychology that is in opposition to natural reason and, as a consequence, to the fundamental doctrines of Catholic morality. It is necessary to protest energetically, categorically, and publicly; man, as a rational human being, and above all, Catholics reject such practices, which are animalistic and inhuman actions [38].

A similar attitude is repeated in other journals. One of these, speaking on family planning in India, concludes: "What exclusive patrimony is left to man today, if, as it seems, the creation of man itself, the most beautiful act in creation, becomes socialized?" [39].

With rare exceptions—such as the publication by some sociologists [40] of newspaper articles in which they request that the subject not be taboo, no matter what the position adopted may be, and especially with regard to the problem of overpopulation in the world—it is normal to read that "in Spain there is no demographic explosion" [41].

Furthermore, the press reproduced in great detail the conclusions of the *Sociological Report on the Social Situation in Spain* regarding the attitudes of Spanish women toward the pill. Thus, the attitude expressing the greatest opposition was reported when the women interviewed were asked if they would take the pill if the church were to authorize Catholics to do so. Only 16 percent would take it, 25 percent were undecided, and 58 percent would persist in their present negative attitude. "Therefore, it is not a matter of formal prohibition by the church that inhibits women on this subject but rather a more deeply rooted attitude" [42, p. 484].

The collection of articles gathered in a recent issue of the magazine *Nuestro Tiempo* from the University of the Opus Dei in Navarra is very significant. In one article, after dedicating the study to the suppression of shame as a characteristic of our time, the author scorns the growth of the world population as a simple slogan [43, p. 28].

In another article, warnings are formulated concerning sex education: "And a well-directed sex education does not necessarily mean wide, exhaustive and even planned information in this context but rather harmonic information dependent on the other educational aspects of the personality: the effective, the intellectual, the social, and so forth" [44, p. 106].

The Opus Dei news agency *Europa Press* published not long ago some statements made by Professor Colin Clark in which he affirms: "Far from creating unsolvable problems, population growth should be seen as something beneficial, since it stimulated man to seek solutions to problems which he would tend to ignore if it were not for this pressure" [45].

The exception to this general rule is expressed by some social scientists, such as the economist José Luis Sampredro, for whom

limitation of birth, even though it impedes the appearance of new lives, has (in the demographic circumstances expressed) the positive side of struggling in favor of existing life. In the underdeveloped countries limitation of birth is not to decide against life but to place more importance on real and daily suffering of the living rather than on the hypothetical future life of those who do not yet exist. For my part there is no hesitation in choosing the hungry living, even though it may affect those not yet existing, since the promise that technology will end up feeding everyone does not today seem more than a hope [46, p. 39].

Along the same lines, the authors of the *Sociological Report on the Social Situation of Spain* wrote as follows: "Birth control is not natural, as is true of all scientific progress which tries not to obey nature but to dominate it. The world we know will not be able to oppose this general tendency, and unconditional resistance to birth control—when dealing with underdeveloped countries—is, therefore, inconsistent with human progress" [42, p. 74].

It is of great interest to review some pronouncements made by the Spanish Catholic church, represented by its bishops, either individually or collectively. Before this, it should be pointed out that, within the five-year period 1968–1972, the number of episcopal documents regarding subjects of faith and morals has been small: 34 in a total of 418, or 8.2 percent [47]. Nevertheless, the complete solidarity of the Spanish bishops in the traditional doctrine of the church on birth is continuously registered. We reiterate the statement of Pius XII that "marriage as a natural institution in virtue of the will of the Creator does not have as its primary and intimate goal the personal perfection of married couples, but rather the procreation and education of the new life" [48].

The present Cardinal Archbishop of Madrid, while Bishop of Solsona, wrote:

The practices of eugenics, birth control, etc., are defended in our days by technological and economic reasons. And these contraceptive practices sanction pleasure as the supreme standard of life. Marriage loses all of its sacred character, before a purely natural order. For this reason the institution of the family continues losing sacredness and even consistency . . . [49, pp. 29–30].

Some years later, the Bishop of Ciudad Real dedicated a long pastoral to the disjunctive between birth control and large families, stating that, "the defense and protection of large families constitutes one of the great needs of the modern era" [50, p. 26].

When the encyclical *Humanae Vitae* was published, the Spanish Episcopacy formulated a declaration in which they reiterated their total support of the encyclical [51, para. 1]. Among the aforementioned pastoral pronouncements, we can cite an exhortation by Monsignor del Campo y de Las Bárcenas, Bishop of Calahorra, regarding the difficulties in carrying out the *Humanae Vitae* [52] and a pastoral from the present Cardinal Archbishop of Barcelona, written while Bishop of Gerona [53].

Highly significant is the recent collective declaration of the Episcopacy concerning morality, in which it is stated expressively:

> We consider it a duty to reaffirm . . . the traditional doctrine of the Magistery of the Church regarding the grave illicitness of extramarital sexual relations and even premarital relations and of the original sin and the unnatural character and sinfulness of homosexuality, a vice which so energetically stigmatized Saint Paul. As regards birth control, we reiterate our declaration of November 1968 in conformity with the teachings of Pius XII in his encyclical *Humane Vitae* [54].

The "diagnosis of faith and morality in Spain" of the Episcopal Commission for the Doctrine of Faith states the following about the illegality of modern contraceptive means and the low moral standards:

> It is a fact that the birth index has notably decreased. After reflecting on this fact, the following are indicated as its causes: environmental hedonism and the resulting decline in moral standards; anovulatory means consciously authorized; contraceptive means consciously immoral [55, p. 330].

Monsignor Escrivá de Balaguer, founder of the Opus Dei, also cautions against inhibiting fertility:

> As regards marital chastity, I assure all married couples that they should not be afraid to express love; on the contrary, because that inclination is the basis of your family life. What God asks is that you have mutual respect and be mutually loyal, that you act delicately, naturally and moderately. I will say also that marital relations are deserving when they are proof of true love, and they are therefore open to fertility, to children.
>
> To cut off the sources of life is a crime against the gifts that God has granted to humanity, and it is egotism, not love, which inspires their conduct [56].

Other similar manifestations have been made by Monsignor Escrivá; for example, he once responded in an interview that "those theories that make the limitation of births a universal or simply general ideal or duty are criminal, anti-Christian, and inhuman" [57].

Only some authors disagree with this uniform religious view. Thus, Miret Magdalena states: "We must not be parents irresponsibly. For this we must measure what we do and govern ourselves by authentic and true love, which is the dynamic goal of marriage" [58].

The "Dossier of Rome,"[11] which appeared in the magazine *Triumph,* collected the report of the majority of the pontifical commission charged with studying the religious view. On another occasion, *Triumph* stated that the *Humanae Vitae* was edited against the majority opinion of the pontifical commission [60, pp. 140–147].

With different religious arguments, Gonzalez Ruiz has said that "the multiplication of human beings should not be done mechanically, but rather should assume conscience and responsibility of contributing effectively to the multiplication of free and responsible human beings" [61, pp. 22–23]. According to him, the Christian perspective of marriage should abandon the closed ghetto of the family.

Passing now to the legal aspect, we should note that the diffusion, sale, and even information on contraceptive means has been gravely prohibited in the penal code for some time. Article 416 of the official penal code states:

Those who carry out any of the following acts relating to medication, substances, objects, instruments, devices, means or procedures capable of causing or facilitating abortion or preventing procreation will be punished with maximum imprisonment and a fine of from 5,000 to 100,000 pesetas:

(1) Those who in possession of a medical or health degree merely suggest them, as well as those who, without said degree, do so for profit.

(2) The manufacturer or dealer who sells them to persons not pertaining to the Medical Corps or to merchants not authorized to sell them.

(3) He who offers them to the public, sells, expends, supplies or announces them in any form.

(4) The divulgation in any form of information regarding the prevention of procreation, as well as public exposure and sale.

(5) Any type of contraceptive propaganda.

In spite of such a strong prohibition, contained in the law of January 24, 1971, some contraceptives are sold in Spain. An Order of the Ministry of the Government of August 14, 1965,[12] established as an indispensable requirement a medical prescription signed by the doctor (in which he must

---

[11] Later published as a book; see [59].

[12] The order dictates standards for the dispensation of medication [62]; see also the resolution of the Department of Health in which the contents of parts 1 and 14 of the annex of the order are modified [63].

state his physician's number and the date of the prescription) for medication serving to prevent conception.

Furthermore, birth control and the use of contraceptives have a very long tradition in Spain. Jutglar reports that, in October 1815, the Vicar General of the Diocese of Barcelona told about the "apprehension . . . of 120 dozen condoms and of the person who had introduced them into the city, a tragedy so contrary to Religion and Nature." On March 23, 1816, a trial was set, and the civil and religious authorities were charged with "employing all zeal and vigilance for the purpose of halting the use and knowledge of such artifacts, and this Royal Audience was advised to at the same time destroy and render unusable the apprehended condoms" [64, p. 254].[13]

More recently, Severino Aznar, Ros Jimeno, and others, this author among them, have commented on the high level of birth control in Spain.[14] In 1963, the author made a survey of 161 doctors in Barcelona in which some questions that related to the subject of birth control were included [69, pp. 27–38]. The proportion of doctors who thought that their patients were using certain contraceptive methods—excluding rhythm—were as follows:

Method	Percentages
Withdrawal	34.0
Preservatives	25.0
Chemical methods	14.1
Douches	9.6

A survey has also been conducted on the basis of indirect questions to women about the methods they believe are most used for birth control [70]. The principal results, compiled in Table 4, show that the most well-known method is the pill but that the most used in Spain, in the opinion of those interviewed, are preservatives and withdrawal.

The data regarding the use of the pill in Spain vary considerably. Thus, a recent exposition of the government has shown that:

The total number of contraceptives manufactured during 1969 rose to 1,739,544. It is calculated on the basis of the length of treatment necessary, that

---

[13] Another example is the affirmation of Livi Bacci with regard to standards of conduct relating to the limitation of birth since the eighteenth century; "the center of diffusion was Catalonia, a region open to French influence which experienced an early decline in mortality and an accelerated process of industrialization" [65, pp. 230–231]. See also [66, p. 556].

[14] See also [67; 68].

TABLE 4.

Women's Knowledge about Contraceptives, Spain, 1973 (in percents)

Knowledge of Those Interviewed	With-drawal	Preser-vatives	Vaginal Douche	Rhythm (Ogino)	Pill	Diaphragm	Other	No Answer
Have heard about	35	42	29	58	72	16	2	21
Believe are the most used in Spain	11	11	2	23	20	0	0	40
Believe are the most efficient	5	8	1	6	35	1	0	46
Believe are the least efficient	5	2	5	29	2	1	0	57
Believe are dangerous	6	3	2	1	41	4	0	49
Believe are the most difficult to find	0	1	0	0	27	6	0	67
Believe are permitted by the church	3	3	2	38	3	0	1	58

SOURCE: See [70, p. 90].

TABLE 5.

Use of the Pill, Spain, 1966–1971

Year	Units Used
1966	789,000
1967	1,262,000
1968	2,716,400
1969	2,837,100
1970	3,029,200
1971[a]	3,221,900

SOURCE: Department of Health data.
[a] Until November.

the number of women who used them in 1969 was 120,000. At the present time, it is proven that the production figure during 1970 and 1971 is simply equal to or very slightly more than that for 1969 [71].

The author was given other figures of units sold by the Department of Health, which appear in Table 5. At the present time, there are on the Spanish market fifteen pharmaceutical specialties. It therefore can be estimated that a little less than 300,000 women in Spain legally acquire contraceptives; one authority placed the number of consumers at no less than 1 million [72].[15] This would mean that approximately 12.2 percent of all women between the ages of fifteen and forty-nine use contraceptives.

Abortion.

There is total condemnation of abortion in Spanish society. In late 1972, the press published a speech by Pope Paul VI to the twelfth congress of Italian Catholic lawyers, in which he defended the right to birth of all human beings and attacked the "social plague of abortion" [73]. Not long afterward, a large daily newspaper in Madrid dedicated an editorial to the condemnation of abortion, formulated by the North American Episcopacy, and concluded the following:

It is surprising and alarming at the same time that while the advocates of modern freedom and the proclaimers, rather nominalists, of the rights of man do not hesitate in legally protecting the possibility of assassination of the unborn, the Catholic Church alone . . . in a unanimous voice of believers and even of all humanity, comes to the defense of indefensive human life [74].

[15] The discussion followed a speech by Professor J. Botella Llusia at the Congress of Women Physicians.

There are many other manifestations. For example, in a very recent session of the Royal Academy of Medicine, it was said: "Abortion is rejected as a means of birth control, the same as abortion carried out for social, psychological, eugenic reasons, etc. For this reason, in a Christian conscience a new life cannot be instrumentalized by directly destroying it in order to obtain an end, no matter what the reason may be" [75].

The same Royal Academy of Medicine later released the conclusions of a roundtable discussion on "Moral and Medical Problems surrounding Abortion," which were sent to the government and the Attorney General of the Supreme Court. Among the conclusions are the following:

> From the moral principles . . . it is deduced . . . that in no way can direct abortion be admitted as legal for social, demographic, eugenic, or medical reasons. . . .
> From the legal point of view and the medical ethics point of view it seems monstrous to concede to the woman the right to abortion, as has been done recently in some countries [76].

In a discussion held in the offices of the daily newspaper *Pueblo* of Madrid, it was concluded that "abortion is always immoral. But a legal ordinance should also exist for conflicting cases. It is very important to rely on legal ordinances which clarify ideas to doctors and patients; above all, because the classical idea of abortion has suffered great changes" [77].

Antonio Soroa is trying to create in Spain a "Pro-Defense Committee for Life" for the purpose of informing the world that "abortion is always a brutal assassination, since it cuts off the life of a potential being" [78].

The position adopted by José Botella Llusiá, a renowned gynecologist and former rector of the Complutense University of Madrid, is rather unequivocal:

> Neither is the argument valid that the mother is already a human being and the embryo is not. . . .
> I do not know if some day, and I think not, abortion will be justified in the light of moral theology. But if this unimaginable day arives, we biologists will have to continue defending that new life, which nobody seems to want to protect, because the fear falls upon us that in an overpopulated world humanity is beginning that "unconscious suicide" which has caused myriads of species to be erased from the face of the earth [79].

In the legal sphere, abortion is penalized gravely in title 8, "Crime against Persons," chapter 3, "On Abortion," of the official penal code, approved by the decree of December 23, 1944, in articles 411–417 inclusive [80]. They are reproduced below, except for article 416, which has already been transcribed:

Article 411: He who purposely causes an abortion will be punished:

(1) By a maximum prison sentence, if done without the consent of the woman.

(2) By a minimum prison sentence, if the women consents. If violence, intimidation, threats or deceit were employed in carrying out the abortion, the first sentence applies, or if they were employed in order to obtain consent, the prison sentence will be imposed at its highest level.

When, as a consequence of an abortion or abortive practices carried out on a woman who is not pregnant but believes herself to be so, or when inadequate means to cause the abortion are used, the death of the woman or injuries referred to in article 420 result, the sentence of minimum imprisonment will be imposed, and if accused of other grave injuries, the sentence of maximum imprisonment will be imposed.

Article 412: Abortion done violently, knowing the state of pregnancy of the woman, when there has been no reason to cause it, will be punished with the minimum prison sentence.

Article 413: When the woman causes her own abortion or gives her consent for another to do it in order to hide her dishonor, the maximum prison sentence will be imposed.

The same penalty will apply to parents who, for the same purpose and consent of the daughter, cause or cooperate in her abortion. If death or grave injuries result to the pregnant woman, the minimum prison sentence will be imposed on the parents.

Article 415: The doctor who, abusing his art, causes abortion or cooperates in it, will incur the greatest level of the penalties stated in the above mentioned articles and a fine of from 25,000 to 250,000 pesetas.

The sanction of the physician includes doctors, *matronas, practicantes,* and persons in possession of health degrees, and the sanction of pharmacists to their subordinates.

Article 417: Those guilty of abortion, whether or not in possession of a physician's or health degree, will be condemned to the penalties stated in the above mentioned articles, and moreover to special disqualifications, including those of giving any kind of services in clinics, gynecological consulting and health establishments, public or private.

These harsh sanctions already existed in the precepts of the law of January 24, 1941 [81], in which the following was affirmed:

Demographic policy is one of the fundamental preoccupations of our State. An effective demographic policy is not conceived without undertaking the problem of the thousands and thousands of lives which are frustrated before birth by criminal acts. The experience and evaluation of experts through competent scientific entities show this. . . . The Government, conscious of its responsibility, decides to combat the social crime which abortion represents and which impedes many thousands of Spaniards from being born annually.

Not long ago, a rigorous statistical study of abortion in Spain was carried out; it showed that abortion is much more frequent than official figures show [82]. According to official sources, the variation since 1941 has been:

Year	Legal Abortions	Abortions per 100 Live Births
1941	16,605	3.27
1950	18,753	3.35
1960	24,140	3.68
1970	16,810	2.56

Deleyto has complemented the official data with calculations about the number of abortions annually attributable to prostitution, a maximum of 40,000 and a minimum of 36,000; to extramarital relations, a maximum of 15,000 and a minimum of 10,000; and in marriage, between 12,000 and 14,000—concluding that it is not unrealistic to estimate a maximum figure of 114,000 abortions annually, that is, between six and seven times greater than the number of legal abortions and between 10 percent and 18 percent of all live births each year. The minimum, in his opinion, can be estimated at 73,000 [82, p. 23].

These data have awakened interest in the question. Among the multitude of commentaries it has stirred, it is fitting to remember the affirmation that "the practice of abortion occurs more among married women than among single women" [83].

There is a precise mandate on sterilization in the penal code. Article 418 states: "He who purposefully castrates another will be punished by penalty of minimum imprisonment." More specifically, part 2 of Article 420 of the same penal code (revised text of 1963, decree 691 of March 28, 1963) states that:

He who wounds, beats or mistreats another will be punished, guilty of grave injury, with the penalty of minimum imprisonment and a fine of from 5,000 to 50,000 pesetas, if as a result of the injury the offended party lost an eye or some principal member or became incapacitated due to the injury, or incapable of doing the work to which the injured party had been customarily dedicated prior to that time.

Illegitimacy and Adoption

In Spain, illegitimacy constitutes a less serious problem than in some Latin American countries. The number of illegitimate births for each 100 live births was 3.63 in 1901, 5.67 in 1930, 5.20 in 1950, and 1.36 in 1970. Thus, from a rather moderate proportion at the beginning of the century, which could be caused, in part, by defects in the Civil Register, the proportion of registered illegitimate births increased after 1915 until 1955, when it began to decline.

The Spanish law recognizes two kinds of illegitimate children: "natural children," that is, children of single or widowed parents who could have married with or without dispensation at the time of conception but who did not marry by their own choice; and those of second-, or inferior-, class parents (adulterers, incestuous partners, and the sacrilegious). There are differences in civil rights between legitimate and illegitimate children and between the two classes of illegitimate children [see 84].

In Spain, two kinds of adoption exist: simple and complete. The basic kind is complete adoption. The only ones who can adopt completely are conjugals who live together, who make a unanimous decision, and who have been married for more than five years. In complete adoption, the adopted child is on a par with the legitimate one. Adoption is a rarely used legal institution in Spanish society, as is shown by the annual number of adoptions in 1958–1967 [85, p. 103]:

Year	Number of Adoptions
1958	1,646
1961	1,568
1964	1,541
1967	1,515

In December 1969, under the High Council of Protection of Minors, a Spanish Association for the Protection of Adoption was established, which is beginning to function.

¶ MORTALITY AND HEALTH

Between 1930 and 1970, the main causes of mortality have been as follows:

Causes (per 1,000 deaths)	1930	1970
Infectious diseases	224.6	57.8
Heart diseases	92.8	214.4
Cancer	41.8	162.9

The number of persons per doctor has decreased from 882 in 1960 to 749 in 1970. The number of persons per health professional, not including nurses, dropped from 375 in 1960 to 347 in 1970. On the other hand, the percentage of hospital beds per 1,000 inhabitants rose from 44.4 in 1963 to 46.4 in 1970. The number of persons protected by health care under the scope of the Department of Social Service was 9,427,979 in 1953, and 18,264,542 in 1970, or 53.6 percent of the total population.

The Spanish Health Administration was founded with the law of November 23, 1855, and its fundamental complementary order, the General

Health Order, approved by Royal Decree on January 12, 1904. At that time, health care was of a preventive nature, and the administration acted through typically political means. The execution of technical services was charged predominantly to local entities.

The organization of the Department of Social Service marked the beginning of the state's assumption of health activity of a curative nature—an activity which had formerly been the concern of the church. The state initiated assistance to the needy on the basis of the law of 1822. The Royal Decree of May 14, 1852, which regulated the Law of Social Service of June 20, 1849, contains an initial planning of curative care. Concludes Morell Ocaña:

> Thus the Departments of Health and Social Service have taken different bases as points of departure. On the one hand, health administration tries to centralize its duties around a supraindividual aspect of health, assisting the individual when the problem is not specifically his but rather is or could be of the community: common hygiene, contagious disease. On the other hand, social service contemplates, atomistically, singular needy situations, combating them with a system of services indispensable to the reparation of an injiury that has already been produced; for this, of course, medical care is fundamental" [86, p. 146].

Three of the fundamental Spanish laws establish the right to health care. Thus, the Law of Principles of the National Movement, part 9, affirms that "all Spaniards have the right to benefits of social assistance and security." Article 28 of the Rights and Privileges of the Spanish People states: "The Spanish State guarantees workers the security of protection from misfortune and gives them the right to assistance in the cases of old-age, death, illness, maternity, labor accidents, crippling, unemployment and other risks which could be the object of social security." Finally, the Rights and Privileges of Labor, part 9, declares: " (1) The worker will be provided with the security of protection from misfortune. (2) Social security will increase for old age, crippling, maternity, labor accidents, professional illnesses, tuberculosis, and unemployment, tending toward the implantation of total security. It will primarily be responsible for giving a sufficient retirement to elderly workers."

The situation of health in Spain was studied and described on the occasion of the Second Economic and Social Development Plan (1968–1971), which contains very significant data about the subject of assistance in Spain. It affirms, for example, that "only 43.3 percent of the hospital beds in the country were inaugurated after 1900. Between 1900 and 1949 the total number increased to 1,561 beds, that is, an annual average of approximately 171. From 1949 to 1963 a notable acceleration in the growth rate was produced, reaching a yearly average of 2,100 beds, of which one-third corresponds to the Department of Sickness Security" [87, p. 28].[16]

The fundamental plan of the Law of Principles of National Health of November 25, 1944 [89], is now considered outdated. Its introduction states:

For the attainment of health and the strengthening of citizens, as well as for the physical betterment of the Spanish people, the State will be able to impose partial obligations and limitations. Therefore, for those cases and conditions which the laws and regulations anticipate, the following can be ordered: vaccinations, the use of preventive measures, individual recognition, isolation, hospitalization, vigilance, and other preventive sanitary measures and treatment; also, the confiscation of medication and other means of health care, the timely inspection of locales and means of transportation, the utilization of services, the carrying out of work and labor in unhealthy terrain, and the appointment of commercial activities for sanitary purposes.

Morell Ocaña made the following comments about this introduction:

Besides contemplating curative health measures by regulating some institutions dedicated to the struggle against very socially relevant diseases, the point of departure of the health law now in effect is the idea that the State, for reasons of public health, can impose limitations on the liberty and property of citizens and, moreover, help combat certain socially transcendent illnesses.

Opposing this concept of public health is, in the realm of true belief, . . . the affirmation that the so-called social activity of the State must amplify, against man, its sphere of action; that the center of gravity of that activity has been displaced from the idea of need to the idea of solidarity among all members of the community; that the primitive action of power, tending toward establishing an equilibrium between unequal individual situations, gives way to another in which all the members of a community are protected by means of a unified and group action of all citizens [86, pp. 158–159].

The present health law has aptly been classified as a "mixture of directives." In reality, it is a law of principles to which the organization and functioning of the state and local health administrations are to accommodate themselves. It traces an organic scheme and provides a fundamental program of action. It contains principles referring to the organization of the central services, the National Health Council, central health institutions, health personnel, and so forth. It is very important that its principles be directed against infectious diseases; health in ports, border towns, and means of transportation; tuberculosis; rheumatism and cardiopathology; malaria; trachoma; venereal diseases; leprosy and skin diseases; cancer; maternal and infant health; mental hygiene; veterinary health; medical

[16] See also [88].

assistance in relation to medical security; health propaganda; medical mineral baths and waters.

The Spanish Department of Health has begun acting by means of other important instruments. Thus, article 28 of the text of the Law of Social Security establishes the coordination of health activities in the field of preventive medicine. It states in part:

Along the lines of coordination, social security will be able to carry out the preparation and development of programs of preventive medicine which affect, totally or partially, the protected population, either exclusively or by collaborating in programs extending to the people of the country, of a general or limited nature.

We must also cite the Law of Hospitals of July 21, 1962, for the purpose of coordination in the area of curative assistance. Its express purpose was that of "coordinating the hospital situation in the country . . . interested above all in the functional connections of the various hospitals" [90, p. 13].[17]

The Third Economic and Social Development Plan (1972–1975) has attempted to establish a health policy. Thus, article 24 of decree 1541 of June 15, 1972, establishes that the action of the state in matters of health and social assistance will be oriented toward establishing a hospital policy that permits one to obtain optimal efficiency of the available resources and installations, and also to reform, order, and plan national and local health.

In the text of the development plan, there are some indicators of infant death and the proportion of doctors per 10,000 inhabitants. It notes that the participation of the health services in the gross national product represented 1.4 percent in 1970 as opposed to 1.1 percent in 1968 [4, p. 18].[18]

The guidelines of the development plan specify, on the one hand, the promotion of rural and commercial health and, on the other, the coordination of hospital care [4, p. 149]. In his recent speech before the Spanish Parliament [92], the Minister of the Interior, on whose department the Spanish health department depends, made it known that a new law overruling the outdated Law of Principles of National Health of November 25, 1944, would be necessary, but that, in his opinion, the creation of a Ministry of Health was not absolutely necessary, in spite of the fact that various sides of the medical profession have criticized the lack of unity of action in health matters, because of the many competing organizations. With regard to the organization of the Spanish Department of Health, a recent order creating an autonomous organization depending on the Department of Health

---

[17] This is cited in [86, pp. 163–164].

[18] A monograph on the papers of the third plan has been published; see [91].

was published, which groups together a series of activities that previously were separate [93].

¶ LABOR AND EMIGRATION

Labor.
Decree 1541 of June 15, 1972, by which the revised text of the law of the Economic and Social Development Plan was approved (*Official Bulletin of the State* of June 16, 1972), dedicates various articles to labor and social promotion policies. Specifically, Article 30, part 1, affirms that

The action of the State in matters of labor policies will be directed toward guaranteeing full employment, toward progressive incorporation of female labor, toward giving to workers access to property in its various forms and toward a greater participation of salaries in the national revenue. Also, the adaptation of invalids and abnormal persons to the labor force will be promoted.

In the same article (part 3), it is determined that a series of measures for maintaining full employment will be taken. Among them are: intensify plans for professional attainment; facilitate the placement of elderly workers; direct and assist internal and external migratory movements; and promote the creation of child care centers in order to permit an increase in the economically active female population. These are the principal aspects of the Spanish labor policy that influence demographic policy and, therefore, deserve some consideration. The Ministry of Labor presented to the Syndical Executive Committee a decree on employment policy that appeared in the *Official Bulletin of the State* on November 15, 1972, in which the means for implementation of the labor policy are established [94].

The standards are a continuation of what had been established in the Rights and Privileges of Labor Act of March 9, 1938, modified on January 10, 1967. Part 2 established that "the State is obliged to exercise a constant and efficient plan of action in defense of the worker, his life, and his job. It will suitably limit the length of the working day so that it is not excessive and will grant to the worker all types of guarantees along defensive and humanitarian lines. Especially, it will prohibit night work for women and children, will regulate work at home, and will free the married women from workshops and factories." The law is very precise in stating that "all Spaniards have the right to work. The execution of this right is a primary aim of the State."

The growth of the economically active population in Spain throughout the twentieth century is shown in Table 6. Since 1900, the active population has increased by some 5 million persons. Nevertheless, the growth of

TABLE 6.

Growth of the Economically Active Population, Spain, 1900–1970

Years	Active Population (in thousands)	Activity Rate (percent)	
		Men	Women
1900	7,546.8	67.83	14.51
1910	7,581.5	67.42	9.98
1920	7,962.4	66.81	9.37
1930	8,772.5	66.25	9.16
1940	9,219.7	65.28	8.29
1950	10,793.1	67.44	11.78
1960	11,816.6	64.24	13.49
1965	12,065.2	60.19	18.18
1966	12,044.6	59.78	17.81
1967	12,161.6	59.31	17.64
1968	12,263.5	59.38	17.44
1969	12,363.5	59.14	17.45
1970	12,854.5	58.90	18.10

SOURCE: See [1, tables 21 and 22].

the active population has been less than the growth of the total population of the country, which means that the total activity rates—that is, the percentages of active persons in the total population—are decreasing constantly.

An increase in the dependent population occurred largely because of the greater decrease in the death rate than in the birth rate. At the same time, the extension of social security benefits has permitted the retirement of a larger number of persons and, together with the increase in the rate and age limit for schooling, has collaborated in reducing the population involved in productive work. The provinces and regions whose dependency rate is greatest are those that show the lowest activity rate, examples of which are the Canary Islands and Andalusia [95].

The distribution of the active population by age groups shows that 82.97 percent in 1965 were aged twenty-five to sixty-five years, indicating the aging of the active population.

The active population aged fourteen to twenty-nine years of age is decreasing, even in absolute figures, but the group between twenty and twenty-four is experiencing an important increase, which reveals that the individuals begin work at age twenty-one or twenty-two, or upon completion of military service. Also, it is this age group that exhibits a greater activity rate and, at the same time, a greater rate of growth of the activity rate.

Parallel with the delay in the age of incorporation into the labor force is the loss of the traditional preponderance of the primary sector in the Spanish economy, accompanied by a corresponding change in the composition of the active population [96]. This indicates that the process of industrialization appeared rather late in Spain and seems to have become consolidated in recent years. It must not be forgotten that a great part of the surplus of the agricultural population is absorbed by those industrial sectors that require less skill, such as mining and construction, and that many subsectors of services pertain to occupations related more to economic underdevelopment than to an increase in the industrial sector.

On the other hand, it is necessary to take into account the composition by age of the active population in the principal economic sectors. The extraordinarily older age of the agrarian population is undoubtedly related to the phenomenon of the rural exodus of the younger population. The population active in the tertiary sector is also older, although less so. This may be because the life expectancy for those in this population is higher and, therefore, so is the average age. Moreover, in this sector, retirement is less frequent or nonexistent. Thus, the population dedicated to commerce is younger than the total working population, but the age group sixty-five and over also is greater, which seems to indicate that commerce constitutes one of the few occupations in which a person may continue working to an advanced age. The population of the industrial sector is clearly the youngest, but the subsectors in which skill is lower absorb an older population. Such is the case with mining and construction, sectors filled primarily from the agricultural population.

The analysis of the composition of the active population by sex introduces us directly to the problem of the work of the Spanish woman. Generally, Spain still has a rather small proportion of women in the economically active population. It is stabilized at about 18 percent of the total female population, whereas the countries in which the active population in the primary sector is low normally have rates of active female population that vary between 25 percent and 35 percent [97]. In the socialistic countries, industrial as well as agricultural, the proportion of women who work also surpasses that of Spain and is estimated at 40 percent or more.

The difficulties that women have in finding rewarding jobs are related to age and civil status. Mir de la Cruz estimates that "at the present time 64% of the single women over 15 years of age work, but only 7% of the married women and 12% of the widows do so" [98].

Finally, it should be noted that the average unemployment estimated in 1971 of the total active population was less than 2 percent (240,582 persons), of which 70 percent of unemployed were registered in industry.

All of this information should be placed in relation to legal standards that regulate labor in Spain. Thus, as regards the minimum work age, the labor contract of minors is regulated in Spain by the Labor Contract Law, which prohibits all work, except agriculture and family care, to those less than fourteen years of age. The law also establishes that those between fourteen and sixteen cannot accept night jobs (between 8:00 PM and 6:00 AM) or underground or dangerous jobs. Those under eighteen cannot accept jobs that could endanger their morals. The ages of this latter group were raised in July 1957 to twenty-one, for various kinds of work.

Many of the labor standards for minors allow for a wide margin of arbitrary decisions on the part of the labor or governing authorities. Article 176 of the Labor Contract Law states that work in public entertainment may be performed by those under sixteen, with prior authorization from the Labor Commissioner and permission from the Police Department; and those under fourteen may work in public shows for children's functions if there is no physical or moral danger. At the same time, the decree of 1957 established labor prohibitions that are absolute at some times and relative at others. Article 1 prohibits "work which is detrimental to the health of the workers, if it implies excessive physical strength or are prejudicial to personal circumstances." Article 4 establishes administrative discretion for prohibiting certain unanticipated work as well as for reducing or palliating certain legally established prohibitions.

Although the estimate of those who break these regulations is very unreliable, it is calculated that there are about 60,000 minors who are working and that there must be many more than 100,000 under eighteen who are in passive violation of the laws. The predominant trend is in the opposite direction, influenced by the International Labor Organization, which is trying to raise the minimum work age to fifteen instead of fourteen.

In regard to workers over forty, a decree of April 30, 1970 prohibits discrimination for reasons of age, sets the criteria that must be followed with jobs reserved for them, and assists in professional retraining. In 1971, an order was passed that established appropriate standards and procedures for obtaining jobs by workers over forty years of age [99].

As for protection of abnormal persons, the decree of April 9, 1970 sets adequate measures for their adaptation to professional work. Special consideration was given to the fact that, in other countries, there are Spanish families with abnormal members who cannot benefit from any help or assistance in the country in which they reside, and therefore, protection is extended to them.

A ministerial order of November 24, 1971 established standards of employment for the disabled. Another order of the same date regulated the social services concerned with the rehabilitation and recuperation of invalids; recognized and classified these persons, their medical rehabilitation, orientation, formation, and readaptation; and assisted invalids in health, social, and family areas.

In 1970, sex discrimination was outlawed; the new laws concerning labor rights of the working woman were based on the ideal of complete equality with men in employment. According to the decree, a woman has the legal right to the same job as a man for the same pay, although this does not always occur in reality. As for a married woman, her services can be contracted with the authorization of her husband, which it is presumed will be granted if she has been previously employed.

Besides benefits awarded by social security to women in specific cases, the labor laws have established a series of measures pertaining to the reduction of heavy work and the regulation of time schedules.

Since 1919, the maximum normal work week in Spain has been established at forty-eight hours, distributed eight hours per day. Nevertheless, when the type of work does not permit a uniform daily distribution, or for the convenience of employers and employees, with prior authorization from the Provincial Labor Delegation the work schedule can be distributed differently, under the condition that the workday not exceed nine hours.

A law of July 26, 1957, sets those industries and jobs—very numerous— prohibited to women as well as to minors, by reason of danger or health. In regular work, women have the same right to overtime pay as men. Moreover, it is higher for women. In December 1971, the National Commission of Female Labor was established with a wide range of functions (study, consultation, and evaluation) in matters of labor policy.

Emigration.

In the nineteenth century, emigration was understood as a phenomenon that had to be channeled to put an end to profiteering [*100*]. In the Constitution of 1869, for the first time, the freedom of immigration and emigration was recognized (Articles 25 and 26); the Constitution of 1876 returned to the principle of prohibition, recognizing, nevertheless, freedom of immigration. Finally, the Constitution of 1931 returned to express recognition (Article 31).

The law of December 21, 1907, attempted to terminate illegal activities, watch over ships, require the fulfillment of contracts made with emigrants, and establish a service and repatriation fund, principles that were later reiterated by the Royal Decree of November 6, 1914, which established that "tutelage and protection of the emigrant should be sought, considering him as an economically and intellectually weak human being." The most radical indirect measure for reducing emigration was set forth in the Law of Colonization of August 30, 1907, whose Preamble stated that the objective was that of "giving roots to those families in the nation deprived of means of work and capital in order to meet their needs, decreasing emigration, populating the country areas, and cultivating uncultivated or deficiently exploited public lands, by means of dividing public lands among the families of poor laborers."

In 1953, Gonzalez-Rothvoss summarized the available data on emigration of the Spanish population between 1850 and 1950 [101]. As has been noted, the period witnessed great legislative activity in support of promoting emigration. Between 1853 and 1903, according to the historian Nadal, "Spanish legislation passed from one extreme to another, successively eliminating all obstacles which opposed the exit of citizens" [6, p. 680].

The period immediately preceding World War I (1914–1918) witnessed a continuation of emigration at a high level. In the 1930s, the traditional currents of Spanish emigration were halted but began to flow again in 1946. After 1906, Spanish emigration was directed especially to the European countries. The evolution of emigration to Europe is shown in Table 7. The statistics do not take into account illegal emigration which, although it may not have much importance in overseas emigration, does account for a minimum of 35 percent to 37 percent of emigration to Europe, according to the most conservative estimates [102].

TABLE 7.

Continental Emigration, Spain, 1959–1971

Year	Total	Emigration	
		Permanent	Temporary
1959	31,272	7,217	24,055
1960	44,050	12,712	31,338
1961	125,937	59,243	66,694
1962	155,949	65,336	68,624
1963	165,573	83,728	76,180
1964	205,278	102,146	103,496
1965	180,453	74,539	106,562
1966	155,232	56,795	98,437
1967	124.530	25,911	98,619
1968	169,721	66,699	103,022
1969	207,268	100,840	106,428
1970	203,887	97,657	106,230
1971	213,930	113,702	100,228
Total	2,056,358	866,525	1,089,833

SOURCES: Ministry of Labor. *Report on Emigration, 1967–1968*. Madrid, 1970. And *Controlled Spanish Emigration: 1970 Statistics*. Madrid, 1971.

Permanent emigration grew continuously until 1964. Between 1965 and 1967, emigration declined but began to increase again in 1968, 1969, 1970, and 1971. Temporary emigration reached its height in 1965 and stabilized after this date. Nevertheless, the drastic decline in real permanent emigration, according to the statistics of the receiving countries, did not occur until 1967, whereas the total temporary emigration continued growing until 1965 and experienced a slight decrease in 1966 and 1967. In accordance with the latest data, the emigratory trend continued until November 1971, when it reached 5.8 per 1,000 active persons, whereas in the same month in 1970, it affected only 3.7 per 1,000 active persons.

The statistics on emigration of the receiving countries differ substantially from those furnished by the Spanish Institute of Emigration. Thus, between 1960 and 1967, whereas the institute estimates a total of 480,410 permanent emigrants, the receiving countries set the figure at 1,031,683. These latter figures are always higher, and it can be assumed that real Spanish emigration is approximately 214 percent over that of the official number. As for temporary emigration, there were 649,878 persons in 1960–1967 according to the Spanish Institute of Emigration and a total of 847,641 according to the receiving countries.

Naturally, incorrect data make an interpretation difficult, but we can see a certain relationship between the expansive economic situation of 1964 and after and the decrease in emigration, which later increased again. It can be affirmed that emigration has affected more than 2 million persons during the past thirteen years, although it must be kept in mind that more than 1 million persons have been temporary emigrants. Real emigration is probably much greater.

Continental emigration has centered in three countries: France, Germany, and Switzerland. These three presently absorb more than 90 percent of the total Spanish emigration. The growth of emigration to Switzerland is the most important, although Holland and France also show a growth rate higher than the average.

Emigration to countries in the Americas and Europe has characteristics derived from the peculiarities of the demand for labor in both groups of countries. Overseas emigration, because of geographic distance, has been and continues to be permanent. The demand for work in those countries has been linked to agricultural and commercial needs, since these occupations require a long period of adaptation and maturation. On the other hand, emigration to Europe always is viewed as temporary in nature, which makes it possible to take vacations to the homeland and which responds to a demand for salaried work, especially in industry.

The data from a survey taken by the Spanish Institute of Emigration concerning factors affecting Europe emigration support some of the affirmations. Thus, 99.3 percent of a sample of 6,802 interviewees in 1966 answered that they intended to return to Spain. Furthermore, 46.7 percent had no intention of being emigrants for more than a year, and 24.2 percent did not wish to be so for more than two years [103].

The contrast between overseas emigrants and those to Europe according to age, sex, and other variables also confirms our conclusions since, as we have already seen, emigration to Europe is composed basically of males, whereas overseas emigration is of the family type in which the wife and children accompany the male. Children under fifteen accompany their parents overseas, but not to European countries.

We have indicated previously that the number of Spaniards residing outside of Spain in 1970 reached 3,360,895; in the meantime, the influx of foreign currency coming from our European emigrants has been a great economic aid to Spanish development [104].

As we have mentioned, after 1959, the process of Spanish emigration increased in volume and varied in geographic destination, for which reason the approval of a new law was necessary, which has governed migration for a relatively short time. Law 33 of July 21, 1971, had the following effect [105]:

(1) Stated the agreement of the state to exercise protective action during the entire emigratory process, giving to the Ministry of Labor the general task of developing the government's policy.
(2) Regulated in detail the entire contractual and operational process of programmed emigration internally and gave considerably more assistance externally.
(3) Endeavored to strengthen state intervention in emigrant transportation.
(4) Emphasized the importance of international agreements as the only instruments through which Spanish workers can be guaranteed equality or assimilation of labor rights and of social security abroad in respect to the nationals in the receiving country by means of government agreements to supply any insufficiency in the coverage of risks.
(5) For the purpose of strengthening the ties that bind all nations of the Spanish community and of contributing to the impetus of their economic and social development, created a Qualified Emigration Service and encouraged social and technical cooperation agreements.
(6) Introduced specific modifications in the structure and functions of the Spanish Institute of Emigration.

In reply to a Member of Parliament, the government recently stated that "the total number of workers in Europe at the end of 1972 reached 824,000 including those in France, of which some 200,000 correspond to a previous, older emigration, completely integrated into the country" [106]. For its part, the Report of the OECD (Organization for Economic Cooperation and Development) on the Spanish economy (1973) shows the great paradox between the high growth rate during the 1960s caused by money sent to Spain by the emigrants and the fact that Spain has not created any jobs for its emigrants.

One last point should be made. For every 200 Spaniards, one foreigner lives in Spain, according to the latest official data from the National Statistics Institute. The number of foreigners who live in Spain has increased in the five-year period 1968–1972 by 20 percent, reaching 131,000 in 1968 and approximately 160,000 in 1972 [107].

By nationalities, the majority are Portuguese (26,000), followed by the French (16,000), Germans (14,500), British (a little more than 14,000), Cubans (11,000), North Americans (more than 9,000), Italians (9,000), Venezuelans (almost 8,000), and Argentinians (about 6,000). By continents, the Europeans lead with almost 100,000, equal to 86 percent of the total number of foreign residents. It is calculated that over 57,000 foreigners now work in Spain, excluding illegal workers. The largest number of permits is given to the English.

The existence of a great number of illegal workers should also be remarked on, among which at least 30,000 Portuguese have been mentioned, and according to newspaper articles, there are some 30,000 North Africans in Barcelona. The living conditions of these workers are not very humane and their legal situation is not determined in any concrete manner [108].

¶ REGIONAL POLICY
As Professor Garcia Barbancho has shown [109], the phenomenon of internal migration is not new in Spain, although its average intensity has increased greatly, as the following figures for *partidos judiciales*[19] show:

Years	Emigrants
1901–1910	94,903
1911–1920	87,819
1921–1930	116,893
1931–1940	80,365
1941–1950	105,412
1951–1960	229,527
1961–1970	369,200

The decade 1921–1930 also recorded a large rural exodus. However, there have been other changes—apart from intensity—in internal migration, such as the generalization of the phenomenon, since the southern

[19] A *partido judicial* is a territorial division composed of one or more municipalities but less extended than a province.

regions of Spain are now in first place: "Emigration," writes Garcia Barbancho, "seems to have mobilized those persons who were traditionally more sedentary."

The statistics on internal migration were not collected systematically in Spain until 1962; since this date, it has been possible to conduct more rigorous analyses of the process. The figures of internal emigration in the decade of the 1960s (as shown in Table 8) record maximum numbers in 1964 and 1965 and a minimum in 1966. In all, it can be estimated that, in the nine years before 1970, nearly 3.5 million Spaniards changed residence, not counting external emigration.

In the decade 1960–1970, the major immigration centers of the country were the three large urban nuclei of the interior: Madrid, Zaragoza, and Seville—to which was added, in the period 1966–1970, Valladolid—and the peripheral provinces of Catalonia, Valencia, the Basque Provinces, and Navarra (whose migratory balance, although very low, is increasing).

On the other hand, those provinces with a definitely negative migratory balance also stand out. Of these, in 1950–1960, four provinces had a natural growth rate so intense that it compensated for the drain of the emigrant population and produced for them a growth rate higher than the average. These provinces were Cadiz, Huelva, Seville, and Las Palmas.

The relationship between population loss in absolute figures and emigration is clearer if analyzed by municipalities, which show the depopulation of rural in favor of urban areas (see Table 9).

TABLE 8.

Internal Emigration, Spain, 1962–1970

Year	Number of Emigrants	Index of Variation (1962 = 100)
1962	347,279	100
1963	442,104	127
1964	495,202	142
1965	445,548	128
1966	227,608	80
1967	379,916	109
1968	366,957	106
1969	384,644	111
1970	380,351	110
Total	3,519,609	

SOURCES: Banesto. *Spanish Market Yearbook, 1971.* Madrid, 1971, p. 489. National Statistics Institute. *Spanish Statistical Yearbook, 1970.* Madrid, 1971.

TABLE 9.

Migratory Balances of the Municipalities, Spain, 1961—August 1969
(according to population size)

Municipalities	Net Migration	Percentage of Total
Less than 100,000 inhabitants	979,976	30.76
From 10,000 to 100,000 inhabitants	262,079	8.23
More than 100,000 inhabitants	717,895	22.53
Total emigrants	3,186,141	100.00

SOURCE: See [42, p. 578].

The most urban provinces receive emigrants from the most rural provinces. This is the case in Andalusia, Aragon (except Zaragoza), Castille (except Madrid), Extremadura, Galicia, Leon, and Murcia. However, of these regions and provinces, even the following capitals are losing population: Almeria, Granada, Jaen, Malaga, Huesca, Teruel, Ciudad Real, Cuenta, Guadalajara, Toledo, Avila, Zaragoza, Badajoz, Caceres, Albacete, and Murcia; except for Malaga and Murcia, these are the smallest capitals of Spain.

Naturally, the most important point is the measure of how such migratory movements have been affected by regional policies. When migration began between 1950 and 1960, the first reaction of the government was to contain it by a parallel initiation of a series of development schemes for some geographic zones, which differed from a general program of economic development on a national scale. Thus, there arose the plans of Badajoz and Jaen, that of Badajoz approved by the law of April 7, 1952, and that of Jaen by the law of July 7, 1953. A similar plan was approved by the law of May 12, 1956, for the islands of Hierro and Fuerte Ventura in the archipelago of the Canary Islands.

Inasmuch as the demographic dynamics of internal settling negated the effectiveness of the partial plans, other significant laws were passed. For example, the Decree of August 23, 1957, of the President, regarding illegal settlement in Madrid, stated the following:

The constant flow to Madrid of families from other capitals and towns in the nation generally lacking economic means, a specific profession, and a place to live, carries with it a systematic construction of shanties, caves and similar structures in the periphery of the population, occupying areas next to approved or projected urban developments and transportation [110].

In view of the facts, Article 1 states that "all persons or families who wish to move to the capital of the nation will inform the Civil Governor of the province through the Mayor of his town that he has adequate housing in Madrid."

During the same year, in the Plan of Social Urgency of Madrid, approved by the law of November 13, 1957, the Ministry of Housing ordered the construction of 60,000 houses in Madrid. The ministry

... must limit the uncontrolled growth of the capital, which on the one hand should be directed toward impeding immigration and on the other toward putting a halt to the formation of inhumane suburbs. The future of Madrid's expansion should be in satellite cities and not in an indefinite prolongation of its urban core [111].

Regional development became one of the four basic objectives of the First Plan of Economic and Social Development, approved by law 194 of December 28, 1963, for the four-year period 1964–1967. The preferred plan of action during the period of the first plan was implemented through a policy of development poles, or zones.* The law established two kinds of zones: (1) promotional, located in Burgos and Huelva, cities in which industry was practically nonexistent but which contained natural and human resources for conversion into nuclei of industrialization; and (2) regional development zones, situated in regions with low revenue levels, with excessive dependence on agriculture, and with strong emigration. In this manner, the zones of La Coruna, Vigo, Valladolid, Zaragoza, and Seville were created. The benefits of the Industrial Law of Preferential Interest of December 2, 1963, were applied to the new industries and activities situated in the zones, as well as another group of incentives. The technique of poles, or zones, was complemented by a policy of structuring some regions in which development was inferior to the national level and was dependent on the primary sector; these plans were specifically for Tierra de Campos and Campo de Gibraltar.

The Second Plan of Economic and Social Development, corresponding to the four-year period 1968–1971, created the zones of Oviedo, Logrono, Cordoba, and Granada. With the creation of the zone of Villagarcia de Arosa (decree of August 22, 1970), there were twelve zones of industrial development. The last five are of ten years' duration.

The regional policy followed during the first and second plans of development has been the object of much criticism. There are those who feel that true regional planning began in 1959 and materialized and became consolidated with the First Economic and Social Development Plan, before

---

* Note from translator: A large area benefitting from facilities (fiscal, administrative, transportation, and so on) for the installation of industries and thus promoting development.

which time there were only scanty and dispersed emergency measures. Others feel that, since 1939, there has existed an authentic policy of regional development, although this is contrary to the official texts [112]. Something of this is revealed in the correct observation of H. W. Richardson that the most outstanding fact about the poles is that they are not concentrated in the most backward regions. The poles are conceived as an extension of the national and sectorial planning strategy but not as an instrument for the development of the poorest regions [113].

Not long ago, the Bank of Bilbao, in an estimate of provincial distribution of the national revenue of Spain, formulated the following conclusions:

The results of this investigation show how in the past two years we have tended toward concentrating the product and the population in provinces with the highest level of development. Nevertheless, the internal migratory movements, causing a decrease in the population level of depressed provinces, have given rise to a reduction in the disparities between productivity and revenue per person of the most and least developed provinces. Those provinces located nearer to the most developed ones are those that have shown a greater growth rate. The most depressed, as a consequence of the migration of part of the population, have obtained average production levels and higher revenue levels, even when their total participation in the national picture has remained visibly deteriorating. In conclusion, we are heading toward a greater concentration of population, production, and rent from an overall point of view and toward a decentralization of personal revenue from a relative point of view [114].

These results clearly contradict the policy of regional development in Spain and imply failure as an operative instrument of regional development in the zones of development and promotion established by the first plan. The conclusions recently reached by Richardson reveal the need to do a more detailed analysis of this complex policy, in which practice has contradicted promises.

A recent study of the OCED pointed out some additional difficulties of the system of promotion zones, development zones, and decongestion areas. First, the numbers of years devoted to each program are too short to permit a profound change; second, it is necessary to establish a delicate balance between size and variety of undertakings, paying particular attention to a potential decrease; and third, the procedure for attracting people entails great delays in development [115].

In the Third Economic and Social Development Plan for the period 1972–1975, the bases for a new regional development policy were established, in which it was "conceived as a channel for avoiding excessive differences in the standard of living of the various Spanish provinces and for overcoming discrimination between the ways of life in the country and in the city, using the territory as the protagonist of development and pushing for an optimum reevaluation of space" [116]. The plan proposed to give to each one of the regions and districts the means necessary for stimulating and accelerating growth and for permitting their inhabitants to live a life of dignity. The stated objectives of the policy of regional development were as follows:

(1) To obtain the greatest possible growth of the national product by means of the best allotment of productive resources in the territory.
(2) To reduce interregional differences in economic and welfare levels.
(3) To improve the integration of regional economies among themselves for the purpose of obtaining more solid economies.
(4) To diminish the inequality of job opportunities among the different regions in Spain.
(5) To facilitate a closer integration of Spain with international markets.

In order to reach these objectives, a series of measures of regional development were established, which may be listed in four major groups:

(1) The restructuring of the territory, meaning a reevaluation and new set of priorities.
(2) Productive development, by encouraging each one of the areas of national territory to be perfected and developed in accordance with its specific vocation.
(3) The attainment of an infrastructure, services, and equipment adequate for present needs.
(4) Selective regional programs.

The third plan publicly favors and recommends, therefore, regional and urban development seeking, through a hierarchical system of cities and towns, a more human and rational settlement of the population. The policy of segmentation of the territories seeks the formation of an urban system so that the spatial organization of the country is transformed into a union of metropolitan areas intimately related among themselves and with dependent urban and rural areas. For the purposes of programming the urban framework of the nation, the rural nuclei are the last link in a chain that allows the inhabitants of the rural areas to take advantage of the process of development begun in the metropolitan areas.

The diffusion of the benefits of economic and social development is stated through a selective policy of population nuclei which, by geographic situation, economic resources, human potential, and possibilities for the future, permit the extension and diffusion to all areas of the country the life that is normal in the metropolitan and urban nuclei. The objectives of selection can be stated as follows: Acknowledgment of a hierarchy of population settlements, concentration of services, and coordination of investments.

As a consequence, six large metropolitan areas and seventeen other urban and metropolitan areas have been chosen. Each of the large metropolitan areas (Madrid, Barcelona, Valencia, Bilbao, Seville, and Zaragoza) will reach a population of more than 750,000 inhabitants by 1980. The other urban and metropolitan areas will reach 250,000 inhabitants by 1980. Furthermore, cities of an average size were defined as those whose estimated population by 1980 will be between 75,000 and 250,000 inhabitants, as well as large tourist zones, which will house more than 150,000 persons including permanent and temporary residents. The rural nuclei are classified in three levels: main districts, nuclei for expansion, and dependent nuclei.

In the opinion of the work group of the OECD that has examined the Spanish regional policy, the promotion of a regional plan of action in the field of development policy in Spain is an important element, and the third plan constitutes a step forward in relation to the previous plans. Nevertheless, the present situation is in great confusion because, although it recognizes the failure of the previous regional policies, concrete means that should permit the restructuring and orderly arrangement of the territory have yet to be formulated by the Third Economic and Social Development Plan. Perhaps the most exact and authoritative description of the present situation was presented by the Director General of Industrial Promotion of the Ministry of Industry in a recent symposium: "We are in a vacuum regarding the availability of instruments of regional development" [117].

REFERENCES

1. Salustiano del Campo. *Analysis of Population in Spain.* Barcelona: Ariel, 1972. (In Spanish.)

2. Juan Antonio Lacomba. "Demographic structure and social dynamics in the Spain of the nineteenth century." In J. L. Aranguren et al. *Social History of Spain, Nineteenth Century.* Madrid: Guadiana, 1972. (In Spanish.)

3. Adolfo Serigó. *The Evolution of Infant Mortality in Spain.* Madrid, 1964. (In Spanish.)

4. *Third Economic and Social Development Plan, 1972–1975.* Madrid, 1971. (In Spanish.)

5. Office of the Development Plan. *Study of Spanish Population.* Madrid, 1972. (In Spanish.)

6. Jorge Nadal. "History of the population of Spain." Appendix to M. Reinhard and A. Armengaud. *History of World Population.* Barcelona: Ariel, 1966. (In Spanish.)

7. William J. Leasure. "Factors involved in the decline of fertility in Spain, 1900–1950." *Population Studies,* no. 3, 1963.

8. André Mounier. "The Spanish population." In *Readings on the Spanish Economy,* Juan Velarde Fuertes (ed.). Madrid: Editorial Gredos, 1969, pp. 255–269. (In Spanish.)

9. M. Artola. *Origins of Contemporary Spain.* Madrid: IEP, 1959, "Introduction." (In Spanish.)

10. J. Mercader. "Bourgeoisie, industrialization, the working class." Book 1, volume 4 of *The Social and Economic History of Spain and America,* edited by J. Vicens Vives. Barcelona, 1958. (In Spanish.)

11. Thomas R. Malthus. *Essay on the Principle of Population.* Translated by José María Noguera and Joaquín Miguel, under the direction of Dr. Eusebio María del Valle, Professor of Political Economics at the University of Madrid. Madrid, 1846. (In Spanish.)

12. J. Ros Jimeno. "The decline in the birth rate and its causes." *International Journal of Sociology,* September 1944. (In Spanish.)

13. J. Ros Jimeno. "Birth and the future development of the population in Spain." *International Journal of Sociology,* no. 1, 1943. (In Spanish.)

14. J. Ros Jimeno. "Some aspects of birth in Spain." *International Journal of Sociology,* no. 67, September 1959. (In Spanish.)

15. *Words from the Caudillo, April 19, 1937–December 31, 1938.* Second edition. Barcelona: Editorial Fe, 1939. (In Spanish.)

16. *Official Bulletin of the State,* no. 42, February 17, 1968. (In Spanish.)

17. Manuel Ramírez Jiménez. *Pressure Groups in the Second Spanish Republic.* Madrid: Tecnos, 1969. (In Spanish.)

18. *Pueblo.* Madrid, January 15, 1972. (In Spanish.)

19. *Official Bulletin of the State,* no. 95, April 21, 1967. (In Spanish.)

20. Erasmus. "Marriage: Problems." *Pueblo.* Madrid, June 20, 1972. (In Spanish.)

21. Joint Pastoral Letter Entitled "Christ Is Our Peace." *Ya.* Madrid, December 28, 1972. (In Spanish.)

22. Juan Diez Nicolás. "Evolution and foresight of birth in Spain." *Annals of Social and Economic Morals,* vol. 14. (In Spanish.)

23. Publications Service, Ministry of Labor. *Large Families; Law Regulations; Complementary Dispositions.* Madrid, 1972. (In Spanish.)

24. *Ya.* Madrid, October 1 and 3, 1972. (In Spanish.)

25. Miguel Hernainz Márquez. *Elementary Treatise on Labor Law,* vol. 2. (In Spanish.)

26. *Economic Information.* Madrid, December 2, 1972. (In Spanish.)

27. *General Rules of Social Security 2: Rules of Protection to the Family.* Madrid, 1967. (In Spanish.)

28. *Ya.* Madrid, October 6, 1972. (In Spanish.)

29. V. G. Leronés. "The family movement in Spain." *Social Documentation,* vol. 3, no. 4 (October–December 1971). (In Spanish.)

30. Gabriel Elorriaga. *The Family in Spain.* Madrid: SIE, 1965. (In Spanish.)

31. "Interview with D. Vicente Soriano Garcés, President of the National Federa-

tion of Associations of Large Families." *Ya.* Madrid, March 15, 1973. (In Spanish.)

32. *Ya.* Madrid, March 14, 1973. (In Spanish.)

33. *Ya.* Madrid, March 18, 1973. (In Spanish.)

34. *Ya.* Madrid, February 23, 1973. (In Spanish.)

35. "A serious problem: Abortion and contraceptives in Spain." *Sábado Gráfico,* March 17, 1973. (In Spanish.)

36. Questions of attorney D. Antonio Castro Villacañas. "Official Bulletin of the Spanish Parliament," no. 1271. *Ya.* Madrid, April 17, 1973. (In Spanish.)

37. *Ya.* Madrid, February 20, 1973. (In Spanish.)

38. *Ya.* Madrid, January 17, 1973. (In Spanish.)

39. Daniel. "Family planning." *Pueblo.* Madrid, August 18, 1970. (In Spanish.)

40. Amando de Miguel. "The subject should not be taboo: The demographic explosion continues." *Madrid,* December 12, 1970. (In Spanish.)

41. J. A. Echague. "The myth of overpopulation: In Spain there is no demographic explosion." *Nuevo Diario,* December 12, 1968. (In Spanish.)

42. FOESSA. *Sociological Report on the Social Situation in Spain.* Madrid: Euramérica, 1970. (In Spanish.)

43. Manual Ferrer Regales. "The slogan of world population growth." *Nuestro Tiempo,* no. 205–206, July–August 1971. (In Spanish.)

44. Salvador Carvera Enguix. "Sexual and educational conditioning." *Nuestro Tiempo,* no. 205–206, July–August 1971. (In Spanish.)

45. *Informaciones.* Madrid, December 18, 1972. (In Spanish.)

46. José Luis Sampedro. *The Economic Forces of Our Times.* Madrid: Guadarrama, 1967. (In Spanish.)

47. Father Jesús M. Vazquez, O.P. *The Contemporary Spanish Church.* (Forthcoming.) (In Spanish.)

48. Pius XII. "Speech to Catholic Midwives." October 29, 1951. (In Spanish.)

49. Vicente Enrique Tarancón, Bishop of Solsona. *The Family Today.* Madrid: Euramérica, 1958. (In Spanish.)

50. Monsignor Juan Hervás, Bishop of Ciudad Real. *Birth Control or Large Family? Criteria for Keeping Up-to-Date.* Madrid: Folletos Mundo Cristiano, 1965. (In Spanish.)

51. *Ecclesia,* no. 1418, November 30, 1968. (In Spanish.)

52. "Is it impossible to comply with the provisions of the *Human Vitae?*" *Ecclesia,* no. 1415, November 9, 1968. (In Spanish.)

53. "Conjugal love and responsible transmission of life." *Ecclesia,* no. 1417, November 23, 1968. (In Spanish.)

54. *Ya.* Madrid, June 18, 1971. (In Spanish.)

55. "Diagnosis of faith and morality in Spain." *Pentecostas,* no. 27, September–December 1971. (In Spanish.)

56. *ABC.* Madrid, December 13, 1970. (In Spanish.)

57. *Telva,* no. 105, February 1, 1968. (In Spanish.)

58. Enrique Mirst Magdalena. "Responsible parenthood." *Triunfo*, February 23, 1967. (In Spanish.)

59. *Birth Control and Regulation: The "Dossier" of Rome*. Barcelona: Nova Terra, 1967. (In Spanish.)

60. Enrique Mirst Magdalena. "1968 religious panorama." *Spain, 1969*. Madrid: Guadiana, 1969. (In Spanish.)

61. José María González Ruiz. "Image of God and the demographic explosion." *Tauta*, no. 8, March 20, 1973. (In Spanish.)

62. *Official Bulletin of the State*, September 28, 1965. (In Spanish.)

63. *Official Bulletin of the State*, November 25, 1965. (In Spanish.)

64. Antoni Jutglar. *Ideologies and Classes in Contemporary Spain, I (1808–1874)*. Madrid: Edicusa, 1968. (In Spanish.)

65. Massimo Livi Bacci. "Fertility and nuptiality changes in Spain from the late eighteenth to the early twentieth century," part 2. *Population Studies*, vol. 22, no. 2 (July 1968).

66. D. Vicens Vives. *Manual of the Economic History of Spain*. Barcelona: Teida, 1959. (In Spanish.)

67. Severino Aznar. "The average of the birth differential in the social classes of Madrid and Barcelona." *International Journal of Sociology*, no. 20, 1960. (In Spanish.)

68. Pedro Bustinza Ugarte and Angel Sopeña Ibáñez. "Analysis of Spanish birth." *International Journal of Sociology*, no. 60, October–December 1957. (In Spanish.)

69. Salustiano del Campo. "Doctors and the problem of the limitation of birth." *Spanish Journal of Public Opinion*, no. 1 (May–August 1965). (In Spanish.)

70. Juan Diez Nicolás. "The Spanish woman and family planning." *Tauta*, no. 8 (March 20, 1973): 86–97. (In Spanish.)

71. *Ya*. Madrid, April 17, 1973. (In Spanish.)

72. *Pueblo*. Madrid, May 25, 1971. (In Spanish.)

73. *Ya*. Madrid, December 10, 1972. (In Spanish.)

74. "No to abortion." *Ya*. Madrid, February 21, 1973. (In Spanish.)

75. Speech by Father Diaz Moreno. *Informaciones*, March 21, 1973. (In Spanish.)

76. *Ya*. Madrid, April 4, 1973. (In Spanish.)

77. *Pueblo*. Madrid, March 22, 1973. (In Spanish.)

78. *Pueblo*. Madrid, January 8, 1973. (In Spanish.)

79. *Ya*. Madrid, April 15, 1973. (In Spanish.)

80. *Official Bulletin of the State*, January 13, 1945. (In Spanish.)

81. *Official Bulletin of the State*, February 2, 1941. (In Spanish.)

82. José María Deleyto. "Abortion in Spain." *Medical Tribune*, December 1, 1972, pp. 20–23. (In Spanish.)

83. *Pueblo*. Madrid, December 15, 1972. (In Spanish.)

84. Enrique Jiménez Asenjo. "The children are not guilty." *Ya*. Madrid, December 15, 1972. (In Spanish.)

85. INE. *Legal Statistics in Spain, 1968.* Madrid: National Statistics Institute, 1971. (In Spanish.)

86. L. Morell Ocaña. "The evolution and present configuration of health administrative activity." *Journal of Public Administration,* no. 63 (September–December 1970): 131–165. (In Spanish.)

87. Commission of Social Security, Health, and Social Assistance. *Second Economic and Social Development Plan.* Madrid, 1967. (In Spanish.)

88. F. J. Jiménez. "Directives of health policy." *Bulletin of Documentation of the Ministry of Government,* no. 44. (In Spanish.)

89. *Official Bulletin of the State,* no. 331, November 26, 1944. (In Spanish.)

90. Sanz Boixeres. "The Law of Hospitals as a law of coordination." *Administrative Documentation,* no. 185, September 1966. (In Spanish.)

91. *Social Security, Health, and Social Assistance.* Madrid, 1972. (In Spanish.)

92. *Medical Tribune,* December 1, 1972. (In Spanish.)

93. *The Spanish Vanguard.* Barcelona, December 27, 1972. (In Spanish.)

94. *Informaciones.* Madrid, November 15, 1972. (In Spanish.)

95. *Second Economic and Social Development Plan: Report on Regional Development.* Madrid, 1968, table 18, p. 161. (In Spanish.)

96. Salustiano del Campo. *Analysis of Population in Spain.* Barcelona, Ariel, 1972, table 24, p. 98. (In Spanish.)

97. Figures from Maria de los Angeles Durán Heras. *Female Labor in Spain: A Sociological Study.* Madrid: Tecnos, 1972 (in Spanish). See also Spanish Labor Organization. *The Rights of the Working Woman.* Madrid, 1970 (in Spanish); and Eliseo Bayo. *Hard Labor for Women.* Barcelona: Plaza y Janes, 1970 (in Spanish).

98. Rafael Mir de la Cruz. "The Spanish woman in the active population." *Labor Journal of Statistics,* no. 99, 1970, p. 78. (In Spanish.)

99. The minimum retirement age in Spain is sixty-five years, except for certain jobs of special danger or with high mobility or mortality indexes. See M. Hernainz Marquez. *Elementary Treatise on Labor Rights.* Eleventh edition. Madrid, 1972, vol. 2, pp. 408–409. (In Spanish.)

100. J. A. García-Trevijano Fos y Francisco de Blas García. *Spanish Emigration Legislation, 1936–1964.* Madrid: Spanish Institute of Emigration, 1965, p. 7. (In Spanish.)

101. Mariano González-Rothvoss. "Influence of emigration on population growth in Spain in the last 100 years, 1850–1950." *International Sociological Journal,* no. 41, January–March 1953, pp. 61–84. (In Spanish.)

102. Jesús García Fernández. *External Emigration from Spain.* Barcelona: Ariel, 1965, p. 16. (In Spanish.)

103. Spanish Institute of Emigration. *Survey on the Determinants of Emigration, 1966.* Madrid: Ministry of Labor, 1966. (In Spanish.)

104. Spanish Institute of Emigration. *Emigration in 1970.* Madrid, 1971, pp. 85–86, 96. (In Spanish.)

105. Spanish Institute of Emigration. *Emigration in 1971.* Madrid, 1972, pp. 116–117. (In Spanish.)

106. *Official Bulletin of Parliament.* Madrid, June 15, 1973. (In Spanish.)

107. *Ya.* Madrid, July 1, 1973. (In Spanish.)

108. *Informaciones.* Madrid, March 6, 1973, and April 6, 1973. (In Spanish.)

109. Alfonso García Barbancho. *Spanish Migrations in 1961–1965.* Studies of the Institute of Economic Development. Madrid, 1970, pp. 16 and 20. (In Spanish.)

110. *Official Bulletin of the State,* nos. 239 and 240, September 20 and 21, 1957, p. 1270. (In Spanish.)

111. *Official Bulletin of the State,* no. 286, November 14, 1957, p. 1522. (In Spanish.)

112. See *Informaciones,* Madrid, May 25, 1973 where a session of the Symposium on Regional Policies is summarized. (In Spanish.)

113. H. W. Richardson. "Regional development policy in Spain." *Urban Studies,* vol. 8, no. 1 (February 1971), p. 46.

114. Banco de Bilbao. *National Revenue in Spain and Its Distribution by Provinces, 1969.* Bilbao, 1971, pp. 14–15. (In Spanish.)

115. See "Regional policy in Spain." *Reports of OECD,* no. 64, June 1973, p. 12. (In Spanish.)

116. Third Economic and Social Development Plan. *Regional Development.* Madrid, 1972. (In Spanish.)

117. Intervention of José María Castane Ortega, Director General of Industrial Promotion and Technology of the Ministry of Industry in a symposium on regional policy in Deusto. *Informaciones,* May 25, 1973. (In Spanish.)

CHAPTER 19

France

Jean Bourgeois-Pichat

ABSTRACT

The ideas on population matters in France during the last hundred years have evolved into three currents of thought. First, a movement in favor of birth control that started in the last quarter of the nineteenth century and presently continues to act. It may be considered as the origin of the recent developments in favor of contraception. This movement is not directly linked to demographic considerations; birth control is advocated mainly as a means of liberating women. A second movement, free also from demographic goals, originated just after World War I out of the concept of social justice for families. It still plays an important role, and most new legislation tries to achieve social justice. Finally, a third movement, based on demographic concern, gathered people afraid of the consequences of a decline of natality. It started more or less at the same time as the movement in favor of birth control. It was particularly active just before and just after World War II. Under this impulse legislation on family allowances, social security, and immigration was adopted. During the last few years, this movement seems to have lost momentum.

These sometimes conflicting movements of ideas molded the present legislation, which can be characterized as follows:

(1) A set of laws and decrees providing various allowances to be paid to families (for the last ten years, the total amount represented 4 or 5 percent of the gross national product).

(2) A very restrictive law against abortion (voted in 1920). Recently, strong

545

movements of opinion have developed to replace this law by a more
tolerant one.

(3) A relatively liberal law on contraception (voted in 1967) organizing the
sale of contraceptives and setting up the bases for informing the public
on contraceptive matters.

(4) A set of laws and decrees regulating the entry of foreign workers into
France. One special feature of the French legislation is that it facilitates
the reunification of families.

(5) An elaborate organization aimed at remodeling the industrial framework
throughout France which, as a by-product of its action, precipitates
internal movement of workers and their families.

INTRODUCTION

As in many countries, there is in France no population policy if we mean
by that a set of coordinated laws aimed at reaching some demographic
goals. There is a complex system of legislation protecting the family. This
system of legislation evolved in the course of time mainly to achieve better
social justice.

Legislation on immigration was adopted essentially for economic reasons
except for a short time just after World War II when demographic considerations were taken into account. But the hope of achieving a demographic goal through immigration failed, and the government rapidly
returned to the economic point of view.

Legislation on internal migrations, as we shall see later, is concerned
with population only indirectly. The application of this legislation is to the
development of new plants, and the movement of the labor force is only a
by-product.

Only legislation on contraception and abortion has been adopted for
demographic reasons. The purpose of the law of 1920, which until recently
was the basis of the legislation, was to slow the decline of fertility. Its
effects are doubtful, and a new law on contraception was enacted in 1967
in which no reference was made to demographic factors.

The abortion legislation remained the same as it was in the 1920 law,
and from a legal point of view, at least, one of its purposes is to prevent
the decline of fertility. As for the new legislation on contraception, its
effects are doubtful, and movements are developing that favor a further
liberalization of the law.

We shall examine successively the legislation on family, abortion, contraception, immigration, and internal migrations. But first, it may be useful
to examine the trend of ideas on population during the last one hundred
years.

THE DEVELOPMENT OF IDEAS
ABOUT POPULATION IN FRANCE

¶ PRINCIPAL DEMOGRAPHIC CONCERNS BEFORE 1900

The movement initiated in England by Malthus and developed by Francis Place during the course of the nineteenth century had delayed reverberations in France. Fifty years after Place, Paul Robin,[1] a revolutionary and one-time friend of Karl Marx, espoused the cause of birth control in the last quarter of the nineteenth century. To publicize his cause, he founded the League for Human Reproduction and published a periodical entitled *Régénération*.

Another current of thought developed during the same period. Noting the continued decrease in the French birth rate, certain persons became alarmed about the demographic future of France and formed the National Alliance against Depopulation to refute the ideas disseminated by Robin. Also founded at this time were Family Associations, whose essential purpose was to defend the rights of the family. Although often in agreement with the goals of the alliance, the family associations based their program on different principles. For them, the problem was not so much depopulation as the injustice against the family. From the start, therefore, the defenders of demographic growth included in their numbers both the pronatalists and the supporters of social justice. These two tendencies can be found throughout the history of demographic policy in France. Considerations of social justice are predominant in legislation, but there are also some purely pronatalist measures.

In the last quarter of the nineteenth century, political parties were as divided as public opinion on demographic development in France, although for different reasons. Socialists, with a strict allegiance to Marxist doctrines, opposed any propaganda in favor of contraception. Arguments developed then are encountered again in today's Marxist countries when there is any question of supporting contraception in the third world. According to these arguments, the poverty of the proletariat (of the people in today's third world) is caused not by the excessive increase of its population but

---

[1] Paul Robin (1837–1912) began his professional life as a teacher (1861). He soon gave up this activity (1865) for a political life as a revolutionary. In 1880, he returned to his previous field to become director of a boarding school for boys and girls in the neighborhood of Paris where he tried to apply daring ideas on education. He was dismissed from this post in 1894 mainly because he had been advocating the practice of birth control as a means of achieving happiness. He devoted the last part of his life to propaganda in favor of birth control. He attempted suicide on August 31, 1912, and died the next day (for further details see [1]).

by the defects of the capitalist economy. Some socialists in France, nevertheless, recognized the disadvantage of an overpopulated labor force and called on workers to stop having large families which provide cheap labor for capitalists. This controversy between partisans and opponents of growth has continued until the present, with one or the other tendency dominant at various times.

¶ BEGINNING OF THE TWENTIETH CENTURY
For a long time, the state adopted a neutral position between these two factions. It is possible to take the view, a posteriori, that compulsory education, enacted in 1882, and the creation in the same year of a High Council of Health, for the purpose of organizing public health in France, were population policy measures. At the time, however, no demographic consideration was invoked to justify either action.

The first measure adopted under pressure from the pronatalists and supporters of the family appeared in 1900; mailmen and telegraph operators received the first family allowances. In 1913, the measure was extended to the army and, in 1916, to all civil servants.

During this period, the Senate on two occasions, in 1902 and 1912, ordered that a Commission on Depopulation be established. On November 22, 1901, the Senate adopted a draft resolution requesting the government to create an extraparliamentary commission whose aim would be "to study the whole of the questions related to depopulation and to try to find the appropriate means to counteract it" [2].

The commission, which was effectively created by a decision of the Ministry of Internal Affairs on January 21, 1902, was composed of sixty-seven members and four secretaries. It was convened regularly during 1902 and then remained idle until 1905. After 1905, it again stopped working until June 1908 when it was asked to present its final report, which appeared in private reviews.

In 1912, again following the advice of the Senate, the Ministry of Finance took the initiative of proposing to the President of the republic the creation of a new commission. In the report to the President, the reasons for the failures of the previous commission were stated: "The [population] problem is not only a national and social concern, it has essentially fiscal and financial implications. It is because the previous commission did not take sufficiently into account this aspect of the question that its work remained sterile" [2].

In creating a new commission attached to the Ministry of Finance, it was hoped that the financial and fiscal aspects would take the lead. The commission was created on November 5, 1912. Its size[2] was impressive: 315

² Decree of November 15, 1912.

members. Four subcommittees were created in charge, respectively, of the following aspects: fiscal, military, social, and administrative and judicial. A fifth committee had the task of coordinating the work of the four others. At the opening session, July 1913 was proposed as the end of the mandate of the commission and the Ministry of Finance agreed to this deadline.

The start of the commission's work also was impressive; for example, the subcommittee on fiscal aspects decided to meet every Saturday afternoon. But the concrete realizations fell short of the wishes. The commission was unable to present its report before the outbreak of the war, and it was dismantled by the world conflict.

During the aftermath of World War I, in January 1920, the government set up the Ministry of Hygiene, Assistance, and Social Providence. This was the consummation of efforts begun in 1882 with the creation of the High Council of Health. On January 27, 1920, a decree of the President of the republic created a High Council on Births attached to the newly established ministry. Contrary to the two previous commissions, this high council was a permanent organism. But it was dealing only with births. Composed of thirty people, it was required to meet once a month, and it was instructed to find ways of increasing the birth rate, developing child care, protecting and honoring large families, and in a more general way, to prepare such legislative proposals, decrees, and memorandums as they thought should be presented for the approval of the Ministry of Hygiene, Assistance, and Social Providence. The decree also created in each of the ninety departments a commission on births made up of thirteen people representing the academic world, the fathers of big families, and other circles chosen by the local elected body and the prefect who was chairman of the commission. Each commission had to present a report every six months to the High Council on Births.

The work of these departmental commissions was unequal. Periodically, they organized regional conferences on births in which their work was discussed. This system, that is, High Council on Births and departmental commissions, lasted until 1940 when the high council was suppressed. In the meantime a new organism—the Chief Committee on Population—had been created in 1939. This will be studied later.

There is often a gap between intention and implementation, and indeed, the positive measures taken by the government to increase fertility as a result of the work of the High Council on Births were not significant. The most important legislative action had been the passage of the law in July 1920 forbidding abortion and the sale and dissemination of contraceptive products. (This law is discussed in detail later.) But at that time, the High Council on Births had just begun its work.

In a parallel private initiative, the Chamber of Commerce decided to hold congresses on the birth rate. The first one took place at Nancy in 1919. The second, at Lille in 1920, formulated the "Declaration of Rights of the Family." This declaration was an effort to state the point of view of the family-life supporters as opposed to that of the natalists in the High Council of Births.

At the instigation of the family associations, management and corporate associations decided to make family allowances to employees working in the private sector who had dependents. (As has been mentioned, family allowances had existed in the public sector since 1916.) A law passed on March 11, 1932, made the measure official and obligatory. During the same period, the government created, under the name of social insurance, measures that later became the social security system for wage earners (law of April 30, 1938).

The current of opinion favorable to birth control did not vanish with the suicide of its leader in 1912. In fact, as early as 1908, Paul Robin gave up any real action, and his team of followers was regrouped under the leadership of Eugene Humbert, who had previously been the editor of the review *Régénération.*

A new review, *Génération consciente (Conscious Generation)*, was launched and lasted until August 1, 1914. At that time, the team of *Génération consciente* was dispersed by the war. Its leader, Humbert, had to fly to Spain. One of his followers, George Hardy, continued the work and began to publish in 1916 another review: *Le Néomalthusien.* The government censored it almost immediately.

After the war, Humbert returned from Spain, and Hardy again started to publish the *Néomalthusien* in which he tried in vain to fight against the passage of the 1920 law. As a consequence of that law, the police launched an investigation at the headquarters of *Génération consciente*; Humbert was arrested and sentenced to two and one-half years of imprisonment.

Ten years later in 1930, the tireless Humbert launched a new Malthusian review, *La grande réforme (The Great Reform)*, but the war again stopped the efforts of the neo-Malthusian group. As we will see later, the Vichy government enacted new legislation against abortion. Again Humbert was arrested, and he died in prison.

In the 1930s, a new current of ideas emerged in the path of the world movement for sexual reform. In 1933, three medical physicians—Dalsace, Mal, and Toulouse—began publishing a review entitled *Le problème sexuèl*, and in 1935, Jean Dalsace opened the first medical center on birth control in Suresnes, a town in a suburb of Paris.

The two movements were fighting for the same cause but from different angles. Humbert and his followers had a global approach to the problem, whereas Dalsace was considering the individual aspect or, at least, that of the couple. This way proved to be more fruitful than the other. All the developments of family planning that took place in the 1950s came from the efforts of Dalsace. We will come back to this matter.

¶ A TURNING POINT: THE FAMILY CODE

On February 22, 1939, the president of the Council of Ministers appointed a Chief Committee on Population, composed of five members (this was increased to seven in 1940) to coordinate and stimulate action in ministerial departments to counteract depopulation and to provide France with a family code.

The creation of this committee was a decisive turning point in the government policy on population matters. The small number of members of the committee contrasted with the membership of the previous commissions and councils: first commission in 1902, 71 people; second commission in 1912, 315 people; High Council on Births, 30 people plus 90 departmental commissions of 13 people each (in all, 1,200 people); Chief Committee on Population, 5 people. Moreover, the committee was close to the head of government and had an importance that no similar organization had enjoyed previously. Obviously, this time the government had decided to act.

On June 30, 1939, the chief committee transmitted its report to the head of government, who promulgated on July 29 the "family code." The action placed French legislation of the period ahead of all other legislation of this type. Chapter headings of the code were as follows:

(1) Family aid: premiums on the first born and general family allowances, loans for the establishment of young rural households, contracts for extended payments, and family assistance.
(2) Protection of the family: maternal protection (prevention of abortion, establishment of maternity homes, reduction of infant mortality), protection of children.
(3) Human protection (against social offenses, toxic substances, alcoholism).
(4) The family and instruction (demographic teaching, medical supervision of educational establishments).
(5) Fiscal arrangements.

¶ THE HIGH CONSULTATIVE COMMITTEE ON POPULATION AND THE FAMILY: THE ORGANIZATION OF DEMOGRAPHIC RESEARCH

After World War II, a new organization, the High Consultative Committee on Population and the Family, responsible directly to the Prime Minister, was established by decree on April 12, 1945. In the course of eleven sessions, of which seven were presided over by General Charles de Gaulle himself, the committee elaborated formulas designed to complete the existing measures in support of the family. It prepared a project on the status of foreigners in France and critically reviewed the texts in preparation of the organization of social security. Finally, two ordinances were passed by the government on October 4 and 19, 1945, that completed the body of texts regulating the social policy of France and set up the framework in which this policy subsequently developed.

In the preparation of these ordinances, the need for further research and study became increasingly obvious. This led to the creation of the *Institut national d'Études démographiques* (INED) (Ordinance 45-2499, October 24, 1945) and the *Institut national d'Hygiène* (INH) (Article L-785, *Code de la Santé publique.*) [3]

Finally, an ordinance of November 2, 1949, established the "conditions for entry and residence in France for foreigners."

POLICIES CONCERNING THE FAMILY

From a demographic view, the social policy of France is characterized by:

(1) A body of laws that are "natalist" and (or), more particularly, family oriented.
(2) Health and maternity insurance, extended to members of workers' families.
(3) Old-age pensions extended to spouses of workers.

The pronatalist and family oriented measures include payments calculated on a hypothetical base salary. The salary varies according to the various allowances. These salaries are reevaluated periodically according to the increase in the cost of living but generally not to the increase in the standard of living. This means that the allowances represent a diminishing part of the total income. The hypothetical salaries are not uniform throughout France. The territory is divided into five zones numbered 0–4, and the salaries diminish by 1 percent from one zone to the following one.

For the purpose of these payments, children are considered as dependents until they have completed their compulsory education.[4] However, four categories of children are considered to be dependent beyond school-leaving age[5] as follows:

---

[3] The institute has been reorganized recently under a new name: *Institut national de la Santé et de la Recherche médicale* (INSERM) by Decree 64727 of July 18, 1964.

[4] Fourteen years of age for children born before January 1, 1958; sixteen years of age for children born thereafter. In practice, the allowances are given until six months after these ages.

[5] These four categories combined represented, in 1970, about 13 percent of child beneficiaries.

(1) Apprentices until their eighteenth birthdays.
(2) Students until their twentieth birthdays.
(3) Handicapped children until their twentieth birthdays.
(4) Girls in the home until their twentieth birthdays (that is, girls not engaged in the labor force).

The following basic allowances have been paid since 1945. Recently, new allowances have been created, different in nature and, at least for some, in the way they are paid. These new developments will be examined later.

(1) *Family allowance*: This consists primarily of payments according to the birth order of the child and his age.

(2) *Allowance for single income*: This is given each month to each household in which there is a single income. It varies according to the economic activity of the head of the household (salaried employees and independent workers outside of agriculture, nonsalaried workers in agriculture) and to the age of children.

(3) *Prenatal allowance*: This is an allowance for anticipated dependents and all pregnant women are entitled to receive it. It consists of three payments, at the end of the second, sixth, and ninth months of pregnancy, in zone 0 in 1973, respectively, 193.82, 387.64, and 290.73 francs.[6]

(4) *Maternity benefit*: The mother of a newborn child is entitled to a maternity allowance if she complies with one of the following conditions: If it is a first child, the mother must be less than twenty-five years old or have been married for less than two years. For a child after the first born, the birth must take place less than three years after the previous birth. The benefit is given in two equal payments (of 572.65 francs in zone 0 in 1973), the first at birth and the second six months after birth. Finally, the child must be French or become French within three months of birth.

(5) *Housing allowance*: The housing allowance is given to the head of the family to help him finance his principal dwelling, when he is entitled to receive family allowance, allowance for single income, or prenatal allowance. To qualify for the allowance, the conditions of the dwelling place must comply with certain regulations about crowding and sanitation. In addition, the family must spend a certain fraction of their income on their lodging. This fraction varies with the number of children and the level of income.

¶ MISCELLANEOUS MEASURES
In addition to the family benefits described above, there are measures aimed at alleviating the costs of rearing children: social welfare payments

---

[6] On January 1, 1973, 100 francs equaled approximately US$19.55.

for the neediest, scholarships for students, reductions in transportation fare for families with more than two children, extension of social security benefits to children and to mothers not engaged in the labor force, sick leaves for pregnant working women before and after birth. Finally, income tax is calculated according to the size of the family (quotient familial).

¶ RECENT DEVELOPMENTS

The following allowances, established recently, seem to indicate a new orientation in the policies regarding aid to families:

(6) *Allowance for specialized education* (law of July 31, 1963): A monthly allowance is given for each handicapped child under twenty who needs, in addition to special care, special education or special professional training adapted to his case.

(7) *Allowance for handicapped children under age twenty years*: This allowance cannot be cumulated with the previous one.

(8) *Allowance for orphans* (law of December 2, 1970, and decree of July 22, 1971): A monthly allowance is given to any person who permanently takes care of an orphan. For an orphan of both parents, the allowance is given regardless of the income of the foster family. For an orphan of only one parent, there is an income limit beyond which the allowance is not paid. A single woman with children is classified as a widow.

(9) *Allowance for care of children* (law of January 3, 1972): This allowance is given to the working mother to help her to pay for the care of her children under the age of three when she is away from home. The allowance for single income (mentioned earlier) was created as an incentive to keep the mother out of the labor force so that she could concentrate on the rearing of her children. The new allowance departs from this position. To be entitled to receive this allowance, a family must have income below a certain limit.

The amount of the allowance is equal to the real cost of care within a maximum limit which, at present (February 1973), represents 194.50 francs per month. Part of this limit will follow the increase of both the cost *and* standard of living. This is new. The amount of the allowances mentioned so far vary, if at all, only with the cost of living.

(10) *Complementary single income allowance* (law of January 3, 1972): Payment of the single income allowance [see item no. (2)] has been modified recently. First, the allowance is not paid above a certain income limit. This limit varies with the number of children.[7] An estimated 300,000 families are excluded from the benefit as a consequence of this

---

[7] For a family of two children, 4,050 taxable francs per month, and 5,000 for a family of six children.

limit. Second, for families with low income (not taxable according to the income tax schedule) and for families with one child below age three or with four children, it is supplemented by a *complementary single income allowance*. It is estimated that 1,110,000 families benefit from this complementary allowance, defined as a percentage of base salary because the allowances for care of children increase with both the cost and the standard of living. Moreover, for families receiving the complementary single income allowance, the years spent by the mother in childrearing will be taken into account for the calculation of retirement benefits.

The new elements in the allowances listed [see items (6), (7), (8), (9), and (10)] can be summarized as follows:

The new allowances serve specific needs (specialized education, handicapped children, orphans, care of children).

Most of the new allowances are paid only if certain conditions of income are fulfilled. Generally, the families have to be exempt from income tax. This has reduced the impact of these allowances and encounters the opposition of family associations. Members of these associations feel that by such measures the government tends to reduce the role of family benefits to welfare payments for the neediest.

For the first time, the rule for the payment of the allowance for care of children and the complementary allowance when there is only one income in the family takes into account the increase of the standard of living.[8]

Finally, the housing allowance has also been modified. First, a new kind of housing allowance has been created (law of July 16, 1971) for young workers (less than twenty-five years of age), for old people (more than sixty-five years or more than sixty years old if unable to work), and disabled people more than fifteen years old. Second, the system of housing allowance for families has been extended to new beneficiaries (law of January 3, 1972):

(1) People entitled to the new allowances for specialized education, for orphans, for care of children, and for the complementary single income allowance.
(2) Young couples without children, during the first five years of the marriage provided that the spouses are less than forty years old at the time of the marriage.
(3) Households and persons having a sixty-five-year-old dependent.
(4) Households and persons having a dependent unable to work as a consequence of physical disability.

[8] A confirmation of a new trend can be found in the fact that in recent years the percentage increase of the theoretical salary used for calculating the family allowances has been greater than the percentage increase of the cost of living.

Table 1 summarizes the above indications and gives some additional information, particularly on the amount of the various monthly allocations.

¶ NEW INSTITUTIONAL FRAMEWORK

Changes in the principle have been accompanied by changes in the institutional framework. The High Consultative Committee on Population and the Family, which had jurisdiction over all population-related matters, has been replaced by three committees on population, the family, and health, respectively. A special committee has been created for working women. Rather than reporting directly to the Prime Minister, each committee is under the jurisdiction of the relevant minister: the Minister of Labor, Work, and Population for the High Committee on Population (Decree 70-355, April 20, 1970) and the Committee on Working Women (decision of the minister, April 16, 1971); the Minister of Health and Social Security for the High Consultative Committee on the Family (Decree 71-768, September 17, 1971) and for the High Medical Committee on Health (decision of the minister, September 23, 1971).

The transformation of one single committee into four committees is indicative of the waning interest of the high-level governmental sphere in population problems. The single committee directly attached to the Prime Minister had and frequently exercised the power to advise on subjects that the various ministers might not be able to broach as easily. This freedom and access to the Prime Minister were lost when the committees became dependent on each minister. Each committee now deals only with problems accepted in advance by its minister. The committees are consultative bodies only.

For program implementation, three new organizations have been created: (1) the National Agency for Employment (Ordinance no. 67-578, July 13, 1967), an organization with regional branches whose aim is to help jobless workers return to the labor force; (2) the Center for the Study of Employment (Decree no. 70-1087, November 25, 1970), a research institution within the INED; and (3) the Center for Information on Population Problems (Decree 68-534, May 30, 1968).

¶ THE LEGAL STATUS OF THE FAMILY

We have dealt so far mainly with measures to improve the economic situation of families. Other measures are directed at changing the legal status of the family by altering such laws as those regulating marriage and divorce, inheritance, and the status of illegitimate and adulterine children. The demographic effects of these laws are negligible. The common tendency of the new legislation is to increase the rights of minors. (On the question of abortion, the legal right of the fetus had been alleged by the High Con-

TABLE 1.

Assistance to the Family, France, 1973 (Monthly allowances paid in January 1973 in the zone zero, in French francs; France is divided into five zones. The allowances diminish by 1 percent from one zone to the next.)

	(1)		(2)					(6)	(7)	(8)		(9)	(5)
			One Income Only in the Family[g]							Orphanhood			
			No Child Less than Two Years Old			At Least One Child Less than Two Years Old							
Number of Children[a]	Family Allowance[b]	Compensatory Allowance[d] (salaried only)	Single Income (salaried)	Mother at Home (employers and independent workers)	Mother at Home, Agri. Sector (non-salaried)		Complementary Allowance[h]	Specialized Education Allowance	Handicapped Children Allowance	of Both Parents	of One Parent[i]	Care of Children Allowance	Housing Allowance
1					19.45								
2	96.91	9.81	38.90	19.45	48.68				52.86				Variable[k]
3	259.89	24.90	77.80	38.90	47.25	97.25[f]	97.25[f]	229.25		132.15	66.08	194.50[j]	
4	422.88	39.99	97.25	58.35	97.25								
5	568.24	55.08	97.25	77.80	97.25								
6	713.61[c]	70.17[e]	97.25[f]	97.25[f]	97.25[f]								

NOTE: Numbers in parentheses refer to text explanation. Allowances (6), (7), (8), (9), and (5) are not related to the size of the family. They are paid for each child entitled to receive them.

a Children less than sixteen years old, or less than eighteen years old if apprentices, or less than twenty years old if students.
b For each child 10–15 years old, add 39.65 francs, except for the oldest child of families with fewer than three children. For each child above fifteen years old, add 70.48 francs, except for the oldest child of families with fewer than three children.
c Add 145.77 francs for each additional child.
d No zoning for this allowance.
e Add 15.00 francs for each additional child.
f The allowance remains at this level after six children.
g This allowance is not paid for families with high income (see text).
h Subject to certain conditions for the income and the composition of the family.
i Subject to certain conditions for the income and the composition of the family.
j This represents a limit within which the real expenses are paid.
k Subject to certain conditions for income, composition of the family, the rent and composition of the lodging.

sultative Committee on Population and the Family as grounds for refusing complete freedom for the right to abortion.) These changes of legislation are noted in the review *Population* in a special chronicle appearing one or two times a year and entitled "Legislation."

The amount of the allowances allocated to help the family represents a sizable part of the gross national product: 4.5 percent since 1960. It is larger than the budget of the state for education: 3.3 percent since 1965.

POLICY ON ABORTION

In France, the legislation concerning abortion is based on the Napoleonic code of 1810, which defined abortion as a murder for which the woman was subject to trial by jury in an "assize court." For many years, the number of accused women was very small (approximately 100 per year), and most of the juries rendered verdicts of not guilty.

A series of revisions in the law were enacted with the objective of making it more rigorously enforced. Just after World War I, on July 31, 1920, a law was promulgated prohibiting abortion and any incitement to abortion.[9]

The main purpose of the law was to set different rules for the various people involved in an abortion. The woman who aborts was considered with the greatest indulgence, and strictly speaking, only the woman who aborts *herself* must be punished.[10] The accomplices are much more severely punished, and the more it is a common practice for them, the more severe the punishment.

A law of March 27, 1923, relegated abortion to a lower level in the hierarchy of offenses, but at the same time, proscribed that the sentence be given directly by a judge without a jury. It was felt, at that time, that the judge would be less indulgent than a jury. This did not prove to be the case, however; the number of women found guilty remained small (200 to 300 per year).

As a result, the "family code," published as a governmental decree on July 29, 1939, specified the penalties for all related offenses, proscribing fines and imprisonment for anyone assisting in an abortion, having an abortion, selling or possessing items represented, falsely or otherwise, as abortifacients, or propagandizing about abortion.

Under the government of Vichy, a law promulgated on February 15, 1942, returned[11] to the position of the Napoleonic code, again defining

---

[9] The law also dealt with contraception (see later).

[10] This explains why the aborting woman sometimes is found not guilty whereas the other people involved are punished.

[11] As explained above, the imprisonment of Humbert was a consequence of this new legislation. He died in prison.

abortion as murder to be sentenced by jury in an assize court. The decline of fertility between the two world wars was held responsible, at least partly, for the loss of the war in 1940, and the government was determined to punish severely people convicted of facilitating abortion.[12]

The law promulgated by the Vichy government was abolished in 1945, and the dispositions contained in the family code were upheld. They are still valid at the present time.[13] They are described in more detail below.

¶ PRESENT LEGISLATION

According to *Article 317 of the penal code*, anybody who performs or tries to perform an abortion on a woman, pregnant or supposed to be pregnant, with or without her consent, by using food, beverages, drugs, physical action, violent or otherwise, or any other means will receive a punishment of one to five years of imprisonment, a fine of 1,800 to 36,000 francs, and possibly an interdiction to remain in certain areas. The penalties are increased for the abortionist who makes abortion a common practice (five to ten years of imprisonment and a fine of 18,000 to 72,000 francs). People belonging to medical and paramedical professions (medical physician, midwife, dentist, nurse, pharmacist, physiotherapist, and students in these various fields, herbalist, trussmaker, seller of surgical instruments), in addition to the above penalties, are forbidden to practice for a duration from not less than five years to the remainder of their lives.

The woman who aborts herself receives six months to two years of imprisonment and a fine of 360 to 7,200 francs.

According to *Articles L. 645 to L. 647 of the public health code:*

(1) Anybody who offers, sells, or distributes abortive remedies or substances or surgical specialized apparatus without a medical prescription receives three months to two years of imprisonment and a fine of 1,800 to 18,000 francs.

(2) Any speech, writing, poster, or other form of advertising by a medical or paramedical office with the aim of promoting abortion, even when abortions are not being carried out, is punishable by six months to three years imprisonment and a fine of 360 to 18,000 francs. The same punishments are given for the offering, sale, or distribution of equipment[14] for performing an abortion, even if the equipment is revealed to be insufficient for the purpose.

---

[12] In one assize court in Paris, a laundry woman responsible for twenty-six abortions received a capital punishment and was executed on July 30, 1943.

[13] The vote of the law of December 1967 on contraception did not change any part of the legislation concerning abortion.

[14] And also probably possession of such equipment. However, the law does not mention possession explicitly.

Article 378 of the penal code relieves physicians and their assistants from professional secrecy in all matters concerning abortion.

Finally, *Article L. 161.1 of the public health code* gives the conditions for a therapeutic abortion:

When in order to save the life of a mother gravely endangered, a medical physician or a surgeon is obliged to perform a surgical operation or use a treatment which might stop pregnancy, he is obliged to take the advice of two consulting medical physicians, one of whom being listed among the experts of the court of first instance. After examining the expecting mother, these consulting medical physicians will testify that the life of the mother can be saved only by an abortion.

The annual number of therapeutic abortions is very small (a few hundred).

Although the judicial apparatus to repress abortion in France is potentially very strong, the number of judicial actions is very small compared to the estimated number of induced abortions. In recent years, the number of persons convicted was as follows:

Year	Convicted Abortionists
1960	289
1961	500
1962	462
1963	569
1964	700
1965	588

By comparison, a conservative estimate of the annual number of induced abortions is 300,000; thus, there are only one or two sentences for each 1,000 abortions. The cases that are prosecuted are mainly those in which a death has been recorded.

¶ PROPOSAL OF THE HIGH CONSULTATIVE COMMITTEE ON
POPULATION AND THE FAMILY

The report of the High Consultative Committee on Population and the Family on birth control, published at the beginning of 1967, discussed the problems raised by an unenforced repressive legislation and examined the alternatives. They addressed themselves to the problem as follows: The state and, consequently, the law is the guardian of certain ethical rules commonly accepted by the society. One of these rules is the respect of human life. An abortion is the suppression of a human life. Therefore, the fundamental question is: "Do we have to apply to the child before birth the rules applied to any human life after birth?"

If the reply is "yes," the repressive laws must obtain, at least in principle. If the reply is "no," it is necessary to establish new legislation defining the rights of the society, the couple, and the mother.

The committee discussed first the arguments in support of a negative reply. Two sets of arguments are generally put forward:

(1) The rights of the couple and the mother. The committee pointed out that to honor these rights would be contrary to the general trend of the progress of civilization, which has consistently limited the rights of parents in order to protect the child.
(2) The threat to the equilibrium of the society and the family that the birth of a child can pose. Such a position also appeared to the committee to be contrary to the tendency of the society to confront a difficult situation and to solve the corresponding social problems rather than to suppress the people affected by them.

Therefore, the committee decided that the same rules regarding the respect of life have to be applied before and after birth. The case of self-protection is, therefore, the only situation in which an abortion is permitted. The committee considered the present legislation that allows abortion only when the life of the mother is *immediately* endangered by the pregnancy too restrictive. It proposed to modify the present legislation to include, as grounds of self-protection, the case in which birth could be expected to have an adverse effect on the health of the mother, shortening her life expectancy.

¶ THE PROPOSAL OF ANEA

The association[15] Happy Motherhood—French Movement for Family Planning has always pursued the study of abortion as part of its activity. A special committee established within this association composed of such professionals as lawyers, medical physicians, sociologists, economists, and social workers tried to reconcile the existing repressive legislation with the almost complete lack of enforcement. In Paris in 1966, this committee organized an international colloquium on the problem.

A group of medical physicians was formed to study fecundity and the prevention of abortion under the auspices of Happy Motherhood. This college of medical physicians wanted to promote experimentation on the various techniques of birth control, their failures, and the reasons for their acceptance or rejection by couples.

The law of December 28, 1967, on contraception authorized, among other things, the manufacture, import, and sale of contraceptives. The

---

[15] The creation of this association and its work will be discussed later, when policy on contraception is reviewed.

association announced it would fully cooperate with the administration in the implementation of the law, but it pointed out that the law dealt only with contraception and left untouched the present legislation regarding abortion, and announced that it would continue to lobby for a law liberalizing abortion.

For this purpose, ANEA, the National Association for the Study of Abortion, was created in July 1969. After one year of work, the association presented a proposal to modify the present legislation, based on the following principles:

(1) From an ethical viewpoint, the association suggested the principle: choose the lesser of two evils.

(2) Abortion concerns not only the mother but also the child, the family, and the society. It follows that a complete freedom of abortion is not possible. The state must retain a certain kind of control.

(3) Women should be persuaded to use contraception to avoid repetitive abortion. In both cases, too many facilities for abortion would be dangerous.

The ANEA proposed the following grounds for abortion: present or future threat to the life of the mother; serious impairment of the physical or mental health of the mother; damage to the fetus resulting in probable permanent impairment; rape; incapacity of one parent through hereditary disease or mental illness to care for the child; and economic and social conditions that would seriously compromise the well-being of the child or the family. Table 2 compares the present legislation, the proposal of the high committee, and the proposal of ANEA.

¶ A LEGISLATIVE ACTION: THE PROPOSED PEYRET'S BILL
The work of ANEA was examined by the parliamentary study group of UDR[16] (Health and Social Affairs). After hearing various experts, the group concluded that it could not accept the whole proposal of ANEA, and it drafted Peyret's bill, accepting all but three of ANEA's recommendations (see Table 2). The bill was submitted to the Assembly for discussion in June 1970 but has not yet been discussed. The proposal brought the whole question of abortion into the open and was the starting point for a series of public discussions on abortion.

¶ REACTION TO PEYRET'S PROPOSAL
The first reactions came from ANEA, whose recommendations had initiated the parliamentary action. ANEA was disappointed by the final text

---

[16] *Union démocratique républicaine*, the political party of the majority of the Assembly.

TABLE 2.

Comparison of the Various Proposals Concerning the Legislation on Abortion and of the Opinions of Various Groups of People on this Matter, France, 1970

Indications for Abortion	Present Legislation	Present Legislation and Proposals for Modifications				Opinion of Various Groups of People ("yes" means that a majority approves, "no" means that a majority disapproves)			
		High Consultative Committee on Population and the Family	Peyret's Bill	ANEA's Proposals	Cavaillet's Bill	Total Population (July 1970) ANEA[a]	Medical Physicians		Total Population (November 1970) SOFRES[c]
							The Whole Profession (July 1970) ANEA[b]	Council of Order (October 1970)	
		1	2	3	4	5	6	7	8
Life of the pregnant woman endangered at the present moment	Yes	Yes	Yes	Yes	Yes	Yes	Yes	Yes	Yes
Life of the pregnant woman endangered in the future	No	Yes	Yes	Yes	Yes	Yes	Yes	Yes	Yes
Physical and mental health of the pregnant woman seriously impaired	No	Yes	No	Yes	Yes	Yes	Yes	No	Yes
The fœtus has been seriously impaired, and there is a strong probability of abnormality at birth (serious sickness, malformations, psychotic troubles)	No	No	Yes	Yes	Yes	Yes	Yes	Yes	Yes
The pregnancy is the result of violence	No	No	Yes	Yes	Yes	Yes	Yes	No	[d]
The pregnant woman is single and less than 21 years old	No	No	No	No	Yes	No	No	No	No
One parent is mentally sick or is suffering from a hereditary disease making him unable to take care of the material and moral needs of a child	No	No	No	Yes	Yes	No	No	No	[d]
Pregnant woman already has three children	No	No	No	No	Yes	No	No	No	No
Economic and social conditions of pregnant woman are such that full development of child and family seriously compromised	No	No	No	Yes	Yes	No	No	No	No

[a] Gallup poll (IFOP) of 3,000 people representing the whole population of France.
[b] Gallup poll (IFOP) of 499 medical physicians.
[c] Gallup poll (SOFRES) of 1,000 people representing the whole population of France.
[d] The question has not been asked.

which only retained the more conservative aspects of their proposal (see Table 2). ANEA released the results of two surveys, one showing that most French people favored more liberal legislation on abortion than that in Peyret's bill, the other showing that the position of physicians vis-à-vis abortion closely paralleled the proposals of ANEA (Table 2).

¶ OFFICIAL POSITION OF THE MEDICAL PROFESSION

The National Council of Medical Order gave the official position of the medical profession with respect to the present legislation and to the proposal of the High Consultative Committee on Population and the Family on the concept of "self-protection." The extension of this concept to circumstances endangering the *life* of the mother in the future was in its view permissible, but the statement stressed that the life of the mother had to really be endangered and that grounds of impairment of health or social and economic difficulties were not acceptable.

The council did not feel that the interruption of pregnancy resulting from violent action was justified as a case of self-protection. If Parliament voted a law favorable to such abortions, the National Council of Medical Order would oppose the presence of medical physicians on the commission responsible for authorization.

The council did not find malformation of the fetus a case of self-protection but accepted the possibility of an abortion in such a case because of the undue strain on the pregnant woman that the situation would cause.

The most interesting proposal of the National Council of Medical Order was that the best course perhaps would be to avoid any legislative action and to give full responsibilities about rules on abortion to the medical professional, provided the "deontological code"[17] be modified to avoid too great laxity.

¶ POSITION OF LAWYERS

An antiabortion association of lawyers was created in November 1970. Its aim is to inform members of the bar that, by remaining silent, they sanction the violation of essential human values represented by Peyret's bill 70/ 1347. In June and July 1971, the association published statements warning the general public against the bill and requesting Parliament to vote against it and to seek new legislative measures to relieve the burdens of unwanted pregnancies.

---

[17] The *deontological code* is the set of rules that medical physicians agree to apply in the exercise of their profession. For the time being, according to these rules, abortion is authorized only when the life of the mother is endangered. If full responsibilities on abortion were given to the physicians, the code would have to be modified, but the medical order is not proposing that the new code give to the physicians complete freedom to decide on abortion.

¶ POSITION OF THE CHURCHES

The Catholic church took a stand as soon as Peyret's bill was submitted to the bureau of the Assembly. Several bishops issued statements rejecting the proposal. In February 1971, the Episcopal Commission on the Family published a booklet reaffirming the church's categorical opposition to abortion.

In March 1971, the Protestant Federation of France issued a statement. After noting that society is entering increasingly into a stage in which the ethic of responsibility is replacing the ethic of respect for nature including its abnormalities, the Protestant Federation pointed out that no legislative action can relieve parents and medical physicians from their responsibilities in the matter of abortion. A legislative frame can only guide them in decision making. A little reluctantly, the federation accepted the following framework: Abortion would be permitted if the pregnancy represents a very serious danger to the physical and mental state of the mother, if there is a high probability that the child will be born with a malformation, if the pregnancy is a result of violence, or if the mother is less than sixteen years old. The federation also recommended that the law provide some procedure to help mothers who were granted permission for an abortion.

¶ OTHER REACTIONS

A number of other associations traditionally opposed to abortion also took official positions. Although Peyret's proposal was quite moderate and fell far short of the proposals of the High Consultative Committee on Population and the Family, the supporters of the status quo felt, from reading the introductory note to the bill, that the sponsors of the project considered their proposal as a first step toward more extended modifications.

Speaking of the diversity of opinion, the introductory note says, for example, that "the group was convinced by the hearing that *at this moment*[18] it was premature to try to reconcile these various opinions." Later on, the note states that the proposal represents "a change of position, *perhaps limited but nevertheless of a fundamental nature.*"[19]

The Human Life Association, created in 1968, had in May 1970, before Peyret's bill was submitted to the bureau of the Assembly, expressed its regret over the action of the supporters of contraception who had succeeded in passing the law of December 1967 and who were now trying to change the legislation regarding abortion.

The Federation of Couples and Families, a conglomerate of fifty-four associations spread throughout France, indicated that Peyret's bill was unable to solve the multiple problems raised by abortion.

Finally, a new antiabortion association entitled Let Them Live was created at the end of 1970.

[18] Italics mine.
[19] Italics mine.

In November 1970, a public discussion on the problem was held on television. On this occasion, the results of a Gallup poll of the whole population of France were made known. They confirmed the previous survey of ANEA showing that the public favored liberalization of abortion. Table 2 gives the various opinions expressed on the subject.

¶ NEWCOMERS AND NEW MEANS OF ACTION

The year 1971 marked the entry into the debate of advocates of complete freedom of abortion. These advocates used manifestos, public debates, and open letters to propagate their stance.

At the initiative of the Women's Liberation Front, the weekly newspaper *Le Nouvel Observateur* published on April 5, 1971, a manifesto in which 343 French women known to the public (writers, actresses, singers, movie stars, political leaders, and so forth) declared that, at least once in their lives, they had had recourse to abortion.

Three weeks later, the same newspaper organized a public debate when the results of a new Gallup poll were made public. The questions asked in this survey differed from those in the previous surveys and, consequently, so did the answers. The main results of the survey are shown in Table 3.

Some people were annoyed by the fact that the Women's Liberation Front was purely feminist. The need for a movement in which women and men could militate led to the creation of a Movement for the Liberalization of Abortion, which created a new association—Choice—with the aim of obtaining complete freedom for abortion.

From the ethical point of view, these movements based their claims on the woman's freedom to control her own body.

Some medical physicians signed the manifesto published on April 5 in *Le Nouvel Observateur* but not in their capacity as physicians. A special manifesto signed by 500 medical physicians was published in *Le Nouvel Observateur* on May 3, 1971. These physicians declared that they favored complete freedom of abortion and invoked the respect of individual rights, as did the previous manifesto of women. But they added a new justification for legalized abortion linked to their professional activities: They stated that the present legislation placed physicians in a position contrary to the code of medical deontology by making them guilty of "not rendering assistance to persons in danger."

Gynecologists refused to sign the manifesto, explaining in a separate manifesto that they favored liberalization but were against a complete freedom of abortion. As physicians qualified to perform abortion, they stressed the dangers of repeated abortions. They felt that contraception was safer than abortion and that complete freedom of abortion would impede the use of contraceptive methods.

TABLE 3.

Survey on the Opinion of the Population on Abortion, France, 1971

Questions	Replies (in percents)		
	Yes	No	Do Not Know
Has a woman, bearing an unwanted child, the right to be aborted by a medical physician?	55	38	7
It is sometimes said that an abortion is a murder. Do you agree?	47	42	11
Do you think that abortion is a personal concern for each woman (reply yes) or a concern for the whole society (reply no)?	66	27	7
Do you agree with the opinion that couples ought to be free to make decisions regarding abortion?	87	7	6
Do you think that now that the pill is authorized, if abortion is also authorized, the number of births will be insufficient in France?	35	48	17
Do you think that it is hypocritical to forbid abortion when it is well-known that this problem is the concern of many French people?	62	24	14
Do you think that, if rendering contraception becomes easier, the problem of abortion will disappear?	57	29	14
Do you think that abortion is not a serious problem in France because any woman looking for an abortion can get one?	50	37	13

SOURCE: See [3].

Of course, the publication of these manifestos drew strong reactions from those opposed to liberalization of abortion. A manifesto against abortion signed by 100 known personalities of the medical, social, judicial, and cultural circles was published by the Confederation of Catholic Family Associations.

¶ A NEW BILL

In the middle of this hot discussion, Senator Cavaillet proposed to the Assembly a bill much more liberal than Peyret's. His proposed bill permits abortion on almost all grounds, as can be seen from Table 2. It represented the translation into parliamentary action of the manifestos published by *Le Nouvel Observateur.*

¶ THE POSITION OF THE GOVERNMENT

The government made known its position through a private letter sent by Minister of Health and Social Security Robert Boulin in June 1971 to Prime Minister M. Jacques Chaban-Delmas, explaining that the government was studying new legislation regarding abortion. The letter did not give many details but mentioned that the government was prepared to authorize abortions on the first four grounds in the ANEA proposals (mentioned in Table 2). The letter was disclosed to the public two months later, and then its contents were only partially revealed. In reaction to the letter, the president of the Confederation of Catholic Families Association wrote a letter to the President of the Republic, M. G. Pompidou, protesting the terms of Boulin's letter.

At the same time, the association Let Them Live announced a congress in Versailles on November 6, 1971.

Finally, in May 1971, the French Communist party published its position on the problem of abortion, endorsing the proposals made by ANEA (see Table 2).

¶ FURTHER DEVELOPMENTS

This concludes the account of the situation on the eve of 1972. Figure 1 shows clearly that, in 1971, the controversy grew and, with it, the pressure for a resolution. The general consensus was that the situation was ripe for a fruitful discussion by the Parliament, and everybody was waiting for an initiative from the government. Surprisingly, the pressure cooled in 1972, and discussions on a revision of the law almost disappeared from the press.

On March 31, 1972, the Communist party submitted to the bureau of the Parliament a bill permitting abortion along the lines of the proposals made by ANEA.

On April 27, the association Let Them Live held a press conference on its activities,[20] and at the beginning of May, ANEA held for two days its second international conference on abortion. These various events were mentioned by the press with almost no commentaries.

The "fire" started again in 1973. On February 4, a manifesto signed by 330 medical physicians was made public. The physicians were advocating complete freedom for abortion and explained that during the last few

---

[20] The association is running centers to help parents with physically handicapped children.

months they had performed abortions. Three days later, on February 7, a declaration signed by 206 important personalities belonging to various circles was published. These persons explained that, taking into account the absence of any governmental action in the matter of abortion, they decided to move by themselves. They elaborated a "charter" of abortion, corresponding more or less to the previous proposals of ANEA, with commissions set up to examine requests for abortion transmitted by physicians. When a commission decided that a case met the conditions of the charter, abortion was performed by one gynecologist chosen from the 206 signers free of charge if the woman was too poor to pay.

Both groups were acting illegally, but no action was taken from the judicial side. The government declared it was a problem to be solved by the National Council of Medical Order, and this order declared it was a case to be treated by the courts.

The time for the publication of the manifesto of the 330 and the declaration of the 206 was purposely chosen close to the legislative elections. Candidates were urged by ANEA to take a position on the subject. In fact, the political circles did not react and carefully avoided making abortion a case to be discussed in the election campaigns.

Public opinion itself did not take fire. The associations opposed to a liberalization of abortion made critical statements and produced other manifestos also signed by physicians who condemned the action of their colleagues.

However, the Minister of Health and the Prime Minister declared that they agreed on the necessity to revise the law of 1920 and pledged that they would take proper actions for such a revision after the elections, provided they continued to be in power.

No doubt the measures taken in other countries for a liberalization of abortion influenced the decision. In this connection, it is worthwhile to mention the publication in January 1973 in the review *Études* (a monthly review established in 1856 by the Jesuits) of a study entitled "For a Reform of the French Legislation on Abortion." For the first time, a group of Catholic people were opening the door to a more liberal interpretation of the Christian dogma on abortion. It is difficult to summarize in a few words a study of thirty pages in which almost every word is important. Let us say that the authors make a distinction between a human being and a humanized human being, that is, a human being who enters into relations with other people. The goal of procreation is to produce humanized human beings, and when the condition of humanization does not exist, the pregnancy may be interrupted by an abortion. They proposed that commissions be established whose aim would be to discuss with the parents the condi-

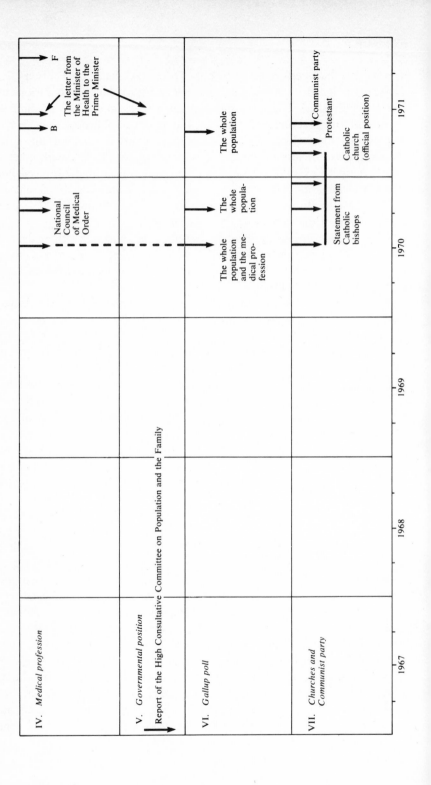

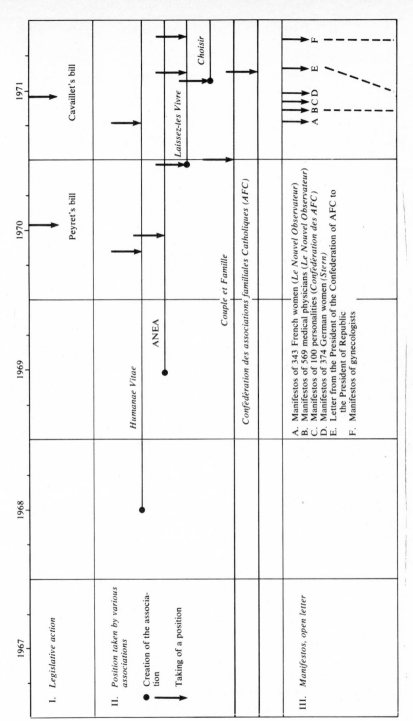

FIGURE 1

The Problem of Abortion in France: List of Various Events
That Took Place in France from 1967 to 1971

tions of "humanization" and decide if the abortion should be permitted or not. Such a system is very close to the one put into action by the 206 signers of the charter of abortion.

Since abortion generally is presented as a solution to unwanted pregnancies, it seems worthwhile to describe the ways in which French law presently deals with unwanted pregnancies. In each department in France, there is a Maternity Home where any pregnant woman can stay from the time her pregnancy becomes visible until after the birth of the child. The state facilities are free of charge, although there are also private clinics that provide the same service at a charge (with partial reimbursement from the social security system). In any public or private maternity home, any pregnant woman is entitled to ask to be hospitalized anonymously.

In each department, there is an office open day and night where it is possible to abandon anonymously any child less than one year old. The child becomes the ward of the government which may look for a foster family for him. Thus, a pregnant woman who, for whatever reasons, does not want to have a child can give birth and then legally ask the society to take charge of her child.

These arrangements, however, are no solution to the problems of abortion. They work only because few women make use of them: In 1970 in Paris, only 236 children were abandoned. If all women resorting to abortion decided to bring their pregnancies to term and to give the children to society, the social and economic burden represented by these abandoned children would be tremendous, and the legislation would have to be modified.

POLICY ON CONTRACEPTION

Until 1920, there was no official policy in France on contraception. The only legal bases against contraception were the dispositions of the penal code punishing affronts to decency. Although these regulations were invoked during the nineteenth century against contraceptive propaganda, Paul Robin was able in 1870 to open a clinic in Paris where advice on contraception was given to poor women because no legislation prohibited the functioning of such clinics.

The law passed by Parliament in 1920 prohibiting promotion and practice of induced abortion also prohibited the dissemination of contraceptive propaganda and the diffusion of information on and the sale of contraceptives or any devices supposed to be contraceptive in nature. This law was interpreted stringently by the courts during the following years.

The two articles dealing with contraception read as follows:

Article L. 648: Anybody who describes, discloses or offers to disclose contraceptive methods or facilitates the practice of these methods by using any of the means enumerated in Article L. 647[21] as a part of a propaganda in favor of contraception shall be punished by six months of imprisonment and a fine of 360 fr. to 18,000 fr. The same punishment shall be given to anybody having an activity of propaganda in favor of contraception or against natality.

Article L. 649: The same punishment shall be given for infractions listed in Articles L. 517, 518, 556[22] when the secret remedies are said to have the power of preventing a conception even if this power is an illusory one.

Several criticisms of the form of the law might be offered. First, the law deals with two different matters, abortion and contraception, and it is unfortunate to establish a connection between the two fields in the mind of the public. Second, the passages forbidding any propaganda in favor of contraception and forbidding sales of contraceptive devices are subject to misinterpretation; for example, the High Consultative Committee on Population and the Family made the following comment:

When reading Articles L. 648 and L. 649, one could argue that the law had in mind only to repress any propaganda in favor of contraception. Article L. 648 (first paragraph) would repress only actions taking place as a part of an activity of propaganda in favor of contraception. The second part of the same article deals with pure propaganda. . . .

Article L. 649 seems to repress the sale and offer of . . . secret remedies supposing to have a contraceptive action even if it is pure illusion. The text is not very clear, but seems however to be dealing again with advertising [4, p. 23].

¶ THE APPLICATION OF THE LAW

In fact, the court of justice decided not to interpret the law in such a liberal way. The basic decision was made by the court of cassation (supreme court of appeals) in 1925, under the following circumstances: The court of appeals of Paris rendered a judgment of not guilty for a seller of contraceptive devices, arguing that the sale was made without any outside act of propaganda. The public prosecutor asked the court of cassation to void the decision, and the court complied on December 10, 1925. One week earlier, the same court of cassation had rendered a judgment ruling that

---

[21] Article L. 647 enumerates in detail the means which are forbidden. These are: the public speeches—the sale, the organizing of sale or offering for sale, even in private, or through exhibits, posters, distributions on the streets or in public locations, home distributions, distributions in wrappers or in envelopes opened or closed through the post office or any agent distributing or transporting books, writings, printed matter, advertisements, posters, drawings, pictures, badges—the advertising through a medical or so-called medical officer.

[22] The infraction concerns the making and selling of drugs.

the *practice* of contraception was not forbidden by the law. These two judgments decided the practical application of the law until a new law was voted in 1967. Thus, the situation was as follows in France from 1925 to 1967:

(1) Propaganda for contraception was forbidden.
(2) Sale of contraceptive devices was forbidden even if no propaganda was attached to it.
(3) The practice of contraception was permitted.

The application of the law went, therefore, beyond the initial intention of the lawmakers.

A movement started in the 1950s finally led to the abrogation of the 1920 law and the vote of a new law by Parliament in December 1967. The events leading to the ruling can be classified on three levels: private, legislative, and governmental.

The private activities were dominated by one person, Dr. Marie André Lougroua-Weill-Hallé, and one association, the French Movement for Family Planning. In 1953, Dr. Lagroua-Weill-Hallé published an article urging a revision of the 1920 law. In 1955, she submitted a statement at the Congress of Medical Ethics in Paris in which she explained that the law of 1920 was difficult to reconcile with the medical ethic. Later the same year, in a communication to the Academy of Ethics and Political Sciences, she cited reasons why the law of 1920 endangered the equilibrium of the family and the health of women.

In March 1956, the association Happy Motherhood was created with the aim of promoting family planning in France, taking its name on September 28, 1960.

In 1960, Dr. Lagroua-Weill-Hallé published a report on her experiences in giving contraceptive advice to 218 women who came to consult her for gynecological problems. In June 1961, Dr. H. Fabre, a medical physician, arguing that the law of 1920 only prohibited propaganda in favor of contraception, opened a center of information on family planning in Grenoble. His interpretation of the law of 1920 did not contradict the language of the laws, but it contradicted the interpretation adopted by the court of justice. No judicial action was taken against Dr. Fabre, and a second center was opened in Paris in October 1961. Many others followed and when, at the end of 1967, a new law on contraception was voted, 300 centers provided information on family planning. As is explained later in this report, the new law, in its Article 4, recognized the usefulness of such centers and requested the government to establish a special ruling of public administration for their creation and functioning.[23]

---

[23] This ruling has been published, and the centers are gradually being organized.

In 1963, the association Happy Motherhood changed its title to National Federation of Happy Motherhood. It became a member of IPPF (European region).

¶ THE FUTURE

The main, if not the only, objective of the National Federation of Happy Motherhood was to obtain from the Parliament the vote of a new law abrogating the 1920 law. The law of December 27, 1967, fulfilled the aims of the federation at least with regard to contraception. The new law did not modify the dispositions of the 1920 law concerning abortion. The federation announced immediately after the passing of the new law that it would continue to fight for a liberalized abortion law. With regard to contraception, the federation was uncertain how to define its program of action. There was no guarantee that the 300 centers of information on and guidance in contraception it had established would be accepted by the government. Pending the government publication of rules for the creation and functioning of such centers, the federation continues to administer them.

Recently, at its eighth congress, the federation published the basic principles of its action. Centering its activities on the problems raised by sex, the federation cited three broad fields of action: sex and the institutional framework, sex and social conditions, and sex and the cultural environment. It reiterated its fight for the liberalization of abortion.

¶ LEGISLATIVE ACTION

The first move in the legislative field occurred in 1956 when four bills were submitted to the bureau of the Assembly aiming at modifying the 1920 law. The sponsors of the bills were members of the opposition, and their proposals were not discussed. Nine years later in 1965, during the campaign for the presidency of the republic, most of the candidates openly favored the passage of a new law. In October 1965, the Minister of Health, when questioned in the Assembly on the matter, decided to initiate a commission to report to him on oral contraception, and he asked INED to report on the possible demographic consequences of a liberalization of contraception in France.

Various new bills were proposed by members of the opposition at the Chamber of Deputies. They were not discussed. On May 18, 1966, a member of the majority group in the Assembly, M. Neuwirth, presented a draft bill which, after some revision, was voted on December 28, 1967. In the first draft, parental authorization to receive contraceptive devices was required only for persons under eighteen years of age. In the final text, authorization for oral contraceptives also is needed for people under age twenty-one. The first draft requested the creation of a special institute—

Institute for Biological and Medical Studies on Procreation—and a National Office on Information and Education Regarding the Family. Neither proposal was retained; only the creation and functioning of centers of contraceptive information were authorized by law.

¶ GOVERNMENT ACTION

In 1961, the French government created a special committee on the family to study the various aspects of birth control in France. The committee recommended that a working group be established to examine in detail how the 1920 law could be modified.

The working group initially proposed a more liberal interpretation of the 1920 law rather than abolishment of the law.

The High Consultative Committee on Population and the Family, in its 1967 report on birth control, opposed retention of the 1920 law because it was subject to misinterpretation. The committee further recommended separate laws governing abortion and contraception.

As mentioned above, a deputy of the majority group submitted a draft bill to Parliament. A working group was established in the Assembly which, after hearing many people (medical physicians, sociologists, demographers, theologians, political leaders, and so forth) submitted a bill to the bureau of the Assembly. Finally, on December 27, 1967, the new law containing nine articles was adopted.

Article 1 nullified Articles L. 648 and 649 of the law of 1920 which prohibited birth control information and the distribution and sale of contraceptives.

Articles 2 and 3 authorized the manufacture, sale, and import of contraceptives to be distributed solely by pharmacies. Each contraceptive was to be authorized by the government (subject to conditions to be fixed by a special ruling of the public administration). Contraceptive drugs can be sold only by medical prescription, and the pharmacist must keep a record of such sales. IUDs must be inserted by medical physicians in clinics or hospitals under conditions to be fixed by a special ruling of the public administration. For people under eighteen years old, a written authorization of one parent is necessary to buy contraceptives. For contraceptive drugs, a written parental authorization is necessary for people less than twenty-one years old. A special ruling of public administration will define implementation of these matters.

Article 4 stated that a ruling would determine conditions for the creation and functioning of special centers to give information and advice on contraception. Such centers would not be authorized to dispense contraceptives or to work for money.

Article 5 forbade any propaganda against natality or in favor of contraception and permitted advertisements about contraceptives in medical publications only. Here again, a special ruling of public administration is foreseen.

Article 6 stated that special measures would be taken in France's extraterritorial holdings, according to the individual situations.

Article 7 listed sanctions to be incurred by violators of the law.

Article 8 assigned the government the responsibility of preparing annual reports on the demographic trends in France.

Finally *Article 9* stated that the various rulings of public administration referred to in the previous articles must be published within six months following promulgation of the law.

The basic similarities and differences between the law of 1920 and the law of 1967 can be summarized as follows:

Law of 1920	*Law of 1967*
(1) Propaganda against natality or in favor of contraception is forbidden.	(a) Propaganda against natality or in favor of contraception is forbidden.
(2) Sale of contraceptives is forbidden even if it is not linked to a propaganda activity.	(b) Manufacturing, import, and sale of contraceptives are authorized under certain conditions and provided that they are not part of propaganda activities.
(3) The practice of contraception is legally permitted.	(c) The practice of contraception is legally permitted, and in order to facilitate this practice, special centers of information and advice will be created.

The law announced the publication of six special "Rulings of Public Administration." As of February 1973, five rulings have been published. The pending ruling concerns the application of the law to the departments of Guadeloupe, Martinique, and Reunion.

¶ THE OVERSEAS DEPARTMENTS

Regarding the three departments of Guadeloupe, Martinique, and Reunion, a decree of October 4, 1968, dealing with the financing of certain social actions pointed out that the expenses for the implementation of a policy tending to control population growth would be paid by the social security budget. This represents a liberal application of the 1967 law. Even reimbursement of expenses related to abortion is accepted by the social security system (but, of course, under a different denomination). In Guadeloupe and Martinique, the existence of a small dependency of Guadeloupe—the island of St. Martin, half of which is under Dutch administration, the other half, French—facilitates the import of oral contraceptives and IUDs.

The leaders of the Catholic church on these islands favor this liberal policy, although there is some opposition to it among parish priests.

There is a fourth overseas department: French Guiana. It was not mentioned in the 1967 law, but the decree of October 4, 1968, is applicable there. No detailed information is available on the situation in this department, but the policy is probably as liberal as in the three others.

In addition to the four overseas departments, France administers seven overseas territories: the Comoro Islands, French territory of the Afars and the Issas, and the French Southern and Antarctic territories near Africa; Saint Pierre and Miquelon in North America; and French Polynesia, New Caledonia, and Wallis and Futuna Islands in Oceania. Finally, the archipelago of New Hebrides is a French-English condominium (that is, a territory jointly administered by France and the United Kingdom).

These territories are mentioned neither in the 1967 law nor in the decree of October 4, 1968. The position in these territories regarding contraception and abortion is difficult to ascertain.

In spite of a restrictive legislation on contraception, France was the first country in the world to start its demographic revolution by diminishing its fertility in the second half of the eighteenth century. Fertility in the other countries of western Europe began to decline only three-quarters of a century later. But the decline was more rapid than it was in France, and on the eve of World War II, most of the countries of western Europe had more or less the same fertility (a crude birth rate of around 16 percent). After the war, an increase of fertility occurred in western Europe, but since 1964, a decline can be observed. So far, France has not participated too much in this decline, and as a result, as of 1972, fertility in France is the highest among the western European countries, the United States, and Canada. Perhaps this is the result of the French policy on the family. The natural increase is approximately equal to 330,000 each year.

POLICY ON INTERNATIONAL MIGRATION

Until the beginning of the nineteenth century, emigration exceeded immigration in France. In the nineteenth century, this trend was reversed, perhaps as a consequence of the decline of fertility. From 1851 to 1968, the population of foreign origin has been multiplied by 100 (Table 4). These data represent a minimum. For a more accurate estimate, it is necessary to add to the number of naturalized citizens and foreigners those people who

TABLE 4.

Foreign Population, France, 1800–1968 (in thousands)

Year	Naturalized	Foreigners	Total
1800		100	100
1805		110	110
1810		130	130
1815		160	160
1820		200	200
1825		220	220
1830		240	240
1835		270	270
1840		300	300
1845		330	330
1851	14	381	395
1861	15	497	512
1866	16	635	651
1872	15	741	756
1876	35	802	837
1881	77	1,001	1,078
1886	104	1,127	1,231
1891	171	1,130	1,301
1896	203	1,052	1,255
1901	222	1,034	1,256
1906	222	1,047	1,269
1911	253	1,160	1,413
1921	256	1,532	1,788
1926	249	2,409	2,658
1931	361	2,715	3,076
1936	517	2,198	2,715
1946	853	1,744	2,597
1954	1,068	1,765	1,833
1962	1,284	2,170	3,454
1968	1,316	2,664	3,980

SOURCES: Estimates for 1800 to 1845 taken from [5, p. 94]. Figures for 1851 to 1968 from census data.

automatically obtained French citizenship by marriage or birth. Presently, the order of magnitude of the latter would be 1 million, which gives therefore a total population of foreign origin of 5 million, that is, 10 percent of the entire population.

For a long time, there had been no special legislation on nonnationals. During the last quarter of the nineteenth century, measures were passed to restrict the free movement of foreigners on French territory and to curb the entry of foreigners. A law of 1888 required foreigners to declare to the local authorities their place of residence within fifteen days of their arrival. A ruling of 1893 required foreigners to register change of residence and prohibited an employer from hiring nonregistered foreigners. In 1899, percentage limits were established for employment of foreigners by the state, the departments, and the communes. During the same period, a special tax on foreigners was proposed but never passed.

There was no legislation to prevent the entry of foreigners. The first attempt to organize the entry of foreign workers was undertaken by the Federation of Agricultural Societies of the North West which began to encourage the immigration of Polish agricultural workers in 1907. In 1908, the Committee of Iron Masters organized the immigration of Italian workers. At the same time, the coal mining societies of the north of France organized the hiring of Polish miners.

The outbreak of World War I brought significant changes in government policy. The French economy needed foreign manpower to replace the French workers called by the army. At the Ministry of War, a service recruited workers from colonial territories and China, mainly employed by the state in private establishments producing arms and munitions. A service at the Ministry of Agriculture imported workers for agriculture. A service at the Ministry of Army Supplies imported laborers from other areas.

In 1917, the government decided to establish a special residence permit for foreigners aged fifteen years and over. By the end of the war, the government was directing the entry of foreign workers through the following framework:

(1) A service of the agriculture manpower (Ministry of Agriculture).
(2) A service of the foreign manpower outside agriculture (Ministry of Labor).
(3) An interministerial commission linked to the Ministry of Foreign Affairs and dealing with diplomatic problems. Its name was Permanent Interministerial Commission on Immigration.

Outside of this framework, other ministries took charge of specific aspects of immigration such as special residence permits, naturalization and civil status, international agreements, and special problems raised by foreigners. This structure continued until the outbreak of World War II in 1939.

Private enterprises, in 1924, created a General Society of Immigration which took care of all concrete problems related to the immigration of foreign workers: recruitment, professional and medical selection, transportation, welcome in France, and so on.

Although the responsibilities in matters of immigration were spread among a great number of groups, the results were quite satisfactory in that the entry of foreigners increased rapidly after 1921 and reached a peak in 1931.

At that time, the effect of the world economic crisis began to be felt in France. Confronted with increased unemployment, the government decided to stop the flow of foreign workers. A law of 1932 limited the number of foreign workers in each sector of the economy. The law also specified a complicated procedure for the entry of foreign workers which tended to discourage candidates. At the same time, the various services dealing with immigration were centralized under the direction of the Ministry of Labor, and in 1936, a Secretariat of State for Immigration Matters was created. It lasted only a few months.

¶ THE END OF WORLD WAR II

At the end of World War II, mass immigration of foreign workers appeared necessary not only for economic reasons, as was the case after World War I, but also for demographic reasons. The provisional government of France adopted two ordinances: the Ordinance of October 19, 1945, dealing with the *French nationality*; and the Ordinance of November 2, 1945, regulating the *conditions of entry and stay in France of foreigners* and creating the National Office of Immigration. These ordinances have been modified during the last twenty-five years, but the basic framework they established remains valid. They were based on the following four principles: (1) large immigration was necessary; (2) immigration must be controlled; (3) the state must take charge of all recruiting operations; and (4) the assimilation of foreign people by the French society must be facilitated.

The old Permanent Interministerial Commission on Immigration created in 1920 was reorganized. Instead of being attached to the Ministry of Foreign Affairs, it was put under the direction of a new Ministry of Population (later the Ministry of Health and Population).

A National Office of Immigration was created as an autonomous organism, under the authority of the Ministries of Labor and Population.

The Interministerial Commission on Immigration continued to take charge of fixing the principles and the broad lines of the governmental policy on immigration. The task of the national office was to carry out this policy, replacing private organizations which, between the two world wars, were in charge of solving concrete problems raised by immigration. At the beginning, the office did not deal with family members of foreign workers, but soon, at the request of the Ministry of Population, it took charge of these people.

¶ THE PROCESS OF ENTRY INTO FRANCE

In principle, an employer willing to hire a foreign worker had to send a request to the National Office of Immigration which recruited abroad a suitable candidate to whom a firm offer was proposed. The office took charge of transportation of the immigrant from the point of departure in the foreign country to the point of arrival at the work place. If the foreign worker was accompanied by his (or her) family, a lodging for the family had to be provided by the employer.

The office had to establish branches abroad in agreement with foreign countries. Medical and professional selection of candidates took place at these branches.

The ordinances in 1945 and 1946 established regulations regarding residence permits and work permits. A residence permit is compulsory for every foreigner. A work permit, delivered by the Ministry of Labor through the National Office of Immigration, is necessary only if the foreigner wants to work.

A foreigner with a residence permit who decides later on to work must pass through the National Office of Immigration just as a foreigner coming directly for work. This means that, in theory, he is obliged to return to his country to be taken in charge by the authorities legally entrusted for the entry of workers in France. However, a special process—the process of regularization—has been established that permits foreigners to obtain work permits without leaving the country. This process was only to be resorted to in exceptional circumstances.

¶ THE RESULTS

Starting in 1946, the institutional framework was, therefore, ready for a mass immigration. In fact, such an immigration did not materialize.

The process of regularization became increasingly common and soon constituted a substantive part of the work of the immigration office. In 1951–1955, a period in which the economy had little demand for foreign workers, regularization represented 38 percent of the total entries. After 1961, when economic demand increased, the rate of regularization also increased dramatically.

Regularization was associated with bad material and moral conditions for the workers. They were brought to France as tourists by illegal organizations that demanded a lot of money for their services. Arriving with debts, the workers were generally hired at reduced salaries which they were forced to accept because of their illegal status. They had no permits, and often they lived in very bad conditions.

This led the government to try to reverse the trend. A working group was created in January 1965 with the aim of proposing a new policy on immigration. The report of this working group was made public in June 1965.

¶ THE REASONS FOR THE FAILURE

Before examining the proposals of the group, it seems worthwhile to come back to the functioning of the whole institutional framework put into action just after World War II. Besides the National Commission of Immigration, which was in charge of establishing the government policy on immigration, other organizations were created which also advised on these problems.

A decree of April 12, 1945, had created at the presidency of the provisional government a Permanent Interministerial Commission on Immigration and a High Consultative Committee on Population and the Family.[24] Both dealt with immigration.

The members of the interministerial committee were ministers, whereas the members of the immigration commission were only high civil servants of various ministries. It was, therefore, in fact the interministerial committee that defined the policy on immigration, taking into account the advice of the High Consultative Committee. The immigration commission gradually lost power, and it ceased to meet after 1958.

The primacy of the interministerial committee was sanctioned in 1964 by the decree of June 25, 1964 (no. 64-628), which clearly stated that this committee had to deal "with policy on population and family, particularly in the field of . . . migratory movements both internal and external."

But there was no organizational link between the interministerial committee and the National Office of Immigration, which was supposed to follow instructions from the Permanent Interministerial Commission on Immigration. In the absence of such instructions, the two ministers who had authority in the office—the Minister of Public Health and Population and the Minister of Labor—gave instructions to the office. As the economic aspects were becoming prominent, the Ministry of Labor took the lead and alone practically ran the National Office of Immigration. In fact, the creation in January 1965 of the working group referred to above was due to the initiative of the Ministry of Labor.

[24] The High Consultative Committee on Population and the Family was reorganized in 1970. It no longer deals with the family, but it continues to deal with migration (see section on family policies for more details).

¶ THE NEW PRINCIPLES

The proposals of the working group were as follows: The policy would be established by the High Consultative Committee on Population and the Family, after consulting with a group of high-level civil servants. The National Office of Immigration would continue to carry out the policy, but it would be reorganized in such a way as to have better collaboration between the state, the employers, and the unions.

The government accepted in principle the proposals set up by the working group but was reluctant to modify the existing legal scheme. It preferred to reinforce the effects of the actual legislation by way of circular letters sent to the executants.

On July 29, 1968, a circular letter, issued by the Ministry of Labor, stated that the only foreigners eligible for regularization were those who were (1) of Portuguese nationality; (2) willing to work in personal services; (3) skilled workers, performing a job not listed in a document established quarterly by the Ministry of Labor.

Members of workers' families could continue to be "regularized if necessary."

The circular letter was quite efficient. The proportion of regularized situations dropped rapidly.

On July 29, 1971, a protocol was signed with the Portuguese authorities (effective September 1, 1971) aimed at normalizing the introduction of Portuguese workers.

A new circular letter recently has been published. It concerns (1) simplification of the delivery of permits of residence and permits of work; (2) a requirement that the employers find a dwelling for each foreign worker they employ; (3) a requirement that the employers seek a French worker in the National Employment Agency before hiring a foreigner; (4) creation of new mechanisms improving collaboration of the state with the professional organizations and the unions; (5) provision of fellowships for school children of foreign workers;[25] and (6) decentralization at the local level of certain activities relating to immigrants.

¶ EXCEPTIONS

Three categories of foreigners remain outside the legislation: The citizens from former European territories which have been members of the

---

[25] The creation of fellowships deserves an explanation. According to the existing system, the fellowships are given only to children of French citizens (except for Algerian children). Some private organizations dealing with the social problems of the migrants have tried to fill the gap by distributing a small number of fellowships to the most promising children of foreign workers, and the state has subsidized these private organizations for that purpose. But the circular letter in the making wants to include the children of foreigners in the regular channels of the educational system.

Communauté and which now represent fifteen independent countries in Africa. According to the multilateral agreements signed on June 22, 1960, they are not considered as foreigners in France, and they do not need a permit of residence or a permit of work to be engaged in an economic activity. Since the signature of these basic agreements, special bilateral agreements have been signed to control medically and professionally candidates from these countries. In any case, the number of people from these fifteen countries is small—about 40,000—and during the last few years, the number has stabilized.

Citizens from Algeria also receive special treatment. The cease-fire agreements recognized the principle of free movement for French and Algerian people between the two countries. Consequently, a huge immigration of Algerian workers took place after Algerian independence, and the French authorities soon established a medical control which was performed by the services of the National Office of Immigration.

On April 14, 1964, a protocol was signed between France and Algeria to regulate immigration. New immigrants had to obtain a special permit delivered by ONAMO, the National Algerian Office of Manpower, and to be cleared by French medical physicians attached to the Algerian authorities. In addition, quarterly throughout the year, the number of immigrants would be fixed by agreement between the two governments. Many immigrants continued to enter France illegally, and a new agreement was signed between Algeria and France on December 27, 1968 (Decree no. 69-243 of March 18, 1969).

The agreement confirmed the previous restriction of the free circulation and introduced two new provisions: the Algerian workers presently in France would receive a residence certificate which would serve as residence permit and work permit; the number of new immigrants would be limited to 35,000 each year for the next three years.[26]

Also under this agreement, a new immigrant with a permit from ONAMO and medical clearance can stay in France for nine months to look for work. When hired by an employer, he receives a residence certificate (valid for five years). If at the end of the nine-month period he has been unable to find work, he must return to Algeria. The members of an immigrant's family follow the same rules. They are authorized to come to France only if the employer is providing a lodging for them. It is too early to evaluate the curbing effect of this agreement.

Finally, the third category of immigrants with special status comprises citizens from the countries of the European Economic Community (EEC). In accordance with the Treaty of Rome, a free circulation of people has been established starting on October 15, 1968 (Rule no. 1612 of the EEC).

---

[26] In December 1971, the annual limit was reduced to 25,000 for 1972 and 1973.

Any person from a member state is free to move inside the EEC member countries in order to perform an economic activity as a *salaried* worker. All discriminations based on citizenship and concerning employment, salaries, and other working conditions are abolished for the salaried workers of the EEC.

For France, all dispositions tending to protect French manpower are not valid for citizens from EEC countries. The residence permit and the work permit have been replaced for EEC members by a single permit delivered on presentation of a passport (or an identity card) and a certificate from the employer.

Few people in France have been affected by this legislation because immigration from the EEC countries is at a low level. But it might be different in the years to come. In any case, this new legislation is very important because it represents the first attempt to limit the power of a state over its own territory.

¶ SUMMARY AND CONCLUSION

In seventy years of seeking the best policy on immigration, the primacy of economic factors is clear. Immigrants come mainly to work, and the migratory streams remain sensitive to fluctuations in the economic conditions. The state has on hand a variety of legal dispositions which permit action in almost any direction according to the economic situation of the moment. No disposition has ever been abolished. For example, the law of 1932, voted after the economic crisis of 1929 to curb the introduction of foreign manpower, is still in force. It is not applied, but it could be if it were necessary.

The concern for the members of the family of the foreign workers is a distinct feature of the French policy. The legislation has always favored the entry of all members of a family if one member is already present. In 1970, for example, for a total of 216,010 permanent immigrants controlled[27] by the National Office of Immigration, there were 80,952 members of families. The distinction between workers and their family members is based on activity. The members of the family are not workers. In addition, there are members of families in the demographic sense who are working, particularly married women. They have to be counted to estimate family immigration. This means that, in 1970, almost half of the immigrants were people coming into France to reunite a family.

Some aspects of the policy on immigration have been omitted from the discussion. We have said that the National Office of Immigration worked

[27] This means that Algerian immigrants and black immigrants from Africa and French-speaking countries are not counted in that figure.

under a bilateral agreement signed by the French government and governments of the countries of emigration. These agreements organized the recruitment and assigned quotas on immigrants, but they also regulated the application of the social security legislation to the immigrants (family benefits, health, retirement, and so forth). Some laws still have to be enacted permitting immigrants to send their savings to their own countries.

Finally, we did not comment on the dispositions provided by the nationality code to become a French citizen. It is a complicated legislation which changes from time to time. Since World War II, the tendency has been to favor the acquisition of French citizenship (roughly 30,000 to 35,000 foreigners each year become French citizens).

Special legislation has evolved for people banned from their fatherland and willing to settle in France.

Foreigners represent an important asset for France. For an economically active population amounting to roughly 20 million, there are 350,000 permanent and seasonal workers entering France each year (including workers from Algeria and black Africa). They have to be compared to approximately 800,000 French citizens entering the labor force each year.

The effect of immigration on the increase of population is more difficult to estimate. The return of workers to their country of origin is not registered, and the net immigration is estimated by the comparison of successive censuses. For the recent years, it has been estimated to be 200,000, which, with a natural increase of 330,000, gives a total increase of 530,000.

The foreign population also participates in the birth rate. Each year, there are approximately 100,000 births for which at least one parent is a foreigner. They are included, too, in the number of deaths—40,000 each year, which gives an excess of 60,000 births over deaths.

This excess would disappear if there were no immigration. The 200,000 net immigrants would also disappear. Of a total increase of 530,000 people, 260,000 are the result of immigration, that is, roughly 50 percent.

POLICY ON POPULATION DISTRIBUTION

France has no legislation restricting internal migration of citizens. (A 1941 law requiring compulsory declaration for a change of residence was abrogated in 1954.) But there are incentive measures for the creation of new jobs in certain parts of France. Since the economically active population is determined in part by the availability of new jobs, these incentive measures have an effect on the internal distribution of people in the French territory. There are five categories of incentives for mainland France and one category for the regions around Paris, as follows:

(1) *Premium for industrial employment* and (2) *premium for industrial adaptation.* The aim of these two premiums is to favor localized investments for the creation of new plants or the adaption of existing facilities to new industrial activities. The premiums are paid under the following conditions:

(a) The investment must exceed 300,000 French francs.
(b) In case of a new establishment or a total adaptation, thirty new jobs must be created.
(c) In case of an extension or a partial adaptation, the number of jobs must be increased by 30 percent.
(d) The premiums cannot exceed 13,000 French francs for each new job.
(e) The project must be executed within three years.

The rates are shown in Table 5 with some indications of the areas in which the various rates apply.

(2) *Premium for the localization of specific tertiary activities.* The goal of this premium is to facilitate the creation of new tertiary activities or the transfer of such activities outside the region of Paris to certain specified cities (twenty-two cities). This premium cannot be combined with the two previous premiums. It is paid under the following conditions:

(a) One hundred jobs must be created as a result of the new investment (or fifty in the case of study or research activities).

TABLE 5.

Premiums as Percent of Expenses of Investment, France, 1973

Areas (rate[a])	Industrial Development		Industrial Adaptation	
	New Creations	Enlargement of Existing Facilities	Complete Transformation	Partial Transformation
Highest[b]	25	15		
Increased[c]	15	6[d]		
Normal[e]	12	6[d]		
Industrial adaptation[f]			25	15

[a] If the project involves an investment of 10 million French francs or more, the rate can be settled without reference to a rule within a maximum of 25 percent.
[b] Applied in the urban agglomeration of Brittany, the southwest of France, and the center of France.
[c] Applied in Brittany.
[d] Raised to 10 percent in areas dominated by rural economy. There are two areas dominated by rural economy: Brittany and the center of France.
[e] Applied in the center and southwest of France and in Corsica.
[f] The areas in which the legislation on industrial adaptation is applied are scattered around the center and in the northeast of France.

(b) The premium cannot exceed 13,000 French francs for each new job.

(c) The project must be executed within three years.

The rates are as follows: The allowance amounts to 5–15 percent of the expenses of investments depending on the interest and the importance of the operation. For projects of very high interest, the rate can reach 20 percent. Finally, the expenses of investments cannot exceed 40,000 French francs for each new job.

(3) *Payment for the transfer outside the region of Paris of an industrial activity.* An owner of an industrial establishment in the region of Paris who wants to transfer outside this region receives reimbursement for the expenses of moving equipment (dismantling, transportation, reassembling). The allowance amounts to 60 percent of the expenses, and at the new location 500 square meters of industrial premises must be available for new equipment. The region of Paris in which this transfer obtains includes eleven entire departments.

(4) *Tax reliefs.* An enterprise that is carrying territorial reorganization can be relieved of four forms of taxes: (a) license duty, (b) duty for transfer of property, (c) exceptional amortization, and (d) tax on unearned increments, with the following stipulations: The reliefs are not applied uniformly throughout France. The reduction of license duty is variable within a maximum of 100 percent during five years. Reduction of duty on transfer of property applies to the buying of businesses and plants built during the last five years. The rate is reduced from 13.2 percent (plant) or 17.2 percent (business) to 1.4 percent.

A special amortization of 25 percent can be applied to the cost of new buildings. The tax on unearned increments can be reduced from 10 percent to 5 percent. The necessary conditions to qualify for these tax reliefs are indicated in a series of circular letters sent by the Minister of Economy and Finance. The tax reliefs are also applicable to tertiary activities under certain conditions.

¶ BUILDING PERMIT

A building permit must be obtained for all construction. In the case of industrial premises representing more than 2,000 square meters, the High Commissioner for the Remodeling of the National Territory[28] must be consulted to obtain a permit. If the project is contrary to the plan of remodeling the industrial framework (development goals set forth above), the building permit can be rejected or given only under exceptional conditions.

---

[28] A kind of high commissioner for the remodeling of the industrial framework throughout the territory of France.

¶ AID TO MANPOWER

In addition to these measures concerning building and equipment, there are different arrangements concerning manpower:

(1) Financial aid is supplied for the development of manpower to work on an enterprise creating or transferring an establishment outside the region of Paris.

(2) The same aid can be given in order to facilitate a conversion of a declining activity.

(3) Salaried workers accompanying the transfer of an enterprise can receive partial reimbursement for the expenses of moving furniture. Their transportation can be reimbursed. They can also receive an installment allowance. Finally, they will be assisted in finding a new lodging.

There is no precise zoning for the granting of these aids; the administrative authorities grant them in areas where the government wants to favor industrial development.

¶ SPECIAL RULES CONCERNING THE REGION AROUND PARIS

The region around Paris is not the same as the region of Paris defined above. The region around Paris includes seven departments: Paris, Hauts de Seine, Seine Saint-Denis, Val de Marne, Val d'Oise, Essonne, Seine et Marne, and five "cantons" of the South of Oise. Two rules regulate every industrial development in that region:

(1) A ministerial permit must be obtained (Ministry of Equipment) in order to create 500 square meters of industrial premises (1,000 square meters when the extension takes place on the spot). A similar permit is necessary for building office space of more than 3,000 square meters.

(2) Construction of new buildings for workshops or offices is penalized by a charge, and the destruction of similar spaces is facilitated by the grant of a premium. The rates of the charge and the premium vary according to the geographical location.

A special committee is in charge of implementing this legislation: the Committee of Decentralization. This regulation concerning the region around Paris is to be revised soon. A bill placed by the government on the agenda of the Parliament raises the limit for which a ministerial agreement is necessary from 500 to 1,500 square meters for industrial premises and from 500 to 1,000 square meters for offices. It also increases the charge for new buildings and changes the zoning. The premium for destruction is voided.

¶ INSTITUTIONAL FRAMEWORK

For policy formulation, legislation, and for supervision of the legislation, the government created in 1963 a special unit directly attached to the

Prime Minister, the Division for the Remodeling of the National Territory and Regional Planning (DATAR). The unit is gradually building with the collaboration of private and public sectors a "Study Scheme for the Remodeling of France," known under the name of SESAME.

The various aids are not given automatically. In each case, the granting of the aid is decided by the Minister of Economy and Finance. To guide the minister in his decisions, a special unit has been created: the Governing Council of the Fund for Economic and Social Development.

This concludes the study of population policy in France. As explained at the beginning, there is, strictly speaking, no population policy in France but only policies in various fields influencing indirectly the trend of population. From this point of view, almost any policy has demographic consequences, and to be complete, it would be necessary to comment on all the matters on which a country has legislation.

For example, in its effort to lower mortality, the state has always produced a complex set of laws for the protection of the health of its people. Housing policies may have an effect on family size and on internal migrations. Employment policies, particularly policies concerning the work of women, may modify the level of fertility. Policies affecting accidents have an obvious bearing on mortality.

There are three direct ways of influencing the trend of population: mortality, procreation, and migration. Only the last two are subject to the human will and can be affected by policies. This explains why we restricted our analysis to policies linked to procreation and migration.

REFERENCES

1. Gabriel Giroud. *Paul Robin—His Life—His Ideas—His Acts.* Paris: G. Mignolet et Soiz éditeurs, 1937. (In French.)

2. *Bulletin of the National Alliance for French Population Growth,* January 1902 and January 1913.

3. *Le Nouvel Observateur,* April 20, 1971. (In French.)

4. *Family Planning.* Report of the High Consultative Committee on Population and the Family. Paris: La Documentation française, January 1967. (In French.)

5. "Demographic studies, no. 3: Naturalization in France." *Statistique générale de la France.* Paris: Imprimerie Nationale, 1942. (In French.)

CHAPTER 20

Great Britain

John Simons

Acknowledgments: I am indebted to David Glass for guidance, and for encouraging me to write this paper. I received invaluable help from Kay Bispham and William Brass.

ABSTRACT

Population policy in Great Britain[1] has consisted largely of attempts to influence the geographical distribution of people rather than to influence their numbers. After the end of World War II, ambitious policies were undertaken to remedy urban congestion and unsatisfactory use of land. Building construction and most other forms of development were made subject to official approval and conformity with physical planning policy. New towns were established to draw people from urban areas. To restrain migration to the south, businessmen were given incentives to expand in areas where employment was needed.

In 1962, restrictions were imposed on immigration from within the Commonwealth in response to a substantial increase in the number of non-white immigrants from the Caribbean, India, and Pakistan. As a result of immigration and the persistence of an upward trend in fertility, the projected population of the United Kingdom at the end of the twentieth century rose considerably—from 64 million (projected in 1960) to 75 million (projected in 1965). In the early 1960s, the fact that world population was growing rapidly became widely known. Eminent scientists referred to environmental hazards and scarcity of resources as justification for a policy to reduce population growth. Skeptics accused them of exaggerating the problem. It was pointed out that population policy was not a

---

[1] Great Britain comprises England, Wales, and Scotland. The United Kingdom comprises Great Britain and Northern Ireland.

substitute for pollution control and that average family size (about 2.5 per married woman) was already low. In 1971, a parliamentary committee urged the government to adopt a population policy without delay. Inside and outside Parliament, advocates of population policy placed particular stress on the need to extend birth control services. In 1973, a panel of experts established by the government recommended a strengthening of birth control services and a number of measures to increase the information available on population trends, their causes, and their implications. Meanwhile, fertility had declined; the projected population at the end of the century had fallen to 63 million.

One of the best-known characteristics of the British population is that it occupies a relatively small space. Only the Netherlands, Belgium, and a few island states are more densely populated. In Table 1, the population densities of Belgium and the Netherlands are compared with those of Great Britain. Densities are also shown for England and southeast England. It is more realistic to compare the Low Countries with these parts of Britain because, in their case, topography does not restrict development to the extent that it does elsewhere in the country. The southeast region is relatively densely populated and compares most closely in size to the Netherlands and Belgium [1].

Problems attributed to excessive density have been the principal concern of population policy in Britain.

TABLE 1.

Area, Population, and Density of Great Britain with Selected
International Comparisons, 1969

Item	Great Britain	England	South-east Region	Nether-lands	Belgium
Area (in thousands)					
Square kilometers	229.9	130.4	27.4	40.8	30.5
Acres	56,808	32,213	6,774	10,093	7,540
Population (in thousands)	54,022	46,102	17,295	12,873	9,646
Density					
Persons per					
square kilometer	235	354	631	315	316
Persons per acre	0.95	1.43	2.55	1.28	1.28

SOURCE: See [1].
NOTE: Population figures are based on 1969 midyear estimates.

PROJECTED GROWTH

Projections of the population of the United Kingdom and its constituent countries by sex and age have been made by the Government Actuary's Department, in consultation with the Registrars General, since the 1920s. Since World War II, these projections have been used increasingly as a framework for governmental planning in a number of sectors. Since 1955 new projections have been made every year.

Over the decade 1960–1970, projections of the population by the end of the twentieth century moved from 64 million to 75 million (1964–1965-based) and back to 63 million (1971-based). These projections, especially the higher ones, have often been deployed in arguments for a population policy. Projections made for various periods every year since 1955 are shown in Table 2.

TABLE 2.

Estimated Future Total Population, United Kingdom, 1968, 1980, 1990, 2000 (in millions)

Base Year for Projection	Estimated Population in Year			
	1968	1980	1990	2000
1955	52.5	53.3	53.1	
1956	53.2	54.7	55.4	
1957	53.8	55.8	57.1	
1958	54.0	56.5	58.3	
1959	54.1	56.6	58.5	
1960	54.5	57.7	60.6	63.8
1961	55.6	60.1	63.6	67.5
1962	55.9	60.6	65.2	71.1
1963	55.8	60.7	65.4	71.6
1964	55.9	61.4	67.0	74.7
1965	55.8	61.2	66.8	74.6
1966	55.4	60.0	65.1	72.1
1967	55.5	59.5	64.2	70.3
1968	55.4 (actual)	59.3	63.2	68.2
1969		58.6	62.0	66.1
1970		58.6	61.9	66.0
		1981	1991	2001
1971[a]		57.7	60.3	63.1

SOURCES: See [2; 3].
[a] There is a discontinuity in the base populations of the 1970- and 1971-based projections. See text.

¶ ASSUMPTIONS AFFECTING PROJECTIONS

The ways in which assumptions concerning fertility and migration affect projections have been emphasized by the departments responsible for them [2; 3; 4]. Compared with variations in assumptions concerning future fertility, the effects of variations in migration assumptions were relatively small. The variations in mortality assumptions had a negligible effect.

The 1955-based projection was made at a time when births had been falling from their postwar peak in 1947; it was assumed that fertility would fall to roughly the immediate prewar level, with an average family size of little more than two children. The 1960-based projections were made when births had been increasing in number for four or five years. The 1964-based projections were made when births had increased in number for nearly a decade and it seemed reasonable to assume that family size would continue to increase; also, there had been heavy immigration from Commonwealth countries. The 1968-based projections were made after four years of decreasing births but when there were indications that the fall might have been halted; it was assumed that average family size would stabilize at 2.5 children or a little less. For the 1969 projections, changes in assumptions were made about the average family size that would be achieved by women marrying before age twenty. It was thought that, with the growing proportion of women marrying at these young ages and a greater willingness to adopt more reliable forms of contraception, there was likely to be a fall in their fertility and, thus, a narrowing of the differential between this group and women marrying in their early twenties.

The 1970 population projection of 66 million by the end of the century was made after six years of decreasing births. This was a 10-million increase over the estimated population in 1970.

The mid-1971 population projection of 63.1 million by the year 2001 took into account the preliminary findings of the 1971 census, which showed that the existing population was 0.4 million smaller than the estimate carried forward from the 1961 census, by allowing for births, deaths, estimated net migration, and changes in armed forces in the intercensal period. As well as being affected by the use of a new base population, projections were also modified by changes in the assumptions made concerning future fertility and migration [3; 5]. The projected annual rate of increase averages 0.4 percent over the period of the projection, 1971–2011.

The number of births in future years was reduced (from the 1970-based figures) by about 60,000 a year in the early years of the projection, the reduction rising to more than 170,000 a year by the end of the projection period. The reductions were in response to a persistence of the fertility decline and evidence of deferment of childbearing, together with survey data suggesting that young married women would have an average completed family size of 2.3 or a little less. For a comparable sample interviewed in 1967, the figure had been 2.4 to 2.6 [6].

With regard to migration, it was assumed that future net emigration would be 20,000 per year higher than the figure assumed for the 1970 projections. By reducing the expected number of potential mothers, the new migration assumption also contributed to the reduction in expected births.

¶ AGE STRUCTURE

An analysis of the results of the projection in very broad age groups is given in Table 3, which shows the projected number of children under age fifteen, the number of people at the main working ages, and the number older than the normal retiring ages of sixty-five for men and sixty for women. Despite a steady increase in the projected *number* of children in the population in the future, the *percentage* of children declines from 24.2 to 22.8 over the projection period. After an increase initially, the percentage of elderly people also declines from 16.0 to 15.2. Thus, the "dependent" age groups (under fifteen and over sixty-five) constitute 40 percent of the total for the first half of the projection period and 38 percent by the end of the period.

¶ USES OF POPULATION PROJECTIONS

Advice and information concerning projected changes in population are provided by the Government Actuary's Department and the Registrars General. The statistics are provided to departments of central government, local government, and many academic and research institutions and representative groups of individuals. Regional and local projections use current fertility and mortality differentials appropriate to the areas concerned. Assumptions concerning regional migration patterns are based on interdepartmental discussions on the likely effects of current governmental policies on the distribution of population, for example, the effects of policies to foster the economic development of areas. The only data of real value on internal migration is derived from the census [4]. The 1971 census sought migration data over a five-year and a one-year period in an attempt to improve the quality of the statistics.

According to the Government Actuary, planners can rely on the accuracy of national population projections for a period of seven years, subject to government intervention in migration. The largest source of doubt is in the estimation of future births, but even wide fluctuations in births have a relatively small overall effect within a seven-year period. It is reasonable

TABLE 3.

Age Structure of Projected Population, United Kingdom, 1971–2011 (numbers are in thousands)

Age Group	1971		1981		1991		2001		2011	
	Number	Percent	Number	Percent	Number	Percent	Number	Percent	Number	Percent
0–14	13,499	24.2	13,400	23.2	14,219	23.6	14,840	23.5	15,151	22.8
15–29	11,897	21.4	12,851	22.3	13,492	22.4	13,594	21.5	14,547	21.9
30–44	9,749	17.5	10,936	18.9	11,985	19.9	13,031	20.7	12,952	19.5
45–64 males	11,624	20.9	10,841	18.8	10,735	17.8	12,171	19.3	13,597	20.5
45–59 females										
65+ males	8,899	16.0	9,711	16.8	9,832	16.3	9,452	15.0	10,089	15.2
60+ females										
All ages	55,668	100.0	57,739	100.0	60,263	100.0	63,088	100.0	66,336	100.0

SOURCE: See [3].
NOTE: The dotted line approximately divides those born before mid-1971 (below the line) from those born after that date.

to assume, for planning purposes, that recent projections of total population size at the end of the twentieth century are accurate to within ±3 million [4].

DISTRIBUTION OF THE POPULATION

Changes in the distribution of the population of Great Britain since 1801 are summarized in Table 4. The changes have been associated with changes in the nature and location of economic activity. The decline of traditional industries (such as coal mining, shipbuilding, heavy engineering, textiles, and agriculture) in this century has been associated with rates of economic expansion below average and a level of unemployment above average in Scotland, Wales, the northeast, the northwest, and parts of the southwest. In England's south and midlands, on the other hand, fast-growing industries have created a sustained demand for labor. Despite the partial success of efforts to promote new employment in northern England, Scotland, and Wales, their population has grown less rapidly than has the population of the south and midlands. The difference has been caused by migration between regions and, more recently, by migration to and from overseas.

TABLE 4.

Regional Distribution of Population, Great Britain, 1801–1969 and Projection to 2001 (in percents)

Area	1801	1851	1901	1951	1969	2001 (projected)
Northern	6.0	5.6	6.8	6.4	6.2	5.6
Yorkshire and Humberside	7.8	8.7	9.5	9.3	8.9	8.4
Northwest	8.4	12.1	14.3	13.2	12.5	12.3
East midlands	6.1	5.5	5.4	5.9	6.2	6.9
West midlands	8.2	8.2	8.1	9.1	9.5	9.7
East Anglia	6.0	5.0	3.1	2.8	3.1	3.5
Southeast	23.8	24.6	28.4	31.0	32.0	32.2
Southwest	12.8	10.8	6.9	6.6	6.9	7.3
Wales	5.6	5.6	5.4	5.3	5.0	4.8
Scotland	15.3	13.9	12.1	10.4	9.6	9.1
Great Britain (millions)	10.50	20.82	37.00	48.85	54.02	64.43
Northern regions, Wales, and Scotland	43.1	45.9	48.0	44.6	42.3	40.3
Midlands and south	56.9	54.1	52.0	55.4	57.7	59.7

SOURCE: See [1, tables 1.4, 1.7, 1.15, and 3.7].

Governmental action to maintain employment and retain population in "problem" areas began in the 1930s, at a time of acute economic depression. World War II brought new industries to these areas, and their employment situation improved. Under the Distribution of Industry Acts of 1945–1950, the areas were designated "development areas" and enlarged. New and more flexible powers were obtained under the Distribution of Industry (industrial finance) Act of 1958, which permitted the Treasury to give financial assistance to undertakings that would provide employment in some places with high unemployment outside the development areas.

Another sphere of policy concerned with population distribution has been land-use planning. The proportion of the British population who lived in large towns increased from 20 percent to 80 percent during the nineteenth century when there were no controls over land use. Growth of industrial towns led to congestion and poor housing and, later, to suburban sprawl.

From early in the nineteenth century, these conditions prompted the development of ideas for new, functional settlements. Among the innovators was Ebenezer Howard who, in 1898, put forward detailed plans for "garden cities": new, self-contained communities, surrounded by open country, complete with factories, houses, schools, shops, and other amenities. In 1899, the Garden City Association (which later became the Town and Country Planning Association) was founded to promote these aims. Two garden cities, Letchworth (1903) and Welwyn Garden City (1920), were established within 65 kilometers of London. The idea of garden cities attracted considerable support and strongly influenced policy development in the 1940s, when land planning became mandatory.

In 1940, the report of the Royal Commission on the Distribution of the Industrial Population (the Barlow Report) recommended decentralization or dispersal of both industry and population from congested urban areas and the encouragement of a reasonable balance of industrial development throughout Great Britain [7]. The report urged that urban growth be restrained by a positive policy of developing new towns and expanding existing ones. In 1944, Sir Patrick Abercrombie's Greater London Plan proposed that a series of new towns should be established, each accommodating 60,000–80,000 people and industry from the overcrowded capital. A "green belt" should intervene between them and the London built-up area. In 1945, a New Towns Committee was established under the chairmanship of Lord Reith to consider all aspects of the planning and development of new towns.

The wartime studies led to the Town and Country Planning Act of

1947 and subsequent legislation. The aim was to preserve a balance between the competing claims made on the environment by homes, industries, transport, and leisure. The legislation established a centralized planning system, imposed compulsory planning duties on local authorities, and made most building construction and other forms of development subject to the authorities' consent. Essentially, the planning arrangements affected the distribution of population by establishing areas where development was restricted or even prohibited and by supporting the creation of homes and jobs in areas where, it was hoped, people would prefer to live and work.

In a recent review of regional population trends since 1951, an Interdepartmental Study Group concluded that, at a very high level of generalization, the country could be said to fall into four broad territorial groups [1]. In Scotland and Wales, the highlands and uplands have been generally characterized by population declines resulting from outward migration greater than natural increase. In the subdivisions that showed growth, the cause has generally been a natural increase, often accompanied by net migration loss. Northern England, roughly north of the Humber/Mersey, constitutes the second group. There the overall growth attributable to natural increase has more than compensated for migration loss. The third group comprises the midland regions, including northern parts of the more southerly regions. The subdivisions in this area typically have experienced population growth by migration and natural increase, the latter being dominant. The exceptions are mainly conservation hinterlands, which fall into the fourth territorial group, the south. With the principal exception of Greater London (which has had an overall decline), this area has been characterized strongly by population increase, caused by both natural increase and migration, principally the latter. The Sussex coasts, however, like the Lancashire and north Wales coasts, have experienced natural decrease caused by the unbalanced age structure of the population of the area that resulted from the inward migration of the elderly. Within the four groups, large towns typically have experienced outward migration from inner and central areas to the peripheries and beyond.

¶ RECENT DEVELOPMENTS IN REGIONAL POLICY

In a comprehensive account of the development of regional policy in Britain (on which this section draws heavily), Gavin McCrone describes the marked changes in direction and emphasis that began to occur in 1960 [8]. In the 1960s, regional unemployment rates worsened, and the government accorded higher priority to regional policy than it had in the 1950s. The regional problem began to be seen as a problem of economic growth rather than as primarily a social problem. Emphasis was placed on contributions the regions might make to the achievement of a higher national rate of growth. McCrone points out that the subject of economic growth was receiving much greater attention than ever before because of Britain's low rate of growth in comparison with other countries and "increasing frustration over the stop-go cycle."

The Local Employment Act of 1960 gave the Board of Trade power to schedule what were known as "development districts": localities in which, in the opinion of the board, a high rate of unemployment existed or was imminent and was likely to persist. Firms that were willing to use these areas could obtain building grants and special loans or grants for expansion schemes, on the advice of a Board of Trade Advisory Committee. Another inducement was discrimination in favor of the districts by the use of Industrial Development Certificates, which were introduced by the Town and Country Planning Act of 1947. A certificate was required for any new industrial development of more than a specified size.

The 1960 legislation had two major defects. First, frequent changes in the scheduled districts upset industrialists' plans for expansion and made it difficult for public authorities to make long-term plans. Second, the use of unemployment rates to identify districts meant that assistance was not necessarily related to an area's economic potential for development.

In 1963, the building grants were increased to 25 percent of actual construction costs from a figure that varied between areas but averaged 17 percent. Grants were offered for new plant and machinery in development districts at the rate of 10 percent of costs. The most important innovation of the 1963 legislation was the provision for "accelerated depreciation." Under this scheme, manufacturers in the development districts could amortize investments in plant and machinery against profits at any rate they chose. A Location of Offices Bureau was established to encourage the voluntary movement of office workers and jobs away from London. The bureau claims to have helped transfer some 90,000 jobs away from central London by the end of 1971.

In 1963, the first steps were taken toward establishing "growth areas" and undertaking regional economic planning. Eight growth areas were designated in central Scotland, and a growth zone was established in northeast England. These were to have all the benefits currently available for development districts and could retain them regardless of the subsequent employment situation. Further, the areas were to be built up as centers of economic growth by a program of public investment.

The next developments occurred after a Labour government came to power. The Industrial Development Acts of 1966 abolished the development districts, replacing them with development areas—the largest areas yet scheduled for special assistance, encompassing over 40 percent of the land area of Britain and 20 percent of the population. (Only about 17 percent of the employed population had been covered by development districts.) Previous types of assistance with investment in plant and machinery were replaced by investment grants favorable to the development areas. The availability of the grants did not depend on employment created or on the commercial soundness of the investments.

In September 1967, a regional employment premium was introduced as a weekly subsidy for employees to employers in manufacturing industries in the development areas. According to McCrone, the justification was not primarily the need for labor-intensive industry but an extension of Keynesian techniques of economic management to the regional level. Firms in the development areas were also given generous assistance toward the cost of training employees, to ease problems of obtaining suitably skilled personnel for expansion schemes. The building of government factories for rent or sale in advance of demand (a source of factory space since the end of the war) was increased. In 1970, "intermediate areas" were established. These, too, were eligible for assistance but on a lesser scale than were the full development areas.

The government's measures had been criticized by the Conservatives on the ground that the help given was not sufficiently related to profitability as an estimate of viability. When the Conservatives came to power in 1970, they abandoned Labour's investment grants. The Investment and Building Grants Act of 1971 replaced grants with complete first-year depreciation allowances for investments in plant and machinery in assisted areas for both manufacturing and service industries. Notice was given that the regional employment premium would be phased out over a period from 1974. In 1972, the Finance Act extended the depreciation allowance and the tax allowance on new industrial buildings to the whole country. The Industry Act of 1972 supplemented these incentives with a return to the system of investment grants. The new incentive system was considered to give a greater regional differential in favor of investment in assisted areas than had been achieved by previous systems. Another claim was that the system was profit related: that proportionately more of the total value of incentives was represented by tax allowances, the benefit of which depended on a firm's profit position, and less by the grants, the availability of which was unaffected by whether or not a firm was profitable. On this point, a Labour party study group argued that tax concessions had less effect than grants at the decision-making stage and gave less help to a company in its early years when it most needed help [9].

The Industry Act also provided for selective financial help, including loans and removal grants, to projects likely to provide, maintain, or safe-guard employment in any part of the assisted areas. An Industrial Development Executive was established within the Department of Trade and Industry under a Minister for Industrial Development. The minister was given special responsibility for private sector industry generally and for industrial development in the assisted areas. Regional Industrial Development Boards were created in a number of regions, to advise generally on industrial opportunities and on applications for selective financial assistance for the development of industry in their regions.

¶ EFFECTIVENESS OF REGIONAL POLICY
In McCrone's view, the increased assistance to the problem areas in the 1960s had the effect of decreasing out-migration. For most regions, the loss in the period 1961–1966 was small; much less than it was in the periods 1951–1956 and 1956–1961. Wales, which had a net loss of 47,000 in the period 1951–1961, actually had a net gain of 5,000 in the period 1961–1966. An exception was Scotland, where annual loss in net migration rose from about 25,000 in the mid-1950s to 47,000 in 1965. The southeast experienced a net loss to other regions (especially to the southwest and East Anglia) throughout the 1960s, "striking evidence of the effects of regional policy" [8].

In 1965, the Department of Economic Affairs invited the National Institute of Economic and Social Research "to build up a theoretical and empirical framework for the analysis of regional economic development and the consideration of regional policy in the United Kingdom, especially in relation to problems of national economic development." Reporting results of the study in 1972, A. J. Brown summarized the United Kingdom's regional problem as a mismatch between regional rates of natural increase of population and regional rates of growth of employment opportunities. This mismatch was allied with the necessarily imperfect mobility of enterprises and people and with the sense of attachment that people felt to communities and places. The mismatch had been mitigated "quite powerfully" by the extremely close commercial connections of the regions ("far beyond anything yet demonstrated by State members of Common Markets") and by the powerful pooling and stabilizing machinery of progressive taxation and centralized public expenditures. It had also been mitigated powerfully since the beginning of the 1960s by deliberate regional policy [10].

However, there is general agreement that regional policy has not been adequate for the problems, and that the problems are not likely to become more tractable. The requirements of more effective policy have been the subject of many studies and proposals. In a report issued in 1970, a Labour party study group favored the idea of "growth complexes" within wide development areas [9]. The growth complex would comprise a group of complementary firms or industries, related or mutually dependent. The complex of electronic firms in Scotland was cited as a successful British example. The actual character of the growth complex would depend on the nature of the region and its problems. It could be designed to be a generating point for economic expansion in an underdeveloped region or, in a prosperous region, as a countermagnet to the attraction of the congested metropolis. The authors stressed that theirs was not a proposal to concentrate aid in a small area. National controls and aid to regions as a whole would remain essential. Another point stressed was that the planning of growth complexes, and regional planning in general, required improved statistics and better techniques of industrial planning, together with more sophisticated and flexible policy measures. An improvement in policy measures favored in the report was the use, in conjunction with more conventional measures, of payroll subsidies and taxes to encourage firms to move from congested areas to areas where employment was needed. The tax would be levied on all employment, except for very small businesses, in the congested zones. The subsidy, replacing the regional employment premium, would be paid at its highest rate in those areas with severe economic problems. It would be paid to all employers, service as well as manufacturing. The idea of growth complexes and the idea of payroll subsidies and taxes were endorsed in the Labour party's policy proposals in 1972 [11].

Britain's entry into the European Economic Community (EEC) poses new questions about regional problems. The government is optimistic. Its White Paper on the terms of entry said, in July 1971: "Because of the new opportunities for the economy as a whole, we shall be able as members of the Community to deal more effectively with our problems of regional development." In contrast, dominant groups in the Labour party have been apprehensive, believing that entry might exacerbate regional problems while, at the same time, imposing restrictions on policy. For example, in a commentary on the White Paper, the party's research department complained that the document did not attempt to examine which regions might benefit and which might suffer as a result of membership or discuss whether or not a measure such as the regional employment premium could be reintroduced by a future Labour government [12]. In a paper on the subject, Harold Lind suggested that the use of measures such as the regional employment premium might well prompt objections from other EEC members, on the grounds that it was an export subsidy [13].

He thought it was unlikely, however, that serious difficulties would arise with most forms of regional aid.

¶ NEW AND EXPANDED TOWNS

Within regions, population distribution has been more directly influenced by such means as the creation of new and expanded towns, the establishment of green belts, and the provision of residential land for commuters and retired people.[2]

The term "new town" is used to designate developments that take place under the New Towns Acts of 1946–1972. What chiefly distinguishes the new town from other schemes is that it is planned and managed by a development corporation appointed by the appropriate minister. The development corporation is a publicly constituted estate developer that appoints its own architects, engineers, and other staff. In England today, many new towns are situated relatively near London and are designed to help relieve housing problems in the Greater London area. Other new towns are providing a similar service for conurbations in other regions.

The original purpose of creating new towns was to provide for the gradual dispersal of industry and population from urban areas. Owing to sustained population growth and continued migration into the southeast, new towns have become increasingly important as outlets for the expansion of population generally. They also have been used to further the aim of distributing employment more evenly by acting as catalysts of industrial growth.

The Labour party has come to regard the planning of the new town program as an integral part of regional planning policy. "Future Labour Governments will extend the new and expanded towns programmes, and particular attention will be paid to the need for more towns to be designated in the poorer regions where they have proved effective as generators of the type of growth that is of especial value to these regions" [11].

Most of the early new towns were expansions of relatively small existing communities. In the past few years, many of the new towns have already become important in their own right. The scale of planned development also has increased substantially. A population of between 50,000 and 60,000 was envisaged for the first series of new towns, although these figures were raised subsequently. Some of the more recent new towns are intended to be much larger; it is envisaged that the population of Milton

---

[2] For further information about town and country planning legislation and policy in Britain, see [14].

Keynes eventually will approach 250,000. A progression toward much larger new towns reflects a recognition of the advantages of size: a wider choice of employment opportunities; the ability to support a greater range of facilities for shopping, education, and leisure; and the attraction to early migrants of existing facilities.

By the end of 1969, 175,000 dwellings had been built in the new towns in Great Britain since the war. A further 72,000 dwellings had been provided by town expansion schemes. The total—about 0.25 million dwellings—is only 4 percent of the 6 million or so dwellings built in that period. However, since all public and private housing has been subject to planning control, the total impact of physical planning policies on population distribution within regions has been very much greater than that of the new and expanded towns alone.

About 800,000 people have been accommodated in new towns and town-expansion schemes. Under present plans, an additional 1 million will be accommodated in this way by 1981. The possibility of considerably larger numbers in some additional schemes is under consideration.

¶ DEVELOPMENT PLANNING

Responsibility for the physical environment in England now rests with a single department—the Department of the Environment. Responsibility formerly was divided among the Ministry of Housing and Local Government, the Ministry of Public Building and Works, and the Ministry of Transport. General responsibility for British industry, including control of its location, rests with the Department of Trade and Industry. Regional planning (see the next section) requires cooperation between this department, the Department of the Environment, and many other departments.

Locally, town and country planning is the responsibility of local government. Local authorities are required to survey their areas and to prepare and submit development plans to the appropriate secretary of state for approval.

A new type of development plan for Great Britain was established by the Town and Country Planning Acts of 1968 and 1969. It is based on a survey of the area and comprises a "structure plan" and one or more local plans. The structure plan requires the minister's approval. It outlines policies and general proposals for the future use of land in the local planning authority's area, including measures for the improvement of the physical environment and the management of traffic. The proposals must be prepared in their regional context. For example, they must show the implications for investment and employment. The actual nature and location of future development are the subjects of the local plans. Almost all new construction and other forms of development require the prior consent of the local planning authority; normally, the proposed development must be consistent with the provisions of the development plan.

Local authorities have been urged to adopt comprehensive land-use and transport policies in their development plans, for example, by dispersing markets, sports stadiums, and other traffic attractions and by introducing measures for the control of parking. In 1968, the government asked local authorities responsible for relatively large communities to prepare traffic and transport plans showing how they intended to relate traffic and parking policies to available road capacities to the mid-1970s.

The problems of development planning have prompted a substantial amount of research, much of it conducted or sponsored by the Center for Environmental Studies. The government is the center's principal source of funds [15].

¶ REGIONAL PLANNING ARRANGEMENTS

In recent years, the individual local planning authority has been regarded as too small a unit for the adequate planning of development and other land use. In 1964 and 1965, the government established a system of regional economic planning councils and boards in Great Britain. The councils comprise about thirty part-time members appointed for their experience and wide knowledge of their regions. They are advisory bodies with no executive powers. Their main tasks are to study and advise on the needs and potentialities of their regions and to advise the government on long-term planning strategy. The boards consist of senior civil servants representing the main governmental departments concerned with aspects of regional planning in their respective areas. Their functions are to coordinate the regional economic planning work of the government departments and to cooperate with the regional economic planning councils.

In order to restrict the physical expansion of urban areas, eight green belts have been established in England. They comprise areas where it is intended that land should be left permanently open and free from new development. A number of new green belt areas have been proposed. The government regards the green belt policy as an integral part of strategic regional planning.

The Town and Country Planning Association believes the government has failed to appreciate the requirements of effective regional planning. The association, which has been a prominent pressure group, believes that developments implied by the new regional plans are different "not only in scale, but in kind and in urgency . . . from those for which the Government's 'conventional' planning procedures were conceived." Essentially, the association's argument is that it is not realistic to believe that regional planning and its implementation can be a shared task of local authorities within a region. What is required is some form of regional development agency—a regional version of the development corporation that plans and organizes new towns. This regional agency would provide the competence, the sensitivity to social as well as private needs, and the powers necessary for adequate regional planning [16].

SHORTAGE OF LAND FOR URBAN DEVELOPMENT

The postwar plans to move people and industry from London to new towns and expanded towns assumed that there would be very little increase in population. It was also assumed that the distribution of industry policy would be sufficient to restrain migration to the south. Both assumptions were incorrect. There was rapid natural increase and continued migration, together with substantial net migration to Greater London and other conurbations[3] from overseas from the mid-1950s onward. The increase in numbers was accompanied by a continuous rise in real income. This had the effect of increasing the amount of space individuals regarded as an acceptable minimum in their dwellings. It also had the effect of increasing the individual's range of movement.

In 1965, the prospect of a further substantial population increase led the government to ask an Interdepartmental Study Group of officials to examine population trends, patterns of settlement, and other relevant factors to the end of the century. The study group was asked to report on areas suitable for large-scale development in the longer term. The aim of the work was to ensure that any new major developments that might be necessary were planned in such a way as to make the best possible contribution to national economic growth and the improvement of the natural environment. According to their report, the area of land in urban use in Great Britain grew from 3.8 percent of the total area in 1901 to 8.6 percent in 1970 [1]. They estimated that, by the end of the century, the figure would rise to 11 percent, given the persistence of current trends in urban development and population growth. There would be the growing population to accommodate and the persistent movement of population from the inner areas of towns and cities to their peripheries and beyond. It was also expected that acceptable standards of urban space per person would continue to increase.

¶ REGIONAL SHORTAGES
There is nothing obviously alarming about the prospect that one-ninth of the total area might be in urban use. Problems emerge when one con-

[3] Seven areas are designated as conurbations: builtup, economically interdependent areas, including developing suburbs of the towns within them.

siders the likely regional distribution of the increase in relationship to the amount of land available for development. The study group's projection[4] shows a rate of increase in the northwest over the thirty-one years 1970–2001 almost double that over the twenty years 1950–1970. In the southeast, on the other hand, the rate of increase is approximately the same. The discrepancy occurs despite a projected growth of population between 1970 and 2001 of some 20 percent in the southeast, compared with 17 percent in the northwest. The latter's greater projected rate of urban growth is accounted for by the continuance of a steep increase in the amount of urban land required for the same number of people: from 26.32 hectares (65 acres) per 1,000 population in 1950–1951 to a projected 38.07 hectares (94 acres) in the year 2001. In the southeast, the ratio shows little change; the increase in urban area is proportional to population growth. According to these projections, the northwest will have nearly 40 percent of its area urbanized by 2001. The southeast will follow with 22 percent.

These proportions are much more substantial than they might seem because they are proportions of total regional areas and not of the total available for urban development. For Great Britain as a whole, it has been estimated that about 50 percent of total area is either physically unsuitable for development or consists of areas such as national parks and green belts that are deliberately preserved from development. The proportion for the northwest is 47 percent, and for the southeast it is 40 percent.

The study group concluded that land shortages could become acute by the end of the century, especially in the northwest. The problem of resolving competing demands for land around major urban areas is complicated by the fact that much high-quality agricultural land adjoins them. In addition to the demand for urban land, undeveloped land will also have to meet growing demands for space for recreational activities. Many otherwise suitable areas are too remote from existing population centers for day and weekend leisure excursions. Housing shortages constitute another demand for new urban land, and these shortages are most acute in the conurbations.

The population capacity of urban areas depends in part on the rate at which substandard dwellings are replaced and the residual density standards adopted for replacements. Although a large program of slum clearance has been completed since the war, the problem is much bigger than was foreseen in the 1940s. A considerable program of urban renewal,

---

[4] The study group pointed out that, since no comprehensive official figures exist of the amount of land in urban use at any date or of changes over time, all estimates must be regarded as tentative.

extending to the end of the century, will be required. As well as the replacement of housing, the replacement of schools, hospitals, and commercial and industrial buildings is also a necessary part of urban renewal.

The extent to which urban renewal will displace population from existing urban areas cannot be predicted. However, displacement is expected for a very long time into the future; it is assumed that rising real incomes are likely to maintain the increase in per-capita space requirements.

¶ PROBLEMS OF SPONSORED LONG-DISTANCE MIGRATION

In view of the prospective shortage of land for urban development, the Interdepartmental Study Group considered the possibility of accommodating major planned developments at a substantial distance from existing concentrations of population. Their conclusions are summarized below.

The number of jobs that can be provided in new towns in a given period broadly determines the level of population that can be accommodated there in the same period. For at least a considerable period of their initial planned growth, new and expanding towns are dependent for most of their additional employment needs on the introduction of new industry. Therefore, the future availability of mobile industry dictates the scope for influencing the future distribution of population by the creation of new major planned-expansion schemes.

The supply of mobile manufacturing industry has been, and is likely to continue to be, limited. It has been governmental policy to give first priority to mobile industry for those areas where it was needed to replace jobs lost in traditional industries. The needs of these areas for new employment are likely to remain substantial for many years. Spare mobile industry to support further planned population movement is not likely to be available until the early 1980s. In the period 1981–2001 there should be sufficient mobile industry to support, if necessary, the development of new population growth areas on a somewhat larger scale than the current program, provided that measures similar to those aimed at securing redistribution of industry at present are used to assist the development of new growth areas.

¶ UNSPONSORED MOVEMENT

The study group emphasized that, although planned migration from London and other conurbations had made an important contribution toward reducing congestion in London, most population movement out of urban areas had taken place on the initiative of individuals. The outward spread of population from central and inner areas to the periphery and beyond had been shown to be typical of large towns. This effect had been most marked in the southeast, where it had been strongly associated with a greatly increased net outflow from Greater London to East Anglia and the southwest.

Much of the unsponsored movement had been to areas within sixty-five kilometers of the conurbations, roughly the same distance as most of the planned expansion schemes. Although some of the migrants had obtained work locally, many commuted back to the main conurbations to work. As population in the inner areas of towns and cities had fallen, rapid population growth had taken place beyond the green belts. This new pattern of development, the "city region," was similar in many respects to a city. It retained most of the general advantages of cities, while mitigating some of the disadvantages. However, it presented new planning problems and could impede planned migration schemes. For example, movement often took the form of small local developments that, individually, did not warrant local capital investment to meet additional calls on services. When taken in aggregate, however, they often called for carefully coordinated planning between local planning authorities.

¶ PROSPECTS

The Interdepartmental Study Group concluded from their work that population distribution changes rather slowly; that the broad regional distribution pattern of population at the end of the twentieth century might not be strikingly different from the current pattern; that the greater part of the increase in population would probably be accommodated by the growth of existing centers and in overspill developments around the conurbations; and that there would be less emphasis on the development of major new areas of population and industrial growth at considerable distances from existing conurbations.

As a consequence, the most important planning problems of the next thirty years are expected to arise in and around existing conurbations. The study group pointed out that, because the areas surrounding the conurbations now contained substantial and rapidly growing populations, it was important to consider each conurbation and its surrounding area as a whole. More than half of the additional housing required would have to be provided in and around the city regions, based on the major conurbations. Other urban areas with large populations were likely to face similar problems.

Population pressures in the areas surrounding conurbations were likely to be severe, especially since these areas provided the conurbations with the most readily accessible recreational land. Comprehensive planning would be needed to determine the optimum pattern of development. Especially necessary was a definite regional strategy for the northwest region of England, where future land pressures were likely to be the most acute.

IMMIGRATION AND EMIGRATION[5]

Immigration became regarded (by some) as a problem in the late 1950s, owing to a considerable increase in the number of non-white immigrants from the Caribbean and other Commonwealth countries. Until 1962, Britain was alone among Commonwealth countries in admitting citizens of other Commonwealth countries without restrictions.

Table 5 summarizes the demographic effects of immigration since 1951. The estimated immigrant population of Great Britain was over 2 million in 1961 and about 2.5 million in 1966. The New Commonwealth[6] component increased from 256,000 in 1951 to 853,000 in 1966. Depending on assumptions made concerning future immigration, the New Commonwealth population may increase to 1.75 million or 2.6 million in 1985 [20].

In order to improve statistics on the ethnic composition of the population, the 1971 census included a question on the parents' country of birth in addition to that of the individual himself. Also included for the first time was a question on the year of first entry into the country for persons born overseas. A mid-1971 official estimate put the population of New Commonwealth ethnic origin at about 1.5 million, or 2.7 percent of the home population of Great Britain. Of this number, about 0.5 million were children born in Great Britain; of these, some 100,000 were the children of mixed marriages [21].

Supporters of immigration control have drawn particular attention to estimates of the extent to which the fertility of non-white immigrants exceeds the national average. According to a recent estimate, the fertility of women born in the New Commonwealth may currently exceed the national average by 50 percent [21]. This estimate was based on birth registration data for 1970 and statistics from the advance analysis of the 1971 census. (In 1969, the particulars required at birth and death registration had been extended to include the birthplace of the child's parents.) Because the estimate is based on an analysis of current fertility, it may, of course, be biased by a variety of factors such as the reuniting of families after some years of separation.

Although the non-white population is a modest proportion of the total

---

[5] Much of the material for this section is taken from the book, *Colour, Citizenship, and British Society* [17]. This is a short version of a report published in 1969 on a survey on race relations in Britain which comprised nineteen major studies and twenty-two smaller projects [18]. The survey was sponsored by the Institute of Race Relations, an independent body. A useful summary of statistics on immigration is given in a booklet published by the institute [19].

[6] The term "New Commonwealth" refers to all Commonwealth countries with the exception of Canada, Australia, and New Zealand.

TABLE 5.

Population Born Abroad, Great Britain, 1951–1966
(in thousands and percents)

	New Commonwealth	Australia, New Zealand, Canada	Irish Republic[a]	Other Immigrants	All Immigrants	Total Population of Great Britain
Residents in 1951	256	93	533	695	1,577	48,854
1951–1961						
Deaths[b]	(21)	(14)	(59)	(70)	(164)	
Immigration[c]	306	31	252	219	808	
Residents in 1961	541	110	726	844	2,222	51,284
1961–1966						
Deaths[b]	(14)	(5)	(29)	(52)	(100)	
Immigration[c]	326	20	42	95	483	
Residents in 1966	853	125	739	887	2,603	52,304[d]
Immigration (annual averages)						
1951–1961	31	3	25	22	81	
1961–1966	65	4	8	19	96	
Annual growth rates (in percents)						
1951–1961	7.7	1.7	3.1	2.0	3.5	0.5
1961–1966	9.5	2.6	0.3	1.0	3.2	0.4
1951–1966	8.3	2.0	2.2	1.6	3.4	0.5

SOURCES: 1951 census, general tables; 1961 census, birthplace and nationality tables; 1966 sample census, summary tables; Annual Abstract of Statistics, 1965, No. 102; NIESR estimates reproduced from [20].

[a] Includes all those born in Ireland unless Northern Ireland stated.
[b] Estimated from the death rates for England and Wales.
[c] Net of re-emigration.
[d] Sample census, probably deficient by 1–2 percent.

population, it is concentrated in the cities, especially London. The highest concentrations are in London boroughs. Often the availability of work has attracted the immigrants to areas that have severe housing shortages, and the majority of immigrants have fared badly in competition for the housing that was available. The 1966 census showed that, for Great Britain as a whole, under 2 percent of households had densities of over 1.5 persons per room in 1966; but the figure was 12 percent of households when the head of the household or spouse was New Commonwealth born. Immigrants also have obtained a disproportionate share of unpopular jobs. Many of their difficulties in this and other respects have been attributed to racial discrimination [22].

The Race Relations Act of 1965 made discrimination on racial grounds an offense in a variety of public places. The Race Relations Act of 1968 extended the legislation to prohibit discrimination on grounds of color, race, or ethnic or national origins in the provision of goods or services and in employment and housing.

¶ CAUSES OF INCREASED IMMIGRATION

There were several reasons for the increase in immigration in the 1950s. The McCarran-Walter Act passed in the United States in 1952 restricted migration from Jamaica to the United States. This act made Britain the only major industrial country open to large-scale migration from the British West Indies. Unfavorable employment conditions there, combined with reports of easily obtainable jobs in the United Kingdom, prompted much of the increased flow. Further, employees were recruited actively by London Transport and other British employers. The migration level showed itself responsive to labor demand in Britain, varying with the level of registered unfilled vacancies.

Toward the end of the 1950s, immigration, especially from the New Commonwealth, increased again and now included large numbers from India and Pakistan. Net arrivals increased from 45,000 in 1958 to 172,000 in 1961. In 1963, the year following imposition of controls, net arrivals fell to 10,000. The precontrol increase has been attributed to rising labor demand and to the expectation that control of Commonwealth immigration was imminent. "A paradoxical conclusion is that the proponents of control created the very situation that they most feared by inducing a far higher rate of migration than has occurred before" [17]. It also has been argued that control and the threat of control gave a new impetus to permanent settlement, by prompting families to join migrants in Britain.

A new flow of non-white immigration was created when east African countries achieved independence from Britain. Many people of Asian origin living in east Africa, especially in Kenya and Uganda, retained their citizenship of the United Kingdom and colonies. In 1967, there was a heavy increase in the number of these citizens who left east Africa for Britain.

¶ THE DEVELOPMENT OF IMMIGRATION POLICY
Demands for restriction on the entry of non-white immigrants, which had been made since the 1950s, were pressed strongly in the 1960s by members of Parliament from the Birmingham area, where housing shortage was an acute problem. A pressure group, the Birmingham Immigration Control Association, was also established in the area. Later in the 1960s, the "cause" of immigration control (including proposals to encourage voluntary repatriation) was championed with particular vigor by Enoch Powell, Member of Parliament for Wolverhampton. As a result of his widely publicized views, "Powellism" became a shorthand description of a doctrine that saw non-white immigration as the import of an alien and unacceptable way of life. Particular emphasis was given to the immigrants' contribution to the rising birth rate. After one speech in Birmingham, Powell received 100,000 letters of support and 800 of dissent [23].

Powell has been accused of encouraging racism. His views have been countered by the arguments that the economy needs the immigrants' labor; that Britain should respond compassionately to the desires of people in poor countries with long historical ties; that Britain has a tradition of admitting peoples of other nationalities; that fears of "the aliens" are understandable but misguided; and that the British have a duty to treat immigrants fairly and to take positive measures to remove the underlying causes of tensions [24]. The National Institute of Economic and Social Research concluded that the economic cost of an unduly restrictive immigration policy could well be high "especially since the natural demographic forces in this country are such that, certainly up to 1980, the rate of increase of the labour force will be even less than the small expansion experienced between 1960 and 1965" [20].

Immigration policy has varied with the immigrants' country of origin. There have been no controls on immigration from Ireland. Until recently, immigration from other non-Commonwealth countries was subject to controls based on the Alien Restriction Acts of 1914 and 1918. An alien who wished to work in Britain needed a work permit, which was issued to the prospective employer in Britain for a specific period of time. Aliens and their dependents were admitted at the discretion of the Home Secretary. After four years, aliens could be admitted to permanent residence in Britain unconditionally. In 1969, this status was achieved by 9,598 alien workers.

The Commonwealth Immigrants Act of 1962 was the first measure to control immigration from the Commonwealth. It made entry into Britain subject to the possession of an official employment voucher. From the standpoint of the Conservative government that introduced the act, its justification was "that a sizeable part of the entire population of the earth is at present legally entitled to come and stay in this already densely populated country . . . and at present there are no factors visible which might lead us to expect a reversal or even a modification of the immigration trend."[7] The government had tried to avoid legislation by attempting to persuade governments of the countries concerned to restrict the numbers leaving for Britain, but the necessary cooperation had not been forthcoming.

The election campaign of 1964, which was won by the Labour party, provided evidence that Commonwealth immigration had become an important policy issue. A prospective minister in the Labour government lost his place in Parliament to a Conservative who had made the need for much stricter immigration control a major issue in his campaign.

The Labour party had opposed the 1962 act. Once in power, the Labour party strengthened the provisions of the act by imposing, in 1965, an upper limit of 8,500 on the issue of employment vouchers; 1,000 of these were earmarked for Malta. In 1968, the number of new entrants actually granted vouchers from all the Commonwealth was less than 5,000, although, with dependents and others, the total admitted for settlement exceeded 50,000, excluding United Kingdom passport holders from east Africa.

After the 1962 act, Commonwealth migration was made up mainly of families arriving to join worker-immigrants. By 1967, over 90 percent of all Commonwealth immigrants were dependents. The definition of a "dependent" has been narrowed several times and has been narrower for Commonwealth citizens than for aliens. Since 1969, dependents have been required to obtain entry certificates from British high commissions and consular posts overseas before embarking. The Conservative party claimed that this requirement had an immediate impact upon immigration from India and Pakistan; in July 1969, arrivals from India were 352 compared with 1,791 in July 1968 [25].

After the general election of 1966 when the Labour party was returned to power, it seemed that the immigration issue had ceased to be important politically. It was revived, however, by the increase in the number of non-white immigrants from east Africa—immigrants of Asian origin but with British passports. The government's response to the increase, and to the clamor by Powell and others for restriction, was the Commonwealth Immigrant Act of 1968. This act extended restrictions to citizens of the United

---

[7] R. A. Butler, then Home Secretary, in a debate on the act, November 16, 1961.

Kingdom holding British passports but having no substantial family connection—personally or through one of the parents or grandparents—with the country. An upper limit of 1,500 heads of households plus dependents, per annum, was established.

A Select Committee on Race Relations and Immigration was established in 1968. After its first report on the problems of non-white school leavers it began an enquiry into immigration control procedures. The evidence was published, but no final report appeared before the committee was dissolved in 1970 when the Labour government was defeated. Two members who served on it prepared a short summary and analysis of the evidence [26]. The committee was reconvened by the incoming Conservative government.

Controversy over British policy suddenly flared again in 1972 when all Asians with British passports were summarily expelled from Uganda. There was some angry debate over whether or not Britain should accept the large number (first estimated at 50,000) of Asians affected. The government decided that, in fact, the country was legally and morally obliged to accept them. Other countries offered to ease the problem by accepting some of the refugees. Eventually, a total of 28,000 arrived in Britain. In January 1973, the Home Secretary made it clear that the government would not accept a repetition of the situation. In a speech in the House of Commons on January 25, 1973, he said, "To have a similar burden thrust on us again would impose unacceptable strains and stresses on our society and, not least, would endanger our ability to carry out our duty to those immigrants already resident here."

A new system of immigration control was created by the Immigration Act of 1971, which came fully into force in January 1973. The act introduces the idea of a single system of immigration control for both Commonwealth and alien immigrants. It removes from control a large number of Commonwealth citizens who can prove parental links with Britain. On the other hand, it establishes for those subject to control a system of regulations based on that in force for aliens. Introducing revised immigration rules, the Home Secretary said he wished to make it clear, in particular to employees, that work permits would be issued very sparingly indeed, and that this stringency would apply to Commonwealth and non-Commonwealth countries alike.

The act has attracted much criticism. The director of the Runnymede Trust[8] said it would introduce "a new element, with unmistakable racial overtones, into Britain's relationships with other countries." It worsened

---

[8] The Runnymede Trust is an independent body established to provide information and education in race relations.

the situation of aliens and made Commonwealth citizens already here subject to new types of insecurity [27]. A Labour party study group declared that the act would stimulate prejudice among the majority in the community and would intensify the feelings of insecurity of the minorities [28]. The Labour party's current position is summarized in the statement: "We have no objection in principle to immigration control, but the criteria must be rational and non-racial and must be seen to be so" [11].

Britain's entry into the European Economic Community (EEC) has created the possibility of a type of immigration that cannot be unilaterally controlled. Membership in the EEC confers on nationals of member states the freedom to move to any other EEC country at any time to seek work. No work permit, entry clearance, or other special document is required.

¶ EMIGRATION

It has been estimated that between 1815 and 1914, over 20 million people emigrated from the United Kingdom to destinations outside Europe. After the 1914–1918 war, the volume of emigration dropped sharply and virtually ceased in the 1930s when the dominions ceased to encourage immigration. After World War II, emigration increased again. It has been estimated that emigration from the United Kingdom to the Commonwealth reached 200,000 or more in each of the years 1952 and 1957. In 1964, a net outward migration balance of 60,000 replaced the inward balances of the peak immigration period 1958–1963. There has been an outward balance each year since 1964. It was approximately 44,000 from mid-1971 to mid-1972.

The Commonwealth Migration Council was formed in 1946 to encourage British migration to the Commonwealth. "The Council has consistently asserted that Britain's population is too large for present or future security or comfort, and that emigration is vital for enabling surplus population to start elsewhere" [4]. Apart from wartime restrictions and a small subsidy to an "assisted passage" scheme for emigrants to Australia, there have been no official attempts to influence emigration.

In a report published in 1973, a panel of experts set up to advise the government on population policy[9] rejected the possibility that emigration could solve problems associated with population pressure. Since the majority of emigrants were younger adults, whose contribution to society was lost for the rest of their productive lives, emigration on a scale sufficient to have significant effects on total numbers would involve a substantial real cost.

[9] Further information about the panel and its work is given in later sections of the paper.

NATURAL INCREASE

Current debates about the control of natural increase had their origin in 1798 when Thomas Malthus produced the first edition of *Essay on the Principle of Population*. Marx condemned him for attributing to individual improvidence what Marx regarded as the inevitable consequence of capitalism. Similar conflicts of view about causes and therefore about remedies were to become divisive themes of later controversies about population increase and its effects. However, the fertility decline that began in the 1870s diminished the relevance of the issue for a time. Attention turned instead to problems of insufficient childbearing.

In 1913 the English Socialist Sydney Webb offered some evidence to support his view that the decline was taking place primarily among those sections of every class where there was most providence, foresight and self-control. He foresaw the prospect of either national deterioration, or a loss of the country to the Irish and the Jews [29]. Such speculations were less influential, however, than were widely publicized forecasts made in the 1930s of an absolute decline in numbers. According to one estimate, the population of England and Wales would fall to 4.426 million by the year 2035, assuming a continued decline in fertility until 1985. The seriousness with which such estimates were taken was probably reinforced by the adoption in Germany of a comprehensive pronatalist policy. Similar policies had been pursued in France, Belgium, and Italy for several years. The Population (Statistics) Act of 1938 was indicative of the increased interest in population trends. The act changed the vital statistics system, making possible the calculation of precise reproduction rates and the analysis of current changes in fertility [30].

Suggestions that population growth should be the subject of an official enquiry were made before World War II. In 1944, a Royal Commission on Population was appointed, assisted by three specialist committees. The commission's enquiries, which lasted five years, included a fertility enquiry and a special family census. The final report, published in 1949, was reassuring to those who had feared that population was shrinking [31]. After falling continuously for half a century, family size had been comparatively stable for twenty years, at about 2.2 children per married couple. This was only about 6 percent below the level needed for replacement at prevailing mortality rates. The total population of Great Britain would probably continue to grow for at least one or two decades, but only by a few million. Although sanguine about general prospects, the commission had no hesitation in concluding that

A replacement of family is desirable in Britain at the present time. It is impossible for policy, in its effects as distinct from its intentions, to be "neutral" in this matter since over a wide range of affairs policy and administration have a continuous influence on the trend of family size [31].

The principal recommendation was that the economic and social disadvantages of having a large family should be reduced by a number of social policy measures. It also was recommended that the newly established National Health Service should include facilities for advising on contraception to married persons.

The report was never debated in Parliament, and most of its specific recommendations have been ignored by successive governments. On the other hand, the report and the work of the specialist committees shaped much of the subsequent study and discussion of population trends.

Events since 1949 have revived concern with population increase. A boom in births starting in the mid-1950s led to major upward revisions in projected population growth. Immigration increased substantially shortly afterward. Finally, the implications of world population growth secured a prominent place in discussions of national problems.

¶ MORTALITY CONTROL

As in other advanced countries, the prevention of death is no longer the dominant concern of medical care. In Great Britain, expectation of life at birth in 1969 was sixty-nine years for men and seventy-five years for women, some twenty-one and twenty-three years, respectively, greater than at the beginning of the century. Although by the start of the twentieth century substantial declines in mortality had taken place (largely as a result of improved living standards and public health measures rather than specific medical developments), the infant mortality rates had remained at about 150 per 1,000 live births since the middle of the nineteenth century. During the twentieth century, the most marked feature of the continued mortality decline was the reduction of infant mortality. In 1970, the rate was 18.1 per 1,000 live births per year.

There were a number of reasons for the further reduction of death rates in the twentieth century. General improvements in nutrition and living conditions and the further expansion of measures to control environmental hazards continued to be of great importance. Another factor was the improvement in the delivery of medical care to the population. Developments in medical science and staff training improved hospital services substantially. The role of central government in the field of health care was considerably expanded, first through the National Health Insurance scheme and direct provision of health services for selected "high risk" groups, and eventually in the establishment in 1948 of a National Health Service to protect the whole population.

Because of the concern over the high infant mortality rate, attention was first focused on mothers and small children. In 1902, the first legislation in the personal health field was passed—the Midwives' Act. This established standards for training, made provision for the maintenance of a register, and prohibited untrained women from practicing midwifery. In 1918, the Maternity and Child Welfare Act established local authority services for expectant and nursing mothers and for children under five years of age. Under this act, the care of large numbers of mothers and infants could be undertaken by local authority midwives, doctors, and health visitors working from infant welfare clinics. A school health service and a school meals service were instituted.

Many factors were involved in the development, from services aimed at specific sections of the population to the National Health Service. One powerful influence was involvement in the world wars. The needs of the war periods established the beginnings of the administrative framework for health services and revealed the uneven distribution of medical care throughout the country. The National Health Service Act laid a duty on the Minister of Health not only to provide free medical, nursing, and ancillary services for everyone needing them but also to aim for improvements in the physical and mental health of the people. An individual could choose a general practitioner as his "family doctor." Midwifery and other supporting services were provided by the local authority. A Hospital and Specialist Service was available for those receiving in-patient and out-patient treatment. A concise account of the development of the health services in England and Wales has been published by Olive Keidan [32].

Accompanying the advances in the organization of medical care and public health were advances in the control of disease through vaccines and chemotherapy. Over half the total fall in childhood deaths between 1931 and 1960 was the result of a decline in mortality from five diseases: pneumonia, tuberculosis, diphtheria, measles, and whooping cough. By 1960, these diseases, with the exception of pneumonia, had virtually ceased to cause childhood deaths [33].

Considerable attention has been paid to social-class differentials in mortality. Census data have been used to establish populations at risk for each of the five social-class groups used, so that registration figures for the groups could be compared. Sample survey enquiries have also been made. For general mortality and infant mortality, a social-class gradient from top to bottom has been a persistent finding.

¶ FERTILITY TRENDS

In retrospect, the decade of the 1930s was a period of temporarily depressed fertility. Since then, changes in several demographic characteristics have contributed to a recovery. First, there has been an increase in marriage rates: the proportion of women not marrying within the childbearing period (that is, before age forty-five) has fallen to 8 percent. The proportion unmarried in the first four decades of this century was 19 percent. Second, there has been a trend to earlier marriage: about 30 percent are now married by age twenty years, compared with 10 percent in 1931. More marriage and earlier marriage would tend to increase overall fertility even if average family size remained constant. In fact, there has also been a small but important increase in the number of children couples are having. It has been estimated that the average family size of those marrying in the late 1950s and early 1960s will be nearly 2.5 live-born children, a substantial increase over the average of 2.1 in the 1930s. The increase in marital fertility is explained by a substantial reduction in childlessness and by a shift from the one-child family to families of two or three children. Finally, generation replacement rates have been rising as women experience the lower death rates achieved during the past thirty years.

The increase in total births in the postwar period has been mainly accounted for by births within marriage, but an increase in both the number and relative proportion of illegitimate births has also occurred. The increase in the illegitimacy rate roughly coincided with a trend to early marriage. In about a third of cases, illegitimate births are registered by the fathers as well as by the mothers.

There has been a continued reduction in the number of large families. Among English and Welsh women married 15–19 years in 1961 (uninterrupted first marriages, wife's age at marriage under forty-five years), those who had had five or more live births amounted to only 6.3 percent of the total, and those with seven or more live births represented only 1.6 percent of the total. The percentage distribution of births by parity of mother in 1971 is shown in Table 6.

Numbers of births declined after 1964, and the decline has persisted. It

TABLE 6.

Percentage Distribution by Parity of Legitimate Live Births to Women Married Once Only, England and Wales, 1971

Number of Previous Live-Born Children	Births (in percents)
0	40.1
1	33.7
2	15.3
3	6.1
4+	4.7

SOURCE: See [34].

has been associated with a lengthening of the average intervals between marriage and the birth of the first child and between first and second births. The proportion of premaritally conceived births has fallen, and there has been a marked fall in the proportion conceived in the first three months of marriage. All these changes are indicators of a relative delay in child-bearing.

A recent development in Great Britain is the attempt to use surveys to determine the family size women expect to have. A family intentions survey was undertaken in 1967 by the Government Social Survey [6]. A sample of married women was asked both what they expected would be the size of their completed family and what they considered to be an ideal family size. It was officially inferred from the answers that "an average family size of about 2.5 children is regarded by parents today as a desirable level, and realistic in the sense that this is roughly what they expect (on average) to achieve." The "ideal" in the sense of that which parents would like to have if they had no financial problems was about 3.5 children per family. More recently, information on the subject was obtained in the course of the General Household Survey, which indicated that recently married women expected to have a mean completed family size of under 2.3. An average completed family size of "rather under 2.4" for the United Kingdom was assumed for the mid-1971 projections [3].

It is not difficult to suggest ways in which policies might have influenced fertility trends. For example, the number of dwellings completed by local authorities and new towns dropped from 69,000 in 1966 to 55,000 in 1971 [35]. During the same period, prices of homes soared. However, the effect, if any, that social policy in this and other spheres has had, or could have, on fertility remains unknown.

THE CAMPAIGN FOR POPULATION CONTROL

During the 1960s, it became public knowledge that world population was growing rapidly. At first, the growth was presented as constituting a particular problem for poor countries. Agencies and individuals responsible for overseas aid emphasized the view that rapid population growth was impeding attempts at economic development. Voluntary aid organizations began to support family planning projects in some of these countries. The importance of giving official aid was the subject of debates in the House of Lords. In 1968, a Population Bureau was established at the Ministry of Overseas Development. The government started to give grants to the International Planned Parenthood Federation.

From about the mid-1960s onward, greater emphasis was given to the view that not only poor countries but the world as a whole was threatened by the effects of rapid population growth. It was suggested that developed countries such as Great Britain would fare badly in the struggle for survival. At the same time, it was also argued that Britain's own population was already larger than could easily be supported; that projected population growth would outstrip the nation's resources and impose hazardous demands on the environment; and that the country should have a positive population policy, directed toward a substantial reduction in numbers.

Probably the single most effective stimulus to the discussion of such a policy was the presidential address given in September 1966 by Sir Joseph Hutchinson to the British Association for the Advancement of Science. In this widely publicized speech, Hutchinson told his audience:

> Make no mistake, this country already carries a population as great as the environment can support without degeneration, and it will call for all the knowledge and skill we can command to prevent irreparable damage before we achieve a stable population, even if we set about stabilization without delay [36].

He suggested that Britain should aim for a stable population of 40 million.

Concern with these issues led to the creation of the Conservation Society in November 1966. One of its past chairmen, Sir David Renton, a Conservative Member of Parliament who has been a prominent campaigner for policies to stabilize population size, has given somber accounts of the implications of population growth [4]. Britain was already one of the most densely populated countries in the world, yet a child born in 1969 was likely to see the country's population nearly double in his lifetime. The possibility of bringing about a major shift in the distribution of population appeared to be slight. As well as increase in numbers, it was necessary to take into account the increase in leisure time, and the increase in mobility that wider car ownership would bring. Further decreases in the average amount of land per head of population would lead to further overcrowding, high land values, shortage of land to meet recreational purposes, and reduction in the area of agricultural land. Already the country grew only one half of its requirements in food and feedstuffs. World demand for food, especially proteins, would increase owing to world population growth. The increasing purchasing power that industrialization would give to developing countries would make it difficult for Britain to import all the food she needed by the end of the century. The country had to import most of the minerals, raw materials, and energy sources on which her industries and her whole way of life depended. She was therefore in the vulnerable position of having to export a large proportion of manufactured goods to pay for imports, although her economy was extremely sensitive to world trade. Should the terms of trade move in favor of primary producers and against producers of manufactured goods, it would become more difficult to pay for imports. Home agricultural production was being expanded, but to the detriment of the country-side. Continued population growth would adversely affect the balance of payments, would be inflationary, and would accentuate the problems of air, water, and land pollution. It would overtax investment resources required to maintain and improve standards of infrastructure and social capital. There would be a continuous increase in constraints on personal freedom, and a continuous deterioration in the natural environment. People should be told, Renton said, about the dangers of overpopulation so that they would be put "into the frame of mind in which they will consider what size their family should be." It was also essential and urgent to make family planning services, including sterilization, available without charge within the National Health Service. After a few years, he concluded, it might be necessary to abolish family allowances for children or children's tax allowances, if voluntary birth control failed to reduce the birth rate substantially.

In September 1969, the Institute of Biology convened a symposium on the optimum population for Great Britain. Most of the audience were professional biologists. Ninety percent of them registered the opinion that the optimum population for Great Britain had already been exceeded. The most vivid contribution to the symposium was a paper by P. R. Ehrlich. He contemplated the position of Britain in a world made increasingly prone by population growth to nuclear war, worldwide plague, and "eco-catastrophe." If these calamities were avoided but current trends continued, he predicted that, by the end of the century, the United Kingdom would "simply be a small group of impoverished islands, inhabited by some 70 million hungry people, of little or no concern to the other 5–7 billion people of a sick world" [37]. Views of this kind have been presented with increasing frequency since the late 1960s. Newspapers and television programs have treated the subject as a matter of major public interest. For some time, *The Observer*, one of the more sophisticated weekly newspapers, labeled features on the subject "Spaceship Earth."

The Research Department of the Labour party published a pamphlet on the implications of world population growth, as a discussion document for the National Conference of Labour Women in 1971 [38]. A section entitled "A Population Policy for Britain" referred to a resolution passed at the Labour party's 1970 annual conference calling for the mandatory provision by all local authorities of a family planning service. The pamphlet proposed that the next Labour government should have a specific commitment to provide a comprehensive service under the National Health Service.[10] The section concluded with the suggestion that the most signifi-

---

[10] Resolutions favoring full and free family planning services were passed at the annual conferences of the Labour party and the Liberal party in 1972.

cant step toward achieving a slowing rate of population growth might be the expansion of educational and employment opportunities for women. "Once they can achieve satisfaction and status outside the home equally with men, many women who are temperamentally inclined to be childless would feel much less pressure to have children."

Public debate on these issues was given further momentum in January 1972 with the publication of a special issue of *The Ecologist* entitled "A Blueprint for Survival" [39]. It comprised a series of radical proposals for reducing pressure on the environment. They included the proposal that Great Britain should try to reduce its population to a size that could be fed from its own agricultural resources: approximately 30 million. It was also proposed that instead of trying to increase gross national product, countries should strive to reduce it.

Early in 1972, T. R. E. Southwood and 137 other "scientists concerned with ecology" signed a letter to *The Times* (January 25, 1972) about the "Blueprint." The letter explained that portions of the "Blueprint" contained scientifically questionable statements of fact and highly debatable short- and long-term policy proposals, but nevertheless these scientists welcomed the document as a major contribution to current debate and affirmed the gravity of the growing crisis.

Specifically we agree that it is a matter of urgency to stabilize the world population and for the British Government to formulate a population policy for this country, not only in our own interests but also because developed countries such as ours make far greater demands on scarce resources and create far greater pollution per capita than do the peoples of the rest of the world.

Further support for population policy came at the same time in the form of a letter to *The Lancet* signed by fifty doctors [40]. The letter referred to "the British disease of overpopulation" and held that "doctors, as an informed and highly educated section of the community, are in a particularly strong position to influence society on this all-important topic." The letter received editorial support from *The Lancet* itself.

In 1965, the president of the Royal Society, the late Lord Florey, brought together a group of eminent demographers, economists, geneticists, family planning experts, and others to examine population questions from various points of view. A report of their discussions was published in May 1970 as a supplement to *Population Studies* [41]. The report did not recommend a specific population policy. Its authors took the view that policy might need to change with changes in actual and prospective circumstances. But the report pointed out that the absence of specific measures constituted a form of population policy: the implicit assumption that population growth should be taken as given. It recommended an end to the comparative neglect of demographic considerations in the design of Great Britain's policies and institutions, whether the aim was to influence or to anticipate population trends. Action in a number of spheres was proposed: the promotion of research and development in contraceptive techniques; the incorporation of training in contraceptive advice in the medical services to this end; improvements in the collection and analysis of statistical information about relevant demographic, social, and economic developments; the formulation and initiation of research into the factors affecting motivations in family building; and the explicit recognition of demographic considerations in the discussion and formulation of social and economic policies.

In 1972, the Conservation Society published a document stating its proposals for a population policy for Britain [42]. The preamble stressed that explicit acceptance of population policies by advanced Western countries would have much more influence on the Third World's policies than would the giving of technical advice and help. Another benefit would be that of minimizing the dangers posed by underprivileged groups who sometimes resented and resisted family planning programs aimed specifically at them. Suitable opportunities should be created for the many women who would be glad to have only two children and then return to work. As a general rule, tax concessions should be given in respect of the first two children only. The family allowance system should be reviewed with a view to giving benefits in kind rather than cash, to ensure that the system did not encourage large families. The Society also urged population education and relevant research.

In 1972, a pamphlet urging the government to adopt a population policy was published by Stanley Johnson, a former member of the Conservative party's research department [43]. He noted that the party's annual conference held in October 1971 had accepted, by an "overwhelming majority," a motion put forward by the Young Conservative National Advisory Committee: "that this Conference expresses its concern at the problem of population growth in Britain and the world and calls upon Her Majesty's Government to aid practical schemes of population limitation." Johnson favored the idea of "trying to create a climate of opinion in which small families were considered right." He pointed out that, at the 1972 party conference, the Secretary of State for Social Services had spoken of the need to extend family planning services "even to those who may not seek it for themselves without being persuaded."

¶ OBJECTIONS TO THE CASE FOR POPULATION CONTROL

The case for sponsored population reduction has not been without skeptical opponents. Prominent among these has been the prestigious journal *Nature*. In a leading article entitled "The Case against Hysteria," it derided the

628 POPULATION POLICY IN DEVELOPED COUNTRIES

scientists who had supported *The Ecologist*'s "Blueprint for Survival" and the doctors who had written to *The Lancet*. They were accused of taking part in a reprehensible attempt to fan public anxiety about problems that either had been exaggerated or were nonexistent [*44*].

Skeptics were also present at the Institute of Biology's symposium. A. J. Boreham[11] pointed out that, although Britain's population density was 11 times that of the United States, it was 60 percent lower than that of Holland; that the rate of growth of population in Britain was just over 0.5 percent per year; and that, if the average family was 2.25 instead of 2.5 children, the population would eventually stop increasing. Since the required changes were small and would take a long time to reveal themselves and since, in his view, the economic arguments for and against change were finely balanced, he thought it would be misguided to attempt to influence population changes. While the social costs of population growth increased more than linearly with population size, he did not believe they would place unmanageable burdens on Great Britain's resources [*45*].

In his paper at the symposium, David Eversley[12] said that he thought it very likely that, within a very few years, the birth rate would drop below replacement level and that there would then be "a new wave of pro-populationist hysteria." Family size was already controlled by a majority of parents at a level determined by their living standards. Therefore, short of extreme bribes or deterrents to parents, it was unreasonable to expect policy to have much effect on fertility [*46*].

A particularly vigorous polemic against advocates of zero population growth was published by David Wolfers, director of the Population Bureau at the Overseas Development Administration. In his view, the attainment of zero growth, if it were possible, would do nothing to improve the quality of human life, pollution of the environment, or consumption of non-renewable resources. The zero growth movement had romantic, not scientific, origins. Wolfers argued that policies in different countries had to be determined in the light of local conditions [*47*].

The case for population control was also skeptically examined by Geoffrey Hawthorn, a sociologist engaged in research on the social and economic determinants of British fertility. In a pamphlet for the Fabian Society, he accused the campaigners of fostering an immoral denial of the right of individuals to determine their own fertility. Population control would not solve the problem of depletion of resources if the remaining population continued to live at a higher standard of living. While conges-

---

[11] Then head of Economic and Statistical Analysis Division, Ministry of Technology.
[12] Then Professor of Population Studies, Sussex University, and Chief Planner (Strategy), Greater London Council.

tion might be alleviated in the short term, road traffic, the most serious form of congestion, would continue to increase. The road system was going to seize up within the next generation whatever happened demographically. A concentration on the contribution of population growth drew attention away from "the real issues," which were ones of the distribution of material resources within the population, and the freedom of some to restrict the freedom of others [48].

Although not opposed to a population policy, David Glass [4] pointed out that, according to the 1961 census, those who had five or more live births amounted to only 6.3 percent of the total population. Those with seven or more live births represented only 1.6 percent of the total. Glass remarked that this was scarcely evidence of irresponsible parenthood on a substantial scale. The most striking feature of the present situation was that family size was relatively small and fairly uniform. Economic circumstances since the 1940s had not been such a barrier to desired family size as they had been in the economic depression of the 1930s. A shift from one to two or three children entailed less hardship than would have been the case earlier. Further, the reduction in childlessness was associated with a fall in the age at marriage.

The Conservation Society and other advocates of fertility reduction have suggested that tax concessions and family allowances for dependent children are pronatalist in their effects.[13] It has not been the aim of family policy to encourage parents to have more children. The purpose of the allowances and concessions has been to help parents provide for their children's welfare. Critics of family policy have protested that the extent of family assistance has been quite inadequate for low-income families. The issue was considered in a book on family policy by Margaret Wynn [49]. She conceded that some of the measures needed to relieve child poverty could have a pronatalist effect, but she argued that it was not logical to oppose such measures in a country that retained a wide range of laws and institutions with a heavy pronatalist bias. In her view, a more certain way to reduce fertility would be to expand women's opportunities for education and satisfying employment. She also argued that a tradition of high stand-

---

[13] Parents receive a weekly family allowance of 90 pence for the second child and £1 for the third and subsequent children. No allowance is given for the first child. The part of annual income not subject to tax is increased by amounts varying from £155 to £205, according to the age of the child. (As of January 1, 1973, £1 equaled approximately US$2.35; there are 100 pence to £1.) In most cases, family allowances are regarded as part of taxable income, so that the main benefit of the allowance is received only by those who pay no tax. In addition, needy parents not in full-time employment receive benefits based on the number and ages of their children. A family income supplement has been available since 1970 for those in full-time employment who are earning very low wages.

ards of child care could tend to reduce the number of large families. "No mother will, however, be convinced of the country's concern by exhortation, but only by the quality of the child-care services."

From her analysis of family policy in Great Britain, Wynn concluded that, far from being excessively well-treated, families with dependent children generally had a substantially lower standard of living than families without dependent children; that parents spent very much more than the state on bringing up their children, even taking fully into account the state's expenditure on education.

¶ THE GOVERNMENT'S RESPONSE

In June 1966, Sir David Renton asked Prime Minister Harold Wilson what steps were being taken by the government to predict future trends of population, to influence such trends, and to ensure that social policies were planned in accordance with a realistic and acceptable policy of controlling immigration and encouraging emigration. Wilson invited Renton to write to him about it. In November 1966, Renton accepted this invitation and subsequently published the correspondence [50]. From this, it emerged that, not only was the Prime Minister unmoved by Renton's arguments, he rejected most of them. Wilson wrote:

A key point I think is that we must take into account that an expanding population besides raising problems also means an expanding market and that this should induce investment and technological development as well as help to solve our longer-term manpower shortages [50].

Wilson thought the problem of population pressure could be resolved largely by policies directed toward securing more balanced regional population growth. Influencing family sizes was a very delicate matter for any government; nor would it be easy to achieve any marked effect. Wilson believed that Britain would be able to support a population of about 75 million at a rising standard of living. He did not pretend that there would be no loss of amenity. But, "Would this alone justify a policy of attempting to influence family sizes?"

Many members of Parliament were more sympathetic to Renton's views. In February 1968, he and five other members presented a motion on the issue, signed by 326 members. It called on the government "to establish permanent and adequate machinery for examining the difficulties to which population growth would give rise, and for giving early warning to Parliament of such difficulties and to advise what steps should be taken to overcome them well in advance of crisis point."

In January 1970, a subcommittee of Parliament's Select Committee on Science and Technology began an enquiry into the consequences of population growth in the United Kingdom. In his evidence to the committee, Sir Solly Zuckerman, then the government's chief scientific adviser, revealed that the government was planning to create a central population study unit in the Cabinet office [4]. He said that a broad survey of social, economic, and other implications of economic growth had been carried out in 1969 by the staff of the Cabinet office, in consultation with interested departments. In his view, the projected population growth at the end of the century would greatly intensify pressures on the physical environment. A continuing increase in the size of the population would require a parallel increase in social investment for the maintenance of equivalent standards of housing, schools, medical treatment, road space, and so forth. He thought the problem was a manageable one. But if population seemed likely to continue to increase, "then one ought to start considering what measures could be adopted by the Government in order to restrain the growth of population."

From the evidence given to the committee, it was clear that spokesmen for government departments were by no means alarmed by population growth. The Ministry of Agriculture, Fisheries, and Food said that there were no grounds for assuming that the trading position of the country was going to worsen as years went by. And even if it did, this was unlikely to happen suddenly. There would be time to adapt. The Ministry of Housing and Local Government thought that, given adequate regional planning, there should be no problem in accommodating the expected increase in population. The Department of Employment and Productivity did not foresee population increase exceeding the number of jobs that would be available.

The general election of 1970 brought the enquiry to a premature end, but a report was published in May 1971 [51]. In this, members of the committee said that they did not share the complacent views expressed by many of the departmental witnesses. They were convinced of the need to act twenty years in advance in order to influence the trend in population figures. Their report stated their conclusions as follows: "The Government must act to prevent the consequences of population growth becoming intolerable for the everyday conditions of life." The committee recommended the creation, as an integral and permanent part of the machinery of government, of a special office directly responsible to the Prime Minister. This new office would study British and world population trends and their implications for resources and services. It would advise the government on population policy and publicize the results of its studies. It would also publicize the role of family limitation and socially responsible parenthood.

In July 1971, the government published "Observations" [52] on the report. These may be summarized as follows: the study of the implications for policy of actual and foreseen population trends was a continuing process involving many departments and was now being coordinated centrally by Cabinet office machinery. With regard to population policy, what was required was an assessment of available evidence about the significance of population trends. To achieve this, the government had decided to appoint a small panel of experts "from outside the Government machine as well as inside. The members of the panel will not be experts in a narrow sense, but will have broad and relevant experience of the subject and the necessary qualities to tackle its analysis effectively and dispassionately." They were required to report within one year.

In July 1972, the Select Committee on Science and Technology decided to investigate the progress of the Population Panel. They heard evidence from the chairman of the panel, the Secretary of State for Social Services, and the Lord President of the Council. The Lord President had been made responsible for answering questions in Parliament on the work of the panel and on matters arising from coordinating work within the government on population questions.

In their report on the investigations, the committee members were strongly critical of what they regarded as the government's "leisurely and disinterested attitude to the question of population growth" [5]. They were "astonished" that the Secretary of State for Social Services had no plans or policy for relating family planning to population size or trends. The panel was not influential enough, and the terms of its formation did not provide for it to make recommendations on the implementation of a particular policy. The committee repeated its recommendation that a special office should be set up to advise the government on population policy. The government was also urged to take immediate steps to provide comprehensive family planning and birth control services as a normal part of the National Health Service.

Answering questions in the House of Commons on November 23, 1972, the Prime Minister said he did not think a single minister could cope with the problem of population policy, and therefore did not propose to appoint one. Replying to one questioner, he said that "doomwatchers" had been in existence for more than a century—in fact since the time of Malthus. "I do not think we should pay them any more attention now than was paid to them then."

¶ REPORT OF THE POPULATION PANEL

The *Report of the Population Panel* [65] was published by the government in March 1973. The panel was skeptical of much of the case for population policy, but granted that the time had come for the government to consider whether, and if so how, to act to influence the rate of population growth. Population might well increase by 20 percent over the ensuing thirty to forty years but the situation did not require immediate policy initiatives to reduce dramatically the rate of increase. The panel did not know the optimum size of Britain's population, nor could they see how any such optimum could be calculated on the basis of existing knowledge. However, they had concluded that Britain would do better in the future with a stationary rather than with an increasing population, since problems of accommodating a further 10 or 20 million people, in addition to the 10 million or so already in prospect, were likely to be progressively more difficult.

The panel was opposed to fiscal measures to provide disincentives to childbearing, and to nonfiscal measures involving any interference with individual liberty or family life. The possibility of increased emigration was also rejected. It neither should nor could provide a major contribution to the relief of population pressure. Immigration policy should be decided on social and humanitarian grounds, and in the light of more definite and immediate factors than speculative long-term assessments of the future size of population.

However, the panel did recommend the institution of measures to reduce the number of unwanted pregnancies. Policy in regard to family planning services should take account of population implications instead of being decided entirely in terms of its effects on health and social welfare. "The first positive step towards a population policy should be the development of comprehensive family planning services as an integral part of the National Health Service, so that everyone knows of their existence and is free to use them." Further, the facts about population size and growth should be made widely known, so that people could make decisions about family size knowing the implications of their decisions not only for themselves but also for the country as a whole.

The panel recommended that since existing knowledge was an inadequate basis for policy, much more work should be done to increase the information available on population trends, their causes and implications. Population affairs should become the responsibility of a senior nondepartmental minister. There should be a small executive unit and an interdepartmental committee in the Cabinet office, responsible for organizing, coordinating, and ensuring implementation of the work program.

"INVOLUNTARY" NATURAL INCREASE

The Population Panel was adopting a familiar position in recommending measures to reduce the number of unwanted pregnancies, as part of population policy. It has been frequently asserted that every year large numbers of births (up to 150,000) are "unwanted"; they occur contrary to the wishes of the parents [4; 5; 53; 54].

Sometimes the estimated number of unwanted births is referred to as a measure of the failure of birth control services to prevent personal and family distress. The number is also used, often by the same people, as the measure of a population burden which could be avoided simply by improving the family planning services. In fact improving the services, together with public education on population issues, has become the population policy usually urged on the government. Often the essential problem is seen as that of enabling and encouraging people to use reliable methods of birth control. For example, according to Hawthorn: ". . . with 100 per cent effective contraception in 100 per cent of marriages more than 20 per cent of births at present occurring would not occur" [48].

Little attention has been paid publicly to reservations about such arguments. They often appear to be based on an ingenuous use of "unwanted" and similar terms. In general they ignore the way the strength and character of an individual's inclinations with respect to pregnancy may affect choice of birth control method and effectiveness of use. In some cases the figures for avoidable births have been inflated by the inclusion of births (for example, many illegitimate births) which might have been inconveniently timed but which were not likely to increase the ultimate total. Finally, it has been generally assumed that improved family planning services would inevitably act to reduce fertility. In their report the Population Panel mentioned the possibility that comprehensive family planning services could also be an influence making for higher fertility, either by changing attitudes to family formation or by tending to encourage promiscuity.

¶ BIRTH CONTROL PRACTICE

There have been three national surveys of trends in birth control practice in Britain since 1947. The most recent was undertaken in 1967–1968 by the Population Investigation Committee [55; 56]. It found a steady increase over time in the percentage of women who claimed to be using or to have used birth control by the time they were interviewed. For recent marriage cohorts, the combined figure for actual and prospective use had reached 95 percent. The findings are summarized in Table 7. Glass has pointed out that a figure of 95 percent implied practically total coverage of all married women. Further, "ever use" was now almost as widespread among working-class as among middle-class couples, although the latter were much more likely to use birth control appliances and to obtain professional advice. The middle class was also more likely to practice birth control before the first pregnancy. However, pregnancies reported as having occurred despite the use of birth control remained fairly frequent, even among relatively recent marriage cohorts. This applied to 24 percent of third pregnancies of women married in the period 1956–1960. In Glass's view, it was probable that many of the "accidents" were related to the timing of the births rather than to the total number but that, if more effective contraception were used, ultimate family size "might well be modified and perhaps reduced." However, in the short run, it was changes in marriage and in the timing of birth that were likely to have the major effect on natural increase. And "given the present narrow range of family sizes— predominantly in the range of 1–3 live births per couple—relatively small changes could have a considerable effect on average family size" [4].

¶ DEVELOPMENT OF BIRTH CONTROL POLICY

In 1930, the Ministry of Health gave permission for Child Welfare Centers to give contraceptive advice to married women for whom a further pregnancy would be detrimental to health. Previously, the government had neither assisted nor hindered the use of contraceptives. The 1930 concession was interpreted liberally by most local authorities, who subsidized voluntary clinics through the provision of rent-free premises and financial grants [57]. In 1949, the report of the Royal Commission on Population recommended that contraceptive advice and treatment should be available to all married women who required it, as part of the newly established National Health Service. The recommendation was ignored.

A voluntary body, the Family Planning Association (FPA), has built a national system of birth control clinics. In 1970, it provided at least 90 percent of the available clinics. From the mid-1960s, the FPA began to press for more official support of birth control services. The cause was given enthusiastic support by most newspapers. To be against it became a sign of gross ignorance or religious fanaticism. The pressure for improvement of services was reinforced by the activities of the abortion law reform movement (see below).

The government's first response was a circular to local authorities in 1966 requesting all local health authorities to make arrangements for birth control advice and treatment (including supplies) for all women who requested them. Service could be provided either directly or through a voluntary body such as the FPA. In the following year, the National Health Service (Family Planning) Act of 1967 came into force. It had been sponsored by a Member of Parliament, Edwin Brooks, but its passage through Parliament was accomplished with the help and encouragement of the government. The act enabled local authorities to provide (directly or through voluntary bodies) free advice on contraception and free contraceptive supplies to any person who needed them, on social as well as med-

TABLE 7.

Birth Control Practice, Britain, 1967–1968

Year of Marriage	Number of Women	Professional Advice and the Use of Contraception, by Marriage Cohort			
		Of These Women, the Percentage Who Have Ever:		Of Women Who Have Ever Obtained Professional Advice, the Percentage Who Have Ever Used Contraception	Of Women Who Have Never Obtained Professional Advice, the Percentage Who Have Ever Used Contraception
		Used Contraception	Obtained Professional Advice		
		A	B	C	D
1941–1950	647	84.6	21.6	99.3	80.5
1951–1960	626	90.2	37.9	99.6	84.6
1961–1965	359	91.4	41.1	99.3	85.8
1941–1965	1,632	88.2	32.1	99.4	83.0

NOTE: Includes the pill, chemical and appliance methods, coitus interruptus, douching, breast-feeding, abstinence, and the rhythm method. In fact, douching, breast-feeding, and abstinence were reported by very few women, and these "methods" had little or no effect on the level of "ever use" of birth control.

Use of Individual Methods of Contraception
by Advice and Marriage Cohort for Women
Who Have Ever Used Birth Control

	Year of Marriage							
	All		1941–1950		1951–1960		1961–1965	
	Advice	No Advice	Advice	No Advice	Advice	No Advice	Advice	No Advice
Number of women who have ever used birth control	521	918	139	409	236	328	147	181
Of these women, the percentage who have ever used:								
Pill	42.2	4.4	19.0	1.7	45.7	5.2	58.4	9.4
Condom	58.2	63.2	60.6	58.4	59.0	68.4	54.6	64.5
Diaphragm	48.1	1.6	55.8	1.5	51.0	1.8	36.4	1.7
IUD	4.9	0.0	2.2	0.0	4.4	0.0	8.2	0.0
Jelly (spermicides)	52.9	11.7	60.1	15.2	55.6	10.4	41.6	6.1
Rhythm	12.9	10.5	11.8	8.1	14.8	10.7	10.9	15.5
Withdraw	33.7	50.6	27.8	54.0	38.9	52.1	31.0	40.3
Other methods	4.6	4.2	8.9	4.2	3.6	4.0	2.0	4.4

SOURCE: See [56].
NOTE: Since each woman may have used more than one method, the sum of the percentages shown is greater than 100.

ical grounds. No distinction was to be made between married and unmarried persons. The act and subsequent Scottish legislation enabled the 232 local health authorities to provide services, but it did not insist that they should do so. At the beginning of 1972, 40 of the authorities were running their own clinics, and 169 were using the FPA as their agent.

In 1969, the Department of Health and Social Security (DHSS) gave the FPA its first grant specifically for training purposes. Also in 1969, hospitals were asked to review their arrangements for providing family planning advice and service. The department sponsored a national survey on the provision and use of contraceptive services. In 1971, it was announced that the government would sponsor two pilot experiments in "saturation" provision of contraceptive services. In 1972, male sterilization was added to the services that could be provided by the local health authorities as part of their family planning services.

Meanwhile, most people have used alternative sources for their contraceptives. Over 80 percent of prescriptions for oral contraceptives were being issued by general practitioners in 1971 [53]. Doctors have been encouraged officially to provide this service, but they have not been allowed to give a free service, except where there are medical grounds. The most popular appliance method, the condom, and spermicides and pessaries are available from chemists. The condom is also available from vending machines and in many barbers' shops. Condoms or oral contraceptives are chosen by the great majority of those who use a contraceptive method. Trends in the use of methods are shown in Table 7.

In 1969, the Royal College of Obstetricians and Gynecologists established a working party to study and report on "unplanned pregnancy." It was intended that the working party should investigate the causes of the increase in requests for abortion. Evidence was taken from numerous organizations and individuals. In its report, published in 1972, the working party recommended that a comprehensive contraceptive service should be established within the National Health Service [58]. There should be no financial disincentive to the provision of advice and service by any doctor working within the service. Sex education in schools should be given as an integral part of health education programs designed to include the principles of healthy living and responsibilities in all human relationships. More research should be undertaken into the problem of motivating couples to seek advice on family planning. The laws on paternity with respect to illegitimately conceived pregnancies should be modified. With regard to abortion, there was an urgent need to make Parliament's intentions clearer, in the interests of both the public and the medical profession. A population policy should be established by the government and implemented by intensive propaganda and (perhaps) financial inducements to influence attitudes on family size.

On December 12, 1972, the Secretary of State for Social Services announced in the House of Commons an expansion of services, intended to reduce the number of unwanted pregnancies. The advisory services would be extended to make advice readily available free of charge to all who wished to have it. The number of clinics would be increased, and the domiciliary services would be expanded. Facilities in hospitals would be improved, particularly for abortion and maternity patients. A way would be sought to avoid charging patients for consultations with general practitioners in cases of nonmedical need; already, no charge was made for cases of medical need. Extra funds would be made available to the Health Education Council to inform the public about the services available and to encourage people to use them. Free contraceptive supplies would be available to those who had a special social need and who would otherwise be unlikely to undertake effective contraception, as well as for those with a financial need. It was expected that the total cost of family planning services would grow to about £17 million per year over the ensuing four years, compared with the current annual expenditures of about £4 million.[14]

The fact that free supplies were not to be available to everyone caused much dismay, especially as some local authorities were already providing a free supplies service. A parliamentary critic, Dr. Shirley Summerskill, complained that: "Free advice without free supplies is totally illogical and is a serious deterrent to those in the lower income groups to seek advice."

The House of Lords voted for an amendment calling for free birth control. Conservative sympathizers in the Commons tabled a motion of support for the amendment.

On March 26, 1973, the Secretary of State for Social Services announced a change of plan. Contraceptive supplies would not be free, but they would be fully available under the normal conditions of National Health Service prescriptions. This meant that supplies would be available for the standard prescription charge of 20 pence.

¶ DEVELOPMENT OF ABORTION POLICY

Before 1938, abortion could not be performed legally except to save a woman's life. In 1938, an English gynecologist was tried at the Old Bailey for terminating the pregnancy of a girl of fourteen who had been raped by a group of soldiers. He was acquitted on the grounds that it was impos-

[14] Total public expenditure on health and personal social services, 1971–1972, was about £2.800 million.

sible to distinguish between a woman's life being in danger and her health being in danger. It was in this way that a tenuous precedent was established for lawfully terminating pregnancy on grounds of health. But there was much opposition at the time, especially from Roman Catholics.

For nearly three decades, the opposition successfully prevented attempts to liberalize the law. But in 1966, a young Liberal, David Steel, introduced a bill in Parliament that, unlike its seven predecessors, survived to reach the stage of a free vote. The result was the Abortion Act of 1967, which became effective in April 1968 in England, Wales, and Scotland. The act permits abortion if two physicians certify in good faith (1) that the continuance of the pregnancy would involve risk to the life of the pregnant woman or injury to the physical or mental health of the woman or any existing children in the family greater than if the pregnancy were terminated; or (2) that there is a substantial risk that, if the child were born, it would suffer from such physical or mental abnormalities as to be handicapped seriously. In determining whether or not the continuance of a pregnancy would involve risk of injury to health, "account may be taken of the pregnant woman's actual or reasonably foreseeable environment." The abortion must be performed in a National Health Service hospital or in an officially approved clinic.

According to two students of the reform, Madeleine Simms and Keith Hindell, the fact that liberalization of the law occurred when it did should be attributed primarily to efforts of the Abortion Law Reform Association [59; 60]. The association was founded in 1936. Between the end of the war and the early 1960s, its efforts were mainly educational rather than directly political. According to Simms and Hindell, it was public reaction to the fetal deformities caused by the drug thalidomide that produced the stimulus for a vigorous campaign in the 1960s. From 1961, the association was increasingly successful in recruiting supporters among members of Parliament. In January 1967, an opposing organization, the Society for the Protection of the Unborn Child, was launched. This society and the Catholic church led sustained and vigorous opposition to the 1967 act. The church and the society have continued to oppose the implementation of the act.

The number of legal abortions reported in England and Wales increased from 54,157 in 1969 to 126,774 in 1971—one for every eight live and stillbirths to English and Welsh women [61]. The total is close to that quoted as the total number of induced abortions in Britain of all kinds—"legal, illegal and semilegal"—that may have taken place each year in the period before reform [62].

There is a marked regional variation in the number of abortions carried out by the National Health Service. For example, in the first half of 1971, the ratio of abortions to live births was 2.7 in Birmingham but 8.8 in

Newcastle. One reason for the disparities is the regional differentials that exist in the supply of hospital beds and gynecological resources; another is variation in the attitudes of senior consultants, a number of whom have been strongly opposed to the implementation of the act. In England and Wales, the proportion of abortions carried out in private nursing homes increased from 39 percent in 1969 to 57 percent in 1971. Part of this increase is accounted for by private abortions taking place under the auspices of Pregnancy Advisory Services. These are charitable agencies that came into existence in response to the shortage of facilities. About a third of private abortions (about 30,000) were carried out on foreign women in 1971. In the same year, nearly 50 percent of abortions were performed on single women [61].

In February 1971, the Secretary of State for Social Services announced the creation of a committee of enquiry, under Mrs. Justice Lane, to evaluate the implementation of the abortion act. Its underlying principles were not in question. The committee has yet to report.

¶ "COSTS" OF THE "SURPLUS"

Since the mid-1960s, the reported number and social cost of surplus births have been the subject of considerable publicity, much of it generated by the director of the Family Planning Association, Caspar Brook. In a characteristically forthright expression of his views, he said: "We are building three or four new towns every year just to house and provide services for people whom nobody wanted and who are, in many ways, disadvantaged on coming into the world. In economic terms this is absolute lunacy to my mind" [4]. As a body, the FPA has not been much concerned with population policy as such, although it does profess the view that the government should, at present, have a policy to stabilize population size. The FPA has used the birth-surplus issue to buttress its campaign to persuade the government and local authorities to improve official birth control services.

In April 1971, a new pressure group was established—the Birth Control Campaign. The president of the campaign is Lord Gardiner, Lord Chancellor in the last Labour government. Its chairman is Alastair Service, one of the leading activists in the Abortion Law Reform Association. The goal of the Birth Control Campaign is a comprehensive birth control service (including provision for abortion) within the National Health Service. The latter is to undergo extensive reorganization in 1974, and the campaign's proposals are based on the plans for this. One of its specific aims, adopted on the initiative of Sir David Renton, is "to persuade the Government to recognise and study the problem of Britain's population growth." In March 1972, the campaign published *A Birth Control Plan for Britain* [53]. According to this, about 150,000 live births result from unwanted pregnancies each year in Great Britain. The total, based on 1969 figures, was calculated as follows:

(1) Total live births: 890,000
(2) Total deaths: 640,000
(3) Excess of live births over deaths: 250,000
(4) Pregnancies thought to be unwanted:
    (a) 66 percent of 74,000
        illegitimate live births: 50,000
    (b) 50 percent of 90,000
        live births conceived
        before marriage: 45,000
    (c) 20 percent of 129,000
        third children;
    (d) 25 percent of 57,000
        fourth;
    (e) 40 percent of 26,000   60,000
        fifth;
    (f) 50 percent of 26,000
        subsequent children
        conceived within marriage:
(5) Total from unwanted
    pregnancies: 155,000
                   (approx.) 150,000
(6) Excess of live births from
    probably wanted pregnancies over deaths: 100,000

The report concluded that births could be made roughly equal to deaths (1969 figures) if the former were reduced by the 150,000 unwanted pregnancies plus 100,000 live births "of other third or subsequent children."

In these calculations, the percentage of unwanted illegitimate children was the percentage not born to stable unions. The percentage of unwanted premarital conceptions was "a rough estimate only." Apparently, no allowance was made for the proportion of "unwanted" illegitimate children and premarital conceptions which, though perhaps inconveniently timed, would be unlikely to add to the ultimate family size of the women concerned. The percentage of third and subsequent children is based on a study of contraceptive services and practices carried out in 1967 and 1968 by the Institute of Community Studies. As part of this study, mothers of a random sample of legitimate births were asked whether they were sorry the pregnancy had occurred. In about 15 percent of cases, the women said that when they first heard that they were pregnant they were "sorry it happened at all" [63].

With the help of a grant from the FPA, Political and Economic Planning recently made a study of "the extra demands for health and welfare services which are likely to be made by the unwanted child and its family, over and above those made by the average child" [64]. The study calculated the expected costs of excess usage of health and welfare resources by "unwanted" children. It was assumed that there would be neither a demonstrable gain nor a loss in terms of the child's eventual productivity. The Birth Control Campaign report used these calculations to estimate the possible savings from births resulting from unwanted pregnancies in Britain each year (1969 figures) as follows:

50,000 illegitimate children (£4,350 each):	£217,000,000
14,000 fourth children (£500 each):	7,000,000
10,000 fifth children (£500 each):	5,000,000
13,000 sixth and subsequent children (£500 each):	6,500,000

Using a figure of £2000 per child to include costs not in the above calculation, the BCC report stated:

For every year that we continue to allow perhaps 150,000 live births as a result of unwanted pregnancy through lack of an efficient birth control service, we are committing ourselves to an expenditure of somewhere in the neighbourhood of another £300,000,000 of tax payers' and rate payers' money during the following two decades. That money is well spent once the children are born, but most of it could have been saved by better birth control provision and publicity [53].

The cost of a free comprehensive birth control service was estimated to be a maximum of £40 million a year.

Claims concerning the number and costs of unwanted births intensified support, inside and outside Parliament, for legislation to improve birth control services. However, these services have continued to be officially regarded as part of health care and not as an instrument of population policy.

REFERENCES

1. Department of the Environment. *Long-Term Population Distribution in Great Britain: A Study.* Report by an Interdepartmental Study Group. London: HMSO, 1971.

2. Office of Population Censuses and Surveys. *Population Projections, 1970–2010.* London: HMSO, 1971.

3. Office of Population Censuses and Surveys. *Population Projections: No. 2, 1971–2011.* London: HMSO, 1972.

4. Select Committee on Science and Technology. *Minutes of Evidence and Appendices Taken before Sub-Committee C, Session 1969–1970.* H.C. 271. London: HMSO, 1969–1970.

644 POPULATION POLICY IN DEVELOPED COUNTRIES

5. *Population Policy.* Fifth Report of the Select Committee on Science and Technology, Session 1971–1972. H.C. 335. London: HMSO, 1972.

6. M. Woolf. *Family Intentions.* London: HMSO, 1971.

7. Royal Commission on the Distribution of the Industrial Population. *Report.* Cmnd. 6153. London: HMSO, 1940 (reprinted 1963).

8. G. McCrone. *Regional Policy in Britain.* London: Allen & Unwin, 1969.

9. Labour Party. *Regional Planning Policy.* London, 1970.

10. A. J. Brown. *The Framework of Regional Economics in the United Kingdom.* London: Cambridge University Press, 1972.

11. Labour Party. *Labour's Programme for Britain.* London, 1972.

12. Labour Party, Research Department. *Regional Policy and the Common Market.* Information Paper no. 12. London: October 1971.

13. H. Lind. *Regional Policy in Britain and the Six.* European Series no. 15. London: Chatham House, 1970.

14. J. B. Cullingworth. *Town and Country Planning in Britain.* Fourth edition. London: Allen & Unwin, 1972.

15. Center for Environmental Studies. *Fifth Annual Report.* London, 1972.

16. *Statement by the Town and Country Planning Association on Implementing the Developments Proposed in Regional Plans.* London, January 1972.

17. N. Deakin, et al. *Colour, Citizenship, and British Society.* London: Panther, 1970.

18. E. Rose, et al. *Colour and Citizenship: A Report on British Race Relations.* London: Oxford University Press, 1969.

19. Institute of Race Relations. *Facts Paper on the United Kingdom, 1970–1971.* London, 1970.

20. K. Jones and A. D. Smith. *The Economic Impact of Commonwealth Immigration.* National Institute of Economic and Social Research. London: Cambridge University Press, 1970.

21. C. A. Moser. "Statistics about immigrants: Objectives, sources, methods, and problems." *Social Trends*, no. 3, 1972.

22. Political and Economic Planning. *Racial Discrimination in Britain.* London, 1967.

23. D. Spearman. "Enoch Powell's postbag." *New Society*, May 1968.

24. D. Stephen. *Immigration and Race Relations.* Fabian Research Series 291. London: Fabian Society, 1970.

25. Conservative Party, Research Department. *Immigration.* Notes on Current Politics no. 7. April 1971.

26. A. Bottomley and G. Sinclair. *Control of Commonwealth Immigration.* London: Runnymede Trust, 1970.

27. G. Bindman and R. Evans. *The Immigration Bill, 1971.* London: Runnymede Trust, 1971.

28. Labour Party. *Citizenship, Immigration, and Integration.* London, 1972.

29. W. Petersen. *The Politics of Population.* London: Gollancz, 1964.

30. D. V. Glass. *Population Policies and Movements in Europe.* London: Cass, 1940 (reprinted 1967).

31. Royal Commission on Population. *Report.* London: HMSO, 1949 (reprinted 1964).

32. O. Keidan. "The health services." In *Penelope Hall's Social Services of England and Wales.* Edited by A. Forder. London: Routledge & Kegan Paul, 1971.

33. Office of Health Economics. *Infants at Risk.* London, 1964.

34. *Registrar General's Statistical Review of England and Wales, 1971.* London: HMSO, 1973.

35. *Social Trends,* no. 3. London: HMSO, 1972.

36. J. Hutchinson. "Land and human populations." *The Advancement of Science,* vol. 23 (1966): 241–254.

37. P. Ehrlich. "Population control or Hobson's choice." In *The Optimum Population for Britain.* Edited by L. R. Taylor. London: Academic Press, 1970.

38. Labour Party. *Population.* London, 1971.

39. *The Ecologist,* vol. 2, no. 1 (January 1972).

40. *The Lancet,* January 8, 1972.

41. D. V. Glass, et al. *Towards a Population Policy for the United Kingdom.* Supplement to *Population Studies,* May 1970.

42. The Conservation Society. *A Population Policy for Britain.* Walton-on-Thames, 1972.

43. S. Johnson. *A Population Policy for Britain.* Old Queen Street Paper no. 18. London: Conservative Party, Research Department, 1972.

44. "The case against hysteria." *Nature,* vol. 235, 1972: 63–65.

45. A. J. Boreham. "Economics and population in Britain." In *The Optimum Population for Britain.* Edited by L. R. Taylor. London: Academic Press, 1970.

46. D. E. Eversley. "The special case: Managing human population growth." *The Optimum Population for Britain.* Edited by L. R. Taylor. London: Academic Press, 1970.

47. D. Wolfers. "The case against zero growth." *International Journal of Environmental Studies,* vol. 1, 1971: 227–232.

48. G. Hawthorn. *Population Policy: A Modern Delusion.* Fabian Tract 418. London: Fabian Society, 1973.

49. M. Wynn. *Family Policy.* London: Penguin, 1972.

50. *The Population Problem.* Correspondence between the Prime Minister and Sir David Renton, November 1966–October 1967.

51. *Population of the United Kingdom.* First Report from the Select Committee on Science and Technology, Session 1970–1971. H.C. 379. London: HMSO, 1971 (reprinted 1972).

52. *Population of the United Kingdom.* First Report from the Select Committee on Science and Technology, Session 1970–1971, Observations by the Government. Cmnd. 4748. London: HMSO, 1971.

53. Birth Control Campaign. *A Birth Control Plan for Britain.* London, 1972.

54. Department of Health and Social Security. *On the State of the Public Health.* Annual Report of the Chief Medical Officer of the Department of Health and Social Security, 1968. London: HMSO, 1969.

55. C. Langford. "Birth control practice in Britain." *Family Planning,* January 1969.

56. C. Langford. "Family planning trends: The British study." *Proceedings of the Sixth Conference of the Europe and Near East Region of the International Planned Parenthood Federation.* London: IPPF, 1970.

57. J. Peel and M. Potts. *Textbook of Contraceptive Practice.* London: Cambridge University Press, 1969.

58. *Unplanned Pregnancy.* Report of the Working Party of the Royal College of Obstetricians and Gynaecologists. London: RCOG, 1972.

59. M. Simms and K. Hindell. *Abortion Law Reformed.* London: Peter Owen, 1971.

60. K. Hindell and M. Simms. "How the abortion lobby worked." *The Political Quarterly,* vol. 39, no. 3, 1968.

61. Department of Health and Social Security. *On the State of the Public Health.* Annual Report of the Chief Medical Officer of the Department of Health and Social Security, 1971. London: HMSO, 1972.

62. M. Simms. "The future of the abortion act." *Midwives Chronicle and Nursing Notes,* January 1972.

63. A. Cartwright. *Parents and Family Planning Services.* London: Routledge & Kegan Paul, 1970.

64. W. A. Laing. *The Costs and Benefits of Family Planning.* London: Political and Economic Planning, 1972.

65. *Report of the Population Panel.* Cmnd. 5258. London: HMSO, 1973.

CHAPTER 21

Italy

Massimo Livi Bacci

Acknowledgments: I am very much indebted to Dr. Guido Ferrari for his help throughout the preparation of this chapter. The sections "Procreation and Family Planning" and "Measures affecting the Family" are partly taken, with the author's consent, from Dr. Ferrari's report on Italy for the October 1972 meeting of the Joint Working Group for the Study of Legislation Directly or Indirectly affecting Fertility in Europe, an affiliate of the International Union for the Scientific Study of Population and the European Center for Coordination of Research and Documentation of Social Sciences.

ABSTRACT

Italy's main demographic problems can be summarized as follows: (1) a decreasing but still considerable emigration; (2) a moderate level of fertility which is the result of very different regional fertility levels, too high in the south and too low in the north; (3) differentials in mortality; (4) a very intense process of internal migration under the pressures of rapid economic and social change and of regional differentials—especially in the recent past—of the rates of population growth.

After the fall of Fascism, with its consistent pronatalist policy, postwar political concern and action in the field of population was dominated by the problems of unemployment, and one of the solutions envisaged was an active stimulation of emigration. But, generally speaking, during the last quarter of a century population has never been considered a major problem. Population growth has been thought of as a datum largely unaffected by public intervention. Public concern, although very sensitive at all times to the problems posed by unemployment, emigration, the exodus from the south and from the rural areas, and the congestion of the cities, has always failed to acknowledge that these factors are greatly affected by differential demographic growth and the delayed process of modernized procreation in the south.

Relevant legislation and social policy measures are reviewed with reference to marriage and divorce; procreation and family planning; the family, its welfare and economy; female work and working mothers; and infrastructures for children. The repressive legislation prohibiting birth control propaganda was abolished by the Supreme Court in 1971; however, no public support is given to family planning programs. Abortion and sterilization are considered criminal offenses. The family allowance scheme, the relatively comprehensive system of medical care, and the fairly modern labor legislation are, in principle, favorable to the welfare of the family, but, on the other hand, lack of infrastructures for the children and an inadequate public housing policy certainly have a negative impact.

In the last section, policy on migration is considered. The provisions of various economic plans call for a more rational process of internal migration, but no adequate policy has been devised. Internal and international migration may be affected in the future by an active policy of the European Economic Community for regional development, as well as by the agricultural policy (Mansholt plan) that calls for a radical reduction of employment in the primary sector and, therefore, perhaps an impact on the rate of migration from the rural areas.

INTRODUCTION

Perhaps the fact that Italy does not have a population policy—either expressed or tacit—is a reaction against the demographic policy of the Fascist regime. The government, the political parties, and other opinion and pressure groups do not seem to put much emphasis on the nature and desirability of current demographic trends or the need to modify or control such trends. The population variable generally is considered as a datum, an exogenous factor, which we have to recognize and come to terms with but which cannot be modified or controlled, at least not at the national level.

Considered in this light, it would appear that there is no real need to treat the subject. It could be argued that the apparent lack of concern for population growth explains the lack of a population policy, and Italy could easily be defined as "agnostic"—unmoved and uninterested by the worldwide debate on the population issue.

But this is not entirely true. In the first place, a growing concern has been expressed regarding the tendencies of the redistribution process of the population over the national territory through internal migration. In the second place, the complex legislative system governing marriage, divorce, procreation and contraception, the family, the status of women, and the complex social policy (influenced by internal migration) undoubtedly has an impact on population. It is certainly worth an attempt to describe and interpret this situation.

A few remarks are, however, necessary. Legislative and social measures that "influence" population are, at times, contradictory and uncoordinated. Their impact on population, which is always difficult to assess, is obscured further by the lack of a deliberate intention on the part of the legislature. The measures are either the consequence of the natural historical evolution of the law or the results of the enforcement of the principles of social justice and social equality; they are certainly not dictated by population concerns. But the entire legal system plays an important role in determining the economic, social, and psychological framework in which, for instance, a couple may make decisions regarding marriage or divorce, procreation and contraception, internal or external mobility. After cursory consideration, it may be thought that no social or legislative measure has the power to modify the long-term historical demographic trends. After all, the European countries, irrespective of their political and social systems—whether capitalist or socialist, industrial and urban or still largely rural—seem to have experienced the same demographic trends. But this is not strictly true. We certainly do not believe that an analysis of legislation and social policy will provide the key to an interpretation of population trends. But this field is worthy of systematic investigation, since its influence may become apparent only in the long run, and changes in the legislative framework made today may only start to have effect a generation later.

The purpose of this paper is, first, to give a brief history of the main population trends and of the emerging population problems, and second, to attempt an analysis of the official views on population during the Fascist period and in the last twenty-five years. We will then try to give a brief account of the main legislative and social measures that affect marriage, fertility, the family, and public health. Particular attention will be given to the policies that concern external and internal migration and the problems that arise from the integration of Italy in the European Economic Community.

OLD AND NEW POPULATION PROBLEMS

An integrated statistical balance of population movements is given for the country as a whole in Table 1. A few observations will be sufficient for our purposes.

First, the Italian population has grown at a rather steady rate, the only exception being the decades affected by the consequences of World War I. The annual rate of growth has fluctuated between 6 and 8 per 1,000. Birth-

TABLE 1.

Births, Deaths, Vital, and Growth Rates of the Population, Italy, 1862–1971

Period	Births (1)	Deaths (2)	Migratory Balance (3)	Birth Rate (per 1,000) (4)	Death Rate (per 1,000) (5)	Rate of Natural Increase (per 1,000) (6)	Rate of Net Migration (per 1,000) (7)	Rate of Increase (per 1,000) (8)
1862–1871	10,016	8,116	− 78	37.4	30.3	7.1	−0.3	6.8
1872–1881	10,500	8,422	− 378	36.9	29.6	7.3	−1.3	6.0
1882–1891	11,381	8,227	− 845	37.2	26.9	10.3	−2.8	7.5
1892–1901	11,182	7,732	−1,378	34.2	23.7	10.5	−4.2	6.3
1902–1911	11,241	7,449	−1,417	32.2	21.3	10.9	−4.1	6.8
1912–1921	10,065	8,076	− 903	27.2	21.8	5.4	−2.4	3.0
1922–1931	10,829	6,402	− 898	27.5	16.3	11.3	−2.3	9.0
1932–1941	9,864	5,963	− 242	23.0	13.9	9.1	−0.6	8.5
1942–1951	9,215	5,843	− 631	20.1	12.8	7.3	−1.4	5.9
1952–1961	8,793	4,687	−1,305	18.0	9.6	8.4	−2.7	5.7
1962–1971	9,475	5,126	− 483	18.2	9.8	8.4	−0.9	7.5

rate and death-rate trends have proceeded on a parallel, with the decline in mortality starting in the 1880s, preceding by one or two decades the decline of natality and both leveling off in the 1950s and 1960s. Net emigration has been partially responsible for the relatively uniform rate of increase, tending to rise with the rising rate of natural increase.

The statistics for the last two decades bring Italy well into the European average for levels of fertility and mortality. During the last two decades, the mean number of children per marriage has remained constant: about 2.4–2.5 children. The mean number of children of the most recent marriage cohorts, for which an estimate of the final family size has been possible, attain similar levels. For the youngest cohorts, there is an evident tendency toward an increase of duration-specific fertility at the low durations of marriage, in large part imputable to a change in timing, although a slight recovery in the final family size cannot be ruled out.

Nuptiality also has increased slightly, because of both a slow but continuous fall of the age at marriage and a decrease in the proportion of individuals who remain single.

Finally, the drop in mortality, as measured by expectation of life at birth, has been considerable but leaves room for further improvement. Infant mortality, in particular, is still well above the European average (28 per 1,000 in 1971), and infectious diseases are probably above the level one would expect in a country of a relatively high per-capita income, given the present state of medical technology and desirable standards of medical care.

Summing up, if one considers the Italian population as an aggregate, without mentioning the regional level, there would appear to be two major population problems: (1) a very high emigration rate and (2) a mortality that is not as low as it should be. On the other hand, fertility is moderate and the growth rate is on a par with the average level of the more-developed parts of Europe. Certainly, various opinions could be expressed as to the optimum level of population growth but this seems—at least in the Italian context—to be a very minor problem.

¶ REGIONAL POPULATION PROBLEMS

The nature of Italy's population problems cannot be understood by viewing them at the national level. One source of the many tensions—political, economic, and social—that have been plaguing the country since unification in 1861 is the difference in regional development. Different demographic trends have played an important role in deepening the social and economic gap between the south and the rest of the country. Italy, even excepting the north-south differences, is a nation full of contrasts. But there is no doubt that the north-south contrast is at the root of the major problems of the country. Two factors are at the basis of this contrast:

(1) The mass emigration from the south, which began in the last two decades of the last century.

(2) The late decline of fertility in the south, where fertility control began between the two world wars, several decades later than in the rest of the country where—in some regions—fertility control began as early as 1870.

These differentials also have characterized the more recent development of the two areas, as is shown by the integrated demographic balance in Table 2. As may be seen, the higher birth rate in the south is responsible for the relatively high rate of natural increase, about 1.3 percent a year. Much of it has been wiped out by the net out-migration of over 2 million people (over 11 percent of the average population) during the decade. Over 75 percent of these Italians migrated to other parts of the country.

Table 3 gives a more precise idea of the difference in fertility, as measured by the total fertility rate, since 1931. Southern fertility is, throughout the whole period shown in Table 3, some 30 percent to 50 percent above the total fertility needed for replacement, while the fertility of the north and the central area is, with the exception of 1931 and 1966, below replacement (about 15 percent short of the replacement level during the 1950s). It is worth noting that the low fertility areas include both the heavily industrialized regions of Piedmont, Liguria, and Lombardy, and areas that are still mainly rural like Umbria and Marche, and until the mid-1950s, the Venetias, Emilia, and Tuscany. Column (8) shows the proportion of the total Italian population below replacement: This proportion grows from 35 percent in 1931 to a record of 51 percent in 1956, dropping again to 32 percent in 1966. This drop is a consequence of the recent increase in fertility in the north and central region and of the further decrease in the south, as shown in Table 4. The figures for more recent times are shown in Table 5. However, the recent drop of the birth rate in the south is largely the consequence of the deteriorated age and marital structure of the population, which is the result of heavy out-migration. Fertility control, as will be discussed later, is still far from being efficient. Table 6 shows the distribution of legitimate live births, by parity, in 1969.

Although less important for their consequences on the dynamics of the population, differences in health conditions are still very evident. Although in 1960–1962, the expectation of life at birth for the south was higher than the Italian average, the health conditions of the southern population were and still are generally poor. This is apparent from the few indicators reported in Table 7.

It is almost unnecessary to say that the differentials described in this section project their consequences into the future. For the coming decade, Table 8 shows the projected rate of increase of the total population and

TABLE 2.

Demographic Balance between North and South, Italy, 1961–1971

Area	Population at Mid-Period	Births	Deaths	Excess of Births Over Deaths	Birth Rate	Death Rate	Net Migration Rate	Rate of Natural Increase	Rate of Increase
North and central	33,643	5,454	3,510	1,566	16.2	9.9	+ 4.7	6.3	11.0
South	18,194	4,051	1,638	−2,057	22.3	9.0	−11.3	13.3	2.0
All Italy	51,837	9,505	5,148	− 491	18.3	10.4	− 0.9	7.9	7.0

TABLE 3.

Differential Development of Fertility, Italy, 1931–1966

| | Total Fertility Rate (TFR) | | | | | | |
| | | | Index nos. 1931 = 100 | | | | |
Year (1)	North and Central (2)	South (3)	North and Central (4)	South (5)	South, North, and Central = 100 (6)	Needed TFR for a NRR of 1,000[a] (7)	Approximate Percent of Population below Replacement[b] (8)
1931	2,679	4,198	100	100	157	2,659	34.9
1936	2,429	3,912	90.7	93.2	161	2,593	42.2
1951	1,883	3,240	70.3	77.2	172	2,279	46.6
1956	1,881	3,072	70.2	73.2	163	2,215	50.6
1961	2,010	3,105	75.0	74.0	154	2,182	46.8
1966	2,296	3,090	85.7	73.6	135	2,166	32.0

SOURCE: See [1, B.2.3 14, table 14].
[a] On the basis of the national life table.
[b] Considering the regions.

TABLE 4.

Changes in TFR, Italy, 1931–1966

Area	1931–1951	1951–1966
North and central	−29.7	+21.9
South	−22.8	− 4.6

TABLE 5.

Changes in Birth Rate, Italy, 1966 and 1971

Area	1966	1971	Change (in percents)
North and central	15.8	15.1	− 4.4
South	23.7	20.2	−14.8

TABLE 6.

Distribution of Live Births by Parity, Italy, 1969 (in percents)

Area	1–2	3–4	5+	Total
North and central	77.7	18.5	3.8	100.0
South	56.6	28.4	15.0	100.0
All Italy	68.9	22.6	8.5	100.0

TABLE 7.

Indicators of Health Conditions, Italy, 1971

Area	Infant Mortality	Still- Births	Death Rates for Infectious Diseases (per 100,000)
North and central	23.2	11.8	16.0
South	35.6	20.3	21.6
All Italy	28.3	15.1	17.9

TABLE 8.

Population Forecast, Italy, 1971–1981

Area	Population Ages 15–64			Total Population		
	1971	1981	Percent Increase	1971	1981	Percent Increase
North and central	22,363	22,672	+ 1.4	34,031	35,288	+ 3.7
South	13,296	15,073	+13.4	21,120	23,830	+12.8
All Italy	35,659	37,745	+ 5.8	55,151	59,118	+ 7.2

SOURCE: See [2].

the population of working age, in the absence of migration, according to a recent population forecast.

The population of working age, as well as the total population, will increase quite rapidly in the south, as opposed to the very modest rise in the rest of the country. It is not difficult to predict the continuing pressure on mobility resulting from the differential increase of the two large areas of the country.

¶ INTERNAL MIGRATION AND DEPOPULATION
One of the main demographic problems we have mentioned is the rapid redistribution of the population over the territory. Italy, like most European countries, is a land of very old settlement. The distribution of the population over the territory in the late Middle Ages was very similar to the distribution found in this century. In many instances, the settlement of the population has resulted from factors that have long since ceased to be important. Villages were built away from the malaria-ridden plains and away from the coasts, to escape from pirates, or on the tops of hills or mountains, for defense. With the pressure of change and, in particular, the transition from a mainly rural to a mainly industrial population over the last twenty years (in 1951, 42.5 percent of the labor force was engaged

in agriculture, compared to 17 percent in 1972), an age-old situation has been shaken radically. Population movements have been mounting and exerting an increasing pressure on the system of infrastructures that are less adaptable to change.

It has already been shown that, during the 1961–1971 decade, net out-migration from the south amounted to 2.1 million and net immigration into the rest of the country to 1.5 million. But this figure is the result of flows of different signs between the various regional or provincial areas. Taking the 8,056 *comuni* (the smallest administrative unity) into which the country is subdivided, 5,330—or two-thirds of them (accounting for 28 percent of the total population)—experienced a population decline. In six regions— four of these in southern Italy—the *comuni* with a population decline represented the majority of the regional populations. This means that more than half the territory is undergoing a more or less marked decline in population. Concentration in the large urban areas is rapidly increasing; those *comuni* with 100,000 inhabitants or more have gained over 3.3 million people during the last decade. From 1962 to 1969, Turin and Milan have gained, through net immigration, 27,000 inhabitants every year; Rome's annual gain is 38,000. The eleven largest urban areas have grown from a population of 6.9 million in 1951 (14.5 percent of the total) to 9.8 in 1961 and to 11.2 in 1969 (20.6 percent).

These few data indicate how serious and rapid is the process of internal migration and, as a consequence, the redistribution of the demographic weight over the nation's territory. This process has been more sudden and rapid than in other more advanced European countries where development, and the necessary adjustment to it, has taken place more gradually.

¶ CONCLUSIONS

Summing up the considerations of the preceding paragraphs, modern Italy faces the following demographic problems:

(1) A decreasing, but still considerable, net outflow of emigrants.
(2) An unbalanced fertility, which is still too high in the south, where control is far from efficient, and too low in the north and central region,
which have remained constantly below replacement for several decades.
(3) The persistence of differentials in mortality.
(4) An intense process of internal migration—partially as a consequence of
the differential rate of growth of certain areas—and a rapid process of
population redistribution, under the pressures of social and economic
changes.

Basically, the four main problems derive from the unbalanced regional development of the country, which is the cause and the effect of differential population trends. It is against this background that legislation and social policies concerning population have to be measured and considered.

FROM FASCISM TO MODERN TIMES:
GENERAL CONSIDERATIONS

Between the two world wars, during the Fascist regime, population was an important element of the government's policy. Fascist policy advocated a fast increase of the population as a means of increasing power, in view of the many potentially declining European populations. Thus, emigration was discouraged, nuptiality and fertility stimulated, and the unity of the family sustained by an attempt to prevent the emancipation of women. People were discouraged from leaving the rural areas. From 1926 to World War II, a set of coordinated legislative and social measures were adopted in an effort to achieve a sustained growth or, at least, to check the fall of the rate of increase. It would be impossible to give a complete picture of the various aspects of this deliberate policy, ranging from economic incentives to continuous propaganda at all levels; we will merely recall some of its main traits [3; 4; 5].

The first set of measures was aimed at increasing nuptiality. A nuptiality allowance was introduced for those marrying before the age of twenty-six. Loans also were available for young couples at a very low interest rate. The loan was partially extinguished with the birth of the children and completely canceled with the birth of the fourth child. These measures were coupled with several discouragements against celibacy. All unmarried males above the age of twenty-six and below the age of sixty-five were subjected to a special tax, increasing progressively with the increase of the income. Married persons took precedence over unmarried persons in public employment, with respect to both hiring and promotion. Later, in 1938, the state of marriage or widowhood was an essential prerequisite for being elected to an honorary or eminent public office, such as mayor (*podestà*), full professor in the universities, or dean or principal in the public school system.

Another important set of measures had, as an object, the stimulation of fertility and the unity of the family. These measures were inspired by a commission, nominated in 1926, one of whose objectives was to ensure that "the order of the family system could be maintained against the many menaces of neo-Malthusianism, scientific and empirical." The ban against the spreading of contraceptives and birth control propaganda was instituted in 1926 and reinforced in the new penal code of 1931, together with severe penalties for induced abortion.

Many were the fiscal facilitations for large families, both in the case of personal income tax and inheritance tax. In 1934, the family allowance system was introduced, with allowances that increased with every additional child. A bonus also was given at the birth of a child, and the sum increased with every additional birth. The number of children was a preferential factor in hiring and promotion for public employment. A few limitations to the employment of women also were introduced in an effort to protect the role of the woman in the family. Special public honors were granted to mothers of large numbers of children.

Fascist policy discouraged emigration, which was also made difficult, if not impossible, by the Great Depression and, before it, by restrictions on immigration introduced in the United States. Schemes were, however, produced for emigration and settlement in the Italian colonies, particularly in Libya. The clearing of the malaria-ridden areas was followed by an effort to populate the once deserted areas. The regime followed a policy of slowing internal migration and the exodus from the rural areas. Citizens were prohibited from taking residences in *comuni* with 25,000 inhabitants or more or in *comuni* of special administrative or industrial importance, unless they could demonstrate that they had found permanent employment there.

It is impossible to assess the effects of Fascist demographic policy. Fertility continued to decrease: The final family size of the couples married between the late 1920s and the beginning of World War II continued to decrease steadily. Some effect could, perhaps, be detected in the "period" measures as a result of the changes in timing of childbearing.

It would, however, be very superficial to judge the effects of the demographic policy—so apt in a system of conservative values—on the basis of the consideration of parallel demographic trends, which apparently were unaffected. The twenty years of the Fascist regime undoubtedly delayed the process of modernization and partially are responsible for the widening gap between the demographic trends of the south and the rest of the country. We will try to prove this assertion later.

WORLD WAR II AFTERMATH

¶ RECONSTRUCTION, UNEMPLOYMENT, AND EMIGRATION

After the war, Italy faced the complex problems of reconstruction. The country still was mainly rural, with a very low productivity. Its industrial system had been shattered by the war; a large share of its infrastructures had been destroyed; and in the views of many contemporary observers, it stood little chance of a sustained development. In spite of the effects of the war, the natural rate of increase during the 1940s was about 7 percent. Among the many points of concern was unemployment, which was to have a direct demographic effect [6]. In the late 1940s, a figure estimated at between 2 and 3 million—from 10 to 15 percent of the labor force—was unemployed. Emigration was considered as one of the main remedies, at least for a short period; actually, during the decade 1947–1956, net emigration amounted to 1.7 million, almost two-thirds of which went to non-European countries. Following a century-long tradition, emigration would have helped to solve the problem of the surplus of manpower and, in the meantime, would have greatly helped the balance of payments.

There is no trace, however, in political, parliamentary, or other public debates and statements of the notion that population growth could be slowed by means of an adequate policy or that a decreasing rate of population growth could have helped to solve the problem of unemployment, at least in the long run. Still, in 1950 (once the temporary recovery of the birth rate was accomplished) the rate of natural increase in the southern regions was between 1.5 percent and 2.0 percent (against 0.5 percent in the northern and central regions), with a birth rate of 25–30 per 1,000. Effects of the high birth rate were to be felt on the labor market during the 1960s.

Population growth, therefore, was taken for granted as a phenomenon that cannot be influenced by policy. Whether as a reaction to the negative experience of the Fascist policy or as a result of the heavy influence of the Catholic morality (unfavorable to family planning), the fact is that never, or at least never significantly since the end of the war, has the population growth issue been contemplated.

In spite of the successful efforts of reconstruction, the first steps toward industrialization, and mass emigration, unemployment still plagued the country. A Parliamentary Commission of Enquiry into the Problems of Poverty and Unemployment was created in 1952 [7], and the problems were debated widely. The only results were a few timid suggestions for slowing the rate of population increase and many statements to the effect that the current population trends, with respect to unemployment and poverty, were of no consequence. Many of the legislative measures enacted by the Fascist regime have survived (for example, it is a criminal offense to disseminate birth control propaganda, according to the penal code).

The first scheme for a national plan (*Piano Vanoni*) for the decade 1954–1964 reflected the general concern over high unemployment. The plan forecast that the acceleration of industrialization would not be enough to eliminate unemployment and that an annual net emigration of 70,000 should take place, or, in other words, between one-third and one-half of the annual increase of the labor force should emigrate. The benefits of emigration also included the considerable contribution of remittances to the balance of payments.

¶ THE NEW INDUSTRIAL SOCIETY
AND THE LACK OF A GENERAL POPULATION POLICY

During the 1950s and the early 1960s, an unexpected and very sustained economic growth took place, considerably reducing unemployment, with the help of emigration, which changed from predominantly non-European to predominantly European.

Several official bodies, during the early 1960s, prepared the groundwork for the Five-Year Plan. These acts, combined with public statements made by the responsible persons in the economy, increased the awareness of the problems created by the differential development of the country, especially in the south [8]. The problem of the *Mezzogiorno* has been at the center of public attention since unification of the country in 1861; but during the 1950s and the early 1960s, the extraordinary level of emigration from the south (abroad but, principally, to the rest of the country) made its human implications felt brutally.

The 1966–1970 plan made provisions for a more balanced growth, and one of its goals was the equalization of the growth rate of the labor force in the various regional areas [9]. This meant that, during the five-year period, the net increase in the labor demand in each area had to be proportional to the population. The necessary means to reach this goal were considered to be adequate investments, particularly public, in the regions of the south. Concern also was expressed for the increasing congestion of the urban and metropolitan areas, but the means for reequilibrating the situation were insufficient and, in any case, only vaguely outlined.

Emigration no longer was considered essential for solving the depression of the labor market, and the plan simply forecast the gradual decrease in this phenomenon following a more or less spontaneous trend. It also should be said that the role of the emigrants' remittances in the balance of payments was no longer indispensable as it was in the late 1940s and the 1950s.

There is little doubt that, during the last quarter of a century, population has never been considered a major problem. Growth has been thought of as a datum, largely unaffected by public intervention, very much like climate, the nature of the soil, or mineral resources. Public concern, although very sensitive at all times to the problems posed by unemployment, emigration, the exodus from the south or from the rural areas, and by the congestion of the cities, has always failed to acknowledge that these factors are affected greatly by differential demographic growth and by the delayed modernization of procreation in the south. In this sense, population has been left to the improperly defined "spontaneous" forces or tendencies, and policy has been directed, if at all, at the consequences rather than the determinants of such tendencies.

LEGISLATION AND SOCIAL POLICY
THAT AFFECT MARRIAGE

Legislation concerning marriage does not differ greatly from one country to another in Europe. Its connections with fertility and population growth, in populations where fertility control is relatively strong, are weak. An extensive treatment of legislation that concerns marriage would, therefore, be out of place in this chapter, but one must comment on a few points.

The first notable point is the minimum age at marriage, which is sixteen for the groom and fourteen for the bride and which, with special dispensation and the parents' consent, can be reduced to fourteen and twelve, respectively. The age limits are among the lowest in Europe, roughly corresponding with puberty. The main concern of the legislature seems to have been to make the legitimization of a child conceived out of wedlock possible through an intervening marriage, thus confronting the very young parents with grave obligations that, it is now generally accepted, they are in no condition to undertake at such young ages.

A proposal to raise the minimum age at marriage to eighteen has been put before Parliament. However, should this proposal be approved, very few marriages would be prevented. In 1968, only 0.32 percent of the grooms and 6.05 percent of the brides were below eighteen years of age, accounting for 6.14 percent of the marriages performed in that year.

Considering that many of the very young marriages take place to regularize premarital conceptions, it is to be supposed that the raising of the minimum age to eighteen would have the following consequences:

(1) A rise in illegitimacy with, in view of current legislation, the consequent unfavorable effects on the status of the newborn child.
(2) A shift of the timing of fertility to a later age but with unappreciable consequences on the final family size.

The second relevant point consists in the need for parental consent for minors. The proposal to lower the age of majority from twenty-one to eighteen would free a large number of young people from the need for parental consent. In 1968, there were 85,544 brides (22.8 percent) and 14,230 grooms (3.83 percent) in this age group, forming a total of 93,622 marriages (25.0 percent) dependent on parental consent. Although, in the absence of parental consent, the marriage can be authorized by a judge, this procedure is resorted to by a very limited number of people (213 in 1968). The abolition of parental consent probably would result in an increase of early nuptiality and a shifting of the timing of fertility to an earlier age, although with little or no impact at all on the final family size. Any change in the regulations concerning the age at marriage would affect the various regions of the country differently, since early marriages are much more frequent in the south.

A final point: In Italy, after the Concordat of 1929, marriages performed according to canon law have full civil effects; the civil status official is replaced by the parish priest. Very few weddings in Italy take place with a civil ceremony alone; in 1951, they consisted of 2.4 percent of all marriages, but the proportion decreased to only 1.4 percent in 1968.

¶ SEPARATION

Until December 1970, the date of the introduction of divorce into the Italian system, legal separation was the only way of attenuating the reciprocal obligation contracted by the spouses with marriage. In the frequent case of the *de facto* separation, the two parties decide to live apart without any formal procedure; their situation is not recognized by the law and has no juridical consequences. A legal separation, on the other hand, has direct juridical consequences and may take one of the following forms:

(1) Judicial separation (Articles 151, 152, 153 of the civil code) on the grounds of adultery, willful abandonment, threats, excess, violence, serious sentences, refusal of the husband to fix a suitable residence, mental cruelty. The judge establishes where the fault lies, and the parties are provided for, accordingly, as far as the custody of the children or the economic arrangements are concerned.

(2) Mutual agreement separation, or consensual separation, which becomes effective on ratification by the court.

In both cases, the president of the court attempts the reconciliation of the parties.

The main effect of separation is the end of the obligation of cohabitation; the parties are obliged to remain "faithful" to each other and, in case of need, to provide financial support.

The direct effects of legal separation are probably zero, since it usually constitutes the formal recognition of an existing situation in which relations between the parents virtually have ceased. However, legal separations involve a large number of children whose legal status is changed greatly as a result of their parents' separation.

Legal separations are increasing in number; there were 5,212 in 1951, 6,296 in 1966, 7,459 in 1968, and there will be about 12,000 in 1972, or about 3 percent of the marriages performed in one year. However, they represent only a fraction of the *de facto* separations, as shown indirectly from the census data and more directly by daily experience.

¶ DIVORCE

Divorce legally was introduced for the first time in Italy in December 1970. The law defines the instances in which marriage can be dissolved. According to the law, a judge can dissolve a marriage and pronounce the termination of all its civil effects in the following circumstances:

(1) When the other party is sentenced to imprisonment for a term of fifteen years or more or—no matter the length—for incest, rape, inducement to prostitution, and so forth, when the victim is a direct descendant or an adopted child. There also are grounds for divorce when the other party has been acquitted of the offenses just mentioned on the grounds of insanity.
(2) After an uninterrupted period of five years (six in the case of the other partner's opposition) of judicial or consensual separation.
(3) If the other party, being an alien, has obtained annulment or dissolution of the marriage abroad or has contracted a new marriage.
(4) When the marriage has not been consummated.

When marriage is dissolved, the wife resumes her maiden name and one of the partners is obliged to give an allowance to the other in proportion to his or her income and possession; this obligation ceases when the beneficiary remarries. As far as the children are concerned, the obligation to support, educate, and raise them continues even after a new marriage. When necessary, the court may appoint a legal guardian.

During 1971, 55,439 proceedings were begun; about one-third of them (16,988) actually ended in divorce. In the first eight months of 1972, the number of divorces was triple the amount during the corresponding period of 1971 (23,840 instead of 7,930), but new applications for divorce fell from 44,432 to 13,799. Not all applications are handled speedily; many are held up by a lengthy procedure, and others are abandoned in the course of the procedure. However, it may be supposed that, after a period of adjustment, the annual number of divorces will approach that of the legal separations, which, in 1972, will reach a figure of 12,000.

The introduction of divorce marks an important change in the Italian system. Since Fascism and the Concordat, the marriage ceremony has been strongly controlled in its formal structure, substance, and morale by the Catholic Church. We have seen that civil marriages have been diminishing; annulment of marriage, although rare, was more easily granted by canon than by civil law. The introduction of divorce—although not an act of demographic policy—will probably prepare the ground for further steps in the direction of a more secularized family life. It has had, therefore, an impact that goes far beyond its direct demographic effects.

PROCREATION AND FAMILY PLANNING

¶ DISTRIBUTION AND AVAILABILITY OF CONTRACEPTIVES

Until very recently, the distribution, sale, and advertising of contraceptives were prohibited by the following laws and decrees:

(1) Royal Decree of June 18, 1931, no. 773, which prohibited the production, purchase, holding, import, and export of contraceptives and the circulation of writings, drawings, and images which publicize or illustrate the use of direct measures for the prevention of procreation.

(2) *Testo Unico* of public security, Article 114, which prohibited the insertion of advertisements or letters that refer to direct measures for the prevention of procreation in newspapers or periodicals.

(3) *Decreto Legge*, May 1946, which contained norms regarding the confiscation of papers and other publications or printed matter that publicize or illustrate the use of direct measures for the prevention of procreation or that contained advertisements or correspondence on the subject.

(4) Article 553 of the penal code (incitement of persons to the use of measures against procreation) stated: "Whoever publicly incites others to adopt measures against procreation, or disseminate propaganda in favor of those practices, will be punished by up to one year's imprisonment, or by a fine of eighty thousand lire. Both these penalties will be inflicted if the offense has been committed for the sake of gain."

It is well known, for example, that the contraceptive pill could be prescribed only for therapeutic purposes and that all publicity and sale of it as a contraceptive was prohibited. In point of fact, this legislation never constituted a serious obstacle to the use of the pill, but it, nevertheless, created certain problems that were not always easily resolved.

The situation has undergone a radical change (although certain obstacles and prejudices remain), after the verdict of the *Corte Costituzionale* which, on May 16, 1971, declared the above-mentioned laws to be unconstitutional, on the basis of Article 21 of the Constitution. The court accepted that the norm expressed under Article 553 was a result of the general principles and demographic policy that was in force between the two world wars and aimed at increasing the population as a power factor.

On the other hand, the problem of birth control has become so important socially and has such far-reaching effects that, in the light of public awareness and the gradual widening of health education, it can no longer be considered an offense to decency to discuss certain aspects of the problem publicly, to provide information, and to circulate propaganda in favor of contraception. That public opinion feels the need for a greater social awareness on the subject, is demonstrated by the fact that Article 553 seldom is enforced and that bills have been presented repeatedly for its abrogation.

By declaring the publicity, encouragement, and all relevant propaganda of contraceptive measures as illegal, these acts are subject to criminal law. But it should be remembered that the high number of abortions that take place is one of the most eloquent arguments in favor of the dissemination of information regarding contraceptive measures.

¶ ABORTION

Willful abortion is considered a criminal offense and, as such, is severely punished by the law in the following ways:

(1) The woman who obtains it is punished by imprisonment for one to four years (Article 547).
(2) The person who performs it with her consent is punished by imprisonment for two to five years (Article 546).
(3) The person who performs it without her consent is punished by imprisonment for seven to twelve years (Article 545).

If one leaves aside the last case, which unquestionably constitutes a serious offense, and just considers the cases of abortion with the woman a consenting party, it will be realized how severe the law is, in spite of the many arguments in favor of abolition and numerous examples offered by other countries.

¶ STERILIZATION

Sterilization is dealt with essentially by Article 552 of the penal code (induced incapacity to procreate) that states the following:

Whoever performs acts on persons of either sex, with their consent, with the intent of rendering them incapable of procreating, is punished by imprisonment from six months to two years and a fine of 8,000 to 40,000 lire.

¶ CONSIDERATIONS OF LEGISLATION REGARDING
CONTRACEPTION, ABORTION, AND STERILIZATION

As far as Italian legislation regarding contraception, abortion, and sterilization is concerned, it may be stated, generally speaking, that it has always been almost exclusively repressive and negative. There are three apparent reasons for this particular state of affairs:

(1) The strong influence of the Catholic church on the subject of family morals; civil law has fully accepted these principles and, indeed, reinforced them.
(2) The Fascist demographic policy, which strictly prohibited the propaganda and circulation of birth control methods and, thus, provided the basis for an active populationist policy.
(3) A generally passive and neutral postwar attitude to population problems (partly as a reaction against the Fascist demographic policy), which were regarded as inherent in the social framework of the time. This is why repressive norms, frequently contrary to the constitutional regime, have only recently been abrogated.

As a result of this situation, social behavior has, in the last few decades, tended to deviate more and more from the law that had become archaic and no longer relevant. In all the central-northern regions, with one or two exceptions, period and cohort reproduction rates have gone down for long periods to values well below replacement. Thus, the number of children has obviously been limited sharply by family planning. It might be said that the lack of information and guidance in family planning, caused by excessive caution on the part of couples, may have reinforced a neo-Malthusian attitude. Throughout the central-northern area, there has been a strong tendency to limit the number of children among couples married during the last thirty years. It is not to be excluded that these couples may have compensated for the lack of qualified or medical assistance by excessive caution. In other words, confronted with the risk of not producing the desired number of children and the risk of producing more than the desired number, they preferred to run the former risk.

This statement, which may appear somewhat paradoxical, really requires investigation—not always simple—into the factors and motives of fertility by areas and geographic sectors. Unfortunately, at present, no such detailed surveys are available. The point we wish to make is that in particular circumstances, highly repressive legislation may defeat its own ends.

In many parts of the south, fertility is still relatively high (recently wed couples at the end of their married life will have produced about three children), and the decline is more recent and gradual than in the rest of the country.

The cultural climate, with its strong bias on tradition, is less favorable to the generalization of family planning; the woman is still very much in a subordinate position to the man, and the mistrust of new ideas that go against tradition is very marked. The southern area is far behind the central-northern region as far as family planning is concerned.

This is demonstrated not only by the higher fertility rate (three children per couple as opposed to two), but by the still high frequency of large families in the south (see Table 6).

It is, as yet, too early to establish whether or not the modification of the laws regarding contraception, made a year ago, has led to any changes in the demographic behavior of the population. However, the following observations may be made:

(1) The situation regarding the diffusion of contraceptives has not changed; the only difference is that now they are sold as "contraceptives" instead of on the pretext of a medical prescription.

(2) Nothing has changed in the policy of public health and social security bodies, which do not consider as their prerogative the organization of adequate assistance in the field of family planning. The same goes for educational authorities.

(3) Apart from a very few but praiseworthy exceptions, nonpublic initiatives in the field of family planning are practically nonexistent.

Nevertheless, the abolition of restrictive laws is the first essential step toward a more rational approach on the part of families and public bodies to problems that concern fertility and the family.

MEASURES THAT AFFECT THE FAMILY

¶ INTRODUCTION

In this section, we shall try to give an idea of the legislative and social provisions that affect the family, its economy, and its welfare. The idea certainly is not to determine the effects of the various provisions such as the family allowances scheme but to find whether or not the social and legislative system favors procreation and the raising of children. A system in which housing is inadequate, education and medical care expensive, and working mothers hardly considered is one in which—other factors being equal (degree of modernization, income, and so forth)—procreation and raising of children are less favored than in a system that does not have these disadvantages.

It is, of course, impossible and probably of little use to mention all measures which, one way or another, are related to the welfare of the family. We shall try only to mention a few points which, either because they are inspired by demographic reasons or are loosely related to prolification and childhood, seem to be important.

¶ THE FAMILY ALLOWANCE SCHEME

Introduced in the 1930s, the family allowance is regulated by a body of laws approved in 1955 and modified subsequently in 1961, 1967, 1969, and 1971. The family allowance scheme covers all workers, or all those persons, independent of age, sex, or nationality, who are in another's employment and who receive a wage or a salary in exchange for their work, including partners in companies and in cooperatives. Wives, relatives (including relatives by marriage to the third degree), those who work at home, farmers, and crop-sharemen are excluded from the scheme, although they may benefit from it.

The payments are collected by the head of the family; benefits may be claimed during the period of employment, holidays, when notice has been given, in the case of labor accidents, sickness, and military service, or— if the head of the family is the woman—in the case of absence caused by pregnancy or puerperium.

Those eligible for the scheme are all family members dependent on the worker for maintenance: children, wife, and other dependent relatives. The age limit for children is fourteen, which may be raised to eighteen if the child is without gainful occupation and, therefore, supported by the parents; the limit may be raised to twenty-one or twenty-six years if the child is receiving higher education.

In the sectors of industry and commerce, the monthly allowance was 5,720 lire[1] for each child, 4,160 for the wife, and 2,340 for the ascendants. The category of the worker (that is, blue or white collar) in no way influences the amount. In 1965, the scheme covered 5,176,000 family heads for a total of 13,144,000 dependents, practically covering the totality of those falling within the scheme's prerequisite.

A few remarks have to be made here. In the first place, the monthly allowance is very low, because the amount has remained fixed for a long time, its true value has been eroded by inflation, and its utility has been lessened by the general increase of real personal income. In 1960, the sum allocated in family allowances accounted for 4.9 percent of total earned income; this proportion fell to 3.8 percent in 1968. Given the modesty of the additional family income provided by the scheme, it is evident that its impact on the demography of the family is probably very small, with the exception of those families "at the margin" with many children and a very low family income.

The second remark concerns the nature of the scheme. Conceived, in the 1930s, as an incentive to fertility (progressive allowances with the increase of the parity), it has changed its nature, becoming perhaps a rather inadequate instrument of social justice, intended to help those families whose living conditions are made more difficult by the presence of dependent members. The amount of the allowances is fixed at an invariable sum, no matter how many children there are in the family. It is clear that, unlike other European countries, in which the scheme is designed to stimulate or to guide fertility to certain targets, no aim of this kind is present in the Italian situation.

In addition to the benefits derived from the family allowance scheme, the taxation system provides a few minor advantages for large families. National income tax (*Imposta complementare sul reddito complessivo*) is based on the income of the family and is calculated on the basis of income or revenues of any sort on exterior signs of wealth. The tax is levied on an annual income exceeding 900,000 lire. Husband's and wife's income are considered joint for taxation purposes. On the total net income, a deduction of 240,000 lire is admitted, plus 100,000 lire for each dependent member of the family. The families who have seven dependent children may deduct, instead of the sum of 240,000 lire, the sum of 5,000,000, quite apart from the deductions for dependent children. This sum is reduced by 50 percent for families with five or six dependent children. The same benefits apply

---

[1] US$1 equaled 580 lire as of January 1, 1973.

to the other forms of income tax—the communal one (*imposta di famiglia*) —to which the families are subjected.

In the case of taxation, the legislators' intention of favoring large families is apparent. But the limits, set in times when fertility was still relatively high, are so high (seven surviving children and all dependent) that we doubt there are an appreciable number of beneficiaries. It is also to be remembered that in countries like Italy, where a large part of taxation revenue comes from "indirect" taxation, benefits of the kind just described have a much smaller impact than in countries where direct taxation plays a more important role.[2]

¶ WORKING WOMEN AND PROCREATION

The working conditions of mothers can certainly influence the demography of the family. In all industrialized countries, the fertility of the married working woman is far below the fertility of the married woman who is not economically active. In Italy, according to an estimate based on the 1961 census data, the fertility of the former was 30 percent lower than the latter. There are many factors responsible for these differentials and all are evident, but the main one is certainly the difficulty of reconciling motherhood with an active life. The problem is all too familiar, and does not need to be gone into extensively here.

Among the principal regulations governing a working mother are the following:

(1) The law prohibits dismissal both during the gestation period, which must be medically certified, and during the period of compulsory abstention from work following confinement and, lastly, until the child is one year old.

(2) The woman may not be assigned heavy or dangerous or unhealthy tasks during gestation or during the three months after confinement (seven months if nursing the child).

(3) It is forbidden to employ women for a certain period before and after confinement. The period varies from six to thirteen weeks (industry) before confinement to eight weeks after confinement.

(4) During the period of abstention from work (which may be prolonged by the labor inspectorate), the woman receives 80 percent of her salary. The period must be counted as full employment for the purposes of seniority, holidays, and so forth.

(5) When the period of compulsory abstention from work has ended, the woman retains the right to remain at home until the child is one year old, receiving 30 percent of the pay; her place must be kept by the employer, and the period is valid for the computation of seniority.

---

[2] On the other hand, current legislation does not favor the family, since the income of husband and wife is assessed jointly. This fact tends to discourage working women, thereby driving them out of the labor market.

The legislation, as far as the protection of the working mother is concerned, is rather advanced. But the demographic effects of the growing protection of motherhood are difficult to recognize. We may, however, make a few points. In the first place, the increasing legislative protection and welfare has also increased the cost of the working mother who, for the same cost, has, on an average, a lower productivity than the man. This has made it less worthwhile for the employer to hire female labor. From 1959 to 1971, mainly owing to the exodus from agriculture, female employment in this sector fell by 1,190,000; in the same period, a fall also took place in the industrial section (166,000 units) counterbalanced by an increase in the tertiary sector (200,000).

Is there a plausible interpretation of the demographic consequences of labor legislation? With the information available at present, any hypothesis is the result of mere speculation. However, the present tendencies may have two cumulative consequences. On one hand, the easier the conditions of pregnancy, puerperium, childbirth, and so forth, the smaller these differences in fertility will be between working and nonworking women. On the other hand, these easier conditions may result in a lower productivity on the part of women and, therefore, in a decrease in the demand for female labor as has been the case during the last twenty years. Theoretically, it may be imagined that both consequences favor fertility: the first, by reconciling economic activity with the role of the mother in the family; the second, by driving out more and more women from the labor market back into an anachronistic exclusive role of mother and housewife. But we believe that this tendency is incompatible with a modern and rational organization of society, since it creates a sharp distinction between a privileged and modern sector of the female population, able to work and to procreate, and the other sector, constituted by women exclusively tied to the traditional family role, with little interchange between the two groups.

¶ THE NEED FOR INFRASTRUCTURES

Once a mother has given birth to a child, to what extent does society help her? We have noted that she gets several benefits if she is gainfully employed. She also gets free medical care for herself and for the child and free hospitalization. Although the health system leaves much to be desired, the law is generally in tune with the times. Mother and child are, therefore, relatively protected.

Where legislation and social policy are backward is in the field of assistance to children until school age. A mother without any help in the house is in severe difficulties if she wants to resume her economic activity or if she wants to enter the labor market.

Although statistics on the subject are few and fragmentary, it appears that, in 1968, 1,316,193 children (23.5 percent) under the age of six attended preschool institutions. This proportion varies considerably according to geographical area: 29.8 percent in the north, 23.6 percent in central Italy, and 17.4 percent in the south.

As regards the under three year olds, the public assistance body ONMI (*Opera Nazionale Maternita col Infanzia*) (which is, at present, going through a period of crisis and has been strongly criticized), responsible for this sector, assisted in its nurseries only 4 percent of children under three in the north, 2.9 percent in central Italy, and 1.4 percent in the south.

It should, however, be remembered that, of the 23.5 percent of children under six in kindergartens and nurseries, just under half (629,545, or 47 percent) attended institutions belonging to public bodies, which were, therefore, practically free, while the rest (686,648, or 52.2 percent) went to private institutions, for the most part religious ones. The statistics examined here do not include nurseries attached to industrial enterprises or belonging to private bodies and not under direct public control.

Nevertheless, the general picture shows that much progress must still be made in this sector and that the far from efficient organization of child welfare is reflected, first, by the low proportion of women with employment and, second, by the serious difficulties that working women have to face in raising their children.

MORTALITY

The existing problems in the field of mortality can be summarized as follows:

(1) Infant mortality has strongly marked regional differentials.
(2) Incidence of infectious diseases is higher than normal, with large regional differentials.
(3) There is a lack of coordination among the many institutions of public health and an insufficient and, in some instances, irrational distribution of infrastructures.

Public opinion is aware of the many problems posed by the present situation and of the necessity to reform the whole system. Unfortunately, although the main points of reform already were indicated in the preparatory studies for the First Five-Year Plan in 1966–1970 (about a decade ago), the plan itself, in its final formulation, is very vague concerning the objectives of the policy and the instruments for reaching such objectives. According to the plan, the principal objective is the creation of a comprehensive national health system to include all categories of citizens, providing preventive medicine, treatment, and rehabilitation. The plan also formulates the vague objective of "reducing the incidence of those causes of death which are of greatest social importance and infant mortality, and of achieving a rise in the general health level of the population" [9, p. 116]. Little has been done in this sense, and these statements have remained nothing more than wishful thinking. The Ministry of Health has had little power to change the situation.

Growing concern has been expressed by opinion and pressure groups, political parties, and trade unions. The preparatory studies of the Second Five-Year Plan seem to have delineated the objectives of a reform in a more precise and operative manner [10, pp. 164–165].

But the experience of the last decade raises many doubts as to the realization of a reform that encounters serious obstacles in the form of the present health organization, well-entrenched in its traditional and often privileged position. This once more confirms the lack of a studied policy on the objectives: better health and lower mortality.

MIGRATION AND EUROPEAN INTEGRATION

¶ THE CONCERN FOR INTERNAL MIGRATION

We have illustrated briefly the importance of migration as a factor of population redistribution over the territory. Of particular concern is the progressive depopulation of many areas, especially, but not exclusively, in the south. The large internal flows of the last two decades have been determined partly by the differing levels of regional development and, of course, by the differential rates of natural increase—very low (when not negative) in the north and central regions, still high or moderately high in the south.

Within certain limits, mobility of labor represents a factor of progress, but the increasing social costs of the congestion of some urban, industrial, and metropolitan areas since the beginning of the 1960s has started to worry the government and the local administrators more and more. On the other hand, many areas, deprived of their young people, of a large fraction of the labor force, and of the more qualified workers, seem to be heading toward a natural death. This process also has a high monetary and social cost.

Since 1962, the administrators who are responsible for economic policy, the various bodies concerned with planning and, later, the 1966–1970 plan have insisted on the need to increase employment opportunites in the south through concentration of private and, especially, of public investment. Among the five main goals of the 1966–1970 plan was the aim to locate

40–45 percent of the newly created jobs in the south, in order to stabilize the proportion of the total labor force in that area [9, p. 65]. The creation of the giant steelmill plant in Puglie, various petrochemical plants in Sicily, and a new automobile industry in Campania are the tokens of this effort.

In 1971, with the new law financing the activity of the *Cassa del Mezzogiorno*, the special agency created in 1950 for the development of the south, the sum of 3,000 billion lire was allocated to be invested over the period 1971–1975.

The law raises from 60 percent to 80 percent the proportion of the total investment on the part of public owned or controlled industries that must be located in the south. The law also confirms that at least 40 percent of the investments directly made by the public administration must be located in the south.

Local administration—the *comuni*—and regional governments also may affect the internal redistribution of the population through local planning, but it is impossible to say to what extent and in which direction.

¶ INTERNATIONAL MIGRATION

As has been stated earlier, emigration had, for a long time, been considered a partial solution to the heavy unemployment of the country during the immediate postwar decade. Fascism had discouraged emigration—with the exception of the settlement in the colonies—and encouraged repatriation. A radical change in policy marks the return to normality at the end of the war. Mass emigration started again, for the most part controlled and assisted by the government. In 1944, the General Board for Emigration was created at the Ministry of Foreign Affairs, and an ad hoc service was created (1948) at the Ministry of Labor. Several facilities were granted to emigrants; bilateral agreements with the various countries were reviewed and many stipulated anew; an advisory council for the Italians abroad was created [11, p. 106ff]. During the 1960s, full employment seemed to be within reach: Official statements reflected this hope, as did the 1966–1970 plan in which net emigration was supposed to be falling rapidly. In 1963, Italian Premier Moro declared before Parliament:

The Italian government intends to make a special effort to solve the questions which concern our workers abroad. The government is convinced that the basic problem is to give all Italians the opportunity of working in their own country. The aim is to eliminate from emigration (of workers) the element of necessity, leaving freedom of choice, as the expression of the right of the worker to develop his capacity whenever he may wish to do so. While waiting for this to become a reality, the government intends to continue to intensify its actions in order to obtain the best working and living conditions for our workers abroad, by adopting every necessary measure and by pursuing the most worthwhile bilateral and international agreements. The government is fully conscious of the high human, social, and political values of such action [11, p.49].

Unfortunately, subsequent events have shown that full employment is still far away and not within easy reach. The idea that the element of necessity may be eliminated from emigration, leaving absolute freedom of choice, is a romantic dream and scarcely realistic. One also has the impression that Italy has not exerted all the necessary strength and political power in the conclusion of bilateral agreements. And, after all, the country of emigration is always the weaker party. Unilateral decisions on the part of immigration countries may cause serious troubles for foreign workers and shatter any attempt at programming emigration; this is shown, for instance, by the various restrictive measures enforced by Switzerland during the 1960s.

In spite of all the good intentions, during the 1960s, the government was able to plan and guide emigration less and less. The proportion of emigration assisted by the Ministry of Labor fell to a very low figure. The European destinations assumed an increasing importance, and emigration of the 1960s became temporary and recurrent as far as duration is concerned and more and more individualistic in its structure, composed mainly of workers who left their families behind. The increased mobility has meant less control and assistance on the part of the government. On the other hand, the labor market of the more-advanced European economies has shown a persistent excess of labor demand over labor supply, and Italian migrants have been quick in filling the gaps. The principle of free circulation of manpower within the European Economic Community (EEC) has, in theory, increased the chances of Italian emigration although in practice it has had a contrary effect, other factors being equal. Italian labor has become more costly than labor from extracommunitarian countries. In a few years, the competition of Spanish and Portuguese workers in France and of Yugoslavs and Turks in Germany has displaced the Italians as the main foreign nationality. In the meantime, the rising per-capita income, progress in education, and a general, although not easily achieved, advancement have raised the expectations of the young. Emigration, at the beginning of the 1970s, seems to be less attractive, even in the presence, as in 1971 and 1972, of growing unemployment [12].

On the other hand, the government has not yet made up its mind, torn between, on one hand, an old conception of emigration and, on the other, the new developments. The major problems that the government is called upon to face in the field of migration arise from three sources: the need for better protection of the emigrant abroad, the policy of repatriations, and the strategy for the development of the emigration areas within the EEC. Better protection of the emigrant abroad means:

(1) The emigrant must be able to profit from the migratory experience.
(2) The emigrant must be able to be followed by his family.
(3) He must have equality of rights with the nationals not only in the labor market but also in daily life (acquisition of political rights, for instance, in local matters).

A repatriation policy is, at present, completely lacking. The idea that the emigrant, on his return home, brings new skills and capital which contribute to the development of the area of origin is, unfortunately, far from being true. Whatever skills the emigrant may acquire during his temporary and recurrent expatriations (few in most cases), they are rarely put to use upon return. Remittances and savings are, for the most part, used for the current needs of the family or, at the most, invested in a piece of land or in a small business, activities with very low productivity and a very grim future.

A coherent and forceful policy is, therefore, needed in order to help the emigrant who returns to his country of origin; he must be efficiently advised as to the labor opportunities, provided with supplementary training, and assisted in using and investing his savings profitably. The traditional structures, which subdivide the responsibilities between different ministries (mainly those of Foreign Affairs and Labor) are not equal to the task. After all, the Italian community abroad amounts to some 5 million people, who deserve a more watchful assistance.

¶ ITALY AND THE EUROPEAN ECONOMIC COMMUNITY
The third source of problems mentioned in the preceding section derives from Italy's relations with the partners in the EEC. The principle of the free circulation of manpower—in spite of the principle of priority, or the preference that has to be given to workers of the EEC in filling the openings—has increased the competition in the labor market and, instead of favoring Italian labor, has, in practice, favored the workers coming from the Mediterranean countries, who are less costly, less mobile, and more easily controlled.

The Italian government in 1971 took steps to promote a stronger concern for a regional development policy in the EEC. In a "memorandum" submitted to the Council of Ministers of Social Affairs of the EEC [13, p. 43ff, and 14, p. 39ff], Italy took a critical attitude toward the discrimination—in terms of salaries, social insurance, and so forth—against the immigrants from the noncommunitarian countries, which, making Italian labor seem more costly, in fact, represents an escape from the clause of priority and results, in practice, in the preference of employers for other immigrants. The memorandum, noting that the differential regional development is one of the EEC's main weak points, called for a different course in the EEC policy, proposing that the EEC should take a 50-percent share in the industrial investments to be made in the south in order to create 400,000 additional jobs over a ten-year period.

Some of these suggestions were, in principle, accepted at the Paris summit meeting between the nine partners (the six plus Great Britain, Ireland, and Denmark) held in October 1972. The partners agreed that a fund should be established for regional development, with a view to reduction and eventual elimination of the gap between the less-developed and the more-developed areas of the EEC [15, p. 40].

A second important aspect of the policy formulation by the EEC is the so-called Mansholt Plan for the rationalization of agriculture, proposed in late 1968 and accepted in early 1971 [16].[3] The plan begins on the basis of the consideration that the output of agriculture increases faster than consumption; that the sector is subdivided into a very large number of concerns with very low productivity; that although the policy of political prices for foodstuff guarantees a minimum income to farmers, it does not ensure them against the rises in production costs and puts a burden on the shoulders of consumers. In view of all this, the Mansholt Plan calls for a more rapid decrease of the labor force engaged in the primary sector through a system of incentives for the aged farmers who are willing to retire or to move to other activities; it makes provisions for financing the reorganization of farms on the basis of more rational criteria.

According to the plan, the 10 million workers in the primary sector in 1970 (in the Benelux countries, France, Germany, and Italy) will be reduced to 5 million in 1980. A net exodus of 5 million workers will be the result; one-half will be aged workers taking advantage of the welfare measures designed by the plan, and the other half will shift to the extra-rural sector.

It is evident that, if this line of policy is followed consistently by the EEC, Italy will be greatly affected by the rural exodus. The application of the Mansholt Plan will certainly speed up the reduction of the rural population and, therefore, stimulate internal migration, possibly worsening the many problems posed by immigration into the urban areas.

CONCLUSION

This chapter's aim was merely to illustrate the Italian situation. It has not attempted to assess the impact of legislation and social policy on population.

[3] See also [17, p. 15, and 18, pp. 9, 15].

After the fall of Fascism, with its consistently pronatalist policy, the rate of growth of the population has never been an issue in the political debate. The problems of unemployment, of emigration, of the depopulation of vast territories, of congestion of the metropolitan areas, and of the relatively high infant mortality, although often at the center of the public attention during the last quarter of a century, have never been considered a consequence of population trends which could be modified or guided toward certain targets. Population growth is a datum, an exogenous factor. All the complex legislation concerning the family—marriage and divorce, procreation and abortion, children and parents, and so forth—has been discussed more from an abstract point of view (right or wrong, morality and social justice, and so forth) than from its demographic and social implications.

Even in the field of emigration which, since the second half of the nineteenth century has been the object of continuous concern, the attitude of the country is uncertain and, in some instances, contradictory.

Italy badly needs a reconsideration of the population problems that exist (although they are certainly not the most important ones), and a coherent reformulation of its social policy and legislation that concern problems of demographic relevance. Contradictions and inconsistencies have to be eliminated; priorities have to be studied. Although personally in favor of further rationalization of procreation, we consider a grave mistake the announced campaign for the liberalization of abortion in a country where traditional family planning is almost nonexistent. The impression is that influential people, no matter whether they are agnostic or concerned with respect to population problems, seem to be macroscopically misinformed.

REFERENCES

1. M. Livi Bacci. *Recent Trends of Italian Fertility.* IUSSP General Conference. London: IUSSP, 1969.

2. M. Livi Bacci and F. Pilloton. *Population and Labor Force of the Italian Regions to 1986.* Rome: SVIMEZ, 1970. (In Italian.)

3. C. Curcio. *The Demographic Policy of Fascism.* Milan, 1939. (In Italian.)

4. F. Savorgnan. "New and old orientations of the demographic policy of Fascism," *Assicurazioni Sociali,* 16, no. 2 (1939). (In Italian.)

5. D. V. Glass. *Population Policies and Movements in Europe.* London: Oxford, 1940, chapter 5.

6. P. Saraceno. *Elements for an Economic Plan, 1948–1952.* Rome, 1948. (In Italian.)

7. Parliamentary Commission of Enquiry on Unemployment in Italy. *Unemployment in Italy.* 15 volumes. Rome, 1954. (In Italian.)

8. Ministry of the Budget. *Economic Planning in Italy,* vols. 1, 2, and 3, 1967. (In Italian.)

9. Ministry of the Budget. *National Economic Plan for 1966–1970,* vol. 5, 1971. (In Italian.)

10. G. Berlinguer and F. Terranova. *The Massacre of the Innocents.* Florence, 1972. (In Italian.)

11. *Observations and Proposals on Italy's Migration Problems.* Rome; CNEL, 1970. (In Italian.)

12. M. Livi Bacci (ed.). *The Social and Economic Pattern of Emigration from the Southern European Countries.* Florence: Department of Statistics and Mathematics, 1972. (In Italian.)

13. "The Italian memorandum on employment policy in the European Economic Community," *Mondo Economico,* no. 26, 1971. (In Italian.)

14. "First answer of the European Economic Community's Commission to the Italian memorandum on the employment policy," *Mondo Economico,* no. 19, 1972. (In Italian.)

15. *Mondo Economico,* no. 43, 1972. (In Italian.)

16. "The Mansholt plan for agriculture in the community to 1980," *Mondo Economico,* no. 51, 1968. (In Italian.)

17. *Mondo Economico,* no. 16, 1971. (In Italian.)

18. *Mondo Economico,* no. 13, 1971. (In Italian.)

CHAPTER 22

West Germany

Hermann Schubnell

ABSTRACT

Since the founding of the Federal Republic of Germany (West Germany) in 1949, numerous measures have been taken that may directly or indirectly influence population. However, population policy has not yet been developed. The concept of "population policy" is still encumbered by overtones of the National Socialist ideology. Current consciousness of demographic facts and population studies has hardly been awakened.

Policies affecting the institution of the family are regarded as social policy. The Constitution of the republic places marriage and family under special state protection and guarantees free development of personality in all spheres, including reproduction. State protection includes allowances for children, but because the allowances are far less than the costs of raising children, they have not influenced a couple's decision on the number of children to have.

The discussions outside government and Parliament continue, mainly on the two outstanding events of recent years: the arrival of over 3 million aliens and a remarkable birth decrease. Notwithstanding the high fertility of alien women in Germany, the total population in 1972 had, for the first time, 29,000 more deaths than births. As in-migration exceeded out-migration by 300,000, population increase was caused entirely by the migration surplus.

Conservatives tend to favor population growth, social-liberalists to favor stabilization, which also seems to be favored by the trade unions. Scientific discussions are limited to a small group of experts, some of whom regard further population decrease as necessary in view of the present density and to revive the ecological balance. While the Catholic church opposes any family planning—within the context of contraception by effective modern means such as the pill, or chemical or mechanical contraceptives—the Protestant church considers it a private matter. So far, neither of the two churches has commented on population policy. Lately, the German branch of the International Planned Parenthood Federation had been granted government subsidies, but these subsidies were far from adequate to enable a nationwide family planning program to be created. In February 1973, the first Federal Institute for Population Research was established under the Ministry of the Interior. Besides providing information and advice to the government, the institute will do research work in international cooperation.

These very recent developments regarding population and environment problems may urge the government and central administration to develop a population policy concept.

GENERAL REMARKS

The six parliaments and governments that have been in office since the establishment of West Germany in 1949 have not developed specific objectives for population policy. Several steps have been taken, however, by the federal government and the eleven "land" governments of the federated states that directly or indirectly affect the development of population.

The basic law, or Constitution, of Germany regards human freedom and dignity as the highest legal values (item 1) and guarantees freedom in the reproductive sphere (item 2). This means that the state is not allowed to intervene directly with the freedom of individuals or couples to decide on the number of children they wish to have. Men and women have equal rights according to constitutional principles (item 3). A special Law on Equality was passed in 1957 to coordinate contradictory regulations at that time still inherent in civil law. The Constitution also places marriage and family and mother and child under the special protection of the state (item 6). It forbids state actions that might be contrary to the welfare of marriage and family. The basic law does not contain any statements that might be construed as population policies.

The protection of marriage and family guaranteed by item 6 of the Constitution served as a basis for a distinct family policy. Since 1953, there has been a special Ministry for the Family, in particular for problems related to the relief of economic burdens to families. Family policy, however, is regarded as part of social policy. In government statements, parliamentary inquiries, or debates only very rarely have problems of family policy been connected with changes in trends and structure of the population.

The most significant demographic events since the beginning of the 1960s have been:

(1) The admission of a growing number of aliens, in particular aliens of working age. At the beginning of 1972, 3.5 million aliens, 5.7 percent of the population (61.7 million), were living in Germany.
(2) The decrease in births after 1965. The crude birth rate decreased from 17.7 per 1,000 inhabitants in 1965 to 11.3 in 1972, the birth surplus during the same period from 6.2 to −0.5. An excess of deaths over births of about 29,000 occurred first in 1972. While, in 1965, there had been 1.044 million live births, there were only 700,000 in 1972. From 1965 to 1972, the net reproduction rate decreased from 1.165 to 0.81.

These two trends have been for years the focus of public discussions—among representatives of the political parties, the family associations, and the trade unions—on population problems. But they have, so far, not led Parliament and the government to develop a population policy or to take any legal action. The report on the family, which the government had intended to submit to Parliament in 1972, in its first part includes a detailed analysis of development, causes, and consequences of the birth decrease. After repeated delays, the government had to renounce this intention as a new Parliament was elected in November 1972. It is difficult to assess whether party policy played a part in this delay. It may well be that the coalition parties (Social Democratic party and the liberal Free Democrats) did not want to give the opposition (Christian Democratic Union and the more conservative Christian Social Union in the federal land of Bavaria) arguments for election by presenting a clear statement on population policy.

BRIEF HISTORY OF MEASURES RELEVANT TO POPULATION POLICY

Historically, there has been a lack of direct governmental action related to population policy. Thus, a picture of policy development in this area is limited to those measures whose objectives are by no means based on population policy but are, or can be, of indirect influence on development and structure of the population.

¶ MARRIAGE AND DIVORCE
Regulations on marriage and divorce may change the role of marriage in society and, thus, indirectly influence population. The trends and the strength of the effects of these regulations are hard to estimate, for many variables are involved, such as the general attitude toward the institution of marriage, the social and legal status of illegitimate children, female post-

marital economic activity, the economic status, and many other circumstances. No analysis has been made of the effect of laws concerning family status on demographic behavior.

There are no marriage restrictions except for the regulation on marriageability. A male may marry at the age of twenty-one; a female must be sixteen. Exceptions are possible: A young man could be married at age eighteen and declared of age. Females under twenty-one years of age need the consent of their legal guardian. The Parliament is debating a bill that proposes reducing majority from age twenty-one to age eighteen. It remains to be seen whether a decrease in the age of majority will mean earlier marriages and, consequently, increases in the number of married persons and possibly in the number of births. Average age at first marriage for males has varied little during the last decades: In 1970, it was 25.6 (in 1950, it was 28.1; in 1960, it was 25.9). The age at first marriage has somewhat decreased for females: In 1970, it was 23 (in 1950, it was 25.4; in 1960, it was 23.7).

Divorces have increased greatly during the last decade. In 1960, about 36 of 10,000 marriages ended in divorce; in 1970, this number was 51 of 10,000. This increase occurred in spite of the fact that the present law is based on the principle of guilt—that is, one party to a divorce must be guilty of the act that brings about divorce. There are strong movements to replace the guilt principle with the mere request for divorce based on broken marriage. It is not possible to judge the extent to which this change would have indirect effects on demographic behavior.

¶ REGULATIONS ON BIRTH CONTROL

Legislation on dissemination and availability of contraceptives, abortion, and sterilization influences fertility directly. Discussions of these issues, and of abortion in particular, have focused on their implication for public health, ethics, and social policy rather than their population policy implications. Pregnancy, birth, and medical care benefits for mother and child may influence demographic behavior but generally are regarded as health or social policy.

According to present regulations, hormonal contraceptives must be prescribed. IUDs are used less than pills, since many physicians hesitate to insert IUDs. They risk punishment under the Medicaments Act that prohibits the dissemination of means which, if properly used, may cause harmful side effects. (It is doubtful, however, whether IUDs come under medicaments and, consequently, under this law.) Besides, other and more harmless means of contraception are available. All other nonhormonal contraceptives are available, even through mail-order firms. No final legal decision has been made about the sale of contraceptives by vending machines.

Since 1960, sale by vending machines has been allowed if the machine is not located in the streets or other public places. Opposed to this form of availability are the Catholic church, family associations, and others. On the other hand, physicians and sociohygienists recommend this kind of sale since it protects the privacy and freedom of the individual by ensuring continued availability of contraceptives. The supporters of public sale of contraceptives consider it a shortcoming that vending machines may not be located in public places, especially such places as ports and barracks. The main reason for the promotion of vending machine sale is that use of condoms can help prevent transmission of venereal disease. The opposition is difficult to understand because newspapers and periodicals advertise mechanical and chemical contraceptives that—with the exception of the pill, which may only be sold in pharmacies upon prescription—are freely on sale in drugstores, pharmacies, and at hairdressers. Every large town has special shops that sell both literature on sexual problems and family planning and contraceptives (other than the pill). Persons must be over eighteen years of age to enter these shops. One mail-order firm for sexual advice with sales branches in all large towns shows films on sex education.

The national medical insurance does not pay for prescribed contraceptives. According to insurance regulations, methods used purely for contraceptive purposes are not covered, whereas physicians define hormonal contraceptives as prophylactic treatment, which is medically insurable. Contraceptive coverage, it is argued by many, would by no means be as costly to the insurers as treatment for complications of illegal abortions, which is covered by insurance. It is estimated that, in 1971, about 25 percent of the women of reproductive age used hormonal contraceptives. Use of these contraceptives is increasing constantly; they have been sold in West Germany since 1963. According to one interpretation of the German marriage law, use of contraceptives against the will of the spouse can be called "marital failure," and, as such, is grounds for divorce.

In Germany, the illegality of induced abortion has long been a controversial issue. Although the penal code's prohibition of induced abortion often protected a woman's health and life, it also was often responsible for sterility, sickness, and death resulting from the resort to illegal abortion.

Prior to 1945, political policies led to a ban on abortion; today, the ban continues for ethical and religious reasons. The present, much-disputed legislation punishes the woman involved and the performer of the abortion, with up to five years imprisonment for the woman and up to ten years for the agent or supplier of means. Attempted abortion is punishable. The only exception is that, if the woman's life or health is severely threatened by pregnancy, abortion can be approved by a board of experts, with the agreement of the woman concerned.

Reform of the penal law, which has been under way for some time, includes also Article 218 on abortion. Two solutions are being discussed which are fundamentally distinct from each other. The one proposal wants to allow abortion only in case of certain conditions whereby the presently allowed medical indication should be supplemented by social indication. Abortion remains punishable as a rule, but exceptions will be allowed if the case comes under an indication. The second proposal differs completely and wants abortion to be nonpunishable if it is performed during the first three months of pregnancy.

Opinions within the government and among the public are split. The Catholic church turns violently against any abortion except in the case of a medical indication. Conservatives are in favor of indications; liberals, of the three-month period. Opinions differ within the Social-Democratic party. Of course, it shall be up to the conscience of each physician whether or not he will take the responsibility to interrupt a pregnancy.

During the disputes on whether or not to alter abortion legislation, it has often been contended that in West Germany the number of abortions equals the number of births. Although the actual number of illegal induced abortions cannot be determined, the relationship is definitely lower than 1 to 1. It may well be assumed that there are hardly more than 30 abortions per 100 live births, and probably even less. Because of an even broader dissemination of contraceptives, the number of abortions will certainly decrease in the future.

In 1970, 771 abortions were reported by the police; in 1960, there were 4,000. In 1970, 882 persons (women and helpers) were judged to have been involved in abortions, but only 319, or 36 percent, were sentenced, compared to 42 percent sentenced in 1960, when 4,310 persons were involved and 1,823 persons were sentenced. It is possible—although it cannot be proved—that the reduction of abortion cases known to the police is caused by a real decrease in abortions because of greater dissemination of contraceptives. It is possible, also, that the decrease of persons sentenced is caused by a more liberal handling of penalties or a more tolerant attitude of the judges, who may be influenced by discussions of reform.

From 1933 to 1945, sterilization was permitted where medical opinion indicated that sterilization would "prevent offsprings' suffering hereditary disease." Today it is doubtful whether or not this regulation is still valid. Moreover, there is an increasing uncertainty about it, as interpretation and practice differ among the federal *Laender*. In the beginning of the 1960s, a physician was sentenced for deliberate severe bodily injury after undertaking many voluntary, but unlawful, sterilizations. He was acquitted by the federal Supreme Court, the highest appellate court, which held that sterilization in general and in accordance with present-day development of law no longer constitutes an act of bodily injury. The public accepted his acquittal, apparently believing sterilization to be a matter of personal conscience. Many jurists and physicians were surprised by the acquittal.

In formal terms, sterilization is not allowed on strictly social grounds, although some physicians approve of it. As to eugenic sterilization, opinions go from "en marche" to "allowed" as not offending morals and customs. Compulsory sterilization is illegal. In February 1972, the government proposed a bill on voluntary sterilization, which allowed the operation for men and women over twenty-five years of age. The Parliament at that time did not pass the bill, so discussions start anew during the next legislative period.

¶ REGULATIONS ON IMMIGRATION

After the birth decrease, the most important demographic event during the 1960s was the inflow of aliens. The 1961 census enumerated approximately 700,000 aliens, or 1.2 percent of the population; at the beginning of 1972, there were 3.4 million, or 5.6 percent. Of these, two-thirds were employed. Of all employed males in West Germany, 10.3 percent were aliens; of all employed females, 8.4 percent belonged to that category.

Many legal regulations and administrative measures control admission of, employment of, and accommodations for aliens. A law on aliens was enacted in 1965 before the onset of the great flow during the second half of the 1960s. In 1969, a law on entry and residence of nationals of European Economic Community member nations followed. The regulations on employment permits are numerous. There are agreements between West Germany and other nations on the recruitment of foreign labor; the first was with Italy in 1954, and after 1960, others followed with Spain, Greece, Turkey, Portugal, and Yugoslavia. Finally, special agreements exist with Morocco and Tunisia.

At the end of 1965, a coordinating commission on "alien workers" was established in the federal Ministry of Labor and Social Affairs. Members of the commission represent the administration, Parliament, foreign workers, employers' associations, trade unions, care-taking organizations, and the churches. The commission is to deal with all problems concerning the care and integration of alien workers and to coordinate measures to be taken by the national government, the *Laender,* and communities. For example, the commission tackles problems of disseminating information on living and working conditions in West Germany and teaching the German language to aliens in their home countries before they migrate. As for steps to be taken in Germany, the commission deals with such problems as providing lodgings and dwellings, improving the knowledge of the German language, educating the alien children, health maintenance, vocational education, arousing understanding of alien problems with the German population, and so forth. In inquiries submitted to the Minister of Labor or during hearings, members of Parliament repeatedly have requested information on the work done by the coordinating commission. These inquiries and their answers never refer to aspects of population policy.

The growing influx of aliens has changed the structure of the population, due to the distribution of aliens among the federal *Laender* and, consequently, the different degrees of regional changes. In Baden-Württemberg, for example, employed aliens represented 16 percent of all employed persons; in Hessia, about 13 percent. The lowest figure (4 percent) was in Schleswig-Holstein. The flow of aliens also influences population growth markedly. In 1971, the only reason for a birth surplus was the fact that the birth deficit of native mothers had been compensated by the birth surplus of alien mothers. In 1972, there was, for the first time, an excess of deaths of about 29,000. While the native population totaled − 109,000, alien births had a surplus of about 80,000, which reduced the birth deficit of the total population to 29,000. As a matter of fact, without migration into federal territory, the population of West Germany would have decreased in 1971. In 1972, there were 80,000 more births than deaths among aliens. In the German population in the same year, there were 109,000 more deaths than births.

In light of these factors, it is striking that, during both official and public discussions of these problems, the population policy approach is practically missing. Political objectives and administrative measures are expressed entirely in the field of economic policy and, in particular, labor policy, social policy, health policy, and educational policy. The long-term effects of alien migration and alien residence on population development in West Germany as well as in the countries of origin have not yet been discussed officially. Only scientific circles have been considering the problems. A study meeting of the German Association for Population Science in April 1972 had as its subject "Aliens in the Federal Republic of Germany: Causes and consequences of their mobility and its meaning for population processes." The representatives of the federal government present did not comment on questions of population policy. A high official of the labor ministry discussed the social and economic problems that accompany alien employment.

There are comprehensive regulations on recruitment and employment of aliens. Based on intergovernmental agreements, West Germany sends commissions into the home countries to report on the number of workers acceptable for recruitment, working conditions, and qualifications requested. The home countries, as contracting parties, make a preliminary

selection; the final decision is left to the German employer. Additional
legal regulations settle entry permit, residency permit, and employment
permit. Special regulations govern aliens who are nationals of the European Economic Community member countries; they have claims on the
granting and extending of their residency permits as well as on free movement. They also have claims on employment in another member nation if
they merely prove their employment by having employers certify they
work for them.

¶ FAMILY POLICY

Although it may appear reasonable to seek a close connection between
family policy and population policy, any connection of this sort is denied.
On the one hand, the denial is based on the argument that family policy
is part of social policy and not population policy and, on the other hand,
family policy has been ineffective in influencing the decision couples make
regarding the number of children they desire.

Family policy is broadly understood and defined by the Ministry of
Youth, Family, and Health. The primary government efforts aim at a
social policy to expand individual opportunities in education, profession,
family, and leisure time. Consequently, family policy is a very broad offer
of aids that are granted certain families under certain conditions, in particular, families with several children.

Uppermost within the scope of family policy are two measures with
economic appeal. The first, the Children Allowance Act of 1964, enables
persons with two or more children to receive tax-free allowances for the
second child and each additional child. If there are only two children in
a family, the allowance is granted only if the joint income of the spouses
does not exceed 1,250 DM per month.[1] A comparison between the monthly
allowances and the real costs of children shows that, at least, this measure
of family policy alone will not affect population policy. Child allowances
amount to 25 DM per month for the second child, 60 DM each for the
third and fourth child, and 70 DM for the fifth and each additional child.

The second measure prescribes tax-free grants for children, including
1,200 DM for the first child, 1,680 DM for the second child, 1,800 DM
for the third and each additional child. Child allowance and tax-free
amounts are, in principle only, granted for children under eighteen years
of age. However, in case of incomplete school or vocational education paid
by the taxpayer or in case of physical or mental handicaps of the children,
allowances are granted to age twenty-seven years.

The coalition government (Social-Democrats and Liberals) has com-

[1] Approximately US$403; as of January 1, 1973, US$1 equaled 3.10 DM.

pleted reform proposals to abolish this dual system of allowances plus tax-free amounts. Allowances beginning with the first child and a greater equalization of socially induced inequality are also being suggested.

Measures in the field of family policy also include special benefits to families with children through old-age insurance, accident insurance, unemployment insurance, and home-building loans. From 1949, when West Germany was established, to 1972, about 12.8 million dwellings were built; about 3.6 million are family-owned houses. Various government measures, in particular, loans and reduced interest, facilitate the building of homes for families.

A direct connection between living conditions and numbers of marriages or births cannot be proven. Between 1945 and 1960, when millions of destroyed buildings had to be reconstructed and the housing shortage was tremendous, the birth rates were high. After 1960, when residential construction expanded, the number of births decreased. The present birth rate is the lowest ever in German history, though at the same time (estimates for 1973), there are about 100,000 more dwellings (22.5 million) than private households (22.4 million). Also, the quality of dwellings has increased during the last decade. On the other hand, government-sponsored dwellings average four rooms with a total space of 60 square meters. In the opinion of many families, this is not enough space to house more than two children, in particular, because there is a tendency toward a large family living room. Certainly, there has been no postponement of marriage because of housing shortages; many young couples stay with their parents for some time. Here, now, is a connection between dwelling size and the number of children desired, whereby it is not the actual available space that is decisive but the space one wants and regards as an absolute standard.

The government provides allowances for the education of children, special savings arrangements for engaged couples and young couples, savings premiums based on the number of children, railway fare deductions for families with three or more children, recreation facilities for mothers alone and for families, free general and precautionary medical examinations for all family members, and rent subsidies based on maximum income figures and in accordance with family size.

The heterogeneity of family aids reveals that family policy combines those objectives inherent to financial, social, health, and educational policy. It is doubtful that these measures are regarded as population policy. Until recently, there have not been analyses of the effects of family policy on qualitative or quantitative population development.

The thesis of family policy as social policy (not population policy) has been defended repeatedly by the family organizations and the responsible politicians. The two ministers responsible for family policy from 1953 to 1968 have pointed out that family policy seeks to maintain the child's natural sphere of living and to create a better basis for the family's irreplaceable function as a center of education. The shaping of inner family life could not be a matter for the state but is solely a matter for the family, and this distinction would separate family policy from National Socialist population policy. The ministers criticized the fact that, in the past, this distinction was not made. They incriminated population policy as subject to the collective interests of state and society; more children were seen as the bearers of future collective functions.

Even today, the German public associates the term "population policy," with the ideologies of the National Socialist era where the goals were a population by eugenic measures ("racial hygienics"). The progress reports of postwar family ministers used graphs on birth decrease and changing age structure of population to justify family policy. The only report on the family ever published, which was submitted to Parliament in January 1968 but never discussed there, includes a detailed description of the process of population growth. A report on population has been neither presented by the government nor requested by Parliament.

The situation is conflicting: Family policy is regarded as social policy. There is no population policy. A collective interest of state and society in population would arouse suspicion. It is the individual and the family that are to have priority; their economic and social situation is to be relieved. Doubts exist that present family policy affects the number of births; at the same time, however, it is argued that birth decrease and age structure made family policy necessary.

This contradictory opinion prevailed until 1969. In connection with the birth decrease and after the Social-Liberal coalition assumed control of the government, interest in population problems and insight into the necessity of population policy began to increase.

MEASURES OF INDIRECT SIGNIFICANCE
TO POPULATION POLICY

In addition to the regulations and measures mentioned so far, several others may indirectly influence population trends and population structure without being seen primarily as population policy objectives. As there is no intention to influence demographic processes with these measures, politicians and administrative officials often forget that they may have unintentional demographic effects.

¶ MEASURES IN THE FIELD OF HEALTH AND SOCIAL POLICY

In compliance with the 1952 law for the Protection of Employed Mothers, working is prohibited for at least six weeks prior to and eight weeks following childbirth. The working place must not endanger the pregnant or nursing mother or the child. Termination notice is not permitted during pregnancy or to four months after confinement. Other regulations settle the type of reasonable work, time off for medical examinations, nursing, and so on. The national social insurance pays fully for the medical care of the pregnant woman from the diagnosis of her pregnancy through confinement at the hospital or at home, for medicine, dressing material, and other medications. Employed women are paid maternity benefits by the social insurance in the amount of net wages for the total period of their permissible absence from work (six weeks prior to and eight weeks following confinement).

The health insurance is part of the national social insurance, which is under the auspices of the federal Ministry of Labor and Social Affairs. Eighty-nine percent of the population are insured in the national health insurance; about ten percent are insured with private insurance companies. All persons with a monthly income of, presently, not more than 1,725 DM are subject to obligatory insurance; those with higher incomes may maintain their membership with the national health insurance.

Maternity care starts with precautionary checkups. A medical examination is provided at a very early stage of pregnancy and repeated every six weeks and, during the last two months, every two weeks. Additional checkups are provided after confinement.

Children of insured persons are eligible for free medical examinations to ensure early diagnosis of physical or mental handicaps and, on followup treatment, to the age of four.

Finally, advisory centers for mothers have been created at public health offices, and maternity courses are offered as well as child education. They offer advice and therapy with the assistance of physicians. These various activities are not administered centrally by any one government agency.

The motive to have many children—because some of them may die—to be safeguarded in case of old age or incapacity to work no longer exists. For one reason, more and more children reach adult age because of the rapid decline in infant and child mortality (96 out of 100 children born alive reach age thirty years). For another reason, the old-age insurance, already in effect at the end of the nineteenth century, secures the livelihood of old and sick persons. Around 92 percent of employed persons aged nineteen and over are members of the national social insurance, which means that they can claim state support during old age. In addition, the wives of employed men are insured, and social insurance has been extended to cover craftsmen, farmers, and other self-employed persons during recent years. Actually, very few persons in West Germany would be entirely dependent in their old age on the financial help of children or other relatives.

Combat against childbed and infant mortality is motivated by social and health policy. Improvements naturally affect population. Compared internationally, childbed mortality in West Germany was very high in 1971, with 50.5 deaths per 100,000 live births. (In 1960, it was 106.3.) Most European countries show much lower figures. Also, infant mortality in 1971, with 23.2 deaths per 1,000 live births during the first year of life (in 1960, it was 23.9), is much higher than in most other European countries and in the United States. Though there was a decrease in both childbed and infant mortality during the last decade, the causes for this high mortality are still being argued. The ministers of health of the federal *Laender* appointed a study group to examine the causes. The group proposed special analyses for childbed as well as for infant mortality. It is assumed that part of the differences with other countries is due to varying definitions.

To date, it is not yet possible to judge how far precautionary medical examinations for mothers and infants will help to reduce mortality. It has only been for a short time that these examinations are made more widely. Both the federal Ministry of Youth, Family, and Health and the medical associations devote great attention to this problem. Explanatory pamphlets and radio and television broadcasts draw the public's attention to special health dangers.

¶ EDUCATION

Because of the federated structure of the government, the federal *Laender* are responsible for all measures in the field of education. Compulsory elementary education lasts nine years.

Compulsory education and subsequent additional training are financial responsibilities of the family. Expenditures involve the livelihood of the child during school years, teaching aids, and foregoing income of juveniles who attend school full time instead of being employed. The increasing duration of education is regarded as one reason why couples want to have fewer children. Direct or indirect government assistance to extend education could affect population trends. School attendance is free in all federal *Laender*, and teaching aids are partially free. Gainful occupation of children is not allowed. Children over twelve years of age may do light agricultural work within exactly determined, narrow limits. There are government allowances for certain types of second grade (that is, higher level) schools (law on the Promotion of Education and Training of 1971). As a means of providing equal opportunities for children of all social strata, measures in the field of education also could be regarded as part of family policy in a broader sense.

THE EFFECTS OF POPULATION POLICY RELEVANT TO MEASURES ON BIRTH DEVELOPMENT

Politicians, administrative officials, and scientists largely agree that family policy should improve the social situation of the family and ensure for all children optimal conditions for their socialization and their educational opportunities. There is agreement that family policy, in particular those measures to provide economic relief, has had practically no influence on the number of children couples decide to have. Child allowances and tax advantages are far below the real costs necessary for raising and educating a child, the more so as these costs are inflated by the average high living standard. Little would be changed by far-reaching reform proposals to improve government aid to the family. Also, the necessary financing would only be available if drastic changes in the present income distribution and, consequently, in the system of social policy could be enforced. Political reasons most probably would prevent this change.

The inability of family policy to influence reproductive behavior arises, at least in part, from societal attitudes formed during the social and economic postwar development. One aspect of this development has been the vocational education for women that was promoted and supported by public opinion. Seventy women of one hundred aged 20–25 and fifty-three women of one hundred aged 25–30 presently are employed. These numbers include 80 percent of the single women and about half of the married women in these two age groups. Employed women tend to have smaller families.

From 1961 to 1971, the number of married women employed (outside of agriculture) increased by 44 percent. The highest increase was observed among women with children under fifteen years of age. On the one hand, this situation has arisen because a woman wants to perform in a profession in which she was trained and to be financially independent to a certain extent; on the other hand, it is caused by the chronic lack of manpower, in particular in the services, and the excess of jobs. Employers compete for each qualified worker who, in turn, bargains for special working conditions and favorable wages. Three-fifths of the married women with children are not employed full time, but hold part-time jobs or work a few hours a week. Thus, they attempt to coordinate their vocations and their duties as housewives and mothers.

Another indication of the relative inefficiency of the family allowances with regard to increasing births can be seen in the fact that families forego the children for which they would receive higher allowances and tax reductions, that is, the third, fourth, and additional children.

From 1960 to 1971, the number of births decreased for all female age groups. The decrease was most marked (by nearly one-half) among women aged 40–44. The decrease among women aged 25–29 was about one-third. With the youngest married mothers, fertility has increased somewhat over the decade; after 1966, however, it decreased in this age group as well.

The trend toward smaller average family size is demonstrated even more clearly in classifying live births by parity (see Table 1 and Figure 1).

The decrease in births arises mainly from a decrease in births at third and higher parities. The decrease in families with four children, that is, the large families, started as early as 1964; beginning in 1966, there was a tendency for three-child families to stop reproduction before a fourth child; and after 1968, the two-child families became more prevalent. The trend toward a smaller family with two children is clear.

TABLE 1.

Legitimate Live Births, Germany, 1964–1971
(by birth order and by actual numbers and percents)

Year	Total	1st	2nd	3rd	4th	5th+
		Legitimate Live Births of Which Born as ... Child				
Actual (rounded, in thousands)						
1964	1,012	404	316	156	69	67
1965	995	398	312	153	68	64
1966	1,002	399	316	156	68	63
1967	972	387	310	151	65	60
1968	924	370	295	143	60	55
1969	858	349	275	131	54	49
1970	767	321	244	113	47	42
1971	733	316	233	103	43	38
Percents (1964=100)						
1965	98.3	98.6	98.7	98.3	97.8	95.2
1966	99.0	98.8	100.0	100.2	98.4	93.6
1967	96.1	96.0	98.0	97.0	93.4	88.4
1968	91.2	91.6	93.3	92.0	87.2	81.7
1969	84.8	86.4	87.0	84.0	78.4	72.7
1970	75.7	79.6	77.1	72.3	67.8	62.0
1971	72.4	78.3	73.6	66.2	62.3	56.4

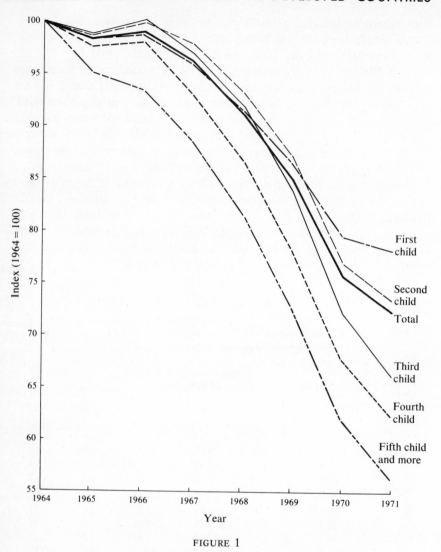

FIGURE 1

Legitimate Live Births by Birth Order, West Germany (1964 = 100)

At the same time, family formation is being delayed. In 1971, a first child was born on the average slightly later in the marriage than was the case in 1964; the intervals between births of second and third children increased, with the third child by one year compared to 1964 and the fourth child somewhat more than one year. Fifth, sixth, and further children, by 1971 data, are born about 1.5 years of marriage later than was true in 1964.

These findings point to an increasingly pursued and successful planning of the number of children, although married women of different age groups reveal differing intensity or efficacy of planning. Although there are no figures from surveys, it may be estimated that 80 percent of all women aged 20–45 practice family planning.

A couple's decision on the number of children they want or on the birth of another child is influenced by a series of factors in the microsphere of the family and the macrosphere of the society. It is not known how the single factors must be weighted because there has, as yet, been no survey in West Germany on the motives that caused birth decrease. Differences by religion no longer exist; yet there are differences by income. For all social denominational strata, couples with higher incomes have more children than do couples with lower incomes. After income, female employment and, perhaps, living conditions are probably most influential in determining family size.

OFFICIAL COMMENTS ON POPULATION PROBLEMS

As was pointed out earlier, there is an apparent discrepancy in the government position on population. The federal government has taken a large number of steps and enacted many laws that influence the size and structure of population, but has avoided, as has Parliament, developing an explicit population policy. This avoidance of policy may arise partly from a failure to analyze actions and conditions in a demographic context and partly from a reluctance for political reasons to formulate policy that might be construed as interfering with the freedom of the individual. The popular misconception that population policy is to be identified with National Socialist ideology is still widespread.

Konrad Adenauer was the only Chancellor who, in a government statement made before the second German Parliament in 1953, spoke of the necessity of population policy because of the constantly growing proportion of older persons, the declining proportion of the economically active, and the danger that declining production would make it impossible to care for the aged. Adenauer spoke of a "destructive process" that his government wanted to counteract by steps of family policy, housing policy, and educational policy. Part of such a "population policy" was the establishment of a new middle class. He further emphasized that the importance his government would attribute to these aims could be seen in the establishment of a special new Ministry of Family Affairs.

The first Minister of Family Affairs, who presided over the ministry for nine years, has, contrary to Adenauer, repeatedly stressed in speeches and articles that family policy and population policy are completely different matters. He has argued that family policy would only be harmed by being associated with population policy. Population policy was practiced in the prewar and war periods because state and society were interested in more children as the bearers of future collective functions. This, however, was not the objective of the federal government. The government would oppose this by saying that the children were not children of the state but children of the family. Society and state assist only insofar as parents could no longer master their duties alone. Evidently the minister did not follow his Chancellor's advice, for Adenauer is said to have stated that family policy should be aligned with population policy rather than with social ethics.

Actually population structure is always—although inconspicuously—incorporated in the reviews of the Ministry of Family Affairs. The annual reports of the minister regularly depict the birth decrease and the "worsening" of population structure. A 1968 government report on the situation of the family treats the demographic and sociocultural structures and tendencies in a detailed manner.

In 1970 and 1971, the political opposition (Christian Democratic Union) addressed Parliament several times and requested the government to make a statement on the extent and effects of the birth decrease. The opposition asked whether the government construed child allowances as an expression of population policy. The government evaded the question by replying that even family allowances as high as those in France played no significant role in determining reproductive behavior.

A first, though negative, approach in the field of population policy was found in a government statement of August 1972. Later that year, however, the Minister of the Interior made a much clearer statement. To the persistent questioning by the opposition about which steps the government intended to take to ensure an ample number of births, the government responded:

The federal government does not aim at a certain number of births in the future. The couple's freedom of decision should be maintained. A temporary birth decrease does not yet question population replacement as it is the long-term development which is relevant and which cannot be overlooked as yet.

In the last section of this statement, the government comments on its efforts to support the family unit. It was necessary to create the basic conditions in accordance with the fundamental ends of the Constitution to help the family best fulfill its pedagogic and social duties.

It is therefore necessary that definite measures to promote the family orientate themselves at this objective, not at aspects which intend to influence the natural population development in a certain tendency. Though consequently population policies and family policies each are independent spheres, the federal government does not deny their interrelations. Consequently long-term objectives as to population development and steps taken in the field of family policy, if any, should not be opposed in their effects.

As yet, there are no long-term objectives for population development. The reply emphasizes once more that the reform of child allowances was to better family economics.

Given that family policy is considered entirely as social policy, it appears only logical that child allowances are paid to aliens who are employed in West Germany. Arrangements have been made with the home countries (1959 with Spain, 1961 with Greece, 1964 with Turkey and Portugal, recently also with Italy and Yugoslavia). The allowances in German currency are also granted for children who still live in the home country. To the extent that these allowances are transferred to the home countries, the existing differences in currency and purchasing power may well effect relatively greater social compensation than in West Germany, possibly even at a level that may alter reproductive behavior in the home countries of aliens. Many of the alien workers in West Germany are paid child allowances. In June 1972, the 2,317,000 aliens employed in West Germany were from the following countries:

Turkey	497,300
Yugoslavia	471,900
Italy	422,200
Greece	269,700
Spain	184,000
Austria	99,300
Others	372,600

PARTY, TRADE UNION, AND SCIENTIFIC UNDERSTANDING OF POPULATION PROBLEMS

Although the government avoids a population policy stand in its official statements, the discussion outside government and Parliament does not come to an end. It has two focuses: the birth decrease and its possible effects, and employment of a growing number of aliens. In addition to the opposition party (Christian Democratic Union), the press, scientists, and recently, the trade unions are the primary participants in this discussion.

In former years, when the Christian Democratic Union was in power, it pursued family policy as a social goal. Recently, members of this rather conservative party, while giving family objectives first priority, have recommended efforts to alter population growth trends. They believe that family policy should, at least, attempt to stop the decrease in the birth rate and possibly increase the birth rate. Christian Democrats point out an inconsistency in that, on the one hand, a long-term reduction of the native population was encouraged by restricting births; whereas, on the other hand, employment of alien workers including family members was recommended to maximize economic growth. Future population development would have to secure a "balanced population figure," a term that is not further explained. It may be assumed from the discussion, though, that it is meant to, at least, maintain the present level of population.

A statement by groups close to the Christian Democratic Union cautions that, due to the high population density in West Germany and in the urban areas in particular, population expansion should, by no means, be advocated; however, such birth figures would be considered desirable as would assure population replacement. This aim should be within reach if the child allowances are increased so that each couple is able to raise and educate as many children as desired. From this point of view, the incorporation of population objectives and motives in the family policy is being advocated.

Besides these rather moderate voices, there are others in this public discussion who regard birth decrease as a danger to the nation and request steps to ensure the growth of the German population. Advocates of growth question whether it was necessary to secure population by immigration of aliens or by the birth of alien children. This position, which has its origins in nationalist ideology, overlooks the fact that further growth within an already densely inhabited country cannot but lead to a worsening of the quality of life. The deterioration of the environment originates not only from the growing number of people who use air, water, and other natural resources and who produce waste but also from the relatively great increase in the number of households. From 1961 to 1971, the population of West Germany grew by 9 percent, but the number of households grew by 17 percent.

Until now, the trade unions have not shown great interest in population problems in their programs on social policy. However, the employees' union, in its program of November 1971, commented on these questions—characteristically enough, in connection with family policy. The union requested that all steps taken to promote families should be based on obtaining "a balanced growth of population figures"; the development of wealth was not dependent on a growing population but on people trained in a modern and optimal manner. Without entering further into the problem of population development, the union appears to tend toward population stabilization.

Scientific discussion on population problems is limited to a small group of demographers assembled in the German Association for Population

Science. During their 1971 meeting, they discussed the problems of the birth decrease, its causes and consequences. Though this discussion brought more attention to the subject of population, no statement by politicians or administration officials was made.

In August 1972, a group of scientists—sociologists, behavioral scientists, environment experts—formed a group "Ecology" to deal in an interdisciplinary manner with the relationship between population and environment. Several members are of the opinion that, not only is it mandatory to stabilize population growth at its present level, but it is necessary to strive for a reduction of the number of people to regain ecological balance.

Representatives of the Christian churches have commented only very cautiously so far on the question of population growth and the interrelationship between population and environment. The conservative position of the Catholic church is known, in particular, with regard to contraceptives (interdiction to take the pill and to use other chemical and mechanical means) and refusal of abortion and sterilization. The representatives of the Protestant church are more tolerant. To them the question of family planning is a matter of personal choice. Population objectives have not been expressed by any religious group.

PRIVATE FAMILY PLANNING EFFORTS

The German branch of the International Planned Parenthood Federation was established in 1952 and started to work under the name "German Association for Marriage and Family, Pro Familia," with great difficulties. It was intended that this name would disguise the actual goal of the association, since at that time, particularly from the Catholic side, there was great opposition to dissemination of family planning information. Later on, Pro Familia called itself the "German Association for Family Planning," and today, it is called the "German Association for Sexual Advice and Family Planning," which points to a shifting of its functions. There is a branch association in each of the eleven federal *Laender*. It was only in 1969, when the coalition of Social Democrats and Liberals came into power, that the federation granted financial aid to Pro Familia and recognized it as an important advisory institution. This financial support of 120,000 DM per year does not suffice, and for this reason, family planning in West Germany has not yet found universal acceptance as it has in Great Britain, for example. What is missing, above all, is a good motivation for family planning in all social strata and a positive sexual attitude. The present forty advisory offices are, by no means, sufficient for comprehensive sex education of the population. Besides, there are shortages of well-trained social workers, physicians, psychologists, and psychotherapists. Nevertheless, the government has recognized Pro Familia as worthy of advancement and as important for family formation.

POPULATION DISTRIBUTION

In 1965, Parliament enacted a law on physical planning. One goal of urban and rural planning is the development of the federal territory in the optimum way to serve the individual within the community. Above all, living conditions are to be improved and environmental damages removed. Planning and measures by federal, land, and local authorities are to be coordinated. Every two years, the government is to submit a report on physical planning to Parliament.

To date, reports are available for the years 1966, 1968, and 1970. They include an abundance of material on population and employment opportunities; regional development trends projected to the year 1980; the federal program for physical planning; agglomeration areas within federal territory; human environment; traffic; training of regional planning experts; and international cooperation, to name only the most important items. The 1970 report states that technical and social developments have led to disproportions in use of space. Development strategy to influence population redistribution provides for two possibilities, the active reorganization of a region and the passive reorganization. Active reorganization involves stimulating capital and qualified workers to flow into a certain region. Under passive reorganization, people living in areas that can be developed no further are offered training to facilitate their migration into other regions, while a minimum of public services is ensured for the remaining population. The objective is to arrive at a regional redistribution of the population based on voluntary decisions to migrate into developing areas. The basis for physical planning, especially urban and rural planning, is the ecological capacity of a region. More recreation and leisure-time services are to be established in the vicinity of agglomeration areas; settlements and working places are to be regionally concentrated; an ecological balance between rural regions and agglomeration areas is to be generated; and urban renewal is to keep distributing industries away from living and recreation districts. Public investments, then, serve to improve the infrastructure of one region and the traffic among several regions. Neither in the law on physical planning nor in the reports mentioned can direct population objectives be found.

All measures intended to effect population redistribution are of an indirect nature. Enforcement is not possible as the Constitution grants every German citizen the right to live wherever he chooses. Considering the freedom for everybody to choose his place of residence, it is doubtful whether the measures for the active and passive reorganization will be successful. There is still an increasing agglomeration in those areas which offer especially good working and living conditions, an attractive landscape, and leisure-time activities. Since the steps taken for reorganization have only become valid during the last few years, their success remains to be seen.

In 1970 (last population census), 32.4 percent of the population lived in cities with 100,000 or more inhabitants, 18.8 percent in towns from 20,000–100,000 inhabitants, and 48.8 percent in communities with less than 20,000 inhabitants. From 1960 until 1970, the proportion of persons living in large- or medium-sized towns decreased; the proportions for communities with less than 20,000 inhabitants increased. There is generally a tendency to move into the outskirts of towns or into metropolitan areas and to use a daily commutation to work. The proportion of commuters among the active population has increased constantly; in 1971, it was 28.3 percent. The stagnating growth of the large cities contrasts with the extension of the smaller communities which continuously lose their rural atmosphere and, together with the cities, grow into one agglomeration area.

FINAL REMARKS

Population development in West Germany during the last decade has raised numerous questions and efforts at solution. Although there are a clear labor market policy, a family policy, a social policy, and physical planning policies, objectives and measures concerning population policy are almost completely missing. Not least among the reasons for the absence of population policy is the disbursement of responsibility for population-related problems among too many ministries and agencies.

In the nineteenth century, the interior administration was responsible for population; logically, today, it is the responsibility of the federal Ministry of the Interior. However, it is not possible for the Minister of the Interior to have the sole responsibility, and consequently, problems relevant to health policy and family policy are handled by the Minister of Youth, Family, and Health; those relevant to labor market policy and social policy are handled by the Minister of Labor and Social Affairs.

In 1971, for example, the latter formed an ad hoc commission to analyze the effects of the birth decrease. Members of the commission were representatives of the federal Ministry of Labor and Social Affairs. They were to examine to what extent birth decrease and the resulting shifts in the age structure might later jeopardize the payment of rents and pensions by the economically active population. Although problems of employment and rent development were foremost, this commission was called the "pill commission" by the public. Its findings were published, but they were not submitted to Parliament. The committee concluded that the birth decrease then recognized would endanger neither the economic development nor the social security of the old. Now that the birth decrease continues, these findings are considered out of date by the public, and new analyses have been requested.

Latest developments indicate that the federal government is gradually discarding the standpoint of laissez faire in population. After several years of planning, the Federal Minister of the Interior established the Institute for Population Research. The institute belongs to the Ministry of the Interior but cooperates closely with the federal Statistical Office. The functions of the institute are:

(1) To conduct scientific research in the field of population and related family questions as a basis for the work of the federal government.

(2) To collect, evaluate, and in particular, publish scientific findings in this field.

(3) To inform the federal government about major developments and research results and to advise it on individual problems.

Focal points of the institute's work will be analyses of the following:

(1) Changes in the number of births and the possible influence on, among others, educational planning, labor force potential, and old-age insurance.

(2) Changes in age structure and the influences on the economic and social situation of the aged.

(3) The economic significance of child allowances for families of different social strata as well as the effect of the family equalization of burdens.

(4) The connection between population developments in developing countries and the efficiency of developing aid.

(5) Changes of population development caused by the admission of alien workers and consequences for the labor market, intensified infrastructure (schools, and so forth), integration, and assimilation.

The institute will keep close contact with scientific institutions at home and abroad.

It is remarkable that it was the federal government that established a research institute for population problems and not the scientific sector or the universities. The backwardness of West Germany in the field of demography still exists. Only two university professors teach demography, and none of the universities has a special research institution.

Though it will be difficult in a pluralistic democratic society to reach consensus on population policy objectives—even if such objectives can be substantiated rationally by facts and trends—recently, there has been the deepening opinion that it is necessary to both limit and stabilize population growth. During a television broadcast after the elections to Parliament in November 1969, when the Social-Liberal coalition won majority, the federal Ministry of the Interior for the first time formulated population policy objectives, based on the proposition that the legal order of West Germany places marriage and family under its special protection. The following proposals for government population policy have been made:

(1) The freedom of couples to decide on the number of children they want to have and on the time they want to have them must be guaranteed.
(2) The state has to guarantee to all its citizens the right to a life that maintains the dignity of man.
(3) The protection of marriage and family does not oblige the state to aim at the family with many children as a population policy objective.

It is the opinion of the Ministry of the Interior that this framework for government population policy should not rigidly eliminate other desirable developments. A stationary population would appear to suit the conditions of a densely populated country with its environment problems, more so than a heavily increasing population. Consequently, the aim of government population policy should consider this problem.

It appears that the stage of government ignorance in the field of population policy has come to an end. The problems of birth decrease and its consequences, the employment of alien workers, the air and water pollution, the disproportion between ecological conditions and population development, the growing understanding of quality of life being more important than the number of people and, finally, the awareness that the growth ethic can no longer exist with a densely populated industrial society—all this will compel politicians and administrators to develop a population concept that guarantees a worthy life in the future.

CHAPTER 23

Japan

Minoru Muramatsu
Toshio Kuroda

The views presented in this document are not necessarily the official
views and opinions of the government of Japan. The authors
prepared this paper in their individual capacities.

ABSTRACT

In Japan, as in other countries, the reduction of mortality has been an
unquestionably important policy, although it is treated independently and
not as part of population policy.

The control of fertility has been primarily a matter of individual concern. With regard to the numerical growth of population, a number of
programs with demographic implications have been adopted in the past,
but no "explicit" population policy has ever been enforced. The only
exception was the clearly pronatalist policy effected in 1941.

During the 1920s and 1930s, in some quarters of society, there emerged
concern over population growth in relationship, first, to food, and later,
to employment. However, with the nation's move toward the preparations
for war, the subject became severely suppressed.

The devastation of the whole country after the war caused a grave concern about Japan's overpopulation among the general public as well as
official bodies, and the awareness of the necessity for population control
grew rapidly. Between 1945 and 1960, a series of population-related programs were put into effect, such as the liberalization of induced abortion
in 1948 and the implementation of a national family planning program in
1952. In a sense, these may be regarded as demographic measures, but
official statements indicated that the main considerations were not directly
related to population control.

With the completion of demographic transition and the rapid growth of the national economy by 1960, the focus of attention in the population field showed a conspicuous shift from the problems of number to those of structure. Interest in family planning waned considerably, and such issues as the declining young labor force or the aging of the population came to the fore. In 1969, the Population Problems Advisory Council recommended a slight upsurge of birth rates. In 1971, the council emphasized the need for social development policies as they saw numerous difficulties arising from the one-sided concentration on economic development. Also, the imbalance of the distribution of population is now drawing the keen attention of those concerned with national planning and the so-called regional development program is underway, aiming at the dispersion of industries so that, in turn, population may be properly redistributed on a voluntary basis.

Quite recently, more people have begun to see population growth in relationship to problems characteristic of developed countries: environmental degradation, depletion of natural resources, and the impingement on space. This may lead to an eventual change in growth ideology of population and foster a recognition of the global nature of population—no country can remain free from the impact of the population problems of others on the surface of this already shrunken earth.

FERTILITY AND THE GROWTH OF POPULATION

¶ TOKUGAWA PERIOD

It is accepted generally by Japanese demographers that the population of Japan accelerated during the first half of the Tokugawa period (1603–1867) but that the growth slowed down during the second half approaching a standstill. There were many reasons for this stagnant population growth: famines, epidemics, abortion, infanticide, and the postponement of marriage. Widespread practice of abortion and infanticide was particularly characteristic of the late Tokugawa period. Poverty in rural areas not only increased abortion and infanticide but also precipitated out-migration of farmers into towns and cities. The Tokugawa Shogunate and local feudal clans were concerned with these events and took measures for encouraging marriage and birth, prohibiting abortion and infanticide, restricting the out-movement of farmers, and sending town people forcibly back to farms. These measures were not effective, but it should be noted that as early as two centuries ago, a population policy in its broad sense, including both aspects of fertility and spatial distribution, actually was adopted in Japan. The Japanese people indicated in the seventeenth century a "demographic multiphasic response" [1].

¶ PRIOR TO WORLD WAR II

After the Meiji Restoration (1868), population problems came to be a major interest of a few scholars, but they were not a matter of national concern until 1918 when the so-called Rice Riot occurred. Protesting against high prices of rice, the traditional staple food of the Japanese, a large number of underprivileged people rioted in many parts of the country, destroying rice shops and public establishments. The government policy was criticized, and the population problem was gradually brought to the attention of many individuals. As a result, during the 1920s, a number of social scientists entered into a debate over the population growth in Japan, with some favoring Malthusian and others leaning toward Marxian doctrines. The visit of Margaret Sanger in 1922 gave a strong stimulus to advocates of birth control, although she was not allowed to talk about the subject in public.

In 1927, a Commission for the Study of the Problems of Population and Food Supply was organized by the government. Eight reports were submitted on the following items to the government by this commission between 1927 and 1930: internal and external colonization, adjustment of the labor supply, population policy in the colonies, population control, promotion of industry, improvement of the distribution and consumption of national wealth, and the establishment of a government social affairs department.

The commission was abolished in 1930. During its three-year term, however, the central issue shifted from the problem of food to that of employment. Unemployment and underemployment increased greatly as a result of the world economic depression in the late 1920s.

In the early 1930s, Professor T. Ueda became seriously concerned with population problems [2]. He established a private group to study the problems, and he pointed out that the increase in the productive age groups could not be accommodated by reduction in the current fertility and that unemployment in cities and underemployment in villages would create a social danger unless employment opportunities were rapidly enlarged. His policy conclusions included further industrialization and urbanization, together with the spread of contraceptive practices.

During the 1930s, however, the general political atmosphere of the country became increasingly antagonistic to birth control. Rapid population increase was thought essential for the future of the nation. Voluntary birth control movements were suppressed; during the period 1935–1945, their activities were practically nonexistent. Dissemination of birth control information was considered to endanger the national interest.

In January 1931, the Regulations for the Control of Harmful Contraceptive Devices were put into effect. Intracervical pins and stems were the main target for control, but later in 1936, intrauterine devices which had gained in popularity also were included.

In 1940, the National Eugenic Law was promulgated. It provided a legal basis for the performance of induced abortion and sterilization, but its overall purpose was to enforce official restrictions on them as far as possible.

In January 1941, a national policy of expanding population size was adopted. The policy statement urged strongly that all the efforts be directed toward increasing the birth rate in order to carry out the war and set a target of 100 million population in Japan proper by 1960. The statement recommended a broad range of maternal and child care services. This was the only occasion in the modern era when the government adopted an explicit population policy in its strictest sense. It represented the culmination of all the pronatalist attitudes that prevailed during the decades prior to the end of the war. The effectiveness of the policy, however, was much in doubt; at least it could not significantly reverse the long-range downward trend in fertility that had been under way in association with economic development, urbanization, and the common desire for a small family.

¶ AFTER WORLD WAR II, PHASE 1: FROM 1945 TO ABOUT 1960

The defeat in World War II was accompanied by a complete turnabout in the general attitude toward birth control and population growth. In 1946, 1947, and 1948, a large number of Japanese nationals returned to Japan either as demobilized soldiers or as repatriates. Even offsetting emigrants against immigrants, a net gain of some 5 million was recorded over the three years. This in itself was a significant factor in population increase, but the resultant "baby boom" in the postwar years gave an additional burden to the war-devastated economy. The general public realized that overpopulation of the country was posing a serious threat to their daily life as well as to the nation's future economic recovery.

During these years, a large number of debates and discussions about population took place among both leading circles and the general masses. Daily newspapers carried articles related to population and birth control; public forums were held from time to time; and radio programs discussed the problems. Some observers, because of their political ideologies or religious beliefs, violently opposed the adoption of birth control as a solution to postwar difficulties, but by and large, people reacted favorably. Gradually the number of births began to decline while the number of induced abortions increased.

In 1949, two American demographers, Warren Thompson and P. K. Whelpton, visited Japan as consultants to the General Headquarters of the Occupation Forces. Their recommendation of birth limitation received wide publicity through news media and magazines. In the same year, Margaret Sanger was denied a permit to enter Japan on the grounds that her visit would be used for political purposes [3, p. 370, footnote 25].

In 1950, the Mainichi Newspapers Service conducted its first KAP (knowledge, attitudes, and practice) survey on birth control. To the question, "Do you think a slowdown in population growth is beneficial to our country?" 34 percent replied "yes" and 28 percent answered "no." (The remaining 38 percent gave "don't know" answers.) In 1952 and also in 1954, Margaret Sanger paid further visits to Japan. Her oral testimony before the Diet as to the possible benefits derived from the widespread practice of birth control, the audience she was given by the Emperor, and her advice to create a voluntary planned parenthood group in the country were reported in the mass media. In 1955, the Fifth International Conference on Planned Parenthood was organized by the IPPF and convened in Tokyo. The real significance of this event, perhaps, lay more in the psychological influence it exerted over the Japanese people than in the various technical particulars presented during the deliberations, although they included the first substantial report on oral pills by Gregory Pincus.

On the official side, during the period under consideration, a number of expert committees or councils on population were established. Some were attached directly to a ministry; other were more autonomous. Also, small "study groups" on population-related matters were organized in the upper and lower houses of the Diet. These committees and councils functioned mostly as advisory bodies, with the responsibility of submitting necessary recommendations or resolutions but without the power to enforce the measures and programs they suggested.

In 1946, a Population Planning Committee established with the Foundation Institute for Research on Population Problems submitted a proposal on the fundamental course and aim of population policy to the government [4]. It stated that the balance between the population and the carrying capacity of the country had been lost and that the unprecedented overpopulation was an undeniable problem. Two countermeasures were to be explored: one, an increase in the capacity for supporting population, and the other, the regulation of population growth. As to the possibility of increasing the capacity, the committee was pessimistic. Its members feared that surplus population would continue and that there might be no way left except requesting the sympathetic cooperation of foreign countries in peaceful emigration from Japan.

The postwar baby boom accelerated the gravity of the problem. In 1949, a Population Problems Advisory Council was established at the request of the Prime Minister. It was organized into two subcommittees: one, on population supporting capacity, and the other, on population control. On November 29, 1949, the council made interim recommendations to the government after a month's deliberations [5]. Its general conclusion was as follows: "The solution of our problems demands not only the suppression of population expansion through birth control but also emigration overseas coupled with the rehabilitation of domestic industry and restoration of foreign trade for enhancing the country's population supporting capacity" [p. 2].

The council realized that the implementation of its recommendations in the economic field or with reference to emigration was severely limited. Those recommendations that were concerned with the "adjustment of population," on the other hand, contained the following four items:

Recommendations in Respect to
Adjustment of Population

In order to prevent a sharp increase in the population which will have adverse effects on the economic reconstruction and promotion of public health in this country, and to bring a sound and cultural life to realization, it is considered necessary to furnish married couples with necessary information on contraception by teaching reasonable methods and to give guidance of conception control to all classes of our nation so that married couples can regulate the number of births freely and voluntarily by means of conception control.

It is essential to take into consideration the following points in order to attain the said objects. These are necessary:

(A) Immediate improvement of the equipment in health centers, Eugenic Marriage Consultation Offices, and other similar organizations throughout this country and mobilization thereof for the said purpose; education and training for those who take charge of the actual business of the above organizations; education by nation-wide medical training institutions on the population problem, family planning, eugenic protection, and the techniques of conception control.

(B) It is particularly desirable that efforts be made to enlighten those classes among whom contraceptive information and means are most difficult to spread and that positive measures be taken at the same time to enable them to secure the proper means of contraception free of charge through a partial revision of the Daily Life Security Law.

(C) It is necessary to establish a government office exclusively in charge of administrative affairs concerning the population problem in order to give nation-wide guidance in family planning and eugenic protection enterprises. It is also desirable, in this connection, to expand the work of the Institute of Population Problems and the Institute of Public Health with a view to collective operation of population administration.

(D) It is essential to exercise precaution to maintain good social customs and morals when information on conception control is furnished and when efforts are made to popularize this control [5, pp. 11–12].

This Population Problems Advisory Council, however, was terminated in March 1950. No concrete action was taken pursuant to these recommendations immediately afterward, but they were of value in the sense that they laid a foundation for the subsequent 1951 Cabinet decision on birth control that, in turn, resulted in the establishment of a national family planning program in Japan.

In August 1951, the Foundation Institute for Research on Population Problems, a quasi-governmental organization charged with the task of examining the population situation and advising the administration, issued an official document, the "Population White Paper." The need for rapid widespread dissemination of birth control was emphasized again.

The Foundation Institute for Research on Population Problems further continued its study on comprehensive national population policies. Two subcommittees were established within the institute: one, on population and the standard of living, and the other, on the quantitative adjustment of population. The former was responsible for the problems of under-employment and unemployment. Pointing to the fact that the number of new entrants in the labor market would exceed 1 million each year, it called for the adoption of every possible measure to alleviate the grave situation of employment as part of population policy. The latter subgroup considered the diffusion of family planning most essential for the reduction of population pressure in Japan and resolved that it should be promoted as a population policy.

On the basis of the work by these two subcommittees, another Population Problems Advisory Council, which was created in 1953 at the request of the Minister of Health and Welfare, submitted two recommendations in 1954 and 1958. The 1954 recommendation, concerning the quantitative adjustment of population, recognized the persistent overpopulation of the country and emphasized the need for family planning to be regarded explicitly as a population control measure, as indicated in the following resolution they issued:

Resolution in Regard to the Quantitative Adjustment of Population
(Passed August 24, 1954)

In order to solve the grave population problems which this country is facing nowadays, it is needless to say that measures should be taken to increase the capacity to support the population. In view of the present situation, however, where the heavy pressure of population is detrimental to the successful accumulation of capital as well as to the rationalization of industries, it is necessary for the government to adopt policies to curb the population increase.

The movement for the popularization of the practice of conception control, which thus far has been put into operation, should be conducted not only from the standpoint of the protection of mother's health but also from the standpoint of family planning as part of overall population policies. Steps should be taken so that adequate means and facilities are afforded to all individuals who desire to limit childbirths, and also that all the obstacles and frictions which are making difficult the successful dissemination of family planning are removed. It is necessary for the government to adopt these measures.

Induced abortion, which is widely prevalent today, very often is followed by another pregnancy. Therefore, the operation usually must be repeated frequently if it is to be effective for the limitation of births. This necessarily incurs undesirable effects upon the health of the mother. For these reasons, the government is recommended speedily to take necessary measures not to let the present situation follow its natural course.

In regard to the dissemination and popularization of the practice of family planning, due attention must be paid to possible changes in the eugenic quality of the population, which may occur as a result [6, pp. 37–38].

Attached to this resolution, the council submitted nine recommended procedures which contained even such a strong statement as: "In relation to wage payments as well as the taxation system, measures should be taken to avoid provisions which may be interpreted as encouraging large families" [p. 39].

Thus, a series of recommendations and resolutions came forth from committees and councils, all calling for the intensification of fertility limitation programs. However, in almost no instance did the government take decisive action as a direct response to the suggested policy recommendations. A national family planning program was initiated in 1952, but it was primarily from the viewpoint of health. As far as birth control as a population control measure is concerned, no explicit implementation of policy was enforced. On the whole, the most significant role played by these advisory groups was to alert the public to population problems and thereby speed up the process of nation-wide diffusion of birth control practice.

Liberalization of Induced Abortion.

In 1947, three Diet members initiated a bill liberalizing regulations on induced abortion and contraception to replace the outmoded National Eugenic Law. The bill did not qualify on procedural grounds for discussion in the Diet.

In 1948, six other Diet members joined the movement to liberalize the laws. The main focus was placed on induced abortion, and the consideration of contraception was omitted. The Eugenic Protection Law of 1948 was established, setting an example of extreme liberalism toward induced abortion. With the subsequent amendments, especially those of 1949 and 1952, the treatment of induced abortion was broadened to include economic indications (in conjunction with health reasons) and to leave the performance of an abortion to the discretion of one medical practitioner.

The primary purpose of the Eugenic Protection Law remains a subject of debate to this day. Since its creation, some have maintained that the law was clearly meant to be an explicit population control policy; others have emphasized the health components contained in it. Typical of efforts to interpret the intent of the law is the following abstract from a professional book published in 1950:

In general, a law always has an ultimate aim beyond what is written in the book as its direct purpose. The Eugenic Protection Law, too, has its ultimate aim in addition to the two primary purposes as given in Article One: the "prevention of the birth of genetically inferior offspring" and the "protection of the health of mothers."

What then is the ultimate aim? To this question, many mention the solution of population problems and regard the Law as a means to cope with the problem of overpopulation.

At the time when the Law was submitted in the Diet, overpopulation was becoming an overwhelming issue among the public, and our journalists made it a rule to describe the Law in association with population. Partly because of this influence, there are many who believe that the primary intention of the Law was to try to solve the problem of overpopulation.

If, however, we look closely into the way in which the Law was discussed in the Diet, we must remember the fact that the proponents of the Law repeatedly emphasized the absence of such association between the two issues. From this standpoint, we somehow have to conclude that the Law was not related to demographic considerations.

On the other hand, the situation as we see it today after one year's operation of the Law, has undergone some changes. A few official groups such as the Population Problem Advisory Council established this year (1949) are recommending actively the widespread use of birth control for population control. In accordance with these developments, the Law was recently amended in part, and it is being proposed that the birth control guidance be carried out by a network of government agencies.

If viewed by such a recent trend, it appears undeniable that what was expected of the Law was its possible contribution to the solution of our population problems, no matter what the stated purpose of the Law may have been or no matter what explanations the original proponents may have offered [7, pp. 122–123].

That induced abortion is a delicate issue for policy makers is well illustrated in these passages. We would have to conclude from this description that the probable demographic effects of the law were taken into account when it was passed, but that the legislators and the government avoided any overt acknowledgment of them.

Authorization of the Manufacture and Sale
of Contraceptive Devices and Drugs.
With the enforcement of the new Constitution in 1947, many laws and regulations established prior to 1945 became subject to review and revi-

sion. In the field of contraceptive devices and drugs, a set of new standards was formulated along with the creation of new pharmaceutical laws.

The new standards for contraceptive devices, announced in September 1949, authorized the manufacture and sale of condoms, diaphragms, and sponges as long as the devices met specifications. The official prohibition of the use of intrauterine rings, which was introduced in 1936, remained valid on the ground that the devices were medically harmful. By the end of 1949, a total of twenty-six brands of contraceptive drugs were authorized by the Ministry of Health and Welfare. However, many contained materials of inferior quality, and in 1950, when a system of national assay was put into effect, only a few passed the examination.

These official actions illustrate the positive attitude of the government toward birth control in sharp contrast to the negative policy before the war. As was mentioned, the government avoided supporting birth control as a population control policy per se. But when a decision was required on practical matters, as with contraceptive materials, the administrative authorities showed little hesitation in responding to public demands.

Government-Sponsored Program
for the Promotion of Contraception.

In October 1951, in a Cabinet meeting discussion of induced abortion and contraception, the members expressed concern at the increase in induced abortions and associated health problems. The following is the statement issued on that occasion:

> The number of abortions is increasing each year. These are often necessary to protect the life and health of the mother. Occasional damage to the mother's health, however, makes the dissemination of the knowledge of contraception desirable to eliminate the bad influence of abortions on the mother's health. To accomplish this, the government has already provided the Eugenic Marriage Consultation Offices and trained instructors in the teaching of contraception, etc. For the welfare of the people, however, this information should be more widely disseminated and means for making it more effective should be studied.
> *Recommendation*: Abortion has undesirable effects on maternal health. It is therefore necessary to disseminate contraceptive information to decrease these undesirable effects [6, pp. 35–36].

Pursuant to this statement, the Ministry of Health and Welfare compiled in 1952 a document elaborating an official program for the promotion of contraception. Contraceptive methods recommended were of the type commonly called traditional. Midwives (with fairly high education, distinct from "granny" midwives) were assigned responsibility for teaching contraception.

Neither the Cabinet statement nor the program for contraception mentioned population control as a purpose. Administrators from the Ministry of Health and Welfare, when speaking to local officials about the program, emphasized repeatedly the program's objective as a health measure for the protection of mothers. The fact that the execution of the program had been assigned to the Ministry of Health and Welfare was, in itself, indicative of the purpose, they asserted. However, it was again obvious that the program had other implications. When the Minister of Health and Welfare, the chief of the governmental department in charge of the program, instructed local health officers on this particular duty, he stressed the program's importance "because of its influence on population growth." As was the case when the Eugenic Protection Law was introduced in 1948, the justification for the policy was to improve public health, but its effect was also demographic.

¶ AFTER THE WAR, PHASE 2: A DECADE FROM ABOUT 1960
The late 1950s can be regarded as a turning point in socioeconomic and demographic developments in Japan. The so-called demographic transition was almost completed by then, and both birth and death rates began to fluctuate at low levels, resulting in an annual growth rate of 1 percent. A norm of two, or at most three, children per couple was widespread throughout the country.

Enormous progress was recorded in the economy during the 1960s. Throughout the decade, the annual rate of economic growth was almost always higher than 10 percent. Capital investments expanded at an un-precedented pace, and industries grew tremendously. Aided by the slow-down of birth rates and the resultant decrease in population growth, the level of per-capita income and the standard of living rose significantly.

These striking developments in the economic sphere of society were accompanied by a gradual shift in the emphasis on population matters. In a word, the shift can be summarized as one from concern about growth to concern about structural and distribution aspects of population. More stress was placed on the problems associated with the change in age composition, spatial distribution, regional development planning, the need for social development, and the enhancement of the quality of human resources in order to support the desired economic growth.

A "White Paper on Population" was published in 1959 by the Popula-tion Problems Advisory Council. In its conclusion, it listed three major points: (1) employment problems arising from the rapid increase in work-ing age groups, (2) further promotion of contraception to replace the wide-spread resort to induced abortion, and (3) high incidence of physical and mental diseases among the economically less privileged.

Subsequent discussion in official circles began to emphasize the improve-ment of "population quality" as a basis of population policy. Economic growth policies could not achieve their objectives without manpower endowed with high physical, mental, and intellectual ability. The proportion of young adults to the total population would inevitably decline, and the quality of the next generation who would become responsible for society in the future was a matter of concern. So far, the overall policy had been prejudiced to economic growth without due regard to social development. The need for social development to ensure the qualitative improvement of the population was urgent, they maintained. In addition, the imbalance of population distribution between urban and rural areas began to cause various problems on both sides. When the Population Problems Advisory Council submitted its resolution to the Minister of Health and Welfare in 1963, they urged the adoption of regional development and population redistribution planning from the standpoint of population policy.

Along with such a shift in emphasis on population matters, interest in population growth and fertility also underwent a change. In contrast to the overwhelming concern about overpopulation during the preceding decade, increasing numbers of individuals, especially those holding important positions in the economy, started to express misgivings about the fluctuation of birth rates at low levels. The labor shortage—the shortage of young workers in particular—became a serious problem in enterprises of medium or small size. A tendency for more graduates from middle or high schools to seek higher education contributed to the shortage. Also, statistical evidence that Japan's net reproduction rates fell below the replacement level in several years gave rise to concern that the population of the nation was diminishing.

Thus, in some quarters of society, the feeling grew that the continuation of low fertility was not advantageous. Although not advocating pronatalist policies and program immediately, supporters of this position hoped that an increase in births would be brought about in some way in order to secure a labor force large enough to maintain economic growth.

With reference to the national family planning program operated by the Ministry of Health and Welfare, the budgetary appropriations allocated to the program during the 1960s were generally lower than those during the late 1950s. One might say that the official family planning activities actually were reduced even more significantly than the smaller amounts would indicate because of inflation. The government-sponsored family planning program is still being carried out today, but its scope and coverage have been on the decline.

Until 1960, the emphasis in family planning was on limitation of births; after 1960 and especially during the latter half of the 1960s, those working for family planning promotion stressed that the true meaning of family planning was not to limit births but rather to have as many children as a couple wanted.

In April 1969, the Mainichi Newspapers Service conducted its tenth survey on birth control. Although the vast majority of respondents endorsed the practice of family planning as a matter of individual concern, only 15 percent expressed the opinion that a slowdown in population growth was favorable for the nation, whereas 35 percent felt that it was disadvantageous. In the 1950 survey by the same newspapers, more respondents had favored lowered population growth rates than opposed them; in the course of two decades, public opinion swung to the opposite direction according to survey results.

1969 Interim Report by the Population Problems Advisory Council.
In August 1969, the Population Problems Advisory Council submitted its interim report at the request of the Minister of Health and Welfare, focusing its attention on the low fertility levels [8].

Stating that the reproduction rates of the Japanese people now were among the lowest in the world, and also that the below-unity net reproduction rates observed during the preceding ten years would, if continued, suggest a "decrease in the size of the population of Japan after a generation or so," the report urged the restoration of the nation's fertility. Because of the already large population and high density in Japan, the report did not advocate boundless expansion in numbers; instead, it recommended a "stationary population" as a desirable goal. As a means to attain the goal, the report proposed social development programs rather than explicit pronatalist programs, in the hope that if socioeconomic deterrents to childbirth and childrearing were decreased, the number of births would rise. Further, the report cautioned that any abrupt change in fertility was not advisable since it would bring about unfavorable distortions in the age structure of population.

In essence, the report of this Population Problems Advisory Council (1) expressed concern over Japan's low fertility levels, (2) urged the recovery of fertility slightly but not substantially, and (3) suggested indirect measures to attain the goal of stationary population.

The impact of the report lay in two major areas. The first is the sensational treatment accorded the report in some of the Japanese mass media. Editorials described the low birth rates as shocking and implied that the population of Japan was already declining. The mass media may have misunderstood the report because of its lengthy treatment of such technicalities as net reproduction rates and its failure to explain sufficiently that these figures were only projections based upon certain assumptions and that the population of Japan was bound to increase in size for several decades even if the current near-replacement rates were maintained. At the same time, the hope for more births entertained by some influential groups of society was reflected significantly in such reactions as well as in the report itself.

The second point of impact lies in the report's position as the first official document on population policy in a developed country to recommend zero population growth. Unfortunately, this point was not given due publicity, because it was overshadowed by the "depopulation scare."

Since the report was issued, no explicit measures or programs to encourage more births have been enforced in direct response to it. As with the recommendations and resolutions of the previous committees and councils, the report mainly served to inform and advise the government, but the council has had no definite power for program implementation.

¶ CURRENT SITUATION

In 1970, a total of 1,934,239 live births was registered. Of this total, the first born accounted for 45.4 percent; second born, 39.0; third born, 12.7; and the remaining 2.9 percent was for the fourth and over.

According to the information obtained by the 1971 Mainichi Newspapers Service's survey on birth control, the proportion of those practicing contraception and the methods employed are shown in Table 1.

The ratio between the reported number of abortions and that of live births for 1971 was 739,674:2,022,204 = 37:100.

The estimation of the real number of abortions (reported plus unreported) varies widely among researchers. If we take the lowest and the highest estimates and recalculate the above ratio, abortion:live birth = 50:100 − 140:100.

IUDs and Oral Pills: Laws and Practice.

Although a few Japanese medical people started their own work on IUDs as early as the 1930s, current legal regulations do not approve the general use of IUDs, since the 1936 prohibitions are still in force. However, there is a saving clause attached to the prohibitions to the effect that IUDs may be used under proper medical supervision for experimental purposes. It is because of this provision that about 8 percent of those practicing contraception reported the use of Ota ring (a Japanese IUD) in 1971, as noted in Table 1. Late in 1971, a special committee, established within the Japanese Association of Obstetrics and Gynecology for the study of the devices, submitted its recommendation to the Minister of Health and Welfare and stated that the ban on IUDs should be removed. Since then, however, no official action has been effected.

With regard to the use of oral pills, no official sanction has been accorded by the Ministry of Health and Welfare, though several applications for authorization have been put forward. Fear of possible harmful effects after long-term administration and a peculiarly loose system of sales of drugs in

TABLE 1.

Survey on Birth Control, Japan, 1971
(data from 3,223 married women under fifty years of age)

Item	Percent
Practicing contraception	
Currently	52.6
Ever practiced	20.2
Never practiced	16.8
No answer	10.4
Methods used	
Condoms	72.7[a]
Safe period	32.9
Intrauterine rings[b]	8.1
Withdrawal	5.8
Foam tablets	5.5
Jellies	5.3
Sterilization	3.9
Diaphragms	3.2
Oral pills[b]	1.5

SOURCE: The Mainichi Newspapers Service, 1971.
[a] Some women gave more than one method and all the entries were enumerated. Thus the total exceeds 100 percent.
[b] Rings and oral pills are not permitted officially. But they may be prescribed by physicians on their own decision and judgment.

Japan are said to be major reasons for disapproval. However, a number of practicing physicians deem it their professional right to prescribe the pills when they believe in their necessity and value. The fact that the same compounds are being sold as remedies for female disorders (not as contraceptives) also accounts for a small number of women who actually depend on oral pills.

Changing Views on Population Growth.

Until recently, there has been relatively little discussion about policy consideration of population growth in Japan. Occasionally news media have reported population statistics released by official agencies and other related topics, but in general, one has not encountered serious policy discussions about the size and future growth of the population of Japan. On the whole, it has been understood that birth control and family planning are matters of individual concern, not subject to external intervention.

Nothing is more heavily charged with individual values than the growth of human population. And the values are so divergent. At present, views apparently are divided among individuals and groups as to whether Japan is overpopulated or still has room to accommodate more inhabitants. Accordingly, whether it is advisable to encourage more births or to limit them is a matter of opinion.

On the one hand, it appears that the growth ideology is still deeply rooted in the minds of many individuals, as indicated, for example, in the survey findings of the Mainichi Newspapers Service, in which most people thought a slowdown in population growth was disadvantageous for the nation.

On the other hand, more recently, there is growing evidence of a gradual emergence of concern over population growth as related to the problems of environmental degradation, depletion of natural resources, and the ultimate limits of available living space. During 1970 and 1971, air and water pollution became of critical concern to every citizen. Newspapers and magazines were filled with pollution stories, and the need to redirect the technology was voiced repeatedly. Serious doubts were cast on the merits of continued increases in the gross national product, and the meaning of what GNP's indicate was questioned. Also, the alarming situation of ever-dwindling natural resources, particularly of oil, has been given grave warnings. The vital importance of the conservation of natural ecosystems has been recognized as well.

A series of events, mostly typical of developed countries, such as the publication of "Spaceship Earth," a Japanese version of the Club of Rome's "The Limits to Growth," the Second Asian Population Conference held in Tokyo in November 1972, and debates on the proposed amendments to abortion laws, have significantly affected the thoughts and views on population at least among some sections of society. In general, the Japanese people as a whole have not fully recognized the impact of population growth on social, economic, and ecological problems. Slowly but steadily, a view that population must inevitably halt its growth in the interest of the quality of human life is gaining momentum. In particular, a good many intellectuals are beginning to see population size and density as possible threats to the future of the economy, the society, and the environment. More time must elapse before we know if these views now emerging will become definite and lead to concrete policy consideration of stationary population. But at least the trend is noteworthy since it represents an entirely new attitude toward population in this country. As a matter of fact, the Population Association of Japan is planning to hold a symposium on "Problems Associated with a Stationary Population" in May 1973, the first treatment of such a subject in its history.

There are some critics who observe that the present situation is characteristic in its lack of consistency in population policy. On the one hand, there are antinatalist measures, such as the continuation of the national family planning program and the liberal induced abortions laws; on the other hand, there is the recent child allowance with its possible aim of increasing births.

Under the circumstances of today, in which population is a controversial subject, it appears that it is extremely difficult for any organization or individual to advance explicit population policies, be they pronatalist or antinatalist. In all likelihood, no substantial population programs will be enforced in the near future as far as growth aspects are concerned. Even if policy makers felt the need for modification of growth trends, they would probably try to provide socioeconomic conditions conducive to the desired change rather than propound an explicit population policy.

1971 Report of the Population Problems Advisory Council.
The Population Problems Advisory Council, which submitted its interim report on fertility trends in August 1969, issued another report in October 1971 addressed to the Minister of Health and Welfare.

The introductory part of the report states as follows (abstract):

On April 26, 1967, the Minister of Health and Welfare requested the opinions on "Population Problems of Particular Concern in View of the Recent Population Trends." In response to it, the Population Problems Advisory Council has looked into the subject through an ad hoc committee organized for that purpose. In August 1969, following the studies on population reproduction, an essential aspect of population trends, the council issued an interim report. Since then, studies have also been made of the changes in age structure and regional population distribution. The present report is herewith submitted as a result of these studies.

The population of Japan is now undergoing an unprecedented rapid change in its age structure. This change became remarkable during the period 1955–1965 when the nation's economic activity reached its highest level. Shortage of young laborers and of technically well-trained workers came to recognition, and the improvement of the quality of population was called for. The nature of our population problems has shifted from overpopulation and unemployment to the qualitative consideration.

In view of the growing importance of population quality, the council resolved in 1962 on the "Measures for the Improvement of Population Quality," suggesting the need for social development in balance with economic development as an urgent proposition.

Due to the intensified economic activities and the accompanying population migration, the problems of imbalance of population distribution came to the fore. In August 1963, the council submitted its opinions concerning the matters of special significance in regional development planning as viewed from the standpoint of population.

The above statements all called for welfare-oriented official policies and programs and drew attention to the importance of social development. Among the measures suggested by the council, the child allowance scheme has already been realized. But many other suggestions remain unexecuted. The economic growth in recent years has certainly brought about material affluence, but at the same time, deterrents to the well-being of our people, including environmental problems, have been created.

The 1969 interim report dealt with the quantitative aspect of population. In the present report, we submit our opinions on the qualitative aspect of population, paying major attention to changing age composition and internal distribution. Measures we suggest here are all based on the humanity-centered ideology. It is hoped that systematic, comprehensive national measures and programs will be adopted along the suggested lines [9].

The text of the report discusses such subjects as: eugenic measures, general health care, marriage counseling, sex education, increased health services for infants, maternal health care, promotion of family planning in lieu of induced abortion, child welfare programs, development of human ability in the young-age population, increased utilization of those with special talents, measures for laborers working away from home, balancing women's participation in labor and their responsibility for children, maternal health for working mothers, chronic disease control, old-age pensions, reconsideration of retirement age, social support for helpless old people, encouragement of old people's participation in social activities, measures for the physically or mentally handicapped, promotion of regional planning, environmental protection, improvement of housing situations, betterment of urban development, economic and social development of depopulated areas, conservation of nature, and the development of community organizations for increased participation of citizens in local affairs.

In its conclusion, the report lists seven recommendations: (1) healthy development of young-age groups, (2) care for the aged, (3) building of healthy and sound families, (4) housing programs for better family life, (5) measures to control traffic accidents, (6) measures for environmental betterment, and (7) promotion of community organizations.

Thus, the report contained all-round policy consideration. Welfare programs and social development were the main concern. The government's welfare programs are being given much higher priority in the overall budgetary appropriations, but this may be more appropriately interpreted as a result of people's demand for the enrichment of the quality of life rather than as a specific response to the recommendations made by a population problems study group.

Child Allowance.

Effective January 1, 1972, a child allowance scheme was implemented by the Ministry of Health and Welfare. The scheme, as announced, is somewhat complicated in its operation: a sum of 3,000 yen (about US$10)[1] per

[1] As of January 1, 1973, 1,000 yen equaled US$3.32.

month is provided to a couple for each child after the second aged less than five years, if a family has more than two children aged under eighteen years and a total income of no more than 2 million yen (about US$6,640) in the previous year. It is estimated that a total of 936,000 children (not families) were eligible to receive the allowance as of January 1972.

The child allowance scheme has long been studied in Japan. As early as 1947, an official committee made a proposal for establishment of such a scheme. More recently, social welfare people and the Population Problems Advisory Council actively supported it. After overcoming difficulties in fiscal arrangements, the government decided to put the long-hoped-for program into effect.

Within Japan as well as in other countries, some critics hold the scheme as a pronatalist measure, but nowhere in the official documents concerning the child allowance program can be found a hint of its relationship to the restoration of birth rates. It has been presented clearly as a welfare measure. If the measure was intended to increase births, it seems unlikely that such a small amount of money distributed on such a limited scale could significantly alter fertility practice. To ensure the full development of human ability once a child is born is regarded as the nation's responsibility to the future generation.

Housing.

In its eleventh survey on birth control conducted in 1971, the Mainichi Newspapers Service looked into associations between birth limitation and available dwelling space. With regard to the relationships between the practice of contraception and dwelling space, no correlation was found. On the other hand, a significant relationship was observed between the number of children and the space available for the family. The sample size in the survey admittedly was small, but nevertheless, the findings seemed to endorse the anticipated conclusion: the smaller the space available, the less the number of children in general (Table 2). For example, among wives aged 25–29, 28 percent had no children when the space was extremely limited, while the corresponding proportion was 7–10 percent when the space was relatively large. Among wives aged 35–39, the proportion of those with three children was significantly less when the space was seriously small. Among wives aged 40–44, couples with no children or with one child were relatively more numerous when their dwelling units were small.

Thus, the shortage of houses is believed to be a most significant reason for family limitation and, to some extent, also for late marriage (age at marriage: twenty-four years for women, twenty-seven for men).

There is a comprehensive official housing project being conducted in order to provide for such shortage of dwelling units. Areas adjacent to large

TABLE 2.

Percentage Distribution of Families by Dwelling Space,
Japan, 1971 (by wife's age and number of living children)

Number of Children	Space Available (in units)					
	5–10	10–15	15–20	20–25	25–30	30+
Wife's Age: 20–24						
0	58.3	25.6	42.9	27.3	28.6	50.0
1	29.2	67.4	42.9	50.0	57.1	46.2
2	12.5	7.0	14.3	9.1	14.3	3.8
3	0	0	0	9.1	0	0
Wife's Age: 25–29						
0	27.7	15.6	8.2	9.9	7.9	6.4
1	44.6	37.6	44.7	42.0	33.3	40.4
2	23.1	38.5	40.0	43.2	49.2	45.0
3	1.5	7.3	7.1	3.7	9.5	8.3
Wife's Age: 30–34						
0	11.1	4.9	4.1	3.5	4.4	3.5
1	18.5	22.3	20.3	16.7	8.8	15.7
2	53.7	60.2	61.8	57.0	57.5	51.2
3	14.8	9.7	12.2	22.8	25.7	26.7
Wife's Age: 35–39						
0	12.2	5.6	3.7	4.3	1.9	2.5
1	36.6	16.7	18.7	16.4	13.5	7.2
2	36.6	56.9	45.8	53.4	56.7	52.1
3	9.8	18.1	26.2	22.4	18.3	33.9
Wife's Age: 40–44						
0	7.4	7.0	2.4	3.7	2.4	3.7
1	37.0	19.3	12.9	14.0	14.1	9.8
2	18.5	50.9	48.2	49.5	44.7	42.9
3	29.6	17.5	24.7	23.4	29.4	31.8

SOURCE: The Mainichi Newspapers Service, 1971.
NOTE: Percents may not add to 100 because "number of children unknown" has been excluded.

cities, such as Tokyo and Osaka, are showing enormous in-migration, and in these areas the pressure of housing is most acutely felt. Construction of new housing has been far behind the demand.

Recent Debates on Abortion Laws.

The movement to repeal the Eugenic Protection Law or to amend it by placing rigid restrictions on legal abortion has been in existence over the past several years. Two religious bodies (the Catholic church and Seicho No Ie, a Japanese religion created in 1929) have figured in the movement, joined by a few political leaders. The harmful effects of abortion, the decay of public morals due to the liberalization of abortion, the excessive control of fertility, the shortage of young laborers, the international disgrace because Japan is considered the "abortion paradise"—altogether these have been the bases for their disapproval of the Eugenic Protection Law. Against this group, medical practitioners and other workers in direct contact with women who wish abortions have emphasized that the restriction of legalized abortion leads to black market practice, produces unnecessary ill effects, and is, in any event, untimely in view of the prevailing adverse conditions of housing and other aspects of living standard.

Toward the end of May 1972, a proposal was advanced in the Diet to amend the law. Among other things, it included (1) the removal of economic consideration from the legal indications for abortion, and (2) the addition of a "mental health" aspect when the mother's health is to be considered. According to this proposal, an abortion would be permitted when the mother's physical or mental health is thought to be seriously impaired by the continuation of pregnancy or by delivery, whereas in its existing form, an abortion is approved when the mother's health is threatened because of her physical or economic conditions.

The Ministry of Health and Welfare stated that the only intention was to modify the indications for abortion to make them better conform with the current social conditions. Twenty years ago when the law was first established, it may have been necessary to consider the economic reasons, but they are no longer valid today in view of the remarkable economic progress the country has made. The proposed amendments, it was explained, would merely rationalize the legal bases for abortion; they had nothing to do with demographic intention.

When the proposal was reported in the newspapers, the medical profession as a whole was silent, but a strong reaction came from various sections of society, including a number of voluntary family planning and women's organizations and a few geneticists. Notwithstanding the neutral position toward population expressed in the official statement, they suspected its pronatalist implication as they were versed in the background of the whole movement. They seriously cautioned of the possible danger involved if the growth of the population of Japan was deliberately accelerated. Also, some urged actively that modern contraceptives should be permitted officially for general use before any legal modifications of the abortion laws were made if the government genuinely was to aim at the reduction of induced abortions.

Thus, the proposal of amendments to the Eugenic Protection Law gave occasion to heated debates on abortion, contraception, and population growth in Japan. As a result, the decision on the matter was postponed until the next Diet session for the reason that enough discussions were not held. The proposal may or may not be submitted again, but if it is placed on the agenda once more, in all likelihood its opponents will criticize the move violently.

Population Education.

Population education as part of general school education has not been given much attention so far. There are some programs under consideration whereby family planning and sex education will be incorporated, but by and large, they are still in their infancy.

A small number of individuals and private organizations, which are concerned about population explosion, have begun to point to the need for population education, for both school children and adult groups. Toward the end of 1972, a national television station presented several programs relating to the growing global concern over population on the occasion of the Second Asian Population Conference. With a World Population Conference in 1974, mass media will, of necessity, increase their interest in the subject, and this may significantly enhance the "population awareness" among the general public. Indifference to population may well be the result of ignorance. Population education in Japan could make a good start by the presentation of hard facts about the present and future situations.

¶ CONCLUDING REMARKS

Since the Meiji Restoration of 1868, only one explicit policy has been adopted in Japan regarding the growth of population in size; in 1941, a policy was propounded by the government that was clearly pronatalist. After World War II, induced abortion was accorded liberal legal limitations, a national family planning program was formulated, and a number of family planning fieldworkers were trained. All of these measures, however, have been presented primarily as health and welfare programs. Underlying the whole course of events, a concept seems to have prevailed widely: a deliberate control of population, particularly its growth, is a highly "delicate" issue. Population policy remains controversial, and family planning is a matter of each individual's decision.

Growing concern over the increasing density of population, the environment, and the critical situation of natural resources during the past few years has gradually affected the value system of the Japanese people. Growth ideology is questioned, and the change is beginning to show its impact also on attitudes to population.

The ever-shrinking world is calling for a broader view on world affairs by the Japanese citizens. People have tended to concentrate their attention only on domestic affairs, but inevitable close contacts with other peoples, especially in Asia, are making them aware of Japan's position among different human races. This contributes to a better and easier understanding of the global nature of population problems.

If population education ever reaches significant proportions among the general public in a convincing manner, a time may come when a consensus of opinion can be found in regard to a national population policy that is in harmony not only with the general interests of the Japanese people themselves but also with the environment, nature, and the interests of other peoples in the world.

MORTALITY

This disproportionately short discussion on mortality in no sense implies that much less importance is attached to the subject as compared to fertility. On the contrary, policies and programs to reduce mortality have been a very major concern of the government at any time.

Characteristically, health and medical care programs are conceived and promoted in their own right. In 1941, when a pronatalist policy was adopted, improvements of health conditions were proposed. Recently, the lowering of mortality and morbidity rates among mothers and children has been recommended in the report of the Population Problems Advisory Council for the enhancement of the quality of the next generation. These demographic considerations are rather secondary, however, and the more basic rationale for health and medical measures always lies in their importance as humanitarian policy. Because of this fundamental goodness, people do not question the validity of the programs. Reduction of mortality is not subject to controversy.

Until fifteen years ago, major causes of death among the Japanese people were acute infectious diseases. Nowadays, the picture has been altered substantially. As in other developed countries, degenerative diseases and accidents are central issues. Also, maternal mortality rates are peculiarly high in Japan, and the strengthening of maternal health services is much in need.

With the increasing aging of the population of Japan, an important but difficult task lies ahead. Mere prolongation of life in numerical terms does not satisfy people; how to improve the quality of life, medically, economically, socially, and psychologically, for those who have survived their "three score and ten" remains to be studied. (According to the 1970–1971 life table, the expectation of life at birth is seventy years for men and seventy-five for women).

MIGRATION AND REDISTRIBUTION OF POPULATION

¶ POPULATION POLICY CONSIDERATIONS
AND SOCIOECONOMIC DEVELOPMENT

In spite of the persistence of severe population problems and vigorous discussions among social scientists in prewar modern Japan, no policy explicitly designed to influence population was adopted by the government except in wartime. Some measures taken by the government may be considered as population policy in the sense that the solution of a problem concerning population was the direct goal, but this goal was reached by adopting economic measures, while leaving population factors untouched.

The considerations of policy always had two aspects: one economic, the other demographic. The demographic aspect concerns fertility, mortality, and migration. Recommendations to reduce mortality have been included in all policies. Population policy considerations in the postwar period are characterized by a shifting of emphasis from fertility reduction to redistribution of the population. In the first decade after the war, the major concern was with fertility control.

The mid-1950s was probably a turning point in a socioeconomic and demographic context. The demographic transition was completed, with birth and death rates stabilizing at a very low level. At that time, too, the rapid postwar economic growth was at its incipient stage.

A so-called double income program was initiated by the government in 1960 to achieve rapid industrial growth based on local development programs and heavy and chemical industrializations. Public and private investment was greatly expanded. Economic growth rates continued to exceed those expected by the government. However, predominant emphasis was placed on economic development in order to approach as quickly as possible the advanced level already attained in the more highly developed countries. Consequently, population aspects of social development tended to be neglected by the government.

The rapid economic growth that began in about 1957 was made possible by concentrating and accumulating population and industries in a few limited urban areas, primarily in the three giant cities—Tokyo, Osaka, and Nagoya—and in the large metropolitan areas surrounding these cities. The heavily crowded urban areas inevitably began to produce environmental disruption. Rural areas were characterized by depopulation and a high proportion of older people, because of the heavy migration of young people to urban centers. More and more, after 1960, government attention was concentrated on various diversified development plans and programs at national, regional, and local levels. The Population Problems Advisory

Council, upon the request of the Minister of Health and Welfare, submitted opinions concerning regional development from the standpoint of population problems in August 1963.

The council emphasized two basic objectives. One is that the eventual goal of regional development is to increase the actual welfare of the population, either of the nation as a whole or of people in a region. Another objective is the necessity of balanced growth of regional economic and social development. From these standpoints, and also taking into account the serious emerging effects on human welfare of massive migratory movements, an adequate population redistribution policy achieved by adjusting the volumes and speed of migration was recommended by the council. For that purpose, implementation of regional policies designed to locate and develop industries that would require the employment of many people in local areas was suggested as the most desirable solution.

Also mentioned were other important points to which attention should be paid in connection with the regional development policy: (1) the shrinking trend of increment of productive-age population and the increasing trend of middle- and high-age population accompanied by the change in age composition of the population; (2) the necessity of modernizing agriculture and small-sized enterprises in cities; (3) the creation of urban areas with a high-quality environment; (4) the promotion of health and welfare; and so on, including another five points.

¶ DEVELOPMENT PLANNING AND POPULATION POLICY

In the postwar period, population problems changed in their nature and emphasis as economic progress and social change proceeded. Basically there were two changes: the shift from the quantity to the quality problems of population, and the transition from the economic-oriented problem to the equilibrium-oriented problem between economic and social development. Unprecedented demographic and socioeconomic transformation overlapping each other produced population problems of a different nature, and policy also shifted from simple fertility control to quality improvement and, more recently, to migration and redistribution factors.

As rapid growth started about 1957 and accelerated year after year, rural to urban migration increased quickly and heavily. Nationwide migratory movement brought a tremendous young labor-force population into great cities like Tokyo and Osaka from all rural and agricultural areas. The average annual number of migrants in the country as a whole was 5.2 million during the second half of the 1950s; this increased to 6.5 million in the first half of the 1960s and reached 7.6 million in the second half of that decade. Since 1969, the migrants have exceeded 8 million per year.

The country, then, was polarized into two distinctive areas, one heavily crowded and another heavily depopulated. Both public and private sectors and also central and local governments have become keenly aware of the serious effects on people's welfare of an extremely imbalanced population distribution.

As early as 1962, the government recognized that excessive concentration of population and industries in great cities should be prevented and that balanced regional development should be promoted. In 1962, a National Overall Development Project was adopted, and a New Industrial Cities Promotion Law was enacted. The law, in particular, aimed at establishing several new industrial cities that were expected to be growth points in local areas and, consequently, to slow down the migratory flow into great cities.

At the same time, various measures to stimulate industrialization in underdeveloped areas were adopted, including the passage of a law for this purpose. In this way, local employment opportunities gradually began to increase. The location of industries outside of the large cities also had the effect of increasing decentralization.

In 1969, a new National Overall Development Project was adopted. Its basic principle is that regional development should give priority to the welfare of the citizenry rather than to the advancement of industrial production alone.

Finally, in 1971, a law to stimulate the reallocation of industries was enacted in order to accelerate decentralization of industries to local areas. To implement duties prescribed in this law, a new organization was established in 1972.

The people's increasing awareness about environment disruption in great cities—for example, air and water pollution, traffic congestion, inadequate housing, noise disturbances, and all the rest—and increasing employment opportunities in local cities and towns seemed to function as incentives causing return migration.[2] The results of the 1970 census also indicate that major transformations in redistribution of population are under way. During the quinquennial period 1965–1970, great cities showed for the first time depopulation or a remarkable slowing of increase. Population increase rates in the last intercensual period in the three great metropolitan areas were the lowest of those in the postwar period. The fastest growth rates for urban entities were registered by medium-sized cities with populations between 200,000–290,000 persons and not by the larger cities. However, it is also true that heavy accumulation of population is still continuing even though the rapidity has been reduced. Various expert committees [12] of the Economic Advisory Council to the Prime Minister came to the

---

[2] For more detailed information and analysis of the newly noted migration patterns, see [10] and [11].

same conclusion, namely that the decentralization policy of population and industries should be adopted in order to attain maximization of people's welfare. The effective implementation of the redistribution policy is a formidable task for the government. The policy extends over various fields of social, economic, and fiscal arrangements and of urban, rural, and environmental problems. The expectations and desires of people concerning space selection of residence and work are basic factors for formulating redistribution policy. It seems to be clear that the migration and redistribution of population is now the most urgent population policy facing present-day Japan.

REFERENCES

1. Kingsley Davis. "The theory of change and response in modern demographic history." *Population Index*, vol. 29, no. 4 (October 1963): 345–366.

2. Teijiro Ueda. "Current problems of unemployment and population in Japan." *Population Studies in Japan*, edited by Ueda. 1933. (In Japanese.)

3. Irene B. Taeuber. *The Population of Japan*. Princeton, N.J.: Princeton University Press, 1958.

4. *Proposal on the Fundamental Course and Aim of Population Policy*. Tokyo: Foundation Institute for Research on Population Problems, Population Planning Committee, November 30, 1946. (Typescript, in Japanese.)

5. *Recommendations of the Population Problems Advisory Council*. November 29, 1949. (In Japanese.)

6. The Population Problems Research Council, the Mainichi Newspapers Service. *Some Facts about Family Planning in Japan*. Population Problems Series, no. 12, Tokyo, September 1955.

7. Katsuyoshi Takahashi, and Yoshitome Ushimaru. *Problems of Induced Abortion*. Tokyo: Nihon Iji Shimpo-sha, March 1950. (In Japanese.)

8. Population Problems Advisory Council. "Interim report." *Studies in Family Planning*, vol. 1, no. 56 (August 1970): 1–4.

9. Report of the Population Problems Advisory Council. *Population Problems of Particular Concern in View of the Recent Population Trends*. Tokyo, October 1971. (In Japanese.)

10. Toshio Kuroda. "A new dimension of internal migration in Japan." English Pamphlet Series, no. 69. Tokyo: Institute of Population Problems, 1969.

11. Toshio Kuroda. "Migration, distribution of population, and development." Presented as a working paper for the Second Asian Population Conference held in Tokyo, November 1–13, 1972.

12. *Location and Transportation System in New Era: Report of the Expert Committee on Location and Transportation, Economic Advisory Council*. Overall Planning Bureau of the Economic Planning Agency, 1972. (In Japanese.)

CHAPTER 24

United States

Charles F. Westoff

Acknowledgments: The author thanks Elise Jones of the Office of
Population Research, Princeton University, for library research
assistance.

ABSTRACT

The United States does not have any explicit population policy, if that term
is interpreted to imply objectives of either growth or geographic distribution. Like any other nation, the government has laws and programs that
affect population directly and indirectly. Among the direct influences are
the subsidization of family planning services for the poor and, more recently, a court interpretation that, in effect, permits abortion on request
throughout the nation. Immigration is limited; modern immigration policy
has not been sensitized to demographic considerations until perhaps quite
recently. Although the government has experimented with some programs
of diverting migration away from large metropolitan areas, there is no
coherent policy, and the distribution of population has been influenced
largely by the determinants of the location of economic activity.

In 1970, a two-year Commission on Population Growth and the American Future was created by Congress at the request of President Richard
Nixon. The commission analyzed the population question in the United
States and concluded that, for the most part, no benefits—economic, environmental, governmental, or social—would result from population growth
continued beyond that which our past growth implied and that, therefore,
eventual population stabilization was desirable. The commission made a
large number of recommendations about population education, sex education, child and maternal health, status of women, research in contraception,
and so forth that aimed toward maximizing freedom of choice in reproductive decisions.

The final report has been largely ignored by the President, but some other parts of government have utilized it, and it has received wide coverage in the press. But, nevertheless, the birth rate continues to decline, and a national population policy seems even more unlikely than it did a few years ago.

INTRODUCTION

A review of population policy in the United States indicates clearly that the most conspicuous recent development, both in terms of visibility and level of government involved, was the creation in 1970 of the Commission on Population Growth and the American Future.

In 1972, the commission released its final report—*Population and the American Future*—which includes both an analysis of the problems of population growth and distribution in the country and a series of recommendations on issues associated with population. The report is the closest the nation has come to considering the formulation of a national population policy. The very short history of population policy in the United States testifies to how radical a development the commission represents.

SCOPE OF INQUIRY

Every government has generated laws that affect population directly through the regulation of movement in and out of the country, marriage, divorce, abortion, contraception, and less directly, through a variety of policies governing public health, land settlement, military service, housing, and the status of women. Most such laws, even those closely connected with reproduction, are designed for nondemographic reasons reflecting the underlying sacred and secular values of the culture. It is probable that population policies in the modern sense have existed only when population was perceived as a problem, and even then, the rationales for governmental action invoke mainly nondemographic considerations. The interplay of legal forces with the underlying social norms governing the reproductive patterns of a society are complex and beyond the scope of this review; our concern here is primarily with official governmental policies more or less directly affecting population and the attitudes and reactions of the public and various constituencies. Thus, we shall concentrate on the formal rather than the informal processes, on the direct rather than the indirect influences, and on those policies that are "more or less" intended to produce demographic effects. The emphasis will be on population growth at the national level and, only secondarily, on the internal distribution of population.

POPULATION TRENDS

¶ NATURAL INCREASE
The United States has experienced, with some variations, the demographic history of Western civilization in general and the English-speaking "overseas" colonized countries in particular. In the eighteenth and early nineteenth centuries, there was a very high mortality and fertility and a rapid rate of growth. Even by 1800, the total fertility rate was between 7 and 8 births per woman; by 1900, this rate had dropped to between 3 and 4, and by 1970, to between 2 and 3 births. In 1900, life expectancy was forty-seven; today, it is seventy. The birth rate has dropped from 32 (per 1,000) to below 16, and the death rate, from 17 to 9. The rate of growth, adding in the immigration rate of 2 per 1,000, is now below 1 percent per year. The population of the United States has grown from 76 million in 1900 to 205 million by 1970 so that even the fairly low annual growth now adds considerably to the total population.

The mortality rate has declined uninterruptedly with only few exceptions, and the fertility rate similarly has declined with, however, one major exception—the post-World War II "baby boom." In 1947, following a marriage boom after demobilization in 1946, the birth rate climbed to 27, a spectacular increase from the low of 18 reached in the 1930s. And fertility remained high for a decade, with the birth rate averaging about 25 and the total fertility rate reaching a high of 3.7 by 1957. By the end of that decade, the baby boom had run its course, and the decline of fertility resumed with dramatic force. The birth rate reached a new historic low of 17.5 in 1968 (with a total fertility rate of 2.5). Although the birth rate reversed itself as expected because of the swelling numbers of persons entering reproductive age and moved to 18.2 by 1970, it unexpectedly dipped again in 1971, dropping to 17.3, reflecting a considerable decline in fertility. And in 1972, the birth rate dropped still further to a new all-time low with an (unofficially) estimated total fertility rate of 2.06, slightly below replacement. A 1972 Census Bureau study indicates a decline in the total number of children expected by (white) married women under thirty from 3.2 in 1955 to 2.3 in 1971. The widespread distribution of the pill and other effective methods of fertility control have contributed greatly to the ability of couples to avoid unplanned and unwanted fertility.

Despite the radical change in fertility in recent years, the United States population has such a builtin demographic momentum because of the baby boom, which is now moving into the active reproductive years, that it will continue to grow for another half century or so even if American women reproduce only at replacement—and although we are in sight of that level, we have not reached it. Thus, quite aside from immigration, we are probably committed to, at least, another 75 million persons. It is possible, of course, that fertility might continue below replacement which would reduce the ultimate size of the population.

¶ SETTLEMENT AND IMMIGRATION

At the beginning of the colonization of America, there were less than 1 million estimated aboriginal population—the so-called American Indians. Land grant and other settlement policies determined the initial patterns of European colonization in the eastern region of the country. With a vast continent to explore and exploit, with the high mortality rates typical of the seventeenth and eighteenth centuries, and with the competition among European powers to gain ascendancy in the New World, the attitudes of the day were progrowth. The early tides of European settlers soon were supplemented by the importation of black slaves from west Africa as the agricultural development of the south created a demand for cheap labor.

The settlement of the western part of the country was stimulated greatly by the Homestead Act of 1862 which came as close as any nineteenth-century legislation to having an explicit intended demographic purpose. This act opened vast tracts of virgin land in the interior to settlement by the increasing populations of the eastern states.

Although the chances to acquire land and to seek opportunities created by new frontiers continued to attract immigrants, the nineteenth-century immigration from Europe was stimulated by conditions and policies abroad —economic crises, political unrest, and religious persecutions underlay the waves of migration from northern and western Europe in the nineteenth century. Until 1882, these immigrants and refugees found an open door in the United States. The Immigration Act of 1882 represented the first governmental restrictions—in this case, to the entry of certain peoples from Asia.

The first decade of the twentieth century saw a renewed wave of immigration, this time from southern and eastern Europe. Some 6.3 million immigrants are estimated to have arrived during the decade. The impact of new languages and customs, especially when coupled with the nationalistic sentiments provoked by World War I, led to a series of postwar laws regulating the volume of immigration and establishing quotas based on estimates of the ethnic composition of the population prior to the recent immigration of the early years of the new century. These quotas heavily favored the populations of northern and western Europe and discriminated against those from Italy, Poland, and Russia.

Thus, the explicit population policies of the United States government during the nineteenth and early twentieth centuries can best be described as those characteristic of a youthful nation with a seemingly ever-expanding frontier, a rapidly growing industrial economy demanding cheap labor, and a growing sense of national identity and ethnic preference.

During the past decade, because of the sharp decline in the birth rate, the relative demographic significance of immigration has increased to the point where it currently accounts for about a quarter of annual growth, some 400,000 net immigrants per year. The rate of immigration has been much greater in the past: In 1900, the immigration rate was 8 per 1,000 population, but in 1970, it was 2 per 1,000. However, because of its increasing demographic importance, the subject has become involved in the recent population policy debate.

There are different ways to view the demographic role of immigration. If the United States population reproduced at replacement from 1970 to the end of the century, the population would grow by some 60 million persons, 25 percent of whom would represent new immigrants and their descendants. Viewed from this perspective, the demographic contribution of immigration seems not inconsiderable. There is a contrary perspective this is possible, however. If the fertility rate were to average slightly below replacement—2.0 rather than 2.1 births per woman—the population eventually would stabilize anyway with a continuous annual flow of 400,000 net immigration. Therefore, the "costs" of continued immigration—assuming population stabilization to be the desirable national goal—are a slightly lower level of increase, a slightly later arrival at zero population growth, and a somewhat larger (8 percent) ultimate population size.

Immigrants do not distribute themselves in the same way as the native population. They tend to concentrate in the metropolitan areas of a few, mostly coastal states.

There is also a serious problem of illegal aliens in the United States, mostly in the areas near Mexico. There are estimated to be between 1 million and 2 million illegal aliens in the country.

There are, of course, many nondemographic components to the subject of immigration including our cultural heritage, a long tradition of hospitality, foreign policy questions, economic interests, and attitudes of minority groups which make the subject much more complex and sensitive than a mere matter of numbers.

¶ DISTRIBUTION AND INTERNAL MIGRATION

Americans have become a metropolitan people in a short period of time. In 1900, 60 percent of the population lived on farms or in villages; by 1970, the figure had declined to 26 percent. Today, nearly 70 percent live in metropolitan areas. The historical process of urbanization has been transformed into one of metropolitanization as the density of urban areas has actually declined with suburbanization and the territorial expansion of the metropolitan area. Population growth has involved a dual process of increasing concentration at the national scale with dispersion and expansion at the local level.

Within metropolitan areas, 75 percent of the growth between 1960 and 1970 was from natural increase, and the remainder was net migration, both from abroad and from nonmetropolitan areas. As the reservoir of nonmetropolitan areas diminishes, the role of natural increase and international migration will grow more important.

Despite the diminishing role of internal migration as a source of growth for metropolitan areas, there is a great amount of physical mobility in American society—one in five persons changes residency every year. The main streams of migration have been from depressed areas to areas with economic opportunity—historically from rural to urban—migration has also occurred from central cities to suburbs and between metropolitan areas.

Migrants tend to be younger and more educated, and the great mobility of the United States population reflects an ever-shifting adjustment to the changing distribution of economic activity and the search for opportunities. One consequence of internal migration has been the depopulation of many small towns and rural areas; nearly half of all counties in the nation lost population during the 1960s, creating many social, governmental, and economic problems, which are greatly exacerbated by the selectivity of the migration.

While, in 1970, nearly 70 percent of the population was metropolitan, by the end of the century, the figure is expected to grow to 85 percent (between 225 and 273 million people, depending on whether fertility averages two or three births per woman).

LAWS AND PRACTICES DIRECTLY AFFECTING POPULATION GROWTH

Legislation on marriage, divorce, contraception, and abortion in the past has been primarily the province of individual states rather than the federal government, but until very recently, a federal law on contraception was still on the books. Laws that govern access to contraception and abortion were consistent with the growth ethos of the times and were motivated by moral and medical reasons rather than demographic rationales. The Comstock Law, enacted in 1873, was directed broadly at obscenity. It prohibited the importation, transportation in interstate commerce, and mailing of "any article whatever for the prevention of conception." The prohibition of abortion, except under extreme danger to a woman's health, was regulated by state laws enacted at different times. Again, these laws reflected medical and moral, not demographic, considerations.

Marriage and divorce also have been regulated by state rather than federal laws, and there is some variation in age requirements and extreme differences in the permissiveness of divorce laws in various states.

The general trend in the laws that affect natality and nuptiality has been from restrictive to permissive, in a direction that has reduced their pronatalist impact. Variations in laws that govern age at marriage have probably had little demographic impact in recent years in view of the ability of people to move across state lines. Increasing the minimum legal age at marriage might produce demographic effects, but there is no evidence of any change in this area.

There is no widespread revision of divorce laws under way, but there are several states that have made significant changes in their laws, such as permitting divorce after one or two years of separation. It is still difficult to obtain divorces throughout most of the country, which explains the continuing popularity of divorces obtained in some foreign countries.

Many countries feature family allowance programs that are promoted mostly for general welfare purposes and occasionally for pronatalist reasons. In the United States, although income tax laws favor parents with larger families, there are no family allowance programs that offer direct payments to parents in relation to their number of children. Some claim that welfare programs, which increase payments with the size of the family, are pronatalist, but the evidence is nonexistent, and the increments of payments with increasing size, as in the case of income tax deductions, typically do not seem sufficient to affect motivation.

For all legal intents and purposes, contraception is now widely available, although there remain obstacles for minors and medical prescriptions are required for the oral contraceptives. The Comstock Law was repealed in 1971, but restrictions remain on the display and advertising of contraceptive products in some states. There are few remaining legal inhibitions, however. This is not to suggest that effective contraception is universally practiced; the incidence of unplanned and unwanted fertility in the country testifies to great variations in information, motivation, access, and practice.

There is evidence, however, that the spread of the more effective methods of contraception has reduced the rate of unwanted fertility. Comparisons of data from the 1965 and the 1970 National Fertility Studies reveal a drop of about one-third in the rate (defined as the number of unwanted births per person-years of exposure to such risk) between 1961–1965 and 1966–1970. About 15 percent of all births in the latter period were classified as unwanted. In theory, these births would never have occurred; their mothers reported never having wanted any more children prior to their conception.

There seems little doubt that the reduction in unwanted fertility has resulted, in major part, from the increasing popularity of the most effective methods of contraception. The three most effective methods—surgical sterilization for contraceptive reasons, the pill, and the IUD—were used collectively in 1970 by nearly 60 percent of all married couples of reproductive age, up from just under 40 percent in 1965 (see Table 1). If couples using other highly effective methods such as diaphragm and condom are added, the proportion of all couples highly protected from the risk of unintentional conception in 1970 rises to 80 percent. The pill is, by far, the most popular method among young couples (with the wife under thirty), accounting for about half of all contraceptive practice. Among older couples (wife 30–44), surgical sterilization of either male or female (about evenly divided) has become the single most popular method (25 percent), followed by the pill (21 percent).

Thus, there has been a veritable revolution in contraceptive practice in the United States. This trend toward the use of more effective contraception has occurred among various groups in the population (blacks as well as whites, Catholics as well as non-Catholics) and undoubtedly will continue in the future.

The most dramatic changes have occurred in laws about and attitudes toward abortion. Since July of 1970, the state of New York has permitted abortion on request, a situation that has attracted many out-of-state residents. In the first two years of its existence, some 402,000 legal abortions were performed in New York alone compared with only 20,000 legal abortions in the entire country the year before.

Some other states have also liberalized their laws on abortion, some permitting legal abortion on psychological grounds with medical consent, others permitting abortion on more restrictive grounds. But the most dramatic legal development was the US Supreme Court decision of January 1973 which, in effect, legalizes elective abortion in the United States. For the first three months, the decision to terminate a pregnancy shall be made by the woman and her doctor without further restrictions. In the second three months, additional medical safeguards shall be operative such as requiring the abortion to be performed in a fully equipped hospital. In the last trimester, the state may regulate and even proscribe abortion except where necessary to preserve the life or health of the mother. These different rights and obligations reflect the underlying legal reasoning and philosophy of the court's interpretation. In the early months of pregnancy, the basic issue is the right of the woman to determine, with proper professional advice, the medical treatment of her body. As the pregnancy term increases,

TABLE 1.

Methods of Contraception Used by Married Couples by Age, United States, 1965 and 1970 (in percents)

Method	All Couples		Younger Couples (wife under 30)		Older Couples (wife 30–44)	
	1965 (N=3,032)	1970 (N=3,810)	1965 (N=1,215)	1970 (N=1,800)	1965 (N=1,817)	1970 (N=2,010)
Wife sterilized[a]	7.0	8.5	3.2	3.2	9.5	13.1
Husband sterilized[a]	5.1	7.8	2.9	3.0	6.5	12.1
Pill[b]	23.9	34.2	41.4	49.4	12.8	20.6
IUD[c]	1.2	7.4	1.7	9.2	0.8	5.9
Diaphragm[d]	9.9	5.7	6.2	3.5	12.3	7.6
Condom[e]	21.9	14.2	19.2	11.4	23.7	16.6
Withdrawal	4.0	2.1	2.3	1.7	5.1	2.5
Foam	3.3	6.1	4.8	8.0	2.3	4.3
Rhythm	10.9	6.4	7.5	4.2	13.0	8.3
Douche	5.2	3.2	4.8	2.3	5.5	4.1
Other[f]	7.5	4.6	6.1	4.0	8.4	4.8
Total	100	100	100	100	100	100

[a] Surgical procedures undertaken, at least partly, for contraceptive reasons.
[b] Includes combination with any other method.
[c] Includes combination with any other method except pill.
[d] Includes combination with any method except pill or IUD.
[e] Includes combination with any method except pill, IUD, or diaphragm.
[f] Includes other multiple as well as single methods and a small percentage of unreported methods.

the state has increasing responsibility to be concerned about maternal health. And toward the last third of the pregnancy term, after viability, the state has a legitimate interest in potential human life.

The demographic significance of permissive abortion laws is very uncertain. The demographic experience of other countries which have legalized abortion is of uncertain relevance for the United States because of the difference in the extent of contraceptive practice. It seems clear that such laws will operate to reduce fertility, but the magnitude is uncertain since the extent to which legal abortions substitute for abortions that were formerly illegal is simply unknown. The best estimate is that the universal availability of legal abortion would reduce the annual birth rate by 1.5 per 1,000 in the first year. Any such estimate is complicated further by the unknown increase in willingness to resort to abortion that undoubtedly will accompany its legitimation.

EARLY GOVERNMENT INTEREST IN POPULATION

The first explicit attention paid by the federal government in the modern era to population problems as such was by the subcommittee on population problems of the National Resources Committee in 1938. Opinion in some quarters held that the depressed economic conditions of the time were in some measure caused by the declining rate of population growth. Unlike today, when increasing numbers perceive a stationary population and even a slowing of economic growth as a desirable goal, the characteristic concern of the 1930s was with economic stagnation. Against this background and with a concern for human resources as an enlargement of the concept of national resources, this committee presented its report, entitled *Problems of a Changing Population,* to President Roosevelt in 1938. The report was commended to the consideration of government agencies with a view to appropriate legislation and administration and "to the consideration of the American people in shaping broad national policies regarding our population problems" [1].

The study committee concluded, however, that the slowing of population growth and the prospect of a stationary population should not be viewed with dismay. Although the "change from an expanding to a stabilized or slowly decreasing national population entails new economic and social problems, . . . it also opens up new possibilities of orderly progress" [1]. Indeed, the committee, in its concern for the conservation of natural resources and the improvement of the standard of living, concluded that the "transition from an increasing to a stationary or decreasing population may on the whole be beneficial to the life of the Nation" [1]. This conclusion bears a striking similarity to the main conclusion of the Commission on Population Growth and the American Future which issued its report thirty-four years later against a totally different economic, environmental, and demographic background.

The National Resources Committee's main concern about population distribution centered around the relationship of the location of population and employment opportunities, especially the surplus of population in rural areas. Concern also was expressed for the concentrations in the central cities of population who were completely dependent upon the successful operation of a highly complex technical economy. The committee felt that free movement from agricultural areas of limited opportunity should be encouraged and that, as long as such surplus populations exist, the nation should maintain a conservative immigration policy to limit the competition from the entrance of unskilled workers into the country.

The committee was especially sensitive to the problems of differential fertility—the negative relationship between rates of production and the level of cultural-intellectual development. Their concern was mainly with the reciprocal connections between fertility and poverty and also the dysgenic effects of some of the differentials. Recommendations were made only concerning the necessity for research into the economic, social, and psychological factors affecting fertility, a recommendation, incidentally, that was soon followed in the now-classic "Indianapolis Study of Social and Psychological Factors affecting Fertility."

Enhancement of the opportunity for individual development, on the other hand, was viewed by the committee as offering considerable scope for governmental action. While major advances had been made toward the stated national goal of equality of opportunity, much more could be accomplished in the fields of health, education, and cultural development. The committee urged that medical research and services of a variety of kinds be extended and that private insurance plans be encouraged. Elimination of gross inequalities among the school systems in different parts of the country was considered a matter of prime national importance. Specifically, the committee recommended that the role of the US Office of Education be expanded to coordinate, evaluate, and disseminate new developments in education.

Finally, regarding research on population problems, the committee pointed out the primary responsibility of the federal government for the collection and presentation of basic demographic data. The need for strengthening the regular research agencies in the federal government concerned with population studies was emphasized. Establishment of the federal census on a five-year basis was advised as well as supplementation of the census by sampling studies which would supply information on intercensal population movements and various special topics.

In retrospect, this report appears to be a remarkably enlightened document. As one demographer has commented, it "raised the need and promises of population adjustment to a new analytical level" [2, p. 293]. For better or for worse, however, the basic conditions that led to its being written were already changing by the time it was under way. These processes gathered momentum during World War II, and in those years, national attention was diverted to the immediate problems of the war. Largely for these reasons, the report apparently never received the legislative and administrative consideration which it might have otherwise, although some of its recommendations on research and data collection eventually were adopted.

Professional demographic opinion of the time varied between the views of the committee (which included among others William F. Ogburn, Warren S. Thompson, and Frank Lorimer) and a concern for the possible necessity of developing pronatalist population policies. The latter emphasis was one of the rationales advanced for the Indianapolis study and was evident in the 1943 Milbank Memorial Fund roundtable discussion on the "Implications of Population Trends for Postwar Policy." Soon after World War II, however, the main focus of professional interest in population policy turned toward the underdeveloped world. It was not until the 1960s that domestic population problems regained attention.

OFFICIAL VIEWS IN THE 1960s

The new interest in population matters began inauspiciously with President Dwight Eisenhower's oft-quoted statement that:

> I cannot imagine anything more emphatically a subject that is not a proper political or governmental activity. . . . This government will not . . . as long as I am here, have a positive political doctrine in its program that has to do with the problems of birth control. That's not our business.

This response evidently was occasioned by the opposition of the American Catholic bishops to a recommendation in 1959 by the Committee to Study the Military Assistance Program, chaired by William Draper, to "assist those countries with which it is cooperating in economic aid programs, on request, in the formulation of their plans designed to deal with the problem of rapid population growth."

Eisenhower's reaction only stimulated further debate, and President John Kennedy, after resisting United States birth control aid on the grounds of paternalism, eventually supported United Nations population activities and the need for research and debate; Kennedy also established a National Institute of Child Health and Human Development which included a research program on human reproduction.

In 1965, President Lyndon Johnson opened the door further in his State of the Union Message with the statement that he would "seek new ways to use our knowledge to help deal with the explosion in world population and the growing scarcity in world resources."

Several years later, money began to increase for the population program of the Agency for International Development, and in 1968, President Johnson established a Committee on Population and Family Planning. This committee recommended rapid expansion of federal government family planning programs for indigent women, acceleration of research and training programs in the biological and social sciences, government support for population studies centers, expansion of international assistance in population and family planning, and finally, the appointment of a commission on population.

The most significant population legislation of the period grew partly from the Johnson committee report and partly from President Nixon's 1969 message to Congress proposing that: "We should establish as a national goal the provision of adequate family planning services within the next five years to all those who want them but cannot afford them" [3]. In response, Congress enacted the Family Planning Services and Population Research Act of 1970. This legislation authorized additional funds for family planning services and for population research and established an Office of Population Affairs in the Department of Health, Education, and Welfare. The act specifically prohibited the use of any funds in programs where abortion is a method of family planning.

POPULAR VIEWS

The public's views on population also were developing and changing during this period. Questions to determine the accuracy of popular information about population and attitudes toward population as a problem have been asked in several national opinion polls or sample surveys in the United States since 1965. The most recent poll was conducted in 1971 for the Commission on Population Growth and the American Future. In general, the American public is now overwhelmingly in favor of the government's providing birth control, is split on the question of abortion, and favors high schools' offering information on ways of avoiding pregnancy. The public is quite uninformed about numbers or rates of population growth. Nonetheless, in 1971, about two-thirds regarded the growth of the United States population as a serious problem (up from 54 percent in 1965), and a slight majority felt that the government should try to slow the population growth. Some two-thirds replied that they would not be concerned if population growth slowed down and leveled off.

It is difficult to evaluate how much importance the public attaches to population since most of the questions ask only about population. One approach to assessing its relative importance on the public's agenda of problems is to compare the "population problem" with other leading social problems of the day. In the 1971 poll, a much higher proportion of the public felt that crime would be a greater problem than population growth over the next thirty years; somewhat more thought pollution would be a greater problem. Racial discrimination and poverty were regarded almost equally as serious as population growth. More than half felt that population growth is causing the country to use its natural resources too quickly, and about half felt that population growth is the main reason for air and water pollution. Only one-third agreed with the statement that population growth helps keep our economy prosperous, while two-thirds felt that population growth is producing a lot of social unrest and dissatisfaction. About three-fifths of the American public disagreed with the statement that "population growth is important in keeping up our nation's strength."

In general, the American public appears definitely committed to family planning and their government's responsibility for providing necessary programs. They know little about population, but the majority seems to feel that population is something of a problem and that slower growth would be desirable. In all probability, population growth is not very high on the list of national problems in the minds of most Americans.

THE ENVIRONMENTAL MOVEMENT

Considerable momentum has been, and still is, gathering behind a new concern in the United States: the environmental movement. This ideology not only has captured the imagination and energies of many young people, especially students, it also diverted the interests of many college campuses away from a concern with United States involvement in southeast Asia and from other radical political concerns. The concerns of this movement centered around problems of environmental deterioration, as evidenced by air and water pollution, and the consumption of natural resources at a rate that seemed to threaten their exhaustion by an ever-growing demand for greater material affluence. Some also hold the view that the disproportionate American consumption of the world's resources is at the expense of the rest of the world. Population growth in the United States is seen to multiply the problems of both pollution and resource depletion and has been indicted as one of the leading culprits in the environmental crisis.

Such views were paramount in a national organization created in 1968: Zero Population Growth, Inc. (ZPG). The name reveals the goal. The high priest of this organization, and, indeed, the man primarily responsible for linking the environment and population in the popular mind, is Paul Ehrlich. A professor of biology at Stanford University, his sensationalistic paperback book, *The Population Bomb*, fast became a best seller and the gospel of the movement.

Today, ZPG is an organization of approximately 35,000 mostly white, middle-class, and well-educated young people, who actively campaign for a variety of legislative bills consistent with reducing population growth and promote their cause with buttons, bumper stickers, and written materials. Their early zeal for immediate zero growth and for demographic solutions to environmental problems has become tempered by the complexities of knowledge. The leadership of the organization is now well-aware of the demographic realities of the situation and has become more tolerant of the lead time required to arrest the momentum of recent rapid growth.

The influence of these concerns of young people is evident also from data collected in the 1970 "National Fertility Study"; among married women under thirty with one or two births, those concerned with population growth intend to have only about half as many additional births as unconcerned women—a relationship that is not a matter of differences in education.

The debate about the role of population growth in environmental deterioration continues, although it has lost some of the dramatic sharpness of earlier less-sophisticated arguments. There are still those who ascribe major significance to the population factor as well as some who are unwilling to assign it any major importance. In part, these debates frequently have pitted different professional myopias against each other. On the one hand, biologists view the problem in long-term perspective; this involves interrelationships among organisms in a sensitive, interdependent ecosystem, whose delicate balances are being gravely threatened by population growth, combined with insensitive technologies and increasing economic growth and consumption. On the other hand, the economists view the world in shorter time horizons in terms of the supply and demand for products and services, governed by a pricing system that protects against the depletion of scarce resources but requires adjustments to charge the costs of pollution to the polluters. Proponents of this view have faith in technological solutions to environmental problems and in the desirability of economic growth, in part as a means of providing a better standing of living for deprived people throughout the world.

As would be expected, the extremes of both of these views also have been modified as a consequence of the debate itself and the research it has stimulated. Concessions are visible on both sides. The biologists acknowledge the potentialities of market adjustments and technological approaches. The economists have become much more aware of the fragility of the environment and less sanguine about the ability of the economic system to correct automatically for environmental problems. And both have moderated their views on the role of population growth in the United States, moving toward each other, perhaps with a growing orientation toward seeing population growth as a concern but not a crisis.

Regardless of the actual role of population growth in environmental deterioration, there seems little doubt that the debate played a very important part in increasing public awareness of population and in accelerating governmental activity in the population policy area.

THE BUSINESS COMMUNITY

There are two constituencies that, for different reasons, have historically supported population growth or opposed its limitation—the business community and certain conservative religious bodies, notably the Catholic church. The traditional view of the business community has been progrowth, although most such sentiments have been expressed as local chamber of commerce encouragements for increased business opportunity. In short, the belief has been simply that more people mean more customers, more workers, and more consumption. This point of view probably still exists in many of the growing suburbs and the smaller towns and cities in certain sections of the country. But aside from local merchants and small-town chambers of commerce, such sentiments rarely find their way into national statements. Indeed, the chief economist of the National Chamber of Commerce, in testimony presented at a public hearing of the Commission on Population Growth and the American Future—although careful to indicate that he was speaking as an individual—came out clearly for the stabilization of national population growth in part because:

In our society rapid population growth contributes to added effective demand and thus to increased economic growth, it intensifies existing problems of increased taxation to finance needed social investments in public facilities of education, transportation, public health, of increased urban congestion and crowding, of increased demands on and pollution of the environment. Rapid population growth thus may stimulate economic growth, but it also preempts much of the growth increment to be used for maintaining the existing quality of life for more people rather than improving it. . . . The U.S. population issue, viewed domestically, is whether we wish for added numbers of U.S. people to preempt the resources of ours and the rest of the world to meet the demands for larger quantities of facilities [4].

Another indication that the business community has altered its view on the subject comes from a 1970 poll of the executives of the country's 500 leading corporations, sponsored by *Fortune* magazine. Eight out of ten of these executives favored some sort of effort to curb further population growth. Such opinion reflects both a growing collective sense of social responsibility by business as well as sensitization to their newly perceived environmental responsibilities.

THE CATHOLIC CHURCH

Catholics constitute about 25 percent of the population of the United States. By virtue of the size of its constituency and through its organizations and hierarchy, the Catholic church plays an important role in the nation's political life and, hence, in questions of population policy. Although liberalizing if not radical changes have occurred in the past ten years in the attitudes and practices of Catholics and their clergy in connection with fertility control—a fact that makes it increasingly difficult to generalize about Catholics or the church—the Catholic church, nevertheless, continues to exert a strong conservative influence on social change in the area of population policy. It should be emphasized, however, that this current conservative position, especially if we think of actual Catholic practices and attitudes, would have been regarded as quite radical by the standards of only a decade ago.

The orthodox or traditional view, still held by many if not most clergy, especially the bishops, is that the primary purpose of marriage is procreation. Official church teaching on contraception was stated in the 1968 papal encyclical, *Humanae Vitae*, which reiterated this view and held all methods of fertility control illicit except the rhythm method. In 1965, before the encyclical, research revealed that the majority of Catholic couples were using various methods of birth control. In 1970, after the encyclical, the proportion of Catholics who were using contraception other than rhythm had grown even higher. In 1970, about 75 percent of young married Catholic women were no longer conforming to church teaching on birth control.

This deviation from official teaching has been buttressed by and reflected in the growing liberal views of some clergy who hold that companionship and affection are equally valid purposes of marriage and have to be balanced against the procreative function. Thus, contraceptive practice does not interfere with, and indeed can contribute to, the proper fulfillment of marriage. In this respect, the liberal Catholic theologians and clergy are moving toward the positions taken earlier by many Protestant and Jewish spokesmen who have incorporated a growing sense of social responsibility into traditional moral theology.

While cracks in the official Catholic position on contraception are visible, there is no evidence that liberalization of thought has occurred on the subject of abortion. Whereas many Protestant and Jewish religious leaders have supported the liberalization of abortion laws—although conservative wings of both groups have opposed the trend—the Catholic hierarchy has maintained unbroken ranks in opposition. In fact, some of the softening of resistance to contraception may well be a result of the closing of ranks on the abortion issue.

One manifestation of the opposition to relaxation of abortion laws occurred in 1972, when 237 American Catholic bishops unanimously denounced the recommendations of the Commission on Population Growth and the American Future, the most unacceptable of which was the commission's endorsement of the New York State statute which permits abortion on request. The most recent examples were the cries of moral outrage, in response to the Supreme Court ruling, from leading United States cardinals, using such language as "unspeakable tragedy" and "horrifying" decision.

Nonetheless, the attitudes of the Catholic population have shifted significantly in the past five years, although the great majority still remain opposed to unrestricted availability of abortion services. Between 1965 and 1970, the proportion of Catholic married women who endorsed the idea of abortion in case of rape increased from 43 percent to 63 percent; because of the possible deformity of the child, from 40 percent to 59 percent; in the event the woman was unmarried, from 9 percent to 22 percent; in case the couple could not afford another child, from 8 percent to 16 percent; and if the couple simply did not want another child, from 5 percent to 14 percent.

Catholic views on population growth and population policy are more diffuse and varied. The recent denunciation of the report of the Commission on Population Growth and the American Future by the American bishops is the most conspicuous and explicit indication of the church's attitude. It would have been interesting to observe the reaction of the church if the commission report had not included the abortion recommendation. But unless the report had unequivocally repudiated the liberalization of abortion laws, it is likely that it still would have met with suspicion.

Catholic public opinion is not really crystallized as Catholic except when it invokes the abortion issue. Thus, on such questions as whether or not United States population growth or distribution is considered a serious problem, whether or not the slowing and gradual leveling off of national population growth should be a concern, and even whether or not birth control should be made available by the federal government to all on request or whether or not high schools should offer information on how to avoid pregnancy, Catholics generally are indistinguishable from non-Catholics, according to the 1971 public opinion poll.

ETHNIC GROUPS

Blacks, Chicanos, and other deprived minority groups in the United States attach less importance to problems of national population growth than to their more immediate problems. Indeed, discussion of population policy appears increasingly to provoke indifference at best and suspicion and even hostility in some quarters. Even family planning programs have met with some resistance.

In the black community, the deepest emotional source of this attitude is the apprehension that population policy and fertility control programs are genocidal attempts by the whites to eliminate the blacks. Such an attitude is reinforced by the appearance in ghettoes of birth control clinics without pediatric or maternal health clinics or by occasional public proposals for compulsory sterilization of women on welfare having an additional child. Another related source is the concern that the dominant white community is trying to substitute population control for economic development—an attitude not dissimilar to that voiced occasionally by representatives of some developing nations. Still another expression takes the form of connecting increased population with increasing political power—a view strengthened by recent elections to office of black mayors and other government officials.

Differences between black and white popular views of the subject, though not great, do exist. Half of the black population compared with two-thirds of the white population, according to 1971 public opinion data, regard the growth of the population as a serious problem. When asked if they would be concerned if United States population growth slowed down and gradually leveled off, some 42 percent of the black compared with 26 percent of the white population expressed concern. And although the great majority (77 percent) of blacks are in favor of the government's making birth control available to all men and women who want it, their support for such services is somewhat lower than that of whites (88 percent). When this comparison is confined to women, however, no difference obtains. To a considerable extent, in fact, ideological objections are made by men, while the black women who are more directly involved with the problems and responsibilities of unwanted births are much more receptive to family planning. Black women who have been interviewed in fertility surveys are very similar to white women in their concern about the control of fertility, although their ability to exercise effective control has, until recently, been handicapped by lack of information and access to effective methods. There has been a 56-percent reduction in the incidence of unwanted fertility among blacks between 1961–1965 and 1966–1970, a dramatic indication that black women are acquiring the knowledge of and access to modern methods of fertility control. Nonetheless, the rate of unwanted fertility among blacks still runs considerably higher than among whites. The attitudes of blacks toward abortion have also grown increasingly permissive, although in 1970, they are still more opposed to the idea than are whites.

The picture of the attitudes of black leaders is thus diverse, ranging from indifference to animosity. In the black population at large, however, the average person, especially the woman, is just as anxious to regulate her childbearing as is her white counterpart.

WOMEN'S LIBERATION MOVEMENT

Women have an obvious special stake in the matter of birth control. The women's liberation movement has been particularly outspoken in the cause of permissive abortion laws and the right of the women to control childbearing. This view is simply an extension of the position taken decades ago by the early feminist movement. It is now more strident and demanding and accompanied by more resentment of the fact that the male seems to escape much of the responsibility for preventing conception.

Aside from their position on the rights of women with respect to childbearing, the main relevance of the women's liberation movement for population is the drive for equal economic opportunity. Legislatively, this has assumed many forms, including the proposed Equal Rights Amendment and demands for child care centers and tax deductions for the costs of child care. There is some belief that policies such as day care centers and tax deductions for child care would be, in effect, pronatalist, since by subsidy they make it easier for the woman to have children *and* work. Whether or not exposure to alternative interests competitive with childbearing will outweigh the financial subsidies of childbearing is an empirical question that only time and observation can resolve.

POPULATION GROWTH POLICY

These, then, are some of the main forces influencing the development of population policy in the United States. In the summer of 1969, President Nixon gave the impression in his message to Congress that a national population policy might actually be in the offing. At that time, he said:

If the present rate of growth continues, the third hundred million persons will be added in roughly a thirty-year period. This means that by the year 2000, or shortly thereafter, there will be more than 300 million Americans.

This growth will produce serious challenges for our society. I believe that many of our present social problems may be related to the fact that we have had only fifty years in which to accommodate the second hundred million Americans. . . . Where, for example, will the next hundred million Americans live? . . . Are our cities prepared for such an influx? . . . Are there ways, then, of readying our cities? Alternatively, can the trend toward greater concentration of our population be reversed? . . . Are there ways of fostering a better distribution of the growing population? . . . What of our natural resources and the quality of our environment? . . . How can we better assist American families so that they will have no more children than they wish to have? . . . Perhaps the most dangerous element in the present situation is the fact that so few people are examining these questions from the viewpoint of the whole society. . . . It is for all these reasons that I today propose the creation by Congress of a Commission on Population Growth and the American Future. . . . One of the most serious challenges to human destiny in the last third of this century will be the growth of the population. Whether man's response to that challenge will be a cause for pride or for despair in the year 2000 will depend very much on what we do today. . . . When future generations evaluate the record of our time, one of the most important factors in their judgment will be the way in which we responded to population growth [3].

In March 1970, Congress reacted with legislation creating the Commission on Population Growth and the American Future and assigned it several tasks: to inquire into the most probable course of population growth, internal migration, and related demographic developments between now and the year 2000; to examine the public economic resources required to deal with anticipated population growth and the probable impact of population growth on government activities, on natural resources, and the environment; and finally, to assess "the various means appropriate to the ethical values and principles of this society by which our nation can achieve a population level properly suited for its environmental, natural resources, and other needs."

After two years of research, public hearings, and deliberations, the commission issued its final report. The first part of the report was organized into an analysis of the nature of the population issue in the United States, the impact of growth and distribution on the economy, government services, resources, and the environment, and implications for the family, minority groups, and the aged. The second part of the report developed a series of recommendations on diverse subjects related to population: education, child care, adoption, the status of women, family planning, contraceptive research, abortion, immigration, and different aspects of population distribution. The report concluded with a series of recommendations concerning the improvement of population statistics, the expansion of population research, and the organization of population activities by the federal government.

The commission's basic conclusion was that the nation "can no longer afford the uncritical acceptance of the population growth ethic that 'more is better' " and "that no substantial benefits would result from continued growth of the nation's population" [5]. It reached this conclusion from an examination of the impact of the two-child versus the three-child family between 1970 and 2000 on various aspects of the quality of life in America. It concluded that slower population growth and, eventually, the stabilization of population size would raise per-capita income in the short run, have no deleterious effects on business or industry, ease the pressures on resources and the environment, and in theory, permit the investment of public funds in the improvement of the quality of education and other government services rather than in the continuous expansion of facilities. Similarly, further population growth is seen as essentially irrelevant to national security. The benefits, thus, seem overwhelming, but there also may be some costs associated with a stationary population, notably an increase in the proportion of persons sixty-five and over (from 10 percent to 16 percent) and a reduction by about one-third in the proportion under eighteen (from 34 percent to 24 percent). An older nongrowing population might be less innovative and provide less opportunity for upward social mobility, but such possibilities are much less grounded in evidence than are the numerous benefits associated with reduced growth.

The commission concluded that the nation would not benefit from population growth continued beyond that which the past momentum of growth implies, but it did not set zero population growth as a national goal toward which all its policy recommendations were aimed. The commission developed recommendations worthwhile in themselves which, at the same time, aimed at population issues. These recommendations sought to maximize information and knowledge about human reproduction and the responsibilities of parenthood, to improve the quality of the setting in which children are raised, to neutralize social and institutional pressures which historically have been pronatalist in character, and to enable couples to avoid unwanted childbearing, thereby improving their chances to realize their own fertility preferences. Although the analysis of the population question showed the advantages of slower growth for the society as a whole, the actual recommendations made by the commission to the President and Congress concentrated on enhancing the freedom of individuals to have the number of children they want. It is, of course, true that fertility had been declining and that the elimination of unwanted childbearing would contribute significantly to the achievement of zero growth. Nevertheless, certain recommendations were offered which might just as easily increase fertility. The stabilization of population was viewed as a welcome consequence of maximizing individual choice. No important recommendation to reduce immigration was made other than in connection with illegal aliens.

It is entirely possible that the implementation of the commission's recommendations could result in driving fertility below replacement (this might happen anyway, of course), a condition that, if continued, could mean an ultimate loss of population. The commission recognized this possibility and observed: "We are not concerned about this latter contingency because, if sometime in the future the nation wishes to increase its population growth, there are many possible ways to try this; a nation's growth should not depend on the ignorance and misfortune of its citizenry" [5]. In fact, the commission regarded the report, in part, as an educational effort to dispel future anxieties about below-replacement fertility which seem characteristically to arise in countries on the threshold of low fertility.

It is too early to evaluate the basic impact of the report. Initial responses have been mixed—newspaper editorial comment generally has been quite favorable. As indicated earlier, the response of the Catholic church has been hostile; other religious leaders, primarily Protestant, have supported it. Although many individuals in high positions in the government have privately expressed support for the recommendations, the President's response focused mainly on a restatement of his personal opposition to permissive abortion laws and to providing access to contraception for teenagers. Conspicuously absent was any response to the consensus on the desirability of population stabilization or to the many recommendations in connection with population movement. The fact that the report was issued in an election year undoubtedly has contributed to the limited, narrowly political presidential reaction. But most activities in the population field have been initiated and developed by Congress rather than by the Executive Office of the President. These possibilities notwithstanding, however, the United States does not yet have any explicit population growth policy.

POPULATION DISTRIBUTION POLICY

Some students of United States population questions have concluded that the nation's population problem is less the overall rate of growth than the ever-increasing concentration of people in metropolitan areas, the spread of such areas into regional urban centers, and the accompanying depopulation of rural areas. They point to such well-popularized urban problems as congestion, crime, air pollution, ghettoes, noise, and the loss of a sense of community. Defenders of the city point to its superior cultural advantages, its diversity and excitement, and the fact that it has represented opportunity for advancement for millions of migrants from depressed rural areas and abroad. On the other hand, some would try to revitalize rural America and avoid the continued growth and spread of large metropolitan areas.

The attitude of the federal government toward population distribution has not yet crystallized, although programs have existed to redevelop depressed areas. One difficulty is that such policies and programs are inherently political in the invidious sense that they redirect public resources toward one area rather than toward another. No doubt, there is some truth in the cynical observation that when one party (the Republicans) is in power the reconstruction of rural areas seems important, while the administration under the control of the other party (the Democrats) seem typically more interested in urban redevelopment—a characterization that gains its force from the fact that the Republican and Democratic parties traditionally have drawn their support from rural and urban areas, respectively.

The geographic location of people is affected inevitably by many diverse government policies and programs. The interstate highway system, the Federal Housing Administration, and the Economic Development Administration are leading examples of programs with powerful though inadvertent effects on the distribution of population.

In the current (Nixon) administration, there has been considerable talk about "national growth policy" and concern about "balanced growth" but very little consensus on policy or programs. In his State of the Union Message in 1970, President Nixon expressed concern about "rural America emptying out of people and promise" and the "violent and decayed central cities of our great metropolitan complexes." The President concluded:

I propose that before these problems become insoluble the nation develop a national growth policy. In the future, government decisions as to where to build highways, locate airports, acquire land or sell land should be made with the clear objective of aiding a balanced growth for America" [6].

In the Housing Act of 1970, Congress joined the President in stating the need for a national urban growth policy and directed the federal government to assume responsibility to develop such a policy. It required the President to submit a biennial Urban Growth Report to describe the government efforts to those ends, the first one of which was issued just recently. In this first Urban Growth Report, the administration avoided any policy recommendations and seemed, inconsistently, to downgrade the whole concept of a national growth policy.

At the 1970 National Governors' Conference, the fact of "population imbalance" also was deplored and several remedies were offered.

Most proposals organize around four strategies:

(1) To encourage growth in sparsely settled rural areas.
(2) To encourage growth in existing small towns and cities which have a demonstrated potential for growth (the so-called growth center strategy).

(3) To build new towns and cities.
(4) To plan the better use of land, the development of satellite new towns, and the more orderly growth of metropolitan areas.

The four strategies are not mutually exclusive. Recently, the Commission on Population Growth and the American Future recommended a strategy of alternating and simultaneously better accommodating current trends in distribution by encouraging growth in existing small cities and towns and in depressed rural areas and by making new efforts to plan for and guide metropolitan growth.

The basic distribution of population is probably just not easily amenable to government policy and, for that matter, may be an unprofitable lever to manipulate. Several demographic calculations support that view. For example, if all the counties that have lost people were restored to their historical maximum population, they would absorb no more than five years of national growth at the replacement fertility level, or about 11 million people. A national growth center policy also has its demographic limitations. At most, these areas could divert something like one-third of the future growth of large metropolitan areas. Beyond that, one might begin to wonder whether the cure was any better than the disease.

And, finally, considering the large proportion of current and future growth of metropolitan populations due to natural increase, a policy of national population stabilization may be the most effective lever in the long run.

In recognition of these constraints, the commission also recommended policies aimed more at the welfare of "people than places," focused on assisting migration, worker retraining, and employment information services. While the commission, as well as several other groups, has called for national population distribution guidelines, there is no United States policy on the subject, and it is unlikely that one will be developed soon. In the meantime, individual states will become more active in attempts to discourage or encourage population movements.

CONCLUSIONS

We have noted that the United States does not yet have an explicit population policy if that term includes a population growth or distribution goal. Perhaps, there is no need for such a policy if the main concern is the growth rate. If the trend in fertility between 1971 and the first part of 1972 continues, the United States will be *below* replacement by the end of the year. If this happens it will be interesting to observe public reaction.

But population policy is and should be a much broader concept than a rate of growth and the means to achieve it. It should include opportunities for couples to reproduce under optimal circumstances—a nation that includes considerations of the health of the mother and baby and a maximum freedom of choice for the couple concerning marriage and the reproductive decision. In the United States, many developments have occurred in the last decade or so which have enhanced the individual's freedom to exercise better control over his fertility. The collective consequences of these developments have been to slow the rate of population growth considerably, which appears to imply considerable advantages to the society as a whole. Perhaps "population policies" in the explicit sense of the term only develop when the behavior of individuals and the welfare of society are seen as markedly divergent.

REFERENCES

1. National Resources Committee. *The Problems of a Changing Population.* Washington, D.C.: Government Printing Office, 1938.
2. P. Hauser and O. D. Duncan. *The Study of Population.* Chicago: University of Chicago Press, 1955.
3. Richard M. Nixon. "Presidential Message on Population." Message to Congress, July 18, 1969.
4. Commission on Population Growth and the American Future. *Statements and Public Hearings of the Commission on Population Growth and the American Future.* Volume 7. Washington, D.C.: Government Printing Office, 1973.
5. *Population and the American Future.* Final Report of the Commission on Population Growth and the American Future, Government Printing Office, 1972. Available as advance copy in paperback by Signet Books of the New American Library.
6. Richard M. Nixon. Message to Congress, 1970.

BIBLIOGRAPHY

Barnett, Larry D. "Demographic factors in attitudes toward population growth and control." *Journal of Biosocial Sciences,* no. 4 (1972): 9–23.
Blake, Judith. "Population policy for Americans: Is the government being misled?" *Science,* vol. 164 (May 2, 1969): 522–529.
Building the American City. Report of the National Commission on Urban Problems. Washington, D.C.: Government Printing Office, 1968.
Bumpass, Larry, and Charles F. Westoff. "The 'perfect' contraceptive population." *Science,* vol. 169 (September 18, 1970): 1177–1182.
Burch, Thomas K. "Catholic parish priests and birth control: A comparative study of opinion in Colombia, the United States, and the Netherlands." *Studies in Family Planning,* vol. 2, no. 6 (June 1971): 121–136.
Callahan, Daniel (ed.). *The American Population Debate.* New York: Doubleday Anchor Books, 1971.

Coale, Ansley J. "Alternative paths to a stationary population." In Commission on Population Growth and the American Future Research Reports, Vol. 1. *Demographic and Social Aspects of Population Growth.* Edited by Robert Parke, Jr., and Charles F. Westoff, Washington, D.C.: Government Printing Office, 1972, pp. 589–604.

———. "Man and his environment." *Science,* vol. 170 (October 9, 1970): 132–133.

Commission on Population Growth and the American Future. Research reports. Washington, D.C.: Government Printing Office.

Volume 1: *Demographic and Social Aspects of Population Growth.* Edited by Robert Parke, Jr., and Charles F. Westoff, 1972.

Volume 2: *Economic Aspects of Population Change.* Edited by Elliott R. Morss and Ritchie H. Reed, 1973.

Volume 3: *Population, Resources, and the Environment.* Edited by Ronald G. Ridker, 1972.

Volume 4: *Governance and Population: The Governmental Implications of Population Change.* Edited by A. E. Keir Nash, 1972.

Volume 5: *Population Distribution and Policy.* Edited by Sara Mills Mazie, 1973.

Volume 6: *Aspects of Population Growth Policy.* Edited by Robert Parke, Jr., and Charles F. Westoff, 1973.

Volume 7: *Statements and Public Hearings of the Commission on Population Growth and the American Future,* 1973.

Institute of Society, Ethics, and the Life Sciences. *Ethics, Population, and the American Tradition.* Summarized in Commission on Population Growth and the American Future. Research reports, vol. 6. *Aspects of Population Growth Policy.* Edited by Robert Parke, Jr., and Charles F. Westoff. Washington, D.C.: Government Printing Office, 1973.

Irwin, Richard, and Robert Warren. "Demographic aspects of American immigration." In Commission on Population Growth and the American Future. Research reports, vol. 1, *Demographic and Social Aspects of Population Growth.* Edited by Charles F. Westoff and Robert Parke, Jr. Washington, D.C.: Government Printing Office, 1972.

Jones, Elise, and Charles F. Westoff. "Attitudes toward abortion in the U. S. in 1970 and the trend since 1905." In Commission on Population Growth and the American Future. Research reports, vol. 1, *Demographic and Social Aspects of Population Growth.* Edited by Charles F. Westoff and Robert Parke, Jr. Washingon, D.C.: Government Printing Office, 1972, pp. 569–578.

Keller, Suzanne. "The future status of women in America." In Commission on Population Growth and the American Future. Research reports, vol. 1. *Demographic and Social Aspects of Population Growth.* Edited by Charles F. Westoff and Robert Parke, Jr. Washington, D.C.: Government Printing Office, 1972, pp. 267–288.

Kantner, John F. "American attitudes on population policy: Recent trends." *Studies in Family Planning,* no. 30 (May 1968): 1–6.

Kantner, John F., and Melvin Zelnik. "Sexuality, contraception, and pregnancy among young, unwed females in the United States." In Commission on Population Growth and the American Future. Research reports, vol. 1. *Demographic and Social Aspects of Population Growth.* Edited by Charles F. Westoff and Robert Parke, Jr. Washington, D.C.: Government Printing Office, 1972, pp. 355–374.

Kiser, Clyde V. "Implications of population trends for postwar policy." *Milbank Memorial Fund Quarterly,* vol. 22, no. 2 (April 1944): 111–130.

Lamson, Robert W. "Federal action for population policy—what more can we do?" *Bioscience,* vol. 20, no. 15 (August 1, 1970): 854–857.

Lipson, Gerald, and Dianne Wolman. "Polling Americans on birth control and population." *Family Planning Perspectives*, vol. 4, no. 1 (January 1972): 39–42.

Lorimer, Frank, Ellen Winston, and Louise K. Kiser. *Foundations of American Population Policy*. New York: Harper & Row, 1940.

Mayer, Lawrence A. "U.S. population growth: Would slower be better?" *Fortune*, June 1970.

Morrison, Peter A. "Dimensions of the population problem in the U.S." and "The impact of population stabilization on migration and redistribution." In Commission on Population Growth and the American Future. Research reports, vol. 5. *Population Distribution and Policy*. Edited by Sara Mills Mazie. Washington, D.C.: Government Printing Office, 1973.

Noonan, John T., Jr., and Mary Cynthia Dunlop. "Unintended consequences: Laws indirectly affecting population growth in the United States." In Commission on Population Growth and the American Future. Research reports, vol. 6. *Aspects of Population Growth Policy*. Edited by Robert Parke, Jr., and Charles F. Westoff. Washington, D.C.: Government Printing Office, 1973.

Notestein, Frank W. "Zero population growth." *Population Index*, vol. 36, no. 4 (October–December 1970): 444–452.

Piotrow, Phyllis T. "Congressional-executive relations in the formation of explicit population policy." In Commission on Population Growth and the American Future. Research reports, vol. 6. *Aspects of Population Growth Policy*. Edited by Robert Parke, Jr., and Charles F. Westoff. Washington, D.C.: Government Printing Office, 1973.

Pilpel, Harriet F., and Peter Ames. "Legal obstacles to freedom of choice in the U.S." In Commission on Population Growth and the American Future. Research reports, vol. 6. *Aspects of Population Growth Policy*. Edited by Robert Parke, Jr., and Charles F. Westoff. Washington, D.C.: Government Printing Office, 1973.

President's Committee on Population and Family Planning. *Population and Family Planning*. US Department of Health, Education, and Welfare. November 1968.

Presser, Harriet B., and Larry L. Bumpass. "Demographic and social aspects of contraceptive sterilization in the U.S., 1965–1970." In Commission on Population Growth and the American Future. Research reports, vol. 6. *Aspects of Population Growth Policy*. Edited by Robert Parke, Jr., and Charles F. Westoff. Washington, D.C.: Government Printing Office, 1973.

Public Law 91-572, 91st Congress, S. 2108. *Family Planning Services and Population Research Act of 1970*.

Report on National Growth, 1972. First biennial report of President Nixon to Congress as required by Section 703 (a) of the Housing and Urban Development Act of 1970. Washington, D.C.: Government Printing Office, 1972.

Ridker, Ronald. "Resource and environmental consequences of population growth in the U.S.: A Summary." In Commission on Population Growth and the American Future. Research reports, vol. 3. *Population, Resources, and the Environment*. Edited by Ronald G. Ridker. Washington, D.C.: Government Printing Office, 1972, pp. 17–34.

Rindfuss, Ronald R. "Recent trends in population attitudes." In Commission on Population Growth and the American Future. Research reports, vol. 6. *Aspects of Population Growth Policy*. Edited by Robert Parke, Jr., and Charles F. Westoff. Washington, D.C.: Government Printing Office, 1973.

Ryder, Norman, and Charles F. Westoff. "Wanted and unwanted fertility in the United States, 1965 and 1970." In Commission on Population Growth and the American Future. Research reports, vol. 1. *Demographic and Social Aspects of*

Population Growth. Edited by Charles F. Westoff and Robert Parke, Jr. Washington, D.C.: Government Printing Office, 1972, pp. 467–488.

Spengler, Joseph J. "Population Policy in the U.S.: The larger crisis in American culture." *Vital Speeches of the Day,* vol. 7, no. 6 (January 1, 1941): 177–180.

Taeuber, Irene. "Growth of the population of the U.S. in the twentieth century." In Commission on Population Growth and the American Future. Research reports, vol. 1, *Demographic and Social Aspects of Population Growth.* Edited by Charles F. Westoff and Robert Parke, Jr. Washington, D.C.: Government Printing Office, 1972, pp. 17–84.

Teitelbaum, Michael S. "International experience with fertility at or near replacement level." In Commission on Population Growth and the American Future. Research reports, vol. 1. *Demographic and Social Aspects of Population Growth.* Edited by Charles F. Westoff and Robert Parke, Jr. Washington, D.C.: Government Printing Office, 1972, pp. 645–658.

Tietze, Christopher. "The potential impact of legal abortion on population growth in the U.S." In Commission on Population Growth and the American Future. Research reports, vol. 1. *Demographic and Social Aspects of Population Growth.* Edited by Charles F. Westoff and Robert Parke, Jr. Washington, D.C.: Government Printing Office, 1972, pp. 579–588.

United Nations. *Measures, Policies, and Programs affecting Fertility, with Particular Reference to National Family Planning Programs.* Population Studies no. 51. New York, 1972.

US Bureau of the Census. "Birth expectations data, June 1972." *Population Characteristics.* Series P-20, no. 240, September 1972.

US Senate Joint Resolution. "To declare a U.S. policy of achieving population stabilization by voluntary means." *Congressional Record,* vol. 117, no. 82. (June 2, 1971).

Wattenberg, Ben. "The nonsense explosion." *The New Republic,* April 4–11, 1970.

Westoff, Charles F. "Some reflections on population policy in the United States." *Milbank Memorial Fund Quarterly,* vol 49, no. 4, part 2 (October 1971): 230–235.

———. "The modernization of U.S. contraceptive practice." *Family Planning Perspectives,* vol. 4, no. 2 (July 1972): 9–12.

———. (ed.). *Toward the End of Growth: Population in America.* Englewood Cliffs, N.J.: Prentice-Hall, 1973.

Westoff, Charles F., and Larry Bumpass. "The revolution in U.S. Catholic birth control practices." *Science,* vol. 179 (January 5, 1973): 41–44.

Whelpton, P. K. "Population policy for the U.S." In *The Study of Population.* Edited by Joseph J. Spengler and Otis D. Duncan. Chicago: University of Chicago Press, 1956, pp. 462–469.

White House Press Secretary. "Statement by the President on report of the Commission on Population Growth and the American Future," May 5, 1972.

Willie, Charles V. "Perspectives from the black community." *PRB Selection No. 37.* Population Reference Bureau, June 1971, pp. 1–4.

Woofter, T., Jr. "Population trends and recent government policies in the United States." *Congrès International de la Population,* vol. 7, Paris, 1937, pp. 149–160.

CHAPTER 25

Soviet Union

Dmitri I. Valentei

ABSTRACT

The development of productive forces and production relations conditions the development of population. In socialist society, the population policy is directed at the improvement of the conditions of life and work of the entire population.

The demographic policy concerns only the reproduction of population in terms of quantity and quality. The methods of the demographic policy comprise economic, administrative-legal measures, as well as measures relating to sociopsychological impact. It should be emphasized that administrative-legal measures cannot give a desired effect if they are divorced from economic measures. Demographic policy can be successful only if it is one of the elements of the socioeconomic policy of a state.

THE PRESENT DEMOGRAPHIC SITUATION

What are the characteristic features of the present demographic situation in the USSR? In size of population the USSR ranks third in the world. It had 248.6 million as of January 1, 1973. In the level of fertility the Soviet Union holds an average place among industrially advanced states, its mortality rate being one of the lowest in the world (Table 1).

In prerevolutionary Russia the natural growth of the population was characterized by a high level of fertility, by a high general and especially child mortality, by a low life expectancy and short spans between generations. It is known that such a pattern of reproduction is characteristic of economically and socially underdeveloped countries.

At present the natural reproduction of the population of the USSR is

TABLE 1.

Fertility, Mortality, and Natural Growth of the Population, USSR,
1913–1971

| Year | per 1,000 population | | | Infant Deaths up to Age One Year per 1,000 Births |
	Number of Births	Number of Deaths	Natural Growth	
1913	45.5	29.1	16.4	269
1926	44.0	20.3	23.7	174
1940	31.2	18.0	13.2	182
1950	26.7	9.7	17.0	81
1955	25.7	8.2	17.5	60
1960	24.9	7.1	17.8	35
1965	18.4	7.3	11.1	27
1970	17.4	8.2	9.2	25
1971	17.8	8.2	9.6	23

SOURCE: See [1].

characterized by an average level of birth rate, a low mortality level (general and child), and a high life expectancy. As compared with the 1913 figure, the birth rate decreased by 3.9 times, mortality by 2.8 times, and child mortality by almost 12 times. Average life expectancy more than doubled—from 32 to 70 years.

Thus it took the USSR only thirty to thirty-five years to establish the present-day pattern which has prevailed in the USSR approximately since the end of the 1940s–the beginning of the 1950s. It is our profound belief that the prevailing pattern of the reproduction of population has evolved mainly owing to the country's socioeconomic advancement which is reflected in the growth of the national income, the real income of factory and office workers and the collective-farm peasantry, in extensive housing construction, and in the development of health services, education, culture, etc.

The reproduction of the population in the USSR as a whole just as in every constituent republic is of an expanding nature. However, there exist certain regional differences conditioned by the fact that before the Socialist Revolution of 1917 the peoples of what is now the Soviet Union were at different levels of socioeconomic development.

A considerable part of the population of the USSR lives in republics with a relatively low birth rate. These are Latvia, Estonia, the Ukraine, the Russian Federation, Georgia, and Byelorussia. Their population accounts for nearly 80 percent of the total population of the USSR. In 1969–1970, the gross reproduction rate of the population in the USSR was 1.16; while in Byelorussia it was 1.11, and Estonia 1.04. Over the same period, reproduction rates were high in the republics of Central Asia, Azerbaijan, and Kazakhstan. For instance, in Uzbekistan it was 2.73, and in Tadjikistan 2.86 [2].

As a whole, as we mentioned above, population reproduction is expanding in all the constituent republics. The past few years have been marked by a rise in the general number of births which is explained by the fact that the numerous cohorts born in the first postwar years have entered the prime reproductive age. Thus the birth rate of the population of USSR has increased from 17 per 1,000 in 1969 to 17.8 per 1,000 in 1971 [1].

Of course, apart from age-sex and family structures of the population there is a whole complex of other factors affecting the rate of fertility. For instance, in large cities, especially in those with a population exceeding 500,000, the birth rate is, as a rule, much higher than in smaller towns or in the countryside. However, urbanization and the evolvement of certain standards of demographic behavior as a consequence of urbanization do not produce any appreciable effect on the level of fertility, as it was believed before. Urbanization and its impact on fertility should be considered in close connection with many economic, socioeconomic and ethnic factors.

The present demographic situation in the USSR is marked by intensified migrational fluidity—migration from the countryside to the town, as well as interregional and interrepublican migration. The country's intensive industrial development in conjunction with the improvement of the material-technical base of agriculture has contributed to a steady rise in the gross number and share of the urban population in the overall population of the country. In 1972, the urban population of the USSR accounted for 58 percent of the total figure (in 1913 it was 18 percent; in 1940, 33 percent). This increase was mainly due to the migration of the rural population. Thus, in the period of 1959–1970—the years when census was taken—the country's rural population decreased by 3.1 million, while the urban population increased by 36 million. The main factors contributing to this growth were the migration of the rural population to towns, territorial-administrative changes (administrative conversion of rural communities into urban settlements), as well as the natural growth of the urban population itself.

The rapid development of the national economy, above all of industry, has led to a marked growth of urban dwellers. Between 1926 and 1971, 955 new towns and cities appeared. The number of cities with a population over 100,000 each increased from 31 to 222, while the number of their dwellers from 9.5 million to 77.5 million.

Over the period between the censuses of 1959 and 1970, the urban population of the USSR had grown by 14.6 million due to natural growth, by 5 million due to administrative conversion of rural settlements into urban ones because of their industrial development, and by more than 16 million on account of migration from country to town.

There was a 57 percent increase in the number of dwellers in cities with populations from 100,000 to 500,000, and a 78 percent increase in cities with populations from 500,000 to 3 million each. By the beginning of 1972 the USSR contained 10 cities with populations of one million or more.

The development of population and the development of society are interrelated processes. The role of population in social development as well as certain peculiarities of the demographic situation in the USSR—including demographic differentials among different constituent republics, as well as between urban and rural residents—necessitate not only a detailed study of the role of demographic factors in economic development but also a study of interrelationships between economic and demographic phenomena with a view to elaborating a correct strategy of economic and demographic advancement.

Extensive research into interrelationships of migration of the population and the country's economic progress and higher living standards is essential in ensuring success of measures to further improve the labor and living conditions of the population and effective performances of the economy as a whole. The Socialist society is effecting a complex of measures to control processes taking part in it, including those connected with population. This complex of measures can rightly be called population policy.

POPULATION POLICY

Population policy is regarded by us as a system of measures aimed, directly or indirectly, at altering the conditions of the life and work of the population, as well as its quantitative and qualitative characteristics.

In the Socialist society the population policy is designed to improve the conditions of life and work of the population. It is likewise concerned with its physical and spiritual health, higher educational and cultural standards, better professional and vocational training, all-round concern for motherhood and childhood, the creation of necessary conditions for strengthening family ties, and concern for the elderly and old-age people.

¶ HEALTH ADVANCES

In 1971, Soviet doctors accounted for over one-fourth of the world's total of doctors. It had 698,000 doctors in all specialities, or 28 per 10,000 people, while in 1913 the ratio was 1.8 per 10,000. Medical assistance in the

USSR is free of charge. All expenses are borne by the state. During a period of illness, factory and office workers receive money payments from trade-union social security funds.

¶ EDUCATION

Signal successes have been scored in education and culture during Soviet years. Before the revolution three-fourths of the population could neither read nor write. The returns of the 1959 census confirmed the fact that the USSR had become a country of 100 percent literacy. Forty nationalities had developed their alphabets. In 1913, there were only 190,000 people with a higher and specialized secondary education engaged in the national economy, while in 1971 this figure rose to 18 million.

¶ MATERNAL AND CHILD CARE

The state protects the interests of mother and child, provides assistance to mothers with many children and unmarried mothers. An expectant mother is entitled to a paid maternity leave of 112 days (56 days before and 56 days after childbirth). An extensive network of maternity homes, women's consultation and children's preschool centers has been developed to protect the health of mother and child. In 1971 alone, 400 million rubles were spent on various grants to unmarried mothers and mothers with many children. There were 9.6 million children in kindergartens and nurseries.

¶ CARE FOR THE ELDERLY

Under the Soviet pension law men are entitled to an old-age pension at 60, and women at 55. Many categories of people are entitled to special pension privileges, such as larger pensions, an earlier qualifying age or shorter qualifying service record. This applies to people working underground, in hot shops or on other arduous jobs. Women who have borne and raised five or more children are entitled to a pension at 50. In 1972 there were 42 million pensioners, including 26 million people receiving pensions on account of old age.

¶ STANDARD OF LIVING

The effectiveness of the population policy is ensured by society's increasing capability to meet the population's growing requirements, the volume and pattern of which are undergoing substantial changes due to the development of the population and the growth of scientific and technological progress. The present level of productive forces and the nature of social relations enable the society to meet more fully the growing and changing requirements of the population which, in its turn, is also undergoing qualitative and quantitative changes. It is natural therefore that in working out national economic projections the Socialist countries plan the expansion of the scale of social production to ensure greater popular consumption, and establish a more effective ratio between the material, financial, and labor resources of a country, on the one hand, and the population with its growing requirements, on the other.

We strive to establish more feasible optimal variants of correlation between production and requirements, between growing productive forces, the size and sociodemographic structures of the population and the pattern of its requirements. Social production conditions the scale of social consumption and the pattern of the individual requirements of the members of society.

The law of progressively growing requirements serves, in its turn, as a kind of stimulus for the functioning of the law of the steady growth of labor productivity. In the conditions of scientific and technological progress there are growing demands for higher skills called for by modern production. A consequence of this is the law of the development of population. This implies qualitative and quantitative changes in population brought about by those changes which take place in society as a consequence of the development of productive forces and production relations.

¶ MAIN ELEMENTS OF POLICY

The population policy, the aims, intensity, and concrete contents of which are determined by the nature of a given socioeconomic structure, comprises, according to our view, the following main elements:

1. A change of labor conditions and of the limits of working ages depending on the types of employment and changing conditions of labor. The length of the working time of the "able-bodied" population and the length of leisure time. Concern for labor protection, professional, and vocational training, etc.

2. A change of the living conditions of all the strata of the population. This involves real wages, or level of income, housing conditions, access to everyday services and cultural achievements, availability of modern medical services, the scale of recreation time and the pattern of its use. This also involves an exceptionally important drive for better environmental conditions.

3. Control of the processes related to the reproduction of population (social mobility, natural migration, migrational fluidity) with a view to forming a desirable intensity of these processes. This is exactly what we call demographic policy dealing only with the reproduction of the population in terms of quantity and quality.

Demographic policy is a complex of measures controlling demographic processes in the interests of society as a whole and of each of its members in particular. It should be emphasized that we imply namely the complex of measures embracing all kinds of population movement since all of them are closely interrelated and interdependent. For instance, a low natural growth of population in one area or another may be a consequence of not only a change in fertility intensity but also of the migration of young people from a given area into other parts of the country.

In essence or content demographic policy operates in the following three main directions:

1. It promotes social mobility (movement of population from one social group to another).

2. It influences the processes of the natural replacement of generations the nature of which is determined, in the long run, by the rates of fertility and mortaliy. It is namely the rates of fertility and mortality that determine changes in the size and the age-sex structure of the population. Apart from changes in fertility intensity there is another phenomenon—incidental growth of births (particularly first-borns) under the impact of the age-sex structure of the population. For example, this is exactly what accounts for a rise in the rates of nuptiality and fertility recorded in our country in 1970–1972.

3. It exerts influence upon the direction and scale of migration. The migrational policy carried out by the state has a direct bearing on the policy of resettling the population within the country's boundaries.

Having touched upon the contents of population and demographic policies, their correlation and interrelationships, I would like to dwell on the methods employed in carrying these policies into effect.

POLICY IMPLEMENTATION

Specific individuals making up the population live and work in the conditions of certain social relations. They are interconnected by numerous and different ties of economic, political, ethnic, and family nature. Population represents an improved complex of people placed in the conditions of interdependence with regard to the prevailing social relations and the development of the country's productive forces.

The social nature and the methods of implementing demographic policy depend on a degree of effectiveness of a socioeconomic policy pursued by a state, while its social structure predetermines the possibility of using these methods of demographic policy or others.

In dealing with the methods of demographic policy it should be borne in mind that social conditions are characterized by numerous stable or recurrent ties and relations. The recognition of a close connection between the reproduction of population and the conditions of its life and labor is, at the same time, the recognition of the multitude of interdependent ties between the processes of the reproduction of population and other social processes. These ties cannot be studied by demographic methods alone.

We feel that the importance of a complex study of social processes can hardly be overestimated. After defining demographic policy as a complex of measures regulating demographic processes and after emphasizing its objective connection with the socioeconomic policy of a state I would like now to specify the contents or essence of the demographic policy of the USSR. This policy is aimed at developing the type of the reproduction of population that would fully accord with the basic goal of the Socialist society—a fuller satisfaction of the material and spiritual requirements of the entire population. The demographic policy in our society is directed at the all-around development of the population as a whole and of the individual in particular. In other words, this policy can be regarded as managing the reproduction of the population.

Management of demographic processes cannot be understood as elaboration of some kind of compulsory "plan" which .the population should be encouraged to implement. This not only runs counter to the very nature of Socialist democracy but is impossible in essence. With regard to fertility, migration, and social mobility the aim of demographic policy is to help develop in the country's population stable patterns of demographic behavior in accordance with the long-term interests of the society.

But this requires not only much time—tangible results of demographic policy tend to reveal themselves after some time, often many years—but also the application of an extensive range of measures of demographic policy. In studying the practicability of these measures of demographic policy or others it is essential therefore to realize that all of them should represent an extensive and coherent complex of measures designed as a whole to develop such patterns of demographic behavior which would accord with the long-term interests of both the society and individual families.

What kind of measures do we have in mind? The methods of demographic policy can roughly be subdivided into three groups:

1. Economic measures (allowances to big families, reduced taxation of big families, privileges in providing them with housing, the development of the network of children's centers, everyday communal services, etc.).

In the case of migration, migrants receive all kinds of incentive benefits if they move in a direction desired by society. They receive higher wages, and every effort is made to speed up housing construction and development of everyday facilities in the areas they move into. Measures are likewise taken to provide opportunities of work for the "secondary" members of a family, mainly for women.

2. Legal measures (legislative acts with regard to allowing or banning the production and use of contraceptives, family planning, establishment of the minimal marriage age, etc.).

3. Measures of sociopsychological influence comprising the use of all information media—the press, radio, television, as well as all arts to influence the demographic behavior of the population in a direction desired by society and in keeping with the legal, philosophical views and ethical norms prevailing in a given society.

It should be emphasized that desirable results can hardly be achieved by administrative-legal or sociopsychological measures alone without taking economic measures.

In effecting demographic policy which would take into consideration the complexity of a given demographic situation and accord with the interests of a state it is necessary to bear in mind that demographic processes have a certain force of inertia and, as it was stressed before, the results can only be felt after a long period of time.

One of the major practical problems of demographic policy is the estimation of means to be allocated by a state for carrying this policy into effect. There is no need to say that such estimation is rather involved in terms of methodology. The complexity of such estimating also consists in the fact that it calls for determining the size of expenditures for the entire complex of demographic policy measures which are often closely interrelated. For instance, in estimating family allowances it is necessary to take into consideration the actual and prospective distribution of families by the number of children in them. Information on the actual size of families can be obtained from census returns or records wherever they are kept. So far as the projection of family composition is concerned this is a very involved problem from the point of view of methodology since it is closely connected with the projection of such processes as nuptiality, divorce rate, and fertility, in addition to a number of complex social problems.

The size of allowances for children depends on many factors including the determination of a fertility rate desired by society. In other words, there can be different degrees of encouraging the birth of the first, second, third, and all subsequent children in a family, taking into consideration an optimal fertility level. In determining the size of allowances it is likewise necessary to take into account the real cost of maintaining a child in a family; otherwise such allowances can lose their significance as a stimulating factor. Besides, allowances for children are sometimes designed as material assistance to families having children but not as a stimulus to fertility. In such cases the size of allowances increases depending on the number of children in a family. It follows that such estimations call for much effort and detailed information which is not always available. At the same time a scientifically based analysis of the problems of demographic policy should be made by studying the entire complex of the problems of population.

What kind of investigations do we find most appropriate in this connection?

First of all, it is necessary to make a thorough study of the present conditions of the reproduction of population, the actual demographic situation. It is essential to ascertain the reasons determining a given rate of fertility, to study factors influencing it, to investigate relations between the socioeconomic conditions of life and fertility rate.* It is likewise necessary to determine measures which would make it possible to influence the dynamics of population reproduction.

Besides, it is appropriate to investigate reasons for regional differences in mortality rates and their pattern.

Of equally major importance for determining demographic policy is research into migration in its different forms. Without analyzing the demographic characteristics of migrants it is also difficult to identify and solve many problems connected with immigration.

In our view, particular attention in studying population problems should be paid to the analysis of the working population, its employment and distribution in small, average, and large towns as well as in the countryside. The questions of theory and methodology should likewise be given due attention in studying population problems. In this respect three groups of questions for research can roughly be identified as follows:

1. Elaboration of the theoretical foundations and methodology of integral research;

2. Elaboration of the theory of a demographic optimum as an ultimate goal for which we should strive in the course of the development of population;

3. Questions of internal migration as part of a planned method of developing less economically advanced regions.

Of paramount importance is also the analysis of the demographic aspects of the development of the country as a whole as well as of its separate regions. This makes it possible to determine the present economic-demographic balance which should be known in planning the country's socioeconomic development.

It is our profound belief that demographic policy can be successful only when it is carried out as a component part of a socioeconomic policy and

---

* The use of simulation models and the so-called economic-demographic accounts, apart from other methods of analysis, provide certain methodological possibilities. See [3].

promotes the development of population in keeping with social and economic requirements propounded by the Socialist society.

REFERENCES

1. *Narodnoe Khozyaystvo SSSR, 1922–1972 (The National Economy of the USSR).* Moscow, 1972. P. 40 (In Russian.)
2. *Vestnik Statistiki (Statistical Herald),* no. 12 (1971), p. 75. (In Russian.)
3. R. Stone. "Economic and demographic accounts and distribution of incomes." *Economic-Demographic Methods,* no. 5 (1971). (In Russian.)

CHAPTER 26

Summary

That is where population policy now stands in these countries, in the view of these informed observers. What are the common strands?

If one thing is clearer than any other in this array of policy discussion, it is the close relationship of the matter to the national circumstance. Each country reviews its own situation in the light of its own history and tradition, its own values and operating procedures, and determines its position accordingly. Thus the whole issue of population, already complicated in its very nature, becomes involved in a range of economic and social concerns of national importance and becomes progressively defined and decided in that light.

Nevertheless, the elements of population change—being born, moving, dying—are the same everywhere and hence give rise to similar perceptions, problems, and reactions. In this concluding chapter, I try to pull together from the country papers some common aspects in the consideration of population matters. First I summarize the bases of concern with population changes; then I deal with the courses of action used in response thereto; and finally I make a number of observations about the formulation of population policy in the modern world, among these most modernized nations.[1]

---

[1] I particularly wish to acknowledge the help I received on this chapter at the Belgrade meeting from several collaborators on this volume. The first draft was discussed there in considerable detail and I benefitted greatly from the various suggestions received at that time.

BASES OF CONCERN

In the developing countries the concern over population policy is reasonably clear: the problem is undue population growth and the aim is to lower the birth rate. What are the bases of concern in these developed countries?

Let us start with national policy on the central demographic variable of mortality. All these countries have major programs of public health in order to lower mortality and morbidity to the practicable minimum given available resources, both economic and medical-technological: a death rate "as low as possible." As we have noted, the death rates in these countries are markedly low for relatively older populations, and the (female) life expectancy is typically in the early to mid-seventies, or about twenty years higher than in the poor countries. However, some mortality differentials by socioeconomic or ethnic status do remain in many of these countries. Nevertheless, there appears to be little deliberate governmental policy to equalize the mortality rates of various groups within the society, although the health services designed for deprived sectors, where they exist, tend to work to that end. But to sound a common theme throughout this review, the policies of mortality reduction are primarily considered on other than demographic grounds.

In a few countries there is some concern with the differential demographic performance of ethnic groups within the community, and particularly with their fertility. Perhaps the chief examples are Israel, with three demographic subcommunities, and South Africa, with four, plus the past situation in Canada, with two; but the Flemish/Walloon situation in Belgium and the white/black one in the United States are also relevant, as well as several regional and urban/rural differentials with ethnic overtones as in Italy and the Soviet Union. Indeed, it would appear that rich/poor differences in fertility are mainly perceived as publicly troublesome only if simultaneously ethnic in character, as they typically are in nonhomogeneous societies.

Also in a few countries, but only a few, a concern arises over too much growth—concern, that is, with the same phenomenon as in the developing countries but for a different reason, namely, the potential effect of indefinitely continued population growth on the environment and on the amenities of "the quality of life." This point of view is perhaps best represented among these countries by the Netherlands, where density is a special concern, and by the United States and Great Britain, in both of which there has been a certain amount of public debate in recent years on the relationship of population to ecological/environmental problems.[2] These are the

---

[2] Among these countries the environmental issue related to population has arisen mainly in four highly industrialized countries—United States, Great Britain, Japan, and Australia. If this issue has stamina it lies ahead for other countries moving into major industrialization, and eventually for the entire world.

developed countries where the most concern has been expressed to reduce fertility, even though all now have rates of natural increase below 1 percent a year.

In many more countries the concern is to promote fertility from "too low" levels: in Japan, where earlier pressures for population growth are again being felt, largely for economic/employment reasons; in Israel, where there are political considerations in a hostile regional setting with religio-ethnic overtones and where differential fertility among the key social groups is a profoundly complicating factor; in Argentina, where the pro-growth stance vis-à-vis the "encroachment" of neighboring countries tends to unite opposing political factions; in France, where there has been a long history of efforts to stimulate fertility for political/ideological reasons attached to "national glory"; in Romania, where special targets of growth have been adopted, and in Spain, where steps were once taken in the same direction; in Greece and other eastern European countries where, like Japan, there is an effort to move the birth rate up for economic and ideological reasons; and perhaps implicitly in the Soviet Union.

So while most of the developing world is after lower growth and while worldwide discussion of the "population problem" continues to focus on that theme, the majority of these developed countries are seeking to move the other way—not far to be sure, and from a low base, but still in a slightly pronatalist direction. It thus appears that nations in particularly sensitive positions, as perceived locally (for example, Argentina, France, Israel), and nations with birth rates near or below replacement (for example, Bulgaria, Greece, Hungary, Japan, Poland, Romania) are not comfortable in those situations and seek remedies against "demographic decline," as Ireland similarly did under the impact of heavy emigration. Throughout human history, growth has been considered as a sign of health, and nongrowth a sign of stagnation or worse; as a 1954 Irish Commission Report put it, population growth means "buoyancy rather than inertia." On the national level, particularly in a politically competitive world, accepting stabilization in population growth seems to require a deliberate act of will.

Not that any of these countries is facing nongrowth very soon. None of them is likely to decline in population size over the visible future, short of a nuclear catastrophe; and the median country on this list, with constant fertility at 1965–1970 levels, will be about 25 percent larger in the year 2000 and nearly 50 percent larger fifty years from now. Even with fertility at replacement level from now on, the population of the developed countries would grow 10 percent on the average by 2000 and 15 percent by about 2020. As for zero growth by 2000 in these demographically favored nations, that would require on the average over a 25 percent linear decline in birth rates over the next three decades, which would still result in about a 12 percent increase in population. Thus zero growth still is some distance away for almost all these countries (migration aside).

Related to the pro-growth theme is the consideration of immigration either for the purpose of general development (as historically, for example, in Australia, Canada, Israel, South Africa, and the United States; and the reverse side of the coin in Ireland) or for the narrower end of selective employment (as, for example, in Belgium, France, and the Netherlands). In only a few countries is immigration still a major source of population growth—Australia, Belgium, Canada, Israel, the United States—and everywhere it appears to have had ethnic reverberations (for example, the Asians in Australia, the West Indians in England, the North Africans in France, the Oriental Jews in Israel, various groups in the United States). In recent years emigration has become problematic in some of these countries, as labor supply flows from south to north within Europe across national boundaries—from Greece and Italy and Spain to the more industrialized centers.

Finally, there is concern with the internal distribution of population, or more particularly the issues of urban concentration accompanying the historic shift from agricultural to nonagricultural employment. This theme is a prominent consideration in countries with, say, more than 70 percent of the population living in urban centers—and particularly Australia, Canada, Great Britain, the Netherlands, and the United States as well as in the Soviet Union—or with sharply growing metropolitan center(s) as with Great Buenos Aires in Argentina or Madrid-Barcelona-Bilbao in Spain or with major ethnic problems as in South Africa.

Thus it might be summarized that these countries are variously concerned with population policy in order to move toward population stabilization for environmental and "quality of life" reasons, in order to increase the birth rate slightly for political, economic, and psychological reasons, in order to adjust the contribution of immigration to demographic growth and social differentials, and in order to effect a presumably better distribution of population within the country.

But population is not an issue of really high priority in these countries except perhaps in a few cases seeking to increase fertility. "Population policy" is much more likely to surface as one factor in social policy, as illustrated particularly by the Soviet Union, rather than "in its own right"—as incidental to social welfare rather than directly demographic in cause and consequence.

COURSES OF ACTION

Given this definition of the demographic situation, what actions have the countries taken with regard to both growth and distribution?

To begin with, in very recent years, most of these countries have given explicit attention to the matter by appointing an official commission to study and advise on population policy (Table 1). Several of the countries have been "population concerned" in the past—Spain for centuries, France throughout this century, Australia and Ireland for decades, Japan from the early 1920s, Italy in Fascist times, Israel since its founding and before, the United States and Sweden in the 1930s, Great Britain in the 1940s, Poland after World War II. But the current interest appears to constitute the most concerted official attention to population affairs since the depression of the 1930s and perhaps the most concerted attention ever. The commissions have differing mandates, composition, duration, and position within the governmental structure, but they have in common the task of considering the effect of population trends upon the public welfare and pronouncing thereon. A few have already done so in published form, for example, Japan, Great Britain, and the United States,[3] and others are soon to appear, for example, Australia and the Netherlands.

As the countries have identified their demographic concerns, what can they do about them? The opportunities for intervention are not numerous. What are the policies proposed or followed in these countries?

¶ . . . WITH REGARD TO POPULATION GROWTH
Means of Fertility Control.
On the whole these countries have no comprehensive legal inhibitions against the practice of contraception. However: (1) the removal of restrictive laws is only recent and/or partial in Belgium, France, and the Netherlands; (2) the opportunity is only partial in some countries in that there are still medical restrictions against certain means, for example, the pill in Japan; (3) contraceptive services are not included in the public health programs of a few countries, for example, Argentina, Greece, Israel, and West Germany; (4) in some countries, the use of modern contraceptive means is *de facto* permitted whereas their advertising, promotion, import, or sale as such is prohibited or limited; and (5) the more modern means of contraception—the pill, the IUD, and sterilization—are not widely used in a number of these countries, which still rely on coitus interruptus, periodic abstinence, and the condom. Even in these advanced countries, that is, the recent technology of contraception has not advanced very far.

---

[3] Japan: Interim Report of the Population Problems Inquiry Council, "An Opinion on the Reproductivity Trend in Our Country," *Studies in Family Planning,* vol. 1, no. 56, August 1970.
    Great Britain: *Report of the Population Panel* (London: HMSO, March 1973).
    United States: Report of the Commission on Population Growth and the American Future, *Population and the American Future* (Washington: US Government Printing Office, March 1972).

TABLE 1.

National and Official Groups on Population Policy (recent and current)

Country	Dates	Title	Organization Composition	Mandate
Israel	1962–1966	Committee for Natality Problems	Mainly governmental officers	To inquire and advise the government on matters concerning natality policies, and in particular to consider means by which large and deprived families could be assisted.
	1968–	Demographic Center (in office of Prime Minister)	Core staff, with public committee and executive council	To carry out a policy to encourage and stimulate natality, an increase being crucial for the future of the Jewish people.
Bulgaria	1971–	Council for the Population Reproduction Problems (of the State Council)	Government officers	[not specified]
Greece	1968–	Ad Hoc Committee on Demographic Policy	Nongovernmental doctors, statisticians, and directors of social organizations	To study the nature, the dimensions, and the probable causes of the problems of Greek population and to propose ethically, socially, and economically acceptable corrective measures.
Hungary	1970–	Commission for Long-Range Planning of the Labor Force and Standard of Living	[not specified]	To contribute to the gradual increase in the number of births to the extent that at least *replacement* of the population be ensured; to equalize gradually, as far as possible, the age structure of the population.
Australia	1970–1973	Commission on Australia's Population and the Future	A nonparliamentary committee designated the National Population Inquiry, assigned by government to Australian National University; staffed by specialists, with Advisory Council	To inquire into all aspects of population in Australia and to study countries with which Australia has particularly close associations, contemporary population theories, national growth potential, variations in rate and pattern of that growth, distribution of population vis-à-vis the growth of major urban centers and technological advances. The Aboriginal population is to be the subject of a separate substudy.
Netherlands	1972–	Royal Commission on Population Problems (the Muntendam Commission)	Governmental officers, scientific experts, and representatives of women's organizations, trade unions, and employer's associations	To analyze the development, density, and composition of population, and its influencing factors, and the relations between demographic development and public health. To review the incidence of immigration and its social effect.
Czechoslovakia	1971–	Government Population Committee	28 members from ministries, labor unions, women's and youth	To formulate population policy, organize studies, coordinate relevant work, and propose govern-

Country	Year	Body	Composition	Purpose
Romania	1971–	National Commission of Demography (of the Council of State), supported by County Commissions	Governmental officers, demographic experts, representatives of academies and associations	To study the demographic phenomena, to draw up proposals on demographic policy of the party and the State; the effect of social and economic changes; the prospective dynamics of population and effects on education, manpower, consumer goods, etc.; urbanization; preparation of policy proposals and follow-up on implementation.
Canada	1967–	Manpower and Immigration Council	Outside government; appointed by Minister of Manpower and Immigration, after consultation with interested organizations	To advise on all matters pertaining to manpower resources in Canada, including immigrants to Canada, and their adjustment to Canadian life.
	1972–	Council of Resource and Environment Ministers	Federal and Provincial ministers; completed with regional committees and task forces outside and inside government	To facilitate discussion of common problems between governments and to promote public discussion.
Argentina	1971–	Demographic Policies Work Group	Representatives from both government and private organizations	To elaborate projects that would define the national demographic policies with particular regard to slow growth, immigration, regional distribution and internal migration, and social mobility.
France	1970–	High Consultative Committee on Population and the Family	Ministry of Labor, Work, and Population	
	1971–	High Consultative Committee on Working Women		To advise on matters referred by the host ministry.
	1971–	High Consultative Committee on the Family		
	1971	High Medical Committee on Health	Ministry of Health and Social Security	
Great Britain	1970–1971	Subcommittee of Select Committee on Science and Technology	Committee of Parliament	To inquire into the consequences of population growth.
	1971–1973	Population Panel		To assess evidence on population trends.
Japan	1969–1971	Population Problems Advisory Council	Outside and inside government Mainly governmental officers and demographic experts	To study the basic guidelines for population policy.
United States	1970–1972	Commission on Population Growth and the American Future	Congressional and public members	To inquire into population growth and internal migration to the year 2000 and the impact upon governmental, economic, and environmental resources; to assess "the various means appropriate to the ethical values and principles [to] . . . achieve a population level properly suited for . . . environmental, natural resources, and other needs."

As for legal abortion, the countries have both permissive and restrictive policies—permissive in Bulgaria, Czechoslovakia, Finland, Great Britain, Hungary, Japan, Sweden, and the United States; restrictive in Argentina, Belgium, Greece, Ireland, Israel, Italy, and Romania; both in Australia, in different states; and presumably liberalizing in Australia, France, the Netherlands, and West Germany. Induced abortion is always legalized on other than demographic grounds, usually for health reasons, but it has enough (perceived) demographic effect to be withdrawn or limited on demographic grounds, as recently in Romania and continually under discussion in Japan. There is strong religio-moral opposition in several countries, sometimes leading to tacit toleration of the lesser evil of contraception, as in Greece and Poland. In any case, induced abortion is apparently an important means of fertility control in several countries with legal prohibitions that normally are not enforced, for example, Belgium, France, Greece, Israel, Italy.

Actually, there appears to be a rather close relationship between the use of "old-fashioned" means of contraception on the one hand and the incidence of abortion on the other. Almost all the countries that rely on coitus interruptus or condom as their primary method of contraception have very high ratios of abortions to live births, over 1:3 (for example, Belgium, Greece, Hungary, Japan, Poland, and Romania) as compared to Sweden with 1:7. Apparently fertility control is managed by the use of traditional methods of contraception with ready recourse to abortion in case of failure.

Thus even in these developed countries the principle of voluntary fertility control based on modern technology is not fully realized. It is more nearly approximated for couples wanting children, but even there the technologically possible assistance in infertility and subfecundity is probably not universally available in practice. For couples not wanting children, the technologically possible services are even less available. In only about one-third of the most advanced countries in the world is modern fertility control widely available and legally practiced in the full array of technically and medically available means, both pre- and post-conception— only in Bulgaria, Czechoslovakia, Finland, Great Britain, Hungary, Poland, Sweden, and the United States (see Table 2).

Provision of Family Assistance.
Characteristic of these countries is some system of family assistance or "protection of the family." It is normally justified on social welfare grounds but often has a latent demographic intent as well. The system takes various forms and ranges in substance from trivial benefits (for example, in Australia, Canada, Israel, Japan, and the United States) to moderate ones (for

TABLE 2.

Legal Policies on Fertility Control Services

Country	Legal Availability of Modern Contraception (pill, IUD, condom, sterilization)	Legal Availability of Induced Abortion	Legal Fertility Control Services in Governmental Programs of Public Health	Legal Availability of Advertising, Publicity, etc., on Fertility Control Practices
Ireland	No	No	No	No
Israel	Yes	No	No	Yes
Finland	Yes	Yes, with liberal conditions	Yes	Yes
Sweden	Yes	Yes, with conditions	Yes	Yes
Bulgaria	Yes	Yes, with conditions	Yes	
Greece	Yes, but no vasectomy	No	No	No
Belgium	Yes	No	Yes (in different ministry)	No
Hungary	Yes, but IUD recent	Yes	Yes	
Australia	Yes, with limits on sterilization	One state only, conditional; changes appear imminent	Assisted through subsidies to private organizations	Yes, in one state
Netherlands	Yes	Apparently moving in this direction	Assisted through subsidies to private organizations	Yes
Czechoslovakia	Yes	Yes, with liberal conditions	Yes	Yes
Romania	Yes, but pill and IUD only on medical indication and supervision	No, except under restricted conditions		
South Africa	Yes	No	Yes	No
Canada	Yes	Yes, with conditions	Yes	Yes, with restrictions
Argentina	Yes, except for sterilization	No	No	No
Poland	Yes	Yes, with conditions	Yes	Yes
Spain	No	No	No	No
France	Yes recently, except for sterilization	No	No	No
Great Britain	Yes	Yes, with conditions	Yes	Yes
Italy	Yes recently, except for sterilization	No	No	No
West Germany	Contraception yes, sterilization with conditions	Yes, with conditions; liberalization expected	No	No
Japan	Pill and IUD no, others yes	Yes	Yes	Yes
United States	Yes	Yes	Yes	No, in many states
Soviet Union	Yes	Yes	Yes	Yes

TABLE 3.

Family Assistance Programs (in US$ at exchange value in 1972)

Country	Marriage Payment	Birth Payment	Maternity Benefits
Ireland	Small ($24 max.) $240 income tax allowance	About $8	Yes, $45/mo. for 3 mos.
Israel	No	$50	Free delivery
Finland	No	$20	Free prenatal, delivery, and postnatal care
Sweden		$227	Free obstetrical care
Bulgaria		⅙ times average monthly salary for 1st child; 1½ times for 2nd; 4 times for 3rd; then back to ⅙	Free delivery
Greece	5–10% of salary		$40–200 for each delivery
Belgium	No	$240 for 1st child, to $90 for 3rd+	Free delivery (normally)
Hungary		$40 for layette	Yes, incl. $40–65
Australia	Housing loans	$30–35/child	Yes, essentially
Netherlands	No	No	Free delivery and care
Czechoslovakia	Housing loans	About $325	Free prenatal, delivery, and antenatal care; about $80 monthly allowance for 2+ children until youngest is 2
Romania	No	$190 for 3rd+ child	Free delivery
South Africa	No	No	No
Canada	No	No	No
Argentina	$100	$80	
Poland	Yes	Yes	Yes
Spain	$105	$50	Free delivery and ancillary services
France	No.	$160, under certain conditions	Free delivery
Great Britain	No	$65	$16/wk. for 18 wks.; free medical, nursing, and ancillary services
Italy			Yes
West Germany	No	Yes	Free delivery, plus associated medical care
Japan	No	No	Poor only
United States	No	No	Poor only
Soviet Union	No		Yes

Maternity Leave	Children's Allowances	Tax and Other Benefits for Families with Children
Yes, $45/mo. for 3 mos.	For 4 children, about 6% of average industrial worker's salary; progressive with birth order	Taxes and welfare payments tied to dependents
70 da.	Yes, but only 2–3% of income	
12 wks.	$65–90/yr., 1st–3rd child, with special allowances for poor, etc.	Yes, and rent allowances for poor
Up to 6 mos. with compensation somewhat lower than sick leave	$280/yr., below age 16	Yes, and rent allowances too; more for single parent
120 da. for 1st child; 150 for 2nd; 180 for 3rd; then back to 120	Under 5% average monthly salary for 1 child; 16% for 2 children; 44% for 3	Housing preferences for larger families
12 wks.	3–6% of salary, then $17/mo. for 3rd+ child (approx. 17% of average monthly income)	Yes, and substantial for 3rd+ child
14 wks. at reduced salary	From $16–48/mo., by age and birth order	For all low income families
20 wks.	Nothing for 1, $10/mo. for 2, up to $50 for 6, or 10–50% of expenditures on children	Housing preferences
Yes for government employees; minimum of 6 wks.	$2–8 per child/month, increasing with number of children	Tax benefits
12 wks.	$12–35/mo., per child, up with birth order; per term (?)—$50–98 acc. to birth order	Yes
26 wks. for married mothers and 35 wks. for single mothers (90% of net wage). Unpaid leave until child is 2 yrs.	4–70% of average income, from 1–5 children	Rent reductions acc. to birth order (5–50%), housing loans that are reduced acc. to no. of children, social security benefits
112 da. with higher payment for 3rd+ birth	$7–40/mo., from 1–5 children, or 10–60% of average income	Yes
Yes	Yes, below certain income	Yes
Paid maternity leave, 15 wks., for salaried women	Averages $7/mo., for all children	Yes
	For large families, about 20% of average salary	Yes
12 wks.	Recent increase to about 10% of average wages	Yes
12 wks.	$5–6/child/mo., with increase of 25–35% for larger families	Yes, esp. for large families
Sick leave for pregnant working women before and after birth	From $18/mo. for 2 children, to $50 for 3, and up to $135 for 6	Yes
No	After 1st, about $10/wk., or 10% average household income	Yes, progressive with number of children
14–21 wks. (80% salary); 30% salary until child is 1 year.	3.8% income regardless of number of children	Yes
14 wks.	Beginning with 2nd child, amount depending on income	Yes
12 wks.	Below certain income, for 3rd+ child ($10/mo.)	Yes
Generally, no variable	Poor only, as welfare payments	Yes, but slight
Paid maternity leave	After 4th child, lump sum and monthly payments	Yes

example, in Argentina, Belgium, France, Greece, Italy, the Netherlands, Poland, South Africa, Sweden, West Germany) to quite substantial ones (in Bulgaria, Czechoslovakia, Great Britain for the poor, Hungary, Romania) as summarized in Table 3.[4] Particularly noteworthy is a sharp progression in allowances with parity in some countries. Nonetheless, it is difficult, perhaps impossible, to directly attribute fertility behavior to such allowance programs; most informed observers believe they have not been notably successful as pronatalist measures. What can be said is that countries with the lowest birth rates in the world have and have had for some years some of the largest programs of family assistance tied to numbers of children.

Female Participation in the Labor Force.

In almost all these countries women have a substantial place in the (nonagricultural) labor force, with nearly 40 percent of adult women in employment outside the home in the median country. In several, that place is specifically encouraged by governmental policy—either through various benefits provided for working women, particularly with regard to maternity and childrearing (as in the detailed provisions of eastern European countries, including some child care benefits) or through laws and regulations forbidding discrimination in employment by sex (for example, the United States culminating in the proposed Equal Rights Amendment to the Constitution).

However, the relationship between fertility and women's participation in the labor force is extremely complicated. There appears to be a rough relationship between female employment and fertility (Figure 1)—the more of the former, the less of the latter—but the data are far from firm and the temporal direction of influence is unclear (which caused the other?). In any case, many of the related policies, like maternity benefits, are meant to be both pro-employment and pro-natality; but they sometimes backfire by being so generous as to discourage employers.

Manipulation of International Migration.

Opening and closing this particular valve on population growth is not only available to governments; it is also sanctioned by public opinion and historical experience as "legitimate" (even though it is a "coercive" means of affecting population growth) and it can be effective. There are six positions.

> *First*, in some countries, international migration is now a negligible factor in growth (Argentina, Bulgaria, Hungary, Japan, Poland, Romania, South Africa).

---

[4] Where trivial means up to 5 percent of the average monthly income, moderate means of the order of 10–15 percent, and substantial means 20 percent or more.

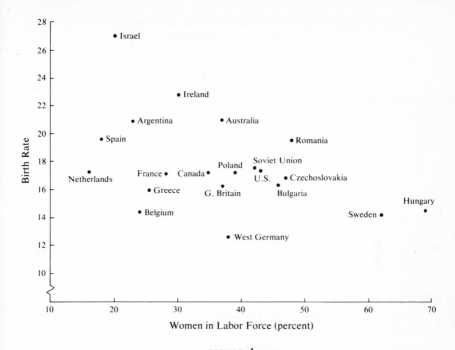

Birth Rate by Proportion of Women in Labor Force (circa 1971)

Second, in a few countries, emigration is larger than immigration and thus exerts a negative effect on overall growth (Great Britain, Greece, Italy).

Third, in some countries of western Europe (Belgium, France, Great Britain, the Netherlands, West Germany), short-term immigration has been used to "fill out" the labor force, typically at the bottom.

Fourth, as the other side of that coin, there are the countries at the sending end of that migration (Greece, Ireland, Italy, Spain) and this intracontinental exchange makes for problems and opportunities at both ends: cultural assimilation and repatriation, the export of unemployment, the balance of payments. Moreover, the relative availability in western Europe of a cheap labor supply from the region may very well soften national concern with the declining birth rate, as compared to a country like Japan; and the declining working population, shortened work hours and longer and more holidays, plus the European Economic Community, will probably keep the flow going.

Fifth, in the United States, the population commission recommended no further increase in legal immigration (already net by far the largest in the world) in view of demographic pressures together with a halt to the presumably large-scale illegal immigration; and suggested that the flow of migrants be continuously monitored on demographic grounds, thus effectively bringing the population situation into the consideration of migration for the first time. And both Great Britain and South Africa are seeking to restrict immigration flows.

Sixth, in a few countries, notably Australia and Canada and Israel where it has contributed between a third and a half of recent growth, immigration has been traditionally encouraged as a population growth measure. However, contemporary public discussions in Israel reveal the first signs of reservations about the continuation of that policy.

Other Policies.

In a few countries, an important determinant of both population growth and population distribution, though not normally intended as such, has been the policy and practice with regard to *housing*: small flats with only one or two bedrooms may tend to keep people from coming to the city but even more they discourage early marriage and large families. Almost certainly the declining postwar birth rates in Japan and eastern Europe show the impact of the housing situation in those countries. At the same time, the allocation of public housing in Ireland to families with at least two children means that the newly married are likely to have the requisite number as soon as possible.

Again in a few countries (Czechoslovakia, Finland, Japan, Sweden, the United States) there is a current movement toward incorporating *population education* in the school system, typically along with environmental or parenthood/sex education as these subjects have pressed upon public concern and claimed the attention of young people in view of their effects into the next generations.

Although they might be quite important with regard to population trends, it is worth noting that relatively little attention is given in these papers to the place of *marital laws* (for example, minimum age at marriage) or requirements with regard to *military or national service* (which could also affect marriage age). Perhaps the major exception is the suggestion that the Irish laws against divorce may have had something to do with the traditionally low rates of marriage in that country and hence with fertility and population growth.

A special case is the policy of *land reclamation* in the Netherlands, a unique response to considerations of population density. The plan in the Netherlands is to enlarge the country by a total of about 2 percent in the decades from now to the year 2000, as compared with a natural increase of the population of just under 1 percent a year.

Finally, a few governments have sought to affect population growth by *exhortation*. Sometimes it takes the form of prizes and awards: monetary awards in Hungary and Spain and formerly in Israel for mothers of large families, medals in Bulgaria, titles in Romania ("Heroine Mother," "Maternal Glory"). Sometimes it is a direct call to patriotism as with an Israeli leader's reference to one's "demographic duty" to increase the birth rate, or a proposed propaganda campaign "that the child is a great value for the Hungarian society and families taking upon themselves to bring up many children deserve the respect of the society." There is no evidence as to the effectiveness of such exhortation to the "correct" demographic behavior in the national interest, in either direction.

¶ . . . WITH REGARD TO POPULATION DISTRIBUTION
In several of the countries the distribution of the population is a substantial concern, and in some, like Japan and Great Britain, it is the major concern of the demographic policy at this time. Many of the countries are concerned with regional distribution or urban concentration, have tried various methods of countering such concentration, and have not been notably successful in doing so.

The methods utilized have been both push-pull: restrictions on immigration to certain urban centers through use of "influx control" and "internal passports" (South Africa), creation of new towns or encouragement of growth centers (France, Great Britain, Japan, South Africa, the Soviet Union, Sweden, the United States), administrative decentralization (Greece, Japan, the Netherlands, South Africa), subsidized dispersal of industry (Argentina, Finland, Great Britain, Ireland, Japan, the Netherlands, South Africa, the Soviet Union, the United States, West Germany), and support to disadvantaged areas (Belgium, Finland, Great Britain, Italy, Japan, the Netherlands, South Africa, Sweden, the United States, West Germany). Meanwhile the trend of the urban centers continues—not always to the central city but outward into the metropolitan area—and governments have found it extremely difficult to stop or lessen the flow.

OBSERVATIONS

Finally, a few residual observations emerge from this survey of population policy in the developed world. Despite the great diversity of national circumstances, some points of general interest can perhaps be identified.

To begin with, what of the very concept of "population policy?" How does a country come to recognize that it has a "population problem" and that something might or should be done by way of national policy?

As is clear from these reports, the answers to such questions are variously given. But in general "population problems" are perceived and defined in a limited number of ways: too little growth, too much growth, the reliance on immigration as against natural increase, the wrong internal distribution, unacceptable consequences of current trends, for example, in environmental cost or unemployment. The particular form may differ from place to place but those are the broad bases of concern. And they become problematic, as one of the authors suggests, when "the behavior of individuals and the welfare of society are seen to be markedly divergent"— seen so, that is, by responsible government officers.

The policies that emerge even then may or may not be "population policies" in an explicit and direct sense. In most of these countries these years, they are *not* explicit for the most part and certainly not adopted exclusively on demographic grounds. More often than not they are seen as part of social policy more generally—part of family or child welfare or health or economic development or environmental balance or some other "larger" concern—and in the case of both growth and distribution.

Thus the criteria by which demographic trends are evaluated have not been solely demographic in character but more broadly social, economic, environmental, political, and humanitarian: the "protection of the family," employment needs, environmental pressures, national power, ethical access to fertility control. The roots of concern and the proposed measures deal not only with the determinants of demographic trends but also, perhaps even more, with their consequences for the public welfare. As a result, there remain what appear to be contradictions and conflicts in some country positions—policies that appear to lead in different directions, as with pronatalist allowances coupled with liberal abortion policies (though when many of the pronatalist programs began in Europe, they were coupled to anticontraception regulations, in full consistency).

And that in turn is testimony to the complicated and pervasive nature of the subject. In several countries it is bound up with the central character of the society: the ethnic divisions in Belgium and Canada and South Africa, the church in Spain, the regional differences in Italy, density in the Netherlands, the role of immigration in the "new" countries of Australia and Israel, Socialist objectives in the Soviet Union. Perhaps even more it is testimony to the priority of such other issues. Population is a concern of most of these countries—witness the several current commissions—but at the same time it does not rank high on the agenda of national problems: it is more given than problematic, more to be adjusted to than changed. Moreover, it seems unlikely that population problems will gain enough priority in these countries over the next years to produce a fully consistent policy position based exclusively or largely on demographic considerations.

As we have noted, many of these countries have a long history of concern with "population policy." Perhaps what distinguishes the present period is the breadth of concern, both internationally and substantively.

With regard to the international scene, these are the population years— that is, a period of great concern with population matters. The rapid population growth of the developing world has been placed on the world agenda as one of the great issues facing mankind for the remainder of this century and beyond. Under present conditions of international relationships, it would be remarkable if the developed world were not brought into such deliberations, not only with reference to assistance to developing countries but also with regard to their own situations. So we have come to recognize that we are all in the same demographic boat, so to speak, and the advanced countries have naturally been led to look at their own situations.

Then, with regard to substance, what several of the countries have seen has been the opposite of the developing countries, namely, in their own perceptions, "too little" growth for national well-being. Particularly is this the response of countries with near or below replacement levels of fertility and, for one reason or another, no real opportunity for growth via immigration. Unlike the current developing world, which is of course in a quite different demographic position, the political interest is to sustain population growth more than to limit growth—but at a low level. Countries do not seem to be at ease with "too low" a growth rate.

Beyond that, the substance of the debate on population issues has both an old and a new ring: still some disputation on religious grounds but coupled now with the environmental implications of continued growth in the most industrialized nations, the fertility role of liberated women, political relations within a region, the powerful momentum of urbanization and, slightly further down the road, metropolitanization.

Moreover, and perhaps increasingly recognized these years, there is the fact of internal demographic division: the existence of different demographic communities within the same society, in fertility as well as mortality, and with the consequent exacerbation of related social and political problems—the periphery and the interior in Spain, the industrialized west and the agricultural east in Romania (now declining), the more prosperous center/north in Italy and the poorer south, the Protestant north and the Catholic south in the Netherlands, the ethnic/regional differences in Czechoslovakia and South Africa and the Soviet Union, the "linguistic problem" in Belgium and Canada, the ethnic groups within Israel, the native/"colored" in Great Britain, the white/black in the United States. Although nowhere is it an explicitly pursued goal of national policy to equalize the vital rates of such internal divisions, nevertheless a rough convergence appears in several of the countries through the general course of social development and the more equitable distribution of medical services.

Thus the issues of population, in dispute virtually everywhere, are not conducive to an easy unanimity—they touch too many deep feelings. Nor are they conducive to easy "solutions" either—partly because they touch too many deep feelings, partly because of their long-term character, partly because they are not very amenable to specific short-term influences. In all the effort to affect demographic growth in recent years, perhaps the two most effective measures, certainly in the short run, have been the manipulation of immigration and of legalized abortion—with major effects in both directions. As for measures to affect population distribution, none of them has worked very well in countering the movement to the metropolitan centers that characterize all these countries.

Where the issue is defined as sufficiently problematic, governments do take steps but they are not always successful. Countries do what can be done, particularly when their policies promise other consequences that are good in their own right, as with the health consequences of liberalized abortion in some countries or the contributions of child assistance payments to family welfare in others. For the most part, it may even be that the impact of demographic-related policies has been greater on the other scores.

In any case, the effectiveness of "population policy" in most of these countries does not appear to be notably high, for example, in encouraging fertility on the one hand or discouraging urban concentration on the other. And because of the need for cooperation on the part of very large numbers of individuals, the objectives of demographic policy perhaps cannot be met very precisely. The data are not very firm, but across the world it may be fair to say that the developing countries have done better in lowering birth rates than the developed countries have done in increasing them; or, perhaps alternatively, that it is easier to lower birth rates by policy measures than to raise them.

In the Introduction to this volume, I noted that these countries represent the whole spectrum of industrialized nations, across culture and politics. It is worth noting here that the major population issues and their treatment appear to be quite similar across countries of different social organization—roughly speaking, across capitalist and socialist/communist. Whatever the economic and political theories, the demographic causes and consequences seem to be essentially similar—problems of urban growth, ethnic and regional differentials, means of fertility control, employment of women, family assistance efforts. In this sense, the demography overcomes or shines through the political and economic overlay.

What of the future? The moderate pace of change in both the demographic facts and their perception makes it hazardous to guess, particularly when one is conscious of the fate of similar forecasts in the past. Still the goal of population replacement as a standard component of the modernized, secularized society may be dimly visible ahead: up to replacement in some countries, down to replacement in others. That goal, leading to population stabilization in a matter of decades, was recommended as national policy first in Japan and supported by the commission in the United States, and may become an important feature of the developed world over the remainder of this century. As we saw in Chapter 1, the fifth child is beginning to disappear in most of these countries; perhaps the fourth is on the way out in several; and some countries are now engaged in the battle for the third.

In any case, the variability of demographic trends is being seen as more of a problem, as against their magnitude: for example, the sharp fluctuations in birth rates, up or down, that leave a legacy of social problems for decades. Many of these countries have experienced that situation in the past quarter century, and are beginning to appreciate the advantages of a more uniform number of births. Beyond that, the stationary population in equilibrium with natural resources is gaining more attention and perhaps, in a somewhat longer view, more familiarity and welcome.

Finally, there appears to be a growing concern with qualitative population issues now that the quantitative range seems to have narrowed—with issues of population distribution, with the amenities and esthetics of space, with environmental cleanliness, with age structure, even with genetic considerations over the long run. So while the developing world struggles with numbers, the developed struggles with the translation of low rates into human values.

The developed world accounts for about one third of the world's population. Given present or likely trends, it will be even less a decade from now, or two or three. Yet the developing world is moving in the direction of industrialization and health and popular education and women's equality and the other building blocks of "modernization." And part of that modern future is the demography as well. Hence the current issues of population policy in the developed countries may well be ahead for the developing. Whatever happens, the developed countries are something of a model for the years ahead, and in that sense, the bases of concern and the courses of action presented in these papers may constitute a picture of the world's demographic future.

Index of Topics*

* Pages given here cover only the *main discussion* of these topics; in most instances, topics are covered in other places in the chapters as well.

This book was set in Life by Cherry Hill Composition. It was
printed and bound by Kingsport Press, Inc. The designer was
Christine Aulicino. The editors for McGraw-Hill were Nancy Tressel
and Laura Givner. Milton Heiberg supervised the production.